LATIN VIA OVID

LATIN
VIA
OVID

A First Course

Norma Goldman
Wayne State University

Jacob E. Nyenhuis
Hope College

Wayne State University Press
Detroit, 1977

Library of Congress Cataloging in Publication Data
Goldman, Norma, 1922–
    Latin via Ovid.
    English or Latin.
    Includes selections from Ovid's Metamorphoses, some of which
have been abridged.
    Includes bibliographical references and index.
    1. Latin language—Readers. I. Nyenhuis, Jacob E., 1935–
joint author. II. Ovidius Naso, Publius. Metamorphoses. Selections.
1977. III. Title.
PA2099.09G6   478'.6'421   77-22501
ISBN 0-8143-1573-9

Grateful acknowledgment is made to Diether Haenicke, Provost
and Vice President, Wayne State University, for his assistance in
publishing this book.

CONTENTS

v

Taped

Taped

Taped

Taped ✳ **XI**
passages only

PREFACE

This text is designed to teach the student to read Latin with ease and enjoyment. To read with ease requires a mastery of basic Latin vocabulary and structure; enjoyment should result from mastery if the reading material is sufficiently stimulating to capture the imagination of a twentieth-century student. We chose abridged versions of Ovid's *Metamorphoses* for the readings, both for their value as background in mythology and for their rich, narrative style, which should impel the reader to continue his pursuit of meaning in a foreign language. The student who already knows the story of Latona and Niobe will be pleased to reread in Latin an already familiar tale, and the one who has never experienced the tragic love story of Pyramus and Thisbe can meet it for the first time in Ovid's own language.

The chapters are divided into sections of Dialogue, Reading, Vocabulary (Verba), Structure, Exercises, and Etymology. Each lesson contains a brief dialogue of a few words of basic communication, not in the foolish notion that twentieth-century students will ever be called upon to speak the language, but so that they can appreciate the beauty of its sound and, through oral repetition, can lessen the tedium of learning. The teacher who wishes to do so may gradually conduct the class in Latin, adding the dialogues as they appear, to greet the class, take roll, give directions for finding page and sentence numbers in the text, open doors and windows, give the assignment, and dismiss the class. After the first twenty chapters are completed, the class can be conducted in Latin for the most part, with English employed only where necessary. Hearing and speaking the language aloud should further an appreciation of its sound and aid in mastery of the forms. To this end a set of tapes excerpting dialogue, reading, vocabulary, drills, and exercises will be available. We hope that students who have facility with language can develop fluency and that students who have had little experience in pronouncing a language—even their own English language—will, in the privacy of the laboratory booth, overcome their fears about making errors and have their "tongues loosed."

The readings begin with abridged and simplified versions of stories from the *Metamorphoses*. We attempted so far as possible to cling to the original not only to illustrate Ovid's imagery and graceful style, but also to employ prose forms that the student will need to recognize when he later encounters the works of other authors. As the readings progress, the vocabulary depends more and more heavily upon Ovid; in the early chapters, the substitution of basic vocabulary was frequently necessary.

The vocabulary is classified according to Nouns, Verbs, Adjectives, and Other Words, so that the student can quickly identify and classify the words acquired with each lesson. The introduction of about thirty new words in each chapter should give the student an adequate vocabulary for reading basic Latin. We included not only vocabulary that would help prepare the student to read Latin prose authors but also some variety to put flesh on the basic skeleton of the language.

For easy reference, the structure sections are numbered consecutively throughout the book. They proceed inductively, with structure material based on the grammar situations that appear in the readings. A more deductive, summary-of-forms method of teaching is introduced in Chapter III to meet the student's need for an over-all view of the material. The grammatical summary and paradigms are repeated in the Appendix. The gradual acquisition of the ideas of structure in Latin is accomplished through a mastery of each lesson's grammatical material. The forty chapters of the text should provide sufficient grammar and reading for the first year of college-level study, along with exercises to give the active drill that learning a language demands. The text has been used profitably several times in experimental form at Wayne State University. It has also been used twice for the summer intensive course where it has proved successful, although the extended vocabulary sections make its use better suited to the work of a normal academic year.

The exercises begin with a series of Latin questions to be answered in Latin sentences, with the aim of teaching the student *to comprehend ideas and to express ideas simply and directly in Latin*. Subsequent exercises provide drill in conjugations and declensions, changing singular ideas to plural, changing cases, supplying the correct cases, changing tenses, changing voice, and changing mood. Although a complete avoidance of drill in forms is impossible, we tried to avoid rote drill and to emphasize *using* knowledge of the material. Where the drills concentrate on conjugations and declensions, we hope they will be rapid-fire.

Each set of exercises includes sentences to be translated into Latin for practice in composition. These often repeat ideas from the reading, with minor changes so that patterns of expression can be rehearsed with some variety. Exercises to teach pronunciation, syllabication, and accent are also included in the first eleven chapters. Before the twelfth is introduced the antepenultimate rule should be an integral part of the student's language experience, from having heard each lesson read aloud by the teacher and by the class, from having practiced in the language laboratory, and from having drilled in the exercises on the means of determining accent. From this point on, oral reading should provide sufficient practice in pronunciation.

The etymology sections are intended to enrich the student's English vocabulary and word-building awareness. Each section works both with the principles of word development in English by means of roots, prefixes, and suffixes, and also with specific words from the lesson which, when doubly acquired through the reading of the Latin story and the English derivatives, make valuable additions to the student's general knowledge. Where appropriate, the Etymology section relates to the story—words from the world of music for the Orpheus episodes and Tombstone Latin for the Achilles' ghost section, for example.

In the sections on Roman life, we expanded the Etymology to add a note on Roman education, names, food, clothing, and housing, as the excitement of explaining *pedagogue, Caesarean* section, *gustatory* experience, *tunic,* and *atrium* spilled over into brief summaries of each of these subjects. The sections on Latin in law, medicine, mathematics, and the sciences have been researched from teachers in the professions who helped select the terms included.

Macrons (the long marks over the lengthened vowels) are a convenience used in teaching elementary Latin for clarity in accent and pronunciation. As the student develops skills in reading, these artificial aids in the text are no longer necessary. The vocabulary and structure sections continue to provide the macrons, but the reading and the exercise sections are presented without the macrons beginning with Chapter XXI. The Interim Readings also appear without macrons. The tapes and classroom drills provide sufficient practice to reinforce the rules learned in the early chapters.

Chapter XXXI introduces a change in format to meet the unique problems encountered in studying poetic content and form. Each page of the text is accompanied by the relevant footnotes and vocabulary. Because it is admittedly difficult to begin reading "real Ovid" in a first year course, the first several sections of Chapter XXXI are adapted as prose; only in 31e do the poetic verses appear. The students will quickly adapt to the new style and feel success in mastering the original. As the format of chapters XXXI–XLV follows that of the series edited by the late Thomas M. Cutt, and revised by Jacob E. Nyenhuis: *Cena Trimalchionis* of Petronius and *Amphitruo* of Plautus (Detroit: Wayne State University Press, 1970), *Latin via Ovid* may serve as a first-year preparation for these second-year readers.

Interim Readings appearing occasionally between chapters provide an opportunity to read an exciting tale without having to master new grammar. Vocabulary is supplied in the footnotes to each page. We selected the tales of Daedalus and Icarus, Phaethon, The Rape of Proserpina, Medea's Evil Deeds, and Ceyx and Alcyone because of the dramatic content and because

Ovid cast the speeches of these vivid characters so excitingly. The teacher can improvise means of extending the stories for exercises if desired, but since the aim is reading for pleasure, no further exercises are provided.

To the students who suffered through early typed editions, making valuable suggestions and diagnosing errors of omission and commission, we owe endless thanks. Particularly, thanks are due to Christine Renaud, who helped in the careful editing of the last twenty chapters. To the secretaries who have helped type both the early and the revised manuscript, we wish to express our gratitude for their secretarial and language skills, their good judgment and common sense: Carol Bartley, Marijo Duprey, M. Jura Kaupas, and Alesia Vaughn. To Emily Batinski, who helped prepare and proofread the vocabulary sections, we wish to express our thanks both for her knowledge of Latin and her careful editing.

Michael Rossi, who twice used the text in experimental form, has offered many valuable suggestions. His skillful teaching, his encouragement and enthusiasm, and his assistance in preparing laboratory tapes to accompany the experimental text deserve a special expression of gratitude. We are also grateful to the late Thomas Cutt, former chairman of the Department of Greek and Latin, Wayne State University, who approved the first experimental use of the book and gave us his encouragement.

To our students and to their pleasurable acquisition of skill in reading Latin we dedicate the textbook.

Norma Goldman
Jacob E. Nyenhuis

INTRODUCTION

The Indo-European Family of Languages

Latin belongs to a language family known as Indo-European. Discussing Indo-European is like talking about the grandfather of a family on the basis of the character of his sons and grandsons. Scholars know little about this single parent language, except that its descendants—Indo-Iranian, Armenian, Albanian, Balto-Slavonic, Hellenic,[1] Italic,[2] Celtic, and Teutonic—share common features that clearly show their mutual relationship. They have a similar system of base or root words, of morphology (the way in which the language changes in its development), and of syntax. The hypothetical parent language is supposed to have been spoken by a people or peoples dwelling in prehistory somewhere between the Baltic and the Black or Caspian seas. By a series of migrations they spread westward into Europe, southeast into Asia to meet Semitic languages already present, and into Russia. Since no Indo-European writing has ever been recovered, it is difficult to postulate absolute rules for the language, but on the basis of the structure and vocabulary of the subsequent descendant "family," the theory of an Indo-European ancestry is widely accepted. Compare, for instance, these basic, common words in several Indo-European languages, which are called *cognate* because they spring from the same stock.

---

[1] Greek, the main Hellenic language, existed in Aeolic, Ionic, Doric, and Attic dialects, depending on the geographical location.

[2] Latin was one of several Italic dialects, which also included Umbrian and Oscan, but Latin eventually prevailed as the dominant language of the Italian peninsula.

Cognate or Related Languages

	Latin	Greek	Sanskrit	Iranian[3]	Anglo-Saxon	Russian
mother	māter	mētēr	matar	matar	moder	mat'
brother	frāter	phrātēr	bhratar	bratar	brothor	brat
is	est	esti	asti	asti	is	est'
ten	decem	deca	daca	dasa	tien	desjat'
me	mē	me	ma	ma	me	menja

A similar growth of distinct but related languages from a common parent is clear in the development of the Romance (from Roman) languages from the parent Latin. In each of the geographical areas of Europe where Latin spread, through Roman conquest and migration, it was first a dialect and later became a separate language. It developed regionally through a process of dropping or changing inflectional endings and adding and intensifying local style, vocabulary, and color. These cognate Romance languages—Italian, Spanish, Portuguese, French, and Romanian—have all derived from the Classical Latin of Ancient Rome.

Cognate Romance Languages

Source

Latin	Italian	Spanish	Portuguese	French	Romanian
amāre (*to love*)	amare	amar	amar	aimer	—
casa (*house*)	casa	casa	casa	case[4]	casă
cognōscere (*to know*)	conoscere	conocer	conhecer	connaître	a cunoaşte
nōn (*not*)	non	no	não	non	nu
mīlle (*thousand*)	mille	mil	mil	mille	mie
nomen (*name*)	nome	nombre	nome	nom	nume
templum (*temple*)	templo	templo	templo	temple	templu
tenēre (*to keep*)	tenere	tener	ter	tenir	a ţine
trēs (*three*)	tre	tres	três	trois	trei
timidus (*timid*)	timido	tímido	tímido	timide	timid
veritās (*truth*)	verità	verdad	verdade	vérité	adevăr

---

[3] As in the older I.E. Avestan or Old Persian language. Modern Farsi (Persian) equivalents are: **madar, baradar, ast, dah, ma**.

[4] Cabin; **maison** is the more familiar French word for house. Also, *cf.* **chez**, related to **casa**.

English is not a Romance language; its base is Teutonic, another branch of the Indo-European family tree. Most of the vocabulary for familial relationships and daily life in England came from Teutonic sources: mother, father, man, wife, son, daughter, brother, sister, home, house, bread, hay, harvest, cow, calf, grass, plow, barn, farm, moon, sun, storm, sea, ice, snow, thunder, summer, winter—short words that say easily what they mean; descriptive words like good, bad, old, young; verbs for daily human activities: eat, drink, talk, laugh, sing, love, hate, buy and sell—these are all of Teutonic origin. Frequently a Latin word came to dwell alongside the Teutonic word: tempest for storm, domicile for house, marine life for sea life, lunatic for moonstruck, bovine for cowlike, fraternal for brotherly, vendor for seller. Notice always the more erudite level of communication in the Latin word. Teutonic words did originally have inflection: declension for nouns and conjugation for verbs, as in Latin; but over the years the endings deteriorated and disappeared, except for tense change in verbs and the third person singular present ending of -s (I, you, we, and they *love*, but he, she, or it *loves*).[5] English still inflects in the change of singular to plural for nouns, but not for adjectives, and not for syntactical relationships within the sentence; word order indicates whether a noun is subject, direct object, possessive,[6] indirect object, or object of prepositions.

Latin and its descendants, the Romance languages, being highly inflected, can express distinctions such as number and gender (for nouns) and tense, person, number, voice, and mood (for verbs) simply by changing the endings of words. Termed "synthetic" by linguistic scholars, Latin may employ a verb consisting of a base or root, carrying the dictionary definition, to which prefixes, tense signs, and personal endings may be affixed; these all "put together" add up to a complex concept of combining many ideas in a single word: e.g., **abripuerat**, *he had carried off* (**ab-**, *off*; **-ripu**, *carried;* **-era-**, *had*; **-t**, *he*). In contrast, English, termed "analytic" by linguists, expresses the same idea by means of independent units with a minimum of grammatical inflection: *he/had/carried/off*, all single words comprising a phrase separable into component parts. If the words **Taurus**, *bull* (as subject) and **Europam**, *Europa* (as object) are added to the statement: **Taurus Europam abripuerat**, *The bull had carried off Europa*, the word order in Latin would be relatively unimportant. **Taurus** usually precedes, but could follow either **Europam** or the verb with only a slight change of emphasis, but with *no change in syntax*. In English, however, the word order is crucial in understanding who had carried off whom; whether *Europa* is subject or object depends entirely upon the word order.

---

[5] We are still familiar with archaic English, kept alive in the King James Bible and in Shakespeare's plays: *thou lovest* and *he loveth* for second and third person singular of the verb.
[6] The book of George (uninflected) or George's book (contraction of George-his-book).

The influence of Latin on English vocabulary is extremely important, the paths from which Latin flowed into English being many and wide. The Roman invasion of England (43–410 A.D.) had left behind a legacy of place names and about eight hundred words referring to housing, clothing, food, education, religion, and the military. The Teutonic language of the Germanic invaders, the Angles and Saxons who settled in England, had borrowed some Latin words from its long pre-invasion contact with Rome. Of much greater influence, however, was the coming of Latin with Saint Augustine,[7] who was sent by Pope Gregory to introduce Christianity into Britain (597). Old English, the language of the Angles and Saxons, was spoken by the common man; Latin was the language of the Church and of learning, since the schools developed within the framework of the Church. Educated people usually were bilingual. After William the Conqueror successfully invaded England from Norman France, French became the official language of the court with a resultant influx of French words, many of Latin origin. Middle English still remained the basic language fabric of everyday life, while French embroidered it from the world of polite and court society, and Latin metered and patterned it from the Church and the Academy. Even during the period of French dominance, however, English was always the language of the people, the vehicle for basic communication in daily life and also the basis for a flourishing literature in the native tongue. By the fourteenth century Chaucer (1340–1400), who has been called the father of English poetry, had available to him a composite English, enriched in vocabulary and subtlety of expression by its long contact with Latin and French. Latin, therefore, tremendously influenced cultural, literary, artistic, religious, and academic English both directly from the Church and the classroom, and indirectly through French.

Added to these influences was the direct absorption of Latin words into the language during the Renaissance with its rediscovering of ancient Greek and Roman literature and during periods of scientific investigation, when Latin words provided the basis for an international science. Thus Latin continually enriched the developing English language; each successive wave of Latin, sweeping over the shore of England, left a rich residue of vocabulary.

This English language transplanted to America has again been enriched with words from all the countries whose emigrants brought their own language traditions with them. Words of Latin origin, through Italian, through Spanish, and again through French entered the language; and Americans also resorted to Latin for the terminology of their science—for chemistry, physics, biology, botany, astronomy, and the new space programs. The process is still going on with Atlas, Apollo, and Jupiter spacecraft; and a Gemini space station whose orbiting rivals that of the planets.

---

[7] This is not the famous patristic Saint Augustine (354–430), but a later missionary.

The Latin Alphabet

The Latin alphabet is the same as the English alphabet, except that there are no *j* and no *w* in Latin.[8] The *v* represented the *w* sound and served as a sign for the vowel *u*. The vowels, *a, e, i, o, u*, are similar to English vowels. The consonant *k* rarely appears, since in classical Latin the *c* is always hard; *y* and *z* were introduced to represent their sounds in words of Greek origin. The long marks, called "macrons," which are placed over the vowels, indicate a lengthening in the quantity and a deepening of the quality (intensity) of the sound.

A brief review of the development of writing may help us better to appreciate the great antiquity of the English alphabetic system of writing. The Egyptians initially employed hieroglyphs or ideographs (picture symbols) to represent each word; eventually they learned to use both syllabic and alphabetic signs in addition to hieroglyphs, but they did not develop a system of pure alphabetism. The schools of Ugarit in Canaan (n. Syria), however, during the fifteenth century B.C., employed an abecedarium after which our own ABC's are patterned. The Phoenicians passed on the alphabetic system to the Greeks; the Phoenicians also may have been the source of the Minoan syllabary of Linear A, which preceded the Greek syllabary of Linear B used on the Greek mainland and at Knossos on Crete c. 1500 to 1200 B.C.[9] Merchant Greeks residing on the Syrian coast probably introduced the North Semitic alphabet to various regions of Greece around the eighth century B.C.[10]

The Romans adopted the Greek alphabet employed by the Greek colonies in southern Italy, such as Cumae; some scholars believe, however, that the Etruscan alphabet supplied the link between the Greek and Roman letters.[11] In addition to engraving on stone, lead pipes, etc., the Romans wrote with reed pens and styli on wax and papyrus at first, then later on parchment and vellum; papyri "books" were on rolls, but the other materials were generally in tablet form.[12]

---

[8] Consonant *i* is written as *j* in many elementary Latin texts. *W* is really a double *u*, the letter originally being pointed at the bottom.

[9] Linear A refers to an ancient syllabary writing used on Crete c. 1700 B.C., as found in clay tablet fragments from the various palace sites on the island. It consists of a cursive system of about seventy-five syllabic signs written from left to right. Linear B is a later Minoan syllabary form of writing, discovered by Sir Arthur Evans in over 3,000 clay tablets and other fragments at Knossos. Deciphered by the British cryptographer-architect Michael Ventris in 1953, Linear B proved that the Minoans of Knossos wrote and spoke an early form of Greek closely related to the language of Mycenae and Pylos on the Greek mainland in the Peloponnesus, where similar finds show that Linear B was also used.

[10] *Cf.* Cyrus Gordon, *World of the Old Testament*, New York, 1958, p. 93; *Before the Bible*. New York, 1962, p. 216; John Chadwick, *The Decipherment of Linear B*, Cambridge, 1958; L. H. Jeffrey, *The Local Scripts of Archaic Greece*, Oxford, 1961, pp. 1–42.

[11] James Hayes, *The Roman Letter*, Chicago, 1951–52, p. 4.

[12] *Ibid.*, pp. 6–9.

English	Latin	Greek		Phoenician	
A a	A a	A α	alpha	āleph	𐤀
B b	B b	B β	beta	bêth	𐤁
C c	C c [K k]				
D d	D d	Δ δ	delta	dāleth	𐤃
E e	E e	E ε	epsilon (short e)	hē	𐤄
		H η	ēta (long e)	chêth	𐤇
F f	F f				
G g	G g	Γ γ	gamma	gīmel	𐤂
H h	H h				
I i	I i	I ι	iota	yôd	𐤉
J j	I i (*consonant*)				
K k	K k	K κ	kappa	kaph	𐤊
L l	L l	Λ λ	lambda	lāmed	𐤋
M m	M m	M μ	mū	mēm	𐤌
N n	N n	N ν	nū	nûn	𐤍
O o	O o	O o	omicron (short o)	ayin	𐤏
		Ω ω	ōmega (long o)		
P p	P p	Π π	pī	pē	𐤐
Q q	Qu qu			qôph	𐤒
R r	R r	P ρ	rho	rêsh, rôsh	𐤓
S s	S s	Σ σ	sigma	shîn	𐤔
T t	T t	T τ	tau	tāw	𐤕
U u	U u	Y υ	upsīlon[13]		
V v	V v [W w]				
W w		(*F*	digamma)	wāw	𐤅
X x	X x	Ξ ξ	xī	sāmekh	𐤎
Y y	Y y	Y υ	upsīlon		
Z z	Z z	Z ζ	zēta	zayin	𐤆

Other Greek and Phoenician Letters

			Phoenician	
th	Θ ϑ	thēta	têth	⊗
			tsade	𐤑
ph	Φ φ	phī		
ch	X χ	chī		
ps	Ψ ψ	psī		

---

[13] The actual sign for *upsilon* seems to be derived from the Phoenician *waw*. See Jeffrey, *Scripts of Archaic Greece*, pp. 24–28, 35.

The debt of the English (and Latin) alphabet to earlier abecedaria can be observed in the table on the opposite page. Since the order of the English and Latin alphabets is the same, a few letters of the Greek and Phoenician alphabets have been removed from their regular order. Although most of the 22 Phoenician letters were employed in the 24-letter Greek abecedarium, a few were eliminated and a few new ones were added. Similarly, a few Greek letters have no direct equivalent in the Latin and English alphabets, and some new letters have been added to the Latin alphabet. The Phoenician alphabet was written from right to left, but the Greek alphabet evolved through *boustrophedon* writing (lit., *ox-turning*, i.e., right-to-left and left-to-right in alternation, like the turning of the Greek oxen when plowing a field) to a strict left-to-right pattern.

Guide to Pronunciation

VOWELS

The following rules are invariable.

Short Vowels			Long Vowels		
a	as in *cart*	**charta**	ā	as in *father*	**fābula**
e	as in *bed*	**est, sed**	ē	as in *they*	**sē, dēsīderat**
i	as in *pin*	**timida**	ī	as in *machine*	**īnsula**
o	as in *domain*	**novus**	ō	as in *note*	**nōn**
u	as in *put*	**nunc**	ū	as in *rude*	**lūna**

y[14] as in French *tu* **cygnus**

DIPHTHONGS

ae	as in *aisle*	**terrae**	eu	e + u in one syllable	**Eurōpa**
oe	as in *oil*	**Phoenicia**	ui	u + i in one syllable	**cui**
au	as in *out*	**laudat**	ei	as in *vein*	**deinde**

CONSONANTS

Latin and English consonants are pronounced alike with the following reservations:

c	is always hard as in *can*	**Cicerō**
g	is always hard as in *give*	**argentum**

---

[14] Both long and short; especially used in borrowed words of Greek origin. Also sounded as Latin **u** to approximate the Greek upsilon.

i	can be a consonant, sounded as *y* in *year* when it occurs in a consonant position[15]	**Iuppiter, iam, iūstus, huius**
r	is tongue-trilled	**vocāre, sonāre**
s	is always hissed as a voiceless consonant, *sea*, never voiced as *z* in *was*	**soror, īnsula, casa**
t	is always sounded *t* as in *tin*, never *sh* as in *oration*	**teneō, initiō**
v	has the sound of *w*	**parva, vocō**
x	has the sound of *ks*	**exemplum**
bs, bt	are sounded *ps* and *pt*	**urbs, obtineō**
ch	is related to Greek *chi* and is close to *kh* in *blockhouse*	**chorus**
ph	is related to Greek *phi* and is close to *ph* in *uphill*	**amphora**
th	is related to Greek *theta* and is close to *th* in *pothook*	**theatrum**

Double consonants: **ss, tt, ll**, etc., are sounded twice the length of time given to the single consonant.

SYLLABLES

A Latin word has as many syllables as it has vowels or diphthongs. The vowel alone or the consonant and vowel together can make the syllable. Divide words according to the following rules:

1. A consonant is pronounced with the vowel that follows it: **a.mā.mus.**
2. When two vowels (or a vowel and a diphthong) occur together, pronounce them separately: **fī.li.a, e.ōs, vi.ae.**
3. When two consonants occur together, pronounce them separately: **por.tō, pu.el.la, ma.gis.ter.** A stop consonant (b, p, d, t, c, g) followed by a liquid (l or r) counts as a single consonant: **ma.tris, fra.tris, ne.glec.tus.**
4. When more than two consonants occur together, the first generally is pronounced with the preceding vowel and the others with the following: **mōn.strum, cas.tra, ex.em.plum.**
5. Separate compound words into the original parts: **trāns.portō, ab.rogō, ex.animō, com.es, in.eō, sub.īre.**

LONG AND SHORT SYLLABLES

1. A syllable is long if it contains a long vowel or a diphthong. Such a syllable is said to be long by nature: **īn.su.la, fā.bu.la, Phoe.nī.ci.a, a.moe.na.**

---

[15] Either at the beginning of a word followed by a vowel, or between two vowels.

2. A syllable is long if it contains a short vowel followed by two consonants (except a stop followed by a liquid).[16] Such a syllable is said to be long by position: **ma.gis.ter, Mi.ner.va.**
3. All other syllables are short.

ACCENT

1. In words of two syllables, accent the first syllable (the penult).

á.mant pú.er cár.ta nó.vus

The last syllable is called the *ultima*, from the Latin **ultimus**, meaning "last." The next to the last syllable is called the *penult*, from the Latin **paene**, meaning "almost" and **ultimus**. The syllable before the *penult* is called the *antepenult*, from the words **ante**, meaning "before," and *penult*.
2. In words of more than two syllables, accent the penult *if it is long*: **habitāre, docḗre, amoénās, magíster.** It may be long by nature or by position. Otherwise accent the antepenult: **ínsula, fábula, fília.** This rule for determining accent is called the *antepenultimate rule*, and it never varies.

Examples

		Antepenult	Penult	Ultima
portāre		por	**tā**	re
rēgina		rē	**gĭ**	na
spectāte		spec	**tā**	te
amoena		a	**moe**	na
taurus			**tau**	rus
terra			**ter**	ra
puella		pu	**el**	la
magister		ma	**gis**	ter
fābula		**fā**	bu	la
insula		**ĭn**	su	la
fīlia		**fĭ**	li	a
incola		**in**	co	la
agricola	a	**gri**	co	la

On what basis do present-day grammarians state the rules for the pronunciation of a language which was never verbally recorded and which is pronounced so differently in various parts of the world? Certainly, Latin

---

[16]The second of these consonants begins the following syllable (**ĭn.su.la**). A syllable containing a short vowel followed by a stop and a liquid may be either long or short.

pronounced by an Englishman and by a German and by an Italian (and by the Church which historically grew within the Italian framework of pronunciation) is quite different from that which we teach as Classical Latin. The sources for our reconstruction of how Latin must have sounded in classical times are many: first, the direct evidence in the writings of ancient grammarians; second, poetry properly scanned to indicate the length of vowels; third, ancient puns and approximations of animal cries; fourth, the spellings on inscriptions; fifth, the spellings in Latin for words borrowed from other languages and the spellings in other languages for Latin words (e.g., **kaisar** in Greek assures us that the **c** was hard); sixth, the pronunciation of the dialects of Latin and of Vulgar Latin; and last, comparative grammar.[17] On these bases, scientific scholarship has reconstructed a pronunciation of Latin which was adopted decades ago in the United States and which tries to reproduce the way Latin was spoken in Classical Rome, c. 200 B.C. to c. 200 A.D.

Publius Ovidius Naso (43 B.C.-17 A.D.): A Biographical Note

The Roman poet Ovid was born at Sulmo, north of Rome, of a family of knights (**Equites**). He went to Rome for his education and there studied rhetoric to prepare for law, which he soon abandoned to become a popular poet. His education included a trip to Athens, much as a modern student might go to Paris or Rome to study. He first wrote love poetry: *Amores, Ars Amatoria, Remedia Amoris*, poems about love affairs and the men and women involved in them. He also wrote the *Heroides*, a series of twenty-one letters written ostensibly by women to their famous hero lovers; for example, Penelope to Ulysses, Dido to Aeneas, Ariadne to Theseus, Medea to Jason. His interest often focuses on an injured female whose situation he is able to recreate and with whose injury he is able to empathize. However, he is best known for his encyclopedic work compiling Greek and Roman mythological themes, *Metamorphoses*, a long series of stories about the gods and humans, and about changes or transformations in the appearance of all forms of life. He seemed fascinated by the mythological background for the holidays of Rome and became engaged in an ambitious project, the *Fasti*, a long almanac calendar with each book devoted to a month of the year, explaining the days which were holidays, how they come into existence, and the ritual associated with them. He had already completed the first six books (through June) at the time of his exile. In 8 A.D. he incurred the displeasure of the Emperor Augustus and was banished to Tomis on the western shore of the Black Sea,

---

[17] Roland G. Kent, *The Sounds of Latin* (Baltimore: Waverly Press, 1940), pp. 31, 43.

where he spent the rest of his life in gloomy exile. His poetry and his letters from this exile period reflect his mood in this cold, barbaric land, separated from all the culture and elegance he had known at Rome (*Tristia* and *Pontic Epistles*). Although privately he may have been reconciled to his exile and may have come to terms with new concepts of deity which he found at Tomis,[18] in his letters and poems he constantly begs for restoration to his former life at Rome and for pardon from Augustus and, later, from the Emperor Tiberius, a boon never granted by either Emperor.[19] Whether or not he believed in the theology he compiled in the *Metamorphoses* is a problem for the literary historian, but certainly he has given an immortality to these anthropomorphic gods of the "changes." From this magnificent body of poetry the stories in our text have been adapted or excerpted.

The choice of Ovid as the author of our abridged tales has made possible the use of the book both as a reader and as a mythology text. Ovid's delight in a well-told tale has made him unexcelled as an elaborate story-teller; this skill, coupled with his psychological penetration into his characters both divine and human, has opened doors to the treasures of the rich mythology of the Greeks now adapted to the Roman scene. These glimpses of a Roman Olympus with its fragmented pantheon of the male and female godhead split into *numina* of specialized powers for particular activities provide an excellent background for study of the literary, musical, and visual artistic creations of western civilization, which have embraced mythological themes. The alert teacher can easily arrange a performance in class of sections from Shakespeare's *A Midsummer Night's Dream* after the story of Pyramus and Thisbe has been translated, and the fine novel by Mary Renault, *The King Must Die*, or Michael Ayrton's *The Maze Maker* might be the subsequent reading after the Theseus episodes. The Trojan War materials should stimulate reading Homer's original epics, as well as the *Aeneid* of Virgil, while *The Voyage of the Argo* by Apollonius of Rhodes would make a fine complement to the

---

[18] See the novel *God Was Born in Exile*, by Vintila Horvia, for a fictionalized account of how Ovid may have adjusted to his life in Tomis, at the very edge of the civilized world.

[19] The cause of Ovid's exile has never been satisfactorily explained and remains an intriguing mystery. The fact that Augustus' granddaughter Julia was exiled about the same time indicates that Ovid may have known some secret indiscretion involving the Emperor's family. In his poetry Ovid refers to two causes for his unhappy situation: a **carmen**, which biographers assume to be the *Ars Amatoria*, the poem on love-making, and an **error** which could have been any kind of indiscreet act. Since Ovid himself was most respectably married and probably was not directly involved in the **error**, it may be that his sympathetic view of the female psyche made him the recipient of knowledge dangerous to the newly reformed Empire of Augustus and the Empress Livia, and dangerous to himself. Or it may be that the moral tone of the earlier poetry did not fit in with the "new morality" in the reforms instituted by the Emperor and Livia. The situation is detailed in *The Mystery of Ovid's Exile* by J. C. Thibault (1964).

xxvi   Latin via Ovid

Jason episodes.[20] It would also be helpful for the student to read a translation of the full Ovidian story from which the initial stories in this text have been excerpted and extensively adapted or abridged.

---

[20]It might be desirable to obtain a copy of *The Odyssey*, a ten-minute shadow puppet film in color which, despite its technical flaws, illustrates how an art class can use these materials most constructively to cross departmental barriers and produce its own creative humanities project. This film may be rented from the Wayne State University Department of Systems, Distribution & Utilization, 5448 Cass Avenue, Detroit, Michigan 48202. A sound and color print can be obtained from Cyril and Arnold Miles, 17711 Hamilton Road, Detroit, Michigan 48203.

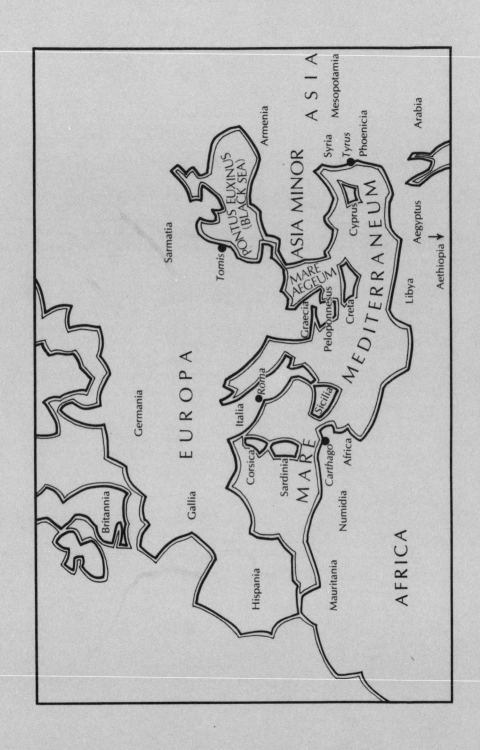

Dialogue
Salvēte! *Greetings!* (addressing more than one)
Salvē! *Greetings!* (addressing one person)

Chapter I
CHARTA GEŌGRAPHICA

Hīc est charta geōgraphica. Est charta parva, sed terrae sunt magnae. Charta est bona. Eurōpa et Āfrica et Asia sunt continentēs.[1] Sunt terrae pulchrae in Eurōpā, in Āfricā, in Asiā.

Spectāte terrās in Eurōpā. Britannia, Gallia, Germānia, Hispānia, Ītalia, Graecia sunt in Eurōpā. Spectāte īnsulās: Siciliam, Sardiniam, Corsicam, Crētam, Cyprum. Ubi sunt īnsulae? Sunt in marī Mediterraneō.[2] Suntne īnsulae magnae? Ita, īnsulae sunt magnae. Peloponnēsus[3] est paene īnsula. Hispānia, Graecia, Ītalia sunt paenīnsulae magnae. Rōma est in Ītaliā.

Spectāte Āfricam. Spectāte terrās in Āfricā: Mauretāniam, Numidiam, Libyam, Aethiopiam, Aegyptum.[4] Carthāgō est in Āfricā. In Āfricā Dīdō, rēgīna Phoenissa,[5] habitat et rēgnat.

Spectāte Asiam. Spectāte terrās in Asiā. Terrae in Asiā sunt Asia Minor, Armenia, Mesopotamia, Arabia, Syria, Phoenīcia. Spectāte īnsulam parvam in Phoenīciā. Est īnsula pulchra—Tyrus.[6] Eurōpa, puella in fābulā prīmā, in Phoenīciā habitat. Estne īnsula magna? Īnsula nōn est magna; est parva.

---

[1] *Continents.*
[2] *In the Mediterranean Sea.*
[3] *The Peloponnesus*, the lower part of the Greek peninsula.
[4] *Egypt.*
[5] *The Phoenician queen.*
[6] *Tyre.*

1

Verba

NOUNS

charta	paper, map
Eurōpa	Europa (*the maiden*); also Europe, the continent
fābula	story
īnsula	island
paenīnsula	peninsula
puella	girl, maiden
rēgīna	queen
terra	land, country, earth

Place names are easily recognized from their English equivalents and from the map, except for **Gallia** (Gaul) and **Hispania** (Spain); also see Etymology, Chapters XXIII and XXIV.

VERBS

est	is
habitat	lives
rēgnat	rules
spectāte	look at (*a command*)
sunt	are

ADJECTIVES

bona	good
geōgraphica	geographical
magna	large
parva	small
prīma	first
pulchra	beautiful, pretty, fair

OTHER WORDS

et	and
hīc	here
in	(*with abl. case*) in, on
ita	yes, thus, so
-ne,	enclitic (*attached to first word in the sentence*): asks a question
nōn	not
paene	almost
sed	but
ubi	where

Structure

1. Omission of the article. There is no word for *a* (*an*) or *the* in Latin. Supply whichever article is needed to express in English the idea most suitable for the context.

Hīc est charta.   Here is a map. (preferable here)
                            Here is the map. (also possible)

2. Word order. The adjective generally follows the noun it modifies.

Terra pulchra est in Eurōpā.   The beautiful country is in
                                    Europe.

The first and last positions are the most important in the Latin sentence. The subject usually occupies the first portion and the verb stands last because of its importance.[7] **Est** and **sunt**, however, do not follow the above rule, but occur in the sentence wherever emphasis demands.

Puella in Phoenīciā habitat.   The girl lives in Phoenicia.
Terra est pulchra.   The land is beautiful.

3. Omission of pronoun subject. The pronoun subject equivalents for *he*, *she*, *it*, *they*, are implied in the verb ending and are not expressed except for emphasis.

Est charta parva.   It is a small map.
Eurōpa est puella. In Phoenīciā Europa is a girl. She lives in
  habitat.   Phoenicia.
Īnsulae sunt pulchrae. Sunt in marī The islands are beautiful. They
  Mediterraneō.   are in the Mediterranean Sea.

The verb contains the pronoun idea within itself in the final letter or letters:

  -t: he, she, it   **-nt:** they

4. Number: singular and plural. The ending of a Latin noun changes to indicate singular (one) or plural (more than one). English-speaking students are familiar with such a change in nouns: girl-girls, boy-boys, island-islands, church-churches. In Latin, nouns in **-a** change to **-ae** to indicate the plural: **terra**, *a land*, becomes **terrae**, *the lands*.

---

[7]Word order is not crucial to the meaning of the sentence, however, since inflected endings indicate the relationship of words. Words or phrases may be shifted for emphasis: **In Phoenīciā puella habitat**. The girl lives *in Phoenicia* (not elsewhere).

Terra pulchra est magna.   The beautiful land is large.
Terrae pulchrae sunt magnae.   The beautiful lands are large.

Note that the verb becomes plural to agree with the plural subject and that the adjective modifying a plural noun must also be plural to agree with its noun, *even when the adjective stands in the predicate.*

5. Case: nominative, accusative, ablative. The ending of a Latin noun also changes to indicate the noun's relationship to other words in the sentence. Names which identify the changes for nouns and pronouns and their modifiers are called *cases.*

   Subject words are in the *nominative case.*
   Object words are in the *accusative case.*
   Many object-of-preposition words are in the *ablative case.*
   Predicate words following a linking verb (**est, sunt**) and referring back to the subject are in the *nominative case.* The case endings are as follows:

	Singular		*Plural*	
Nominative	-a	terra	-ae	terrae
Accusative	-am	terram	-ās	terrās
Ablative	-ā	terrā	-īs	terrīs

Memorize these endings. Note their use in the reading. This change of ending in nouns is called *declension.*

Nominative:	**Terra** est magna.	*The land* is large.
	Terrae sunt magnae.	*The lands* are large.
Accusative:	Spectāte **terram**.	Look at *the land.*
	Spectāte **terrās**.	Look at *the lands.*
Ablative:	Rōma est in **Ītaliā**.	Rome is in *Italy.*
	Puellae pulchrae sunt in **īnsulīs**.	The beautiful girls are on *the islands.*
Predicate Nominative:	Īnsulae sunt **terrae**.	The islands are *countries.*

6. The expletive: there is, there are. The word for "there" is omitted when "there" does not refer to a place, but merely indicates existence. This use of "there" is called *expletive.*

   Sunt terrae pulchrae in Eurōpā.   *There are* beautiful countries in Europe.

   Est īnsula in Phoenīciā.   *There is* an island in Phoenicia.

7. Questions and answers. Interrogative words can ask questions:

Ubi est īnsula?   *Where* is the island?

The syllable ending (*enclitic*) **-ne**, attached to the first word in the sentence, can also be used to ask a question. Usually the verb becomes the first word in a question, because of its importance, but there is no rule, except that the most important elements stand first or last for emphasis.

Suntne īnsulae magnae?   *Are* the islands large?

The answers may be affirmative or negative. If affirmative, the idea is reaffirmed by repeating the words of the sentence:

Īnsulae sunt magnae.   The islands are large.

The affirmation may be stressed by **ita** (*thus, so*) with **est** understood (*it is so*); **ita** has come to mean "*yes.*"

Ita, īnsulae sunt magnae.   *Yes*, the islands are large.

If negative, the sentence is negated by **nōn** placed before the verb.

Īnsulae **nōn** sunt magnae.   The islands are *not* large.
Rēgīna in īnsulā **nōn** habitat. The queen does *not* live on the
                                 island.

8. Apposition. A noun standing next to another noun to explain it is called an *appositive*. It is *in apposition* to its noun and is in the same case as the noun it explains.

Est fābula dē puellā **Eurōpā**. There is a story about the girl
                                  Europa.
Terra **Ītalia** est in Eurōpā.   The country *of Italy* is in Europe.

Pronunciation

Listen carefully to the teacher reading the lesson. Imitate the sounds of the vowels and consonants. A good ear is your best guide for now. The rules will be studied in successive lessons. Note, however, that some vowels are marked with a sign (*macron*) indicating they are long vowels. The others, if unmarked, are short.

Long **i** is pronounced like the *i* in *machine*.	**īnsula**
The diphthong **ae** is pronounced like *ai* in *aisle*.	**terrae**
The **v** is pronounced like *w*.	**parva**
C and **g** are always hard, as in *cat* and *go*.	**Sicilia, Germānia**

Exercises

I. Questions. Answer the following in complete Latin sentences, as in Example 1.

1. Ubi est charta?   1. Hīc est charta.
2. Estne charta magna?
3. Suntne terrae parvae?
4. Ubi sunt Ītalia et Graecia?
5. Suntne Ītalia et Graecia īnsulae?
6. Estne Sicilia paenīnsula?
7. Ubi est Carthāgō?
8. Estne Āfrica magna?
9. Ubi est Phoenīcia?
10. Ubi habitat Eurōpa, puella in fābulā prīmā?

II. Change each *singular* word to *plural*:

1. Terra est parva.   1. Terrae sunt parvae.
2. Charta est bona.
3. Īnsula est pulchra.
4. Paenīnsula est magna.
5. Puella est parva.
6. Rēgīna est pulchra.
7. Terra est magna.
8. Fābula est pulchra.
9. Puella est pulchra.
10. Īnsula est magna.

III. Change each *nominative* form to the corresponding *accusative*, object of **spectāte**. Make the predicate adjective into a direct modifier.

1. Terra est pulchra.   1. Spectāte terram pulchram.
2. Īnsula est magna.   2. Spectāte _____ _____.
3. Puella est parva.
4. Rēgīnae sunt pulchrae.
5. Paenīnsulae sunt parvae.
6. Phoenīcia est pulchra.
7. Graecia est magna.
8. Charta est magna.
9. Īnsulae sunt parvae.

IV. Supply the correct *ablative* form in these prepositional phrases:

1. Ītalia est in ____Eurōpā____.
2. Rōma est in _____.
3. Carthāgō est in _____.
4. Phoenīcia est in _____.
5. Graecia est in _____.

V. Translate into Latin:

1. The island is small.
2. Italy is large.
3. The small island is beautiful.
4. Sicily is a large island.
5. Are the islands small? They are not small.

Etymology

Etymology is the study of the true or original meanings of words or a tracing of the history of a specific word. The word *etymology* itself is derived from two Greek words: **etymon**, *the true sense of a word* (from **etymos**, *true*), and **logos**, *speech, word, reason* (hence, *-logy* came to mean the *science, theory,* or *study of* something). Etymology is also a branch of linguistics which studies the derivation of words.

In this section of each lesson you will examine word origins for selected vocabulary items. The goal of each etymology section is to suggest patterns of development, to stimulate you to apply the principles of etymology to other vocabulary items, and to assist you in the process of acquiring a broader vocabulary in English.

The names of continents, countries, seas, and rivers which have come into English through their Latin equivalents are endless. In this chapter Asia, Asia Minor, Europe, Germany, Britain, Gaul, Italy, Corsica, Sardinia, Sicily, Greece, Crete, Cyprus, Syria, Mesopotamia, Africa, Numidia, Mauritania, Libya, Ægypt, Æthiopia and Arabia all appear as equivalents or nearly so. Note, however, **Hispania** (*Spain*).

In the following paragraph there are many English words which are derived from their Latin cognates. See how many of them you can recognize. Do any English derivatives have different meanings?

The *fable* about the girl of great *pulchritude* who lived on the *peninsula* which extended into the sea which was sailed only by those who had a *chart* of the area is not familiar to everyone. The land is devoid of *habitation* and only a few *spectators* from the ships are able to look through glasses which *magnify* the land and allow the passengers to see the *primate* creatures of the area.

The Romans did not use the word **charta (carta)**[8] for *map* or *chart*. Instead they used **tabula**, which originally meant *plank of wood* or *board*, but later was extended to include any purpose for which the board was subsequently used: *a table* or *a tablet* on which writing was put (usually onto a waxed surface), *a voting list*, *a will*, *a record*, *a painting*, or *a map*. The word

---

[8] Classical Latin **charta** developed into Late Latin **carta**.

came to mean any writing of a permanent nature, e.g., the *Law of the Twelve Tables*. Even today we refer to the *multiplication table* or to a *table of statistics*. The Romans also used the word **forma** (plan) for *map*.

Coming from the equivalent word in Greek, **charta** meant *a piece of papyrus, a paper, a writing material, a page, a roll of a literary work*. Later the word came to mean *a deed* or *a document* and by the late Middle Ages it came to mean *a map*. Actually, the *itineraries* (**itinera**) as maps were more used by travellers and by the army in the ancient world, since scouts and voyagers reported information of a descriptive nature that would enable people to make a trip (**iter**). These itineraries functioned much as an AAA Triptik does, supplying distances along routes, identifying markers, and descriptive details. Copies were kept in libraries, and sections were even exhibited on stone.

Europa and the Bull

Europa, a Phoenician princess, was carried off by Zeus (Jupiter) in the form of a bull from her home in Tyre and taken to the island of Crete where she gave birth to Minos, a name which became the family designation for the subsequent dynasty of this island. The name *Minoan* was then applied to the civilization long considered the cradle of Greek culture (c. 3000–1450 B.C.) when the great palaces such as the one at Knossos flourished. The carrying off of the Near Eastern princess by Zeus, the Greek sky god (later identified with the *Deus-pater*, Jupiter, god-the-father of the Romans) can possibly be considered a most symbolic transplanting and merging of the culture of the Near East, through the subsequent Minoan and Mycenean civilizations, with the culture of Europe and Western civilization; thus her name *Europa* indicates the eventual spread of the ideas of the Near East and Greece to the continent which eventually bears her name. Symbolic also is the form which Zeus assumed to accomplish this act, that of the powerful bull, whose horns decorate the palaces of Crete and whose form appears again in the Minotaur, the half-man, half-bull creature housed in the labyrinth beneath the palace at Knossos.

Europa and Minos are *eponyms* for the lands bearing their names, an eponym being the name of the person from whom a family, race, city or nation is supposed to have taken its name.

Dialogue
Valēte!   *Farewell!* (addressing more than one)
Valē!   *Farewell!* (addressing one person)

Chapter II
EURŌPA ET TAURUS

Eurōpa est puella pulchra. Eurōpa in Tyrō, īnsulā in Phoenīciā, habitat. Agēnor[1] est rēx Phoenīciae, et Eurōpa est fīlia. Eurōpa cum amīcīs Tyriīs lūdit. Amīcae Eurōpae puellam amant, et Eurōpa amīcās amat.

Iuppiter est deus. Deus Iuppiter in Olympō[2] habitat. Olim terram Phoenīciam spectat. Puellam Eurōpam spectat et amat. Deus puellam dēsīderat.

Sed Eurōpa est timida. Ita Iuppiter sē in taurum pulchrum trānsfōrmat. Eurōpa taurum novum diū spectat. Amīcae Eurōpae sunt timidae. Quis est taurus? Taurus cum puellā et amīcīs lūdit. Eurōpa cum taurō lūdit. Nunc taurus nōn est novus; puella nōn est timida. Taurus nunc est amīcus. Taurus puellās in tergō[3] portat. Nunc Eurōpam in tergō portat. Taurus cum puellā in tergō fugitat et puellam ad īnsulam Crētam portat. Deus et puella in īnsulā habitant. Īnsula est in terrā novā. Terra nova nunc est appellāta[4] Eurōpa.

Poēta Ovidius fābulam dē Eurōpā et taurō nārrat.

---

[1] *Agenor* [English pronunciation A.jē.nor], a king of Phoenicia.
[2] *On Mount Olympus.*
[3] *On his back.*
[4] *Is called.*

Verba

NOUNS

amīca	friend (*fem.*)
amīcus	friend (*masc.*)
deus	god
fīlia	daughter
Iuppiter	Jupiter (*king of gods and men*)
Ovidius	Ovid (*the poet*)
poēta	poet
rēx	king
taurus	bull
Tyrus	Tyre

VERBS

amat	loves, likes
dēsīderat	desires
fugitat	flees
lūdit	plays
nārrat	tells
portat	carries
spectat	watches, looks at
trānsfōrmat	transforms, changes

ADJECTIVES

nova	strange, new
timida	shy, timid
Tyria	Tyrian

OTHER WORDS

ad + *acc.*	to, toward, near
cum + *abl.*	with
dē + *abl.*	about, concerning, down from
diū	for a long time, a long while, long
nunc	now
ōlim	once, once upon a time
Quis?	Who?
sē	himself, herself, itself, themselves

Structure

9. Omission of possessive adjective. Though the possessive adjective exists .in Latin, the words for *his*, *her*, *its*, *their* are often omitted when the meaning is clear from the context. Supply the possessive adjective needed in translating into English.

Agēnor est rēx Phoenīciae et   Agenor is the king of Phoenicia
   Eurōpa est **fīlia**.   and Europa is *his daughter*.

10. Word order in transitive sentences. A transitive sentence contains a verb which expresses action carried from the subject to an object: *The poet tells a story*. The word order for a transitive sentence is as follows:

Subject	*Direct Object*	*Verb*
Deus	**Eurōpam**	**amat.**
The god	Europa	loves.

In this sentence, the verb stands last because of its importance in the sentence. Note, however, the following alternatives:

Eurōpam deus amat.   The god loves *Europa*. (*not someone else*)

Amat deus Eurōpam.   The god *loves* Europa.

A change in the word order would make no change in the basic meaning of the sentence, but would change the emphasis, depending on which words stand first and last, the most important positions in the Latin sentence. The word order does not give the meaning; *the endings give the meaning*.

11. The verb: present tense meanings, simple, progressive, emphatic. Each of the verbs in the lesson can have three possible meanings, all contained in the one Latin form:

Poēta fābulam **nārrat**.   The poet *tells* a story. (simple)
                           The poet *is telling* a story. (progressive)
                           The poet *does tell* a story. (emphatic)

Taurus puellam **portat**.   The bull *carries* the maiden. (simple)
                           The bull *is carrying* the maiden. (progressive)
                           The bull *does carry* the maiden. (emphatic)

All present tense verbs, except **est** and **sunt**, can have these three possible English translations.

12. The verb: person and number. You have already learned that final -**t** as a verb ending can mean *he, she, it*. The plural *they* is contained in the Latin ending -**nt**. For all verbs in the lessons so far, except **est** and **sunt**, change the final -**t** to -**nt** to form the plural. These forms are called *third person*, the person spoken of. You will meet the forms for first person (*I-we*), the person speaking, and for second person (*you-you*), the person spoken to, in subsequent lessons.

Singular

amat	he, she, it loves, is loving, does love
portat	he, she, it carries, is carrying, does carry
rēgnat	he, she, it rules, is ruling, does rule
est	he, she, it is
lūdit	he, she, it plays, is playing, does play

Plural

amant	they love, are loving, do love
portant	they carry, are carrying, do carry
rēgnant	they rule, are ruling, do rule
sunt	they are
lūdunt	they play, are playing, do play

13. Genitive case. Possession is shown in Latin by the genitive case. There is no word for *of*. The *of* idea is incorporated into the noun with its genitive endings:[5]

	Singular	*Ending*	*Plural*	*Ending*
Genitive	**puellae**	-ae	**puellārum**	-ārum
	the girl's or		*the girls'* or	
	of the girl		*of the girls*	

Amīca **Eurōpae** est timida.

The friend *of Europa* is shy.
Europa's friend is shy.

Amīcae **poētae** fābulās amant.

The *poet's* friends like his stories.
The friends *of the poet* like his stories.

---

[5] Note that the genitive case can express more than possession. Often its function is to limit or describe another noun; in other words, it also has an adjectival function: John's train was late (i.e., the train he was to board, not his personally owned train).

Est dea **sapientiae**.　　　　She is the goddess *of wisdom*.

Nymphae **silvae** sunt pulchrae.　　The nymphs *of the forest* are beautiful.

Fīliae **amīcārum** sunt timidae.
Poēta **īnsulārum** est fēmina
   Sapphō.

The daughters *of friends* are shy.
The poetess *of the islands* is the
   woman Sappho.

14. Nouns in **-us**. Nouns ending in **-us** in the nominative change to **-um** in the accusative and **-ō** in the ablative case.

    Taurus novus est Iuppiter.
    Puella **taurum novum** spectat.
    Cum taurō lūdit.

    The strange bull is Jupiter.
    The girl looks at *the strange bull.*
    She is playing *with the bull.*

Note that the adjective agrees with the noun it modifies.

15. Preposition **in** with the accusative. The preposition **in** can be followed by either the ablative or the accusative case. If the *ablative* follows, the meaning is *in* or *on*.

    Tyrus est **in Phoenīciā**.
    Tyre is *in Phoenicia.*

If the *accusative* follows, the meaning is *into*.

    Taurus puellam **in terram novam**
      portat.
    The bull carries the maid *into a*
      strange land.

16. Historical present. Many times the present tense is used to tell a story vividly in past time: "Europa lives in Tyre. Jupiter sees the maiden and falls in love with her. He changes himself into a bull and carries off the maiden on his back." Although these events are conceived of as happening long ago, the present tense makes the story more immediate.

Pronunciation Review

The following letters are most likely to cause difficulties in pronunciation. Therefore review the Guide to Pronunciation, pp. xxiii–xxvi, paying particular attention to the following sounds:

VOWELS

    ē   **fēmina**, *woman*
    ī   **īnsula**, *island*
    ae   **terrae**, *lands*

CONSONANTS

c is always hard as in *can*   **amīcus**, *friend*
g is always hard as in *go*   **rēgīna**, *queen*

i is also a consonant pronounced as y in *yet*[6]   **Iuppiter**, *Jupiter*; **iam**, *now*

r is trilled   **nārrat**, *he tells*

s is always hissed as in *sea*   **sunt**, *they are*

t is always as in *tin*, never sh as in *oration*   **portat**, *he carries*

v is always w   **parva**, *small*

ph, **ch**, **th** are almost like p, k, t   **Phoenīciā**, *Phoenicia*;
　　charta, *paper*, *map*
　　theatrum, *theater*

Exercises

I. Answer the following questions in complete Latin sentences, as in Example 1:

　　1. Quis est puella pulchra?　　1. Eurōpa est puella pulchra.
　　2. Ubi habitat Eurōpa?
　　3. Quis est Iuppiter?
　　4. Ubi habitat Iuppiter?
　　5. Quis Eurōpam dēsīderat?
　　6. Quis sē in taurum pulchrum trānsfōrmat?
　　7. Quis cum puellīs lūdit?
　　8. Estne taurus timidus?
　　9. Ubi habitant deus et puella?
　　10. Quis fābulam dē Eurōpā et taurō nārrat?

II. Change each singular to plural:

　　1. Amīca est pulchra.　　1. Amīcae sunt pulchrae.
　　2. Tabula est nova.
　　3. Fīlia est timida.
　　4. Fābula est nova.
　　5. Rēgīna nōn est timida.

III. Change the verbs to plural and translate:

　　1. Puella taurum spectat.　　1. Puellae taurum ＿＿＿＿＿＿＿＿.
　　2. Amīca puellam amat.　　2. Amīcae puellam ＿＿＿＿＿＿＿.
　　3. Poēta fābulam nārrat.　　3. Poētae fābulam ＿＿＿＿＿＿.
　　4. Amīca fugitat.　　4. Amīcae ＿＿＿＿＿＿＿＿＿＿.
　　5. Amīca est timida.　　5. Amīcae ＿＿＿＿＿＿＿ timidae.
　　6. Rēgīna in Graeciā rēgnat.　　6. Rēgīnae in Graeciā ＿＿＿＿＿.
　　7. Deus in Olympō habitat.　　7. Deus et puella in Eurōpā ＿＿＿.
　　8. Puella fābulam dēsīderat.　　8. Puellae fābulam ＿＿＿＿＿＿.
　　9. Fīlia in īnsulā habitat.　　9. Fīliae in īnsulā ＿＿＿＿＿＿.
　　10. Terra nova est pulchra.　　10. Terrae novae ＿＿＿＿＿ pulchrae.

---

[6] Many texts write *i* consonant as *j*, but the *j* did not exist in the ancient Roman alphabet.

IV. Supply the correct form of the genitive case for the noun in the parenthesis:

1. Amīca (*of the queen*) est pulchra.   1. Amīca *rēgīnae* est pulchra.
2. Fīlia (*of the poet*) est parva.
3. Amīcus (*of the girl*) est magnus.
4. Tabula (*of the island*) est parva.
5. Deus (*of the land*) est Iuppiter.

V. Translate into Latin:

1. Once upon a time there was (est) a beautiful girl.
2. Europa lives in Phoenicia.
3. Jupiter desires the beautiful maiden.
4. The god changes himself into a bull.
5. The bull flees with Europa.

VI. Reread the third paragraph of the story aloud, giving the sounds of the long and short vowels carefully.

Etymology

In the following phrases you will find underlined words related to Latin words in the lesson. Find the Latin cognate or source word and give the meanings both of the Latin word and the English derivative; e.g., Jupiter, the Roman sky deity—**deus**, god—any concept of god is called deity.

filial love for a father _____

a poet's fancy _____

amatory poetry _____

desire for the best _____

fugitive dreams _____

to delude oneself_____

a simple narration _____

a portable television _____

making a spectacle of yourself_____

transform the scene _____

a timid animal _____

a novel experience _____

The addition of prepositions as prefixes created many new words from the root or stem **-port-**, both in English and in Latin. We can *import* (carry in), *export* (carry out), *deport* (carry away or down) or *report* (carry back) and *transport* (carry across) goods or ideas.

Minerva and Arachne

Minerva (Athena), goddess of wisdom and war, is also the household deity of spinning and weaving, skills which every Greek maiden and wife once learned and practiced in the home. Ovid's tale of her anger when a mortal, Arachne, rivals her skill, is an example of an aetiological myth, that is one that explains the cause (**aitia**) of a natural phenomenon, the skill of the spider.

Indeed, the Lydian maiden Arachne is a fine weaver, so skillful that she claims that she can weave better than Minerva, the goddess herself. Minerva assumes the form of an old woman and tries to warn the foolish girl against such a display of immoderate false pride (**hubris**), but Arachne, far from acknowledging the goddess as the source of her powers, challenges the goddess to a weaving contest.

Minerva throws off her disguise and orders the looms set up. The goddess weaves into her tapestries the stories about proud mortals who were punished because of their hubris. Impudent Arachne weaves tales about the scandalous behavior of the male gods, another affront. In anger Minerva beats the girl with the shuttle, and Arachne hangs herself on her thread. She becomes smaller and smaller and turns into a spider, weaving eternally.

In zoology the term for spider is *arachnid*.

Dialogue

Salvēte, discipulī!	*Greetings, students!*
Salvē, magister (magistra)!	*Greetings, teacher!* (female teacher)
Valēte!	*Farewell!* (addressing more than one)
Valē!	*Farewell!* (addressing one)

Chapter III
MINERVA ET ARACHNĒ
(Part 1)

Minerva est dea. Est dea sapientiae. Est dea lānae quoque. Arachnē est puella. Est puella perīta in lānā. Pictūrās pulchrās in textilī[1] fōrmat. Minerva cum deīs in Olympō[2] habitat. Arachnē in casā parvā in Lydiā habitat.

Arachnē est superba quod pictūrās pulchrās fōrmat. Saepe nymphae silvae spectant dum puella perīta lānam glomerat et pictūrās in textilī[1] fōrmat. Pictūrae sunt pulchrae. Pictūrae fābulās dē vītā agricolārum et dē vītā incolārum Lydiae nārrant.

Nymphae pictūrās puellae amant et puellam laudant. Deam quoque laudant et clāmant, "Quis est magistra tibi?[3] Certē Minerva pictūrās et fābulās tibi dat. Labōratne Arachnē bene quod est perīta? Puella bene nōn labōrat quod est perīta. Bene labōrat quod Minerva est magistra. Minerva tē bene docet."

---

[1] *Beautiful pictures in weaving, woven tapestries.*
[2] *On Mount Olympus.*
[3] *Your teacher* (lit., *teacher to you*).

Verba

NOUNS

agricola, -ae, *m.*	farmer
Arachnē, *f.*	Arachne (*a maiden*)
casa, -ae, *f.*	house
dea, -ae, *f.*	goddess
discipulī, -ōrum, *m.*	students
incola, -ae, *common* (*c.*)	inhabitant
lāna, -ae, *f.*	wool, spinning
Lydia, -ae, *f.*	Lydia (*a country in Asia Minor*)
magister, -rī, *m.*	teacher (*masc.*)
magistra, -ae, *f.*	teacher (*fem.*)
Minerva, -ae, *f.*	Minerva (*a goddess*)
nympha, -ae, *f.*	nymph
pictūra, -ae, *f.*	picture
sapientia, -ae, *f.*	wisdom
silva, -ae, *f.*	forest
vīta, -ae, *f.*	life

VERBS

clāmat, clāmant	shout, exclaim
dat, dant	give
docet, docent	teach
fōrmat, fōrmant	make, shape, fashion, form
glomerat, glomerant	wind into a ball
labōrat, labōrant	work
laudat, laudant	praise
salvē, salvēte	greetings, hello, Hail
valē, valēte	farewell, goodbye

ADJECTIVES

perīta	skilled, skillful
superba	proud

OTHER WORDS

bene	well
certē	surely, certainly
dum	while
mē	me, myself

quid	what
quod	because
quoque	also
saepe	often
tē (*acc. or abl.*)	you
tibi (*dat.*)	to you, you

Structure

17. Parts of speech. The parts of speech in Latin are as follows: noun, pronoun, adjective, verb, adverb, preposition, conjunction, and interjection. English employs the same parts of speech.

18. Inflection. You have seen how nouns, adjectives, and verbs in Latin change their endings to indicate their use in the sentence.

Puella superba Minervam nōn laudat.	The proud girl does not praise Minerva.
Puellae superbae Minervam nōn laudant.	The proud girls do not praise Minerva.

Puella becomes **puellae** to indicate the plural of the noun. **Superba** becomes **superbae** to agree with its noun. **Laudat** becomes **laudant** in the plural, since the verb must always agree with its subject in number. **Minerva** ends in **-am** to show that it is the direct object. The stem of the word is clearly recognizable to give the meaning of the word, and the ending indicates its use in the sentence. This change of ending is called *inflection*. The inflection of nouns is called *declension*; the inflection of verbs is called *conjugation*.

19. Nouns. As in English, nouns are name words. In Latin they are inflected to show (a) number, (b) gender, and (c) case.

(a) Number (singular or plural) has already been discussed (**Sec. 4**).

> **puella** (*girl*) becomes **puellae** (*girls*) to show plural

(b) Gender (masculine, feminine, or neuter). As in English, nouns are either masculine, feminine, or neuter. Nouns in Latin have both natural and grammatical gender.[4] Natural gender means that nouns referring to males are masculine (**deus, amīcus, agricola**), and nouns

---

[4]We can understand **puella** (*girl*) being feminine, but what logic justifies **fābula** (*story*) or **silva** (*forest*) being feminine? The only parallel in English occurs when we refer to a car or a boat as "she," and thus we can understand the principle of grammatical gender. Learn the gender of each word as it occurs in the vocabulary.

referring to females are feminine (**dea, amīca, nympha**). Grammatical gender means that many nouns which are neuter in English are either masculine or feminine in Latin. **Puella** (*girl*) is, of course, feminine, but so also are **silva** (*forest*), **fabula** (*story*), and almost all of the nouns ending in **-a**. The only exceptions are a few masculine nouns ending in **-a** which demonstrate natural gender (**agricola, poēta, nauta**).

(c) Case (use in the sentence). The names of the cases and their uses follow with the declension of **puella** (**Sec. 21**), the presentation of all the inflected forms.

Case	Use	Example
Nominative	Subject or Predicate Word	The *girl* is *Arachne*.
Genitive	Possession .	The *girl's* house is small.[5]
Dative	Indirect Object	Minerva gives *the girl* pictures.[6]
Accusative	Direct Object	The nymphs watch the *girl*.
Ablative	Object of Preposition	The bull plays *with the girl*.

20. Declension of nouns. There are five declension patterns for nouns in Latin, each with a characteristic vowel.

First	Second	Third	Fourth	Fifth
-a	**-o**	**-i**	**-u**	**-e**

Nouns ending in **-a** belong to the first declension (**fābula, puella**). They are all feminine, except for a few masculines like **agricola**. Most nouns ending in **-us** in the nominative are masculine (**taurus, amīcus, deus**) and belong to the second declension.[7]

21. First declension or **-a** declension.

	Singular	Plural	Endings Singular	Plural
Nominative	**puella**	**puellae**	**-a**	**-ae**
Genitive	**puellae**	**puellārum**	**-ae**	**-ārum**
Dative	**puellae**	**puellīs**	**-ae**	**-īs**
Accusative	**puellam**	**puellās**	**-am**	**-ās**
Ablative	**puellā**	**puellīs**	**-ā**	**-īs**

Henceforth in the vocabulary the nouns will be listed in the nominative

---

[5] Or, the house *of the girl* is small.

[6] Or, Minerva gives pictures *to the girl*. The dative case tells the person *to* or *for* whom something is done. In English the idea can be expressed by a prepositional phrase or by the indirect object preceding the direct, as in the example in the text (see **Sec. 27**).

[7] Later you will meet some nouns in **-us** which belong to the fourth declension.

singular and the genitive singular followed by the gender and the meaning:

silva, silvae, *f. forest*

Practice forming the declension of five nouns from this lesson's vocabulary.

22. Agreement of noun and adjective. The adjective always agrees with the noun which it modifies in *case, number,* and *gender.*

   Est **silva magna** in **īnsulā pulchrā.**   There is a *great forest* on the *beautiful island.*

23. Commands. In the previous lesson **spectāte** (*look at*) was used to express a command. In the dialogue of this lesson appear two more commands, **salvēte** and **valēte,** both ending in **-te,** which is the plural form used in addressing more than one person. Drop the **-te** to form the singular command to address only one individual.

Salvē	*Greetings!* (addressing one) (lit., *be well*)
Salvēte	*Greetings!* (addressing more than one)
Amā	*Love!*
Amāte (*pl.*)	*Love!*
Labōrā	*Work!*
Labōrāte (*pl.*)	*Work!*

Exercises

I. Answer in Latin using complete sentences:

   1. Quis est Minerva?   1. Minerva est dea.
   2. Quis est Arachnē?
   3. Ubi habitat Minerva?
   4. Ubi habitat Arachnē?
   5. Spectantne deae dum Arachnē pictūrās fōrmat?
   6. Spectantne agricolae dum Arachnē pictūrās fōrmat?
   7. Estne Arachnē superba?
   8. Fōrmatne Arachnē pictūrās dē vītā incolārum?
   9. Amantne nymphae pictūrās puellae?
   10. Quid clāmant nymphae?

II. A. Make the following sentences negative:

   1. Arachnē est superba.   1. Arachnē nōn est superba.
   2. Minerva est dea sapientiae.
   3. Arachnē in casā parvā habitat.

4. Arachnē pictūrās pulchrās fōrmat.
5. Nymphae pictūrās spectant.
6. Agricolae pictūrās pulchrās amant.
7. Incolae deam amant.
8. Arachnē fābulās nārrat.
9. Dea hīc habitat.
10. Arachnē deam laudat.

B. Change the number of the subject (and verb) in 5, 6, 7 and 9 in IIA, above.

III. Change the nouns to plural and make the verbs agree.

1. Hīc est magistra.	1. Hīc sunt magistrae.
2. Hīc est fābula.	
3. Hīc est casa parva.	
4. Hīc est puella superba.	
5. Hīc est silva pulchra.	
6. Hīc est nympha perīta.	
7. Hīc est magistra perīta.	
8. Hīc est pictūra puellae.	
9. Hīc est lāna deae.	
10. Hīc est casa pulchra.	

IV. Change each nominative noun and adjective of the first group of sentences into the accusative case, direct object of *spectat.*

1. Puella est superba.	1. Agricola <u>puellam</u> <u>superbam</u> spectat.
2. Pictūra est pulchra.	·2. Agricola _____ _____ spectat.
3. Dea est perīta.	
4. Casa est parva.	
5. Magistra est perīta.	
6. Nympha est pulchra.	
7. Lydia est pulchra.	
8. Silva est magna.	
9. Minerva est superba.	
10. Lāna est parva.	

V. Translate into Latin:

1. Arachne is making beautiful pictures.
2. She is telling stories about the farmers.
3. The nymphs love the stories about Minerva.
4. The stories tell about the life of the inhabitants of Lydia.
5. Minerva is your teacher (**magistra tibi**). She teaches you well.

Etymology

Identify the Latin source for the underlined words, as in the example:
agriculture in the economy—**agricola, -ae**, *m.*, farmer, one who cultivates the fields—field cultivation.

Arachnids are friends!
Christ's disciples
magistrate of the court
a sapient ruler
a sylvan landscape
vital statistics
the docent program at the Museum
a docile animal
formation of rocks
conglomeration of all things (**con** is from **cum**, *with*)
conglomerate stone
laudatory remarks
the chemistry laboratory
the class valedictorian (from **valē**, *farewell*, and **dictum**, *speech*)
expert advice (Note that the prepositional prefix **ex**, *out*, combines with
  perītus, *skilled* or *tried out*: the real source of this word is **expertus**, a form
  of the verb meaning *tried out* or *tested.*)

end of topic 2

Dialogue

Quid est nōmen tibi?

Mihi nōmen est Dominus _____ .

Domina _____ .

Scrībite nōmina hīc, quaesō.

What is your name?

My name is Mr. _____ .

Miss _____ .

Write (your) names here, please.

Chapter IV
MINERVA ET ARACHNĒ
(Part 2)

Sed Arachnē sapientiam nōn habet. Negat Minervam magistram. Puella temerāria sē laudat et clāmat, "Fōrmō pictūrās fābulāsque melius quam Minerva. Nēmō mihi magistra est. Minervam nōn vocō. Nēmō mē docet. Mē doceō."

Dea Minerva fōrmam fēminae simulat et in terrā ambulat. Puellam temerāriam docēre temptat. Dīxit, "Superbia est perīculōsa. Experientia docet." Sed Arachnē iterum affīrmat, "Fōrmō pictūrās melius quam Minerva. Dea dēbet certāre mēcum.[1] Nymphīs pictūrās meās mōnstrāre dēbeō, et dea pictūrās suās mōnstrāre dēbet. Nunc Minervam vocō. Certā mēcum!"

Minerva est īrāta. Sē esse deam mōnstrat. "Arachnē, es stulta. Tē, puella temerāria, docēre temptō," dīxit, "sed es etiam superba. Tē docēre dēbeō. Portāte, nymphae, tēlās hūc, quaesō."

---

[1] **Mēcum—cum mē.** The preposition **cum** with a pronoun object is attached to the pronoun with the order reversed.

Verba

NOUNS

domina, -ae, *f.*	lady, mistress, miss, ms.
dominus, -ī, *m.*	lord, master, mister
experientia, -ae, *f.*	experience
fēmina, -ae, *f.*	woman
fōrma. -ae, *f.*	form, shape
nōmen (nōmina, *pl.*)	name
superbia, -ae, *f.*	pride
tēla, -ae, *f.*	loom

VERBS

affīrmō, -āre, -āvī, -ātum	affirm
ambulō, -āre, -āvī, -ātum	walk
certō, -āre, -āvī, -ātum	contend, vie with, struggle
dēbeō, -ēre, -uī, -itum	ought, owe
dīxit	he, she, it said
doceō, -ēre, -uī, doctum	teach
esse	to be
habeō, -ēre, -uī, -itum	have, hold
mōnstrō, -āre, -āvī, -ātum	show
negō, -āre, -āvī, -ātum	deny
quaesō	please (*lit.*, I ask)
respondeō, -ēre, respondī, -sum	reply, respond, answer
scrībite (*pl.*)	write (*command*)
simulō, -āre, -āvī, -ātum	imitate, copy, pretend, take the form of
temptō, -āre, -āvī, -ātum	try, attempt
vocō, -āre, -āvī, -ātum	call, summon

ADJECTIVES

īrāta	angry, irate
mea	my
perīculōsa	dangerous
stulta	stupid, foolish
sua	his own, her own, its own, their own
temerāria	rash

OTHER WORDS

etiam	still, yet
hūc	to this place, here
iterum	again
melius quam	better than
mihi (*dat.*)	to me
nēmō	no one
-que (*attached to last of two correlative words*)	and

Structure

24. Infinitive. The infinitive of most verbs ends in **-re**. The meaning is usually *to* do something: *to carry, to love, to praise*.

amāre	to love		**dēbēre**	to owe
laudāre	to praise		**docēre**	to teach
vocāre	to call		**habēre**	to have

These verbs which end in **-āre** belong to the *First Conjugation.*[2]

These verbs which end in **-ēre** belong to the *Second Conjugation.*[2]

A. Complementary infinitive. One of the most common uses of the infinitive is to *complete* the meaning of a verb of desire or obligation, a use called "complementary."

Ambulāre dēsīderō.	I desire *to walk*.
Deam **vocāre** dēbeō.	I ought *to call* the goddess.

B. Stem. The stem of the verb is formed by dropping the **-re** of the infinitive.

First Conjugation	*Second Conjugation*
vocā-re	**docē-re**
ā REMEMBER THIS VOWEL	**ē**

The personal endings are added to this stem.

25. Personal endings. Present tense indicative. The indicative mood is the mood or manner of normal communication.

---

[2] There are four conjugations in Latin, each characterized by a different vowel preceding the **re** ending: First **-ā-**, Second **-ē-**, Third **-e-**, and Fourth **-ī-**. We are here concerned only with the first two conjugations.

Person	First Conjugation	Second Conjugation

Singular

1 **vocō**[3] I call, am calling, do call   **doceō**[3] I teach, am teaching, do teach

2 **vocās** you call, are calling, do call   **docēs** you teach, are teaching, do teach

3 **vocat** he, she, it calls, is calling, does call   **docet** he, she, it teaches, is teaching, does teach

Plural

1 **vocāmus** we call, are calling, do call   **docēmus** we teach, are teaching, do teach

2 **vocātis** you call, are calling, do call   **docētis** you teach, are teaching, do teach

3 **vocant** they call, are calling, do call   **docent** they teach, are teaching, do teach

PERSONAL ENDINGS

	Singular		Plural	
1st person is the *person speaking*	I	**-ō**	we	**-mus**
2nd person is the *person spoken to*	you	**-s**	you	**-tis**
3rd person is the *person spoken of*	he, she, it	**-t**	they	**-nt**

Memorize these endings. They are added to each verb stem to indicate person and number. Note that the vowel is short before final **-t** and **-nt**.

Conjugate **amō**, **amāre** (*love*); **spectō**, **spectāre** (*watch*); **respondeō**, **respondēre** (*reply*). Give three possible English translations—simple, progressive, and emphatic—for each form.

26. The linking verb **sum, esse.** The intransitive (having no object) verb *to be* is irregular in most languages, and Latin is no exception.

sum	I am	**sumus**	we are
es	you are	**estis**	you are
est	he, she, it is	**sunt**	they are

The infinitive of **sum** is **esse**, *to be*.
Do not confuse **sum**, meaning *I am*, with the progressive form of the verb: **vocō** can mean *I am calling*.

27. Indirect object, dative case. The indirect object of the verb is the person *to whom* or *for whom* something is done. The indirect object is in the *dative case.*

---

[3] In the first conjugation the two vowels **-aō** merge into **-ō**. In the second conjugation both the vowels appear—**-eō**.

Minerva **puellae** sapientiam dat.

Minerva gives *the girl* wisdom. (*or*)
Minerva gives wisdom *to the girl.*

Nymphīs pictūrās meās mōnstrāre dēbeō.

I ought to show *the nymphs* my pictures. (*or*)
I ought to show my pictures *to the nymphs.*

In English we can expand the indirect object into a prepositional phrase introduced by *to.* In Latin the dative case alone indicates indirect object, and a prepositional phrase is never used.

28. Ablative case. The ablative case is used as object of certain prepositions. The vocabulary will always tell which case the preposition governs:

> **in Lydiā** *in Lydia*
> **dē vītā** *about the life*
> **cum puellā** *with the girl*
> but: **mēcum** *with me*

Cum with a pronoun object is reversed in order and the two words are joined together.

29. Imperative mood. Mood in grammar means manner of expression. So far all of the statements in the book have been in the normal, *indicative* mood, but commands are given in a different tone, in the *imperative* mood.[4] You are already familiar with the forms **spectāte, salvēte,** and **valēte.** These are imperative plural forms. The singular imperative looks like the stem of the verb. The plural imperative adds **-te** (See **Sec. 23**).

Singular

Portā tēlās. *Carry the looms.* (addressing one)
Docē mē. *Teach me.*

Plural

Portāte tēlās. *Carry the looms* (addressing more than one)
Docēte mē. *Teach me.*

30. Vocative case. The person addressed is in the vocative[5] case. The vocative looks just like the nominative and therefore is not listed separately. It usually stands after the first word in the sentence.

Tē, **puella temerāria**, docēre temptō.

Rash girl, I am trying to teach you.

Portāte, **nymphae**, tēlās hūc.

Nymphs, carry the looms here.

Salvēte, **discipulī**.

Greetings, *students.*

---

[4] From **imperāre**, *to command.*

[5] From **vocāre**, *to call.*

31. Enclitic **-que**. The enclitic **-que** is another means of expressing *and*. It is attached to the end of the second of two correlative words: nouns, verbs, or adjectives.

Nymphae puellae**que** pictūrās spectant.	The nymphs *and* the maidens look at the pictures.
Puella sē laudat clāmat**que**, "Mē doceō."	The girl praises herself *and* cries, "I teach myself."
Dea pulchra superba**que**, in terrā ambulat.	The goddess, beautiful *and* proud, walks on earth.

32. Principal parts of verbs. The vocabulary will now list four principal parts for most verbs: the first person singular of the present tense, the infinitive, and two other forms that you will eventually need for later reading (the first person singular of the perfect tense and the perfect passive participle). Learning all the forms now will save having to retrace your steps later:

	Present 1st Sing.	*Infinitive*	*Perfect 1st Sing.*	*Perfect Passive Part*
First Conjugation	**portō**	**portāre**	**portāvī**	**portātum**[6]
Second Conjugation	**habeō**	**habēre**	**habuī**	**habitum**

Almost all first conjugation verbs follow the pattern of **portō**. Many second conjugation verbs follow the pattern of **habeō**, but some differ slightly.

Exercises

I. Answer the following questions in complete Latin sentences:

1. Habetne Arachnē sapientiam?
2. Laudatne Arachnē deam?
3. Quid Arachnē clāmat?
4. Simulatne Minerva fōrmam fēminae?
5. Ubi Minerva ambulat?
6. Temptatne Minerva puellam docēre?
7. Estne experientia magistra bona?
8. Quid dīxit Arachnē Minervae?
9. Estne Minerva īrāta?
10. Quid dīxit Minerva nymphīs?

II A. Conjugate **habitāre**, **portāre**, **dare**,[7] **spectāre**, **habēre** and **dēbēre** in the present tense.

B. Give the principal parts for **vocō, habitō, clāmō, dēbeō, respondeō**.

---

[6]The fourth principal part is given in the neuter (**-um**) to avoid limiting the participle to either masculine or feminine gender.

[7]The present tense of **dare** has short -a throughout: **dō, das, dat, damus, datis, dant**.

III A. Translate into English, giving all three translations—simple, progressive, and emphatic—wherever possible:

1. Portāmus, portās, portō, portant.
2. Laudat, laudant, laudō, laudāmus.
3. Fōrmat, fōrmāmus, fōrmātis, fōrmās.
4. Sumus, estis, est, sum, sunt, es.
5. Amās, amant, amat, amāmus, amātis.
6. Datis, dant, damus, das, dō, dat.
7. Habeō, habēmus, habent, habēs.
8. Negō, negāmus, negant, negātis.
9. Clāmant, clāmāmus, clāmās, clāmat.
10. Docet, docent, doceō, docētis.

B. Supply the correct form of the complementary infinitive and translate:

1. (*To teach*) dēsīderō.
2. Dea fōrmam fēminae (*to take*) temptat.
3. Arachnē cum deā (*to contend*) nōn dēbet.
4. (*To reply*) dēbēmus.
5. Dea Minerva puellam superbam (*to teach*) dēbet.

This infinitive is called *complementary* because it *completes* the meaning of the verb.

C. Translate into Latin:

1. They love, he is carrying, we are praising, we are, you (sing.) do teach.
2. They are, they are carrying, you (pl.) have, you (pl.) are having.
3. He is, he is shouting, I have, I am having, I am, they are giving.
4. She does love, we are teaching, we are having, do they love, we ought.
5. You (sing.) deny, they are working, we praise, he is forming, it is.

IV A. Supply the correct form of the dative case for each indirect object and translate the sentence:

1. Minerva (*to the girl*) sapientiam dat.
2. Puella (*to the goddess*) pictūram dat.
3. Nymphae (*to Minerva*) tēlās dant.
4. Quis est magistra (*to you*)?
5. Agricola (*to the woman*) terram dat.
6. Dea (*to the farmers*) terram dat.
7. Nympha (*to the women*) fābulam nārrat.
8. Agricolae (*to the land*) nōmen dant.
9. Dea (*to the inhabitants*) Lydiae casās dat.
10. Magistra (*to the girl*) lānam dat.

IV B. Supply the correct form of the ablative case after each preposition
and translate the phrase:

1. in (*the house*)   **in casā**   in the house
2. dē (*the life*)
3. cum (*Minerva*)
4. in (*Lydia*)
5. dē (*the pictures*)
6. dē (*the farmers*)
7. in (*the shape*)
8. dē (*the earth*)
9. cum (*the nymph*)
10. in (*earth*)

V.   Translate into Latin:

1. The house is small, but it is pretty.
2. The girls are angry about the story.
3. The stories are new.
4. We are telling tales to the little girls.
5. Minerva walks on earth in the form of a woman.
6. "No one is my teacher; I teach myself," said Arachne.
7. The goddess is trying to teach the rash girl.
8. Experience teaches.
9. The goddess ought to show her pictures to me.
10. Minerva ought to teach the girl.
11. We ought to give houses to the inhabitants of Lydia.
12. Give me wisdom, goddess.
13. What is your name, little girl?
14. Work with me, farmers.

VI.   Referring to the "Guide to Pronunciation," found in the Introduction, pronounce the following words giving the long and short vowels
their accurate sounds:

casa	**vocāre**
est	**fēmina**
incola	**vīta**
agricola	**nōn**
ambulō	**pictūra**

Practice these words with diphthongs:

laudat
quaesō
paene

Etymology

Latin is the basis for the later Romance (from Roman) languages which developed in Italy, Spain, Portugal,[8] France and Romania. Latin has also contributed thousands of words to English, both directly and through French influence (See Introduction, concerning the history of the English language). Study the following table:

Latin	Italian	French	Spanish	Romanian	English
deus	dio	dieu	dios	dumnezeu	deity
filius	figlio	fils	hijo	fiu	filial
magister	maestro	maître	maestro	maestru	master
		magister			magistrate
experientia	esperienza	experience	experiencia	experienţa	experience
fēmina	femmina	femme	hembra	femeia	female
					feminine
casa	casa	case	casa	casa	———
amīcus	amico	ami	amigo	amicul	amicable
vīta	vita	vie	vida	viaţa	vital
nomen	nome	nom	nombre	nume	name
villa	villa	villa	villa	villa	villa

In the column of English words, notice that the cognate is usually a literary word, sometimes a different part of speech, while the familiar, colloquial word is one derived from Germanic: *God* is related to **Gott**, *friend* to **Freund**, *house* to **Haus**, but *deity* comes from **deus**, and *amicable* comes from **amīcus**.

Monstrance, monster, and *demonstrate* all come from the basic meaning of *show* or *point out* in the verb **mōnstrō, mōnstrāre**. The *monstrance* in the Church is the shown sacred image; the *monster* is the oddity in nature which is pointed out; and *to demonstrate* is to point out or show.

The student of Latin can automatically enlarge his English vocabulary by becoming aware of the manner in which both languages form words from a root by adding a prefix and/or a suffix:

Prefix		*Root*		*Suffix*
in	-	**vocā**	-	tion
(*in*)		(*call*)		(a noun)

---

[8] Portuguese equivalents: deus, filho, maestro, experiência, fémea, casa, amigo, vida, nome, vila.

The root gives the basic meaning, usually from a verb stem, and its meaning remains constant. The prefix alters or varies the meaning while the suffix generally indicates the part of speech. By learning the meanings of the prefixes, roots, and suffixes, one can add innumerable words to his vocabulary:

voc- (*call*)

advocate	to call to someone's attention
avocation	something that calls one from his vocation or job (calling)
convocation	a calling together
evoke	to call forth
evocation	the act of calling forth
evocable	able to be called forth
invoke	to call on someone
invocation	the act of calling on someone
provoke	to call forth, summon, excite, incite, stir up
provocation	act of inciting
provocative	tending to provoke or stimulate
revoke	to call back
vocal	sounded (from **vōx, vōcis**, *voice*)
vocabulary	from **vocābulārium**, *a collection of names*, from **vocābulum**, *a name*, from **vocāre**, *to call*
vocalist	a singer (from **vōx, vōcis**)
vocation	a calling, a job
vocative	the case of the person called or addressed

The basic meanings of the prefixes will be studied in subsequent lessons,[9] but for now note the following:

ad-	to, toward
a-(ab)	away, away from
e-(ex)	out of *or* merely intensifying
de-	down from *or* merely intensifying
in-	in, on, into
con-/co-/com- (from **cum**)	with
pro-	forth, in front of
re-	back, again
sub-	under
trans-	across

The suffix *-ion* (invocation) indicates a noun; the suffix *-ive* (provocative) usually indicates an adjective. The suffixes *-or* and *-ist* generally indicate the person performing an act.

---

[9] Consult the drawings in Chapter XX, Etymology, for a helpful memory chart.

Dialogue

Respondē Latīnē, quaesō.	*Answer in Latin, please.*
(**Respondēte,** *pl.*)	
Bene!	*Good! Well* (done)!
Optimē!	*Very good! Excellent!*

Chapter V
MINERVA ET ARACHNĒ
(Part 3)

Minerva et Arachnē bene labōrābant. Prīmō Minerva lānam glomerābat. Fōrmābat pictūrās pulchrās dē factīs bonīs deōrum.[1] Pictūrae fābulās dē vītā deōrum in Olympō nārrant. Deinde Arachnē lānam glomerābat. Sed Arachnē pictūrās dē factīs malīs deōrum fōrmābat. Certē pictūrae deae erant pulchrae; pictūrae puellae quoque erant pulchrae.

Agricolae et nymphae et incolae Lydiae spectābant dum puella et dea labōrābant. Nymphae pictūrās et fābulās puellae amābant; maximē amābant fābulam longam dē rapīnā Eurōpae ā Iove.[2] Sed Minerva erat maximē īrāta neque amābat fābulās dē factīs malīs deōrum.

Itaque dea Minerva puellam in arāneam mūtat. Prīmō puella erat parva; deinde erat minor; dēnique erat minima. Arachnē sē necāre temptat, et in fīlō[3] pendet. Sed Minerva misericordiam habet, et puellam sē necāre prohibet. "Pendē aeternō," dīxit. Ita dea puellam docet et arānea aeternō in fīlō suō pendet.

Poēta Ovidius fābulam dē puellā superbā nārrat.

---

[1] *Of the gods.*

[2] **Iove** is the ablative of **Iūppiter.** What English expression comes from **ā Iove**?

[3] *On a string or cord.*

Verba

NOUNS

arānea, -ae, *f.*	spider
factīs (*abl. pl.*)	deeds
Iūppiter, Iove (*abl.*)	Jupiter, Jove
misericordia, -ae, *f.*	pity
rapīna, -ae, *f.*	carrying off, robbery

VERBS

mūtō, -āre, -āvī, -ātum	change
necō, -āre, -āvī, -ātum	kill
pendeō, -ēre, pependī	hang
prohibeō, -ēre, -hibuī, -hibitum	prevent, stop, prohibit

ADJECTIVES

bona	good
longa	long
mala	evil, bad
minima	very small, very little
minor	smaller
optima	very good, excellent
suō	its

OTHER WORDS

ā (**ab**, *before a vowel*)	by, from, away from
aeternō	eternally, forever
bene	well
deinde[4]	then
dēnique[4]	and then, finally
itaque	and so, and thus
Latīnē	in Latin
maximē	very, exceedingly; yes indeed, especially
minimē	least; not in the least, not at all
neque	and not
optimē	very good, excellent
prīmō	first, at first

---

[4] **Prīmo, deinde,** and **dēnique** (**deinde,** + **-que,** *and*) constitute transition words to signal stages in narration. They will help you to understand the plot as a story develops.

Structure

33. Imperfect tense, first and second conjugations. The imperfect tense, expressing past time, is formed by inserting the tense sign **-bā** between the stem and the personal endings of the verb. The only exception is the first person singular in **-m** instead of **-ō**. This **-m** appears also in **sum**.[5]

First Conjugation

vocābam	I called, was calling, did call
vocābās	you called, were calling, did call
vocābat	he, she, it called, was calling, did call
vocābāmus	we called, were calling, did call
vocābātis	you (*pl.*) called, were calling, did call
vocābant	they called, were calling, did call

Second Conjugation

docēbam	I taught, was teaching, did teach
docēbās	you taught, were teaching, did teach
docēbat	he, she, it taught, was teaching, did teach
docēbāmus	we taught, were teaching, did teach
docēbātis	you (*pl.*) taught, were teaching, did teach
docēbant	they taught, were teaching, did teach

Notice that the long vowel is shortened before final **-m**, **-t**, and **-nt**. The further English translations for the imperfect tense serve to show the incomplete (hence "imperfect") or repeated or customary action of the verb in past time: "I used to call, I kept on calling, I would call (daily), I was accustomed to call." The imperfect tense is also used for simple descriptions in a narrative in past time—"The girl was rash; the house was small; she lived in Lydia; the goddess was angry." The action continues from past tense and is incomplete (still true) as of the present story-telling time. The emphatic *did call* translation is necessary for phrasing questions:

Vocābatne Arachnē Minervam? *Did* Arachne *call* Minerva?

34. **Maximē** and **minimē**. A statement may be intensified by **maximē**, *very much so*, or **minimē**, *not in the least*. Sometimes the adverbs alone or with only the verb constitute an affirmative or negative reply, especially in questions, conversation, or in dialogue in a play.

---

[5] This is the same **-m** that appears in **eram** and in other tenses that you will learn later.

| Nymphae fābulam longam | The nymphs liked the long story |
| **maximē** amābant. | *very much indeed.* |

| Habetne Arachnē sapientiam? | Has Arachne wisdom? (Is she wise?) |
| Sapientiam **minimē** habet. (or) **Minimē**. | She has *very little wisdom.* (or) *Not in the least.* |

35. Imperfect tense of **sum, esse**. The stem for the imperfect tense of **sum** is **era-**. The personal endings are added to this stem.

eram	I was	**erāmus**	we were
erās	you were	**erātis**	you were
erat	he, she, it was	**erant**	they were

36. Further uses of the dative case.

A. Dative of possession. The dative is used to indicate the owner or possessor of someone or something. This use is restricted to sentences employing a form of the linking verb **sum**:

| Sapientia est **tibi**. | *You have* wisdom. (*lit.*, Wisdom is *to you.*) You are wise. |
| **Mihi** sunt magis quam **tibi**. | *I have* more than *you have.* (*lit.*, *To me* are more than *to you.*) |

B. Dative of interest.[6] The dative is also used to indicate the person interested in or affected by the action or event described in the rest of the sentence:

Mihi filius est Marcus.	*My* son is Mark. (*lit.*, The son *to me* is Mark.)
Quid est nōmen **tibi**?	What is *your* name? (*lit.*, What is the name *to you*?)
Nēmō **mihi** magistra est.	No one is *my* teacher.
Mihi nōmen est Marcus.	*My* name is Mark.

Exercises

I. Respondēte Latinē, quaesō. (Answer in Latin, please.)

1. Quis lānam glomerābat primō?
2. Fōrmābatne Minerva pictūrās dē factīs malīs deōrum?
3. Suntne pictūrae pulchrae?
4. Quis deinde lānam glomerābat?

---

[6] This use of the dative is sometimes called dative of reference.

5. Fōrmābatne Arachnē pictūrās dē factīs malīs deōrum?
6. Amābantne nymphae fābulam dē Eurōpā et Iove?
7. Amābatne Minerva fābulam et pictūrās dē Eurōpā et Iove?
8. Mōnstratne Arachnē nymphīs pictūrās suās?
9. Quid Arachnē temptat?
10. Quis fābulam dē Minervā et puellā superbā nārrat?

II A. Complete each verb form in the present tense and translate:

    1. (I) mōnstrā-   **mōnstrō**   I show, am showing, do show
    2. (we) fōrmā-
    3. (she) nārrā-
    4. (you, *pl.*) docē-
    5. (they) da-
    6. (you, sing) temptā-
    7. (he) spectā-
    8. (you, *pl.*) es-
    9. (they) portā-
    10. (we) dēbē-

  B. Change each verb above to the imperfect tense and translate:

    1. mōnstrābam   I was showing, showed, did show

  C. Make each verb above into a question: e.g., **mōnstrābamne?** Was I showing?

III. Change each imperative singular to imperative plural. Remember to make the vocative (person addressed) plural also.

    1. Portā, puella, tēlam hūc, quaesō.   1. Portāte, puellae, . . .
    2. Nārrā, poēta, fābulam, quaesō.
    3. Respondē, magistra, Latīnē, quaesō.
    4. Salvē, dea!
    5. Valē, nympha pulchra!

IV. Change each noun to the case required as object of **spectābam** and make any other necessary changes to make the predicate word agree with the noun it modifies:

    1. Terra erat magna.   1. Spectābam <u>terram magnam.</u>
    2. Dea erat pulchra.   2. Spectābam _____ .
    3. Pictūra erat magna.
    4. Amīca erat bona.
    5. Nymphae silvae erant pulchrae. (Cavē![7])
    6. Minerva erat dea.
    7. Casa erat parva.

---

[7] **Cavē** is the imperative singular of **caveō, cavēre,** *beware.*

8. Puellae erant bonae.
9. Amīcae erant bonae.
10. Magistra erat perīta.

V. Translate into Latin:

1. The pictures about the goddess were beautiful.
2. The girls love beautiful stories.
3. The poet Ovid tells about the goddess and the maiden.
4. Arachne also tells stories about the goddess.
5. The rash girl was proud.
6. Minerva was angry because Arachne told stories about the wicked deeds of the gods.
7. The stories of the poet were long.
8. "I am trying to teach you," said Minerva.
9. Minerva changes the form of the proud girl.
10. Arachne is now a spider and hangs on her thread forever.

VI. Referring to the Guide to Pronunciation, divide each word into syllables. Where does the accent or stress in all two syllable words fall?

casa	laudant	parva	dīxit
bona	spectant	vocant	portō
longa	silva	fōrma	stulta
minor	nympha	terra	Iove
mūtō	pulchra	mea	prīmō

What is the name of the last syllable? It comes from the Latin word **ultimus** meaning *last*.

What is the name of the next to the last syllable? It comes from **paene**, meaning *almost*, and **ultimus**.

Etymology

Explain the meaning of the underlined words in the following phrases by indicating the Latin source word or words:

mutation of genes
impending doom (*in-* changes to *im-* for euphony. Euphony is a word of Greek origin: **eu**, *good, well*; **phony**, *sound*)
prohibit smoking
internecine war (**inter** means *between*)
an optimistic view
malicious gossip
   malpractice is dangerous
   malevolent person (*volent* is from **volens**, *wishing*)

<u>minimum</u> requirements
sent to the <u>minor</u> league
<u>eternal</u> fire from heaven
put forth <u>maximum</u> effort
<u>prime</u> beef, <u>prime</u> rib

*   *   *   *   *

Notice that many first declension nouns in **-ia** appear in English with a
-y ending:

Germānia	Germany	**familia**	family
Ītalia	Italy	**gloria**	glory
Sicilia	Sicily	**memoria**	memory
Britannia	Britanny	**victōria**	victory
historia	history		

Many nouns merely drop the final **-a**: poet(a); form(a); nymph(a);
music(a); urn(a).

Some nouns change the final **-a** to an unsounded *-e* in English:

fāma	fame	**Eurōpa**	Europe
fortūna	fortune	**causa**	cause
pictūra	picture	**statua**	statue
natūra	nature		

Latona and Niobe

Another tale of false pride and boasting (the Greek **hubris**) that causes much grief to a mortal is the story of Niobe, who brags of her good fortune in having seven sons and seven daughters whereas the goddess Latona (whose worship Niobe disparages) has only two offspring, the twin gods of the sun and moon, Apollo and Diana. As in the tale of Arachne, the offended deity, in the form of an old woman, gives a warning, but the foolish mortal only continues her boasting and mocks the goddess, who then reveals herself and her power. Latona summons her two children and instructs each to kill the offspring of Niobe. With deadly arrows, Apollo slays the seven sons and Diana the seven daughters, even though the now humbled Niobe pleads for the life of her smallest daughter. Weeping, the once obdurate Niobe turns to stone—a transformation appropriate to her "hard" line. Even today, tears trickle from the stone.

The dying agonies of the children of Niobe (Niobids) provided ancient artists with challenging subject matter. Perhaps the most famous example was the sculpture at Pergamum.

Learning Numbers

Cardinal Numbers

1	**ūnus**	4	**quattuor**	7	**septem**	10	**decem**
2	**duo**	5	**quīnque**	8	**octō**	11	**ūndecim**
3	**trēs**	6	**sex**	9	**novem**	12	**duodecim**

How many English derivatives can you make from these words?

Chapter VI
LĀTŌNA ET NIOBĒ
(Part 1)

Poēta Ovidius fābulam dē deā Lātōnā et dē fēminā Niobē nārrat. Niobē, rēgīna Thēbārum, erat superba. Erat superba quod septem fīliōs et septem fīliās habēbat. Sē et līberōs suōs laudābat. "Causa superbiae meae nōn est potentia familiae et amīcōrum, sed fāma līberōrum meōrum."

Dea Lātōna quoque līberōs clārōs habēbat. Fīlius erat deus Phoebus Apollō et fīlia erat dea Diāna.

Mantō erat fēmina oppidī Thēbārum. Mantō multam sapientiam habēbat. In viīs oppidī ambulābat et monēbat fēminās ita: "Date dona Lātōnae et līberīs quoque Lātōnae, Phoebō et Diānae. Lātōna est dea fēminārum." Itaque fēminae Thēbārum āram deae in templō ōrnant; ibi dōna deīs deābusque[1] dant et tūra[2] sanctīs flammīs dant.

Ecce Niobē pulchra et superba cum fēminīs in viā oppidī ambulābat. Stat et oculīs superbīs[3] circumspectat; fēminās Thēbārum vocat et clāmat: "Cūr Lātōnam ōrātis? Nēmō mē ōrat. Sum fīlia avōrum clārōrum.[4] Sum rēgīna rēgiae Cadmī.[5] Pulchra sum, digna deae. Sed maximē beāta sum quod septem puerōs et septem fīliās habeō. Rogāte nunc causam superbiae meae. Cūr Lātōna mē praestat? Lātōna ūnum fīlium et ūnam fīliam sōlum habet. Fortūna mihi septem dabat. Fēminae, ōrāte mē, nōn Lātōnam. Date dōna mihi, nōn Lātōnae."

Itaque fēminae Thēbārum dōna rēgīnae superbae, nōn Lātōnae dabant.

---

[1] *And to the goddesses.* **Fīlia** and **dea** have irregular forms in the dative and ablative plural: **fīliābus** and **deābus**, to differentiate them from **fīliīs** and **deīs**, the masculine equivalents.

[2] *Incense, frankincense.*

[3] *With proud eyes.*

[4] *Of famous grandfathers.* Niobe's grandfathers were Atlas and Jupiter.

[5] Cadmus was the founder of Thebes, capital of Boeotia in Greece. Thus he was the builder of the palace.

Verba

NOUNS

āra, -ae, *f.*	altar
causa, -ae, *f.*	cause, reason
Diāna, -ae, *f.*	Diana (*goddess of moon, hunt*)
dōnum, -ī, *n.*	gift
fāma, -ae, *f.*	reputation, report, fame
familia, -ae, *f.*	family
fīlius, -iī, *m.*	son
flamma, -ae, *f.*	flame
fortūna, -ae, *f.*	fortune
Graecia, -ae, *f.*	Greece
Lātōna, -ae, *f.*	Latona (*mother of Apollo and Diana*)
līberī, -ōrum, *m. pl.*	children
Mantō, *f.*	Manto (*a wise woman*)
Niobē, *f.*	Niobe (*a queen*)
oculus, -ī, *m.*	eye
oppidum, -ī, *n.*	town
Phoebus, -ī, *m.*	Phoebus Apollo
potentia, -ae, *f.*	power
puer, -erī, *m.*	boy
rēgia, -ae, *f.*	palace
superbia, -ae, *f.*	pride
templum, -ī, *n.*	temple
Thēbae, -ārum, *f. pl.*	Thebes (*the city*)
via, -ae, *f.*	street, road

VERBS

circumspectō, -āre, -āvī, -ātum	look about, cast a glance
moneō, -ēre, -uī, -itum	warn, advise
ōrnō, -āre, -āvī, -ātum	decorate, adorn
ōrō, -āre, -āvī, -ātum	pray to, beg, implore
praestō, -āre, -āvī, -ātum	stand before, surpass
rogō, -āre, -āvī, -ātum	ask
stō, -āre, stetī	stand

ADJECTIVES

beātus, -a, -um	happy, blessed
clārus, -a, -um	famous, illustrious, bright, shining, clear

dignus, -a, -um + *abl.* or *gen.*	worthy, worth
multus, -a, -um	much, many (*pl.*)
sānctus, -a, -um	sacred
septem (*indeclinable*)	seven
ūnus, -a, -um	one, only

OTHER WORDS

cūr	why
ecce	behold
ibi	there
sōlum	only

Structure

37. Second declension of nouns. The second declension contains *masculine* nouns in **-us** and **-er**, and *neuter* nouns in **-um**. Study the following declension patterns:

Masculine **-us**: *Masculine* **-er**: *Neuter* **-um**:

		Endings			Endings
Nom.	amīcus	-us (er)	puer	templum	-um
Gen.	amīcī	-ī	puerī	templī	-ī
Dat.	amīcō	-ō	puerō	templō	-ō
Acc.	amīcum	-um	puerum	templum	-um
Abl.	amīcō	-ō	puerō	templō	-ō
Nom.	amīcī	-ī	puerī	templa	-a
Gen.	amīcōrum	-ōrum	puerōrum	templōrum	-ōrum
Dat.	amīcīs	-īs	puerīs	templīs	-īs
Acc.	amīcōs	-ōs	puerōs	templa	-a
Abl.	amīcīs	-īs	puerīs	templīs	-īs

Note that the neuter nominative and accusative are alike in the singular (**-um**) and in the plural (**-a**).

38. Agreement of adjectives. You remember that the adjective agrees with the noun it modifies in case, number, and gender. The regular second declension adjective endings are just like the noun endings of the

masculine **amīcus** and the neuter **templum**. Note the following combinations:

	Singular	*Plural*	
Nom.	**amīcus bonus**	**amīcī bonī**	Second Declension Masculine
Acc.	**amīcum bonum**	**amīcōs bonōs**	
Nom.	**amīca bona**	**amīcae bonae**	First Declension Feminine
Acc.	**amīcam bonam**	**amīcās bonās**	
Nom.	**dōnum bonum**	**dōna bona**	Second Declension Neuter
Acc.	**dōnum bonum**	**dōna bona**	

Note, however, the   **puer bonus**   **puerī bonī**
   combination: **puerum bonum**   **puerōs bonōs**

The adjective must agree with its noun in case, number and gender, but does not always have the same ending, as in **puer bonus**.

39. Cardinal numbers. The cardinal numbers are as follows:

ūnus, duo, trēs, quattuor, quīnque, sex, septem, octō, novem, decem, ūndecim, duodecim.

They are indeclinable except for **ūnus**, *one*, **duo**, *two*, and **trēs**, *three*, and they precede the words they modify: **ūnam fīliam, septem fīliōs**.

The most familiar Roman numerals are:

I	V	X	L	C	D	M
1	5	10	50	100	500	1000

Subtracted elements precede and added elements follow the letter:

XL (40), LX (60), LXXIX (79), MCMLXXV (1975)

40. Adjectives with masculine nouns in the first declension. There are only a few nouns in the first (or **-a**) declension which are masculine by natural gender: **agricola** (*farmer*), **nauta** (*sailor*), **pīrāta** (*pirate*), *and* **poēta** (*poet*).[6] *All other first declension nouns are feminine.* These masculine nouns in an otherwise feminine declension are a source of confusion only when they are modified by adjectives, for if the rule about the agreement of adjectives holds (and it does), the adjectives modifying these masculine **-a** nouns must have masculine **-us** endings, as in these examples:

poēta clārus	**pīrāta malus**	**agricolae multī**
a famous poet	a bad pirate	many farmers

---

[6]**Advena** (*stranger*) and **incola** (*inhabitant*) are common (*c.*) in gender; **poēta** may be.

Exercises

I. Respondēte Latīnē, quaesō.

1. Habetne Niobē septem fīliōs?
2. Habetne Lātōna septem fīliōs? duōs fīliōs? ūnum fīlium?
3. Habetne Lātōna septem fīliās? duās fīliās? ūnam fīliam?
4. Quid est nōmen fīliae Lātōnae? (What case is **fīliae**?)
5. Quid est nōmen fīliō Lātōnae?
6. Eratne Niobē superba?
7. Cūr erat Niobē superba?
8. Dantne fēminae dōna Lātōnae?
9. Ubi ambulābat Niobē?
10. Quid dīxit Niobē fēminīs Thēbārum? Niobē dīxit ita: "..."

II. Decline the following nouns:

via	flamma	fāma
oculus	fīlius[7]	līberī (*only in the plural*)
puer	dōnum	Phoebus (*only in the singular*)
templum	fīlia	causa

III A. Change each third person singular into third person plural and translate:

1. temptat	11. circumspectat
2. ambulat	12. habet
3. mūtat	13. docet
4. dat	14. ōrnat
5. glomerat	15. stat
6. est	16. negat
7. dēbet	17. ōrat
8. certat	18. praestat
9. mōnstrat	19. clāmat
10. simulat	20. habitat

B. Change each verb above to imperfect tense, third person singular and translate:

1. **temptābat**—he tried, was trying, did try

C. Translate into Latin:

1. I was carrying	5. you (*sing.*) are
2. he changed	6. they gave
3. we told	7. we are living
4. they were	8. you (*pl.*) walked

---

[7]The genitive singular of second declension nouns in **-ius** and **-ium** keeps both i's: **fīliī**, although originally Latin combined the two into one: **fīlī**.

9. I am having
10. they are decorating
11. do we pray?
12. he was changing
13. she is looking about
14. they were having

15. did we show?
16. he ought to decorate
17. we ought to give
18. I taught
19. they tried to walk
20. it was

IV A. Drill in declensions. Translate: **Niobē habēbat**:

1. one son
2. two sons (**duōs fīliōs**)
3. three sons (**trēs fīliōs**)
4. four sons
5. five sons
6. six sons
7. seven sons

1. one daughter
2. two daughters (**duās fīliās**)
3. three daughters (**trēs fīliās**)
4. four daughters
5. five daughters
6. six daughters
7. seven daughters

B. Decline: **fīlius bonus   fortūna bona   templum magnum**

V.   Translate into Latin:

1. Diana was the daughter of Latona.
2. Niobe had seven daughters.
3. Niobe also had seven sons.
4. Phoebus was the son of Latona.
5. Niobe was proud because she had seven sons and seven daughters.
6. Latona had only one son and one daughter.
7. Latona was irate because Niobe refused (**negāre**) to give gifts to Phoebus and Diana.
8. Niobe said, "Women of Thebes, worship me; give gifts to me, not to Latona."
9. Niobe said, "Fortune is good to me."
10. Behold, Niobe is queen in the palace of Cadmus.

VI.   Divide the following words into syllables:

amīcus   rēgīna   Lātōna
potentia   fortūna   superbia

What is the name of the syllable before the penult? It comes from the word **ante** (*before*) and penult.

Etymology

From which words in the lesson do the underlined words derive their meaning? Give the Latin word, its meaning and the meaning of the English word:

working for a good <u>cause</u>
a generous <u>donation</u>
a <u>famous</u> ballplayer
an <u>infamous</u> wretch (*in-* has a meaning of *not* in both English and Latin)
a <u>familiar</u> quotation
<u>flammable</u> material
<u>inflammable</u>; <u>inflammatory</u> language (the *in-* here merely intensifies the
   meaning)
the arrival of a foreign <u>potentate</u>
<u>regal</u> splendor
Do not <u>deviate</u> from the rule!
<u>puerile</u> behavior
an examination by a competent <u>oculist</u>

*   *   *   *   *

From the Latin **via**, many English words originate: *via*, itself meaning
"by the road of . . ."—We came *via* Niagara Falls; *viaduct*, the road that
leads from one place to another; *deviate*, to go from the general path (*devia-
tion*, the noun and *devious*, an adjective which means both winding from the
straight path and going astray, erring); *voyage* (derived from French);
previous, going before (*pre-* means *before*); *impervious*, not going through
(*im-* is *in-* meaning *not*, changed for euphony, and *per* means *through*).

Many verbs come into English almost identical in form to the Latin verb
with the personal ending dropped or changed to a mute *-e*. Give the English
verb for each of the words below and give the noun meaning the "act of . . ."
by adding *-ion* or *-tion*, except for **respondeō**.

	English Verb	English Noun
accūsō		
adōrō		
cōnfirmō		
(in) habitō		
exspectō		
prohibeō		
respondeō		
occupō		
labōrō		
temptō		
fōrmō		

Some first declension nouns in **-ntia** appear in English ending in *-ce*
meaning the *state of* or the *quality of* or *result of*. What are the English
equivalents of: **experientia, potentia, patientia, scientia, violentia**?

Dialogue

Quot discipulī sunt in scholā Latīnā hodiē?

How many students are in Latin class today?

Sunt trīgintā trēs discipulī in scholā Latīnā hodiē.

There are thirty-three students in Latin class today.

Chapter VII
LĀTŌNA ET NIOBĒ
(Part 2)

Dea Lātōna erat maximē īrāta. Līberōs, Phoebum et Diānam, convocat et longam fābulam dē fēminā superbā nārrat. Dīxit ita māter: "Populus templum meum nōn honōrat. Factum populī est profānum.[1] Ō Phoebe et Diāna, līberī meī, iuvāte mē!"

Deinde Phoebus dīxit: "Satis! Longa querella est mora poenae." Tum celeriter Diāna et Phoebus per aëra ad rēgiam rēgīnae volant.

Campus plānus erat prope moenia rēgiae. Hīc, dum fīliī rēgīnae equōs suōs exercent, Phoebus septem fīliōs necat. Puerōs sagittīs necat. Fāma factī malī et lacrimae amīcōrum rēgīnae fābulam ruīnae nārrant. "Ō Lātōna," dīxit Niobē, "septem fūnera habeō, sed etiam mihi sunt[2] magis quam tibi. Etiam septem fīliās habeō."

Nunc Lātōna erat iterum īrāta. Fīliam Diānam vocat, "Iuvā mē, Diāna!" dīxit Lātōna. Et Diāna sex fīliās necat. Nunc Niobē potentiam Lātōnae videt. Niobē lacrimīs multīs vītam ūltimae fīliae rogat. "Relinque ūnam minimamque," clamat. Sed Diāna ūltimam fīliam quoque sagittā necat. Dum Niobē lacrimat, in statuam congelat; etiam nunc lacrimae mānant.[3]

---

[1] **Profānum** comes from **pro**, *before, outside of*, and **fānum**, *temple*; therefore, *not of the temple, not sacred*, and hence, *wicked, profane*.

[2] *I have* (lit., *there are to me*).

[3] *Flow*, from **mānō, -āre**; not to be confused with **maneō, -ēre**, *stay, remain*.

Verba

NOUNS

aëra, *m. (Greek acc. sing.)*	air
campus, -ī, *m.*	field
equus, -ī, *m.*	horse
fūnera, *n. pl.*	funerals
lacrima, -ae, *f.*	tear
māter, *f.*	mother
moenia, -ium, *n. pl.*	walls, fortifications
mora, -ae, *f.*	delay
poena, -ae, *f.*	punishment
populus, -ī, *m.*	people
querella, -ae, *f.*	complaint
ruīna, -ae, *f.*	ruin, disaster
sagitta, -ae, *f.*	arrow
schola, -ae, *f.*	school, class
statua, -ae, *f.*	statue
verbum, -ī, *n.*	word

VERBS

congelō, -āre, -āvī, -ātum	freeze, stiffen, congeal
convocō, -āre, -āvī, -ātum	call together, summon
exerceō, -ēre, -uī, -itum	train, exercise
honōrō, -āre, -āvī, -ātum	honor
iuvō, -āre, iūvī, iūtum	help, aid
lacrimō, -āre, -āvī, -ātum	cry, weep
relinquō, -ere, relīquī, relictum	leave, leave behind
rogō, -āre, -āvī, -ātum	ask, beg for
volō, -āre, -āvī, -ātum	fly

ADJECTIVES

meus, -a, -um	my
plānus, -a, -um	equal, level, even, flat
profānus, -a, -um	wicked, evil
ūltimus, -a, -um	last

OTHER WORDS

ad + *acc.*	to, toward, near
celeriter	quickly

hodiē	today
magis	more
ō	o, oh
per + *acc.*	through
prope + *acc.*	near, close to
quot, *indecl.*	how many, how much
quam	than
satis	enough
tum	then
ubi	when, while, where

Structure

41. First and second declension adjectives:

	Singular			Plural		
	M.	*F.*	*N.*	*M.*	*F.*	*N.*
Nom.	**bonus**	**bona**	**bonum**	**bonī**	**bonae**	**bona**
Gen.	**bonī**	**bonae**	**bonī**	**bonōrum**	**bonārum**	**bonōrum**
Dat.	**bonō**	**bonae**	**bonō**	**bonīs**	**bonīs**	**bonīs**
Acc.	**bonum**	**bonam**	**bonum**	**bonōs**	**bonās**	**bona**
Abl.	**bonō**	**bonā**	**bonō**	**bonīs**	**bonīs**	**bonīs**

Since the adjective agrees with its noun in any gender, number, or case, all of the above forms must be memorized.

42. Ablative of means. The ablative case is used not only as the object of certain prepositions (**in viā, dē puellā**), but it is used also *without a preposition* to indicate the means or instrument by which something is done.

Phoebus fīliōs **sagittīs** necat.	Phoebus kills the sons *with* (*his*) *arrows.* (*by means of*)
Niobē **lacrimīs** vītam fīliae rogat.	Niobe begs for the life of (her) daughter *with tears.* (*by means of*)

43. Irregular vocative in **-e**. Almost all vocative forms are identical with the nominative forms, and are not listed separately. The only exception occurs in the masculine singular of second declension nouns ending in **-us**. Here the form ends in **-e**, instead of **-us**.

Ō **Phoebe**, ō **Diāna**, iuvāte mē.   Oh *Phoebus*, oh *Diana*, help me.

44. Accusative case with prepositions. There are some prepositions which govern the accusative case; that is, the object of the preposition is in the accusative.

ad rēgiam	to the palace
per aëra	through the air
prope moenia	near the walls
in silvam[4]	into the forest

45. Verb compounds. Many verbs are formed from a single base root with various prefixes, usually prepositions, e.g., from **vocō** (*call*):

advocō	call to, summon, invite
convocō	call together, convoke, assemble
dēvocō	call off, call away, call down
ēvocō	call out, evoke
invocō	call upon, invoke
prōvocō	call forth, summon

Once you recognize the process by which compound verbs are formed, you can add many new words to your vocabulary in both Latin and English. When you meet the combination of prefix and root verb in a single word, attempt to work out a meaning with the best idiomatic English equivalent to fit the context; e.g., **praestat**, *stands before, surpasses, outranks*, and **circumspectat**, *looks around*.

Exercises

I.   Respondēte Latīnē, quaesō.

1. Habēsne casam pulchram?   1. Ita, casam pulchram habeō.
2. Habēsne vītam bonam?
3. Habēsne equum bonum? currum automātum (*automobile*) bonum?
4. Habēsne amīcum bonum?
5. Habēmusne oppidum pulchrum?
6. Habetne Phoebus sagittās?
7. Habēsne sagittās?
8. Habēsne experientiam bonam in scholā?
9. Habēsne lacrimās?
10. Habēsne septem filiās?

II.   Decline the following adjectives like **bonus, bona, bonum**:

1. parvus	3. meus	5. prīmus
2. longus	4. ūltimus	6. multus (What does the plural mean?)

---

[4]Note that **in** (*in, on*) also governs the ablative case, indicating place where (see **Sec. 15**).

III A. Change the singular forms of each case to the plural:

1. *Nom.* vīta bona—vītae 2. amīcus fāmōsus 3. dōnum sacrum
   bonae

Gen. vītae bonae	amīcī fāmōsī	dōnī sacrī
Dat. vītae bonae	amīcō fāmōsō	dōnō sacrō
Acc. vītam bonam	amīcum fāmōsum	dōnum sacrum
Abl. vītā bonā	amīcō fāmōsō	dōnō sacrō

B. Supply the correct case of the noun required and translate (omitting the possessive adjective):

1. Phoebus et Diāna līberōs (*by means of their arrows*) necābant.
2. Lātōna fēminīs (*with proud words*) dīxit.
3. Poēta līberōs (*by means of a story*) docet.
4. (*By her tears*) Lātōna poenam fēminae superbae rogat.
5. (*With her eyes*) Niobē vītam ūltimae fīliae ōrat.
6. Niobē (*with proud eyes*) circumspectat.

C. Supply the correct form of the vocative caṣe:

1. Vocāte, (*women*), fīliōs.
2. Exercēte, (*boys*), equōs in campō.
3. Iuvā mē, Ō (*Phoebus*)!
4. Ō (*people*), spectā ruīnam meam.
5. Honōrā, (*my daughter*), deōs.

IV. Change each imperative singular to the corresponding plural and make the vocative nouns plural also. Then translate:

1. Ōrā deīs, puella superba.   1. Ōrāte deīs, puellae superbae.
2. Dā, fēmina superba, dōna deīs. (The imperative plural of **dā** has a short vowel in the stem.)
3. Spectā, amīce, ruīnam meam.
4. Rogā, agricola, vītam longam.
5. Ōrā, popule, dōnum sapientiae.
6. Dā, rēgīna, equōs incolīs Thēbārum.
7. Stā hīc, nympha pulchra, mēcum.

V. Translate into Latin, omitting the possessive adjectives:

1. Latona summoned (called together) her children, Phoebus and Diana.
2. He said (**dīxit**), "You ought to kill the sons and daughters of the proud woman."
3. Phoebus killed the seven sons with his arrows.
4. Diana killed six daughters with her arrows.

5. Niobe begged for the life of her last daughter.
6. She tried to prevent the evil deed.
7. But Latona was still irate.
8. Diana killed the last daughter.
9. While Niobe weeps, she stiffens (**congelat**).
10. Even now she is weeping.

VI.   Divide the following words into syllables:

	Antepenult	*Penult*	*Ultima*
1. fāmōsus	fā	mō	sus
2. pictūra			
3. puella			
4. laudāre			
5. amāmus			
6. portātis			
7. Lātōna			

Where does the accent fall in each of these words, as you have heard them pronounced?

Etymology

From the word **verbum** (*word*) English derives *verb*, the word which gives the important meaning of the sentence, and *verbal*, meaning communicating by means of words, the spoken language. Also related are *verbiage*, the use of many words, wordiness; *verbose*, abounding in words; *adverb*, the part of speech that stands near (**ad**) the verb; *verbatim*, word for word; *proverb* (from **proverbium**, a word spoken beforehand), a wise saying; and *reverberate*, to sound again (*re-* means back or again).

What is an *equestrian* statue? What is a *lacrimose* farewell?

From **mater** and **pater** English derives its words *maternity* and *paternity*. What is a *paternity* suit? The adjectives *maternal* and *paternal* identify grandparents. In the same manner *matrilineal* and *patrilineal* identify genealogical lines. But there is only one *alma mater*! (**Alma** means *loving* or *fostering*.)

What is a *moratorium*?

What is a *subpoena* to appear in court? (**sub** means *under*)

What is a *querulous* old man

What happens to blood when it *congeals*?

What are *lacrimal* glands?

How can one *relinquish* animosity?

Do you approve of the way in which police *interrogate* suspects? (**Inter** means *between* or *among*.)

What are *ultimate* rites? What syllable is the *ultima*?

The infinitive of the verb **volāre** gives its name to a very popular Italian song, "Volare," which became a favorite American song also. The opening lines are directly from Latin:

> **Volāre** (*to fly*)—oh—oh
> **Cantāre** (*to sing*)—oh, oh, oh, oh—

*   *   *   *   *

Roman numerals began as ideograms with the fingers (**digitus, -ī,** *m.*) used as counters. One held up one finger for one, two fingers for two, three fingers for three, four fingers for four, and the thumb crossing over perhaps was an early form of five (⊞). Then the **V** made by the thumb and little finger when the hand is fully extended wide probably is the source for **V** meaning five. There is a theory that the **X** for ten is two **V**'s, one on top of the other upside down. The **C** for one hundred stands for the indeclinable **centum,** and **M** for one thousand stands for **mīlle, mīlia.** Until the second century A.D., however, one thousand was written **CIↃ** (**D** for 500 represents the right half of this symbol).

The cardinal numbers (**ūnus, duo, trēs, quattuor, quīnque, sex, septem, octō, novem, decem**) are so called because they are the important form of the numbers on which the other forms pivot, and the word *cardinal* comes from **cardō, cardinis,** *a hinge.* The Roman Catholic cardinal is so called because of the importance of his office, but the bird of the same name is so called because of the color of his feathers, the same as that of the garb of the ecclesiastical official.

Pan and Syrinx

The story of the Pipes of Pan is another aetiological myth explaining the musical instrument from the transformation of the nymph Syrinx into reeds by her companion nymphs when the embrace of the satyr Pan became too ardent. The story is one of many involving the pursuit of the female by the male, in this instance the sexually aroused male Pan, whose goat heels identify him with Kinsey's "prancing, leering" animal. The tale is made more romantic by Pan's further use of the maiden whom he cannot embrace in her human form. He binds together the reeds of unequal length, when, as he breathes over them, he finds that they give off the sound of a complaint. Using wax as the adhesive material, he forms the **fistula** or the pipes of Pan which later evolved into the shepherd's pipe, a single or double shaft with holes to provide the corresponding notes of the scale made by the "unequal" length of the reeds.

Learning Numbers

Cardinal Numbers (20–1,000)

20	vīgintī	30	trīgintā	80	octōgintā
21	vīgintī ūnus *or*	40	quadrāgintā	90	nōnāgintā
	ūnus et vīgintī	50	quīnquāgintā	100	centum
22	vīgintī duo	60	sexāgintā	1,000	mīlle, mīlia (*pl.*)
29	ūndētrīgintā	70	septuāgintā		

Except for **mīlle, mīlia**, these numbers are indeclinable.[1]

Chapter VIII
PĀN ET SYRINGA

Ōlim erat nympha pulchra. Nōmen nymphae erat Syringa. In Arcadiā habitābat. Centum deī et satyrī Syringam amābant, sed Syringa eōs nōn amābat. Quamquam Syringa nymphās cēterās et deam Diānam amābat, tamen deōs satyrōsque fugitābat. Sē in silvā umbrōsā et dēnsā cēlābat.

Syringa dīxit, "Diānae vītam meam dēvovēbō. Nūllus vir, nūllus deus mē habēbit."

Deus Pan autem, dum in silvā errat, Syringam videt et statim eam amat. Pān dīxit, "Aeternum tē amābō." Syringa autem dīxit, "Aeternum nympha Diānae erō."

Deinde nympha misera trāns agrōs et per silvās celeriter fugitat dōnec rīpam undārum spectat. Undae fugam prohibēbant. Syringa auxilium nymphās sīc ōrat, "Fōrmam meam mūtāte, nymphae benīgnae." Nymphae eam in papyrōs in rīpā mūtant.

Pān autem putat sē Syringam in bracchiīs tenēre;[2] in bracchiīs nōn eam sed papyrōs habēbat. Dum miser Pān suspīrat trāns papyrōs, papyrī sonum querellae dant. Dēnique Pān dīxit, "Tēcum concilium habēbō. Syringa manēbit." Et cērā septem papyrōs coniungit.[3] Ita Pān fistulam fōrmat, et fistulae nōmen[4] Syringam dat.

---

[1] **Ūnus, duo,** and **trēs** in compound numbers may be declined.
[2] *But Pan thinks that he holds (is holding) Syrinx in his arms.*
[3] *He joins together.*
[4] Accusative, *the name Syrinx.*

Verba

NOUNS

ager, agrī, *m.*	field
auxilium, -iī, *n.*	aid, help
brācchium, -iī, *n.*	arm, limb
cēra, -ae, *f.*	wax
concilium, -iī, *n.*	union
fistula, -ae, *f.*	reed pipe, pipes of Pan
fuga, -ae, *f.*	flight
Pān, *m.*	Pan (*a forest divinity, satyr*)
papyrus, -ī, *f.*	papyrus, reed
rīpa, -ae, *f.*	bank (*of a river*)
satyrus, -ī, *m.*	satyr
sonus, -ī, *m.*	sound
Syringa, -ae, *f.*	Syrinx (*a nymph*)
unda, -ae, *f.*	wave, water, stream
vir, virī, *m.*	man

VERBS

cēlō, -āre, -āvī, -ātum	hide, conceal
dēvoveō, -ēre, -vōvī, -vōtum	devote
errō, -āre, -āvī, -ātum	wander
fugitō, -āre, -āvī, -ātum	flee, avoid, shun
maneō, -ēre, mansī	remain, stay
putō, -āre, -āvī, -ātum	think
suspīrō, -āre, -āvī, -ātum	breathe
teneō, -ēre, -uī, tentum	hold, keep, possess, have
videō, -ēre, vīdī, vīsum	see

ADJECTIVES

benīgnus, -a, -um	kind
cēterus, -a, -um	other, rest of
dēnsus, -a, -um	thick, dense
miser, -era, -erum	wretched, unhappy, miserable
nūllus, -a, -um	no, none
umbrōsus, -a, -um	shady

OTHER WORDS

aeternum	forever

autem (*postpositive*[5])	but, however
dōnec	until, up to the time when
eam (*acc.*)	her
eōs (*acc.*)	them
ōlim	once, once upon a time, formerly
quamquam	although
sīc	thus
statim	immediately
tamen	nevertheless
trāns + *acc.*	across

Structure

46. Future tense, indicative. The future tense is formed by inserting the tense sign **-bi** between the stem and the personal endings of the verb. The characteristic **-ā** of the stem is retained before the tense sign in the first conjugation, the **-ē** in the second conjugation.

First Conjugation		*Second Conjugation*	
vocābō	I shall call	**docēbō**	I shall teach
vocābis	you will call	**docēbis**	you will teach
vocābit	he, she, it will call	**docēbit**	he, she, it will teach
vocābimus	we shall call	**docēbimus**	we shall teach
vocābitis	you will call	**docēbitis**	you will teach
vocābunt	they will call	**docēbunt**	they will teach

N.B. In the first person singular the **-bi** becomes **-bō**.
In the third person plural the **-bi** becomes **-bu**.

47. Two adjectives modifying a single noun. Two adjectives modifying a single noun are usually translated without the "and" conjunction, although **et** connects them in Latin.

in silvā dēnsā **et** umbrōsā   in a dense, shady forest

48. **Tēcum, mēcum.** When the preposition **cum** (*with*) is used with pronoun objects **tē** and **mē** (*you, me*), the preposition is attached to the end of the pronoun.

		Note also the plurals:	
tēcum	with you	**nōbīscum**	with us
mēcum	with me	**vōbīscum**[6]	with you (*pl.*)

---

[5] *Postpositive* means that a word cannot stand first in its clause; these words usually stand second (in an "after" position).

[6] **Dominus vōbīscum.** *The Lord be with you.*

49. Second declension nouns in **-er** and **-ir**. You have already learned that there are a few masculine nouns in the second declension which end in **-er** in the nominative singular. Some like **puer** keep the **-e** throughout the declension; some, however, like **ager** drop the **-e** after the nominative form. The endings are regular in all other cases. **Vir** is the only noun in **-ir**.

	Singular			Plural		
Nom.	puer	ager	vir	puerī	agrī	virī
Gen.	puerī	agrī	virī	puerōrum	agrōrum	virōrum
Dat.	puerō	agrō	virō	puerīs	agrīs	virīs
Acc.	puerum	agrum	virum	puerōs	agrōs	virōs
Abl.	puerō	agrō	virō	puerīs	agrīs	virīs

50. Adjectives in **-er**: **miser** and **pulcher**. The adjective **miser, misera, miserum** differs from adjectives like **pulcher, pulchra, pulchrum** in that **miser** keeps the **-e** in the stem while **pulcher** drops it after the nominative singular masculine. Both declensions are regular thereafter.

Singular

M.	F.	N.	M.	F.	N.
miser	misera	miserum	pulcher	pulchra	pulchrum
miserī	miserae	miserī	pulchrī	pulchrae	pulchrī
miserō	miserae	miserō	pulchrō	pulchrae	pulchrō
miserum	miseram	miserum	pulchrum	pulchram	pulchrum
miserō	miserā	miserō	pulchrō	pulchrā	pulchrō

Plural
Both plurals are regular

The adjective **miser** is declined like the noun **puer**. Retain the **-e**	The adjective **pulcher** is declined like the noun **ager**. Drop the **-e**

51. Future tense of **sum**. The stem for the future is **eri-**

erō	I shall be	**erimus**	we shall be
eris	you will be	**eritis**	you will be
erit	he, she, it will be	**erunt**	they will be

52. Word order, adjectives. Adjectives denoting *size*, *quantity* and *number* generally precede the nouns they modify.

Rēgīna in **magnā** rēgiā habitat.	The queen lives in a *large* palace.
Quīnque equōs in campō vidēbat.	He saw *five* horses on the plain.

Exercises

I. Respondēte Latīnē, quaesō.

1. Quis erat Syringa?
2. Amābatne Syringa virōs et deōs?
3. Ubi Syringa sē cēlat?
4. Quis maximē Syringam amābat?
5. Quid Syringae dīxit Pān?
6. Quid fugam Syringae prohibēbat?
7. Quis fōrmam Syringae mūtat?
8. Quid Pān in bracchiīs habēbat?
9. Quid Pān ita fōrmat?
10. Quid est nōmen septem papyrīs?

II. Decline these nouns with their adjectives:

1. ager plānus   3. vir bonus   5. puer parvus
2. nympha pulchra   4. deus miser

III A. Conjugate in the future tense:

1. vocāre   3. esse   5. dare (*stem vowel is short*)   7. vidēre
2. habēre   4. laudāre 6. stāre

B. Change each verb to the corresponding plural and translate:

1. fugitābit   fugitābunt   *they will flee*
2. eris
3. manēbit
4. habēbō
5. dabit
6. amābit
7. cēlābis
8. mūtābis
9. dēvovēbō
10. vidēbō

IV. Count by tens to one hundred. Count backwards by tens. Supply the accusative plural form of the noun in parentheses to be the direct object of **videō**, as in Example 1:

1. Videō vīgintī (equus).   1. Videō vīgintī equōs.
2. Videō trīgintā (puer).
3. Videō quadrāgintā (papyrus).
4. Videō quīnquāgintā (ager).
5. Videō sexāgintā (satyrus).
6. Videō octōgintā (nympha).

7. Videō nōnāgintā (casa).
8. Videō centum (līberī).[7]
9. Videō decem (magistra).
10. Videō septuāgintā[8] (vir).

V. Translate the following sentences:

1. Syrinx, a beautiful nymph, lived in Arcadia.
2. She did not love the gods and satyrs; she loved only the other nymphs and the goddess Diana.
3. "No man shall have me," she said. "I shall love only Diana."
4. Pan loved Syrinx and said, "I shall love you forever."
5. Syrinx flees through the woods and the fields.
6. Pan holds the reeds in his arms.
7. While he breathes over the reeds, the papyri give (off) the sound of a complaint.
8. Pan binds together (**coniungit**) the reeds with wax.
9. Thus he will have Syrinx forever.
10. Pan forms the pipes and gives to the pipes the name Syrinx.

VI. Divide into syllables and mark the accent on the following words of more than two syllabes:

amābat	**umbrōsa**
vidēbant	**fugitābit**
Diāna	**habēbō**

Notice that in each word the penult contains a long vowel. The accent always falls on the penult if its vowel is long.

Etymology

The words *culture* and *cultivate* come from a form of the verb **colō, -ere, coluī, cultum** which means *cultivate, till the soil,* or *worship.* Compounded with **agrī** (*field*), the word gives us **agricola** (*farmer*) in Latin and *agriculture* in English. Sociologically the word is very interesting for what it tells us about the mystery and importance of the fertility of the soil, a matter of life and death to a farming community whose goddesses of fertility (Juno, Ceres, Proserpina, Diana) all were worshipped and cultivated. How fascinating that the verb for "cultivate or till a field" is the same as the verb for "worship"! Our English word *cult,* the worship of a god or hero, is derived from this same root.

---

[7] Who had a hundred children?
[8] What does "Septuagint" refer to as a Biblical term?

Identify the Latin word in the lesson from which the underlined words in the following phrases are derived. Give the Latin word, the meaning in English and the meaning of the English word, as in the example:

an <u>auxiliary</u> verb—**auxilium**, **-iī**, *n.* (*help, aid*)—a helping verb in a verb
phrase (*have* seen)
<u>reconciliation</u> with my wife
a <u>virile</u> person
tender <u>devotion</u>
<u>error</u> in one's ways
the <u>video</u> on my television
a <u>benign</u> tumour
a <u>miserable</u> existence

*   *   *   *   *

The ending **-ōsus** in Latin means *full of* and was often attached to a noun. **perīculum** (*danger*) became **perīculōsus** (*dangerous*); **umbra** (*shade*) became **umbrōsus** (*shady*); **lacrima** (*tear*) became **lacrimōsus** (*full of tears*); **herba** (*grass*) became **herbōsus** (*grassy*); **fōrma** (*shape*) became **fōrmōsus** (*shapely, beautiful*). *Formosa* in China has this name. What is *umbrage* in English? What is *umbra* in astronomy? What is the *penumbra*?

Some Latin nouns of the second declension come into English with the **-us** ending dropped—e.g., satyr(us) and digit(us)—but many come directly into English intact: *alumnus, campus, locus, circus, papyrus, terminus, mucus* (*mucous* in English), *radius, tumulus, stimulus, virus*. Some of these words form their plurals from their plurals in Latin: *alumni, papyri, stimuli*; but the more common plural is the plural ending in *-es*: *campuses, circuses, viruses*.

Callisto

Of all the myths, the story of Callisto seems the most unfair: the mortal suffering for the indiscretion of the god. The final metamorphosis, however, raising the nymph to a place of honor in the sky along with her son, does compensate for the suffering on earth. This aetiological myth accounting for the Big and Little Dipper is the story of the lovely nymph Callisto whom Jupiter loved and approached in the form of Diana, so as not to alarm the maiden. When the embrace became rather ardent, the poor nymph realized that her companion was not her goddess leader but a male. Months later when her pregnant condition became known, poor Callisto was driven from the band of Diana's nymphs; and after the birth of a son, Arcas, Juno, jealous of her rival, determined to change the beautiful features that had attracted her husband. She cast the nymph to the ground and caused shaggy black hair to grow all over her and gave her a growl for a voice. Now poor Callisto wanders in the woods afraid of the wild beasts, herself a wild animal.

Arcas grown to young manhood and now a hunter comes upon the bear one day in the woods and the mother tries to communicate with her son, but to no avail. Arcas is about to shoot the **ursa** when Jupiter, moved by the impending tragedy, changes Arcas also into a bear and flings both mother and son into the heavens, the two constellations Ursa Major and Ursa Minor.

Dialogue

Quot pāginās spectāvimus?	How many pages have we looked at?
Ūndēseptuāgintā pāginās spectāvimus.	We have looked at sixty-nine pages.
Septuāgintā quīnque pāginās spectāvimus.	We have looked at seventy-five pages.

Chapter IX
CALLISTŌ (Part 1)

Saepe poētae Mūsās[1] invocant dum fābulās nārrant. "Nārrā, ō Mūsa, fābulam dē nymphā Callistō et dē fīliō eius, Arcade."

"Spectāte stellās in caelō," dīxit Mūsa. "Ecce septem stellae, Ursa Maior, et quoque septem stellae, Ursa Minor. Ursa Maior est Callistō, et Ursa Minor est Arcas, fīlius eius. Propter īram rēgīnae deōrum, Iuppiter nympham et fīlium eius in stellās in caelō trānsfōrmāvit."

Callistō erat nympha cuius fōrma erat pulchra. In Arcadiā habitābat. Dum Iuppiter silvās et agrōs in Arcadiā, terrā deō cārā, cūrat, nympham pulchram fōrmōsamque spectāvit et statim eam amāvit. Certē Callistō erat fōrmōsa. Fībula vestīmentum retinēbat et vitta neglectōs capillōs retinēbat.[2] Callistō per silvās cum Diānā et cēterīs nymphīs errābat. Iaculum et sagittās portābat.

Ōlim Callistō sōla erat et in somnō in terrā herbōsā iacēbat; Iuppiter eam vīdit. Nympha erat deō grāta. "Certē Iūnō mē hīc nōn vidēbit," dīxit, "aut sī videt, sunt dēlectāmenta pretiōsa sed digna pretiī." Statim Iuppiter fōrmam Diānae simulāvit et ita ad nympham sēcrētō appropinquāvit. Ita Iuppiter victor erat; Callistō autem, nympha misera, silvās nōtās et amīcās nōtās et deam Diānam ēvītāvit.

---

[1]The Muses were nine goddess of poetry, music and the liberal arts. For their names see the Appendix.

[2]*A band held back her careless locks* (lit., *neglected hair*). **capillus, -ī,** *m., hair.*

Verba

NOUNS

Arcadia, -ae, *f.*	Arcadia (*a region of the Peloponnesus, dear to Jupiter*)
Arcas, Arcadis, *m.*	Arcas (*son of Callisto*)
caelum, -ī, *n.*	sky, the heavens
Callistō, *f.*	Callisto (*a nymph*)
dēlectāmentum, -ī, *n.*	delight
fībula, -ae, *f.*	pin
iaculum, -ī, *n.*	javelin
īra, -ae, *f.*	wrath
Iūnō, *f.*	Juno (*queen of the gods*)
Mūsa, -ae, *f.*	Muse
pretium, -iī, *n.*	price, reward
somnus, -ī, *m.*	sleep
in somnō	asleep
stella, -ae, *f.*	star
ursa, -ae, *f.*	bear
Ursa Maior	Greater Bear
Ursa Minor	Smaller Bear
vestīmentum, -ī, *n.*	garment, clothes
vīctor, vīctōris, *m.*	victor
vitta, -ae, *f.*	fillet, band

VERBS

appropinquō, -āre, -āvī, -ātum	approach
cūrō, -āre, -āvī, -ātum	care for
ēvītō, -āre, -āvī, -ātum	avoid, shun
iaceō, -ēre, -uī	lie (*at rest*)
invocō, -āre, -āvī, -ātum	invoke
retineō, -ēre, -uī, -tentum	keep, hold back, restrain

ADJECTIVES

cārus, -a, -um + *dat.*	dear (*to*)
formōsus, -a, -um	beautiful, shapely
grātus, -a, -um + *dat.*	pleasing (*to*)
herbōsus, -a, -um	grassy
neglectus, -a, -um	neglected
nōtus, -a, -um	familiar, well-known
pretiōsus, -a, -um	costly
sōlus, -a, -um	alone, lone, only

OTHER WORDS

aut	or
cuius	whose (*sing.*)
eius[3]	his, her, its
propter + *acc.*	on account of, because of
sēcrētō	secretly
sī	if

Structure

53. Perfect tense: indicative forms. To form the perfect tense, you must use the third principal part of the verb, the perfect, first person singular. This third principal part appears with each verb listed in the vocabulary.

Present Tense (*1st Per. Sing.*)	*Infinitive*	*Perfect Tense* (*1st Per. Sing.*)
vocō	**vocāre**	**vocāvī**

Using the perfect form (**vocāvī**), drop the **-ī** to obtain the perfect stem and add these personal endings:

	Singular			*Plural*	
-ī	I		**-imus**	we
-istī	you		**-istis**	you
-it	he, she, it		**-ērunt**	they

Perfect Tense of **vocāre**

vocāvī	I called, have called, did call
vocāvistī	you called, have called, did call
vocāvit	he, she, it called, has called, did call
vocāvimus	we called, have called, did call
vocāvistis	you called, have called, did call
vocāvērunt	they called, have called, did call

Observe the following pattern for first conjugation verbs:

laudō, laudāre, laudāvī
nārrō, nārrāre, nārrāvī
amō, amāre, amāvī

Almost all first conjugation verbs follow this pattern.[4]
Memorize the principal parts, the endings, and the meanings in English.

---

[3] See Sec. **58** and **88**.
[4] Three important exceptions are:
 dō, dare, dedī, datum, *give*
 stō, stāre, stetī, *stand*
 iuvō, iuvāre, iūvī, iūtum, *help, aid.*

54. Perfect tense: meanings. The perfect tense refers to time already past, not to continuing action. It often refers to a single, completed action—brief, done once, not a continuous or habitual act. See the difference between the continuous, habitual action of the imperfect tense and the completed action of the perfect in the following sentences:

Imperfect:	Callistō in silvā **errābat**.	Callisto *was wandering* in the woods. (*continuous action*)
		Callisto *used to wander* in the woods. (*habitual action*)
	Callistō in somnō **iacēbat**.	Callisto *was lying* asleep. (*continuous action*)
Perfect:	Iuppiter eam **vīdit** et statim **amāvit**.	Jupiter *saw* her and immediately *loved* her. (*completed action*)

The following story in English has been annotated to illustrate, the tense which would be required in a Latin version.

I was sitting (Impf.) at home one evening. I was relaxing (Impf.) in my favorite chair. The television was playing (Impf.) softly. My son was sleeping (Impf.) upstairs while the dog was sleeping (Impf.) beside me. Suddenly the dog growled (Perf.). He rose (Perf.) and ran (Perf.) to the window. The moon was shining (Impf.) brightly and I tried (Perf.) to peer into the yard. I saw (Perf.) a form as it fled (Impf.) into the night. I was frightened (Impf./Perf.) and I called (Perf.) the police. But I felt (Perf./Impf.) secure because the dog was (Impf.) with me.

The perfect tense can also be translated with the auxiliaries *has/have* or *did*:

Poēta fābulam **nārrāvit**.	The poet *has told* his story.
Mūtāvitne deus fōrmam nymphae?	*Did* the god *change* the form of the nymph?

55. Perfect tense, second conjugation verbs. Second conjugation verbs have several patterns for the perfect. The most common pattern is as follows:

dēbeō	**dēbēre**	**dēbuī**	**docuī**	*I have taught, taught, did teach*
doceō	**docēre**	**docuī**		
habeō	**habēre**	**habuī**	**docuistī**	*you have taught, etc.*
prohibeō	**prohibēre**	**prohibuī**	**docuit**	*he, she, it has taught, etc.*
teneō	**tenēre**	**tenuī**		
			docuimus	*we have taught, etc.*
			docuistis	*you have taught, etc.*
			docuērunt	*they have taught, etc.*

56. Dative with certain adjectives. A few adjectives in Latin are followed by a noun in the dative case to complete the idea. Since the dative noun depends on the adjective, this dative is sometimes called a dependent dative. The "to" idea is usually implied in the adjective:

cārus, -a, -um	dear (to)
grātus, -a, -um	pleasing (to)
Arcadia est **deō cāra.**	Arcadia is *dear to the god.*
Callistō est **deō grāta.**	Callisto is *pleasing to the god.*

57. Subordinate clauses: conditions. A subordinate clause introduced by **sī** (*if*) expresses the condition under which the main clause is enacted. Such possible or "real" conditions may occur in all tenses, present, imperfect, or future.

Sī Iūnō mē videt, dēlectāmenta sunt pretiōsa et digna pretiī.
If Juno sees me, the delights are costly but (and) worth the price.
Sī Iūnō mē vidēbit, dēlectāmenta erunt pretiōsa et digna pretiī.
If Juno sees (will see) me, the delights will be costly but (and) worth the price.
Sī poēta Mūsam invocābat, fābula erat populō grāta.
If the poet invoked the Muse, his story was pleasing to the people.

58. **Suus** and **eius.** Both **suus, -a, -um** and **eius** mean *his, her, its.* Both are possessives: **suus, -a, -um** is an *adjective* declined like **bonus, -a, -um,** agreeing with a noun which it modifies; **eius** is a *pronoun,* the genitive singular of the demonstrative pronoun **is, ea, id** (*he, she, it*). The possessive adjective is generally unexpressed in Latin if it is clear from the context who is the possessor. It is usually not expressed with parts of the body.

Fībula **vestīmentum** retinēbat et vitta **neglectōs capillōs** retinēbat.	A pin held back *her garment,* and a band held back *her careless locks.*

When the third person singular possessive is stressed, however, for emphasis or contrast, **suus, -a, -um** is used to indicate a reflexive possessive, one in which the subject of the clause is the possessor, and **eius** is used if the possessive is not reflexive. **Eius** does not change to agree with its noun, since it is itself a pronoun in the genitive case, meaning literally, *of him, of her, of it.*

Minerva pictūrās **suās** mōnstrāvit, et Arachnē pictūrās **suās** mōnstrāvit.	Minerva showed *her* pictures, and Arachne showed *her* pictures.

Iuppiter nympham et fīlium **eius** in stellās in caelō trānsfōrmāvit.

Jupiter transformed the nymph and *her* son into stars in the sky.

(Arcas was also the son of Jupiter, and therefore the possessive could be reflexive. Note the difference in meaning between the following sentence and the one above.)

Iuppiter nympham et fīlium **suum** in stellās in caelō trānsfōrmāvit.

Jupiter transformed the nymph and *his* (*own*) son into stars in the sky.

If the word or idea *own* can be added after the possessive, then the reflexive **suus, -a, -um** must be used.

Exercises

I.   Respondēte Latīnē, quaesō.

1. Quis est Callistō?
2. Quis est Ursa Minor?
3. Cūr Iuppiter nympham in stellās trānsfōrmāvit?
4. Estne Callistō fōrmōsa?
5. Quid vestīmentum nymphae retinēbat?
6. Quid capillōs neglectōs retinēbat?
7. Quid Callistō in silvīs portābat?
8. Ubi iacēbat Callistō in somnō?
9. Quis spectābat nympham in somnō in terrā herbōsā?
10. Quis erat vīctor?

II A. Conjugate in the perfect tense: **cūrāre, ēvītāre, tenēre, habēre.**

B. Change the singular form to the corresponding plural:

1. docuit   docuērunt
2. exercuī
3. habuit
4. iacuistī
5. prohibuī
6. retinuit
7. portāvī
8. appropinquāvit
9. tenuistī
10. dēbuit

III.   Fill in the correct form of **eius** or **suus, -a, -um**, depending on whether the possessive is reflexive, that is whether the "own" idea is included in the possession:

1. Callistō iaculum (eius, suum) in silvā portābat.
2. Poēta fābulam (eius, suam) nārrāvit.
3. Arcas est fīlius (eius, suus).
4. Arachnē pictūrās pulchrās fōrmāvit, sed Minerva pictūrās (eius, suās) nōn amāvit.
5. Vitta capillōs (eius, suōs) retinēbat. (Possessive may be omitted)

IV. Translate each adverb:

ōlim	statim	ita	maximē	certē	etiam
deinde	iterum	nōn	minimē	hīc	quoque
dēnique	saepe	sīc	aeternum	bene	ibi

V. Translate into Latin:

1. "Look at the stars," said the Muse.
2. The Greater Bear (the Big Dipper) is Callisto, once a beautiful nymph.
3. The Smaller Bear is Arcas, her son.
4. Jupiter changed the nymph and her son into stars because of the wrath of the queen of the gods.
5. Callisto lived in Arcadia, a land dear to the god.
6. Jupiter saw the beautiful nymph and loved her immediately.
7. A pin held back her garment and a fillet bound her careless locks.
8. Jupiter sees the nymph while she is lying asleep, and Callisto is pleasing to the god.
9. Jupiter took on the shape of the goddess Diana and approached the nymph.
10. Callisto avoided her friends and the well-known forests.

VI. Divide the following words into syllables and mark the accent of each. Note that in each case the penult contains either a diphthong or a short vowel followed by two consonants.

neglectus[5]	trīgintā
appropinquō	Callistō
vestīmentum	causa
caelum	dēlectāmentum
amoena	

You are already familiar with the accent falling on the penult if it contains a long vowel:

trānsfōrmō	ēvītō
suspīrō	pictūra

---

[5] A stop (p, b, t, d, c, g) plus a liquid (l, r) count as a single consonant and go with the following vowel (see Guide to Pronunciation).

There are, therefore, three ways in which the penult may be long:

1) if it contains a long vowel (**pictūra**);
2) if it contains a diphthong (**amoena**);
3) if it contains a short vowel followed by two consonants (**neglectus, Callistō**).

Etymology

THE ZODIAC

Like many other myth systems, the signs of the Zodiac were early man's attempts to explain natural phenomena, and they remind us that observance of the order in the sky and star-gazing were part of the science and pseudo-science of ancient man. Actually in both astronomy and astrology, the Zodiac is a zone or belt of the heavens through which the moon and the principal planets travel about the sun. It lies eight degrees on either side of the elliptical path the sun *seems* to travel around the earth. From very early times, the observer from the earth watched the celestial bodies moving in this path (as early as 3100 B.C. in Mesopotamia), and groups of stars called constellations were given names of animals (serpent, goat, bull, etc.). Because the constellations which were crossed by the path of the planets were thought to symbolize animals, the Greeks gave the name **zodiakos kyklos** to the circle or **ta zodia** (the little animals).

Just before the Hellenistic period (about 2300 years ago), mathematical astronomy in Mesopotamia had developed and divided the path into twelve fixed parts of thirty degrees each.

Learning Numbers

Cardinal Numbers 13–19

13	**tredecim**	16	**sēdecim**	19	**ūndēvigintī**
14	**quattuordecim**	17	**septendecim**		
15	**quīndecim**	18	**duodēvigintī**		

Tredecim equōs habeō. (casās, iacula) *I have thirteen horses. (houses, javelins)*

Remember that the numbers are undeclined.

Chapter X
CALLISTŌ (Part 2)

Iūnō rēgīna deōrum erat maximē īrāta. Tempora idōnea poenīs exspectāvit. Cum puer Arcas nymphae nātus est,[1] Iūnō dīxit, "Causa nūlla morae est. Vidē iniūriam meam, adultera! Sed Iuppiter abest. Tē nōn servābit. Figūram pulchram tuam mūtābō."

Dīxit et capillōs nymphae tenuit et eam prōnam in terram strāvit.[2] Cum misera Callistō bracchia in suppliciō tendēbat, bracchia villīs horrescēbant. Nūlla verba in nymphā mansērunt; sōlum vōx rauca. Callistō nunc est ursa fera, sed sēnsa hūmāna in ursā manent. A! Quotiēns in agrīs ōlim suīs[3] errāvit! A! Quotiēns ea, territa, virōs et animalia fera in silvīs fugitāvit, ipsa[4] animal.

Ecce Arcas, post ter quīnque (quīndecim) annōs, paene vir. Est vēnātor et saepe in silvā adest. Dum animalia fera vēnātur[5] Arcas ursam videt. Ursa est Callistō et fīlium suum recōgnōscit.[6] Arcas oculōs immōtōs eius ēvītat et ursam iaculō necāre temptat. Sed Iuppiter omnipotēns[7] erat fīliō benignus. Mātricīdium prohibuit. Ursam et fīlium eius in caelum, stellās vīcīnās, trānsportāvit.

---

[1] *Was born to the nymph.*
[2] *Threw her down (prone) on the ground.*
[3] *Once (formerly) her own.*
[4] *Herself.*
[5] *While he is hunting . . .*
[6] *She recognizes . . .*
[7] *Omnipotent.*

Verba

NOUNS

adultera, -ae, *f.*	adulteress
animal, (*pl.* **-alia**), *n.*	animal
bracchium, -iī, *n.*	arm, branch
causa, -ae, *f.*	cause, reason
figūra, -ae, *f.*	form, shape, figure
iniūria, -ae, *f.*	injury, hurt, wrong
mātricīdium, -iī, *n.*	matricide
poena, -ae, *f.*	punishment
sēnsa, -ōrum, *n. pl.*	sense, feeling
supplicium, -iī, *n.*	supplication
tempora, *n. pl.*	time, times
vēnātor, *m.*	hunter
verbum, -ī, *n.*	word
villus, -ī, *m.*	shaggy hair
vōx, vōcis, *f.*	voice

VERBS

absum, abesse, āfuī, āfutūrum	be absent, be away
adsum, adesse, adfuī, adfutūrum	be present, be near
exspectō, -āre, -āvī, -ātum	await, wait for
fugitō, -āre, -āvī, -ātum	flee, avoid, shun
horrescō, -ere, horruī	grow rough
servō, -āre, -āvī, -ātum	save, protect
tendō, -ere, tetendī, tentum *or* **-sum**	stretch out, extend
trānsportō, -āre, -āvī, -ātum	transport, carry

ADJECTIVES

benignus, -a, -um + *dat.*	kind (*to*)
ferus, -a, -um	wild
hūmānus, -a, -um	human
idōneus, -a, -um + *dat.*	suitable (*for*)
immōtus, -a, -um	unmoving
nātus, -a, -um	born
prōnus, -a, -um	bent over, prone
raucus, -a, -um	hoarse
territus, -a, -um	terrified
tuus, -a, -um	your (*sing.*)
vīcīnus, -a, -um	neighboring

OTHER WORDS

a (interjection)	ah!
cum (*conj.*)	when
ea	she
post + *acc.*	after
quīndecim	fifteen
quotiēns	how often
ter	three times, thrice
ter quīnque	fifteen (3 × 5)

Structure

59. Cardinal numbers 13 to 19. The cardinal numbers, **tredecim, quattuor-decim, quīndecim, sēdecim, septendecim, duodēvīgintī**, and **ūndēvīgintī** are undeclined. **Tredecim** through **septendecim** are obviously compounds of the numbers three through seven and ten, corresponding to English thirteen through seventeen. Eighteen and nineteen, however, are usually expressed by subtracting one and two from twenty. Post-Classical Latin, however, did allow **octōdecim**.

60. Irregular forms in perfect tense, first conjugation. The first conjugation is regular in all tenses, following the pattern for **vocō, vocāre, vocāvī, vocātum**. The following three verbs are exceptions:

   dō, dare,[8] **dedī, datum (dedistī, dedit, dedimus, dedistis, dedērunt)**
   stō, stāre, stetī (stetistī, stetit, stetimus, stetistis, stetērunt)
   iuvō, iuvāre, iūvī, iūtum (iūvistī, iūvit, iūvimus, iūvistis, iūvērunt)

61. Irregular perfect stems, second conjugation. Although many of the second conjugation verbs follow the pattern for **doceō, docēre, docuī**, there are many which do not. Note the third principal part of the following verbs:

videō	vidēre	**vīdī**	*I saw*
maneō	manēre	**mansī**	*I remained*
respondeō	respondēre	**respondī**	*I replied*

The perfect stem in the third principal part of the verb must be learned with each verb as it appears in the vocabulary. To this stem are added the perfect personal endings:

---

[8] **Dō, dare** is also irregular in that the stem vowel is short throughout the present system, except for the form **dās: dō, dās, dat, damus, datis, dant**; Imperfect: **dabam, dabās, dabat, dabāmus, dabātis, dabant**; Future: **dabō, dabis, etc.**

mansī   I have remained, remained, did remain
mansistī   you have remained, remained, did remain
mansit   he, she, it has remained, remained, did remain
mansimus   we have remained, remained, did remain
mansistis you have remained, remained, did remain
mansērunt they have remained, remained, did remain

62. Perfect tense of **sum, esse, fuī, futūrum**. **Esse** is irregular in the perfect tense, changing stem completely to **fuī**. Based on this stem, however, the perfect is regular:

fuī	I have been, I was	**fuimus**	we have been, were
fuistī	you have been, you were	**fuistis**	you have been, were
fuit	he, she, it has been, was	**fuērunt**	they have been, were

63. **Adsum** and **absum**. The verb **sum** can be made into compound verbs by the prefixes **ad-** and **ab-**. **Adesse** means *"to be near"* or *"to be present"*; **abesse** means *"to be away, to be absent, to be lacking."* Both verbs are conjugated like **sum**, but note that the **-b-** is dropped in the perfect stem of **absum—āfuī**.

adsum, ades, adest, etc.	**absum, abes, abest,** etc.
aderam, aderās, aderat, etc.	**aberam, aberās, aberat,** etc.
aderō, aderis, aderit, etc.	**aberō, aberis, aberit,** etc.
adfuī, adfuistī, adfuit, etc.	**āfuī, āfuistī, āfuit,** etc.

Exercises

I. Respondēte Latīnē, quaesō.

1. Quis erat maximē īrāta?
2. Quis nymphae nātus est?
3. Quis abest et nympham nōn servābit?
4. Verbane in nymphā mansērunt?
5. Estne vōx ursae grāta aut rauca?
6. Suntne sēnsa hūmāna in ursā? in ursīs?
7. Eratne ursa Callistō beāta cum in silvīs errābat?
8. Quis ursam necāre temptāvit?
9. Quantōs annōs (*how many years*) Arcas habēbat? (*How old was Arcas?*)
10. Quis mātricīdium prohibuit?

II. Conjugate in the perfect tense: **dare, stāre, iuvāre, respondēre, manēre, vidēre**.

III. Decline the plural after each singular form:

Nom.	pretium idōneum	pretia idōnea
Gen.	pretiī idōneī	
Dat.	pretiō idōneō	
Acc.	pretium idōneum	
Abl.	pretiō idōneō	

IV. Supply the correct form of the dependent dative and translate.

1. Arcadia est (*to the god*) cāra.
2. Iuppiter est (*to his son*) benignus.
3. Callistō est (*to the god*) grāta.
4. Arcas est (*to the nymph*) cārus.
5. Fābulae sunt (*to children*) grātae.

V. Translate into Latin:

1. "I shall change your beautiful form," said Juno.
2. When Arcas was born, Juno gave suitable punishments.
3. Only a hoarse voice and her human feelings remained.
4. Callisto stretched out her arms in supplication.
5. The terrified Callisto, now a wild animal, avoided men and beasts (animals).
6. Arcas is now fifteen years old. (*lit.*, has fifteen years)
7. He is almost a man.
8. He tried to kill the bear with his javelin.
9. Arcas is a hunter in the woods of Arcadia.
10. Juppiter prevented the matricide and transported the bear and her son into the sky (as) neighboring stars.

VI. Divide the following words into syllables and mark the accent. Note that in each case the penult is short, that is,

1) it does not contain a long vowel;
2) it does not contain a diphthong;
3) it does not contain a short vowel followed by two consonants. (except the liquids, *l* and *r*)

Therefore the penult is short and the accent goes back to the antepenult.

animal	retineō	iniūria	supplicium
bracchium	tempora	Iuppiter	territus

Etymology

What is a *persona grata*? A pleasing person who is welcome.
What is a *persona non grata*? A displeasing person who is unwelcome.

The word *person* comes from the Latin **persōna**, a character in a play, who spoke his lines through a mask which both identified the stock character and amplified the sound (**son**) which traveled through (**per**) it. Even today the characters in a play often are listed as *personae*.

Many adjectives have come directly into English from Latin with the **-us** dropped—**long(us)**, **timid(us)**, **benign(us)**—or replaced with a silent **-e**: **dens(us)**, **plan(us)**, **profan(us)**, **irat(us)**.

Many nouns have come into English from neuters of the second declension or from the neuter form of adjectives:

> maximum
> minimum
> praemium   (premium)
> forum
> asylum
> vacuum

Some neuters of the second declension replace the **-um** with a silent **-e**: **templum**-*temple*; **mīrāculum**-*miracle*, **mātricīdium**-*matricide*, **collēgium**, **college**. Some drop the **-um** completely: **verb (um)**; **monument (um)**, **vestiment (um)**; **sacrament (um)**; **ornament (um)**.

Injury comes of course from the Latin **iniūria** which itself is a combination of the negative **in-** and **iūs**, **iūris**, *n.* meaning *right* or *law*. Something that is **in-iūris** is *not right* and hence the compound word **iniūria**. From this word **iūris** comes English *judge, jurisprudence, jurist, juror, jury*, etc. Remember that the letter j did not exist in Roman times and was the i-consonant.

Bracchium meaning *arm* comes into English as *brachi-* and appears in many words such as *brachial, brachiate* (having widely spread branches) and many scientific words all referring to arms. *Embrace* and *bracelet* both are related to this original source word.

Philemon and Baucis

The myth of Philemon and Baucis is a story of piety rewarded. Jupiter and Mercury come to earth as mortals to test the humanity of men. As strangers they are driven out of a village when they seek refuge, but they are kindly received by an old couple, Philemon and Baucis, who share their humble cottage and all their food with the strangers. Old Philemon tries to level the table, as Baucis prepares a hearty meal. The two old folks even try to catch their goose to serve to the guests. In return for such kindness, the gods reveal their "numen," changing the cottage to a grand temple and complying with the request of the two pious old people to be temple guardians as long as they live. Granting also a request that they die at the same time, Jupiter eventually changed the two into trees which flanked the doors to the temple.

In a punishment reminiscent of the Noah story of the Old Testament, the evil village was punished by being flooded by a lake and the people were changed into fish.

Dialogue

Ecce discipulī.	*Here are the students.*
Nōmina vocābō.	*I shall call the names.*
Marce! Adsum.	*Marcus!* *Present.*
Prime! Adsum.	*Primus!* (First) *Present.*
Secunde! Adsum.	*Secundus!* (Second) *Present.*
Quinte! Abest.	*Quintus!* (Fifth) *Absent.*
Sexte! Adsum.	*Sextus!* (Sixth) *Present.*

Chapter XI
PHILĒMŌN ET BAUCIS
(pars prīma)

Potentia caelī est immensa et fīnem nōn habet. Quicquid dī (deī) imperant, factum est. Dubitātisne, discipulī? Nārrābō dē duābus arboribus, dē tiliā[1] et quercō[1] in Phrygiā. Fābula est vēra. Ego ipse[2] locum vīdī; nōn procul est stāgnum, terra ōlim plēna virōrum, nunc undae plēnae piscium. Hūc Iuppiter vēnit et Mercurius caducifer[3] cum patre suō quoque vēnit. Deī fōrmam virōrum simulāverant,[4] et in terrā Phrygiā ambulābant. Requiem in mīlle casīs rogābant, sed mīlle casae erant clausae.

Tamen ūna parva casa erat aperta. Pia Baucis et senex Philēmōn hīc habitābant; duo erant tōta domus.[5] Et servī et dominī erant duo.

Ubi dī parvam casam intrāvērunt, senex Philēmōn deōs sedēre iussit; Baucis vīnum et cibum: carnem et rādīcem et ōva[6] parāvit. Mēnsam quoque parāvit, sed mēnsa plāna nōn erat; ūnum membrum nōn satis longum erat. Testā[7] autem mēnsa plāna facta est. Senēs advenīs benignī erant, et deīs maiōrem partem cibī et vīnī dedērunt.

---

[1] *A beech tree and an oak.*
[2] *I, myself.*
[3] *Carrier of the caduceus.*
[4] *Had assumed*—pluperfect tense (see **Sec. 76**).
[5] *They were the whole household.*
[6] *Meat, radish, and eggs.*
[7] *By means of a tile, a broken piece of pottery.*

Verba

NOUNS

advena, -ae, *c.*	stranger
arbor, arboris, *f.*	tree
Baucis, Baucidis, *f.*	Baucis
cibus, -ī, *m.*	food
dominus, -ī, *m.*	master, lord
fīnis, fīnis, -ium, *m. (or f.)*	end
locus, -ī, *m. (irreg. pl.* **loca)**	place
membrum, -ī, *n.*	leg (*of a table*)
mēnsa, -ae, *f.*	table
Mercurius, -iī, *m.*	Mercury
pars, partis, -ium, *f.*	part
pater, patris, *m.*	father
Philēmōn, -mōnis, *m.*	Philemon
Phrygia, -ae, *f.*	Phrygia
piscis, piscis, -ium, *m.*	fish
requiēs, requiētis, *f.*	rest
requiem, *acc. sing.*	
rēx, rēgis, *m.*	king
senex, senis, -um, *c.*	old man, woman
servus, -ī, *m.*	servant
stagnum, -ī, *n.*	pool
vīnum, -ī, *n.*	wine

VERBS

dubitō (1)[8]	doubt, hesitate
imperō (1)	command, order, bid
intrō (1)	enter
iubeō, -ēre, iussī, iussum	order, command
parō (1)	prepare
sedeō, -ēre, sēdī, sessum	sit, remain, stay
veniō, -īre, vēnī, ventum	come

ADJECTIVES

apertus, -a, -um	open
clausus, -a, -um	closed

---

[8] From now on, first conjugation verbs will be marked (1).

duo, duae, duo	two
factus, -a, -um	done, made
immensus, -a, -um	immense
maiōrem	greater
noster, -tra, -trum	our
pius, -a, -um	pious, reverent
plēnus, -a, -um	full
vērus, -a, -um	true

OTHER WORDS

ego	I
enim (*postpositive*)	for, in fact, truly
et . . . et	both . . . and
nōn procul	not distant, near by
quicquid	whatever
ubi	where, when

Structure

64. Declension of **duo**, **duae**, **duo**. **Duo** is an irregular adjective. Of course it exists only in the plural.

Masc.	*Fem.*	*Neut.*
duo	duae	duo
duōrum	duārum	duōrum
duōbus	duābus	duōbus
duōs	duās	duo
duōbus	duābus	duōbus

65. The numeral **mīlle**. **Mīlle**, *a thousand*, is undeclined, although there is a plural, **mīlia**, meaning *thousands*, which is declined (see **Sec. 107**).

Mīlle puerōs vīdī.	I saw a thousand boys.
Mīlle puellās vīdī.	I saw a thousand girls.
Mīlle oppida vīdī.	I saw a thousand towns.
Mīlle casae erant clausae.	A thousand cottages were closed.

66. Third declension, masculine, feminine, and neuter nouns. Nouns of the third declension follow the patterns listed below.
   Masculine and feminine nouns appear in this lesson; neuter nouns occur in the following lesson. The endings are added to the stem which is formed from the genitive singular by dropping the **-is** ending: **pater**, **patris**; *stem* **patr**.

	Singular		*Plural*	
	Masc. & Fem.	*Neut.*	*Masc. & Fem.*	*Neut.*
Nom.	[See n.⁹]	-en, -us	-ēs	-a (-ia)
Gen.	-is	-is	-um (-ium)	-um (-ium)
Dat.	-ī	-ī	-ibus	-ibus
Acc.	-em	-en, -us	-ēs	-a (-ia)
Abl.	-e	-e	-ibus	-ibus

Study the following examples:

pater, patris, *m.*	**arbor, arboris,** *f.*	**Iuppiter, Iovis,** *m.*	**rēx, rēgis,** *m.*
father	*tree*	*Jupiter*	*king*
pater	arbor	Iuppiter	rēx
patris	arboris	Iovis	rēgis
patrī	arborī	Iovī	rēgī
patrem	arborem	Iovem	rēgem
patre	arbore	Iove	rēge
patrēs	arborēs	[no plural]	rēgēs
patrum	arborum		rēgum
patribus	arboribus		rēgibus
patrēs	arborēs		rēgēs
patribus	arboribus		rēgibus

The third declension endings are added to a *stem formed from the genitive singular* which may resemble or be quite different from the nominative singular. Therefore it is especially important to memorize the form of the genitive when the word occurs in the vocabulary, for it may add a syllable or change the stem vowel or consonant, or do both. Practice with the above nouns until you know the pattern of the declension.

I-STEM NOUNS

fīnis, fīnis, *m.*		**pars, partis,** *f.*	
(sometimes *f.* in sing.)			
end		*part*	
fīnis	fīnēs	pars	partēs
fīnis	fīnium	partis	partium
fīnī	fīnibus	partī	partibus
fīnem	fīnēs	partem	partēs
fīne	fīnibus	parte	partibus

---

⁹A variety of endings in **-er, -or, -s, -x, -ō, -iō** is possible.

The nouns of the second group (called *I-Stems*) add an **-i** before the end-ing in the genitive plural. They are easy to recognize because either they have the same number of syllables in the nominative and genitive singular (**fīnis, fīnis**)[10] or they have one syllable in the nominative singular and two consonants before the **-is** in the genitive singular (**pars, partis**).

67. Adjectives with third declension nouns. When third declension nouns are modified by first or second declension adjectives, the adjective still agrees with its noun in case, number and gender, but the endings frequently differ. Observe the following examples:

DECLENSION PATTERNS

Masculines

good king	*pious father*	*great Jupiter*
rēx bonus	**pater pius**	**magnus Iuppiter**
rēgis bonī	**patris piī**	**magnī Iovis**
rēgī bonō	**patrī piō**	**magnō Iovī**
rēgem bonum	**patrem pium**	**magnum Iovem**
rēge bonō	**patre piō**	**magnō Iove**
rēgēs bonī	**patrēs piī**	[no plural]
rēgum bonōrum	**patrum piōrum**	
rēgibus bonīs	**patribus piīs**	
rēgēs bonōs	**patrēs piōs**	
rēgibus bonīs	**patribus piīs**	

Feminines

beautiful tree	*immense part*
arbor pulchra	**pars immensa**
arboris pulchrae	**partis immensae**
arborī pulchrae	**partī immensae**
arborem pulchram	**partem immensam**
arbore pulchrā	**parte immensā**
arborēs pulchrae	**partēs immensae**
arborum pulchrārum	**partium immensārum**
arboribus pulchrīs	**partibus immensīs**
arborēs pulchrās	**partēs immensās**
arboribus pulchrīs	**partibus immensīs**

Although neuter nouns and adjectives will not appear until the following lesson, the declension pattern is included here.

---

[10]Such nouns are called *parisyllabic*, from **pari-** meaning *equal* and **syllaba** meaning *syllable*.

Neuters

famous name	open mouth
nōmen fāmōsum	ōs apertum
nōminis fāmōsī	ōris apertī
nōminī fāmōsō	ōrī apertō
nōmen fāmōsum	ōs apertum
nōmine fāmōsō	ōre apertō
nōmina fāmōsa	ōra aperta
nōminum fāmōsōrum	ōrum apertōrum
nōminibus fāmōsīs	ōribus apertīs
nōmina fāmōsa	ōra aperta
nōminibus fāmōsīs	ōribus apertīs

68. Partitive genitive (or genitive of the whole). The genitive case is used to denote the whole of something of which a part is discussed. English usage is similar, since we use *of* as the preposition.

maiōrem partem **cibī** et **vīnī**   the greater part *of the food* and (of the) *wine*

69. Ordinal numbers. The ordinal numbers, **prīmus, secundus, tertius, quartus, quintus, sextus, septimus,**[11] etc. are declined like **bonus, bona, bonum.** They were frequently used in names, as the children in the family appeared—first, second, third, etc.

Exercises

I.   Respondēte Latīnē, quaesō.

1. Estne potentia caelī parva?
2. Quis fābulam nārrat?
3. Quī (*who, m. plu.*) ad locum in Phrygiā appropinquant?
4. Ubi est locus duārum arborum?
5. Estne fābula dē duābus arboribus vēra?
6. Simulatne Iuppiter fōrmam deī?
7. Populusne in Phrygiā deīs benignus erat?
8. Quī (*see 3 above*) erant deīs benignī?
9. Quis cibum et vīnum parāvit?
10. Cūr mēnsa nōn plāna erat?

---

[11]Virginia Woolf in her novel *Mrs. Dalloway* uses the name Septimus for one of her characters.

II A. Decline **pater, arbor, fīnis, pars, victor**.

B. Add an adjective and decline:

1. pater noster   2. parva arbor   3. fīnis bona (*but plural*:
4. longa pars   5. victor ferus   fīnēs bonī, *m.*)

III. Add the correct ending to the stem of these nouns and translate the sentences:

1. (Pater) bonum habeō.   1. *Patrem* bonum habeō.
2. Parvam (arbor) habeō.
3. Minimam (pars) habeō.
4. Fābula (fīnis) bonam habet (*This masculine noun is often feminine in the singular*).
5. (Piscis) bonōs habēmus.
6. Pater meus est (senex) pius.
7. Dī longam (requiēs) dēsīderābant.
8. Multum (vīnum) habēmus.
9. (Deus) Mercurium vīdī.
10. Duo (advena) sunt in oppidō.
11. (Dominus) benignum ōrāmus.
12. (Pater) noster est in caelō.
13. (Servus) pium vocāmus.
14. Multum (cibus) dēsīderāmus.
15. Longam (mēnsa) habēmus.
16. Maximam (pars) dēsīderāmus.
17. Longum (piscis) in fīlō (*on the line*) tenēs.
18. (Arbor) pulchram cūrō.
19. Magnum (stāgnum) videō.
20. (Vīnum) bonum parō.

IV. Fill in the blanks with the correct number. Remember that except for one, two and three, the numbers are undeclined.

1. (*One*) fīliam habeō.
2. (*Four*) equōs habeō.
3. (*Seven*) casās habeō.
4. (*Two*) oculōs habeō.
5. (*Two*) discipulī absunt.
6. (*Five*) discipulī absunt.
7. (*Fifty*) discipulī sunt in scholā mathēmaticā.
8. (*Thirty-five*) discipulī sunt in scholā hodiē.
9. Priamus (*a hundred*) līberōs habuit. (**Priamus, -ī**, *m., Priam*)
10. Niobē (*seven*) fīliōs et (*seven*) fīliās habuit.

V.   Translate into Latin:

1. The power of heaven has no end (does not have an end).
2. I shall tell you a story about two old people.
3. It is a true story because I myself saw the place.
4. The lake is now full of fish.
5. Jupiter and his son Mercury approached the place (**ad locum**) and asked for rest in a thousand cottages.
6. Only one small cottage was open to the king of the gods.
7. Philemon bade the strangers (to) sit down (**sedēre**).
8. Baucis gave food and wine to the two gods.
9. The table was not level because one leg was not long enough.
10. The two old people were kind to the gods and gave them (**eīs**) the greater part of the food and wine.

VI.   Mark the accents in the first paragraph of today's reading. Use the antepenultimate rule as your guide:

Accent the penult if it is long (if it has a long vowel)
                                (if it has a diphthong)
                                (if it has a short vowel followed by two consonants)[12]
Accent the antepenult if the penult is short.

Remember that an excellent guide is your ear as you listen and as you imitate the correct sounds and accents, but you can always check the accent by the invariable *antepenultimate* rule.

Etymology

Explain the following words from their Latin sources:

the *arboretum* at Ann Arbor   the *imperative* mood
to *dominate* the situation   *introduce* the speaker
a *final* agreement   *sedentary* animals
a *Requiem* Mass   *aperture* in the rocks
stagnant water   a *pious* priest

Dominus comes into English through many cognate words: *dominate, dominance, dominant, domination, domineer, dominical, Dominican*, the name *Dominic, dominion*, and *domino* meaning costume, mask, and game.

The Senate in Rome consisted originally of older men forming a legislative body, the **senātus**, from which we derive our word *senate*.

---

[12]A stop consonant (**p, b, d, t, g, c, k, q**) followed by **l** or **r** does not always make a long syllable (see Introduction).

Rēx, rēgis, *m.* gives many words both to Latin and to English. Related in Latin are **rēgnum** (*kingdom*), **rēgina** (*queen*), **rēgnāre** (*to rule*), **regere** (*to rule*), **rēgālis** (*kingly, royal*). From the original source word and from the many correlative words come: the name *Rex*, the name *Regina*, *regent*, *regal*, *regicide* (**rēg-** + cide, from **caedō**, meaning *kill*), *regime*, *regiment*, *regimentation*, *regnal*, *regnant*.

What is *patricide*?

What is *matricide*?

Dialogue

Suntne quaestiōnēs?	*Are there questions?*
Quaestiōnem dē Iove habeō.	*I have a question about Jupiter.*
Quis est quaestiō?	*What is the question?*
Quis est Juppiter?	*Who is Jupiter?*
Est rēx deōrum et deus caelī.	*He is king of the gods and god of the sky.*

Chapter XII
PHILĒMŌN ET BAUCIS
(pars secunda)

Sed post cēnam duo, senex et coniunx, mīrāculum vīdērunt. Vīnum et cibus etiam erant in crātēribus! Baucis pia et Philēmōn timidus timent et deōs ōrant. Duōbus senibus ānser erat[1]; Baucis et Philēmōn ānserem prehendere et necāre temptābant, sacrificium deīs.[2] Ānser autem fugitāvit ad deōs quī dīxērunt: "Nōlīte ānserem necāre. Sumus dī, Iuppiter et Mercurius. Malum oppidum vāstāre dēbēmus. Sed vōbīs praemium dabimus."

Iuppiter oppidum malum in stāgnum et hominēs impiōs in piscēs trānsfōrmāvit; casam autem duōrum senum piōrum in templum trānsfōrmāvit. Duōbus senibus dīxit: "Quid dēsīderātis, senex iūste et fēmina pia?" Senēs respondērunt, "Dēsīderāmus sacerdōtēs in templō Iovis esse, et quoniam multōs annōs beātōs inter nōs habuimus, morī[3] dēsīderāmus eādem hōrā."[4]

Itaque Philēmōn et Baucis erant custōdēs templī tam diū quam vīvunt.[5] Sed ōlim dum duo piī prō templō stant, Philēmōn coniugem frondēre et Baucis Philēmōnem frondēre videt. "Valē, ō coniunx," dīxit Philēmōn, dīxit Baucis; deinde arbor ōra cēlāvit. Eōs in arborēs Iuppiter trānsfōrmāverat. Etiam hodiē hae[6] arborēs in Phrygiā stant prō templō Iovis: ego ipse eās vīdī. Multī in templō ōrant et advenae sunt semper bene receptī. Nōmina Baucidis et Philēmōnis sunt nōta in hāc[7] terrā.

---

[1] *The two old folks had a goose.* **Duōbus senibus** is dative of possession (**Sec. 36**).
[2] *As a sacrifice to the gods.* **Sacrificium** is in apposition to **ānserem.**
[3] *To die.*
[4] *At the same hour.*
[5] **Tam diū quam,** *as long as they live.*
[6] *These.*
[7] *This.*

Verba

NOUNS

annus, -ī, *m.*	year
ānser, ānseris, *m.*	goose
cēna, -ae, *f.*	dinner, meal
coniunx, coniugis, *c.*	husband or wife, spouse
crātēr, -ēris, *m.*	bowl
custōs, custōdis, *c.*	guardian, keeper
homō, -inis, *m.*	man, human
mīrāculum, -ī, *n.*	miracle
nōmen, nōminis, *n.*	name
ōs, ōris, *n.*	mouth
praemium, -iī, *n.*	reward
sacerdōs, -dōtis, *c.*	priest (-ess)
sacrificium, -iī, *n.*	sacrifice

VERBS

frondeō, -ēre	put out leaves
prehendō, -ere, -hendī, -hensum	catch, seize, grasp
timeō, -ēre, -uī	fear, be afraid of
vastō (1)	destroy, lay waste
vīvō, -ere, vīxī, victum	live

ADJECTIVES

impius, -a, -um	wicked, impious
ipse, ipsa, ipsum	self, himself, herself, itself, themselves, myself, yourself
iūstus, -a, -um	just, upright, true
receptus, -a, -um	received
timidus, -a, -um	timid

OTHER WORDS

eōs (*m.*); eās (*f.*)	them (*accusative*)
inter + *acc.*	between, among
nōs	us
prō + *abl.*	in front of, before
quī	who (*pl.*)
quoniam	since
semper	always
sine + *abl.*	without
vōbīs	to you (*pl.*)

Structure

70. Common gender nouns. Nouns which logically can be either masculine or feminine are said to be of common gender.

The third declension nouns **sacerdōs**, **custōs**, and **coniunx** can be either masculine or feminine, since the role can be either male or female.

sacerdōs, sacerdōtis, *m. & f.*	priest, priestess
custōs, custōdis, *m. & f.*	guardian, keeper
coniunx, coniugis, *m. & f.*	husband, wife, spouse

71. Neuter third declension nouns. Like all neuter nouns, neuter third declension nouns are alike in the nominative and accusative forms, both singular and plural:

nōmen, nōminis, *n., name*		**ōs, ōris**, *n., mouth*	
nōmen	**nōmina**	**ōs**	**ōra**[8]
nōminis	nōminum	ōris	ōrum
nōminī	nōminibus	ōrī	ōribus
nōmen	**nōmina**	**ōs**	**ōra**
nōmine	nōminibus	ōre	ōribus

72. **Videō** + infinitive with accusative subject. The verb **videō** is often followed by an infinitive *with its subject in the accusative*. In English it is necessary to supply "that" to achieve a smooth translation and to avoid misreading. The infinitive is translated as an indicative verb.[9]

Deōs appropinquāre videō.	I see *that the gods are approaching*.
Hominēs dubitāre videō.	I see *that the men are doubting*.
Coniugem frondēre videt.	He sees *that his wife is putting out leaves*.
Advenās esse deōs vident.	They see *that the strangers are gods*.

73. Third conjugation. The third conjugation infinitive ends in **-ere**.

dīcō, dīcere	say, speak, tell
tendō, tendere	stretch out, extend
prehendō, prehendere	catch, seize
vīvō, vīvere	live, be alive

74. Negative commands. **Nōlī** (singular) and **nōlīte** (plural) are used with an

---

[8] Do not confuse with **ōra, -ae**, *f., shore.*

[9] This construction is closely related to Indirect Statement (**Sec. 128**).

infinitive to give a negative command. These are imperative forms of the verb **nōlle** meaning *to be unwilling*:

Nōlī timēre.	*Do not fear.* (*addressing one*)
Nōlīte ānserem **necāre.**	*Do not kill* the goose. (*addressing more than one*)

75. Adjectives used as nouns: substantives. Many times in Latin the adjective is used as a noun. You are familiar with this use in English in such expressions as, "the blind," "the rich," "the poor," "the brave," "the strong," "the weak," "the old," "the young." The Beatitudes in the Bible employ these adjectives, "the poor in spirit," and "the meek." When the adjective takes the place of the noun or is used as a noun, it is called a *substantive*. In Latin it is also possible to distinguish gender in a substantive.

bonī	the good men
bonae	the good women
bona	the good things (*or* goods)
multī	many men, many people
piī	the pious ones
duo	the two people
duo piī	the two pious ones
malī	evil men

76. Past perfect indicative of verbs (*also called pluperfect*). The past perfect of the verb is formed by adding the imperfect forms of **sum** to the perfect stem of the verb. The auxiliary in English is *had*.

vocāv + eram = vocāveram   *I had called*

First Conjugation		*Second Conjugation*	
vocāv-		**docu-**	
vocāveram	I had called	**docueram**	I had taught
vocāverās	you had called	**docuerās**	you had taught
vocāverat	he had called	**docuerat**	he had taught
vocāverāmus	we had called	**docuerāmus**	we had taught
vocāverātis	you had called	**docuerātis**	you had taught
vocāverant	they had called	**docuerant**	they had taught

Exercises

I. Respondēte Latīnē, quaesō.

1. Quī mīrāculum vīdērunt?
2. Quid erat mīrāculum?

3. Quī ānserem servāvērunt?
4. Quī erant advenae?
5. Cūr dī oppidum vastāre dēbent?
6. Cūr dī praemium dare dēbent?
7. Quid est praemium senibus?
8. Quī sunt custōdēs templī Iovis?
9. Quid nunc est oppidum ubi habitāverant impiī hominēs?
10. Quī sunt arborēs prō templō?

II. Decline:

1. sacerdōs pius   3. coniunx beāta
2. ānser ferus   4. nōmen nōtum

III. Complete each idea by means of an infinitive with an accusative subject: (Omit the word "that" in the Latin sentence.)

1. Videō (*that*) deōs (*are approaching*).
2. (*That*) hōram (*is fleeing*) videō.
3. Videō (*that*) Iovem (*is*) rēgem deōrum.
4. (*That*) Baucidem (*is*) arborem videō.
5. Multī vident (*that*) cēnam (*is*) bonam.
6. Senēs vident (*that*) cibum (*remains*).
7. Senēs vident (*that*) ānserem (*is fleeing*) ad deōs.
8. Dī vident (*that*) bonōs (*are*) laetōs.
9. Dī vident (*that*) senēs (*are*) advenīs benignōs.
10. Philēmōn videt (*that*) Baucidem (*is putting out leaves*).

IV. Fill in the correct case for each object of the preposition in the following sentences:

1. Arborēs prō *templ-_____* stābant.
2. Post *cēn-_____* mīrāculum vīdērunt.
3. Trāns *camp-_____* equus fugitāvit.
4. Dē *vīt-_____* deōrum fābula nārrātur.[10]
5. In *silv-_____* nympha habitat.
6. Nōlīte ambulāre, līberī, cum *adven-_____* .
7. Ursa in *silv-_____* errāvit. (*into*)
8. Inter *arbor-_____* casam parvam videō.
9. Cibus erat etiam in *crātēr-_____* .
10. Sine *homin-_____* terra est vacua et sōla.

V. Translate into Latin:

1. Philemon and Baucis saw a miracle after supper.
2. The bowl was still full of food. (**plēnus, -a, -um**—*full*)

---

[10] *A story is told . . .*

3. They wanted to kill their only goose (as a) sacrifice to the gods.
4. The gods changed the wicked men into fish and the town into a lake.
5. The gods asked the old people, "What do you wish?"
6. The two old folks reply, "We wish to die at the same hour."
7. The gods change the small cottage into a temple.
8. Philemon and Baucis are custodians of the temple.
9. Strangers are always well received in the temple.
10. Two trees stand before the temple of Jupiter, the guardians Philemon and Baucis.

Etymology

WHO INVENTED THE MOTOR CAR?

motor	from **moveō, -ēre, mōvī, mōtum**	move
car	**carrus, -ī,** *m.*	car
battery	**battuere**	beat
accelerator	**accelerāre** (from **ad** + **celer**)	quicken
piston	**pinsō, -ere, pistum**	stamp, pound
cylinder	(Greek) **kylindros, kylindrein**	roll
fuel	(Old French) **fouaille** from **focus**	fireplace, fire
mixture	**misceō, -ēre, miscuī, mixtum**	mix
transmission	**trānsmittō, -ere, -mīsī, -missum**	send across
selector	**seligere, selectus**	gather aside
generator	**generāre**	give birth, bring to life
distributor	**distribuere**	distribute
carburetor	**carbō, -ōnis,** *m.*	coal
air	(Greek) **aër** to Latin **aër, aëris,** *m.*	air, atmosphere
gas	(Greek) **chaos** to Latin, **chaos**	formless
engine	**ingenium, -iī,** *n.*	invention
lubrication	**lubricus, lubricāre**	slippery, slip
universal	**ūniversus**	whole, entire
joint	**iungere**	join
torque	**torquēre**	twist
convertor	**convertere**	turn together, turn with
electric	**electrum, -ī,** *n.*	amber (*associated with electricity*)
differential	**differre**	carry in different directions
suspension	**suspendere**	hang up, hang in

shock absorbers	**absorbere**	suck in
pedal	**pēs, pedis,** *m.*	foot
hydraulic	**hydraulus, -ī,** *m.*	a water organ

Give the source for the underlined words:
annual dues
conjugal bliss
sacerdotal celibacy
a free premium with cereal
prehensile hands
a devastating experience
an impious man (here the *in-* acts as a negative)
a just decision

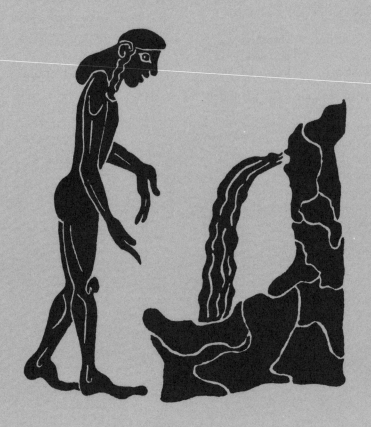

Echo and Narcissus

Echo, another of Diana's nymphs, is robbed by Juno of her power to initiate conversation, in punishment for trying to engage the queen of the heavens in talk while Jupiter philandered in one of his amorous escapades. In an aetiological metamorphosis, the nymph pines away and becomes only an answering voice when she is unable to win the love of Narcissus, a handsome youth who loves only himself. Narcissus, bending over a pool, sees his own reflection in the water and eventually is pulled into the pool by his desire for the handsome youth he sees in the water. In place of the boy only a flower remains. From the youth's name come both the flower and a complex identified by Sigmund Freud as the state of being abnormally absorbed with oneself.

Dialogue

Quis abest hodiē?	*Who is absent today?*
Nēmō abest.	*No one is absent.*
Bene est.	*It is well. (That's good.)*

Chapter XIII
ĒCHŌ ET NARCISSUS

Narcissus erat iuvenis fōrmōsus et superbus. Putābat sē fōrmōsissimum esse.[1] Quamquam multae iuvenem amāverant, tamen Narcissus nēminem praeter sē amābat.

Ubi nympha Ēchō Narcissum in silvā vīdit, statim iuvenem amāvit. Ēchō adhūc et corpus et vōcem habēbat, sed vōx erat nova. Quod Ēchō Iūnōnī, rēgīnae deōrum, dolō[2] nocuerat, nympha Iūnōnī nōn grāta erat. Iūnō dīxit, "Nōn sine poenā mihi nocueris." Ēchō vōcem habet sed sōlum respondēre potest. Verba sōla aliōrum reportāre potest. Sua verba nōn habet.

Ōlim Narcissus cum cēterīs iuvenibus animālia fera in silvīs et montibus sequitur.[3] Forte sōlus errat, et Ēchō iuvenem sēcrētō sequitur. Nox appropinquat et fōrmās obscūrās in silvā cēlat.

"Quis adest?"[4] rogat Narcissus. "Quis adest?"

"Adest,"[4] respondet Ēchō.

"Venī,"[5] clāmat Narcissus magnā vōce. "Venī!"

"Vēnī,"[5] respondet Ēchō, et nympha misera iuvenem superbum bracchiīs suīs tenēre temptat.

"Stā," clāmat Narcissus. "Moriar antequam tibi erō."[6]

"Tibi erō," resonat misera Ēchō. In pudōre sē cēlat—in silvīs, in montibus, in spēluncīs—ūsque fōrma minima est. Vōx sōla manet.

Etiam hodiē haec vōx manet. Sī vōs in montibus spēluncīsque errāveritis et "Ēchō, Ēchō," clāmāveritis, Ēchō verba vestra resonābit.

Narcissus autem potestātem amōris nōn fugitāvit. Ōlim in undīs flūminis sē, iuvenem fōrmōsissimum, vīdit et imāginem suī amāvit. Cum imāginem tangere temptāvit, imāgō fugitāvit. Dēnique pervīdit sē imāginem

---

[1] *He thought that he was most handsome.*
[2] *By means of a trick.*
[3] *Is following, follows.*
[4] *"Who is here?" Echo replies, "Here."*
[5] *"Come!"*: a command (imperative singular); also *I have come.*
[6] *"I will die before I will be yours."*

105

esse.[7] Lacrimīs aquās turbāvit. Imāgō iterum fugitāvit; amor corpus iuvenis dēvorāvit; neque vigor, neque color, neque fōrma mānsit.

"Valē," dīxit Narcissus, et in rīpā flūminis iacuit. "Valē."

"Valē," resonāvit Ēchō.

Sorōrēs Narcissī corpus iuvenis quem amāverant humāre parāvērunt. Sed prō corpore sōlum mānsit flōs—flōs appellātus[8] Narcissus albīs foliīs.

Verba

NOUNS

amor, amōris, *m.*	love
color, colōris, *m.*	color
corpus, corporis, *n.*	body
Ēchō, *f.*	Echo (*a nymph*)
flōs, flōris, *m.*	flower
flūmen, -inis, *n.*	river
folium, -iī, *n.*	leaf
imāgō, -inis, *f.*	image
iuvenis, iuvenis, iuvenum (*gen. pl.*), *c.*	youth, young person
mons, montis, -ium, *m.*	mountain
Narcissus, -ī, *m.*	Narcissus (*a youth*)
nox, noctis, -ium, *f.*	night
potestās, -tātis, *f.*	power
pudor, -ōris, *m.*	shame
rīpa, -ae, *f.*	bank of a river
soror, -ōris, *f.*	sister
spēlunca, -ae, *f.*	cave
vigor, -ōris, *m.*	liveliness, force, vigor
vōx, vōcis, *f.*	voice

VERBS

dēvorō (1)	consume, devour
humō (1)	bury
inquit[9]	he, she says, said
noceō, -ēre, -uī, -itum + *dat.*	harm
parō (1)	prepare
pervideō, -ēre, -vīdī, -vīsum	see through, discern, realize

---

[7] *Finally he realized that he himself was the image* (see **Sec. 72**).

[8] *A flower called . . .*

[9] **Inquit** frequently interrupts the quotation and normally follows the first word in it.

possum, posse, potuī	can, be able
putō (1)	think
reportō (1)	carry back, report
tangō, -ere, tetigī, tactum	touch
turbō (1)	stir, disturb

ADJECTIVES

albus, -a, -um	white
obscūrus, -a, -um	dark

OTHER WORDS

adhūc	until now, up to this point
alius, -ia, -iud	other, another
antequam	before, sooner than
forte	by chance
haec	this
nēmō, nēminem (*acc.*)	no one
praeter + *acc.*	except
prō + *abl.*	in place of, before, for
quamquam	although
quem, *rel. pro.*	whom
Quem, *interrog. pro.*	Whom
suī, sibi, sē, sē, *reflexive pro.*	himself, herself, itself, themselves
tamen	nevertheless
ūsque	as far as, to, until
vester, -tra, -trum	your (*pl.*)
vōs	you (*pl.*)

Structure

77. Superlative of adjectives. Most adjectives form the superlative by adding -issimus, -a, -um to the stem:

> **longissimus   longissima   longissimum**

In English the superlative may be variously translated: *the longest, the most long, very long, exceedingly long.*

beātus, -a, -um	**beātissimus, -a, -um**	happiest
pius, -a, -um	**piissimus, -a, -um**	most pious
sanctus, -a, -um	**sanctissimus, -a, -um**	most holy

78. Subordinate clauses: **quamquam, tamen.** A subordinate clause introduced by **quamquam** (*although*) is frequently concluded by a main clause introduced by **tamen** (*nevertheless*).

> **Quamquam** multae iuvenem amāverant, **tamen** Narcissus nēminem amābat.
> *Although* many maidens had loved the youth, *nevertheless* Narcissus loved no one.

79. Present tense of **posse.** The verb **posse** (*can, be able*) is a combination of **esse** (*to be*) and the stem **pot-** (as in **potentia**, *power*). The **-t** of **pot-** becomes **-s** before another **-s** by a process known as *assimilation*.

possum	I can, am able	**possumus**	we can, are able
potes	you can, are able	**potestis**	you can, are able
potest	he, she, it can, is able	**possunt**	they can, are able

80. Ablative case. The Ablative case originates from three different cases: in the parent Indo-European[10] language, there were eight cases, including a *true ablative* or "from" case, an *instrumental* or "with, by" case, and a *locative* or "in, on" (a where) case. These three cases were merged into one case in Latin, but these three distinct aspects still exist—all as ablative forms. Every use of the ablative in Latin can be reduced to one of these three aspects.

True ablative: separation, source, agent, comparison[11]
Instrumental ablative: means, manner, accompaniment, description

> Means: Phoebus fīliōs rēgīnae **sagittā** necāvit. *by means of an arrow*
> Manner: Narcissus **magnā vōce** clāmat. *in a loud voice*

If no adjective modifies the ablative noun, the preposition **cum** is used, and is sometimes used even when the noun is modified, appearing between the noun and its adjective: **magnō cum gaudiō**, *with great joy.*

> Accompaniment: Mercurius **cum patre Iove** ambulābat. *with his father Jupiter*
> Description: Flōs appellātus Narcissus **albīs foliīs**. *with white petals*

Locative: place where, time when, place or time within which

> Place where: Arachnē **in Lydiā** habitābat.
>   Arachne lived *in Lydia*.

---

[10] See Introduction, The Indo-European Family of Languages.
[11] To be studied in subsequent lessons.

Time when : **Nocte** Pyramus et Thisbē "Valē" dīcēbant.
At night Pyramus and Thisbe said, "Goodbye."

81. Third declension nouns, **-i** stems. You have already met **pars** and **fīnis** (**Sec. 66**) as third declension nouns having **-ium** in the genitive plural. This added **-i** in the stem of the genitive plural is characteristic of the following groups of nouns:

    A.   Parisyllabics ending in
          -is (*nom.*), **-is** (*gen.*)[12] **fīnis, fīnis, fīnium**   (*end*)
          -ēs (*nom.*), **-is** (*gen.*) **aedēs, aedis, aedium**   (*house*)
    B.   Nouns in **-s** or **-x** whose stem ends in two consonants:
          nox, noctis, noctium   (*night*)
          mōns, montis, montium   (*mountain*)
    C.   Neuters in **-e, -al, -ar**: **animal, animālis.**

82. Future perfect tense, indicative. The future perfect tense is formed by adding the future forms of **esse** to the perfect stem of the verb. Note that in the third person plural, however, **erunt** becomes **-erint**. The English auxiliary verbs are *shall have* and *will have*.

	amāv + **erō** = **amāverō**		*I shall have loved*
amāverō	I shall have loved	**amāverimus**	we shall have loved
amāveris	you will have loved	**amāveritis**	you will have loved
amāverit	he, she, it will have loved	**amāverint**	they will have loved
nocuerō	I shall have harmed	**nocuerimus**	we shall have harmed
nocueris	you will have harmed	**nocueritis**	you will have harmed
nocuerit	he, she, it will have harmed	**nocuerint**	they will have harmed

One of the most common uses of the future perfect tense in Latin is in the conditional clause of a real (possible) conditional sentence, when the time or tense is future. The Roman mind conceived of the idea as taking place at a time *preceding* the future time of the main verb:

If you (will have) come home, father will talk to you.

English idiom calls for present or future in the "if" clause.

Sī vōs in montibus **errāveritis** (errābitis) et "Ēchō, Ēchō," **clāmāveritis**, Ēchō verba vestra resonābit.

---

[12] **Iuvenis, iuvenis** *youth* is an exception; its genitive plural is **iuvenum**. Also exceptions are **canis**, *dog*; **senex**, *old man*; and **volucris**, *bird*. For **sedes**, *seat*; **mensis**, *month*; and **vates**, *bard*, both **-um** and **-ium** appear in the genitive plural.

If you *wander* (will have wandered) in the mountains and *shout* (will have shouted), "Echo, Echo," Echo will sound back your words.

83. **Quem** as interrogative and relative pronoun. **Quem** (*whom*) can ask a question, as an interrogative pronoun.

Quem in silvā vīdistī?   *Whom* did you see in the forest?

As a relative pronoun, **quem** within the sentence relates to an antecedent preceding it:

Sorōrēs Narcissī corpus iuvenis **quem** amāverant humāre parāvērunt. The sisters of Narcissus prepared to bury the body of the youth **whom** they had loved.

Quem is accusative, object of the verb **amāverant**. *The relative pronoun takes its case from its use in its own clause.*

84. Reflexive pronoun **sē**. The declension of **sē** is the same both singular and plural:

Gen.	**suī**	of himself, of herself, of itself, of themselves
Dat.	**sibi**	to himself, to herself, to itself, to themselves
Acc.	**sē (sēsē)**	himself, herself, itself, themselves
Abl.	**sē (sēsē)**	with himself, with herself, with itself, with themselves

Sēsē is an alternate form for **sē**.

85. Third declension nouns. Gender.
Nouns denoting human beings are masculine or feminine according to natural gender; the following rules regarding grammatical gender are reasonably consistent:

Masculine
- -or, -ōris (amor, amōris; pudor, pudōris; labor, labōris)
- -tor, -tōris (victor, victōris; scriptor, scriptōris)

Feminine (abstracts)
- -tās, -tātis (vēritās, vēritātis; lībertās, lībertātis)
- -tūs, -tūtis (virtūs, virtūtis; senectūs, senectūtis)
- -tūdō, -tūdinis (multitūdō, multitūdinis; pulchritūdō, pulchritūdinis)
- -tiō, -tiōnis (natiō, natiōnis; ōrātiō, ōrātiōnis)

Neuter
- -us, -o/eris (corpus, corporis, tempus, temporis: genus, generis)
- -e, -al, -ar (mare, maris; animal, animālis, exemplar, exemplāris)
- -en (flumen, fluminis; nōmen, nōminis)

Exercises

I. Respondēte Latīnē, quaesō.

1. Quis erat Narcissus?
2. Quem Narcissus amābat?
3. Cūr Ēchō vōcem novam habet?
4. Estne Ēchō Iūnōnī grāta?
5. Habetne Ēchō sua verba?
6. Quō[13] Narcissus animālia fera sequitur?
7. Cūr nympha misera erat?
8. Ubi Ēchō sē cēlāvit?
9. Quem Narcissus in flumine vīdit?
10. Quid mānsit prō corpore iuvenis?

II A. Conjugate the following verbs in the past perfect and the future perfect:

1. rēgnō (1)
2. parō (1)
3. habitō (1)
4. videō, vidēre, vīdī, vīsum
5. doceō, docēre, docuī, doctum
6. maneō, manēre, mānsī
7. sum, esse, fuī, futūrum
8. tangō, -ere, tetigī, tactum

B. Change the verb to plural:

1. Nympha Narcissum amāverat.
1. Nymphae Narcissum *amāverant.* .

2. Iuvenis in silvīs errāverat.
2. Iuvenēs in silvīs _____ .

3. Soror corpus nōn vīderat.
3. Sorōrēs corpus nōn _____ .

4. Iuvenis silvam amāverat.
4. Iuvenēs silvam _____ .

5. Nox fuerat longa.
5. Noctēs _____ longae .

6. Rēgīna nymphae nōn nocuerat.
6. Rēgīnae nymphae nōn _____ .

7. Dea in terrā nōn mānserat.
7. Deae in terrā nōn _____ .

8. Nympha "Valē," clāmāverat.
8. Nymphae "Valē," _____ .

9. Flumen fuerat longum.
9. Flumina _____ longa .

10. Iuvenis sē in undīs vīderat.
10. Iuvenēs sē in undīs _____ .

C. Supply the correct future perfect in each condition and the future in each conclusion.

1. Sī vōs in montibus, "Ēchō," clāmā _____ , Ēchō respond _____ .

2. Sī Ēchō respond _____ , corpus eius nōn vid _____ .

---

[13] **Quo,** *where, at what place?*

   3. Sī Philēmōn et Baucis in casā fu _____ , senēs deīs
     benignī er _____ .

   4. Sī ā scholā Latīnā āfu _(you,s.)_____ , tibi sententiās[14] report
     _(I)_____ .

   5. Sī poēta Ovidius fābulam nārrā _____ , fābula _____
     mihi grāta.

III A. Practice the declension of these third declension nouns modified by
    second declension adjectives:

    rēx bonus   parva soror   flumen pulchrum   nox longa

  B. Make each adjective in the following sentences superlative:

    1. Narcissus est fōrmōsus.   1. Narcissus est fōrmōsissimus.
    2. Callistō est deō cāra.
    3. Iūnō est īrāta.
    4. Arachnē est superba.
    5. Philēmōn est pius.
    6. Baucis est pia.
    7. Flamma est sancta.
       (What Christmas hymn uses this and the preceding superlative?)
    8. Nympha est nōta.
    9. Lātōna est stulta.
   10. Īnsula est longa.

IV.   Supply the correct forms of **posse**:

    1. Arachnē pictūrās melius quam Minerva fōrmāre nōn

     _____ .

    2. Ēchō fābulam nārrāre nōn _____ .

    3. Narcissus aliās amāre nōn _____ ; sōlum sē amāre

     _____ .

    4. Īnsulam vidēre _(I can)_____ .
    5. _(Can you, sing.)_____ nymphās spectāre?
    6. Iuvenēs Narcissum vidēre nōn _____ .
    7. Ēchō verba resonāre sōlum _____ .
    8. Sorōrēs flōrem vidēre _____ .
    9. Philēmōn et Baucis eādem horā morī[15] _____ .
   10. Nymphae deīs grātae esse _____ .

V.   Translate into Latin:

    1. Handsome Narcissus loved no one except himself.
    2. Echo had a voice up to this time.

---

[14]The sentences.
[15]To die.

3. Juno was angry; the nymph did not please her.
4. Narcissus used to wander (*Imperfect Tense*) with other youths in the forests and mountains.
5. Echo had seen and had loved the youth.
6. Echo can only reply; she can only report the words of Narcissus.
7. The wretched nymph hides in caves until her form is very small.
8. If Narcissus will (have looked) look in the river, he will see himself.
9. He tries to touch the image.
10. (His) sisters see a flower in place of the body.

Etymology

By *assimilation* (**ad** + **similis**) the prefix may change its final consonant to the same letter as the first letter of the root word or to a letter that sounds pleasant (euphonious) with it.

illusion	assimilate
immigration	afferent
irritation	affect
illogical	

Such a change also took place in Latin, producing different spellings for verbs: **adficio** or **afficio**.

Nowhere is this process of assimilation more apparent than in the forms of the verb **possum, posse, potuī**, for the stem **pot-** changes to **pos-** wherever the ending begins with an **-s**: **possum, posse, potest, possunt**. The stem or root, however, is **pot-** (*power*) and from it come many words in both English and Latin: potent, impotent, omni(*all*)-potent, potentate, potential, potency, potentiality, possible, possibly. The last two words come from the infinitive **posse** which itself is a contraction of **potis** + **esse** (*to be powerful*). In Latin the cognate words are **potentia, potēns, potis**, and **potestās**.

*   *   *   *   *

Give the source for the following underlined words and define each one:

vox pop (*populi*)	Monterey (**rey** is Spanish for *king*)
amorous behavior	nocturnal prowlers
the color of his eyes	spelunkers engage in speleology
corporal punishment	my sorority sister
a floral arrangement	tangible evidence
a wild imagination	an obscure poet
juvenile delinquency	Who is Captain Nemo?

Phoebus and Daphne

The theme of the female pursued by the male is reflected in the story of Apollo and Daphne, this time the powerful sun god pursuing the poor nymph of Diana against her will. He begs her to stay her flight, calling out that it is no mere mortal who is seeking her, but the great shining Phoebus, god of music, the arts, and medicine. His arguments are to no avail, and when the god has chased the nymph to exhaustion, the maiden pleads with her river-god father to change her shape. He complies with her request, and Daphne becomes a tree, the laurel, which Apollo embraces even as the nymph disappears into foliage. Since he cannot have the nymph, he wears her leaves as his crown, as do the Roman victors, as a mark of honor to Daphne, the nymph of Apollo and his first love.

Dialogue

Partēs corporis sunt caput et truncus et crūra et bracchia.	*The parts of the body are head, trunk, legs, and arms.*
Partēs capitis sunt capillī, oculī, ōs, nāsum, aurēs.	*Parts of the head are hair, eyes, mouth, nose, and ears.*
Bracchia manūs et digitōs habent.	*Arms have hands and fingers.*

Chapter XIV
PHOEBUS ET DAPHNĒ

Daphnē erat prīmus amor Phoebī. Īra Cupīdinis Phoebō amōrem dedit. Phoebus superbus vīderat Cupīdinem cum sagittīs et dīxerat: "Quid sunt tibi, puer, arma et sagittae? Sagittae sunt mihi. Ego possum dare vulnera hostibus. Tū dēbēs contentus esse cum amoribus."

Fīlius Veneris respondit: "Tuus arcus omnia,[1] Phoebe, fīgit, sed meus arcus tē fīgit." Et in arcū[2] Cupīdō duo tēla tenuit: hoc tēlum amōrem fugat; illud tēlum amōrem facit. Ūnum quod facit est acūtum, alterum quod fugat est obtūsum. Deus Cupīdō hoc tēlum in Daphnem fīgit, illud in Phoebum. Phoebus amat; Daphne nōmen amōris fugitat. Per silvās cum Diānā et cēterīs nymphīs errāre sōlum amat.

Saepe pater nymphae, deus flūminis, dīxit: "Dēbēs coniugem habēre." Saepe dīxit, "Dēbēs fīliōs habēre." Sed Daphnē pulchra patrem ōrat ita: "Cārissime pater, da mihi hoc dōnum—mē esse virginem perpetuam."[3] Pater fīliae hoc dōnum dedit.

Phoebus autem Daphnem amat et flammae amōris in deō crescunt. Deus virginem videt et laudat caput, capillōs, oculōs; laudat digitōs et manūs et bracchia. Daphnē autem nōn manet. Fugitat in silvās.

"Manē, nympha! Nōn sum hostis. Nympha, manē! Amor est mihi causa dolōris. Nescīs quis sum. Sum Phoebus. Iuppiter est mihi pater. Sum deus sōlis, mūsicae, medicīnae, artium."

Daphnē iterum fugitāverat. Phoebus virginem iterum petīvit. Eam superāre temptāvit. Daphnē aquās flūminis patris vīdit et dīxit: "Da mihi auxilium, pater, sī potentiam habēs, mūtā fōrmam meam."

---

[1] *All things.*
[2] *In his bow.*
[3] *That I be a maiden forever.*

Statim pater bracchia pulchra in ramōs mūtat. Daphnē virgō fōrmōsa nunc est laurus, arbor pulchra. Phoebus oscula arborī dat et dīcit: "Sī coniūnx mea esse nōn potes, arbor eris certē mea; stābis prīma in capitibus rēgum ducumque Romae."

Verba

NOUNS

aqua, -ae, *f.*	water
arcus, *m.* (*4th decl.*)	bow
arma, -ōrum, *n. pl.*	weapons, arms
ars, artis, -ium, *f.*	art, skill
caput, -itis, *n.*	head
Cupīdō, -inis, *m.*	Cupid, Eros, Amor (*son of Venus*)
Daphnē, -is, *f.*	Daphne (*a nymph*)
digitus, -ī, *m.*	finger
dolor, dolōris, *m.*	grief
dux, ducis, *m.*	leader
hostis, hostis, -ium, *m.*	enemy
laurus, -ī, *f.*	laurel tree
manus, *f.* (*4th decl.*)	hand
medicīna, -ae, *f.*	medicine
mūsica, -ae, *f.*	music
osculum, -ī, *n.*	kiss
ramus, -ī, *m.*	branch, bough
sōl, sōlis, *m.*	sun
tēlum, -ī, *n.*	weapon, dart, missile
Venus, Veneris, *f.*	Venus (*goddess of love*)
virgō, -inis, *f.*	maiden
vulnus, -eris, *n.*	wound

VERBS

crēscō, -ere, crēvī, crētum	increase, grow
dīcō, -ere, dīxī, dictum	say, speak
faciō, facere, fēcī, factum	make, do
fīgō, fīgere, fīxī, fixum	fasten, affix, transfix
fugō (1)	put to flight
nesciō, -īre, nescīvī, nescītum	not know, be ignorant of
petō, -ere, petīvī, petītum	seek, ask
superō (1)	overcome, conquer

ADJECTIVES

acūtus, -a, -um	sharp
alter, -era, -erum	the other
contentus, -a, -um	satisfied
hic, haec, hoc	this; he, she, it; the latter
ille, illa, illud	that; he, she, it; the former
obtūsus, -a, -um	dull, blunt
tuus, -a, -um	your

OTHER WORDS

eī, eae, ea	they
is, ea, id	he, she, it
quod	which, that
tū	you

Structure

86. Third conjugation. The infinitive of the third conjugation ends in **-ere**.

First Conjugation	Second Conjugation	Third Conjugation
-āre	-ēre	-ere
portāre	habēre	dīcere
vocāre	docēre	petere

Notice how the short **-e** in the stem of the third conjugation infinitive causes the accent to shift to the antepenult. The vowel of the present tense, however, is **-i**, changing to **-u** before **-nt** in the third person plural.

Present Tense		Imperfect Tense	
dīcō	I speak, *etc.*	dīcēbam	I was speaking, *etc.*
dīcis	you speak	dīcēbās	you were speaking
dīcit	he, she, it speaks	dīcēbat	he was speaking
dīcimus	we speak	dīcēbāmus	we were speaking
dīcitis	you speak	dīcēbātis	you were speaking
dīcunt	they speak	dīcēbant	they were speaking

The imperfect is completely regular, though the short **-e** of the stem is lengthened before **-bā**.

The perfect tenses are completely regular, being formed, as in first and second conjugations, from the perfect stem plus endings. Therefore it is important to learn the third principal part with each verb: **dīcō, dīcere, dīxī** but also **petō, petere, petīvī**.

Perfect Tense
Perfect Stem + Perfect Endings

dīxī	I have said, did say	petīvī	I have sought
dīxistī	you have said, did say	petīvistī	you have sought
dīxit	he, she, it has said	petīvit	he, she, it has sought
dīximus	we have said	petīvimus	we have sought
dīxistis	you have said	petīvistis	you have sought
dīxērunt	they have said	petīvērunt	they have sought

Past Perfect Tense
Perfect Stem + Imperfect of **esse**

dīxeram	I had said	petīveram	I had sought
dīxerās	you had said	petīverās	you had sought
dīxerat	he, she, it had said	petīverat	he, she, it had sought
dīxerāmus	we had said	petīverāmus	we had sought
dīxerātis	you had said	petīverātis	you had sought
dīxerant	they had said	petīverant	they had sought

Future Perfect Tense
Perfect Stem + Future of **esse**

dīxerō	I shall have said	petīverō	I shall have sought
dīxeris	you will have said	petīveris	you will have sought
dīxerit	he, she, it will have said	petīverit	he, she, it will have sought
dīxerimus	we shall have said	petīverimus	we shall have sought
dīxeritis	you will have said	petīveritis	you will have sought
dīxerint	they will have said	petīverint	they will have sought

87. **Third -iō conjugation.** There are some third conjugation verbs which end in **-iō** in the present, first person singular. These verbs end in **-iunt** in the third person plural and have **-iē-** before the tense sign **-bā-** in the imperfect. Their perfect tenses are completely regular.

Present Tense	*Imperfect Tense*	*Perfect Tenses*		
faciō	faciēbam	fēcī	fēceram	fēcerō
facis	faciēbās	*etc.*	*etc.*	*etc.*
facit	faciēbat			
facimus	faciēbāmus			
facitis	faciēbātis			
faciunt	faciēbant			

88. Personal pronouns. The personal pronouns are used in all cases in Latin
as in English, except in the nominative case where they are usually omitted
unless the reference is unclear, or unless needed for emphasis; otherwise
the personal endings of the verb absorb the nominative function of the
pronouns. (See **Sec. 25.**)

Personal Pronouns

Singular

	First Person	*Second Person*	*Third Person*		
			Masc.	*Fem.*	*Neut.*
Nom.	ego	tū	is	ea	id
Gen.	meī	tuī	eius	eius	eius
Dat.	mihi	tibi	eī	eī	eī
Acc.	mē	tē	eum	eam	id
Abl.	mē	tē	eō	eā	eō

Plural

Nom.	nōs	vōs	eī	eae	ea
Gen.	nostrum	vestrum	eōrum	eārum	eōrum
Dat.	nōbīs	vōbīs	eīs	eīs	eīs
Acc.	nōs	vōs	eōs	eās	ea
Abl.	nōbīs	vōbīs	eīs	eīs	eīs

Exercises

I. Respondēte Latīnē, quaesō.

1. Quis erat prīmus amor Phoebī?
2. Quis Phoebō amōrem dedit?
3. Cūr Cupīdō erat īrātus?
4. Suntne sagittae Cupīdinis acūtae? Suntne obtūsae?
5. Fīgitne Cupīdō obtūsam sagittam in Phoebum?
6. Quis est pater nymphae?
7. Laudatne Phoebus fōrmam nymphae?
8. Quis est Phoebus?
9. Datne pater nymphae auxilium eī?
10. Mūtatne pater fōrmam eius? Amatne Phoebus etiam eam, nunc laurum?

II A. Conjugate the following verbs in the present, imperfect, perfect, past
perfect, and future perfect.

1. crēscō, crēscere, crēvī, crētum
2. dō, dare, dedī, datum
3. respondeō, respondēre, respondī, responsum

4. petō, petere, petīvī, petītum
5. faciō, facere, fēcī, factum

B. Change these present tense verbs to imperfect:

1. dīcit   dīcēbat   6. iubet
2. facit   7. manet
3. spectat   8. tangit
4. stat   9. petit
5. docet   10. crēscit

C. Change these perfect tense verbs to past perfect:

1. habuērunt   habuerant   6. vīdērunt
2. dīxērunt   7. mānsērunt
3. dedērunt   8. iussērunt
4. tenuērunt   9. ōrāvērunt
5. fēcērunt   10. iūvērunt

Notice the change of accent in the past perfect tense.

III.   Decline the following:

1. magnus amor   4. nōmen fāmōsum
2. coniūnx mea   5. caput meum
3. soror tua   6. hostis novus

IV.   Supply the correct form of the personal pronoun:

1. (*We*), rēgēs, ducibus dōnum dedimus.
2. (*You*), dux, eris rēx Romae.
3. (*I*), nympha, deum amāre nōn possum.
4. (*He*), dux magnus Romae, rēx nōn erit.
5. (*They*), virī Romae, bona consilia habent.
6. (*You*), hostēs, (*her*) nōn nocēre potestis. (**nocēre** takes the dative)
7. (*She*), rēgīna, (*them, f.*) nocēre potest.
8. (*She*) (*us*) nōn nocēre potest.
9. (*They*) (*things*) sunt deō cārissima.
10. (*It*), flumen, (*them, m.*) cēlābit.

V.   Translate into Latin:

1. Cupid gave Phoebus (his) first love.
2. Phoebus had watched Cupid with (his) bow (**arcū**) and arrows.
3. Venus' son had said to Phoebus, "My arrow can transfix you."
4. Cupid holds two arrows in his bow (**arcū**); the one is sharp, the other is dull.
5. Daphne loves only to wander with Diana and her friends in the woods.
6. The father of the nymph is a river god. (god of a river)

7. He gives the nymph a gift—to be an eternal maiden.
8. Phoebus Apollo is the god of the arts, music and medicine; he is also god of the sun.
9. Daphne flees to the river and begs for aid.
10. (Her) father changes the maiden into a tree, the laurel, dear to Phoebus.

Etymology

Aqua (*water*) comes into English in many forms: *aquatic, aquaplane, aquarium, Aquarius* (water-carrier of the Zodiac), *aquatint, aqueduct* (**duc** means *lead*). The famous Pont du Gard in France is one of the most famous aqueducts in the world. Situated dramatically across the Gard River near the town of Nîmes, it spans an enormous valley in three tiers of arches. The trough at the top is about a yard wide and about four feet deep. One can climb the rugged mountainside and walk out into the partially covered aqueduct to view the gorge most advantageously.

The words that come into English from the verb **dīcō, dīcere, dīxī, dictum** are many and varied depending on the root form used: *dictionary, edict, dictaphone, dictate, dictation, dictator, diction, dictum, addict, abdicate, abdication, indict* (**in-** here means *against; to speak against someone, to charge him with an offense*), *indication, indictment*.

Words in English from the stems of **faciō, facere, fēcī, factum** and its many compounds in Latin include the following: *fact, factory, manufacture, faculty, factotum,*[4] *putre(rotten)-faction, putrefy, affect, effect, infect, infection, confection, defect, defective, satis(enough)-fy, amplify, electrify, verify* (*-fy* is from **facere** via Old French **fier**).

*   *   *   *   *

Give the Latin source words for the following underlined words:

"Mono" is an <u>oscular</u> disease.
<u>dolorous</u> sounds
<u>artistic</u> expression
<u>hostile</u> behavior
Il <u>Duce</u>, the name for Mussolini
<u>manual</u> dexterity
a <u>solarium</u> for plants

<u>virgin</u> soil
a <u>vulnerable</u> person
<u>increase</u> in strength
<u>transfix</u> with an arrow
sign the <u>petition</u>
<u>acute</u> reasoning
an <u>obtuse</u> fellow
<u>alter ego</u>

---

[4] *Factotum* comes from the imperative singular **fac** and **totum** (*everything*). The command **"factotum"** (*do everything*) has given English this word for a person who does general service.

Pyramus and Thisbe

Shakespeare took his theme of Romeo and Juliet from Ovid's tale of Pyramus and Thisbe. The story is set in Babylonia. Pyramus and Thisbe live in a duplex, a house with a common wall, and they have fallen in love with each other. Because their parents forbid their marriage, the two meet to converse and send kisses through a crack in the wall, but when love becomes too powerful and the wall too impenetrable, the two lovers decide to meet in the woods at the tomb of Ninus under a mulberry tree. Thisbe comes first and drops her veil in fright as she hides in a cave in fear of a lion all bloody from a recent kill. The lion tears the veil with its bloody mouth and departs. Then Pyramus comes and sees Thisbe's veil all bloody; agonizing over his tardy arrival, he kills himself. Thisbe then comes from the cave, sees the body and bloody garment and realizes that she has been the cause of Pyramus' death. In grief she plunges the dagger into herself. The mulberry tree, which up to then had white berries, now bears purple fruit from the blood-soaked ground near its roots, and the parents bury the ashes of the two lovers in a single urn.

Dialogue
Ad tabulam, quaesō. *To the board, please.*

Chapter XV
PŸRAMUS ET THISBĒ
(pars prīma)

Pȳramus iuvenis pulcherrimus et Thisbē virgō fōrmōsissima domōs vīcīnās tenuērunt. Amantēs erant, et amor tempore crēvit. Parentēs amōrem iuvenum prohibēre temptāvērunt. Sed amor viam facit. Fissum erat in pariete domuum quod[1] nūllī per multōs annōs vīderant. Amantēs hoc fissum prīmō vīderant (quid amor nōn sentit?) et iter vōcis fēcērunt. Pȳramus stābat hinc, illinc Thisbē, et per fissum verba mollia[2] murmurābant. Nocte, "Valē," dīcēbant et utrimque oscula dabant.

Deinde Pȳramus et Thisbē, duo amantēs, consilium habent. Nocte fallere parentēs et domōs relinquere temptābunt. Cum relīquerint domōs et oppidum, ad tumulum Ninī[3] sub arborem convenient. Arbor est mōrus, uberrima pomīs albīs,[4] vīcīna fontī.

Prīmō Thisbē pervenit et sub arbore sedet. Ecce venit leō quī aquās fontis bibere dēsīderat. Quia recēns leō animal necāverat, cruor erat in ōre. Procul Thisbē leōnem videt et in spēluncam obscūram fugit. Ubi fugit, vēlāmina relinquit quae leō ōre cruentō laniat.[5]

Nunc vēnit Pȳramus; vestīgia leōnis et vēlāmina cruenta Thisbēs vīdit. Miserrimus dīxit, "Ūna nox mortem duōrum amantium vīderit. Tū fuistī dignissima vītā longā. Ego sum causa mortis tuī. Ego iussī tē venīre nocte in loca perīculōsa et ego hūc nōn prior vēnī. Ō venīte,[6] leōnēs, dēvorāte meum corpus! Sed est timidum sōlum optāre mortem!" Portāvit vēlāmina Thisbēs ad arborem, dedit oscula lacrimāsque; clāmāvit, "Ego quoque mortem quaeram;" itaque gladiō sē necāvit. Sub arborem iacuit, et gladium ē vulnere traxit. Cruor ēmicat[7] ut fons; ubi herbam tangit, poma alba arboris mōrī[4] purpurea facit.

---

[1] *In the wall of the houses was a crack which . . .*
[2] *Soft words*
[3] *At the tomb of Ninus.*
[4] *A mulberry tree, very heavy with white fruit*; **mōrī**, *of the mulberry*; do not confuse with **morī**, *to die*, the infinitive of the deponent **morior**.
[5] *Which the lion tears with its bloody mouth.*
[6] *Come*, imperative, pl.
[7] *Spurts up.*

Verba

Certain words will appear in the vocabulary with an asterisk (*) beside them. These words will be required to be learned as valuable additions to the student's vocabulary. The others are necessary for the reading, but need not be acquired at this time.

NOUNS

*amāns, amantis, c.	one who loves, a lover
*consilium, -iī, n.	plan, advice
*cruor, -ōris, m.	blood
*domus, -ūs, f.	house, home
fissum, -ī, n.	crack
*fons, fontis, m.	fountain, spring
*gladius, -iī, m.	sword
*herba, -ae, f.	grass
*iter, itineris, n.	road, path, way
leō, leōnis, m.	lion
*mors, mortis, f.	death
*parēns, parentis, c.	parent
pariēs, parietis, m.	wall
pomum, -ī, n.	fruit, apple
*Pȳramus, -ī, m.	Pyramus (a youth)
*tempus, -oris, n.	time
*Thisbē, -ēs, f.	Thisbe (a maiden)
tumulus, -ī, m.	grave, mound
vēlāmen, -inis, n.	garment, covering
*vestīgium, -iī, n.	track, footstep

VERBS

*bibō, -ere, bibī, bibitum	drink
*conveniō, -īre, -vēnī, -ventum	meet, assemble
fallō, -ere, fefellī, falsum	deceive
*fugiō, -ere, fūgī, -itum	flee
murmurō (1)	murmur
optō (1)	wish for, desire
*perveniō, -īre, -vēnī, -ventum	arrive
*quaerō, -ere, quaesīvī, quaesītum	seek, ask, inquire
*quaesō, -ere; quaesō (tē)	seek, beg; I beg (you), please
*relinquō, -ere, relīquī, relictum	leave behind
*sentiō, -īre, sensī, -sum	feel, know, sense

*trahō, -ere, traxī, -ctum	draw, draw out, drag
*veniō, -īre, vēnī, ventum	come

ADJECTIVES

*albus, -a, -um	white
cruentus, -a, -um	bloody
*dignus, -a, -um + *abl.*	worthy (of)
purpureus, -a, -um	purple
*vīcīnus, -a, -um + *dat.*	neighboring, near (to)

OTHER WORDS

*ē (ex) + *abl.*	out of, from, out from
*hinc	here, on this side, hence
illinc	there, on that side, thence
prior, prius	before, earlier
procul	at a distance
*quī, quae, quod	who, which
*quia	because
recēns	recently
*sub + *acc.* or *abl.*	under, beneath
*ut	as, like
utrimque	on each side, on both sides

Structure

89. Fourth conjugation. The infinitive ending of the fourth conjugation is
-īre: venīre. To the stem **venī-** are added the personal endings. Notice how
similar the fourth conjugation is to the third **-io**.

Third -io Conjugation		*Fourth Conjugation*	
fugiō, fugere		**veniō, venīre**	
fugiō	I flee, am fleeing, do flee	**veniō**	I come, am coming, do come
fugis		**venīs**	
fugit		**venit**	
fugimus		**venīmus**	
fugitis		**venītis**	
fugiunt		**veniunt**	

The vowel of the fourth conjugation is **-ī-**, but it, like all vowels, must be
shortened before final **-t** or **-nt**. Notice that the accent is on the penult in

the first and second person plural of the fourth conjugation because of the long vowel.

Imperfect tense: **veniēbam, veniēbās, veniēbat, veniēbāmus, veniēbātis, veniēbant**

Perfect tense: **vēnī, vēnistī, vēnit, vēnimus, vēnistis, vēnērunt**

Past perfect tense: **vēneram, vēnerās, vēnerat, vēnerāmus, vēnerātis, vēnerant**

Future perfect tense: **vēnerō, vēneris, vēnerit, vēnerimus, vēneritis, vēnerint**

90. Future tense, all conjugations. The greatest difference between the first and second conjugations and the third and fourth conjugations is in the formation of the *future tense*. The tense sign for the future in the *first and second conjugations* is **-bi-**,[8] but in the *third and fourth*, the sign is **-e**.[9] The English auxiliary is *shall* (*will*) for the future: "I shall love, you will love, he will love, we shall love, you (*pl.*) will love, they will love."

First	*Second*	*Third*	*Third-io*	*Fourth*
amābō	docēbō	dīcam	faciam	veniam
amābis	docēbis	dīcēs	faciēs	veniēs
amābit	docēbit	dīcet	faciet	veniet
amābimus	docēbimus	dīcēmus	faciēmus	veniēmus
amābitis	docēbitis	dīcētis	faciētis	veniētis
amābunt	docēbunt	dīcent	facient	venient

| **-bi-** | REMEMBER THESE SIGNS | **-e-** |

91. Synopsis of the verb. A short-cut method for reviewing the forms of a verb is the *synopsis*, a presentation of a single person and number of the verb in all tenses. A synopsis of **vocō, vocāre, vocāvī, vocātum** in the third person singular, all tenses, follows:

Present	**vocat**
Imperfect	**vocābat**
Future	**vocābit**
Perfect	**vocāvit**
Past Perfect	**vocāverat**
Future Perfect	**vocāverit**

92. Figures of speech: simile. The comparison of two ideas, using *like* or *as* to introduce the compared image is called *simile*. It is a device much used

---

[8] Note **-bō** for first person singular and **-bu-** for third person plural.

[9] Note that **-e-** becomes **-a-** in the first person singular.

by poets, and although the idea of gore spouting up, fountain-like, may be a bit too graphic for a poetic image today, it is, nevertheless, the simile used by Ovid, although the original compares the spurting up to a jet stream from a broken pipe.

Cruor ēmicat, ut fons . . .
The blood spurts out, like a fountain . . .

93. Superlative of adjectives in **-er**. The superlative of adjectives which end in **-er** is formed by adding **-errimus, -a, -um** to the stem.

pulcher, -chra, -chrum	**pulcherrimus, -a, -um**	most beautiful
miser, misera, miserum	**miserrimus, -a, -um**	most unhappy
sacer, sacra, sacrum	**sacerrimus, -a, -um**	most sacred

94. Declension of **domus**. **Domus** is irregular, being formed in part like a fourth declension noun (see **Sec. 101**) and in part like a second declension noun in the accusative and ablative. Remember also that it is a feminine noun ending in **-us**:

	Singular	*Plural*
Nom.	**domus**	**domūs**
Gen.	**domūs, domī**	**domuum, domōrum**
Dat.	**domuī, domō**	**domibus**
Acc.	**domum**	**domōs, domūs**
Abl.	**domū, domō**	**domibus**
Loc.[10]	**domī**	

Exercises

I. Respondēte Latīnē, quaesō.

  1. Quis est Pȳramus? Quis est Thisbē?
  2. Ubi habitābant?
  3. Quī amōrem iuvenum prohibuērunt?
  4. Ubi fissum erat?
  5. Quid est consilium iuvenum?
  6. Ubi convenient?
  7. Quis vēnit prīmō?
  8. Quis adest quoque?
  9. Quid fēcit leō? Quid fēcit Thisbē?
  10. Quid colōrem pomōrum mūtāvit?

---

[10] Locative is the place-where case: at home—**domī**. It exists also with names of cities, towns, and small islands, resembling the genitive in the singular of nouns of the first and second declensions: **Romae**, at Rome.

II A. Conjugate in all six tenses: **petō, petere**; **fugiō, fugere**; **sentiō, sentīre**.

B. Give a synopsis of: **relinquō**   3rd person singular
                    quaerō   1st person singular
                    faciō   ·   3rd personal plural
                    perveniō   1st person plural

III.   Change each verb to the future tense:

    1. Iuvenēs oscula utrimque dant.   <u>dabunt</u>
    2. Pȳramus vēlāmina Thisbēs videt.
    3. Pȳramus prīmus nōn venit.
    4. Leō Thisbem nōn nocet.
    5. Amor viam facit.
    6. Amantēs domōs relinquunt.
    7. Pȳramus sē necat.
    8. Poma nōn sunt alba.
    9. Cruor colōrem pomōrum mūtāvit.
   10. Leō Thisbem nōn dēvorāvit.

IV.   From the following list of adverbs, choose the correct one for each sentence:

hinc, illinc, hūc, hīc, ibi, ōlim, deinde, dēnique, recens, bene, prior, procul, subitō, utrimque, statim.

    1. Pȳramus (*here*) in herbā iacet.
    2. Leō (*to this place*) nōn venit.
    3. (*On this side*) stābat Pȳramus, (*on that side*) Thisbē.
    4. (*Once upon a time*) erat arbor albīs pomīs in silvā.
    5. Oscula (*on each side*) dabant.
    6. "Ego (*earlier*) hūc nōn vēnī," dīxit Pȳramus.
    7. (*Then*) Pȳramus vēlāmina vīdit.
    8. Thisbē (*from a distance*) leōnem vīdit.
    9. (*Immediately*) Pȳramus vestīgia leōnis vīdit.
   10. (*Finally*) Pȳramus quoque mortem quaesīvit.

V.   Translate into Latin:

    1. Pyramus loved Thisbe, but their parents tried to prevent (their) love.
    2. They spoke through a hole in the wall.
    3. They had neighboring houses.
    4. They have a plan to leave their homes at night and meet secretly.
    5. They will deceive their parents and leave the city.
    6. They will meet at the tree near the tomb of Ninus.
    7. Thisbe is the first to come (comes first) and sees a lion.
    8. Thisbe flees and leaves behind her veil.

9. The lion tears (**laniat**) the veil with his bloody mouth.
10. Pyramus is most wretched when he sees the veil, and he kills himself with his sword.

Etymology

The endings **-arium** and **-orium** mean *a place for*. By adding this suffix to the following roots, English obtains several familiar words:

a place to hear	audit- _____
a place to have the sun	sol- _____
a place for water	aqua- _____
a place for penguins	penguin- _____
a planter holding earth	terr- _____

The Roman baths had three areas for three temperatures of water: a **calidarium** (for hot water), a **tepidarium** (for lukewarm water), and a **frigidarium** (for cold water).

The **-ium** sometimes changes to *-y* in English; what happens to **dormitorium** and **observatorium**?

*   *   *   *   *

Give the English derivatives for the following definitions:

a crack in the rock	f _____
the house one lives in	domi _____
a man who fights with a sword	g _____
the triptik from AAA	i _____
like a lion	l _____
mother and father	p _____
not eternal	t _____
a meeting of salesmen in New York	c _____
drink liquor	imb _____
something sought	qu _____
leave behind, give up	r _____
a Greek mood	o _____
a feeling	s _____

Dialogue

Aperīte librōs, quaesō.	*Open your books, please.*
Claudite librōs, quaesō.	*Close your books, please.*
Legite fābulam, quaesō.	*Read the story, please.*

Chapter XVI
PȲRAMUS ET THISBĒ
(pars secunda)

Ecce Thisbē ex spēluncā venit. Amantem oculīs quaerit quod eī dē perīculīs nārrāre dēsīderat. Locum et fōrmam arboris videt, sed color pomī eam incertam facit. Dum haec dubitat, videt in herbā sub hanc arborem corpus Pȳramī cruentum. Multīs lacrimīs ita clāmat virgō territa, "Pȳrame, quis tē ā mē rapuit? Pȳrame, Pȳrame, respondē, tua tē cārissima Thisbē nōminat!"

Ad nōmen Thisbēs Pȳramus oculōs aperuit; tum iterum eōs in morte clausit.

Ubi Thisbē vēlāmina sua gladiumque Pȳramī vīdit, "Tua tē manus," inquit, "amorque tuus necāvit.[1] Mihi quoque sunt amor et manus. Mē in mortem mittam; sī causa mortis tuae fuerō, comes quoque mortis tuae erō. Ō, parentēs miserī, date nōbis hoc dōnum. Pōnite in hōc tumulō ūnō nōs quōs[2] amor coniūnxit, quōs ūna hōra coniūnxit. At tū arbor, habē semper poma purpurea, monumenta duōrum amantium mortuōrum."

Dum haec dīcit, gladiō Pȳramī sē necat. Et deī et parentēs haec verba audīvērunt, nam color pomī mōrī[3] nōn iam albus semper est purpureus atque cinis duōrum amantium in ūnā urnā requiescit.[4]

---

[1] Latin often uses a singular verb with a plural subject.
[2] *Us whom love has joined together.*
[3] *Of the mulberry tree.*
[4] *Rest.*

Verba

NOUNS

cinis, -eris, *m.*	ashes[5]
*comes, comitis, *c.*	companion, sharer
*hōra, -ae, *f.*	hour
monumentum, -ī, *n.*	memorial, reminder
*perīculum, -ī, *n.*	danger
*urna, -ae, *f.*	urn, vessel of baked clay

VERBS

aperiō, -īre, -uī, -pertum	open
*audiō, -īre, -īvī, -ītum	hear
claudō, -ere, clausī, clausum	close
*inquit	says, said
*legō, -ere, lēgī, lectum	read, gather, choose
*mittō, -ere, mīsī, missum	send
*nōminō (1)	call, name
*pōnō, -ere, posuī, positum	put, place
*rapiō, -ere, -uī, raptum	seize, carry off

ADJECTIVES

*incertus, -a, -um	uncertain, unsure
*mortuus, -a, -um	dead

OTHER WORDS

at (*introducing a contrary idea*)	but, yet, but meanwhile
*atque	and, and also
*nam	for
*nōn iam	no longer
*quōs	whom, *acc. pl.*

Structure

95. The demonstrative pronoun and adjective *this*: **hic, haec, hoc**.[6] **Hic** in its declined forms can function either as a *pronoun* or as an *adjective*:

---

[5] **Cinis** means the ashes of a corpse that has been burned; it is frequently used in both numbers, but occurs in the plural especially in poetry and in post-Augustan prose. Cf. English, *cinerary* urn.

[6] Some dictionaries list **hic** and **hoc** with a long vowel in the nominative, but this text, like most, will consider the vowel short to avoid confusion with the adverb **hīc**, *here*, and the ablative **hōc**.

Pronoun:	**Hoc** est bonum	*This* is good.
Adjective:	**Hic puer** est bonus	*This boy* is good.

Used either way, it agrees with the word or idea it refers to or modifies.

	\multicolumn{3}{c}{Singular (*this*)}	\multicolumn{3}{c}{Plural (*these*)}
	M.	*F.*	*N.*	*M.*	*F.*	*N.*
Nom.	hic	haec	hoc	hī	hae	haec
Gen.	huius	huius	huius	hōrum	hārum	hōrum
Dat.	huic	huic	huic	hīs	hīs	hīs
Acc.	hunc	hanc	hoc	hōs	hās	haec
Abl.	hōc	hāc	hōc	hīs	hīs	hīs

96. The demonstrative pronoun and adjective *that*: **ille, illa, illud. Ille** in all its declined forms can also function either as a pronoun or as an adjective:

Pronoun:	**Illud** est novum.	*That* is strange.
Adjective:	**Illa arbor** est pulchra.	*That tree* is beautiful.

	\multicolumn{3}{c}{Singular (*that*)}	\multicolumn{3}{c}{Plural (*those*)}
	M.	*F.*	*N.*	*M.*	*F.*	*N.*
Nom.	ille	illa	illud	illī	illae	illa
Gen.	illīus	illīus	illīus	illōrum	illārum	illōrum
Dat.	illī	illī	illī	illīs	illīs	illīs
Acc.	illum	illam	illud	illōs	illās	illa
Abl.	illō	illā	illō	illīs	illīs	illīs

The inflected forms of both **hic** and **ille** often function as *substantive pronouns, with the gender indicating whether men, women, or things are being implied.* Since Latin has both natural and grammatical gender, however, the context helps to determine the antecedent.

Hī sunt mortuī.	*These men* are dead.
Illī sunt vīvī.	*Those men* are alive.
Haec venit.	*This woman* is coming.
Hanc videō.	I see *this woman*.
Hic respondit.	*This man* answered.
Hoc videō.	I see *this thing*.
Hī ōrāvērunt.	*These men* prayed.
Hae respondērunt.	*These women* replied.
Illae respondērunt.	*Those women* replied.
Illud nōn est sacrum.	*That thing* is not sacred.
Illam nōn amō.	I do not love *that woman* (*or* her).
Illum nōn vīdī.	I have not seen *that man* (*or* him).
Illī pervēnērunt.	*Those men* arrived. (*or* They arrived.)
Pān haec dīxit.	Pan spoke *these things*.

Hic and ille can also mean *the latter* and *the former*, respectively: Iuppiter Mercuriō dīcit. Ille (*the former*) huic (*the latter*) fābulam dē senibus bonīs in terrā nārrat.

97. Imperative of verbs, all conjugations. The imperative mood regularly gives a command. The singular imperative is formed by dropping the -re of the infinitive form. The plural adds -te to this stem. This third conjugation uses -ite for the plural.

	I	II	III	III-iō	IV
Infinitive:	vocā(re)	docē(re)	mitte(re)	fuge(re)	venī(re)
Imper. Sing.:	vocā	docē	mitte[7]	fuge	venī
Imper. Pl.:	vocāte	docēte	mittite	fugite	venīte

Note the following accents, following the antepenultimate rule:

vocáte   docéte   míttite   fúgite   veníte

Pōnite in hōc tumulō nōs . . .   Place us in this grave . . .
Habē semper poma purpurea . . .   Always have purple fruit . . .
Ōrāte deōs.   Pray to the gods.
Venīte ad tabulam.   Come to the board.
Salvē!   Hello! (*Greeting one person*)
Valēte!   Goodbye! (*Leaving more than one person*)

Exercises

I. Respondēte Latīnē, quaesō.

    1. Cūr Thisbē Pȳramum quaesīvit?
    2. Suntne poma adhūc alba?
    3. Quem Thisbē in herbā vīdit?
    4. Quid clāmat Thisbē?
    5. Cum Pȳramus nōmen "Thisbem" audīvit, quid fēcit?
    6. Quae[8] Thisbē prope corpus Pȳramī vīdit?
    7. Quid est dōnum quod[9] Thisbē parentēs ōrāvit?
    8. Quid est dōnum quod Thisbē arborem ōrāvit?
    9. Quid dēnique fēcit Thisbē?

II A. Supply the correct form of **hic**:

    1. _____ arbor est pulchra.
    2. _____ gladius est acūtus.

---

[7] The imperative singular of **dīcō** and **faciō** is irregular: **dīc** and **fac**.
[8] *What things.*
[9] *Which.*

3. _____ librum in manū habeō.
4. _____ librōs in scholā habēmus.
5. _____ puellam Pȳramus amat.
6. _____ dōnum nōn est tibi.
7. _____ cinis in ūnā urnā requiescit.
8. _____ arborem Thisbē nōn videt.
9. _____ pōma sunt purpurea.
10. _____ ūna hōra duōs amantēs coniunget.

B. Supply the correct form of **ille**:

1. _____ liber est novus.
2. _____ fābula est longa.
3. _____ dōnum est novum.
4. _____ librum novum habeō.
5. _____ longam fābulam amō.
6. _____ dōnum sacrum ōrāvī.
7. _____ pōma sunt purpurea.
8. _____ gladiō sē necāvit.
9. Aperī _____ oculōs pulchrōs.
10. Parentēs erant miserī propter _____ amantēs mortuōs.

III. Supply the correct form of the imperative. The vocative will indicate whether you need the singular or plural.

1. (*Place*), discipulī, librōs in mēnsā.
2. (*Place*), Thisbē, gladium in herbā.
3. (*Hear*), discipulī, verba magistrī.
4. (*Read*), discipulī, fābulam in librōs.
5. (*Open*), Marce, portam (*door*).
6. (*Close*), rēgīna, portās rēgiae.
7. (*Hear*), Marce, mūsicam deōrum.
8. (*Write*), discipulī, nōmina hīc, quaesō. (*Lesson IV, Dialogue*)
9. (*Open*), servī, urnās.
10. (*Send*), parentēs, fīliās fīliōsque ad scholam.

IV. Give a synopsis of the following verbs; translate each form into English:

1. **mittō:** 1st person singular
2. **legō:** 3rd person plural
3. **pōnō:** 3rd person singular
4. **audiō:** 2nd person singular

V. Translate into Latin:

1. Thisbe wants to tell Pyramus (*dat.*) [about] these dangers.
2. She hesitates when she sees the color of the fruit.
3. She sees the body of Pyramus covered with blood (the bloody body).

4. Pyramus did not open his eyes again.
5. Thisbe said, "This great love has killed you."
6. "I shall be your companion in death." (the companion of your death)
7. "O, wretched parents, give us this gift."
8. "Place [our] ashes in a single urn."
9. The gods heard the words of the maiden, and the parents placed the ashes in a single urn.
10. The color of the fruit of the mulberry (**mōrus**) is always purple.

Etymology

Space Age Vocabulary

LATIN

astronaut	**astrum, -ī**, *n.* (*star*) + **nauta, -ae**, *m.* (*sailor*)	
satellite	**satelles, -itis**, *c.*	an attendant, guard, escort
navigation	**navigāre**	to sail
cosmonaut	**cosmos** (*Greek*) + **nauta**	the world + sailor
orbit	**orbita, -ae**, *f.*	track made by a wheel
propellant	**prō** (*forward*) + **pellere** (*to push*)	
rocket	diminutive of (*Italian*) **rocca** (*distaff*)	shaped like a staff
retrorocket	**retrō**	back, backward
Jupiter	**Iuppiter**	king of gods and men, sky god
Juno	**Iuno**	queen of heavens
Mercury	**Mercurius**	messenger son of Jupiter
Delta	**Delta** (*Greek*)	fourth letter of Greek alphabet
Atlas	**Atlās**	mythical giant holding up the sky or the world
Centaur	**Centaurus**	half-man, half-horse creature
Titan	**Tītan**	monumental offspring of Earth and Sky
Saturn	**Sāturnus**	Roman god identified with Cronos, father of Jupiter
Apollo	**Phoebus Apollo**	god of the sun, the arts, healing, and music

Gemini	**geminī**	twins, particularly Castor and Pollux, brothers of Helen and Clytemnestra; one was mortal, the other immortal
Pegasus	**Pegasus**	the winged horse, son of decapitated Medusa
Nimbus	**nimbus, -ī,** *m.*	a cloud
monitor	**moneō, monitum**	warn
communication	**commūnicāre (commūnis)**	communicate (common)
planet	**planēta** from *Grk.* **planētēs**	wandering
lunar	**lūna, -ae,** *f.*	moon
solar	**sōl, sōlis,** *m.*	sun
Mariner	**mare, maris,** *n.*	sea (traveller)
interplanetary	**inter + planēta**	between planets
module	**modulus, -ī,** *m.*	a small measure
command	**commandāre**	command
space	**spatium, -ī,** *n.*	space
station	**stō, stāre, statum**	stand
scientific	**scientia, -ae,** *f.*	science
laboratory	**labōrāre**	to work
umbilical	**umbilicus, -ī,** *m.*	the navel
tower, turret	**turris, turris,** *f.*	tower
liquid	**liquidus, -a, -um**	liquid
trajectory	**trāns** (*across*) **+ iacere** (*throw*)	the path of a moving body

Atalanta and Hippomenes

The maiden Atalanta, exposed as an infant because her royal father wanted a son, had been raised in the woods by animals and had developed into a fine, strapping, beautiful young woman by the time she presented herself to her father. The king was delighted with the splendid, proud girl and accepted her gladly as his daughter and heir. Because of the unusual circumstances of her education, Atalanta conforms to the pattern of the hero who grows up away from parents and, because of the altered conditions, is stronger, wiser, and better able to cope with the world than he would have been had he been reared at home.

Atalanta was so beautiful that many suitors desired to marry her, but hoping to avoid wedlock, Atalanta imposed a harsh restriction on any suitor. "Race with me," she demanded, "and if you lose, you die. As reward, I shall be wife to the victor." And many young princes had died for this prize.

Hippomenes, who first came only to watch, had fallen in love himself with the maiden. Praying to Venus for help, he was given three golden apples which he threw to the side one at a time during the race. Each time Atalanta, delayed by her desire for the golden apple, was slowed down, and Hippomenes raced ahead to win the contest and a wife. Atalanta, who had noticed the courage and manly grace of Hippomenes, was pleased by the outcome.

The two, however, forgot to acknowledge their indebtedness to Venus, and they did not show proper moderation in waiting to consummate their love; therefore they were turned into lions by the offended goddess.

Dialogue

Est prīma hōra.	*It is the first hour.*[1]
Sunt Kalendae Novembris.	*It is the Kalends (first) of November.*[1]
Sunt Nōnae Septembris.	*It is the Nones (fifth) of September.*[1]
Sunt Idūs Martiae.	*It is the Ides (15th) of March.*

Chapter XVII
ATALANTA ET HIPPOMENĒS
(pars prīma)

Forsitan audīvistī dē virgine quae virōs in certāmine cursūs superābat. Illa fābula nōn est rūmor, superābat enim Atalanta. Hominēs dīcēbant hanc esse tam clāram fōrmā quam pedibus.[2]

Ubi haec virgō dē coniuge scīre dēsīderāvit, deus respondit: "Fuge coniugem, Atalanta. Nōn dēbēs coniugem habēre; erit mors tibi." Territa virgō in silvā vīvit innuba et turbam procōrum fugit hīs verbīs dūrīs: "Nōn erō coniūnx, nisi prius victa cursū. Pedibus contendite mēcum. Dabor coniūnx, praemium victōrī. Sed mors erit praemium tardīs. Ea estō[3] lēx certāminis!"

Tamen turba temerāria procōrum ad hanc lēgem vēnit quōs tanta potentia fōrmae amōrisque in audāciam addūxerat. Sēderat quoque Hippomenēs spectātor cursūs; damnāverat procōs: "Petiturne coniūnx per tanta perīcula?" Sed ubi vīdit fōrmam corpusque puellae, dīxit "Mihi ignōscite, quōs[4] culpāvī. Praemia nōndum sciēbam. Ea est vērē pulchra! Ego quoque fōrmā Atalantae capior." Dum laudat, ignēs amōris crescunt; optat victōriam virginī. "Cūr fortūna huius certāminis ā mē nōn temptātur? Deus amantem iuvābit." Dum spectat, virgō pede alite[5] volat. Quamquam vidētur īre nōn tardius sagittā Scythicā,[6] tamen Hippomenēs fōrmam virginis magis mīrātur.[7] Atalanta ad fīnem pervenit; cornū sonātur. Atalanta victor corōnātur. Iuvenibus victīs poena mortis datur.

---

[1] See Appendix for dates and time.

[2] *Men said that this girl was as famous for her beauty as for her (fleetness of) foot.* (Abl. of respect)

[3] *Let this be* . . . (future imperative).

[4] Supply **vōs** as the antecedent of **quōs**, *you whom* . . .

[5] *On swift foot.*

[6] *Not more slowly than a Scythian arrow.*

[7] *Admires*, active meaning with passive ending.

Hippomenēs tamen nōn dēterritus ad certāmen sē parat. Atalantam rogat: "Cūr victōriam facilem[8] quaeris? Contende mēcum! Sī victor sum, nōn pudōrī tibi[9] erit vincī ā mē! Mihi pater est magnus Megareus cui avus est Neptūnus, rēx aquārum." Dum ille dīcit, fīlia rēgis eum spectat et dubitat superārī an vincere malit.[10] Dīcit haec verba: "Quī deus eum iubet coniugem petere? Nōn sum digna pretiī, mē iudice.[11] Sed ille adhūc puer est; nōn iuvenis mē movet, sed aetās. Ō Hippomenēs, relinque loca perīculōsa dum potes. Dēbēs amārī ā puellā meliōre.[12] Sed cūr tamen tū es mihi cūra? Culpa nōn est mea. Ō miser Hippomenēs, erās dignus vīvere!" Sīc dubitat virgō— amat, sed amōrem nōn sentit.

Verba

NOUNS

*****aetās, aetātis,** *f.*	age
*****audācia, -ae,** *f.*	boldness
avus, -ī, *m.*	grandfather
*****certāmen, -minis,** *n.*	contest, struggle
*****cornū, -ūs,** *n.*	horn, end, tip
culpa, -ae, *f.*	guilt, blame, fault
*****cūra, -ae,** *f.*	care, concern
*****cursus, -ūs,** *m.*	running, course
*****ignis, ignis, -ium,** *m.*	fire
*****lēx, lēgis,** *f.*	law
Megareus, -ī, *m.*	Megareus (*a king*)
*****Neptūnus, -ī,** *m.*	Neptune (*sea god*)
procus, -ī, *m.*	suitor
*****rūmor, -ōris,** *m.*	rumor, hearsay
spectātor, -ōris, *m.*	spectator
turba, -ae, *f.*	crowd
*****victōria, -ae,** *f.*	victory

VERBS

*****addūcō, -ere, -dūxī, -ductum**	bring to, draw to, influence
*****capiō, -ere, cēpī, captum**	capture, take
corōnō (1)	crown
*****culpō (1)**	blame

---

[8] *Easy* (**facilem** is a third declension adjective: see **Sec. 112**).

[9] *It will not cause you shame* (double dative; **pudor, -ōris,** *m., shame*).

[10] *She hesitates whether she prefers to . . .*

[11] *If I am any judge* (two words in abl.: lit., *with me as judge*).

[12] *By a better maid.*

*damnō (1)	condemn
*eō, īre, iī (īvī), itum	go
*ignōscō, -ere, -nōvī, -nōtum + *dat.*	forgive
*moveō, -ēre, mōvī, mōtum	move, stir
*sciō, scīre, scīvī *or* sciī, scītum	know
*sonō (1)	sound
*superō (1)	surpass, rise above, conquer
*vincō, -ere, vīcī, victum	conquer, defeat, get the better of, vanquish, be victorious

ADJECTIVES

dēterritus, -a, -um	deterred
dūrus, -a, -um	hard, harsh
innubus, -a, -um	unwed
*tantus, -a, -um	such a great, so great
*tardus, -a, -um	late, slow
*victus, -a, -um	conquered, beaten

OTHER WORDS

an	or
*forsitan	perhaps
*magis	more, bigger
*nisi	unless, if . . . not
nōndum	not yet
*quī, quae, quod	who, which, that
*tam	so
(nōn) tardius	(not) more slowly
vērē	truly

IDIOM

*vidētur	he, she, it seems (*passive of* see)

Structure

98. The passive voice. The active voice of the verb expresses what the subject of the verb *is* or *does*. The passive voice expresses what is *done to* the subject of the sentence (by someone or something).

Active: Agricolae aquam **portant**.   The farmers *carry* the water.
Passive: Aqua ab agricolīs **portātur**.   Water *is carried* by the farmers.

Active: Parentēs dōnum **dant**.   The parents *give* the gift.
Passive: Dōnum ā parentibus **datur**.   The gift *is given* by the parents.

The passive forms in the present, imperfect, and future of the verb are based on the same present stems which you have already learned for all four conjugations, but the *passive endings* are added.

Passive Endings First Conjugation

-r	**portor**	I am carried, am being carried
-ris	**portāris**	you are carried, are being carried
-tur	**portātur**	he, she, it is carried, is being carried
-mur	**portāmur**	we are carried, are being carried
-minī	**portāminī**	you are carried, are being carried
-ntur	**portantur**	they are carried, are being carried

Note how the stem vowel of each conjugation continues to be the characteristic vowel before the passive endings are added.

Remember:

I	II	III	III-io	IV
a	e	e(i)	e(i)	i
	doceor	mittor	capior	audior
	docēris	mitteris	caperis	audīris
	docētur	mittitur	capitur	audītur
	docēmur	mittimur	capimur	audīmur
	docēminī	mittiminī	capiminī	audīminī
	docentur	mittuntur	capiuntur	audiuntur

The *imperfect passive* is formed by inserting between the stem and the passive endings the tense sign **-ba-**, which was also used in the active voice.

portābar[13]	docēbar	mittēbar	capiēbar	audiēbar
portābāris	docēbāris	mittēbāris	capiēbāris	audiēbāris
portābātur	docēbātur	mittēbātur	capiēbātur	audiēbātur
portābāmur	docēbāmur	mittēbāmur	capiēbāmur	audiēbāmur
portābāminī	docēbāminī	mittēbāminī	capiēbāminī	audiēbāminī
portābantur	docēbantur	mittēbantur	capiēbantur	audiēbantur

The *future passive* is formed by inserting the tense sign **-bi-** before the passive ending for first and second conjugations, the vowel **-e-** for third and fourth:

---

[13] I was carried, I was being carried; you were carried, were being carried; *etc.*

-bi-		-e-		
portābor[14]	docēbor	mittar	capiar	audiar
portāberis	docēberis	mittēris	capiēris	audiēris
portābitur	docēbitur	mittētur	capiētur	audiētur
portābimur	docēbimur	mittēmur	capiēmur	audiēmur
portābiminī	docēbiminī	mittēminī	capiēminī	audiēminī
portābuntur	docēbuntur	mittentur	capientur	audientur

99. Ablative of agent. The ablative with the preposition **ā (ab)** is used to indicate the person by whom an act is performed. It is commonly used *with the passive voice.*

Vōx **ā puerō** audītur.	The voice is heard *by the boy.*
Virgō **ā iuvene** vincitur.	The maiden is conquered *by the youth.*
Puer **ā magistrō** docētur.	The boy is taught *by the teacher.*
Fābula **ā poētā** nārrābātur.	The story was being told *by the poet.*
Lēgēs **ab hominibus** fōrmābuntur.	Laws will be made *by men.*

100. The relative pronoun, **quī**, **quae**, **quod**. The relative pronoun agrees with its antecedent in number and gender, but takes its case from its use in its own clause.

	Singular				*Plural*		
Nom.	**quī**	**quae**	**quod**	*who, that, which*	**quī**	**quae**	**quae**
Gen.	**cuius**	**cuius**	**cuius**	*whose*	**quōrum**	**quārum**	**quōrum**
Dat.	**cui**	**cui**	**cui**	*to whom, for whom*	**quibus**	**quibus**	**quibus**
Acc.	**quem**	**quam**	**quod**	*whom, that, which*	**quōs**	**quās**	**quae**
Abl.	**quō**	**quā**	**quō**	*by whom, by which*	**quibus**	**quibus**	**quibus**

Vir, **quī** (*Subject of* **stat**) in certāmine stat, est Hippomenēs.	The man *who* stands in the race is Hippomenes.
Vir, **quem** (*Object of* **vīdī**) in certāmine vīdī, est Hippomenēs.	The man *whom* I saw in the race is Hippomenes.
Nympha **quae** in silvā errāvit est Callistō.	The nymph *who* wandered in the woods is Callisto.
Nympha **quam** Apollō amāvit est Daphnē.	The nymph *whom* Apollo loved is Daphne.

---

[14]I shall be carried; you will be carried; *etc.*

Hī sunt senēs **quibus** Iuppiter dōnum dat.	These are the old people *to whom* Jupiter is giving a gift.
Senēs **quōs** dī amant nihil timent.	Old men *whom* the gods love fear nothing.
Agricola **cui** casa dabātur est laetus.	The farmer *to whom* the house was given is joyful.

In each sentence note how the relative pronoun *agrees with its antecedent in number and gender*, but how *its use in the relative clause determines its case*.

101. Fourth declension. The fourth declension forms are identified by the vowel **-u-** in the stem of the noun, except for dative and ablative plural.

	Masculine		Neuter	
	Singular	*Plural*	*Singular*	*Plural*
Nom.	**cursus**	**cursūs**	**cornū**	**cornua**
Gen.	**cursūs**	**cursuum**	**cornūs**	**cornuum**
Dat.	**cursuī, -ū**	**cursibus**	**[cornū]**[15]	**cornibus**
Acc.	**cursum**	**cursūs**	**cornū**	**cornua**
Abl.	**cursū**	**cursibus**	**cornū**	**cornibus**

Manus and **domus** are two feminine nouns in this otherwise masculine and neuter declension. **Manus** is declined like the masculine **cursus**, and **domus** has been declined in a previous lesson (see **Sec. 94**).

102. Passive infinitives, all conjugations. You are already familiar with the active infinitives of the conjugations:

I	II	III	III-iō	IV
portāre	**docēre**	**petere**	**capere**	**audīre**
to carry	*to teach*	*to seek*	*to take*	*to hear*

The passive infinitives are formed by changing the final vowel (**e**) of the infinitive ending to **-ī**, except in the third conjugation, where the whole ending becomes **-ī**.

I	II	III	III-iō	IV
portārī	**docērī**	**petī**	**capī**	**audīrī**
to be carried	*to be taught*	*to be sought*	*to be taken*	*to be heard*

Spectātōrēs procul **audīrī** possunt.	The spectators are able *to be* (can be) *heard* at a distance.

---

[15] Never used.

Exercises

I.   Respondēte Latīnē, quaesō.

1. Audīvistīne fābulam dē Atalantā, puellā clārā?
2. Estne fābula dē virgine rūmor?
3. Cūr Atalanta coniugem fugit?
4. Ubi Atalanta vīvit?
5. Quis est lēx certāminis?
6. Quī ad hanc lēgem vēnērunt?
7. Cūr vēnērunt?
8. Amatne Hippomenēs spectātor Atalantam?
9. Ubi (*when*) Hippomenēs fōrmam Atalantae vīdit, quid fēcit?
10. Quid Atalanta facit?

II A. Give a passive synopsis: present, imperfect, and future tenses only, of the following verbs (Be sure to translate each form):

1. **laudō:**   3rd person singular
2. **moveō:**   1st person singular
3. **vincō:**   3rd person plural
4. **petō:**   1st person plural
5. **sciō:**   3rd person singular

B. Translate the following passive forms, as in **laudāminī**, *you are praised*:

1. laudābāminī
2. monētur
3. capientur
4. vincēbāmur
5. amāberis
6. mittuntur
7. audiēris
8. audīris
9. vocor
10. **mittar**

C. Translate the following phrases into Latin passive verbs:

1. we are loved
2. you will be killed
3. they were called
4. you (pl.) will be heard
5. he is praised
6. you (sing.) were warned
7. I shall be captured
8. I am being captured
9. we were sent
10. they will be sent

D. Fill in the correct present passive form of the verbs in the following sentences:

1. Templum ā puellīs (ornāre).   1. Templum ā puellīs ornātur.
2. Urna ā parentibus (portāre).
3. Casa ā deīs (petere).
4. Coniūnx ab Atalantā (ēvītāre).
5. Certāmen ā procīs nōn (ēvītāre).
6. Victor ā populō (corōnāre).

    7. Perīculum ā iuvene (<u>petere</u>).
    8. Atalanta aetāte puerī (<u>movēre</u>).
    9. Rūmor ā iuvenibus (<u>nārrāre</u>).
  10. Lēgēs ā virīs (<u>fōrmāre</u>).
  11. Puellae nōn facile (<u>vincere</u>).
  12. Rūmōrēs ā puellīs (<u>nārrāre</u>).
  13. Victōrēs ā rēge (<u>corōnāre</u>).
  14. Cibus ā Baucide (<u>parāre</u>).
  15. Perīcula ā iuvenibus (<u>petere</u>).
  16. Impiī ā deīs nōn (<u>amāre</u>).
  17. Callistō ā Iove in ursam (<u>mūtāre</u>).
  18. Procī ā spectātōribus (<u>laudāre</u>).
  19. Casae impiōrum aquā (<u>cēlāre</u>).
  20. Praemia victōribus (<u>dare</u>).

III. Change these active infinitives to passive infinitives:

    1. Verba deōrum (<u>dubitāre</u>) nōn   1. Verba deōrum <u>dubitārī</u> nōn
       dēbet.   dēbet.
    2. Lēgēs virōrum (<u>ēvītāre</u>) nōn dēbent.
    3. Rēgia rēgis (<u>vastāre</u>) nōn dēbet.
    4. Victor superbus (<u>corōnāre</u>) nōn dēbet.
    5. Verba superba (<u>audīre</u>) nōn dēbent.
    6. Līberī (<u>vidēre</u>) dēbent, nōn (<u>audīre</u>) dēbent.
    7. Lēgēs ab hominibus (<u>scīre</u>) dēbent.
    8. Sapientia ā rēge (<u>petere</u>) dēbet.
    9. Procī ā virgine (<u>vincere</u>) nōn dēbent.
  10. Hippomenēs fōrmā virginis (<u>movēre</u>) nōn dēbet.

IV. Supply the correct form of the relative pronoun:
    1. Virī, (<u>who</u>) in viīs errant,   1. *quī* in viīs errant, . . .
       labōrāre dēbent.
    2. Vir (<u>whom</u>) virgō amat vincere dēbet.
    3. Puella (<u>who</u>) innuba est procōs nōn ēvītat.
    4. Puella (<u>whom</u>) procī laudant est Atalanta.
    5. Lēx (*by which*, *abl. of means*) procī necantur est nōta.
    6. Rēx (<u>whose</u>) fīlia est Atalanta, in rēgiā in Boeotiā habitat.
    7. Dōna (<u>which</u>) ā deīs dantur nōn sunt semper grāta.
    8. Dōnum (<u>which</u>) dea dabit Hippomenem servābit.
    9. Lēx (<u>which</u>) Atalanta fēcit nōn est bona.
  10. Virī (<u>whose</u>) casae sunt in rīpīs flūminum semper aquās (*water*)
       timent.
  11. Atalanta est fīlia (<u>whom</u>) rēx amābat.
  12. Hippomenēs est procus (<u>who</u>) Atalantam amāvit.

13. Lēgem nōn amō (_which_) Atalanta fēcit.
14. Poma (_which_) dea dedit Hippomenem iūvērunt.
15. Poma (_which_) erant pulcherrima Atalantae coniugem dedērunt.

V. Translate into Latin:

1. Have you heard about that famous maiden Atalanta?
2. She surpassed men in a running contest.
3. Let this be the law of the race!
4. If I do not win, I shall be the wife of the victor. But if I do win, the suitor shall be killed.
5. (As a) spectator, Hippomenes condemned the suitors, but when he saw the girl he praised (her) beauty.
6. Hippomenes knows the law of the race, but he will try to win; so great is the power of love.
7. Atalanta says, "Can I be beaten or will I win?"
8. She says, "I am moved by his age, not by the boy."
9. Truly she loves him, but she does not realize her love.
10. Poor Hippomenes, leave while you can!

Etymology

Supply the English derivative from the words in the vocabulary:

bold	au_____
fire produced	i_____
one who watches	s_____
hearsay	r_____
crown (verb)	c_____ (noun)
not able to be conquered	inv_____
late	t_____

*   *   *   *   *

manus, manūs, _f._ hand (_manual_)

sinister, -tra, -trum, _left_   **dexter, dextra, dextrum,** _right_
manū sinistrā, _on the left hand_   **manū dextrā,** _on the right hand_

Since portents on the left were considered unfavorable, the added meaning of threatening or menacing came to be associated with _sinister_, while the sociological evidence here that most people seem to have been right-handed and therefore were more skillful with their right hand gives us the word _dexterous_ in English.

Consulting the _augur_, the priest of a sacred college of prophecy, was generally done before planning activities. The _augury_ (**auspicium, -iī,** _n._ _auspices_) could be in one of many forms: the observation of the flight of birds,[16] the observation of the entrails of recently slaughtered animals, observation of the heavens and interpretation of any unnatural portent or phenomenon—thunder, lightning, earthquake. Since the proclaiming of days favorable (**fās**) or unfavorable (**nefās**) gave the priests great political power, one can see how easily the abuse of the office became prevalent. Ovid's *Fasti* was an almanac of dates in the month, identifying them as being holidays sacred to the many gods of Rome and supplying later generations with a huge compendium of mythological data. Some of the information is labored, but most of it is extremely valuable for what it tells us about the religious observances of the Romans. The work was to be divided into twelve books, originally planned for the twelve months of the year, but only the first six books (through June) were completed.

---

[16]Ovid tells us in the *Fasti* that Romulus observed double the number of birds as did his brother Remus; therefore Romulus became the founder of Rome and gave his name to the city.

Dialogue

Ī (īte) ad tabulam, quaesō.　　　　*Go to the board, please.*

Scrībe (Scrībite) sententiās quae sunt　*Write the sentences which are in the*

　in librō, pāginā septuāgintā.　　　*book, page seventy.*

Chapter XVIII
ATALANTA ET HIPPOMENĒS
(pars secunda)

Iam populus paterque cursum promissum pōscunt. Iam Hippomenēs Venerem hōc modō invocat: "Ō dea Venus, iuvā ignēs amōris quōs dedistī." Venus, hīs precibus adducta et mōta,[1] sine morā auxilium dat.

Est ager in parte optimā īnsulae Cyprī quae est sacra deae Venerī. In mediō agrō stat nōn sōlum templum sed etiam arbor in quā sunt rāmī aureī et poma aurea. Forte Venus tria poma ab hāc arbore carpta portābat quae iuvenī dedit. "Poma sunt pulcherrima," inquit Hippomenēs, "sed quōmodō pomīs vincere possum?" Dea eum pomōrum ūsum docuit.

Nunc dēmum cornua concinunt, quae signum cursūs dant. Duo cursōrēs trāns summum cursum volāre videntur. Spectātōrēs clāmant: "Curre, Hippomenēs, ī, ī, properā sine morā! Nunc vincēs!" Hērōs gaudet; gaudet sēcrētō virgō quoque. Facile virgō eum superāre potest; saepe dubitat, saepe invīta eum relinquit. Mēta longē abest. Hippomenēs est dēfessus. Nunc ūnum dē tribus pomīs eī ā Venere datīs iacit.

Hoc pomum aureum iactum spectat dēsīderatque virgō. Relinquit cursum et pomum manū carpit. Quia intereā Hippomenēs eam superat, spectātōrēs clāmant et plausum[2] dant.

Iterum illa celeriter currit, iterum iuvenem post tergum[3] relinquit. Iterum Hippomenēs virginem secundō pomō remorātam superat. Sed iterum Atalanta eum facile praeterit. Pars ultima cursūs adest. Hērōs dēfessus vix currere potest. "Nunc," inquit, "adēs,[4] dea adōrāta, auctor amōris," et tertium pomum aureum oblīquē in agrum iacit. Virgō dubitāre vidētur; dēsīderat pomum quod in agrō est petere, sed cursum relinquere nōn dēsīderat. Venus superat. Virgō in agrum currit et Venus poma graviōra[5] facit. Propter moram pretiōsam virgō superātur.

Hērōs autem nec Venerī dōna dedit nec in ārā deae tūra[6] posuit. Venus igitur, quae erat magnopere īrāta, duōs amantēs in leōnēs trānsfōrmāvit.

---

[1] *Influenced and moved.*
[2] *Applause* (**plausum dare**, *to applaud*).
[3] *Behind her back.*

[4] *Be near* (*Imperative of* **adesse**).
[5] *Heavier.*
[6] *Incense.*

Verba

NOUNS

*auctor, -ōris, m.	author
cursor, -ōris, m.	runner
Cyprus, -ī, f.	the island of Cyprus
*hērōs, -ōis, m.	hero
*liber, -brī, m.	book
mēta, -ae, f.	goal, post
*pāgina, -ae, f.	page
prex, precis, f. (usually plural)	prayers
sententia, -ae, f.	thought, sentence
*signum, -ī, n.	signal, sign
*tabula, -ae, f.	board, plank, table
*ūsus, ūsūs, m.	use, practice

VERBS

*addūcō, -ere, -dūxī, -ductum	influence
*adōrō (1)	adore
carpō, -ere, carpsī, carptum	pick, pluck
concinō, -ere, -uī	sound in chorus
*currō, -ere, cucurrī, cursum	run
*dūcō, -ere, dūxī, ductum	lead
*gaudeō, -ēre, gavīsus sum[7]	rejoice
*iaciō, -ere, iēcī, iactum	throw
*inquit	says, said
*pōscō, -ere, poposcī	request, demand
praetereō, -īre, -iī, -itum	go past, pass by
*promittō, -ere, -mīsī, promissum	promise
*scrībō, -ere, scripsī, -ptum	write

ADJECTIVES

*aureus, -a, -um	golden
dēfessus, -a, -um	tired, worn out, weary
invītus, -a, -um	unwilling
*medius, -a, -um	middle of
*mōtus, -a, -um	moved, influenced
remorātus, -a, -um	delayed again, hindered
*summus, -a, -um	top of, highest
*tertius, -a, -um	third

---

[7] **Gaudēre** has only *passive* forms in the perfect tenses, but these passive forms have *active* meanings.

OTHER WORDS

dēmum	at last, finally
*facile	easily
*forte	by chance
*iam	now, already
*igitur	therefore
intereā	meanwhile
longē	far away
magnopere	very greatly
nec . . . nec	neither . . . nor
*nōn sōlum . . . sed etiam	not only . . . but also
oblīquē	to the side
*quōmodō	how, in what manner
sēcrētō	secretly, apart
vix	scarcely

IDIOM

*hōc modō	in this manner, thus

Structure

103. Perfect passive participle. The fourth principal part of the verb provides the form needed to make the perfect passive participle. *A participle is an adjective made from a verb*, and this *perfect passive adjective*, declined like **bonus, -a, -um**, appears in the vocabulary listing with the ending **-um**. The use of only this neuter form of the participle resolves the problem of intransitive verbs which lack a passive voice.[8] Learn the fourth principal part for each verb in the vocabulary. *Its ending is either* **-tum** *or* **-sum** *for all conjugations*.

Present Tense 1st Person Sing.	Infinitive	Perfect Tense 1st Person Sing.	Perfect Passive Participle
vocō	vocāre	vocāvī	vocātus, -a, -um
(*I call*)	(*to call*)	(*I have called*)	(*having been called*)
videō	vidēre	vīdī	visus, -a, -um
dūcō	dūcere	dūxī	ductus, -a, -um
capiō	capere	cēpī	captus, -a, -um
audiō	audīre	audīvī	audītus, -a, -um

The perfect passive participle is easy to form for all regular first conjugation verbs, the **-tum** being added to the present stem:

---

[8] This form is identical to the supine (see **Sec. 187**).

parō, parāre, parāvī, **parātum** (*having been prepared*)
cūrō, cūrāre, cūrāvī, **cūrātum** (*having been cared for*)
spectō, spectāre, spectāvī, **spectātum** (*having been watched*)
laudō, laudāre, laudāvī, **laudātum** (*having been praised*)
dō, dare, dedī, **datum** (*having been given*)

The meaning of the perfect passive participle, **vocātus, -a, -um**, is literally *having been called*, but it can be translated simply *called*, depending on the context. In the following examples note that the perfect passive participle agrees with the noun it modifies in gender, number, and case.

Puer ā patre **vocātus** respondit.	The boy (*having been*) called by his father replied.
Puella ā patre **vocāta** respondit.	The girl *called* by her father replied.
Dōnum ā deīs **datum** vīta aeterna est.	The gift *given* by the gods is eternal life.
Cibus ā senibus **parātus** iam in mensā est.	The food *prepared* by the old people is already on the table.
Arcadia est terra ā Iove **cūrāta**.	Arcadia is the land *cared for* by Jupiter.
Atalanta est puella ā iuvene **amāta**.	Atalanta is the maiden *loved* by the youth.
Venus **mōta adductaque** respondit.	Venus *moved and persuaded* replied.
Ad terrās iam **visās** revēnī.	I returned to lands already *seen*.

Maintaining characteristics of both verb and adjective, the perfect passive participle acts in the following manner:

vocātus, -a, -um

Perfect	**having**		
Passive	**been**		
Participle (adjective)	**called**	(by somebody)

In the Latin sentences given above the perfect passive participle is accompanied by an *ablative of agent* (see **Sec. 99**) and is translated by a phrase or clause. Oftentimes, however, the participle is best translated simply as an adjective.

Populus cursum **promissum** pōscit.	The people demand the *promised* race.
Atalanta pomum **iactum** carpit.	Atalanta picks up the *thrown* apple.

| Ades, dea **adōrāta**, auctor amōris. | Be near me, *adored* goddess, author of love. |

104. Interrogative pronoun, **quis, quid**. You have already met most of the forms of the interrogative pronoun in the questions at the end of each lesson. Below is the complete declension:

	Singular			*Plural*			
	M. & F.	*N.*		*M.*	*F.*	*N.*	
Nom.	quis	quid		quī	quae	quae	*Who, What?*
Gen.	cuius	cuius		quōrum	quārum	quōrum	*Whose?*
Dat.	cui	cui		quibus	quibus	quibus	*To whom?*
Acc.	quem	quid		quōs	quās	quae	*Whom, What?*
Abl.	quō	quō		quibus	quibus	quibus	*By whom?*

These forms of the interrogative pronoun can mean *who, what, which, whose, to whom, from whom, by whom*, depending on the gender and case.

Quis est Atalanta?	*Who* is Atalanta?
Quid Hippomenēs fēcit?	*What* did Hippomenes do?
Cui Venus pōma dedit?	*To whom* did Venus give the apples?
Ā quō pōmum iaciēbātur?	*By whom* was the apple thrown?
Cuius arbor in agrō stat?	*Whose* tree stands in the field?

105. Interrogative adjective. The forms of the interrogative adjective are the same as the forms of the relative pronoun (see **Sec. 100**). Note the difference in use between the *interrogative pronoun* and the *interrogative adjective*.

Pro.	**Quis** est Minerva?	*Who* is Minerva?
Adj.	**Quae dea** est auctor amōris?	*What goddess* is the author of love?
Pro.	**Quid** est cōnsilium hostium?	*What* is the plan of the enemy?
Adj.	**Quod cōnsilium** hostēs habuērunt?	*What plan* did the enemy have?
Adj.	**Quam arborem** in agrō vīdistī?	*What tree* did you see in the field?
Pro.	**Quem** Hippomenēs superāvit?	*Whom* did Hippomenes surpass?
Adj.	**Quem iuvenem** Atalanta amāvit?	*What youth* did Atalanta love?
Adj.	**Quam virginem** Pȳramus amāvit?	*What maid* did Pyramus love?

106. Irregular verb: **eō, īre, iī (īvī), itum.** The verb **eō**, a most commonly used verb meaning "go," with its compounds, **ineō, exeō, adeō, abeō, subeō, trānseō, praetereō,** etc., is conjugated as follows in the present tense:

eō	I go, am going, do go	**īmus**	we go, are going, do go
īs	you go, are going, do go	**ītis**	you go, are going, do go
it	he, she, it goes, is going, does	**eunt**	they go, are going, do go

The imperfect and future are regular:

ībam, ībās, ībat, ībāmus, ībātis, ībant   I went, you went, *etc.*

ībō, ībis, ībit, ībimus, ībitis, ībunt   I shall go, you will go, *etc.*

The perfect system can be based either on the stem **i-** or **īv-**:

iī, īstī, iit, iimus, īstis, iērunt   I have gone, *etc.*

(or) **īvī, īvistī, īvit, īvimus, īvistis, īvērunt**

Past Perfect:	**īveram, īverās** *etc. or* **ieram, ierās,** *etc.*
	I had gone, *etc.*
Future Perfect:	**īverō, īveris,** *etc. or* **ierō, ieris,** *etc.*
	I shall have gone, *etc.*
Imperative Singular:	**ī**
Imperative Plural:	**īte**

107. Declension of **trēs** and **mīlia. Mīlia** is followed by the genitive plural (of the whole):

	M. & F.	*N.*	*N.*		
Nom.	**trēs**	**tria**	**mīlia**	**passuum**	thousands of paces
Gen.	**trium**	**trium**	**mīlium**	**casārum**	of thousands of houses
Dat.	**tribus**	**tribus**	**mīlibus**	**feminārum**	to thousands of women
Acc.	**trēs**	**tria**	**mīlia**	**animālium**	thousands of animals
Abl.	**tribus**	**tribus**	**mīlibus**	**sagittārum**	by thousands of arrows

108. Passive of **videō.** The passive forms of **videō** frequently mean *seem* rather than *is seen* or *are seen.*

Duo trāns summum cursum volāre **videntur.**	The two *seem* to fly over the top of the course.

Exercises

I.   Respondēte Latīnē, quaesō.

  1. Quid populus paterque pōscunt?
  2. Quem Hippomenēs invocat?

3. Addūcēbāturne Venus precibus?
4. Ubi stat arbor pomīs aureīs?
5. Quae Venus iuvenī dat? Quid docet?
6. Quae signum cursūs dant?
7. Dēsīderābantne spectātōrēs Atalantam aut Hippomenem vincere?
8. Quōmodō Hippomenēs vīcit?
9. Quis in matrimonium Atalantam, praemium, dūxit?
10. Cūr Venus duōs amantēs in leōnēs trānsfōrmāvit?

II A. Give the principal parts for these verbs:

1. mūtō	6. moveō
2. resonō	7. dūcō
3. parō	8. videō
4. superō	9. iaciō
5. dēsīderō	10. audiō

B. Using the perfect passive participle as an adjective, fill in the blanks with the correct form of the verb above:

1. Venus (*moved*) ā iuvenī auxilium dedit.
2. Pomum (*thrown*) ā iuvenī ab Atalantā spectābātur.
3. Populus cursum (*desired*) pōscit.
4. Auxilium (*prepared*) ā deā est idōneum.
5. Hippomenēs hīs verbīs (*having been heard*)[9] gaudet.
6. Cornua (*having been sounded*) signum cursūs dant.
7. Virgō (*conquered*) ā iuvenī dūcitur.
8. Amantēs ā deā (*changed*) vōcem nōn iam habent.
9. Victor virginem (*conquered*) dūcit.
10. Auxilium ā deīs (*sent*) nōn est sine pretiō.

III. Fill in the correct form of the interrogative pronoun (**quis, quid**):

1. (*Who*) est virgō quae coniugem fugit?
2. (*Whom*) Hippomenēs amāvit?
3. (*Who*) iuvenī auxilium dedit?
4. Ā (*whom*) auxilium dabātur?
5. (*Who*) cursum promissum pōscunt?
6. (*Whose*) arbor ramōs aureōs habet?
7. (*To whom, pl.*) Venus auxilium dedit?
8. (*Who*) est victor in certāmine cursūs?
9. Ā (*whom*) pomum aureum carpitur?
10. (*Whom*) Venus in leōnēs trānsfōrmāvit?

---

[9] When he heard these words (*lit.*, at these words having been heard).

IV.   Fill in the correct forms of the interrogative adjective (**quī, quae, quod**):

    1. (*What*) praemium Hippomenēs quaerit?
    2. (*What*) virgō pomum aureum nōn dēsīderat?
    3. (*What*) dea Hippomenem iūvit?
    4. In (*what*) agrō arbor rāmīs aureīs stat?
    5. (*What*) iuvenem Atalanta relinquit post tergum?
    6. (*What*) virginem Hippomenēs vīcit?
    7. (*What*) dōna hērōs Venerī nōn dedit?
    8. (*In what*) modō Venus Hippomenem iūvit?
    9. (*What*) dea est auctor amōris?
    10. In (*what*) animālia Venus amantēs trānsfōrmāvit?

V.   Translate into Latin:

    1. Hippomenes asks the aid of Venus, goddess of love.
    2. Venus, moved by the prayers of the youth, promises aid.
    3. Venus gave the youth three golden apples picked from her sacred tree.
    4. "How can these apples, even if[10] they are very beautiful, help me to win the race?" asked Hippomenes.
    5. The people seem to wish Hippomenes to be the victor.
    6. Because the people shout the name of the hero, the maiden secretly rejoices.
    7. Hippomenes throws the apples far to the side and Atalanta has to (**dēbet**) leave the course.
    8. Atalanta saw the third apple which was thrown into a field and she wanted it.
    9. The costly delay gave victory to the youth, who led away (**abdūxit**) his prize.
    10. Venus changed the two lovers into animals because Hippomenes had not given her gifts.

Etymology

Many nouns in **-or** are formed from verbs with the meaning of the person performing the act of the verb:

Infinitive	Latin noun	English
spectāre	**spectātor**	spectator
navigāre	**navigātor**	navigator
dēvastāre	**dēvastātor**	devastator
cūrāre	**cūrātor**	curator

---

[10] **Etiamsī** *or* **etsī**.

simulāre	**simulātor**	simulator
ōrāre	**ōrātor**	orator

All of these nouns belong to the third declension: **ōrātor, -ōris,** *m.*

The pronoun-adjective **ille, illa** is the source for the articles **il** and **la** in Italian, **le** and **la** in French, **el** and **la** in Spanish.

Table of Pronoun Cognates in Romance Languages

Latin	*Italian*	*French*	*Spanish*
ego	io	je	yo
tū	tu	tu	tu
mihi	me/mi	moi/me	me
mē	me/mi	me	me
tibi	te/ti	toi/te	te
tē	te/ti	te	te
nōs (*nom.*)/vōs	noi/voi	nous/vous	nosotros/vosotros
nōs (*acc.*)/vōs	ci/vi	nous/vous	nos/os

Suffix Equivalents in Romance Languages and English

-tās, -tātis	-tà	-té	-tad -dad	-ty
lībertās	**libertà**	**liberté**	**libertad**	liberty
gravitās	**gravità**	**gravité**	**gravidad**	gravity
-tor, -tōris	**-tore**	**-teur**	**-dor**	-tor -teur
amātor	**amatore**	**amateur**	**amador**	amateur
spectātor	**spettatore**	**spectateur**	**espectador**	spectator
-iō, -iōnis	**-zione**	**-tion**	**-ción**	-tion
ōrātiō	**orazione**	**oration**	**oración**	oration
natiō	**nazione**	**nation**	**nación**	nation

Midas

Midas, the king of Phrygia, was a man obsessed by greed for gold. Because Midas had done a favor for Bacchus (he had let Silenus, a friend of Bacchus, sleep off a drunken state at his court), Bacchus had offered to grant any favor Midas chose. Like Phaëthon he chose unwisely, asking that everything he touch turn to gold. After rejoicing for a while in the gift, the king tried to eat and drink, but found the hard metal no satisfaction to his appetite and thirst. Then Midas begged to have the gift removed and was told to go to bathe in a river in Sardis. Even today the sands are golden where the touch flowed from the king into the waters and then to the banks along the river.

Foolish Midas also tried to be an unwise and unsolicited judge in a musical contest between Pan playing his pipe and the god Apollo singing and playing the lyre. The mountain god Tmolus was chosen judge and he wisely acknowledged Apollo's superiority, but Midas still claimed that Pan had won. Apollo rewarded such a stupid judgment by giving Midas ass's ears. Midas much ashamed tried to hide his ears in a turban, and only his barber knew the truth. Not able to keep such a delicious piece of gossip, but also not able to tell anyone, the barber dug a hole and whispered the secret into the ground. When the rushes grew up, however, they disclosed the secret when stirred by the wind, "Midas has ass's ears."

Dialogue
Carpe diem. *Seize the day. (Take advantage of each day's opportunity.)*

Chapter XIX
MIDĀS ET VĪS AUREA

Midās, magnus rēx Phrygiae, magnam sapientiam nōn habēbat. Quod Midās fuerat benignus deō Bacchō, Bacchus eī dōnum dedit: "Quicquid dēsīderās," dīxit deus, "tibi dabō." Rēx igitur hōc modō rogat: "Quicquid corpore tangō, id in aurum mūtā, quaesō. Hoc ego maximē dēsīderō." Hoc dōnum rēgī deus magnā maestitiā dedit, quia ille tāle dōnum petīverat.

Rēx autem nōn maestus, sed laetissimus, novum dōnum cupidē temptat. Ūnam et alteram rem digitō tangit; vix fortūnam crēdit. Vērum est. Ubi rāmum viridem ex arbore carpit, rāmum aureum Midās manū tenet. Saxum quoque manū tactum in aurum mūtātur. Dōna quoque Cereris[1] carpta in aurum trānsfōrmantur. Praetereā pomum, quod dē arbore carpsit, nunc est pomum aureum. Ubi digitōs in postibus altīs in rēgiā pōnit, postēs radiāre[2] videntur. Ubi ille manūs liquidīs aquīs lavat, aqua in liquidum aurum mūtātur. Omnia ā manū eius tacta in aurum vī aureā mūtantur.

Ubi Midās satis gavīsus erat[3] servī prō eō mēnsam carne atque dōnīs Cereris[1] onustam posuērunt. Midās cibum dente avidō[4] tangere temptāvit, sed dentēs durum aurum tetigērunt. Ubi Midās aquam et vīnum bibere temptāvit, liquidum aurum in ōre fluxit. Rēs quae prius secundae, nunc adversae vidēbantur.

Miser Midās territus nunc ōdit quod dēsīderāverat, atque hoc dōnum removēre optat. Nūllam aquam bibere potest, nūllum cibum edere potest. Manibus ad caelum tentīs, hōc modō ōrat: "Da veniam, pater benigne, peccāvimus, sed remitte damnōsum dōnum." Bacchus benignus dīxit: "Ī ad magnum flumen Sardibus[5] et carpe viam in montēs Lydiae usque ad ortum fluminis. Lavā caput corpusque. Simul tē in aquīs lavā, simul crīmen lavā."

Hīs verbīs audītīs, rēx ad flumen in Phrygiā īvit, et corpus lavāvit. Cum prīmum rēx flumen tetigit, vīs aurea dē corpore hūmānō in flumen trānsīvit. Etiamnunc terra Lydiae est aurea, aquīs in agrōs vīcīnōs portātīs.

---

[1] *The gift of Ceres, wheat,* and hence *bread.*
[2] *To shine.*
[3] *Had rejoiced.*
[4] *With eager tooth.*
[5] **In Sardibus,** *in Sardis.*

Verba

NOUNS

*aurum, -ī, *n.	gold
*Bacchus, -ī, *m.	Bacchus (*god of wine*)
carō, carnis, *f.*	flesh, meat
Cerēs, Cereris, *f.*	Ceres (*goddess of agriculture*)
crīmen, -inis, *n.*	sin, crime, fault
*diēs, diēī, *m.	day
maestitia, -ae, *f.*	sadness
Midās, Midae, *m.*	Midas (*King of Phrygia*)
ortus, -ūs, *m.*	source, origin
postis, -is, -ium, *m.*	door post
*rēs, reī, *f.	thing, object; *pl.*, situation
*saxum, -ī, *n.	rock, stone
venia, -ae, *f.*	pardon, favor
*vīs,[6] *f.*	force, strength; touch

VERBS

bibō, -ere, bibī	drink
*crēdō, -ere, -didī, -ditum	believe, trust
edō, -ere, ēdī, ēsum	eat
fluō, -ere, fluxī, fluxum	flow
*lavō (1)	wash
ōdī, ōdisse (present system lacking)	I hate
peccō (1)	sin
*remittō, -ere, -mīsī, -missum	send back, let go back, drive away
*removeō, -ēre, -mōvī, -mōtum	remove, take away, put off
tendō, -ere, tetendī, tentum or tensum	stretch out, extend
*transeō, -īre, -iī (-īvī), -itum	go across, pass over, cross

ADJECTIVES

adversus, -a, -um	unfavorable
*altus, -a, -um	tall, lofty, deep, high
damnōsus, -a, -um	ruinous
liquidus, -a, -um	liquid
maestus, -a, -um	sad, gloomy

---

[6] This irregular noun in classical Latin appears in the singular only in nom. (**vīs**), acc. (**vim**), and abl. (**vī**); plural forms are: **vīrēs, vīrium, vīribus, vīrēs, vīribus.** Do not confuse this noun with the second declension **vir,** *man* (see **Sec. 49**).

*omnis, -e	each, every; *pl.*, all
onustus, -a, -um	laden
*secundus, -a, -um	following, favorable, second
*tālis, -e	such (a)
viridis, -e	green

OTHER WORDS

*atque (ac)	and, and also
*cum, *conj.*	when
cupidē	eagerly
etiamnunc	yet, still
praetereā	in addition, further, besides, moreover
*simul	at the same time
simul . . . simul	not only . . . but at the same time

Structure

109. Ablative absolute. The ablative absolute consists of a noun or pronoun and a modifier (usually the perfect passive participle) in the ablative case. This construction is grammatically independent of the subject and verb of the sentence and usually states an adverbial idea telling how, when, where, why, or under what circumstances the main act of the sentence is performed. Note the following examples and their possible English translations:

Mēnsā parātā, Midās cupidē ēdit.   *When the table had been set, Midas ate eagerly (lit., the table having been set.)*

Since the literal English translation is often quite awkward, the ablative absolute is best expanded into a subordinate clause according to the meaning of the sentence. Reread **Sec. 80** concerning the ablative case and note how all of the ablative absolute meanings fit into the pattern for the uses of the ablative.

Aquīs in agrōs vīcīnōs portātīs, terra Lydiae est aurea.   *Because the waters were carried into the neighboring fields, the land of Lydia is golden.*

Virgine victā, Hippomenēs praemium dūxit.   *After the maid had been conquered, Hippomenes led away his prize.*

Pōmō iactō, Atalanta cursum relīquit.	*When the apple was thrown,* Atalanta left the track.
Hīs verbīs audītīs, rēx ad flumen īvit.	*When he had heard these words,* the king went to the river.

Occasionally the ablative absolute consists of two nouns, or of a noun and a pronoun, or of a noun or pronoun and an adjective:

Caesare duce, urbs est tūta.	*With Caesar as leader*, the city is safe.
Atalantā coniuge, Hippomenēs est laetus.	*With Atalanta as his wife*, Hippomenes is happy.
Mē iūdice, nōn sum digna pretiī.	*If I am a judge*, I am not worth the price.
Mē invītā, cornua signum cursūs dant.	*Against my will* the horns give the sign of the race.

110. Principal parts of verbs: perfect passive participles of second, third, and fourth conjugations. There are no rules for the formation of the perfect passive participles of verbs in the last three conjugations, as there is in the first conjugation. There are patterns, however, that are helpful. Learn the following:

habeō, habēre, habuī, habitum
teneō, tenēre, tenuī, tentum
videō, vidēre, vīdī, vīsum
mittō, mittere, mīsī, missum
dūcō, dūcere, dūxī, ductum
faciō, facere, fēcī, factum
audiō, audīre, audīvī, audītum
sentiō, sentīre, sēnsī, sēnsum

111. Fifth declension. The characteristic vowel of the fifth declension is **-e**. All of the nouns are feminine, except **diēs**, which is masculine.[7]

	Case Endings	**rēs, reī**, *f.*	**diēs, diēī**, *m.*[7]
Nom.	-ēs	rēs	diēs
Gen.	-eī	reī	diēī
Dat.	-eī	reī	diēī
Acc.	-em	rem	diem
Abl.	-ē	rē	diē

---

[7] **Diēs** is feminine when it refers to a specific day, e.g., **constitūtā diē**, *on the appointed day.*

Nom.	-ēs	rēs	diēs
Gen.	-ērum	rērum	diērum
Dat.	-ēbus	rēbus	diēbus
Acc.	-ēs	rēs	diēs
Abl.	-ēbus	rēbus	diēbus

112. Third declension adjectives. Thus far all adjectives have belonged to the first and second declensions, declined like **bonus, -a, -um**. There are also *third* declension adjectives which employ the third declension endings you already know. Very common are those which have one ending for masculine and feminine and another for neuter in the nominative singular.[8]

| | Singular | | Plural | |
	M. & F.	N.	M. & F.	N.
Nom.	omnis	omne	omnēs	omnia
Gen.	omnis	omnis	omnium	omnium
Dat.	omnī	omnī	omnibus	omnibus
Acc.	omnem	omne	omnēs	omnia
Abl.	omnī	omnī	omnibus	omnibus

Omnis is frequently used as a substantive. In the plural, **omnēs** means *all (the people)* and **omnia** means *all things*.

The third declension adjective is an **i**-*stem*, in that the characteristic vowel **i** appears in the nominative and accusative of the neuter plural and in the genitive plural. Note also the **ī** in the ablative singular.

Exercises

I.   Respondēte Latīnē, quaesō.

1. Habetne Midās sapientiam?
2. Cui Bacchus dōnum dedit?
3. Estne Midās laetus aut maestus cum Bacchus eī dōnum dat?
4. Quid temptat?
5. Quae tangit?
6. Quōs in rēgiā tangit?
7. Quī mēnsam parāvērunt?
8. Cum Midās edere temptat, quid dentēs tangunt?
9. Potestne Midās bibere aut edere?
10. Quōmodō Midās dōnum damnōsum remittit?

---

[8] Because these third declension adjectives have two endings in the nominative singular, they are sometimes referred to as adjectives of two terminations.

II. Change each clause in column A into an ablative absolute and in-
corporate it into a sentence with the clause in Column B (unchanged)
as the main clause.
Make into ablative absolutes:

1. Mēnsa parātur.   Mēnsā parātā, Midās ēdit.
2. Dōnum datur.   Midās erat laetus.
3. Pōmum tangitur.   Midās novō dōnō gaudet.
4. Verba audiuntur.   Midās ad flumen īvit.
5. Deus movētur.   Midās dōnum remittit.
6. Rēx movētur.   servus līberātur.

III A. Give the principal parts for the following verbs:

1. laudō	6. moveō	11. fugiō
2. vocō	7. dūcō	12. audiō
3. spectō	8. mittō	13. sentiō
4. teneō	9. petō	14. veniō
5. habeō	10. faciō	15. dō

B. Change these imperative singular forms to plural:

1. Cūrā, puella.   1. Cūrāte, puellae.
2. Manē, Marce.   2. _____ , puerī.
3. Pete, pater, fortūnam.   3. _____ , patrēs, fortūnam.
4. Ēvītā, mater, verba dūra.   4. _____ , matrēs, verba dūra.
5. Carpe diem, discipule.   5. _____ diem, discipulī.
6. Fac,[9] iuvenis, aliās rēs.   6. _____ , iuvenēs, aliās rēs.
7. Dūc,[9] rēx, populum laetum. 7. _____ , rēgēs, populōs laetōs.
8. Habē, senex, vītam laetam.   8. _____ , senēs, vītam laetam.
9. Docē, magister, rēs vērās.   9. _____ , magistrī, rēs vērās.
10. Audī, puer, verba mea.   10. _____ , puerī, verba mea.

IV A. Review the five declensions by giving the declensions for the following
nouns:

1. **vīta, -ae,** *f.*   4. **puer, -erī,** *m.*
   life   *boy*
2. **ramus, -ī,** *m.*   5. **oppidum, -ī,** *n.*
   branch   *town*
3. **ager, -grī,** *m.*   6. **rēx, rēgis,** *m.*
   field   *king*

---

[9] The shortened form of the imperative singular occurs only in these commonly used verbs:
dīcō (dīc), dūcō (dūc) and **faciō (fac)**.

7. **color, -ōris**, *m.*
   color
8. **hostis, -is, -ium**, *m.*
   enemy
9. **ūsus, -ūs**, *m.*
   use
10. **rēs, reī**, *f.*
    thing

B. Supply the correct endings for each noun and adjective in the plural:

1. Terra est immēnsa.
2. Amīcus puerī est dēfessus.
3. Lēx hominis bonī est certa.

4. Cīvis[10] tālem lēgem nōn ēvītat.
5. Animal silvae in monte nōn habitat.
6. Diēs longissimus est in Iūniō.
7. Rēs optima nōn est facilis.
8. Cornū signum dat.
9. Dux omnis nōn est pater familiae.
10. Hoc flumen nōn est longum.

1. Terrae sunt immēnsae.
2. Amīc__ puer__ sunt dēfess__.
3. Lē__ homin__ bon__ sunt cert__.
4. Cīv__ tāl__ lēg__ nōn ēvītant.
5. Animāl__ silv__ in mont__ nōn habitant.
6. Di__ longissim__ sunt in Iūniō.
7. Re__ optim__ nōn sunt facilēs.
8. Corn__ sign__ dant.
9. Duc__ omn__ nōn sunt patr__ famili__.
10. H__ flum__ nōn sunt long__.

V. Translate into Latin:

1. Bacchus gave the golden touch to the foolish king of Phrygia with great sadness.
2. Midas however was overjoyed (**laetissimus**) and tried to change all things in the palace to gold.
3. A green branch touched by the king is now golden.
4. In like manner a stone and an apple are transformed by the golden touch.
5. The water with which Midas tries to wash his hands seems to shine.
6. The situation which seemed favorable now is unfavorable.
7. But when the servants place a table laden with food and wine before the king, he can neither eat nor drink.
8. Since the food is now golden (*abl. abs.*) Midas cannot eat.
9. He stretches out his hands to heaven and asks pardon.
10. Bacchus orders him to go to a river in Lydia and wash himself in its waters.

---

[10] **Cīvis, cīvis, -ium**, *c.*, *citizen*.

11. The fields of Lydia are now golden, since (the power of) the golden touch has been carried into the waters of the river (*abl. abs.*).

Etymology

Third declension nouns ending in **-tās, -tūdō, -iō** are all feminine and have the general meaning of the quality of whatever the root means. Many of these words were formed from adjectives:

celer	**celeritās**	celerity
gravis	**gravitās**	gravity
līber	**lībertās**	liberty
antīquus	**antīquitās**	antiquity
sanus	**sanitās**	sanity
secūrus	**secūritās**	security
ūtilis	**ūtilitās**	utility

What does the suffix **-tās** become in English?

Many second conjugation verbs combine their roots with the suffix **-idus**, meaning *quality of* and new adjectives are created in both Latin and English.

timēre	**timidus**	timid
frigere	**frigidus**	frigid
horrēre	**horridus**	horrid
rigere	**rigidus**	rigid
liquēre	**liquidus**	liquid
stupere	**stupidus**	stupid

Many fourth declension nouns which are formed from the fourth principal part of the verb come into English with the **-us** dropped or with a mute **-e**:

cultum	**cultus**	cult
adventum	**adventus**	advent
ūsum	**ūsus**	use
exitum	**exitus**	exit
habitum	**habitus**	habit

Dialogue

Gaudeāmus igitur iuvenēs dum sumus.	*Let us rejoice, then, while we are*
Gaudeāmus igitur iuvenēs dum sumus.	*young.* (Repeat)
Post iōcundam iuventūtem.	*After a joyful youth.*
Post molestam senectūtem	*After a bothersome old age*
Nōs habēbit humus—	*The earth will have us—*
Nōs habēbit humus.	*The earth will have us.*

(The music appears in the Appendix.)

Chapter XX
MIDĀS ET PĀN

Posteā Midās in silvīs habitābat ubi deum Pānem colēbat. Ille autem sē adhūc stultum dēmōnstrābat. Et sapientia et iūdicium rēgī Phrygiae eō tempore dēerant.

Est in Lydiā mōns altus, Tmōlus nōmine, summō quō Pān nymphīs carmina sua cantābat, dum fistulam cērā coniunctam īnflat. Carmina eius quidem erant pulcherrima et grātissima nymphīs Midaeque quī deum maximē laudābat. Pān superbus carmina Apollinis, deī mūsicae, contemnit; vocat Apollinem ad certāmen sub iūdice Tmōlō,[1] deō montis.

Senex igitur iūdex in monte suō sēdit et aurēs ab arboribus līberāvit. Is deum Pānem spectāvit et eum cantāre hīs verbīs iussit: "In iūdice nūlla mōra erit." Quia Midās forte aderat, audīverat Pānem dum sonat fistulam. Rēx hoc carmen barbarum maximē mīrābātur, quod sibi erat grātissimum. Ubi carmen Pānis terminātum est, sacer Tmōlus ōra vertit ad ōs Phoebī, quī gerēbat laurum in capite vestimentumque longum tinctum Tyriō mūricō.[2] Sinistrā manū lyram gemmīs atque dentibus Indīs[3] decorātam, dextrā manū plectrum[4] tenuit. Tum Phoebus ortus est et lyram digitō doctō tetigit. Carmen cantāre coepit. Carmine audītō, Tmōlus iūdex iussit Pānem fistulam lyrae submittere.

Iūdicium autem sacrī montis Tmōlī quod erat omnibus grātum, nōn erat grātum Midae, quī ita loquitur, "Iūdicium est iniustum." Apollō nōn patitur tālēs aurēs hūmānam figūram retinēre. Ille eāsdem longiōrēs[5] et plēnās villīs

---

[1] *Tmolus*, the mountain; also a mountain deity, acting as judge.
[2] *Dyed with Tyrian purple.*
[3] *Ivory.*
[4] *Pick.*
[5] *Longer.*

facit; dat quoque posse movērī. Midās damnātus in ūnā parte corporis aurēs asellī[6] gerit, quamquam cēterae sunt hominis.

Posteā Midās aurēs purpureīs tiārīs[7] pudōre cēlāre cōnābātur, sed servus quī capillōs longōs resecābat aurēs vīderat. Dē quibus īdem nārrāre verēbātur nec tamen retinēre poterat. Effodit igitur terram in quam immurmurat parvā voce dē auribus dominī vīsīs. Terrā repositā, servus tacitus abit. Sed harundinēs tremulae[8] quae ex terrā crēscunt verba humāta remittunt, quia ventō mōtae fābulam dē auribus asellī murmurant.

Verba

NOUNS

*Apollō, -inis, *m.*	Apollo (*god of music and medicine*)
*auris, auris, -ium, *f.*	ear
*carmen, -inis, *n.*	song
gemma, -ae, *f.*	jewel, gem
*iūdex, -icis, *m.*	judge
*iūdicium, -iī, *n.*	judgment
lyra, -ae, *f.*	lyre
*ventus, -ī, *m.*	wind

VERBS

abeō, -īre, -īvī *or* -iī, -itum	go away
*cantō (1)	sing, make music
*coepī, coepisse, coeptum (defective)	began
*colō, -ere, -uī, cultum	till, cultivate, honor, worship
*conor, conārī, conātus sum	attempt, try
contemnō, -ere, -tempsī, -temptum	value little, disdain
decorō (1)	adorn, decorate
*dēsum, -esse, -fuī, -futūrum	be absent, be lacking, missing
effodiō, -ere, -fōdī, -fossum	dig
*gerō, -ere, gessī, gestum[9]	bear, carry, wear, accomplish, do[9]
immurmurō (1)	whisper into
inflō (1)	blow into
*līberō (1)	free, set free, liberate
*loquor, loquī, locūtus sum	speak, say
*mīror, mīrārī, mīrātus sum	wonder at, admire
*patior, patī, passus sum	allow, suffer, permit

---

[6] *Of an ass.*

[7] *In a purple turban.*

[8] *The whispering (quivering) reeds.* The English is also onomatopoetic, "Midas has ass's ears."

[9] Caesar Augustus entitled a book devoted to his accomplishments: **Rēs Gestae** (*Things Accomplished*).

*orior, orīrī, ortus sum	rise
*repōnō, -ere, -posuī, -positum	put back, replace
resecō, -āre, -uī, -tum	cut off
*submittō, -ere, -mīsī, -missum	put down, lower, humble, yield
taceō, -ēre, -uī, -itum	be silent
terminō (1)	end, finish
*vereor, verērī, veritus sum	fear, be afraid
vertō, -ere, vertī, versum	turn

ADJECTIVES

barbarus, -a, -um	rough, rude, foreign
*dexter, -tra, -trum	right, skillful
*hūmānus, -a, -um	human, humane
iniūstus, -a, -um	unjust, unfair
*sinister, -tra, -trum	left, adverse
villōsus, -a, -um	shaggy, hairy
(*from* villus, -ī, *m.*)	(shaggy hair)

OTHER WORDS

*nam	for
*posteā	afterwards, thereafter, after that
*tum	then

Structure

113. Perfect passive system, all conjugations. The perfect passive of all verbs is formed by combining *in a verb phrase* the perfect passive participle and a form of the verb **esse**: **ductus est**, *he has been led*. The perfect passive system is easily distinguished from the active in that the forms consist of *two separate words*. The perfect passive participle agrees with its subject *in number and gender*.

Perfect

Active		*Passive*	
dūxī	I have led	ductus (-a) sum	I have been led
dūxistī	you have led	ductus (-a) es	you have been led
dūxit	he, she, it has led	ductus (-a, -um) est	he, she, it has been led
dūximus	we have led	ductī (-ae) sumus	we have been led
dūxistis	you have led	ductī (-ae) estis	you have been led
dūxērunt	they have led	ductī (-ae, -a) sunt	they have been led

Past Perfect

dūxeram	I had led	**ductus eram**	I had been led
dūxerās	you had led	**ductus erās**	you had been led
dūxerat	he, she, it had led	**ductus erat**	he had been led
dūxerāmus	we had led	**ductī erāmus**	we had been led
dūxerātis	you had led	**ductī erātis**	you had been led
dūxerant	they had led	**ductī erant**	they had been led

(feminine and neuter forms also possible)

Future Perfect

dūxerō	I shall have led	**ductus erō**	I shall have been led
dūxeris	you will have led	**ductus eris**	you will have been led
dūxerit	he, she, it will have led	**ductus erit**	he will have been led
dūxerimus	we shall have led	**ductī erimus**	we shall have been led
dūxeritis	you will have led	**ductī eritis**	you will have been led
dūxerint	they will have led	**ductī erunt**	they will have been led

(feminine and neuter forms also possible)

Notice that the perfect passive participle **ductus, -a, -um** changes to plural **ductī, -ae, -a** depending on the gender of the plural subject.

Vir ab agricolā in casam **ductus** est.	*The man* has been *led* by the farmer into the house.
Virgō ab hērōe in matrimonium **ducta** est.	*The maid* has been *led* into marriage by the hero.
Animal ā nautā in rīpam **ductum** est.	*The animal* has been *led* by the sailor onto the shore.
Virī ā rēge in silvam **ductī** sunt.	*The men* have been *led* by the king into the forest.
Animālia ā puerō in agrum **ducta** sunt.	*The animals* have been *led* by the boy into the field.

114. **Īdem, eadem, idem.** You are familiar with the forms of **is, ea, id** as a personal pronoun from previous lessons (see **Sec. 88**). This word also functions as an adjective, less definite than **hic** or **ille**, in such phrases as:

eō tempore   at *that* (*this*) time
in **ea** loca   into *these* (*those*) places

The enclitic ending **-dem** added to the forms of **is, ea, id** gives an intensive emphasis to the word either as a pronoun or an adjective translated by the English *same*: the same man, the same woman, the same thing.

M.	*F.*	*N.*	*M.*	*F.*	*N.*
īdem	**eadem**	**idem**	**eīdem**	**eaedem**	**eadem**
eiusdem	**eiusdem**	**eiusdem**	**eōrundem**	**eārundem**	**eōrundem**
eīdem	**eīdem**	**eīdem**	**eīsdem**	**eīsdem**	**eīsdem**
eundem	**eandem**	**idem**	**eōsdem**	**eāsdem**	**eadem**
eōdem	**eādem**	**eōdem**	**eīsdem**	**eīsdem**	**eīsdem**

Pro.   **Īdem** est amīcus meus   The *same* man is my friend and
         et comes.   my companion.
Adj.   **eōdem** tempore   at the *same* time
Adj.   in **eadem** loca   into the *same* places

115. Deponent verbs. Deponent verbs are those which have laid aside (**dēpōnere**) their active forms and appear only in the passive; these passive forms must be translated as active. These verbs exist in all conjugations and one from each appears in the lesson:

I	**conor, conārī, conātus sum**	attempt, try
II	**vereor, verērī, veritus sum**	fear
III	**loquor, loquī, locūtus sum**	speak
III-io	**patior, patī, passus sum**	suffer, allow
IV	**orior, orīrī, ortus sum**	arise, rise up

The conjugation of the deponent verb is completely regular (Consult Paradigms in the Appendix), coinciding with the forms for the passive verbs. Below is a synopsis for each verb in the third person singular:

I	II	III	III-io	IV
con**ā**tur	ver**ē**tur	loquitur	patitur	orītur
conābātur	verēbātur	loquēbātur	patiēbātur	oriēbātur
conābitur	verēbitur	loquētur	patiētur	oriētur
conātus est	veritus est	locūtus est	passus est	ortus est
conātus erat	veritus erat	locūtus erat	passus erat	ortus erat
conātus erit	veritus erit	locūtus erit	passus erit	ortus erit

Remember that the sign for the future tense is **-bi-** for first and second conjugation, but **-e-** for third, third **-io**, and fourth conjugations.

116. Figures of speech: onomatopoeia. When the meaning of words is echoed by the sound of the words, the figure of speech employed is called *onomatopoeia*. In the story of Midas the verb **immurmurat** echoes in sound the meaning of the word. Poets are sensitive to the use of onomatopoetic words.

117. The reflexive pronoun **sē (sēsē)**. When the third person subject (*he, she, it,* or *they*) acts upon itself, the cases of **is, ea, id** are not used; the cases of **sē (sēsē)** are used instead for all genders, singular and plural.

> *Gen.* **suī** of himself, herself, itself, themselves; his, her, its, their
> *Dat.* **sibi** to himself, herself, itself, themselves
> *Acc.* **sē (sēsē)** himself, herself, itself, themselves (*Objective*)
> *Abl.* **sē (sēsē)** (by) himself, herself, itself, themselves

> Arachnē sē docet.   Arachne teaches *herself*.
> Narcissus sēsē videt.   Narcissus sees *himself*.
> Vir ā sē necātus est.   The man was killed by *himself*.
> Fēminae sē laudant.   The women praise *themselves*.

Exercises

I.   Respondēte Latīnē, quaesō.

1. Quem Midās colēbat?
2. Habetne Midās nunc sapientiam aut iūdicium?
3. Quibus Pān carmina cantābat?
4. Quem Pān ad certāmen vocat?
5. Quis est iūdex certāminis?
6. Cuius carmen est prīmum? Estne pulchrum?
7. Estne lyra Apollinis decorāta? Quibus?
8. Quis est victor certāminis?
9. Quis iūdicium vocat iniūstum?
10. Quōmodō Midās damnātur?   (**Quō modō**, *in what manner* (how),
11. Quōmodō Midās aurēs cēlat?   is commonly written as one
12. Quis aurēs rēgis videt?   word, **quōmodō**.)
13. Eratne servus tacitus?
14. Quōmodō servus fābulam nārrāre potest?
15. Quae fābulam murmurant?

II A. Give a complete synopsis of the following verbs, active and passive, third person singular:

1. cantō   4. colō
2. submittō   5. audiō
3. retineō   6. gerō

B. Conjugate the perfect passive of the following verbs:

    1. līberō   2. videō   3. repōnō   4. retineō

C. Supply the correct form of the perfect passive in the following:

    1. Iūdicium (*has been made*).   1. Iūdicium factum est.
    2. Verba (*have been spoken*).
    3. Vōx (*has been heard*).
    4. Puer (*has been terrified*).
    5. Fābula (*has been told*).
    6. Terra (*had been abandoned*).
    7. Pomum in aurum (*had been changed*).
    8. Carmen (*will have been sung*).
    9. Clāmor ā spectātōribus (*has been sounded*).
   10. Aurēs asellī ā rēge (*have been hidden*).

D. Translate these deponent verbs (**cavē!** The passive forms must be translated as active):

    1. conantur   6. oriēbātur
    2. verēbāmur   7. loquēmur
    3. locūtī sumus   8. veritus est
    4. passī erātis   9. conābāris
    5. ortus es   10. patiminī

III. Supply the correct pronoun in the following sentences:

    1. (*He*) est rēx, sed rēgēs sapientiam nōn semper habent.
    2. Iūdicium est grātum nymphīs, sed Midās (*it*) iniūstum vocat.
    3. Tmōlus (*him*) spectat dum cantat.
    4. Apollō lyram gemmīs decorātam habuit (*which*) manū sinistrā tenuit.
    5. Nymphīs iūdicium est grātum. Carmen Apollinis est grātum (*to them*).
    6. (*To him*) Tmōlus iūdicium dedit.
    7. Apollō aurēs asellī (*to him*) dedit, sed Midās (*them*) cēlāre temptat.
    8. Servus (*them*) vīdit; quamquam nārrāre fābulam nōn potest, tamen (*it*) retinēre nōn potest.
    9. Fābula dē auribus (*his*) ā ventō nārrāta est.
   10. Asellī aurēs longās habent (*which*) (*they*) movēre possunt.

IV. Supply the reflexive adjective or pronoun where needed:

    1. In summō monte Tmōlō Pān nymphīs carmina (*his*) cantābat.
    2. Narcissus (*himself*) in aquīs flūminis vīdit.
    3. Pȳramus (*himself*) necāvit quod putāvit leōnem Thisbem necāvisse.[10]

---

[10] *Because he thought that the lion had killed Thisbe.* **Necāvisse** is the perfect infinitive.

    4. Pȳramus et Thisbē parentēs (*their*) fallunt.

    5. Midās cibum (*his*) nōn edere potest.

V.   Translate into Latin, please.

    1. Midas, still stupid, now worships the satyr Pan.

    2. Pan sings his beautiful songs to the nymphs on Mt. Tmolus.

    3. He calls Apollo to a contest of songs.

    4. Tmolus has been named (**nomināre**) judge of the contest.

    5. The judgment has been given to Apollo.

    6. Because Midas called the judgment unfair, his ears were changed (perfect passive) into ass's ears.

    7. Midas tried to hide his ears, after he had felt (**sentīre**) his punishment by Apollo. (*use abl. abs. construction*).

    8. The ears had been seen by the slave who cut (imperfect) his hair.

    9. The slave dug the ground and whispered the story into the earth.

   10. Rushes grew in that place, and the rushes, moved by the wind, now tell the tale of Midas and his ears.

Etymology

Piscis in Mari

 **in** + *abl.*
in

 **trans** + *acc.*
across

 **in** + *abl.*
on

 **sub** + *acc.*
under (*or abl.*)

 **in** + *acc.*
into

a (ab) + *abl.*
away from

 **e (ex)** + *abl.*
out of

ad + *acc.*
to, toward,
near

 **inter** + *acc.*
between

ob + *acc.*
against

 **per** + *acc.*
through

circum + *acc.*
around

INTERIM READING

The stories in these sections are designed to give the student reading confidence and pleasure. They employ more of the vocabulary and grammar of the original Ovidian story than was possible earlier. They contain *no new grammar*, but make use of all the forms and constructions of the first twenty lessons. Whatever vocabulary is new is translated in the footnotes to each page. Wherever the note includes a word which would be a valuable addition to the student's vocabulary, the forms of the word are given and the *word is to be learned*; otherwise the word is merely translated.

The story should be read *four* times: once for comprehension with the help of the notes; a second time for a smooth, idiomatic English rendering; then to get meaning from the Latin as it is read; and finally for smooth Latin comprehension and appreciation, aloud if possible. The macrons (the long marks over the lengthened vowels) which have appeared up to now in the readings are no longer provided. The Interim Readings appear without macrons, as do the subsequent reading sections beginning with Chapter XXI, although the macrons appear in the notes, the vocabularies, and the structure sections.

INTERIM READING I: DAEDALUS ET ICARUS

Daedalus in insula Creta longum exsilium egit.[1] Tactus loci natalis amore,[2] diu et magnopere insulam relinquere desiderabat, sed mari[3] clausus erat. "Minos, rex Cretae," inquit, "terras et undas regnat, at caelum certe est apertum. Caelo ibimus. Quamquam omnia Minos possidet,[4] tamen non aëra possidet."

---

[1] **Agō, -ere, ēgī, actum**, *do, drive, spend time*; *spent a long exile.*
[2] *Touched by a longing* (love) *for his native land* (place of birth).
[3] **Mare, maris**, *n.*, *by the sea*; **marī** is ablative singular (see declension in Appendix).
[4] **Possideō, -ēre, -sēdī, -sessum**, *owns, possesses, controls.*

Tum Daedalus animum[5] in artes ignotas dimittit[6] et naturam novat.[7] Nam pennas[8] in ordine[9] ponit a minima usque ad longissimam. Sic quondam[10] fistulam rusticam[11] Pan disparibus[12] papyris quoque fecerat.

Deinde partes medias imasque[13] cera adligat[14] atque parvo curvamini pennas tam compositas flectit.[15] Potes putare has esse alas avium verarum.[16]

Puer Icarus, filius Daedali, ad patrem stat spectatque dum pater laborat. Nescit se sua pericula tangere dum pennas tenet et ceram digito mollit[17] et ludo suo[18] mirabile opus patris impediebat.[19] Denique postquam[20] ultima penna in loco posita est, artifex,[21] duabus alis apertis et motis, in aëre pependit.

Pater filium sic monuit, "Tene viam mediam, Icare. Si ibis prope mare, unda pennas gravet.[22] Si prope solem ibis, ignis pennas vastabit. Te viam mediam tenere iubeo. Vola inter utrumque,[23] mare et solem. Me duce, carpe viam. Praecepta volandi[24] dat dum novas alas umeris pueri accommodat.[25] Manus patris tremunt[26] et oscula ultima filio dat.

Pennis motus pater in aëre volat. Timet et respectat[27] velut[28] avis quae parvam avem ducit et eam volare docet; Daedalus ipse suas alas movet et alas filii respectat.

Homines in terra—piscator, pastor, arator[29]—hos viderunt qui per aëra volare poterant et hos esse deos crediderunt.[30] Et iam insulae Graeciae relictae sunt cum puer gaudere coepit[31] et patrem ducem reliquit. Desideravit

---

[5] **Animus, -ī**, *m., mind.*
[6] *Directs his mind toward unknown skills.*
[7] *He renews nature (invents something new).*
[8] **Penna, -ae**, *f., feather.*
[9] *In order.*
[10] *Once.*
[11] **Fistula, -ae**, *f., a rustic pipe.*
[12] *Uneven.*
[13] **Īmus, -a, -um**, *lowest, bottom of.*
[14] *Ties together.*
[15] *Bends in a slight curve the feathers thus put together.*
[16] *Of real birds* (**avis, avis, avium**, *f.*). *You can imagine that these are the wings of real birds.*
[17] *Softens the wax.*
[18] *By his own play, by his own amusement.*
[19] *Impedes the wonderful work of his father* (**opus, operis**, *n., work*).
[20] **Postquam**, *conj., after.*
[21] *The craftsman, creator.*
[22] *Will wet, weigh down.*
[23] **Uterque, utraque, utrumque**, *each of two; fly between each of two.*
[24] *Rules of flying.*
[25] *Fits the strange wings on the shoulders of the boy.*
[26] *Tremble.*
[27] *Looks back.*
[28] *Just as.*
[29] *The fisherman, the shepherd, the farmer* (he who plows).
[30] *They believed that they* (*these men*) *were gods* (indirect statement).
[31] *Began* (**Coepī, coepisse**) *has no present system, only perfect forms.*

volare altius[32] in caelo et audacia eum ab itinere patris duxit. Sol ceram mollit[33] et pennae liberatae sunt. Puer nudis bracchiis aëra percussit.[34] Aqua quae eum recepit[35] nomen ab illo tenet.[36] At pater infelix,[37] nunc non iam pater, "Icare," dixit, "Icare, ubi es? Quo in loco te quaeram? Icare," dicebat cum pennas notas in undis summis spectavit et damnavit suas artes. Tum corpus carum filii in sepulchrum[38] posuit et terra a nomine pueri dicta est— Icaria.

---

[32] *Higher* (a comparative adverb).
[33] *Melts, softens.*
[34] *Beat.*
[35] *Received.*
[36] *The Icarian Sea.*
[37] **Infēlix, -icis**, *unlucky, unhappy, ill-fated, miserable.*
[38] *Grave.*

Orpheus and Eurydice

Orpheus, the sweet singer of the ancient world, bard of Apollo, was able to soften the spirits of wild beasts and to move harsh stones with his songs. The omens for his wedding day, however, proved unfavorable, for his bride of a day, Eurydice, while walking through a field, was bitten by a serpent and died. Descending to the Underworld, Orpheus begs for her return from Pluto and Proserpina, reminding Pluto in poetic eloquence that he too had been conquered by Love. The king and queen of the gloomy regions of the dead agree to Eurydice's return on the condition that Orpheus not look back at her. Eagerly he leads her out of the Underworld until they are almost at the entrance, the great cave of Avernus. Then Orpheus, anxious for her safety, looks back at Eurydice and she slips back forever to the land of the dead.

Despondent at this double loss, Orpheus shuns the company of women either because his first love had turned out badly or because he had given his pledge to Eurydice. The women, especially the Maenads, the maddened women who worship Bacchus, are angered at being so scorned. They therefore attack the bard and eventually the noise of their shouts and the drums and cymbals drown out the sound of his lyre. Then the rocks run red with the blood of the poet as the women tear him apart.

Orpheus descends again to the Underworld, this time as a shade, where he is finally reunited with Eurydice.

Because of his descent to and emergence from the Underworld, Orpheus has become associated with a cult known as Orphism, which combines features of both Apollonian and Dionysian worship. The literature attributed to Orphism records an early account of the birth of Dionysus.

Sententiae
Omnia vincit Amor.   *Love conquers all.*
Virgil, *Ecl.* X.69

Chapter XXI
ORPHEUS ET EURYDICE

Hymen voce Orphei ad matrimonium cum Eurydice vocatur. Ille deus matrimonii adfuit, sed nec verba laeta nec omen felix attulit. Fax quam tenuit nullos ignes dedit. Matrimonium exitum infelix habuit, nam nupta, Eurydice, dum per herbas cum turba comitum ambulat, dente serpentis in pedem recepto, occidit.

Orpheus, postquam ad superas auras mortem Eurydicis satis ploravit, ausus est ad Stygem descendere et eam inter umbras invenire. Proserpinam et Plutonem tenentem regnum umbrarum adiit et sic ait: "O di positi sub terra, non huc descendi quod Tartarum videre nec canem Cerberum, monstrum ingens, vincere desiderabam. Causa viae est coniunx quam serpens necavit et crescentes annos abstulit. Conatus sum acre vulnus ferre, sine mea coniuge vivere, sed Amor vicit. Hic deus bene notus est in ora supera; forsitan hic de eo audivistis. Si fama rapinae est vera, Amor vos quoque coniunxit. Oro, retexite fata Eurydicis. Omnia debemus vobis; nos omnes ad unam finem properamus. Haec est domus ultima; longissima regna tenetis. Cum Eurydice iustos annos egerit, vobis erit. Poscimus hoc donum; sed si fata negant veniam pro coniuge, certum est mihi[1] hic manere. Gaudete mortes duorum."

Eum dicentem talia animae exsangues[2] audiebant et lacrimabant. Tantalus undam non petivit; orbis Ixionis stupuit; Sisyphus in suo saxo sedit.[3] Eumenides[4] quidem lacrimas non retinebant nec rex Pluto nec coniunx Proserpina ei oranti negare potuerunt; Eurydicem vocant.

Illa erat inter umbras recentes et tardo passu de vulnere ambulabat. Orpheus gaudens eam accipit sed cum hac lege Plutonis; non debet respicere Eurydicem donec ingentem speluncam Avernum exierit; aut donum erit frustra.

---

[1] *I am sure to* . . . (lit., *it is certain to me*).

[2] *Bloodless.*

[3] Tantalus' punishment was always to be thirsty and to reach for water that eluded him, always to be hungry and to reach for food that was out of his reach; Ixion was forever turning on his wheel; Sisyphus was forever pushing a rock uphill.

[4] The Eumenides were the Furies that pursued a man who raised a hand against his parent.

Arduum et obscurum et acre erat iter eorum per muta silentia.[5] Summae speluncae non procul afuerunt. Orpheus timens et avidus magnopere respicere desiderabat; amans oculos revertit et protinus illa relapsa est.[6] Bracchia tendens et certans eam prehendere, nil nisi auras infelix tenuit. Descendens iterum illa dixit supremum "vale" quod iam vix auribus Orpheus accepit, et Eurydice rursus eodem reversa est.

Orpheus gemina morte coniugis stupuit. Charon eum orantem frustra et desiderantem iterum transire flumen Stygiam prohibuit. Septem dies tamen ille sedit in ripa sine cibo. Lacrimae dolorque fuerunt cibum animi. Deinde dicens deos esse crudeles, se domum recepit, et numquam postea amorem feminarum aliarum petivit.

Verba

NOUNS

*anima, -ae, *f.*	spirit, soul
*aura, -ae, *f.*	breeze, air
Avernus, -ī, *m.*	Avernus (*the cave of the underworld*)
*dēns, dentis, *m.*	tooth
*Eurydicē, -is, *f.*	Eurydice (*wife of Orpheus*)
*exitus, -ūs, *m.*	outcome, end, conclusion
*fatum, -ī, *n.*	fate
fax, facis, *f.*	torch
*herba, -ae, *f.*	grass
Hymēn, Hymenis, *m.*	Hymen (*god of marriage*)
*mātrimōnium, -iī, *n.*	matrimony, wedding
*mōnstrum, -ī, *n.*	monster
*nupta, -ae, *f.*	bride
*ōmen, -inis, *n.*	omen, portent
*orbis, orbis, -ium, *m.*	circle (wheel)
*Orpheus, -ī, *m.*	Orpheus (*the singer, bard of Phoebus Apollo*)
passus, -ūs, *m.*	step
*rēgnum, -ī, *n.*	kingdom, rule
*serpēns, -entis, *c.*	snake, serpent
Styx, Stygis, *f.*	the river Styx (*in the Underworld*)
Tartarus, -ī, *m.*	Tartarus (*the Underworld*)
*umbra, -ae, *f.*	shade, spirit, shadow

---

[5] *Total* or *utter silence.*
[6] *Slipped back.*

VERBS

*accipiō, -ere, -cēpī, -ceptum	receive, accept
*adeō, -īre, -īvī *or* -iī, -itum + *dat.*	go to, approach, go near
*afferō, -ferre, attulī, allātum	carry to, bring to, bring in
*ait, *irregular verb*; *pl.* aiunt	he, she says, said
*audeō, -ēre, ausus sum [7]	dare
*auferō, auferre, abstulī, ablātum	carry away, carry off
*exeō, -īre, -īvī *or* -iī, -itum	go out, depart
*ferō, ferre, tulī, lātum	bear, bring, carry
*inveniō, -īre, -vēnī, -ventum	find, discover
*occidō, -ere, -cidī, -casum	die, perish, fall down
*plōrō (1)	weep, mourn for
*recipiō, -ere, -cēpī, -ceptum	receive, take back; return (*with* sē), restore
*redeō, -īre, -īvī *or* -iī, -itum	go back, retreat
*respiciō, -ere, -spexī, -spectum	look back, look behind
*retexō, -ere, -uī, -textum	reweave, unravel
*revertō, -ere, -vertī, -versum	turn back
*stupeō, -ēre, -uī, -itum	be amazed

ADJECTIVES

*acer, acris, acre	harsh, hard, rough, bitter
*arduus, -a, -um	hard, difficult
*avidus, -a, -um	eager
*crūdēlis, -e	cruel, bloody
*fēlix, fēlicis	happy, fortunate
*geminus, -a, -um [8]	twin, double
infēlix, infēlicis	unhappy
*ingēns, ingentis	huge
mūtus, -a, -um	mute, silent, still
*recēns, recentis	recent
*superus, -a, -um	highest, upper

OTHER WORDS

eōdem	to the same place
*frūstrā	in vain
prōtinus	immediately, straightway, directly
rursus	back again

---

[7] The perfect tenses of this verb are passive in form but active in meaning. Therefore **ausus sum** means *I dared.* Such verbs are called semi-deponent.

[8] The space rendezvous project of the United States NASA takes its name from the *Gemini*, the twin stars, Castor and Pollux, named after the twin sons of Leda.

Structure

118. Conjugation of **ferō, afferō, auferō**. The verb **ferō** and its compounds are used so frequently in Latin that its forms and meanings should be thoroughly mastered. The complete conjugation in the active voice is given below:

ferō, ferre, tulī, lātum   *bear, carry*

Present	Imperfect	Future	Perfect	Pluperfect	Future Perfect
ferō	ferēbam	feram	tulī	tuleram	tulerō
fers	ferēbās	ferēs	tulistī	tulerās	tuleris
fert	ferēbat	feret	tulit	tulerat	tulerit
ferimus	ferēbāmus	ferēmus	tulimus	tulerāmus	tulerimus
fertis	ferēbātis	ferētis	tulistis	tulerātis	tuleritis
ferunt	ferēbant	ferent	tulērunt	tulerant	tulerint

Imperatives: *Singular:* **fer**   *Plural:* **ferte**

(See paradigm in the Appendix for the passive forms.)

Notice how the compounds **afferō** (ad + **ferō**) and **auferō** (ab + **ferō**) change in the forms of the principal parts: **afferō, afferre, attulī, allātum** and **auferō, auferre, abstulī, ablātum**. The conjugation of these compounds is patterned on the conjugation of **ferō** given above.

119. Third declension adjectives of one and three terminations. Some third declension adjectives have only one ending for all genders in the nominative singular. These are called *adjectives of one termination*. On the other hand there are several which have separate endings for masculine, feminine and neuter, and these are called *adjectives of three terminations*. You have already studied the adjectives of two terminations (**omnis, omne**) in **Section 112**.

	One Termination		Three Terminations		
	M. & F.	*N.*	*M.*	*F.*	*N.*
Nom.	ingēns	ingēns	acer	acris	acre
Gen.	ingentis	ingentis	acris	acris	acris
Dat.	ingentī	ingentī	acrī	acrī	acrī
Acc.	ingentem	ingēns	acrem	acrem	acre
Abl.	ingentī	ingentī	acrī	acrī	acrī
Nom.	ingentēs	ingentia	acrēs	acrēs	acria
Gen.	ingentium	ingentium	acrium	acrium	acrium
Dat.	ingentibus	ingentibus	acribus	acribus	acribus
Acc.	ingentēs	ingentia	acrēs	acrēs	acria
Abl.	ingentibus	ingentibus	acribus	acribus	acribus

Notice that the accusative has one form for masculine and feminine, and another for neuter, as do nominative and accusative plural. Third declension adjectives are declined like I-stem nouns: acc. pl. **-ia**; gen. pl. **-ium**; and abl. sing. **-ī**.

120. Participles. Participles are verbal adjectives. Like adjectives, they modify nouns or pronouns. Like verbs they express action or state of being, and have tense (present, past, and future), and voice (active or passive).

	Active	*Passive*
Present	**amāns, amantis**	———
	loving	
Perfect (Past)	———	**amātus, -a, -um**
		having been loved
Future	**amātūrus, -a, -um**	**amandus, -a, -um**
	about to love	*to be loved,*
		about to be loved
		(This is the *gerundive* form)

The future participles will be studied in subsequent lessons. Notice, however, that they exist in both the active and passive voices, a condition not echoed in the present (only active) and perfect (only passive). You are already familiar with the forms and the meanings of the perfect passive participle:

Eurydicē, ab Orpheō **amāta**, in Orcō quaesīta est.
Eurydice (*having been*) *loved* by Orpheus was sought in Orcus.

121. Present active participle. The present active participle is a verbal adjective formed from the stem of the verb + **ns**. It is usually translated with "ing" in English: loving, holding, leading, etc.

I	II	III	III-**iō**	IV
amāns	**tenēns**	**ducēns**	**capiēns**	**audiēns**
loving	holding	leading	taking	hearing

These participles are declined like third declension adjectives of one termination, except that they have **-e** in the ablative singular.[9] The present active participle is an adjective capable of modifying a noun in any case, number, or gender.

Orpheus, **tendēns** bracchia et **certāns** eam prehendere, nīl nisi aurās tenuit.

---

[9] Present participles used as adjectives have **-ī** in the ablative singular: **cum amantī coniuge**, *with his loving wife.*

Orpheus, *stretching out* his arms and *struggling* to clasp her, held nothing but the air.

Serpēns[10] **crescentēs** annōs abstulit.

The serpent took away her *growing* years.

Animae eum tālia **dicentem** audiēbant et lacrimābant. (**tālia**, *such things*)

The spirits heard him *speaking* such things and wept.

The verbal aspect of the participle is quite obvious when it takes a direct object (**tālia**) as above.

The irregular **eō, īre** and its compounds have the following present active participle:

iēns, euntis, *going*; **abiēns**, *going away*; **rediēns**, *going back*

Deponent verbs have a present active participle for each conjugation:

hortāns, *urging*; **verēns**, *fearing*; **sequēns**, *following*; **oriēns**, *rising*

Exercises

I.   Quaestiones:

1. Quis vocatur ad matrimonium Orphei et Eurydicis?
2. Cur Hymen vocatur?
3. Quomodo Eurydice occidit?
4. Postquam Orpheus satis ploravit, ad quem locum descendit?
5. Quis deus omnia vincit?
6. Viceratne Amor Plutonem et Proserpinam?
7. Ubi est domus ultima?
8. Quem dei umbrarum vocant?
9. Qua lege Orpheus coniugem in terra duxit?
10. Potestne Orpheus ad Eurydicem non respicere?

II A.   Give the four participles for each verb and translate:

voco   mitto   sentio

B.   Translate these participles:

1. inventum	6. occidens	11. sequens
2. ferens	7. conans	12. loquens
3. recepturus	8. ploraturus	13. abiens
4. revertens	9. redeuntem	14. amata
5. respiciens	10. ablatura	15. daturus

---

[10] The noun **serpēns** (*serpent*) is actually a present active participle formed from the verb **serpō, -ere** (*creep, crawl*).

III A. Decline the following:

    1. Orpheus infelix
    2. canis ingens
    3. fatum acre
    4. coniunx amans
    5. digitus scribens

  B. Fill in the correct form of the present participle of **cantare: cantans, -antis**.

    1. Orpheus _____ carmen sub terra descendit.
    2. Proserpina carmen Orphei _____ audivit.
    3. Dei coniugem Orpheo _____ dederunt.
    4. Eurydice Orpheum _____ audire potest.
    5. Eurydice ab Orpheo _____ per umbras ducta est.
    6. Dei poetas _____ audiverunt.
    7. Dei dona poetis _____ dederunt.
    8. Poetae _____ deis placent (*are pleasing*: **placeō, -ēre, placuī**).
    9. Carmina laetissima a poetis _____ cantabantur.
    10. Carmina poetarum _____ erant laetissima.

IV.   Fill in the correct form of the perfect passive participle of the verb in parentheses:

    1. Carmina __cantata__ deis placent. (cantare)
    2. Eurydice _____ in Orcum descendit. (necare)
    3. Hymen _____ ad matrimonium adfuit. (vocare)
    4. Eurydice dente serpentis _____ in pedem occidit. (recipere)
    5. Coniuge _____ Orpheus ex Orco exire temptavit. (invenire)

V.   Translate into Latin:

    1. Hymen was present at the marriage but the omens were unfavorable (**infēlix, infēlicis**; remember that third declension adjectives are I-stem).
    2. A serpent bit (**momordit**) the foot of Eurydice (while she was) walking. (Express by a present participle in the genitive case.)
    3. Orpheus sang his song of complaint to the gods and they gave the bride back to the rejoicing husband (**vir**).[11]
    4. Orpheus was not supposed to (**nōn dēbēbat**) look back at his bride.
    5. Orpheus was not able to restrain himself, and he gazed back at his wife with loving eyes.

---

[11]Compare the English phrase, "my man," meaning *my husband.*

Etymology

LATIN IN MUSICAL TERMS

The story of Orpheus symbolically represents the power of music over the harsh forces of life. Music was indeed an integral part of Greek life, the natural accompaniment to festivals, public events, marriages, funerals, dramatic presentations, banquets, and social gatherings. Instruction in singing and playing the lyre therefore was part of the education of a citizen. People in general not only could distinguish between music performed well or poorly, they could themselves participate in the performances. At the great games there were contests of musical as well as athletic skills, and prizes were offered for songs accompanied by the **cithara** or the **aulos**.

The **cithara** or lyre was the instrument of Apollo, the shining god of the sun, music, medicine, and the arts. His bard Orpheus also played the lyre and is always so represented in art. The **aulos** was the instrument of Dionysus and of the satyrs, who are usually depicted in vase paintings and on reliefs in a drunken procession honoring this god of the vine. Perhaps the all-pervasive wail of present-day Near Eastern music is descended from the wailing tone of the **aulos** of antiquity.

The Romans never seemed to develop as fully the ear for, the appreciation of, or the ability to perform music, as did the Greeks. The whole field was left to professional musicians who ranked along with actors as a craft or guild. When the Emperor Nero, obsessed with his musical abilities, went to perform at the games in Athens, the event was most unusual. Despite the Romans' neglect of the art, however, Latin has given a rich heritage of musical terms to English, some directly from Latin, but many from the intermediate language of Italian.

fugue (**fuga**, *flight*)
sonata (**sonare**, *to sound*)
invention (**invenire**, *to discover*)
alto (**altus, -a, -um**, *high, deep*)
cantata (**cantata**, *having been sung*)
percussion (**per + cussum**, *beaten*)
plectrum (**plectrum**, *a pick*)
harmony (**harmonia**, *harmony*)
composition (**cum + positum**,
  placed with)

soprano (**supra**, *above, over*)
basso profundo (**pro + fundus**, *bottom*)
tenor (**tenere**, *to hold* basic notes)
lyre (**lyra**, *lyre*)

movement (**movere**, *move*)
opera (**opus**, pl. **opera**, *a work* or *works*)
sound (**sonus**, *a sound*)
dulcimer (**dulcis**, *sweet*)

*   *   *   *   *

Give the Latin source for the following words from the vocabulary of the story:

an *animated* conversation
no *exit*
harsh *fate*
prospect of *matrimony*
a *monster* movie
nuptial bliss
an evil *omen*
put into *orbit*
the Biblical *serpent*
the *penumbra* (**pen** < **paene**) of the sun
a cool *reception*
revert to evil habits
a *stupefying* performance
an *arduous* task
an *avid* reader
felicitations are in order!
a *recent* performance
frustrating experiences

Chapter XXII
MORS ORPHEI

Ter Sol annum finiverat et Orpheus omnem amorem feminarum fugerat, seu quod amor primus male evenerat seu quod fidem Eurydici dederat. Tamen multae feminae ardorem vati se coniungere habebant. Aliquae ab illo repulsae magnopere doluerunt, sed maxime Maenades.

Dum carmine maestissimo dulcissimoque vates Orpheus silvas et animalia fera et saxa dura quidem movet, ecce turba Maenadum irata et insana, pectoribus velleribus tectis, eum de monte vidit. Una e quibus, "en," ait "en, hic est contemptor nostri," et hastam in ora vatis Phoebi misit. Sed hasta ipsa carmine vatis capta sine vulnere pervenit. Altera saxum iecit, quod in aura missum ipsa voce et lyra victum est et veluti supplex ante pedes Orphei iacuit.

Sed enim ira earum crescit et insana Erinys regnat. Omnia tela mota carmine Orphei futura erant innocentia; sed clamor ingens feminarum iratissimarum clamantium et tympana et tibiae et cornua sonum lyrae vicerunt. Tum denique saxa sanguine vatis rubuerunt. Ac primum aves et animalia fera fugerunt et Maenadae vatem rapuerunt et se vertunt circum Orpheum ut aves solent[1] aut ut canes quando cervum, praedam, inveniunt. Vatem petunt et iaciunt tela et saxa et ramos arbore direptos.

Miserrimus Orpheus tendens manus et orans Bacchantes voce movere frustra temptavit; insanissimae eum laceraverunt. Per os ipsum (O Iuppiter!) quod saxa et animos animalium ferorum vicerat, anima eius in ventos exit.

Te aves maestissimae, Orpheu,[2] te turba ferorum, te saxa dura, te silvae ploraverunt. Arbor frondibus positis quasi capillis laceratis[3] te ploravit. Dicunt causa illius[4] flumina crevisse lacrimis plurimis suis et nymphas vestimenta nigra et capillos neglectos habuisse.

---

[1] *As birds are accustomed* (to do). ***Soleō, solēre, solitus sum,** *be accustomed.*
[2] Vocative case.
[3] *As if* (**quasi**) *they were torn hair.*
[4] **Causa illius,** *for his sake,* (lit., *for the sake of that man). They say that for his sake . . .*

Membra eius iacent diversa multis in locis—caput et lyram flumen Hebrus accipit. Dum in summa unda natat, lyra carmen maestissimum dat et ripae respondent. Denique flumine relicto caput in ripa peregrina iacet quod serpens ferus morsurus est. Phoebus autem adest et serpentem in saxum mutat.

Umbra Orphei sub terras ivit et recognovit loca quae antea viderat; quaerens per agros piorum[5] Eurydicem invenit. Bracchiis avidissime eam prehendit. Hic nunc ambo coniunctis passibus[6] ambulant. Orpheus nunc Eurydicem suam tuto respicere potest.

Verba

NOUNS

*animus, -ī, *m.*	soul, spirit, mind; *pl.*, courage
*ardor, -ōris, *m.*	burning, heat, eagerness
Baccha, -ae, *f. also* **Bacchantēs** *for* **Bacchae**	a Bacchante (*female worshipper of Bacchus*)
*causa, -ae, *f.*	cause, sake, reason
cervus, -ī, *m.*	stag
contemptor, -ōris, *m.*	a despiser
Ērīnys, -yos, *f.*	one of the Furies
*hasta, -ae, *f.*	spear, javelin
Hebrus, -ī, *m.*	Hebrus (*a river in Thrace*)
*fidēs, -eī, *f.*	trust, belief, faith, pledge
frons, frondis, *f.*	a leaf, foliage
Maenas, -adis, *f.*	a Bacchante, a maddened woman, a Maenad
*pectus, -oris, *n.*	breast, heart
praeda, -ae, *f.*	booty, prey
tibia, -ae, *f.*	shin bone, pipe, flute
tympanum, -ī, *n.*	tamborine, drum
*umbra, -ae, *f.*	shade, shadow
vātes, -is, *c.* (*gen. pl.,* **-um** or **ium**)	bard, poet, seer, singer
*vellus, -eris, *n.*	fleece, wool
*ventus, -ī, *m.*	wind

VERBS

*dīcunt	they say, people say
dīripiō, -ere, -ripuī, -reptum	snatch apart, tear away
doleō, -ēre, -uī	suffer pain, grieve

---

[5] *The Elysian Fields*; lit., *The fields of the blessed.*
[6] *With their footsteps joined together,* or *walking side by side.*

*ēveniō, -īre, -vēnī, -ventum	turn out, come about
*finiō, -īre, -īvī, -ītum	end, conclude, finish
lacerō (1)	tear to pieces, maim
mordeō, -ēre, momordī, morsum	bite
*natō (1)	swim
*plōrō (1)	weep, wail for
*recognōscō, -ere, -cognōvī, -nitum	recognize, recall
*repellō, -ere, reppulī, -pulsum	drive back, drive away, push, spurn
rubēscō, -ere, rubuī	grow red, become red
tegō, -ere, tēxī, tēctum	cover, conceal, hide
*sē vertere	to turn oneself

ADJECTIVES

amoenus, -a, -um	pleasant
*dīversus, -a, -um	scattered, spread out, turned in different directions
*innocēns, -entis	innocent, harmless
*insānus, -a, -um	maddened, insane
*peregrīnus, -a, -um	foreign
*supplex, -icis	suppliant (*often as substantive*, a suppliant)

OTHER WORDS

*aliquis, aliquid[7]	some, any; some, any one; some, any thing
*ambō, -ae, -ō	both, two, together
*circum + *acc.*	around, about
ēn, *interjection*	lo, behold, see
*male	badly
*quandō	when
*seu . . . seu, *conj.*	whether . . . or
*ter	thrice, three times
*tūtō	safely
velut (velutī)	just as, just like, even as

Structure

122. **Future active participle.** The future active participle, as indicated in **Section 120**, is formed from the perfect passive participle (the fourth principal part) with the **-us, -a, -um** ending expanded to **-ūrus, -ūra,**

---

[7]Consult Appendix for complete declension.

-ūrum. The best way to remember its future nature and forms is to observe the future active participle of **sum**: **futūrus, -a, -um**,[8] from which the English word "future" is formed. The English translation is *about to* or *going to*.

I	II	III	III-io	IV
amātūrus, -a, -um	doctūrus, -a, -um	ductūrus, -a, -um	captūrus, -a, -um	audītūrus, -a, -um
about to love	*about to teach*	*about to lead*	*about to take*	*about to hear*

These participles are declined like **bonus, -a, -um**.

> **Orpheus cantātūrus** ā turbā fēminārum necātur.
> *Orpheus, about to sing, is killed by a band of women.*
> Fēminae **Orpheum cantātūrum** necant.
> The women kill *Orpheus [as he is] about to sing.*
> **Orpheus** Eurydicem ex Orcō **ductūrus** respicit et eam āmittit.
> *Orpheus, about to lead* Eurydice out of Orcus, looks back and loses her.

123. Active periphrastic conjugation. *Periphrasis* means "circumlocution," talking around a subject. The periphrastic construction is a roundabout way of expressing the future tense in a not so definite manner. Compare: **dabit**, *he will give* with **datūrus est**, *he is about to give*. Usually tense, mood, voice, and number are indicated in Latin by inflectional endings on the main verb stem. You have already studied the perfect passive system in which a participle is combined with forms of the verb **sum** to make up what we call in English a verb phrase (**Sec. 113**). The active periphrastic conjugation[9] is also a verb phrase using the future active participle with forms of **sum**: the ending of the participle agrees with the subject of the verb in number and gender. Note the tenses and meanings of the forms of the verb, **do, dare, dedī, datum** in the following sentences:

INDICATIVE MOOD

Pres.:	Pecūniam **datūrus (-a) sum**.	*I am about to give* the money. *I am going to give* the money.
Imp.:	Pecūniam **datūrus (-a) erās**.	*You were about to give* the money. *You were going to give* the money.
Fut.:	Pecūniam **datūrus (-a, -um) erit**.	*He (she, it) will be about to give, will be going to give* the money.

---

[8] When no logical perfect passive participle exists, the future active participle is given as the fourth principal part. The verb **esse** has a fourth principal part that means "about to be," since a "having been" idea would be illogical. Sometimes the supine is given for the fourth principal part: **maneō, -ēre, mānsī, mānsum**, *remain*.

[9] There is also a passive periphrastic, which will be studied in a subsequent lesson.

Perf.:	Pecūniam **datūrī** **(-ae) fuimus**.	*We have been (were) about to give* the money.
Plu. Perf.:	Pecūniam **datūrī** **(-ae) fuerātis**.	*You had been about to give* the money.
Fut. Perf.:	Pecūniam **datūrī** **(-ae, -a) fuerint**.	*They will have been about to give* the money.

INFINITIVE: These sentences are examples of Indirect Statement, which is explained in Chapter XXIII. Supply "that" after the main verb in the following sentences:

| Putō eum **datūrum esse** pecūniam. | I think that he *is about to give* the money. |
| Putō eōs **datūrōs esse** pecūniam. | I think that they *are about to give the money.* |

124. Comparison of adjectives: positive, comparative, superlative. The degree of intensity of adjectives is called comparison. A man may be happy (*positive*), happier (*comparative*) or most happy (*superlative*) both in Latin and in English. Observe the following ending changes to indicate these degrees:

Positive	*Comparative* M. & F. N.	*Superlative*
laetus, -a, -um happy	**laetior laetius** happier, more happy, too happy, rather happy[10]	**laetissimus, -a, -um** happiest most happy very happy exceedingly happy[10] especially happy[10]
The general rule: **-ior, -ius**		**-issimus, -a, -um**

Note the form of these regular adjectives:

avidus, -a, -um	**avidior, avidius**	**avidissimus, -a, -um**
maestus, -a, -um	**maestior, maestius**	**maestissimus, -a, -um**
ingēns (-entis)	**ingentior, ingentius**	**ingentissimus, -a, -um**
fortis, -e	**fortior, fortius**	**fortissimus, -a, -um**

The comparative form is declined in general like a third declension adjective of two terminations.[11] The superlative form is declined like **bonus, -a, -um**.

---

[10]Do not neglect these possible translations for the comparative and superlative.

[11]N.B., abl. sing. in **-e**, neuter nom. and acc. plu. in **-a**, gen. plu. in **-um**. The I-stem nature of the third declension adjective disappears in the comparative declension.

COMPARATIVE DECLENSION

Singular		Plural	
M. & F.	N.	M. & F.	N.
laetior	laetius	laetiōrēs	laetiōra
laetiōris	laetiōris	laetiōrum	laetiōrum
laetiōrī	laetiōrī	laetiōribus	laetiōribus
laetiōrem	laetius	laetiōrēs	laetiōra
laetiōre	laetiōre	laetiōribus	laetiōribus

The most common adjectives, however, are compared irregularly. The easiest way to remember these forms is from the English cognates:

Positive		Comparative		Superlative	
bonus, -a, -um	good	melior, melius	better	optimus, -a, -um	best
malus, -a, -um	bad	pēior, pēius	worse	pessimus, -a, -um	worst
magnus, -a, -um	great	māior, māius	greater	maximus, -a, -um	greatest
parvus, -a, -um	small	minor, minus	smaller	minimus, -a, -um	smallest
multus, -a, -um	much	plūs	more	plūrimus, -a, -um	most
(ulter, -tra, -trum)[12]	far	ulterior, -ius	farther	ultimus, -a, -um	farthest, last

125. Comparison of adverbs. The adverb, the part of speech telling *how* an action is performed usually ends in -ē (-e) or -iter and sometimes -ō.

male (badly)   celeriter (quickly)   multō (by much)
optimē (very good,   (*really an ablative form*)
  excellent)   tūtō (safely)

The adverb can exist not only in the positive form, but also in the comparative and superlative, the endings being -ius in the comparative and -issimē in the superlative, as follows:

Positive	Comparative	Superlative
laetē (*happily*)	laetius (*more happily*)	laetissimē (*most happily*)
avidē	avidius	avidissimē
forte	fortius	fortissimē

---

[12]Positive forms not found except in adverbs: ultrā, ultrō.

male	peius	pessimē
bene (*from* **bonus**)	**melius**	**optimē**

126. Infinitives: present, perfect, future. The infinitive exists in three tenses, active and passive. Its forms are as follows:

	Active		*Passive*	
Pres.:	**amāre**	to love	**amārī**	to be loved
Perf.:	**amāvisse**	to have loved	**amātus (-a, -um) esse**	to have been loved
Fut.:	**amātūrus (-a, -um) esse**	to be about to love	**amātum īrī** (rarely used)	to be about to be loved

Below is a review of the active and passive infinitives for all conjugations:

PRESENT

	I	II	III	III-io	IV
Act.	**amāre**	**tenēre**	**ducere**	**capere**	**audīre**
Pass.	**amārī**	**tenērī**	**ducī**	**capī**	**audīrī**

PERFECT

Act.	**amāvisse**	**tenuisse**	**duxisse**	**cēpisse**	**audīvisse**
Pass.	**amātus esse**	**tentus esse**	**ductus esse**	**captus esse**	**audītus esse**

FUTURE

Act.	**amātūrus esse**	**tentūrus esse**	**ductūrus esse**	**captūrus esse**	**audītūrus esse**
Pass.	**amātum īrī**	**tentum īrī**	**ductum īrī**	**captum īrī**	**audītum īrī**

127. **Eō** compounds. The verbs compounded with **eō**, the verb meaning *go*, are frequent in Latin, each preposition shading and altering the meaning, but the basic conjugation remaining the same. See the Appendix for the complete conjugation.

eō, īre, iī or **īvī, itūrus**	go
abeō	go away, depart
adeō	go toward, approach
exeō	go out of, depart
ineō	go into, enter
obeō	go against, oppose
redeō	go back
subeō	go under
trānseō	go across

Exercises

I.   Quaestiones

1. Cur Orpheus amorem feminarum evitavit?
2. Quae Orpheus voce et lyra cepit?
3. Cur Maenades erant iratae?
4. Quae iacuerunt Maenades?
5. Nocueruntne Orpheum tela et saxa primo?
6. Quid denique Maenades fecerunt?
7. Per quod anima Orphei exivit?
8. Qui Orpheum ploraverunt?
9. Quis serpentem in saxum mutavit?
10. Quem Orpheus sub terram quaerit?

II A. Form the active and passive participles for each of the following verbs and give the English for each.

1. voco   vocans   vocatum   vocaturum   vocandum
2. doceo
3. ago
4. finio
5. capio
6. mitto

B. Form the six infinitives for each verb above and translate each form, following the pattern given below:

Pres.	**finire**	to end	**finiri**	to be ended
Perf.	**finivisse**	to have ended	**finitum esse**	to have been ended
Fut.	**finiturum esse**	to be about to end	**finitum iri**	to be about to be ended

III. Fill in the correct form of the active periphrastic for the verb phrase.

1. Pecuniam puellae (*he is about to give*).
2. Maenades Orpheum (*were about to kill*).
3. Eurydice Orcum (*was about to leave*).
4. Orpheus (*was about to sing*).
5. Fabulam mihi (*you were going to tell*).

IV A. Fill in the correct form of the adjective in the comparative and super-lative.

Positive	Comparative	Superlative
1. amoenus, -a, -um		
2. clarus, -a, -um		
3. fortis, -e		

    4. magnus, -a, -um

    5. bonus, -a, -um

B. Now use these forms in the sentences below:

    1. Haec terra est (*the most pleasant*).

    2. Haec urbs est (*more famous*) quam illa.

    3. (*The bravest*) quidem viri mortem timent.

    4. Ursa (*the larger*) est Callisto.

    5. Ursa (*the smaller*) est filius eius, Arcas.

    6. (*The best*) carmina a vate Orpheo cantabantur.

C. Use adverb forms for the words above in the following sentences:

    1. (*Most bravely*) pugnavit.

    2. (*Very good!*)

    3. Aliqui (*very beautifully*) occidunt, sed Orpheus (*very badly*) occidit.

    4. Haec stella lucem (*most brightly*) dat.

    5. Haec fabula mihi (*very much*) placet.

V.   Translate into Latin:

    1. Many women repulsed by Orpheus desired to love the bard.

    2. Some insane Maenads especially tried to kill him with all the weapons which they could find.

    3. Even the weapons were charmed (**capere**) by the voice and the lyre of Orpheus, but the shouts of the women overcame the sound of his song.

    4. All nature wept the death of the bard of Phoebus who was killed by the very crazed Maenads.

    5. But Orpheus descending again under the earth found his Eurydice and now could look back at her in safety.

Etymology

MUSICAL TERMS

Musical terms in English of Latin (or Italian) origin abound. Traditionally the expressive dynamic markings in the musical score are written in Italian, most of them of Latin origin:

forte (**fortis**, *strong*) loud, strong
piano (**planus**, *even*, *smooth*) soft
con amoroso (**cum amore**, *with love*) tenderly
vivace (**vivere**, *to live*) lively
allegro (**alacer**, *merry*, *gay*) quickly

con espresso molto (**cum expresso
multo**, *with much pressed or forced
out*) with much expression
rhythm (**rhythmus**, *time, harmony*)
regular pulsation
fortissimo (**fortissimum**,
strongest) very loud
pianissimo (**planissimum**,
smoothest) very soft
tempo (**tempus**, *time*) pace
clef (**clavis**, *key*) key
lento (**lente**, *slowly*) slowly
crescendo (**crescere**, *to increase*)
increasing power of tone
diminuendo (**diminuere**, *to lessen*)
decreasing power of tone
cadence (**cadere**, *to fall, agree with*)
harmonic resolution

The number of musicians in a group gives the names to the performing
artists:

solo, duet, trio, quartet, quintet, sextet, septet, octet

Many of the instruments existed in an early form in antiquity or were
given names from Latin as they were invented:

cymbal (um), tuba, tympanum, cornet (a small horn)

What is the Latin or Greek source for these musical terms?

vibrato, accent, meter, sound, note, tone, tune, melody, instrument,
balance, legato, firmata, pulse, triple, rehearse, symphony, concerto,
repeat.

* * * * *

Give the Latin source for the underlined words, taken from the vocabulary, in the following phrases:

a <u>Bacchanalian</u> orgy
the <u>cause</u> of it all
a <u>contemptuous</u> remark
a <u>bonafide</u> guarantee
the <u>fronds</u> of a plant
the <u>members</u> of the body
<u>pectoral</u> muscles

the <u>winds</u> of March
a blessed <u>event</u>
<u>finite</u> forms (<u>infinite</u> forms)
<u>lacerations</u> of the face
only a <u>morsel</u> of bread
a clean, large <u>natatorium</u>
a <u>recognition</u> vocabulary
a <u>repelling</u> remark, a <u>repulsive</u> person
<u>diverse</u> knowledge
<u>innocent</u> blood (**in** + **noceo**)
<u>insane</u> act
a <u>peregrinating</u> hero
<u>suppliant</u> voices
<u>circa</u> (ca., c., C.) 1800
<u>ambiguous</u> terminology
a <u>tertiary</u> source

INTERIM READING II: PHAËTHON

Phaëthon erat filius Phoebi Apollonis, dei solis, et feminae Clymenes.[1] Iuvenis superbus de patre claro Phoebo magnopere dicere solebat;[2] olim amicus autem ait,[3] "Stultus es, si credis omnia quae mater tibi narrat." Phaëthon iram vix retinuit et ad Clymenen matrem it. "Mater, si vere a caelesti patre creatus sum,[4] da mihi signum tanti parentis." Ita puer oravit sibi signa veri parentis.

Clymene, mota precibus Phaëthontis iraque sua, ad caelum bracchia tendit et dicit, "Tibi iuro,[5] puer, Solem quem spectas, qui orbem temperat,[6] esse patrem tibi. Si vera verba non dico, numquam iterum lucem solis oculis meis videam.[7] Sed non longe laborabis, si regiam patris quaerere desiderabis. Si animus est tibi,[8] i et roga, tu ipse, de parente patrem Solem." Phaëthon talibus verbis matris maxime gaudet; deinde terras suas transivit et regno[9] patris appropinquavit.

Regia solis erat alta sublimibus columnis.[10] Duae portae utrimque[11] auro argentoque[12] decoratae sunt. Opus materiam superabat.[13] Nam Mulciber[14] picturas terrarum et caeli in portis fecerat. In picturis terra homines oppidaque tenet silvasque fluminaque animaliaque et nymphas et

---

[1] **Clymenē, -ēs**, wife of Merops, an Ethiopian king; beloved of Phoebus.

[2] *Was accustomed to speak excessively, to brag.*

[3] *Said.* **Dixit, inquit, ait** all are used to introduce dialogue and may be postpositive often interrupting the quotation. Possible word order: **"Stultus es," ait, "sī crēdis. . . ."**

[4] *If I have been created by a heavenly father* (**creō** [1]).

[5] **Iūrō** (1), *swear.*

[6] *Who controls the earth.*

[7] *May I never see the light of the sun again* (**lūx, lūcis,** *f., light;* **numquam,** *adv., never*).

[8] *If you have the spirit* (lit., *if the spirit is to you*).

[9] **Rēgnum, -ī,** *n., kingdom* (dat. with **appropinquāvit**).

[10] *On lofty columns.*

[11] **Utrimque,** *on each side.*

[12] **Argentum, -ī,** *n., silver.*

[13] *The work surpassed the material.*

[14] **Mulciber, -eris,** *m.,* a surname of Vulcan in whose forge the heavenly metalwork was wrought.

ceteras incolas silvae. Super haec posita est imago caeli, decorata sex signis zodiacis portis dextris, sex portis sinistris.

Phaëthon autem non deterritus, missus a matre, regiam parentis magna cum audacia intravit. Phoebus vestimento purpureo velatus[15] in solio sedebat.[16] A dextra sinistraque stabat Dies et Mensis et Annus Saeculaque et Horae; stabat quoque Ver et nuda Aestas et Autumnus et Hiems.[17] Lux erat clarissima; Phaëthon vultus[18] patris non spectare potuit.

Deinde vidit Sol iuvenem oculis illis quibus omnia spectavit et dixit: "Quae causa itineris est tibi, fili Phaëthon?" Hic respondit, "O Lux toti caeli, Phoebe pater, si das mihi usum nominis huius, da mihi quoque dona quibus me filium tibi esse monstrabo.

Pater Sol coronam deposuit[19] et iussit puerum appropinquare. "Es dignus me non negare te esse filium meum. Noli dubitare. Roga donum. Quicquid rogas, illud dabo."

Phaëthon, verbis patris auditis, rogavit currus[20] patris et ius agendi[21] equos solis in diem unum.[22] Pater erat infelix[23] quod puer tale donum rogaverat. "Temeraria," dixit, "est vox mea quae tibi donum infelix dedit. Promisi, sed non est gratum mihi dare quid quaeris. Magna petis, Phaëthon. Pater Iuppiter ipse hos currus agere[24] non potest et quis est maior quam Iuppiter?[25]

"Ardua est prima via caeli; durum et difficile[26] est iter caeli quod equi ascendere[27] debent. Medio caelo est altissima via unde[28] etiam ego ipse timeo mare et terras spectare. Ultima via est prona,[29] et si equi rapidius[30] descendent,[31] portaberis in undis maris vi equorum. Vix ipse ego equos retinere possum ubi animi eorum agitati sunt.[32] At tu, fili, cave, dum tempus

---

[15] *Covered, veiled.*
[16] *Was seated on a throne.*
[17] *Day and Month and Year and Century, and the Hours; also standing there were Spring, naked Summer, Autumn, and Winter.*
[18] *Face, countenance.*
[19] **Dēpōnō, -ere, -posuī, -positum,** *lay aside;* +**corōna, -ae,** *f., crown.*
[20] *Chariot,* here used in the plural with a singular idea (**currus, -ūs,** *m.*).
[21] *The permission to drive* (lit., *the right of driving*).
[22] *For one day* (accusative of extent of time).
[23] **Īnfēlix, -icis,** *unhappy, unfortunate, unlucky.*
[24] *To drive this chariot* (**agō, agere, ēgī, actum:** *do, drive, discuss, live; spend time.* This is a very important verb in Latin and its meanings are quite diverse).
[25] *Greater than Jupiter* (**māior, māius** is the comparative of **magnus).**
[26] *Difficult* (**difficilis, -e** is declined like **omnis, -e, Sec. 112**).
[27] *Ascend* (**ascendō, -ere, ascendī, ascensum**).
[28] *Whence.*
[29] *Straight down.*
[30] *Too rapidly.*
[31] *Descend* (the Latin future tense in the *if* clause of a conditional sentence is usually translated by the present tense).
[32] *When their spirits have been aroused.*

est; muta tua verba. Monstro me esse patrem tuum patrio timore.[33] Circumspecta omnia dona caeli et terrae et maris.[34] Posce aliquid. Noli dubitare;
dabitur (per Stygias undas[35] iuravi) quiquid optas."

Pater admonitum finiverat;[36] tamen Phaëthon poposcit donum iam a
se rogatum; agere currus patris. Ergo[37] pater ducit iuvenem ad altos currus.
Axis erat aureus, rotae erant aureae cum radiis argenteis.[38] In ligno[39] currus
gemmae positae ex ordine[40] luces claras Phoebi reddebant.[41]

Dum Phoebus et Phaëthon omnia ea spectant, ecce Aurora[42] portas
purpureas caeli aperuit. Stellae fugiunt et Lucifer[43] exit e loco suo apud
stellas. Ut Phoebus vidit terras rubescere,[44] Horas iungere[45] equos iussit.

Tum pater ora sui filii sacro medicamine[46] tetigit posuitque coronam
radiarum[47] in caput filii et dixit, "Si haec verba patris audire potes, puer,
tene frena;[48] equi sponte sua properant.[49] Labor est inhibere eos volantes.[50]
Vestigia rotae meae videbis. Tene iter nec dexterius nec sinisterius.[51] Manda[52]
cetera Fortunae quae te iuvabit melius quam tu ipse te iuvare potes, opto.
Sed iterum, puer, tene consilium meum, non currus. Est melius me dare luces
terris."

Phaëthon autem iam in currus ascendit statque superbus gaudetque
frena tangere manibus. Equi viam rapuerunt et celeriter per nebulas[53]
cucurrerunt. Sed equi solis notas manus non cognoscere possunt[54] et quasi
sine frenis[55] ferociter[56] currunt. Cum Phaëthon sensit equos esse feros, ipse
territus est nec scit iter. Tum primum Callisto et filius eius et ceterae stellae

---

[33] *By my fatherly concern* (fear).
[34] *And of the sea.*
[35] *By the River Styx;* such an oath could not be revoked by a god.
[36] *Had finished his warning.*
[37] *Therefore.*
[38] *With silver spokes* (**axis**, *axle;* **rota**, *wheel;* **argenteus, -a, -um**, *silver*).
[39] **Lignum, -ī**, *n., wood.*
[40] *In order.*
[41] *Reflected, gave back.*
[42] *Aurora*, goddess of the Dawn.
[43] *Lucifer* (the morning star, lit., *light-bringer*, son of Aurora) *left his place among* (**apud**)
the stars.
[44] *Grow red.*
[45] **Iungō, -ere, iūnxī, iūnctum**, *join together, yoke.*
[46] *Touched his son's face with sacred salve.*
[47] *Crown of rays.*
[48] **Frēna, -ōrum**, *n., reins.*
[49] *Hasten of their own accord.*
[50] *To stop their flying* (lit., *to hold back them flying*).
[51] *Not too much to the left nor to the right.*
[52] *Trust* (imperative singular of **mandō** [1]) *other things to Fortune* (a goddess).
[53] *Clouds.*
[54] *Cannot recognize.*
[55] *As if without reins* (**quasi**, *as if*).
[56] *Wildly.*

gelidae[57] callescunt.[58] Ut infelix Phaëthon a summo aethere[59] terras spectavit, subito palluit[60] et manus timore tremuerunt.[61] Tenebrae[62] oculos celaverunt. Nunc optat numquam equos aeternos tetigisse;[63] Phaëthon portatur ut[64] navis mota ventis.

Multum caeli post tergum relictum est, sed ante oculos plus est. Equos tenere non potest, nec nomina equorum scit. Territus simulacra[65] ferorum animalium in caelo videt—Scorpionem, Ursam Magnam, Cancerem.[66] Ecce Scorpio bracchia tendit. Puer frena dimittit.[67] Equi currunt quo impetus egit[68] sine lege et stellis nocent. Nunc summum caelum petunt; nunc currus prope terram portantur. Luna[69] viam novam equorum spectat. Terra flammis ardet;[70] altissimae montes, flumina, agri ardentur, arbores cum frondibus et frumentum[71] flammis ardentur. Magnae urbes vastantur. Flammae totas gentes[72] cum populis suis in cineres vertunt. Silvae cum montibus ardent.

Tum facta est Libya arida.[73] Nymphae undas et flumina et fontes lacrimant, sed omnia flumina arida fiunt.[74] Pontus ipse fit campus.[75] Pisces undas imas[76] petunt et delphines in auras saltare non audent.[77]

Tandem alma Tellus[78] ora ad patrem Iovem tollit[79] et causam tantae poenae rogat. "Estne hoc praemium fertilitatis.[80] Si dei Tellurem aridam desiderant, Iuppiter fulmina repente iactare debet.[81] Sed circumspecta terram; ecce—ardet ex polo ad polum.[82] Si ignis ad caelum extendet, domus

---

[57] *Cold.*
[58] *Grow warm.*
[59] *From high heaven.*
[60] *Suddenly he paled* (**subitō**, *suddenly*).
[61] **Tremō, -ere, -uī,** *tremble.*
[62] *Darkness.*
[63] *That he had never touched the immortal horses.*
[64] **Ut,** *as* or *like.*
[65] *Likenesses.*
[66] *Scorpio, the Great Bear, Cancer* (the Crab).
[67] *Lets go the reins.*
[68] *Where their force drives them.*
[69] **Lūna, -ae,** *f., moon.*
[70] **Ardeō, -ēre,** *burn.*
[71] *Trees with their leaves and grain are burned.*
[72] **Gēns, gentis,** *f., nations.*
[73] **Aridus, -a, -um,** *dry.*
[74] The irregular passive system of **faciō,** *make, do,* which has the transposed meaning of *become* (**fīo, fierī, factus, sum; fīō, fīs, fit, fīmus, fītis, fiunt**).
[75] *The sea itself becomes a field.*
[76] *Lowest.*
[77] *Dolphins do not dare to jump in the air.*
[78] *Loving mother Earth.*
[79] *Raises.*
[80] *Fertility.*
[81] *Ought to hurl his thunderbolts* (**fulmen, -inis,** *n.;* **iactō** [1], *hurl*).
[82] *From pole to pole.* It is interesting that the idea of poles should have existed in Ovid's time.

vestrae quoque in periculo erunt. Cape ex flammis quid adhuc superest."[83]
Haec dixit Tellus, et caput celavit; fumos enim tolerare[84] non potuit neque plura dicere. At pater omnipotens deos vocat et Apollonem ipsum qui currus dederat puero; deinde summum caelum petit unde fulmina iactabat. Fulmen dextra tenet et id ab aure misit. Phaëthonem ex curru vitaque expulsit[85] et ignes ignibus exstinxit.[86]

Phaëthon per aëra capillis flammis ardentibus[87] iacitur. Cecidit[88] ut stellae de caelo cadere videntur. Naïdes[89] corpus eius tumulo dant his verbis:

> Hic positus est Phaëthon currus auriga paterni
> Quem si non tenuit magnis tamen excidit ausis.[90]

Pater miser os celavit, sed mater per totum orbem erravit et tumulum quaerit. Denique tumulo invento[91] lacrimas super nomen carum in marmore sculptum[92] dat. Sorores Phaëthonis Heliades lacrimas dant et querellas nocte dieque vocant. In arbores mutantur; ut mater earum ramos manibus eripere[93] temptat, clamant, "Parce, oro, nobis,[94] mater, parce. Corpori nostro in arbore noces, iamque vale"—arbor verba novissima celavit. Interim lacrimae fluunt, et electra fiunt congelata radiis solis.[95]

---

[83] *Take from the flames whatever still is left.*

[84] *Bear, withstand, or endure the smoke* (**fūmus, -ī,** *m.*).

[85] *Drove out, expelled, thrust out of.*

[86] *He extinguished the fires with fires.* Compare modern firefighting methods.

[87] *With his burning hair ablaze.*

[88] **Cadō, cadere, cecidī, casum,** *fall.*

[89] The Naiads, water nymphs.

[90] *Here is buried Phaëthon, charioteer of his father's coach; although he could not drive it, nevertheless he died daring to do great deeds* (**Quem** refers to the chariot or coach of the sun).

[91] *When she had found the tomb.*

[92] *Carved in marble.*

[93] **Ēripiō, -ere, -ripuī, -reptum,** *tear away, snatch away.*

[94] *Spare us;* **parcō, parcere** takes the dative case.

[95] *They became amber, hardened by the rays of the sun* (**ēlectrum, -ī,** *n. amber*).

The Voyage of the Argonauts

The story of Jason and the Golden Fleece is an early tale of the episodic adventures of a great hero. This epic is the first sustained romantic love story, although the hero and heroine do not "live happily ever after." For Medea, the daughter of the king of Colchis, is a witch, related to Circe in Italy, her father's sister, and Medea's evil potentialities become evident when Jason brings his bride home to Greece from the far side of the Black Sea.

Apollonius of Rhodes has written Jason's adventures into a long epic, *The Voyage of the Argo*, which begins with Jason's arrival at Iolcus wearing only one shoe, the token by which he can be recognized by his usurper uncle Pelias. To regain his kingdom the young Jason must bring back to Greece the fleece of a miraculous golden ram which years before had come down from heaven to rescue the young Greek prince, Phrixus. Easily persuaded to show his prowess, Jason assembles the noble heroes of antiquity, pre-Trojan war heroes like Hercules, Orpheus, Theseus, Pelias, Zetes, and Calais, to participate in the expedition of the *Argo*. En route to their destination Jason has a love affair with the Queen of the island of Lemnos; Hercules drops out to search for his young armor-bearer Hylas; the sons of the North Wind, Zetes and Calais, rescue old King Phineas from starvation by driving off the Harpies; and the sailors of the *Argo* are told how to pass safely through the clashing rocks, the Symplegades.

At the far side of the Black Sea the Argonauts see Prometheus hanging on his crag in the Caucasus Mountains, and finally they arrive at the palace of Aeëtes where Medea, the princess, falls madly in love with the handsome Greek hero. In both the story of Apollonius and that of Ovid written several hundred years later, Medea wrestles with herself, torn between her love for Jason and her loyalty to her father. Ovid puts into her words the same idea Job uses to describe mortal frailty:

Video meliora proboque, deteriora sequor.

Medea, succumbing to the passions of love and Jason's promise of marriage, gives him all of her magic potions, her powers, and herself to thwart Aeëtes' trials and conditions for winning the fleece. For King Aeëtes had hoped to kill off the presumptuous Greek adventurer by giving him humanly impossible tasks to perform. By means of Medea's magic charms and her advice, the hero escapes with the fleece and the princess. When Aeëtes sends her brother Absyrtus to pursue the couple, Medea cuts him up, a bloody deed which delays Aeëtes, who stops to pick up the pieces of his son.

Once back at Iolcus in Greece, Medea causes the death of Pelias by pretending to his daughters that they can restore him to youth by cutting him up and boiling him in a pot, a magic trick she has demonstrated to them. For a time she and Jason live happily in Greece. Medea bears Jason two sons, but after the couple go to live at Corinth, Jason considers taking a new bride, the Princess of Corinth, an act which he justifies as expedient. Medea, in a doubly abhorrent act, causes the death of the princess by sending her a poisoned robe that consumes her by fire, and then—final horror—Medea kills her own two sons to revenge herself on Jason. She escapes to the court of Aegeus, king of Athens.

Sententiae
Audentis fortuna iuvat. *Fortune aids those who dare.*
Virgil, *Aen.* X.284

Chapter XXIII
IASON ET ARGONAUTAE

Aeson erat olim rex Thessaliae, sed frater suus, qui Pelias appellabatur, regnum obtinere cupiens Aesonem e regno expulit. Filium praeterea Aesonis, nomine Iasonem, occidere temptavit Pelias, homo scelestus, sed ei, fabula ficta,[1] nuntiaverunt amici Aesonis puerum iam mortuum esse. Nonnullis post diebus nuntius regi novo fidelis Delphos[2] missus ad dominum suum se retulit, cui nuntiavit oraculum. Pythia, nam sic appellata est Delphis[3] sacerdos, ediderat nullum esse periculum eo tempore, sed regem vereri debere iuvenem unum calceum solum induentem.

Paucis post annis, ubi Iason, altero calceo amisso, unum calceum solum induens ad regiam Peliae pervenit, rex ipse periculum statim sensit, nam oraculi memoriam retinebat. Iuvenem igitur ad Colchidem misit, quo loco habitabat quidam rex, Aeëtes appellatus, qui vellere aureo potiebatur. Hoc enim vellus a Phrixo olim in regno Colchidis relictum erat, postquam ariete aureo in illum locum pervenit. Quia iter ad Colchidem erat maxime periculosum, Iasonem hoc iter facere iussit Pelias, eum enim hoc itinere interiturum esse sperabat.

Iason autem sine comitibus ire non desiderabat; quam ob causam[4] quinquaginta viros fortissimos delegit inter quos erant Orpheus et Hercules. Hi viri cum Iasone navem ab Argo[5] perito aedificatam brevi tempore conscenderunt atque solverunt. Post multos dies multaque pericula auxilio deorum ad Colchidem pervenerunt Argonautae (sic enim nominabantur ex nomine navis, quae Argo appellata erat).

Tum Argonautae, multis periculosis rebus gestis,[6] e nave egressi[7] ad

---

[1] *Having made up a story* (lit., *a story having been invented; abl. abs.*).

[2] *To Delphi* (no preposition necessary with names of cities; *acc. of place to which*).

[3] *At Delphi* (no preposition necessary with names of cities; *abl. of place where*).

[4] *For this reason* (*N.B.* postpositive position of **ob** introducing **quam causam**).

[5] Do not confuse with Argus of the hundred eyes.

[6] *After they had accomplished many dangerous tasks* (lit., *many dangerous things having been accomplished*).

[7] *Having disembarked from the ship* (perfect participle of a deponent verb; deponent verbs can also have present participles: **ēgrediēns, -ientis**, *stepping out or disembarking*; both participles are translated actively).

regiam se contulerant, qua[8] habitabat Aeëtes. Ubi autem ab illo vellera aurea Phrixi poposcerunt, primum negabat se ulli vellus aureum umquam traditurum esse, sed deinde legem dedit ad quam hoc donum tradet. Si Iason duobus tauris iunctis agrum quendam araverit atque dentes draconis sparserit, vellera ei tradentur. At hoc negotium erat maxime periculosum, quia tauri ex ore flammam spiraturi erant atque viri armati creaturi e dentibus sparsis erant, sed iuvenis, rem esse malam non putans, haec nescivit.

Aeëtes autem filiam nomine Medeam habebat, quae auxilio magno Iasoni futura erat.

Verba

NOUNS

Aeētēs, -ae, *m.*	Aeëtes (*King of Colchis*)
Aesōn, -onis, *m.*	Aeson (*father of Jason*)
*Argonautae, -ārum, *m.*	Argonauts (*sailors on the Argo*)
Argus, -ī, *m.*	Argus (*the builder of the Argo*)
ariēs, arietis, *m.*	a ram
calceus, calceī, *m.*	shoe
Colchis, -idis, *f.*	Colchis (*on the Black Sea*)
*Delphī, -ōrum, *m.*	Delphi (*the site of Apollo's oracle*)
*draco, -ōnis, *m.*	dragon, serpent
*Iāsōn, -onis, *m.*	Jason
*Mēdēa, -ae, *f.*	Medea (*princess of Colchis*)
*nāvis, nāvis, -ium, *f.*	ship
*negōtium, -iī, *n.*	business, affair
*nuntius, -iī, *m.*	messenger
*ōrāculum, -ī, *n.*	oracle
Pelias, -ae, *m.*	Pelias (*usurper king of Thessaly*)
Phrixus, -ī, *m.*	Phrixus (*who dedicated the fleece*)
*Pȳthia, -ae, *f.*	Pythia (*the priestess of Apollo*)
Thessalia, -ae, *f.*	Thessaly (*a country in Greece*)

VERBS

*aedificō (1)	build, construct
*āmittō, -ere, -mīsī, -missum	lose
*appellō (1)	call, name
*arō (1)	plow
*conferō, -ferre, -tulī, collātum	bring together, collect; (+**sē**, *take oneself to*)

---

[8] *In which . . .* (**quā** is feminine, since its gender is determined by **rēgiam**).

conscendō, -ere, -dī, -sum	go on board ship, embark
*creō (1)	create
dēligō, -ere, -lēgī, -lectum	pick, choose, select
*ēdō, -ere, ēdidī, ēditum	put forth, give out, announce
*ēgredior, -gredī, -gressus sum	step out, go out, disembark
*expellō, -ere, -pulī, -pulsum	drive out, expel
fingō, -ere, finxī, fictum	shape, form, invent
*gerō, -ere, gessī, gestum	do, make, experience, achieve; (+**bellum**, *wage war*)
*induō, -ere, -uī, -ūtum	put on, wear
intereō, -īre, -īvī *or* -iī, -itum	die, perish
*iungō, -ere, iūnxī, iūnctum	join
*morior, morī, mortuus sum	die
*nuntiō (1)	announce, report
*obtineō, -ēre, -uī, -tentum	obtain, get
*occidō, -ere, -cidī, -cisum	slay, kill
*potior, -īrī, potītus sum + *abl.*	get possession of, possess
*referō, -ferre, rettulī, relātum	carry back, take back
*retineo, -ēre, -uī, -tentum	retain; (+**memoriam**, *hold in memory, remember*)
solvō, -ere, solvī, solūtum	set sail, free, loosen
*spargō, -ere, sparsī, sparsum	scatter, sprinkle
*spērō (1)	hope for
spirō (1)	breathe
*trādō, -ere, trādidī, trāditum	hand over, betray, surrender

ADJECTIVES

*armātus, -a, -um	armed
*brevis, -e	short
*fidēlis, -e + *dat.*	faithful (to)
nōnnūllus, -a, -um	some (lit., *not none*)
*paucus, -a, -um; paucī, -ōrum	few; a few
*quīdam, quaedam, quiddam	a certain
*scelestus, -a, -um	wicked
*ūllus, -a, -um	any

OTHER WORDS

crās	tomorrow
herī	yesterday
hodiē	today
*ob + *acc.*	on account of, against
*umquam	ever

Structure

128. Indirect statement (**Ōrātiō oblīqua**). Although we frequently quote the exact words of a speaker or a writer, much more frequently we form a new sentence by incorporating another's words into it. We call direct quotations of another's words "direct statement, or **ōrātiō recta**" and the rephrased sentence "indirect statement, or **ōrātiō oblīqua**." Consider the following examples:

DIRECT STATEMENT

(1) Dīcunt, "Marcus hodiē adest."

(2) Dīcunt, "Marcus herī adfuit." *or* "aderat."

(3) Dīcunt, "Marcus crās aderit."

(1) They say, "Mark is here today."

(2) They say, "Mark was here yesterday."

(3) They say, "Mark will be here tomorrow."

INDIRECT STATEMENT

(1) Dīcunt Marcum hodiē adesse.

(2) Dīcunt Marcum herī adfuisse.

(3) Dīcunt Marcum crās adfutūrum esse.

(1) They say that Mark is here today.

(2) They say that Mark was here yesterday.

(3) They say that Mark will be here tomorrow.

Notice that in English the indirect statement consists of a clause introduced by *that* and quotation marks are no longer used. In Latin there is no word for *that*, and the indirect statement is expressed by an infinitive with its subject in the accusative case. In each example the tense of the infinitive conveys time *relative to the main verb* (present infinitive—same time; perfect infinitive—prior time; future infinitive—subsequent time). The participial element (**adfutūrum**) of the future infinitive agrees with its subject (**Marcum**) *in case, number, and gender*. If one keeps in mind the English idea, "I consider her to be the best woman for the job," one can understand the Latin idea of the infinitive with its subject in the accusative.

Latin uses indirect statement after verbs of saying, thinking, sensing, knowing, hoping, and showing. Some of the verbs that regularly introduce indirect statement are: **ait, dīcō, negō, inquit, nuntiō, nārrō, mōnstrō, sciō, nesciō, crēdō, putō, audiō, videō, sentiō, spērō,** and **dēmōnstrō**.

A. **Tense in indirect statement.** *Since the tense of the infinitive is relative to the tense of the main verb* in the sentence, it is essential that the following examples be studied thoroughly to master this relationship.

PRIMARY SEQUENCE

Dīcit
(Dīcet)

(1) deōs **amāre** poētam.		the gods *love* the poet.
(2) deōs **amāvisse** poētam.	He says that (will say)	the gods *loved* the poet.
(3) deōs **amātūrōs esse** poētam.		the gods *will love* the poet.

The main verb in indirect statement affects the meaning of the subsequent infinitives. The primary tenses of the main verb include the present and future; the secondary tenses are the imperfect, perfect, and pluperfect.

SECONDARY SEQUENCE

Dīcēbat
(Dīxit)

(1) deōs **amāre** poētam.		the gods *loved* the poet.
(2) deōs **amāvisse** poētam.	He said that	the gods *had loved* the poet.
(3) deōs **amātūrōs esse** poētam.		the gods *would love* the poet.

Passively the same idea could be expressed as follows:

Dīcit
poētam

amārī ā deīs.		*is loved* by the gods.
amātum esse ā deīs.	He says that the poet	*was loved* by the gods.
amātum īrī[9] ā deīs.		*will be loved* by the gods.

B. **Reflexive in indirect statement.** If the subject of the infinitive is the same as the subject of the main verb of saying or thinking, the reflexive pronouns are used:

Illa dīcit **sē** hodiē adesse.	She says that *she* is here today.
Ille dīcit **sē** herī adfuisse.	He says that *he* was here yesterday.
Illī dīcunt **sē** crās adfutūrōs esse.	They say that *they* will be here tomorrow.

---

[9]This form of the passive infinitive was seldom used by the Romans.

Dīcō **mē** crās adfutūrum esse.

I say that *I* will be here tomorrow.

Dīxistī **tē** herī adesse.

You said that *you* were here yesterday.

The sentences from the lesson follow the rules discussed above:

Amīcī Aesonis nuntiāvērunt puerum iam **mortuum esse.**

The friends of Aeson reported that the boy *was* already *dead* (*or had* already *died*).

Pȳthia ēdiderat nūllum **esse** perīculum eō tempore.

Pythia had replied that there *was* no danger at that time.

129. The use of **negō.** In Latin one must use the verb **negō** to translate "say that . . . not" instead of using **dīcō** plus a negative word.

Negō nautam adesse.

I say that the sailor is *not* here.

Prīmum Aeētēs **negābat** sē **ūllī** vellus aureum **umquam** trāditūrum esse.

At first Aeetes *said that* he would *never* give (surrender) the fleece to anyone.

Note that with **negō** the negative words **numquam** or **nēmō, nusquam, nūllus,** etc. are not used but **umquam, ūllus, usquam,** etc., since the verb **negō** already contains the negative idea within itself.

130. **Quīdam, quaedam, quiddam.** The adjective **quīdam, quaedam, quiddam** is declined like **quī, quae, quid (quod)** with the suffix **-dam.** The meaning is "a certain."

	Singular			*Plural*	
quīdam	quaedam	quiddam	quīdam	quaedam	quaedam
cuiusdam	cuiusdam	cuiusdam	quōrundam	quārundam	quōrundam
cuidam	cuidam	cuidam	quibusdam	quibusdam	quibusdam
quendam	quandam	quiddam	quōsdam	quāsdam	quaedam
quōdam	quādam	quōdam	quibusdam	quibusdam	quibusdam

quoddam may be used instead of **quiddam**

131. Irregular adjectives: **alter, alius, nūllus, sōlus, tōtus, ūllus,** and **ūnus.** These seven adjectives are irregular in the Genitive and Dative case, Singular only. All the other forms are like those of **bonus, -a, -um.** Study the following example:

Singular			*Plural*		
sōlus	sōla	sōlum	sōlī	sōlae	sōla
sōlīus	sōlīus	sōlīus	sōlōrum	sōlārum	sōlōrum
sōlī	sōlī	sōlī	sōlīs	sōlīs	sōlīs
sōlum	sōlam	sōlum	sōlōs	sōlās	sōla
sōlō	sōlā	sōlō	sōlīs	sōlīs	sōlīs

alter, *other* (of two); **alius**, *other*; **nūllus**, *none*; **sōlus**, *only*; **tōtus**, *whole, all*; **ūllus**, *any*; **ūnus**, *one*.

Exercises

I. Respondete Latine ad interrogata:

1. Quam ob rem expulit Pelias fratrem suum? (**Quam ob rem**, *for what reason, why?*)
2. Quid erat nomen filio Aesonis?
3. Quando misit rex nuntium Delphos?
4. Quid ediderat Pythia?
5. Quomodo erat habitus Iasonis novus? (**habitus, -ūs**, *m., appearance, dress*)
6. Quis potiebatur (habebat) vellere aureo?
7. Quid iussit Pelias?
8. Quisnam navem aedificavit? (**quisnam**, *who?*)
9. Quantum virorum fortissimorum delegit Iason? (**quantum**, *how many?*)
10. Perveneruntne Argonautae ad Colchidem sine auxilio deorum?
11. Quid primum respondebat Aeetes?
12. Quid denique respondebat ille?

II A. Give a synopsis of the following deponent verbs with English meanings:

(consult Appendix for paradigm)

1. miror (3rd person sing.)
2. vereor (3rd person plu.)
3. morior (1st person plu.)
4. potior (2nd person plu.)

B. Give the participles and infinitives of the verbs in A with their English translation. Consult the paradigms in the Appendix for the forms.

C. Translate into English the following deponent verbs:

1. verebatur
2. egressi sunt
3. miramini
4. potitus es
5. mortuus erat
6. locuta est
7. egressi
8. potiebatur
9. mirabar
10. veriti erimus

D. Supply the correct forms of the verbs in the following sentences:

1. Puellis dona (*they are giving*).   Haec dona (*I admire*).
2. Iason tauros (*feared*).
3. Iason tauros (*had to yoke together*). (*had to*—**dēbeō, dēbēre** + infinitive)
4. Iason haec verba (*spoke*).
5. Aeetes vellere aureo (*obtained*).

III. Complete the following sentences in indirect statement by supplying the correct infinitive:

1. Dicunt puerum (*is*) filium regis. (**esse**)
2. Putant puerum (*is fleeing*). (**fugere**)
3. Dicunt puerum (*fled*). (**fugisse**)
4. Nuntiaverunt puerum (*had fled*).
5. Nuntiant puerum iam (*is dead*).
6. Nuntiaverunt puerum (*had died*).
7. Non putat Iasonem ad Colchidem (*will arrive*).
8. Navem ab Argo perito (*had been built*) nuntiavit.
9. Primum negabat nautam (*was present*). (**nauta, -ae,** *m., sailor*)
10. Poeta narrat Argonautas (*were called*) quoque Minyas. (Minyans)
11. Nautae putant ducem (*fears*) tauros.
12. Negat se cras (*will be present*). (**adsum**)
13. Nauta putat navem (*is here*). (**adsum**)
14. Nauta putat navem (*was here*).
15. Nauta putat navem (*will be here*).
16. Nautae putant ducem (*loves*) Medeam.
17. Nautae putaverunt ducem (*loved*) Medeam.
18. Nautae putaverunt navem (*was here*).
19. Nautae putaverunt navem (*had been here*).
20. Nautae putaverunt navem (*would be here*).
21. Scit enim regem vellere aureo (*possessed*).
22. Scivit enim regem vellere aureo (*possessed*).
23. Putavi te loqui (*desired*).
24. Putavi Iasonem (*was dead*).
25. Spero omnes homines (*are*) bonos.

IV. Supply the subject for each of the following infinitives in the indirect statements:

1. Omnes sciunt (*Pythia*) esse sacerdotem.
2. Aeetes negat (*he*) vellus aureum traditurum esse.
3. Nautae non putant (*he*) vellus aureum traditurum esse.
4. Nuntiat (*the friends of Aeson*) fabulam finxisse.
5. Negavit (*anyone*) vereri debere.

6. (*Those women*) fabulas ficturas esse non putavit. (He did not think . . .)
7. (*A ship*) ab Argo aedificatam esse dicunt.
8. Quam ob rem dixisti (*I*) de his rebus locutum esse?
9. Nescivit (*you*) veritos esse.
10. Iason veritus est (*he*) moriturum esse.

V.   In Latinum convertite (Translate into Latin):

1. Aeson's brother wanted to rule (desired the kingdom), but he did not kill Aeson.
2. He was going to kill the king's son, but the messengers announced that the boy was already dead.
3. Jason was wearing only one sandal because he had lost the other.
4. He says that Jason did not choose fifty very brave men.
5. Many days later Jason and the Argonauts arrived in Colchis.
6. Then the Argonauts disembarked and went (took themselves) to the palace.
7. Aeetes said, "I will surrender the fleece on this condition." (**lēx**)
8. If you plow this field and sow the dragon's teeth, I will give you the golden fleece.
9. They did not know that this task would be very dangerous.
10. A few years later the king recalled the oracle which the priestess had uttered.

Etymology

LATIN IN GEOGRAPHICAL TERMS

Perhaps the idea of the earth being so productive, with its fertile valleys and swelling hills, provides the psychological explanation for the Earth being usually feminine in Latin, both in mythology and in grammar (terra, tellus, humus). Whatever the reason, the names of the continents of the earth are also constructed as first declension feminine nouns:

America (North and South)	Asia
Europe (-a)	Arctic (-a)
Africa	Antarctica
Australia (from Latin **australis**, *south*)	

The name America is derived from the name of the Italian explorer Amerigo Vespucci, whose first name was adapted by a cartographer about 1507 to designate the whole of the regions of which Vespucci had explored a part. Europe, Africa, and Asia were names already existing in antiquity, and the naming of the last three continents followed the pattern set by the earlier names.

The names of most Mediterranean lands and adjacent areas, well-known in antiquity, have come into English either intact or with a suffic change -ia to -y or -e. In the word Spain, the rough breathing (Hi-) has been dropped in English. Locate the following countries on the map of the Mediterranean area.

Graecia	Mauretania	Asia Minor	Phrygia
Italia	Numidia	Phoenicia	Lydia
Hispania	Libya	Syria	Thracia
Germania	Aegyptus	Arabia	Thessalia
Britannia	Aethiopia	Parthia	Dacia
Gallia	Cyrenaica	Ionia	Macedonia
		Persia	

The travels of the ancient heroes whose bold adventures provided the events of the epic tales sung in the halls of the great lords were naturally set in the lands and islands of the Mediterranean and its surrounding areas. Some of the lands the travelling bard knew first-hand; some are fancifully described; several of the heroes even make trips to the Underworld to visit departed relatives, former associates, or dead lovers. One entrance to the Underworld was the cave of Avernus near Naples (see Chapter XXXIX).

*   *   *   *   *

Identify the source of the following underlined words from the lesson:

oracle at Delphi	detective fiction
dental hygiene	mortuary science
final negotiations	annunciation to Mary
naval operations	obtain the fleece
a fine edifice for the governor	refer to my secretary
the appellate court	retain the power
collate these pages	solution to the puzzle
send a delegate	sparse population
the last edition of the book	my (in-)spiration
no egress through this door	tradition in the family
a disgrace to be expelled	armed camp
at the junction of the roads	brief encounter
	fidelity in marriage

Sententiae
(me) gravat invitam nova vis, aliudque cupido,
mens aliud suadet: video meliora proboque,
deteriora sequor.
Ovid, *Met*. VII.19–21

Chapter XXIV
AMOR IASONIS

Medea interea, filia regis, ratione furorem et amorem non vincere poterat. "Frustra, Medea, repugnas: nescio quis deus obstat," ait "nisi hoc est quod amare vocatur. Cur iussa patris mihi dura videntur? Sunt durissima. Ne pereat, iuvenis quem modo amo. Quae est causa tanti timoris? Flammae amoris exstinguantur. Quid faciam? Nam me gravat invitam nova vis, aliudque cupido, mens aliud suadet: video meliora proboque, deteriora sequor. Cur, virgo, filia regis, advenam amas et coniugem de terra nova desideras? Haec quoque terra coniugem dare potest. Vivat an ille occidat; in deis est.[1] Vivat tamen! Quid enim commisit Iason? Certe virtus iuvenis mea pectora movit.

"At nisi opem tulero, tauri ignem ex ore spirabunt in eum, aut concurret hostibus armatis tellure creatis, aut avido draconi dabitur. Si hoc patiar, tum me de tigride natam esse et ferrum in pectore habere fatebor! Eum pereuntem spectare non possum: tauros in[2] illum hortari non possum. Di meliora dent! Tradamne ego regnum parentis atque ope mea servabitur nescio quis advena? Forsitan ille per me salvus sine me vela dabit atque vir erit alterius dum ego poenae relinquor? Si hoc facere potest et aliam praeponere mihi, occidat ingratus! Ego autem non arbitror illum haec scelesta et nefaria facturum esse. Antea fidem det, priusquam ego auxilium ei dabo, et di testes sint! Mihi se semper debebit Iason, me in matrimonium ducet. Tum apud Graecos perque urbes eorum honorabor servatrix.

"Ergo ego germanam fratremque patremque deosque et natalem terram ventis ablata relinquam? Pater certe saevus, certe est mea terra barbara. Sed frater adhuc puer est et soror mecum stat, et maximus deus intra me est! Non magna relinquam, magna sequar. Honorabor servatrix iuvenum Graecorum et terram meliorem noscam. Artes colam oppidorum humaniorum et, coniuge Aesonide, felix vivam et dis cara.

---

[1] *Let him live or let him die; it rests with the gods* (lit., *it is in* [*the hands of*] *the gods*).
[2] *Against*; **in** + the accusative has this added meaning.

"Heu me miseram,[3] cur pericula timeo? Dicunt mediis in undis montes concurrere et Charybdem naves vastare et Scyllam periculosam nautis esse. Nihil timeo, salva in bracchiis Iasonis quem amo. Si quicquid timeo, timeo de coniuge solo."[4]

Verba

NOUNS

*ars, artis, -ium, *f.*	art, skill, profession, practice, conduct
Charybdis, -is, *f.*	Charybdis (*a dangerous whirlpool*)
*ferrum, -ī, *n.*	iron, weapon, sword
furor, -ōris, *m.*	madness
germāna, -ae, *f.*	sister
*iussum, -ī, *n.*	order, command
*mēns, mentis, *f.*	mind
nata, -ae, *f.*	daughter
nūbēs, nūbis, -ium, *f.*	cloud
[ops,] opis, *f.*	power, aid, abundance
*ratiō, -iōnis, *f.*	reason, order, account
Scylla, -ae, *f.*	Scylla (*a monster, a rock*)
servātrix, -icis, *f.*	savior (*fem.*)
tellus, -uris, *f.*	earth, land
*testis, -is, -ium, *c.*	witness
*tigris, -idis, *c.*	a tiger
timor, -ōris, *m.*	fear
vēlum, -ī, *n.*	sail
*virtūs, tūtis, *f.*	courage, manliness

VERBS

*arbitror, -ārī, -ātus sum	think, judge
*committō, -ere, -mīsī, -missum	commit, combine, connect
*concipiō, -ere, -cēpī, conceptum	conceive, hold together

---

[3] *Alas, wretched me, . . .*

[4] This lesson's reading passage is a condensation of a much longer passáge in the original of Book 7 of the *Metamorphoses* in which Medea wrestles with her conscience as the daughter of a ruler whom she believes unfair and as a woman in love with a stranger, her father's enemy. Her ability to justify what she knows to be wrong is echoed and reechoed in other stories in the *Metamorphoses*, always in the mind of a woman (Myrrha in the story of Cinyras and Myrrha; Scylla in the story of Nisus and Scylla). Perhaps this understanding of female psychology made Ovid a confidant of women and eventually caused his exile.

concurrō, -ere, -currī, -cursum + *dat.*	meet, come up against
*exhortor, -ārī, -hortātus sum	urge, exhort
existimō (1)	think
exstinguō, -ere, -stīnxī, -stīnctum	extinguish, put out
*fateor, -ērī, fassus sum	confess, say
gravō (1)	load, burden, weigh down
*metuō, -ere, -uī, -ūtum	fear, be afraid
nāscor, nāscī, nātus sum	be born, originate from
*nāvigō (1)	sail
*nōscō, -ere, nōvī, nōtum	come to know, get to know
obstō, -stāre, -stitī, -stitum	block, oppose
pereō, -īre, -īvī *or* -iī, -itum	die, perish
*praepōnō, -ere, -posuī, -positum + *dat.*	place before, prefer
*probō (1)	approve
*repugnō (1)	fight back
*sequor, sequī, secūtus sum	follow
suādeō, -ēre, suāsī, suāsum	persuade
*subveniō, -īre, -vēnī, -ventum	come to the aid of, help, relieve

ADJECTIVES

dēterior, -ius	worse, lower
*ingrātus, -a, -um	unpleasant, unpleasing
*melior, -ius	better
nefārius, -a, -um	impious, wicked, abominable, evil
saevus, -a, -um	cruel, savage
*salvus, -a, -um	safe

OTHER WORDS

*anteā	beforehand
*apud + *acc.*	among
ergō	therefore
*heu	alas
*intrā	inside
*modo	just now, only now
*nescio quis, -quid, nescio quis (advena)	I do not know who or what (stranger), somebody or something, some (stranger)
*nihil (nīl)	nothing
priusquam (*conj.*)	before

Structure

132. Subjunctive forms: present active and passive. Since the subjunctive mood was so frequently used by the Romans (although it is rare in English), it is absolutely essential that its forms and uses be thoroughly mastered. Learning the forms is relatively easy, since their distinguishing characteristics are clearly recognizable. In the first conjugation the characteristic vowel -a- before the personal endings in the present indicative is replaced by -e- in the present subjunctive. In the second conjugation both vowels -ea- are retained in the stem, and in the other conjugations the characteristic vowel in the present subjunctive is -a-. Except for the ending -m in the first person singular, active voice, the personal endings are the same as the ones already mastered in the indicative, both active and passive:

Present Subjunctive Forms, Active Voice

I	II	III	III-io	IV
-e-	-ea-	-a-	-ia-	-ia-
vocem	doceam	dūcam	capiam	audiam
vocēs	doceās	dūcās	capiās	audiās
vocet	doceat	dūcat	capiat	audiat
vocēmus	doceāmus	dūcāmus	capiāmus	audiāmus
vocētis	doceātis	dūcātis	capiātis	audiātis
vocent	doceant	dūcant	capiant	audiant

Present Subjunctive Forms, Passive Voice

vocer	docear	dūcar	capiar	audiar
vocēris	doceāris	dūcāris	capiāris	audiāris
vocētur	doceātur	dūcātur	capiātur	audiātur
vocēmur	doceāmur	dūcāmur	capiāmur	audiāmur
vocēminī	doceāminī	dūcāminī	capiāminī	audiāminī
vocentur	doceantur	dūcantur	capiantur	audiantur

133. Subjunctive forms of **sum** and **possum**. Present tense.

sim	sīmus		possim	possīmus
sīs	sītis		possīs	possītis
sit	sint		possit	possint

134. Subjunctive mood: usage. The moods of a verb are used to express the *manner* (mood) in which the action is conceived, whereas the tenses express the *time* of the action. The *indicative mood* is the mood of direct assertions or questions. The *imperative mood* is used to issue commands, orders, or entreaties. The *subjunctive mood* in Latin derives from a merging of several forms with modal significance in the parent language: the

subjunctive and the optative, expressing actions *willed* or *vividly conceived* and actions *wished for* or *vaguely conceived*. When the two forms merged, further meanings were given to the subjunctive and this development accounts for the many varied independent uses of the subjunctive. Its dependent uses, however, have arisen in every case from the employment of some independent subjunctive construction in coordination with a main statement. In time the two coordinate clauses grew together into a single complex sentence, with the subjunctive clause assuming a subordinate relation to the main statement. In fact, the name subjunctive signifies a subordinate role.

135. Independent uses of the subjunctive. There are three independent uses of the subjunctive, but these constructions are merely different phases of the same use (the negative is **nē**).

1) The hortatory or jussive (from **iussum**, participle of **iubeō**) subjunctive is used to express a milder *exhortation* or *command* than the more direct imperative mood. This is perhaps the most important independent use of the subjunctive mood. Since the imperative mood is also used to issue commands, it is logical that the imperative be used in the second person and the hortatory or jussive subjunctive primarily in the first and third persons.

Vīvat tamen!	Yet *let him live!* (*or*)
	Yet *may he live!*
Flammae amōris **exstinguantur.**	*Let* the flames of love *be extinguished.*
Occidat ingrātus!	*Let* the ungrateful wretch *die!*
Hoc faciāmus!	*Let us do* this!
Nē hoc **faciāmus!**	*Let us not do* this!
But	
Hoc fac.	(You) *Do* this. (*Singular*)
Hoc facite.	(You) *Do* this. (*Plural*)

2) The optative (from **optō**) subjunctive is used to express a wish. It is often preceded by a particle (**ūtī** [**ut**], **utinam** or **ō sī**).

Utinam dī meliōra **dent!**	*Would that* the gods *may give* better things!
Ō sī dī meliōra **dent!**	*O that* the gods *may give* better things! (*or*) *May* the gods *give* better things! (*or*) God *forbid!*
Ita vīvam. (Cic. *Att.* 5.15)	So *may I live.*
Valeant, valeant, cīvēs meī; **valeant, sint** incolumēs. (Cic. *Deiot* 7)	*Farewell, farewell,* my fellow citizens; *farewell* and *may they be* secure from harm.

Utinam falsus vātēs **sim**.
(Livy 21)

May I be a false prophet! (*or*)
Would that I am a false
prophet! (*or*) *Would that I*
may be a false prophet!

3) The deliberate or dubitative (from **dubitō**) subjunctive is used in questions implying doubt or indignation.

Quid **faciam**?
Quid senātuī populōque
  Rōmānō **dīcam**?
Quid **dīcerem**? (*Imperfect*
  Subjunctive, see following
  lesson) (Cic. *Att.* 6.3)

What *am I to do*?
What *am I to say* to the senate
  and to the Roman people?
What *was I to say*? (*indignation*
  expressed)

Exercises

I.   Respondete Latine ad interrogata:

1. Quis erat Medea?
2. Quam ob rem putavit Medea se frustra repugnare? (*For what reason? lit.*, "on account of what thing?")
3. Quomodo sensit Medea amorem?
4. Quid fiet nisi opem tulerit regis filia? (**fiet**, *will happen*)
5. Quid fatebitur Medea, si patietur Iasonem noceri?
6. Quae magna dixit Medea se secuturam esse?
7. Quomodo navigabit illa?
8. Cur nihil verebitur Medea?
9. Quid timet illa, si quid timet?
10. Cur dubitat Medea Iasoni opem ferre?

II A. Convert the following verb forms into their corresponding forms in the subjunctive mood, and translate:

1. laudat	laudet	let him praise
2. ducis	ducas	you may lead
3. capio	capiam	let me take
4. monent		
5. facimus		
6. audiris		
7. docemini		
8. vocant		
9. ducimur		
10. miror		
11. veretur		
12. potiuntur		

13. negat
14. loquitur
15. es
16. potest
17. facio
18. iubemus
19. mittit
20. traditur

B. Locate all first conjugation verbs in present tense in the reading selection and convert indicative forms into the subjunctive and vice versa.

C. Select from the reading selection at least one verb from each conjugation and conjugate each in the present subjunctive, active and passive.

III. Supply the correct form of the verbs in the following sentences, then translate:

1. (*Let them give*) puellis dona.
2. Quid (*is to do*) Iason, si tauri flammam ex ore spiraturi sunt?
3. (*Let us live*), mea Lesbia, atque (*let us love*)!
4. Hoc (*let be*) quod amor vocatur.
5. Quid (*is to be called*) hoc malum factum?
6. Ne iussa patris mihi durissima (*seem*).
7. Non iam (*let us hesitate*), nisi veremur.
8. Falsi utinam vates (*may we be*).
9. Ita (*may you be taught*).
10. Ne (*may we think*) Iasonem haec scelesta ac nefaria facturum esse. (*or*, better English, *Let us not think* . . .)

IV. Supply the correct Latin forms for the word or words in parentheses:

1. Medea putat Iasonem (*loves*) eam.
2. Aeetes putat Iasonem (*will die*). (**moriturum** is fut. act. part.)
3. Iason scit vellus (*is*) in regno Colchide.
4. Iason putat Medeam (*is*) pulchram.
5. Medea credit nescio quem deum (*is opposing*) se.
6. Putantne feminae se (*will be afraid*)?
7. Illa femina dixit (*Jason*) moriturum esse.
8. Scivit enim regem vellere aureo (*possessed*). (**potīrī**) *or* **habēre**
9. Poeta dixit filiam regis (*loved*) iuvenem formosum.
10. Quam ob rem (*for what reason*) dixisti (*she*) de his rebus (*had spoken*)?
11. Nego virginem (*loves*) advenam.
12. Nauta non putat ducem suum tauros (*will fear*).
13. De mortuis nihil nisi bonum (*let us say*).
14. Ne ullus credat (*he*) esse (*happier*) aut sapientiorem quam te.

V.   In Latinum convertite:

1. Let us do even greater and better deeds for our country.
2. Let the daughter of the king be able to overcome her passion with reason.
3. May they not say that my father's commands seem too harsh.
4. A few days later the Argonauts realized that Medea had a great love for their leader.
5. He said that he had never seen a more beautiful girl.
6. Unless you bring help, we shall all die.
7. First let him give a pledge and summon the gods as witnesses.
8. I will say that no one is more faithful than you.
9. Let no one think that he can betray his friends without penalty.
10. Let parents themselves neither allow evil deeds nor commit (them).

Etymology

The adventures of Jason, whose episodic peregrinations are described in the epic of Apollonius of Rhodes, the *Argonautica*, are indeed a geography tour of the ancient world. Jason first crosses the Aegean, probably going along the northern coast by sailing from port to port. He stops at Lemnos, has many adventures while passing through the Hellespont and across the Black (Euxine) Sea to Colchis. After his trials to gain the fleece, Jason returns with Medea across the Euxine to the Danube; the two go up the Danube to strange semi-fictitious lands; somehow or other they get the *Argo* across to the Rhone and come down into the Mediterranean again. They visit "Aunt" Circe on the coast of Italy, see Scylla and Charybdis between Sicily and the toe of Italy, have an adventure on Crete and eventually return to Greece. The following name equivalents from the areas are obvious:

Islands (F.)	Rivers (M.)	Seas (N.)	Cities (F.)
Sicilia	Nilus	Mare Mediterraneum	Roma
Corsica	Danuvius	Mare Aegeum	Ostia
Sardinia	Rhodanus	Mare Euxinum	Athenae
Creta	(Rhone)	Mare Caspium	Syracusa
Cyprus, -i, f.			Delphi (m.)
Minorca (the smaller)			Troia
Maiorca (the larger)			Alexandria
			Sparta
			Mycenae
			Massilia
			(Marseille)

*   *   *   *   *

Explain the Latin source for these underlined words from the vocabulary in the lesson:

blind fury
ferrous oxide
jussive use of the verb
mental anguish
nebular formations
rational powers
tiger, tiger, burning bright
timorous child
testify at a trial (-fy from **fio/facio**)
virtue is its own reward
submit to arbitration
commit yourself to work
a commission chosen by the mayor
such a grand concept

concur with you
my estimation of him
exhort you to work
extinguish the fire
navigate these waters
perish from hunger
repugnant to me
that is a non sequitur
nefarious schemes
the situation will deteriorate
you ingrate!
ameliorate the situation
annihilate the population of the city

Tapped - passage only

Nunc scio quid sit Amor.   *Now I know what love is.*
     Virgil, *Ecl.* VIII.43

Chapter XXV
LABORES IASONIS

Medea nunc ad aras antiquas Hecates[1] ibat ut in silva carmina secreta et artes magicas disceret. Iam fortis erat et amor recesserat, sed cum Iasonem videt flammae amoris revenerunt, quod illa die filius Aesonis tam formosus fuit ut Medeae amanti eum ignoscere posses.[2] Spectat et oculos fixos in vultu eius tenet. Iason loqui coepit et dextram prehendit et matrimonium promisit ut ea auxilium daret. Medea lacrimis multis ait: "Quid faciam? Video me auxilio meo eum servaturam esse. Servatus, promissa det et teneat!" Ille per sacra Hecates triformis deae iurat. Illa herbas magicas et carmina magica ei dat et ille laetus in tecta recessit.

Postero die populi in agrum sacrum Martis convenerunt; rex ipse in medio sedit vestimentum purpureum gerens et notus sceptro eburneo. Ecce tauri appropinquabant qui tantos ignes efflabant ut herbae ignibus tactae arderent. Tamen Iason obvius it. Argonautae terribiles tauros videntes magnopere timent, sed Aesonides nec ignes nec fumos sensit. Tantum medicamina possunt ut sine timore dextra forti iugum grave in umeris taurorum poneret et ferreo aratro campum coleret.

Mirantur Colchi,[3] Argonautae clamoribus gavisi sunt. Tum ex galea aenea dentes serpentis excepit ut eos in agros spargeret. Humus semina mollit et dentes tam celeriter crescunt ut nova corpora hominum fiant. Quod magis mirum est, quisque vir arma tenet. Graeci timent tot homines et tot arma videntes; Medea, quae illum tutum fecerat, ubi vidit unum iuvenem ab tot hostibus peti, palluit et frigida subito sine sanguine sedit.

Iason autem saxum in hostes iecit ut a se bellum in ipsos converteret. Omnes per multa vulnera cadunt; Graeci gavisi sunt et Medea quoque, agens gratias carminibus et dis auctoribus horum.

---

[1] *Of Hecate* (Greek genitive singular) the three-formed goddess of mystic incantations, the crossroads, the secrets of the underworld and the deep forest. Originally a very powerful goddess of all regions in the *Theogony* of Hesiod, Hecate became relegated in later Greek and Roman mythology to the mystical areas of the dark worlds, the places where her worshippers like Medea, one of the few witches in mythology, would go to learn magic spells.

[2] *You could forgive Medea loving him* (**ignoscere** takes the dative case).

[3] *The men of Colchis are amazed.*

Superest herbis in somno ponere draconem pervigilem, qui horrendus custos velleris aurei erat. Iason eum aquis Lethaeis sparsit et ter dixit verba somnos placidos facientia[4] ut somnus in oculos draconis veniret. Heros Aesonides vellere aureo potiebatur. Superbus spolio et portans quoque secum auctorem spolii, ipsam altera spolia, victor ad Graeciam cum uxore nova rediit, effugiens iram patris.

Verba

NOUNS

Aesonidēs	the son of Aeson, Jason
arātrum, -ī, *n.*	plow
bellum, -ī, *n.*	war
***carmen, -inis,** *n.*	song, chant, incantation, charm
***clāmor, -ōris,** *m.*	shout, clamor, noise
***dextra, -ae,** *f.*	right hand
fūmus, -ī, *m.*	smoke
galea, -ae, *f.*	helmet
Hecatē, -ēs, *f.*	Hecate
***humus, -ī,** *f.*	ground, earth
***iugum, -ī,** *n.*	yoke
Lēthē, -ēs, *f.*	Lethe (*a river in the Underworld*)
***Mars, Martis,** *m.*	Mars (*god of war*)
medicāmen, -inis, *n.*	drug, medicine
***prōmissum, -ī,** *n.*	promise
sceptrum, -ī, *n.*	sceptre
***sēmen, -inis,** *n.*	seed
spolium, -iī, *n.* (*usually plu.*)	booty, plunder, spoils
umerus, -ī, *m.*	shoulder
***uxor, -ōris,** *f.*	wife
***vultus, -ūs,** *m.*	expression of the face, the countenance, face

VERBS

***agere grātiās**	to give thanks
***ardeō, -ēre, arsī, arsum**	be on fire, burn with love, glow, burn
***cadō, -ere, cecidī, cāsum**	fall, fall down
***coepī, coepisse** (*defective, no present system*)	began
***convertō, -ere, -vertī, -versum**	turn around, alter, change
***discō, -ere, didicī**	learn
efflō (1)	breathe out, blow out

---

[4] *Words making* (causing) *calm sleep.*

*effugiō, -ere, -fugī, -fugitum	flee, escape from
*fīō, fierī, factus sum (fīō, fīs,	become, be made, happen (*semi-deponent*
fit, fīmus, fītis, fiunt)	*passive of* **faciō**)
molliō, -īre, -īvī *or* -iī, -ītum	make pliant, make soft, soften
palleō, -ēre, -uī	become pale
*recēdō, -ere, -cessī, -cessum	go back, draw back, recede, retreat
*supersum, -esse, -fuī, -futūrum	be left, remain

ADJECTIVES

*aēneus, -a, -um	brass, bronze, brazen
eburneus, -a, -um	ivory
*exstīnctus, -a, -um	put out, extinguished
ferreus, -a, -um	iron
fixus, -a, -um	fixed
frīgidus, -a, -um	cold
*gravis, -e	heavy
horrendus, -a, -um	horrible, terrible
Lēthaeus, -a, -um	Lethean
magicus, -a, -um	magic
*magis, -e	more
*mīrus, -a, -um	wonderful, amazing
obvius, -a, -um	to meet, in the way, against, exposed to
pervigilis, -e	ever-watchful
*placidus, -a, -um	calm, placid
posterus, -a, -um	next
*sēcrētus, -a, -um	secret
*terribilis, -e	terrible
triformis, -e	three-formed
*tūtus, -a, -um	safe

OTHER WORDS

*ipse, ipsa, ipsum	himself, herself, itself; *pl.* themselves
*quisque, quaeque, quidque	each, every, everyone, everything
*subitō	suddenly
*tam	so
*tot	so many

Structure

136. Subjunctive forms, imperfect active and passive. The imperfect forms
are based on the infinitive used as a stem, with the personal endings
added. The translation of the subjunctive varies with each construction:

vocarem could mean *I might call* or [with **si**] *if I called* or [with **ut**] *so that I might call.*

Imperfective Subjunctive Active

I	II	III	III-io	IV
vocārem	docērem	dūcerem	caperem	audīrem
vocārēs	docērēs	dūcerēs	caperēs	audīrēs
vocāret	docēret	dūceret	caperet	audīret
vocārēmus	docērēmus	dūcerēmus	caperēmus	audīrēmus
vocārētis	docērētis	dūcerētis	caperētis	audīrētis
vocārent	docērent	dūcerent	caperent	audīrent

Imperfect Subjunctive Passive

vocārer	docērer	dūcerer	caperer	audīrer
vocārēris	docērēris	dūcerēris	caperēris	audīrēris
vocārētur	docērētur	dūcerētur	caperētur	adīrētur
vocārēmur	docērēmur	dūcerēmur	caperēmur	audīrēmur
vocārēminī	docērēminī	dūcerēminī	caperēminī	audīrēminī
vocārentur	docērentur	dūcerentur	caperentur	audīrentur

137. Dependent uses of the subjunctive: The purpose clause. The Romans used the subjunctive mood to express the purpose or reason for the action of the main verb. The "purpose" appears as a subordinate clause introduced by **ut** (*so that, in order that, to*) or **nē** (*so that . . . not, in order that . . . not, not to*).

Sequence

Primary: Venit **ut** mē **videat**.   He is coming *to see* me (*so that he may see* me).

Secondary: Vēnit **ut** mē **vidēret**.   He came *to see* me (*so that he might see* me).

Primary: Nāvem aedificat **ut** in illā Colchidem **nāviget**.   He is building a ship *so that he may sail* to Colchis in it.

Secondary: Nāvem aedificābat **ut** in illā Colchidem **nāvigāret**.   He was building a ship *so that he might sail* to Colchis in it.

Primary: Dux clāmābit **ut** mīlitēs **moneat**.   The leader will shout *to warn* the soldiers.

Secondary: Dux clāmāvit **ut** mīlitēs **monēret**.   The leader shouted *to warn* the soldiers.

Primary:	Magister venit ut discipulōs **doceat**.	The teacher is coming *to teach* students.
Secondary:	Magister vēnit ut discipulōs **docēret**.	The teacher came *to teach* the students.
Secondary:	Mēdēa ad ārās ībat ut magicās artēs **disceret**.	Medea went to the altars *to learn* magic arts.
Secondary:	Dux clāmāvit **nē** mīlitēs **fugerent**.	The leader shouted *so that* the soldiers *might not flee*.
Secondary:	Iāsōn saxum in mediō iēcit **ut** bellum ā sē in ipsōs **converteret**.	Jason threw a stone into the middle *to turn* the war from himself onto them.
Secondary:	Iāsōn dracōnem aquīs sparsit **ut** somnus in oculōs dracōnis **venīret**.	Jason sprinkled the dragon with water *so that* sleep *might come* into the eyes of the dragon.

138. Sequence of tenses. Note that in each of the sentences above there is a fixed pattern for the tense of the subjunctive following the main verb. This pattern is as follows:

	Main Verb: **Indicative**	Subordinate Verb: **Subjunctive**
Primary:	Present or Future	Present
Secondary:	Imperfect or Perfect	Imperfect

This pattern is repeated for almost all dependent subjunctive clauses.

139. Dependent uses of the subjunctive: Result clauses. When the main clause has a modifying element of *so, such a, so great, so many* (**sīc, ita, tam, tantus, -a, -um,** *or* **tot**), the subordinate clause completing the idea is called a result clause and is expressed with a verb in the subjunctive mood introduced by **ut** (*that . . .* [*as a result*]) or **ut nōn** (*that* [*as a result*] *. . . not*).

Tantus virtūs in Iāsone erat ut Mēdēa statim eum **amāret**.	*Such great* courage was in Jason *that* (*as a result*) Medea immediately *loved* him.
Tot vulnera habuit **ut mortuus esset**.	He had *so many* wounds *that he died*.
Tam celeriter relīquit **ut** rēgem **nōn vidēret**.	He left *so* quickly *that he did not see* the king.

140. Present and imperfect subjunctive forms of **sum, esse, fuī, futūrum** and of **possum, posse, potuī**:

Present	Imperfect		Present	Imperfect
sim	essem		possim	possem
sīs	essēs		possīs	possēs
sit	esset		possit	posset
sīmus	essēmus		possīmus	possēmus
sītis	essētis		possītis	possētis
sint	essent		possint	possent

There are no passive forms for **sum** or **possum**.

Exercises

I. Respondete Latine, quaeso.

1. In quo loco est ara Hecates?
2. Quae (*What things*) Medea ad aram Hecates quaesivit? (*at the altar of Hecate*)
3. Cur potes ignoscere Medeae amanti Iasonem?
4. Quid Iason promisit ut Medea auxilium ei daret?
5. Quomodo potes recognoscere regem Aeetem ubi in medio populo sedit?
6. Qui sunt labores Iasonis quos rex Aeetes iussit eum facere ut ei vellera aurea daret?
7. Cur difficillimum erat iugum in umeris taurorum ponere?
8. Quae debet Iason spargere in humum? Qui crescunt de seminibus sparsis? Quomodo Iason effugit?
9. Quomodo Iason draconem pervigilem in somno ponere potest?
10. Quae altera spolia Iason secum quoque aufert ubi vellera aurea aufert?

II. Subjunctive forms:

A. Write the imperfect subjunctive active and passive for the following verbs (deponent only passive):

1. specto, moneo, mitto, cupio, invenio, sum
2. miror, gaudeo, sequor, potior, pono, disco

B. Translate these verbs into Latin (review deponent verbs!):

1. I urge	6. we shall follow
2. you (*sing.*) follow	7. they had owned
3. we were admiring	8. we did follow
4. they rejoiced	9. he had admired
5. you (*pl.*) admire	10. they will have followed

III. Translate each secondary sequence subjunctive purpose clause verb into Latin and translate the sentence. Do not use infinitives.

1. Vēnit ut me in matrimonium (*to lead*).
2. Vēnit ut me (*to teach*).
3. Vēnērunt ut me (*to see*).
4. Vēnērunt ut regem (*to kill*).
5. Vēnērunt ut vellera aurea (*to carry off*).
6. Vēnit ut me (*to watch*).
7. Mane (*early in the morning*) vēnit ne milites eum (*might not see*).
8. Vēnērunt ut musicam (*to enjoy*).
9. Vēnī ut te linguam novam (*to teach*). (**lingua, -ae,** *f., language*)
10. Vēnistī ut linguam novam (*to learn*).
11. Vēnimus ut (*to enjoy ourselves*).
12. Iason vēnit ut draconem (*to kill*).
13. Vēnistis ut tauros (*to watch*).
14. Vēnī ut me linguam novam (*you might teach*).
15. Medea Hecatem ōrāvit ut dea auxilium (*to give*).
16. Nos Bacchum ōrāvimus ut deus nobis vinum (*to give*).

IV. Write the form of **tam, ita, tantus, -a, -um** or **sic** or **tot** that would best complete these sentences that contain result clauses and translate each sentence.

1. _____ homines et _____ arma videbat ut magnopere timeret.
2. _____ dixit ut omnes homines pallerent.
3. _____ opus habuit ut non finire posset.
4. _____ timor feminis erat ut illae in casis remanerent.
5. _____ tempestas coepit ut nautae in terrore clamarent.
6. Medea _____ amorem habuit ut Iasonem iuvare non recusaret.
7. Tauri _____ ignes efflabant ut herbae arderent.
8. _____ celeriter homines crescebant ut statim pugnare inciperent.
9. Draco _____ horrendus erat ut omnes adire metuerent.
10. Medea _____ Iasonem amabat ut patrem suum traderet.

V. Translate into Latin:

1. Medea asked Hecate (**Hecatem**) to help her with charms and magic spells (**artibus**).
2. Jason promised to marry (to lead in marriage) Medea so that she might give him aid.
3. Medea watches and rejoices while Jason yokes the bulls, which breathe fire.

4. Finally Jason was so brave that he put to sleep (**in somnō ponere**) the ever-watchful dragon and sailed away with the fleece and his new wife, Medea.

5. Jason scattered dragon's teeth in the field, but he was amazed (wondered) when the teeth grew (**crescēbant**) into armed men.

Etymology

LEGAL LATIN

Many of the terms for conducting business within the law courts of England, and subsequently, America came from Latin, including such basic words as:

legal   (**lex, legis,** *f.*)
jury   (**ius, iuris,** *n.*)
judge   (**iudex, iudicis,** *m.*)
justice (**iustitia, -ae,** *f.,* from **iustus**)

Although the words *law* and *lawyer* come from the Anglo-Saxon word **lager**, many of the important terms which the lawyer must use to express ideas and conduct business in the courts have continued to be used in the original language of Latin:

habeas corpus	a writ or document demanding a person's bodily appearance in order to release him from unlawful restraint (*you shall have the body*)
ex parte	on one side only (*by or for one party*)
causa mortis	(a gift) given in contemplation of and conditional upon the approaching death of the donor (*with the cause of death*)
amicus curiae	a party, neutral to the specific action, but not to the issue before the court, who is invited to give advice (*friend of the court*)
inter vivos	during lifetime, while alive (*among the living*)
prima facie	on the face of it (*at first appearance*)
ultra vires	beyond or outside the scope of the powers as defined in a charter (*beyond the powers*)
nunc pro tunc	applies to acts allowed to be done after the time when they should have been done with retroactive effect (*now for then*)
res ipsa loquitur	an obvious inference (*the situation speaks for itself*)
res judicata	an issue already decided (*a matter adjudged*)
mens rea	the basic ingredient for criminal culpability, criminal intent (*a criminal mind*)

quantum meruit	a claim for goods or services unjustly enriching another (*as much as* [*the claimant*] *deserves*)
sua sponte	voluntarily (*of one's own accord*)
subpoena duces tecum	process by which the court commands a witness to produce documents or papers by a threat of punishment (*under penalty you shall produce* [the papers] *with you*)
stirpes	by branches of the family as opposed to per capita (*roots or stalks*)
pari passu	equal participation, equal process (*in equal step*)
in pari delicto	equally culpable or criminal (*in equal fault*)
nolo contendere	no contest (*I do not wish to contend the charge*)
in rem	*in* or of *the thing itself*
inter se	a relationship between partners (*between each other*)
corpus delicti	the body upon which the deed was done (*the body of the crime*)

*   *   *   *   *

Give the Latin source for the underlined words from the vocabulary:

<u>fumes</u> from the fire
<u>clamor</u> from the street fair
<u>dexterous</u> use of his hands
<u>heroic</u> deeds
(ex)<u>hume</u> the body
<u>Martial</u> music
hold the <u>scepter</u>
artificial (in)<u>semination</u>
the <u>spoils</u> of war
heavy loss due to <u>arson</u>

try to <u>convert</u> you
<u>conversion</u> tables
to <u>mollify</u> my parents
cause the waters to <u>recede</u>
<u>antique</u> furniture
a <u>horrendous</u> tale
a <u>magic</u> act
a <u>placid</u> animal
<u>secret</u> signals
a <u>terrible</u> experience

| Nutrix: | **Abiere Colchi, coniugis nulla est fides Nihilque superest opibus tantis tibi** | Nurse: | *The Colchians have left, there is nothing left of your husband and his promises, and of all your great riches nothing remains.* |
| Medea: | **Medea superest.** | Medea: | *Medea remains.* |

Seneca, *Medea*, 164–166.

Chapter XXVI
FACTA MALA MEDEAE

In Graecia patres matresque dona pro filiis receptis ferunt, sed abest Aeson, qui iam morti vicinus est atque defessus multis annis. Tum sic ait Aesonides: "O coniunx, cui me salutem debere confiteor, si hoc facere possunt carmina tua (quid enim non possunt?), aufer a meis annis et annos ablatos adde parenti." Nec retinuit lacrimas. Medea pietate rogantis mota est et "Putasne ergo" inquit, "me spatium vitae tuae transmittere posse? Ne hoc Hecate permittat! Aequa non petis. Sed maius munus dare experiar, Iason. Arte mea ei longiorem vitam dare conabor, annis tuis non revocatis, si modo dea triformis me iuvabit."

Tres post noctes ubi cornua lunae coierunt ut luna plenissima terras spectaret, Medea nuda pede et vestimento aperto et capillis fluentibus egreditur e domu et sola per muta silentia mediae noctis gradus fert. Omnes homines et volucres et ferae graviter dormiunt; stellae in caelo solae micant ad quas tendens bracchia Medea ter se convertit, ter in caput aquas magicas sparsit et ter magnis clamoribus deam oravit.

"Nox," ait, "fidissima et stellae et luna aurea et tu Hecate triformis quae meas artes magicas carminibus tuis iuvas, auxilio vestro ventos voco et nubes moveo; serpentes supero et saxa silvasque moveo; montes tremescere et manes ex sepulcris exire iubeo. Te quoque, luna, ex caelo traho. Nunc opus est mihi sucis per quos senectus in florem redeat et primos annos retineat.[1] Et dabitis hos sucos mihi! Neque enim frustra stellae micant neque frustra currus draconibus pennatis tractus adest."

Ecce adest currus ex caelo dimissus in quem simul ascendit, rapitur in montes summos quo crescunt herbae magicae. Novem post dies et novem noctes, herbis collectis, Medea curru draconibus pennatis ablato rediit; dracones solum odore herbarum tacti pelles senectutis deposuerunt.[2] Pro

---

[1] Subjunctive: . . . through which old age *may return* into the flower (of youth), and *may regain* . . .

[2] *Laid aside the skins of old age*, i.e., *shed their skins.*

valvis regiae duas aras aedificavit, unam dextra parte Hecati et alteram sinistra parte Iuventuti. His sacris factis magnam fossam effodit. Tum in guttur atrae ovis gladium conicit et fossam sanguine perfundit. Deinde crateras vini lactisque simul verba addit et rogat regem umbrarum[3] cum coniuge rapta ne mortem senis regis properent.

Tum iussit corpus defessum Aesonis afferri ad aras quod in plenos somnos in herbis ponit. Hinc procul Aesonidem et hinc procul sacerdotes ire iussit et oculos profanos[4] removere; Medea tum capillis fluentibus in modo bacchantum aras geminas circumit terque senem flamma, ter aqua, ter sulphure spargit.

Interea aeno in igne posito medicamen validum fervet[5] et albet spumis.[6] Addit semina et flores et sucos acres et lapides Oriente extremo petitos. Praeterea in aenum iacit alas et carnes volucrum et membrana serpentis et ova et caput avis. His rebus et mille aliis sine nomine mixtis, Medea omnia in aeno miscuit ramo olivae. Ecce ramus primo viridis fit; brevi tempore frondet et subito gravis erat viridibus olivis. Quae simul ac vidit stricto ense Medea guttur senis secat; Medea veterem sanguinem effundit ut sucis novis eum repleat. Quos postquam Aeson bibit aut ore aut vulnere, barba capillique colorem nigram receperunt. Pallor abit et membra valida fiunt. Aeson miratus iuventutem iterum videt!

Verba

NOUNS

**aēnus, -ī, *m.*	brass pot
**āla, -ae, *f.*	wing
barba, -ae, *f.*	beard
**currus, -ūs, *m.*	chariot
**ēnsis, ēnsis, -ium, *m.*	sword
fossa, -ae, *f.*	ditch, trench
gradus, -ūs, *m.*	step, footstep
guttur, -uris, *n.*	throat
Iuventus, -tūtis, *f.*	Youth
lac, lactis, *n.*	milk
**lapis, -idis, *m.*	stone
**lūna, -ae, *f.*	moon
**mānēs, mānium, *m. pl.*	the shades of the dead
membrāna, -ae, *f.*	thin skin (*of a snake*)
**modus, -ī, *m.*	manner

---

[3] Pluto with Proserpina, his **coniuge rapta** (see Interim Reading IV).
[4] *Profane*, i.e., *not sacred* (to her rites)
[5] *Is boiling.*
[6] *With foam.*

mūnus, -eris, *n.*	gift
*odor, -ōris, *m.*	smell, odor
olīva, -ae, *f.*	olive
*opus est mihi + *abl.*	there is a need of, I need
*Oriēns, -ientis, *m.*	the East (*the land of the rising sun*)
ovis, ovis, -ium, *f.*	sheep
ōvum, -ī, *n.*	egg
pallor, -ōris, *m.*	pallor, paleness
pecunia, -ae, *f.*	money
*pietās, -tātis, *f.*	respect, reverence; piety
prex, precis, *f.*	request, prayer
*salūs, -ūtis, *f.*	safety
*sanguis, -inis, *m.*	blood
*senectūs, -ūtis, *f.*	old age
sepulchrum, -ī, *n.*	grave
spatium, -iī, *n.*	length, space, distance, period, portion
sūcus, -ī, *m.*	juice
sulphur, -uris, *n.*	sulphur
valvae, -ārum, *f. pl.*	folding doors
volucris, -cris, volucrum, *f.*	bird

VERBS

*addō, -ere, -didī, -ditum	add
albeō, -ēre, albuī	become white
*ascendō, -ere, -scendī, -scēnsum	mount, ascend, go up
*circumeō, -īre, -īvī *or* -iī, -itum	walk around
coeō, -īre, -īvī *or* -iī, -itum	go, come together
*confiteor, -ērī, -fessus sum	confess
coniciō, -icere, -iēcī, -iectum	throw, hurl; plunge
dormiō, -īre, -īvī *or* -iī, -ītum	sleep
effundō, -ere, -fūdī, -fūsum	pour out
micō (1)	twinkle, shine
misceō, -ēre, -uī, mixtum	mix, mingle
perfundō, -ere, -fūdī, -fūsum	pour over, fill with
experior, -īrī, expertus sum	test, try, attempt
*reddō, -ere, -didī, -ditum	give back
repleō, -ēre, -plēvī, -plētum	fill up again, refill
*revocō (1)	call again, call back
*secō, -āre, -uī, sectum	cut
*trānsmittō, -ere, -mīsī, -missum	send across
tremescō, -ere	tremble, quake
vīsitō (1)	visit
*vulnerō (1)	wound

ADJECTIVES

*aequus, -a, -um	fair, just
āter, ātra, ātrum	black
calidus, -a, -um	hot
collectus, -a, -um	collected
*extrēmus, -a, -um	furthest, last
*fīdus, -a, -um	faithful
niger, -gra, -grum	black
nūdus, -a, -um	naked
*pennātus, -a, -um	winged
strictus, -a, -um	drawn
*validus, -a, -um	strong
*vetus, veteris	old

OTHER WORDS

*ergō	therefore
graviter	heavily, deeply
quō	where
simul ac	as soon as
*tandem	at last

Structure

141. Perfect subjunctive forms, active and passive. The forms of the perfect subjunctive resemble the forms of the future perfect indicative. Note carefully the difference (in first person singular and in accent):

ACTIVE

I	II	III	III-io	IV
amāverim	docuerim	dīxerim	cēperim	audīverim
amāverīs	docuerīs	dīxerīs	cēperīs	audīverīs
amāverit	docuerit	dīxerit	cēperit	audīverit
amāverīmus	docuerīmus	dīxerīmus	cēperīmus	audīverīmus
amāverītis	docuerītis	dīxerītis	cēperītis	audīverītis
amāverint	docuerint	dīxerint	cēperint	audīverint

PASSIVE

I	II	III	III-io	IV
amātus sim	doctus sim	dictus sim	captus sim	audītus sim
amātus sīs	doctus sīs	dictus sīs	captus sīs	audītus sīs
amātus sit	doctus sit	dictus sit	captus sit	audītus sit
amātī sīmus	doctī sīmus	dictī sīmus	captī sīmus	audītī sīmus
amātī sītus	doctī sītis	dictī sītis	captī sītis	audītī sītis
amātī sint	doctī sint	dictī sint	captī sint	audītī sint

142. Pluperfect subjunctive forms, active and passive. The pluperfect forms are simply the personal endings added on to the perfect infinitive:

ACTIVE

amāvissem	docuissem	dīxissem	cēpissem	audīvissem
amāvissēs	docuissēs	dīxissēs	cēpissēs	audīvissēs
amāvisset	docuisset	dīxisset	cēpisset	audīvisset
amāvissēmus	docuissēmus	dīxissēmus	cēpissēmus	audīvissēmus
amāvissētis	docuissētis	dīxissētis	cēpissētis	audīvissētis
amāvissent	docuissent	dīxissent	cēpissent	audīvissent

PASSIVE

amātus essem	doctus essem	dictus essem	captus essem	audītus essem
amātus essēs	doctus essēs	dictus essēs	captus essēs	audītus essēs
amātus esset	doctus esset	dictus esset	captus esset	audītus esset
amātī essēmus	doctī essēmus	dictī essēmus	captī essēmus	audītī essēmus
amātī essētis	doctī essētis	dictī essētis	captī essētis	audītī essētis
amātī essent	doctī essent	dictī essent	captī essent	audītī essent

143. Contrary-to-fact conditions. One of the most common uses of the imperfect and pluperfect subjunctive is in the contrary-to-fact condition. Imperfect subjunctive is used for the present time, and pluperfect for past time in both the **sī** clause and the conclusion:

Imperfect:	**Sī** rēx **essem,** pecūniam omnibus **darem.**	*If I were* king, *I would give* money to all.
Pluperfect:	**Sī** rēx **fuissem,** pecūniam omnibus **dedissem.**	*If I had been* king, *I would have given* money to all.
Pluperfect:	**Sī** rēx **fuissem,** pācem **fēcissem.**	*If I had been* king, *I would have made* peace.
Imperfect:	**Sī** ālās **habērem,** ad **lūnam volārem.**	*If I had* wings, *I would fly* to the moon.
Pluperfect:	**Sī** ālās **habuissem,** ad lūnam **volāvissem.**	*If I had had* wings, *I would have flown* to the moon.
Imperfect:	**Sī** pecūniam **habēret,** novum carrum **emeret.**	*If he had* money, *he would buy* a new car.
Pluperfect:	**Sī** pecūniam **habuisset,** novum carrum **ēmisset.**	*If he had had* money, *he would have bought* a new car.
Pluperfect:	**Nisi** pennātīs serpentibus in	*If she had not gone* into the sky with her winged serpents,

aurās **īvisset,**	*Medea would* not *have escaped*
Mēdeā poenās	punishment.
nōn **ēvītāvisset.**	

144. Subjunctive perfect and pluperfect forms of **sum** and **possum**.

fuerim	fuissem	potuerim	potuissem
fuerīs	fuissēs	*etc.*	*etc.*
fuerit	fuisset		
fuerīmus	fuissēmus		
fuerītis	fuissētis		
fuerint	fuissent		

145. Dative with certain verbs: Ten verbs whose meaning implies a "to" idea take the dative case as an object. Note the alternate English meaning for each:

crēdō	trust, put faith in	**pāreō**	obey, be obedient to
ignoscō	forgive, give pardon to	**persuādeō**	persuade, be sweet to
imperō	command, give orders to	**placeō**	please, be pleasing to
noceō	harm, do harm to	**serviō**	serve, be slave to
parcō	spare, be lenient to	**studeō**	study, direct energy to

Tibi crēdō.	I trust *you.*
Ignosce **mihi.**	Forgive *me.*
Caesar **mīlitibus** imperat.	Caesar commands *the soldiers.*
Mēdēa **puellīs** persuādet.	Medea persuades *the girls.*
Iuvenēs **parentibus** nōn pārent.	Young people do not obey *their parents.*

146. Dative of compound. Certain verbs whose meaning is altered or compounded by the addition of prepositions at the beginning of the Latin verb take the dative case as an object. The following prepositions often alter the verb meaning to change the object to the dative case: **ante, ob, prae** and **sub,** although compounds of **ad, circum, com- (con)-, in, inter, post, pro, re-,** and **super** may also govern the dative.

Acc. Object	Multa verba dīcō.	I say many things (words).
Dat. Object	**Meīs discipulīs** praedīcō ut audiant.	I instruct *my students* to listen.

Exercises

I.   Respondete Latine, quaeso.

1. Cur Aeson, filio tuto, laetus non erat?
2. Quid est factum bonum quod Medea pro Aesone fecit?
3. Quae dea carminibus Medeae adiuvat?
4. Quo (in) loco crescunt herbae magicae?
5. Quomodo currus Medeae volat?
6. Quibus deabus Medea duas aras construxit?
7. Quo ramo Medea omnes herbas in aeno miscuit?
8. Quid fit ramus?
9. Quomodo Aeson sucos bibit?
10. Quid fit Aeson?

II A. Give the conjugation of **voco, vocare, vocavi, vocatum** in the perfect and pluperfect subjunctive, active and passive.

B. Translate each of the following verb phrases:

1. ut effugerit
2. si effugisset
3. ut pervenerimus
4. si pervenissemus
5. ut repleat

6. ut repleverit
7. si replevisset
8. ut mittat
9. ut miserit
10. si misisset

III.   The following verbs take the dative case for the object. In each case there is the idea of "to" implied in the verb. Put an object in the dative case from the list of pronouns given (**mihi, tibi, ei, nobis, vobis, eis, sibi**) and translate the idea into English.

1. Credo _____ .
2. Ignosco _____ .
3. Impero _____ .
4. Noceo _____ .
5. Parco _____ .

6. Pareo _____ .
7. Persuadeo _____ .
8. Placeo _____ .
9. Servio _____ .
10. Studeo _____ .

IV.   Many verbs which take the accusative direct object or a predicate nominative form take a dative direct object when compounded. Notice the following examples:

Erat imperator.	He was the commander.
Praeerat exercitui.	He was in command of the army.
Hostem pugnavit.	He fought the enemy.
Fratri tuo repugnavit.	He opposed your brother.

Compound the following verbs and change the accusative direct object to a dative:

1. Iason haec verba dixit.

Iason milit _____ praedixit ut pugnent. (*instructed*)

2. Sum magistra.

Praesum discipul _____. (*am in charge*)

3. Sum dux.

Praesum exercit _____.

4. Fecit bellum.

Praefecit milit _____ Marcum. (*put in charge*)

5. Sto primus in pacem.

Praesto omni _____. (*surpass*)

V. Translate into Latin:

1. Medea had left her country and (had) betrayed her father so that she could marry Jason.
2. After a long journey Jason and Medea returned to Greece and Medea gave Aeson back his youth.
3. Medea built two altars, one on the right to Hecate and one on the left to Youth.
4. Medea poured new blood into Aeson and in this manner gave him back his youth.

After the Interim Reading translate the following sentences:

5. With false friendship Medea promised to restore Pelias (**Pelian,** *acc.*) and she persuaded (with dative) his daughters to cut him up.
6. Medea fled in her chariot with winged serpents to the palace of Aegeus after she had killed the daughter of the king of Corinth and also her own sons.

Etymology

MEDICAL LATIN

The medical profession relies heavily on Latin terms for anatomy, for fields of specialization, for directives and for prescriptions:

Anatomical Terms

capillary (**capillus**, *hair*)

nasal, (**nasum**, *nose*)

oral (**os, oris**, *mouth*)

ocular (**oculus**, *eye*)

lacrimal (**lacrima**, *tear*)

aural (**auris**, *ear*)

jugular (**iugulum**, *throat*)

ovary (**ovum**, *egg*)

fertile (**fero**, *bear*)

valve (**valva**, *door*)

disk (**discus**, *a circular plate*)

cerebrum (**cerebrum**, *the brain*)

cerebellum (diminutive of **cerebrum**)

dorsal (**dorsum**, *back*)

bracchial (**bracchium**, *arm*)
flexur (**flexum**, *bent*)
pectoral'(**pectus, pectoris**, *chest*)
intestine (**intus**, *inside*)
foetus, fetus, (**fetus**, *offspring*)

ventral (**venter**, *belly*)
iris (**Iris**, *the rainbow*)
canine (**canis**, *dog*)
incisor (**incisus**, *cut*)
tibia (**tibia**, *leg bone*)

Consult a standard dictionary for the etymology of the following medical terms:

operation
transplant
observation
monitor
cardiac
infarction
coronary
cancer
benign
malignant
formula

convulsion
circumcision
mental
doctor
dentist
internist
podiatrist
pediatrician (Greek, **pais, paidos**, *child*)
dermatologist (Greek, **derma**, *skin*)
npo (**nihil per os**, *nothing by mouth*)
prescription

* * * * *

Identify the Latin words from which these English words are derived:

hold my *camera*
attend the *coronation*
second *grade*
begin to *lactate*
lapidary science
lunatic asylum
Mediterranean Sea
remove the *membrane*
mode of living
all that was *mortal* in him
the *odor* of roses
the *Orient* express (from **orior**, *rise*)
ovulation cycle
pallor of his skin
piety in children
salutary effect
bury him in the *sepulchre*
sanguinary war
sulphuric acid
a *valve* in the heart

addiction to a drug
ascend to the peak
confession of one's sins
emission standards
expert advice
merge on the left
mixture of the old and the new
persuade people to vote
replete with good advice
retention of water
the *transmission* is broken
visit to the hospital
equal to each other
collect evidence
Niger River
a *nude* model
veteran of foreign wars
valid evidence
extreme cold or heat
frustrating experience

INTERIM READING III:
PLURA FACTA MALA MEDEAE

Nunc ut de familia Peliae poenas caperet,[1] Medea querellam falsam cum coniuge Iasone simulat et supplex ad regiam Peliae fugit. Cuius filiae illam magno cum gaudio accipiunt quoniam rex ipse senex est. Parvo tempore Medea amicitia[2] falsa filias cepit dumque fabulam de iuventute Aesonis recepta narrat, eis spem dat parentem eorum arte magica revirescere[3] posse. Idque petunt pretiumque iubent sine fine dari. "Ut sit fides maior huius muneris," ait, "maximus dux ovium feratur ut agnus[4] medicamine meo fiat." Statim hoc ducto, Medea guttur ense secat et in aeno corpus mergit.[5] Subito in medio aeno balatus[6] auditur et sine mora evenit agnus iuvenis qui matrem quaerit.

Filiae Peliae miratae sunt postquam ipsae miraculum promissum viderant; tum vero munus maxime rogant. Tres post noctes filia Aeëtae in ignibus aenum posuit in quo aquas sine herbis ponit. Iam somnus mortis similis[7] corpus regis tenebat ubi filiae cum Medea cubiculum[8] regis intraverunt et circum lectum[9] ambulaverunt: "Cur nunc dubitatis?" ait Medea "gladiis emittite sanguinem ut sanguine iuventutis corpus patris repleam. In manibus vestris est vita parentis." His verbis auditis, quaeque pia filia factum malum facit. Tamen quia nulla ictus[10] suos spectare potest, oculos vertunt ut caeca[11] vulnera dextris dent. Ille sanguine fluens tamen surgere[12] temptat

---

[1] *To inflict punishment on* (**dē**).
[2] **Amīcitia, -ae,** *f., friendship* (**cēpit** here means *took in* or *won over*).
[3] *To grow young again.*
[4] **Agnus, -ī,** *m., lamb.*
[5] **Mergō, -ere, mersī, mersum,** *dip, immerse.*
[6] *Bleating.*
[7] **Similis, -ē,** +*gen., like, just like.*
[8] *Room, bedroom, bedchamber.*
[9] **Lectus, -ī,** *m., bed.*
[10] **Ictus, -ūs,** *m., blow, stroke.*
[11] *Blind.*
[12] **Surgō, -ere, -rexī, -rectum,** *rise, rise up.*

et inter tot gladios bracchia tendens ait, "quid facitis, filiae? Cur in mortem parentem mittitis?" Animi illarum ceciderunt[13] et manus quoque. Sed Medea gutture regis plura verba abstulit et corpus in calidis[14] undis mersit. In hoc modo Medea filiabus Peliae persuasit[15] ut patrem suum necarent.

Nisi pennatis serpentibus in auras ivisset, Medea poenas non evitavisset. Fugit alta super montes et oppida usque Corinthum. Quo in oppido post multos annos Iason alteram uxorem quaerebat. Aesonides in matrimonium filiam regis Corinthii ducere speravit ut (ita dixit) pro Medea et filiis duobus suis domum tutam faceret. Medea hanc iniuriam sine ira non fert et filiae regis vestimenta magica et coronam cum veneno[16] misit quae ignara[17] filia induit. Statim haec et pater qui eam servare temptavit in totis corporibus ardebant.[18] Tum Medea, regia arsa filiisque suis ense suo necatis, Athenas et ad regiam Aegei[19] fugit; ita curru serpentibus pennatis ablato arma iramque Iasonis effugit.

---

[13] Cadō, -ere, cecidī, casum, *fall.*
[14] Calidus, -a, -um, *hot.*
[15] Persuadeō, -ēre, -suāsī, -suāsum (+*dat.*: see Sec. 145).
[16] *A poisonous crown* (corōna, -ae, *f.*, *crown*; venēnum, -ī, *n.*, *poison*).
[17] *Unwittingly, unaware.*
[18] Ardeō, -ēre, arsī, arsum, *burn.*
[19] Aegeus, -eī, *m.*, *Aegeus*, king of Athens.

Theseus

The many tales woven around Theseus, the legendary king of Athens, are richly embroidered with threads of love and adventure on the loom of prehistory and archaeology. The first episodes of his heroic adventures occur at his birthplace, Troezen, as he claims the tokens, the sword and the sandals, left by Aegeus, his mortal father. He then becomes a local folk hero as he travels through the Isthmus, clearing it of fantastic monsters and robbers, his adventures being climaxed by his arrival in Athens to reveal himself to King Aegeus. The inference that Poseidon is also his father-protector is a continuing theme in Mary Renault's two novels of the Theseus myth, *The King Must Die* and *The Bull from the Sea*, the latter based on Theseus' later adventures after he becomes King of Athens. Ann G. Ward's *The Quest for Theseus* reconstructs the Bronze Age archaeological settings both in Crete and in Athens against which the stories are projected.

Aegeus' joy at acknowledging his princely son is short-lived, since the threat of tribute to King Minos of Crete hangs over the city. Theseus contrives to join the young Athenians who are sent to be devoured by the Minotaur housed in the labyrinth beneath the palace at Knossos. Once there, he is befriended and aided by the Princess Ariadne, who teaches him the secret of the labyrinth and the means of escaping from it. In return, Theseus takes her with him after he has slain the monster, but he abandons her on the island of Naxos on the voyage home. As he nears Attica on the return trip, he forgets to raise the white sail, the signal to his father that he is alive. Aegeus, waiting at Cape Sounion, assumes that his son has died and throws himself into the sea which thereafter bears his name, the Aegean.

Theseus then becomes king of Athens and with his friend Pirithous, king of the Lapiths, has many further adventures, including the famous fight which occurs at the latter's wedding when the centaur relatives of the bride get drunk and behave in a most unseemly manner. The ensuing battle is depicted on the metopes of the Parthenon on the Acropolis in Athens. Another of his adventures with Pirithous might have ended in catastrophe, when the two were caught in Hades trying to steal Proserpina, had not Hercules, the mighty kinsman of Theseus, descended to that dreary place and forcibly removed him from the seat of forgetfulness.

Theseus emerges also as the just and wise ruler of the city of Athens, its lawgiver and sagacious prince. He marries the Amazon queen Hippolyta, who later dies fighting at his side in battle after she has borne him his beloved son Hippolytus. When this son has grown to become a handsome youth, Theseus marries again, taking as his bride the young princess Phaedra, sister of Ariadne. Phaedra falls madly in love with the young Hippolytus; and when her love is rejected, she kills herself in shame, after first writing a letter to Theseus accusing Hippolytus of having violated her. Theseus, believing the false accusation, banishes his son from the kingdom. The young Hippolytus, driving along the coast road, is thrown to his death from his chariot when the horses rear at an apparition from the sea. Theseus learns the truth too late and grieves at having caused the death of his only son.

Theseus befriends others in grief, particularly Oedipus, when that tragic figure, now blind, is wandering as an outcast. He is also invited to aid in settling the bloody strife at Thebes, after the princes of Argos have intensified the internecine war between the brother princes of the city. After Theseus' troops have established order, he forbids the soldiers to pillage or sack the city, and in all his later roles he emerges as a peacekeeper, an arbiter, a judge, a wise ruler and lawgiver, as contrasted with his much envied kinsman Hercules, whom he so admired, who represents the hero of physical strength. Tragically, Theseus dies in a foreign land, betrayed by a neighboring king while a guest in his court.

Sententiae

Possunt quia posse videntur.   *They can do it because they believe they*
Virgil, *Aen.* V.231   *can (seem to be able to do it).*

Chapter XXVII
THESEUS TROEZENE

Theseus erat filius Aegei, regis Atheniensium. Aethra, filia regis Troe-
zenii, erat mater ei. Ille quoque proles Neptuni fuisse traditur; quam ob
rem Theseus appellatus est Neptunius heros, et deum maris semper colebat.
Troezene igitur aetatem puerilem in regia matris avique Pitthei egit; nam
pater eius Athenas rediverat. Aegeus autem discedens a Troezene sub
magnum saxum soleas et gladium suum celaverat et Aethrae imperaverat ut
Theseum iuvenem ad se Athenas mitteret. "Ubi puer tam validus crescit ut
saxum removere possit, mitte eum ad me ut se patri demonstret." Ubi tempus
aderat, Aethra prolem ad saxum duxit. Iuvenis rogavit cur Aethra huc
duceret. Tum mater fabulam de Aegeo exposuit. Quamquam erat labor
difficillimus, Theseus saxo remoto soleas et gladium cepit. Gladio induto,
Theseus se paravit ut Athenas proficisceretur.

Avus Pittheus, valde conatus ei persuadere ut iter per mare faceret, ei
navem offerebat; Theseus autem, cupiens similem Herculis cognati[1] se
facere, per isthmum ire constituit ut populos periculo liberaret; nam scivit
illam regionem esse plenam monstrorum et latronum.

Primo die Theseus prolem claviferentem[2] Vulcani superavit; postea
clavam illius semper portabat, memoriam primae victoriae. Deinde ille
occidit Sinem magnis viribus male usum qui tam validus erat ut pinus ad
terram curvare posset. Arboribus solutis corpora hominum late per aera
iaciebat. Eum Theseus eodem modo necavit.

Sequens[3] viam secundum oram, Theseus venit ad montes altas. Nam
scivit in quo loco Sciron latro habitaret et in quo saxo sederet. Hic latro
peregrinatoribus imperavit ut pedes lavarent; sed cum hi se inclinabant ut ita

---

[1] *His kinsman Hercules.*

[2] Compound descriptive participle made up of **ferēns** (*bearing*) and **clāvam** (*club* or *cudgel*):
Cf. **mortiferēns** (*bringing death*) and the name Christopher (*Christ-Bearer*); this monster was
named Periphetes, the son of Vulcan.

[3] Deponent verbs can have present active participles: **sequēns, -entis,** *following.* **See Sec.
121.**

facerent, ille eos in mare ictu pedis demisit. In mari ingens turtur illos devorabat. Theseus autem pedes Scironis lavare recusavit. Quem[4] e saxo sublatum in mare iecit. Prope Eleusinam heros suem feram interfecit ut agricola in illo loco nunc securus ruri agros suos arare posset.

Ceteri tyranni et latrones a Theseo superati sunt, in quibus erat Procrustes qui incolas prope Athenas terrebat. Traditum est eum habuisse lectum ferreum in quo omnes peregrinatores ponebat. Si quis hospes longior erat, aut caput aut pedes secabat. Si quis minor erat, Procrustes eum tendebat ut lecto aptaret. Aegides Procrusten necavit in modo apto.

Multi poetae narrant quomodo Theseus ceteros latrones monstraque superaverit et in quibus regionibus populi vota publica fortissimo heroi suscipiant. Factus erat heros, filius idoneus regi Atheniensium.

Verba

NOUNS

*Aegēus, -eī, m.	Aegeus (*king of Athens*)
*Aegīdēs, -ae, m.	son of Aegeus, Theseus
Aethra, -ae, f.	Aethra (*princess of Troezen*)
Athēniensēs, -ium, m.	the inhabitants of Athens, the Athenians
clāva, -ae, f.	club
Eleusina, -ae, f.	Eleusis (*a very ancient city of Attica*)
hospes, hospitis, c.	a host, a guest
isthmus, -ī, m.	the Isthmus of Corinth
latrō, -ōnis, m.	robber, brigand
*lectus, -ī, m.	bed, couch
*rūs, rūris, n.	the country
*Neptūnus, -ī, m.	Neptune (*god of sea*)
*ōra, -ae, f.	shore, sea shore
peregrīnātor, -ōris, m.	stranger, traveller
pīnus, -ūs or -ī, f.	pine tree
Pitthēus, -eī, m.	Pittheus (*grandfather of Theseus*)
Procrustēs, -ae, m.	Procrustes (*a robber*)
prōles, -is, f.	off-spring, son
*regiō, -ōnis, f.	region, land
rūs, rūris, n.	the country
Scīron, -ōnis, m.	Sciron (*a brigand*)
Sinis, -is, m.	Sinis Pinebender (*a mythical robber*)
solea, -ae, f.	shoe, sandal
sūs, suis, c.	pig, sow

---

[4] See Sec. 160.

Thēseūs, -eī, *m.*	Theseus (*son of Aegeus*)
Troezēn, -ēnis, *f.*	Troezen (*a city in Argolis*)
turtur, -uris, *m.*	turtle
*tyrannus, -ī, *m.*	tyrant
*vōtum, -ī, *n.*	prayer, offering
Vulcānus, -ī, *m.*	Vulcan (*god of fire*)

VERBS

aptō (1) + *dat.*	fit to, adapt to
arō (1)	plow, cultivate
curvō (1)	curve, bend, arch
*dēmittō, -ere, -mīsī, -missum	send away, send down
*discēdō, -ere, -cessī, -cessum	depart, go away
expōnō, -ere, -posuī, -positum	put out, display, show
inclīnō (1)	bend, bend over
*occīdō, -ere, occīdī, -cīsum	kill
*offerō, -ferre, obtulī, oblātum	offer, present
*persuādeō, -ēre, -suāsī, -suāsum + *dat.*	persuade
*proficiscor, -ciscī, -fectus sum	set out
recūsō (1)	refuse
*suscipiō, -ere, -cēpī, -ceptum	undertake, offer
terreō, -ēre, -uī, -itum	terrify
*tollō, -ere, sustulī, sublātum	raise
*trāditur, trādunt	it is said, handed down, people say
*ūtor, ūtī, ūsus sum + *abl.*	use

ADJECTIVES

aptus, -a, -um	fitting, suitable
*ferreus, -a, -um	iron
idōneus, -a, -um	suitable
*publicus, -a, -um	public
*puerīlis, -e	boyish
Troezēnius, -a, -um	of Troezen (*a city of Argolis*)
sēcūrus, -a, -um	secure, free from care
similis, -e + *gen.*	like
solūtus, -a, -um	loosened, freed

OTHER WORDS

*quam ob rem	for this reason
*secundum + *acc.*	after; by, along
valdē	strongly, very hard

Structure

147. Review and synopsis of subjunctive forms: The forms of the subjunctive are most easily mastered when seen as a unit in a synopsis of a single person and number. Notice the rules apparent from these synopses in the third person singular.

ACTIVE

	I	II	III	III-io	IV
Pres.	amet	moneat	dūcat	capiat	audiat
Imp.	amāret	monēret	dūceret	caperet	audīret
Perf.	amāverit	monuerit	dūxerit	cēperit	audīverit
Pluperf.	amāvisset	monuisset	dūxisset	cēpisset	audīvisset

PASSIVE

	I	II	III	III-io	IV
Pres.	amētur	moneātur	dūcātur	capiātur	audiātur
Imp.	amārētur	monērētur	dūcerētur	caperētur	audīrētur
Perf.	amātus sit	monitus sit	ductus sit	captus sit	audītus sit
Pluperf.	amātus esset	monitus esset	ductus esset	captus esset	audītus esset

Easiest, of course, is the imperfect, which consists of the infinitive plus personal endings, active and passive. These forms are very commonly used and they are easy to recognize and to produce. With the present tense forms, the trick to remember is that the first and third conjugation verbs reverse their characteristic vowels:

amā (stem)		duce (stem)	
Subj.: amet	amētur	ducat	ducātur

  -e-   -a-

Second conjugation uses both vowels:

monē
moneat   moneātur

3rd-**io** and 4th conjugations are conjugated like 3rd with an **i** preceding the **a**:

capiat   audiat
capiātur   audiātur

Perfect subjunctive forms resemble the future perfect indicative and differ only in the first person singular (**erim** instead of **erō**) and in accent caused by vowel lengthening.

Pluperfect forms active consist of the perfect infinitive (**-isse**) plus the personal endings. The passive forms in the perfect system consist of the perfect passive participle plus the forms of **sum** *in the subjunctive* written as separate words.

There is, of course, no future or future perfect tense in the subjunctive since the philosophy or logic of this mood lies in the unreal world of future possibility or probability:

Exercitum **dūcam**.	*I may lead* the army.
Exercitum **dūcerem**.	*I might lead* the army.
Exercitum **dūxerim**.	*I may have led* the army.
Exercitum **dūxissem**.	*I might have led* the army.

When?

In some vague or future time. *Therefore there are no future tenses in the subjunctive.*

148. Indirect question. Another very common use of the subjunctive is in a subordinate construction called the Indirect Question. Such indirect questions depend on a declarative verb of telling, knowing (or not knowing), asking, wondering, and the like. They are really noun clauses introduced by interrogative words such as **quis** (*who*), **quid** (*what*), **cūr** or **quam ob rem** (*why*), **quōmodo** (*how*), **ubī** (*when* or *where*), **(in)quō locō** (*where*), and the like.

Scit **quis sīs**.	He knows *who you are.*
Rogant **cūr veniās**.	They are asking *why you are coming.*
Thēseūs Aethram rogāvit **cūr** ea sē hūc **addūceret**.	Theseus asked Aethra *why she was leading* him to this place.
Thēseūs Aethram rogāvit **cūr** ea sē hūc **addūxisset**.	Theseus asked Aethra *why she had led* him to this place.
Multī poētae narrāvērunt **quōmodo Thēseūs** monstra **superāret**.	Many poets have told *how Theseus overcame* the monsters.
Multī poētae narrāvērunt **in quibus regiōnibus populī** vōta Thēseō **susciperent**.	Many poets have told *in what regions the people offered* prayers to Theseus.

149. Sequence of tenses. In all of the above examples there is a fixed pattern for the use of tenses in the subjunctive following the tenses of the main verb in the indicative. The scheme is as follows:

Indicative	**Subjunctive**
(*Main Verb*)	(*Subordinate Clause Verb*)

PRIMARY SEQUENCE

Present or Future	Present (same time as main verb)
	Perfect (time before main verb)

SECONDARY SEQUENCE

| Imperfect, Perfect, Pluperfect | Imperfect (same time) |
| | Pluperfect (time before) |

PRIMARY SEQUENCE

Rogat (rogābit) cūr veniās.   He asks (will ask) why you are coming.

Rogat (rogābit) cūr vēnerīs.   He asks (will ask) why you came.

SECONDARY SEQUENCE

Rogābat (rogāvit, rogāverat) cūr venīrēs.   He asked (has asked, had asked) why you came.

Rogābat (rogāvit, rogāverat) cūr vēnissēs.   He asked (has asked, had asked) why you had come.

This relationship of tenses holds true for most subordinate clause usage with introductory indicative verbs.

150. **Utor** with the ablative case. Several deponent verbs have the peculiarity of governing the ablative case for their direct objects. The logic appears when the verb **ūtor**, *to use*, is understood as meaning *make use of*. In the reading, the perf. pass. part. (translated in the active sense) governs the ablative **magnīs vīribus male ūsus**, *using his great powers evilly* or *making bad use of his great powers*. The verbs **fungor** (*perform*) and **vescor** (*feed on*) also use the ablative case in this manner.

151. Locative case. Place where may be expressed by the preposition **in** with the ablative case: **in marī, in viīs**, *in the sea, on the roads*, but with the names of cities and small islands *no preposition is used and the locative case is used instead*. The locative always expresses place where. Its forms are taken from the other cases. In the first and second declensions the forms resemble the genitive in the singular and the ablative in the plural. Since the names of cities are frequently plural, be prepared to recognize both cases as locative:

Rōmae	*at Rome*	**Athēnīs**	*at Athens*
Corinthī	*at Corinth*	**Thēbīs**	*at Thebes*

In the third declension the forms are like the dative or ablative, both singular and plural:

Carthāgenī or **Carthāgene**   *at Carthage*
Troezēnī or **Troezēne**   *at Troezen*

The words **domī** and **rūrī** (*at home* and *in the country*) are regularly used to indicate place where *without a preposition*.

The accusative case *without a preposition* indicates place to which for cities, small islands and **domum** and **rūs** (*home* and *to the country*).

Rōmam   *to Rome*   **Thēbās**   *to Thebes*

Exercises

I.   Respondete Latine, quaeso.

   1. Quis erat pater Theseo?
   2. Quis erat mater ei?
   3. Quis quoque tradebatur fuisse pater ei?
   4. Ubi Theseus crescebat?
   5. In quo loco Aegeus soleas et gladium celavit?
   6. Quid debebat Theseus facere ut soleas et gladium caperet?
   7. Cur Theseus desiderabat iter facere per isthmum?
   8. Quomodo necavit Theseus Sinem?
   9. Quomodo Procrustes peregrinatores curabat?
   10. Ad quam urbem Theseus proficiscebatur?

II.   Give a synopsis of the subjunctive forms of: **aptare, persuadeo, dimitto, suscipio,** and **offero.**

III A. Construct sentences of your own using the following verbs in the indicative and the subjunctive, illustrating the primary and secondary tense sequence usage:

	cur (why)
Nescio	**quomodo** (how) **rex bellum gerere** (wage war)
(I do not know)	**ubi** (where)

   B. Rewrite the Quaestiones of Exercise I as Indirect Questions introduced by **Scivi**.

   1. Scivi quis esset pater Theseo.

IV.   Review the usage of locative forms and prepositions with names of cities, regions, islands and "home" and "the country." Complete each idea with either **ibam** or **habitabam**.

   1. to Athens   <u>Athenas ibam.</u>
   2. at Athens   <u>Athenis habitabam.</u>
   3. home (going)   _____
   4. in Attica (a region) _____
   5. to Rome   _____
   6. at home   _____
   7. in the country   _____
   8. at Troezen   _____

9. in Marathon   _____

10. in Thebes   _____

V.   Translate the following sentences into Latin:

1. Aegeus, king of Athens, was the father of Theseus, and Aethra, daughter of Pittheus, was his mother.
2. Neptune also is said by many poets to have been his father.
3. Theseus grew up in Troezen, but when he was a strong young man he removed the stone which covered the sandals and sword of his father and set out for Athens.
4. Theseus wanted (**volēbat**) to free the people of Corinth from monsters and tyrants.
5. Sinon used his great strength to bend pine trees to the ground.
6. Sciron killed travellers who had to bend over to wash his feet (purpose clause).
7. Procrustes stretched his guests to fit his bed (purpose clause).
8. Even today poets tell how Theseus freed the isthmus from danger.
9. Theseus asked his mother why she had led him to the rock.
10. Aegeus will ask Theseus how he came to Athens.

Etymology

CHURCH LATIN

The Roman Catholic Church, which used Latin for centuries as a vehicle of communication for ideas in both the spoken and written language, has bequeathed many Latin words directly to English. Within the last few decades sweeping changes within the Church have required that local languages be substituted for previous Latin prayers and liturgy, but there remains a body of terms which remind one of the historical development of the Church via the legacy of its language.

advent (**advenire**, *to arrive*)
angel (**angelus**, *angel*)
ascension (**ascendere**, *to ascend*)
Beatitudes (**beatus**, *blessed*)
benediction (**bene + dicere**, *well + to speak*)
commandment (**commandare**, *to command*)
communion (**communis**, *common, shared*)
congregation (**con + gregare**, *to collect*)

confession (**confessum**, *confessed*)

confirmation (**confirmare**, *to strengthen*)

consecration (**consecrare**, *to consecrate*)

convent (**convenire**, *to come together*)

conversion (**convertere**, *to turn together*)

creation (**creare**, *to create*)

Credo (**credo**, *I believe*)

curate (**curare**, *to care for*)

Dominus vobiscum (*Lord* [*be*] *with you*)

immaculate conception (**immaculata**, *without stain or blemish, pure*, **conceptum**, *conceived*)

missionary (**missum**, *having been sent*)

Consult a standard dictionary for the etymology of the terms below:

resurrection	coronation	providence
sacrament	crucifix	relic
sacrifice	nativity	religion
temptation	excommunication	remission
Trinity	novice	sanctuary
unity	pontiff	vespers
altar	procession	vigil
cardinal	profane	vulgate
ex cathedra	reformation	mass

*   *   *   *   *

Explain the derivation of the following words from the lesson's vocabulary:

Aegean Sea

hospitality in that city

isthmus of Corinth

Marathon runner

regional representation

a *votive* offering

the *tyrant* overthrown

incline his head

terrify all strangers

curve of the earth

use all your powers

puerile behavior

public worship

secure in the confidence of his love

apt to win

second prize; *second* the motion

Sententiae

Quo fata trahunt retrahuntque   *Let us follow wherever the fates take us,*
   sequamur.   *there and back again.*

     Virgil, *Aen.* V.709

Chapter XXVIII
THESEUS ATHENIS

Dum Theseus Troezene crescit, Aegeus Medeam[1] in regnum accipit ad quod haec curru serpentibus pennatis ablato fugit postquam regiam Corinthi accenderat filiosque suos ense necaverat. Aegeus hanc accipit, neque satis hospitium est, sed se Medeae foedere thalami quoque iungit, nam sperabat se arte Medeae filium procreaturum esse. Non adhuc Theseum vivere cognovit.

Iamque Theseus aderat filius parenti ignarus, qui virtute sua bimarem isthmum pacaverat. At tamen Medea eum recognovit simul ac in urbem pervenit; quam ob rem mala invidaque Aegeo persuasit ut Theseum in regiam invitaret ut necaretur. Cum hic in convivium iniret, illa vino venenum miscuit quod Aegeo dedit ut ipse nato ignaro daret. Hoc mortiferum[2] venenum, quod Medea secum attulerat, olim factum est de spumis albis quibus Cerberus agros latratibus sparsit, dum Hercules eum ex Orco[3] aufert. Theseus iam poculum datum ignara dextra sumpserat, cum pater in ornamento eburneo gladii signa sui generis recognovit et ab ore Thesei poculum abiecit. Medea autem cantans carmina magica necem effugit nebulis motis, cum facinus patere videret.

At pater, cum laetus esset nato tuto invento, tamen miratus est se nefas ingens commisurum esse. Di prohibuerunt quin[4] filium suum necavisset! Accendit igitur aras deorum ignibus. Nulla dies fertur[5] celebrior quam illa Athenis. Pater et populus carminibus heroem celebraverunt. "Tu, maxime Theseu, amatus es ab omnibus incolis Isthmi. Tutum iter nunc patet peregrinis. Si desideramus numerare et facta bona et annos tuos, facta superant annos. Pro te, fortissime, vota publica suscepimus; tibi poculum vini bibimus."

---

[1] Fabulam de Medea in Capitibus XXIV–XXVI legistis.

[2] *Death-bearing.*

[3] **Orcus, -ī,** *m.,* is another poetic name for Hades. It is an area in the lower regions.

[4] *The gods prevented him from killing his own son.*

[5] *Is considered.* The passive of **ferō** has this possible meaning.

Regia Athenis plausu precibusque populi sonat. Nec tristis locus ullus est in tota urbe. Tamen (nam nulla est voluptas sine cura) Aegeus nato tuto recepto gaudere magnopere non poterat; nam Minos bellum parabat. Hic filius Iovis et Europae, quamquam milite, quamquam navibus valet, tamen maxime valet ira patria, quod filius Androgeus ut[6] hospes Athenis interfectus erat. Audite quomodo accideret: In regno Aegei erat taurus albus quem Hercules e Creta in Graeciam transportaverat. Hic taurus qui ignes efflabat multos homines necaverat et agros vastaverat. Multi iuvenes eum interficere temptaverunt, in quibus erat Androgeus, filius Minois, sed frustra. Denique Theseus taurum cornibus mortiferis prehensit et per vias Athenarum traxit usque ad templum[7] quo deis sacrificium hunc necavit. Cum Androgeus ab Aegeo missus in periculum interfectus esset, Minos nunc bellum paravit. Minos iussit quoque septem iuvenes et septem virgines sibi Cretam mitti ut Minotauro sacrificarentur. Quod biforme monstrum, taurus cum capite hominis, natus Pasiphaae[8] et tauri albi, sub regia in labyrintho habitabat.

Verba

NOUNS

*Cerberus, -ī, *m.*	Cerberus (*three-headed dog of the Underworld*)
convīvium, -iī, *n.*	banquet, party
Crēta, -ae, *f.*	Crete (*an island*)
facinus, -oris, *n.*	bad deed, crime
foedus, -eris, *n.*	covenant, agreement, treaty
*genus, -eris, *n.*	race, kind, family
hospitium, -iī, *n.*	hospitality
*labyrinthus, -ī, *m.*	labyrinth
lātrātus, -ūs, *m.*	barking
*Mīnōs, -ōis, *m.*	Minos (*king of Crete*)
Mīnōtaurus, -ī, *m.*	The Minotaur
*nebula, -ae, *f.*	cloud
nefās, *indecl.*, *n.*	a wicked deed
nex, necis, *f.*	death
*plausus, -ūs, *m.*	applause, clapping

---

[6] *As a guest.* Ut can mean *as* in this sense, though no word for *as* is necessary. **Androgeus hospes** would have the same meaning with **hospes** an appositive.

[7] The temple was probably located on the Acropolis, the high place of the city.

[8] Pasiphaë, the wife of Minos, conceived an illicit passion for a beautiful white bull (see next chapter). The offspring of this unnatural union was the Minotaur, who was imprisoned by Minos in a labyrinth built by Daedalus beneath the palace at Knossos.

pōculum, -ī, *n.*	drinking cup, goblet
spūma, -ae, *f.*	foam, froth
thalamus, -ī, *m.*	marriage couch, marriage, bedroom
venēnum, -ī, *n.*	poison
*voluptās, -tātis, *f.*	pleasure, delight

VERBS

*abiciō, -ere, -iēcī, -iectum	throw down, aside
accendō, -ere, -cendī, -cēnsum	kindle, set on fire
celebrō (1)	praise, honor
*interficiō, -ere, -fēcī, -fectum	kill
*invītō (1)	invite
pācō (1)	make peaceful
*pateō, -ēre, patuī	lie open, be disclosed, be revealed
prōcreō (1)	beget offspring
sacrificō (1)	sacrifice
*volō, velle, voluī	want, wish (**vel-** is pres. subjv. stem)

ADJECTIVES

*albus, -a, -um	white
biformis, -e	two-formed
bimaris, -e	lying between two seas
celeber, -bris, -bre	celebrated
*ferox, -ōcis	savage, wild
ignārus, -a, -um	unknowing, unaware of
patrius, -a, -um	fatherly, parental
*potēns, potentis	powerful
*trīstis, -e	sad, gloomy

OTHER WORDS

*quam (after a comparative)	than
quīn	but that, from . . . doing (*see note in Lesson*)

Structure

152. **Cum** as a preposition and as a conjunction.
    A. The word **cum** as a preposition can mean "with" or "accompanied by" to express either manner or accompaniment.

cum amōre	with love	(*manner*)
magnō cum amōre[9]	with much love	
cum patre fīliōque	with the father and son	(*accompaniment*)

B. **Cum** as a subordinate conjunction introduces several kinds of subordinate clauses with the following possibilities of meaning:

1. **Cum** *with the indicative* mood indicates time when in simple temporal clauses:

Cum vocās, respondeō.	*When you call*, I reply.
Cum vocābis, respondēbō.	*When you* (will) *call*, I shall reply.

Cum with the pluperfect tense is used to express the idea of "whenever," when the main verb is in a past tense.

Cum Rōmam **vēnerat**, īvit ut mātrem vidēret.	*Whenever he came* to Rome, he went to see his mother.

The past tenses of the indicative with **cum** are limited to expressions of the exact time concurrent with the happening of events in the main clause. More frequently when **cum** is used with the past time, the subjunctive mood is used to indicate the circumstances or cause of the events in the main clause.

2. **Cum** *with the subjunctive* mood indicates the circumstances, cause or concession under which the events of the main clause occur.

   a. **Cum** *circumstantial* (when)

Cum Caesar iter per Galliam **faceret**, ad Rhodanum pervēnit.	*When* Caesar *was marching* through Gaul, he arrived at the Rhone.
Cum Caesar iter per Galliam **fēcisset**, ad Rhodanum pervēnit.	*When* Caesar *had marched* through Gaul, he arrived at the Rhone.

   b. **Cum** *causal* (because or since)

Quae **cum** ita **sint**,[10] Caesar Rōmam ibit.	*Since* these things *are* so, Caesar will return to Rome.
Quae **cum** ita **essent**, Caesar Rōmam rediit.	*Since* these things *were* so, Caesar returned to Rome. (Since this was the situation . . .)
Cum Androgeus **missus esset** ın perīculum ab Aegeō, Mīnōs bellum parāvit.	*Because* Androgeus *had been sent* into danger by Aegeus, Minos prepared for war.

---

[9] **Nota bene**: position of **cum** between adjective and noun. **Cum** may be omitted if the noun is modified by an adjective: **magnō amōre**.

[10] Frequently the **cum** is postpositive, especially after **Quae**.

c. **Cum** *concessive* (although)

Cum laetus **esset** nātō tutō
inventō, **tamen**[11] Aegeus
mirātus est . . .

Although he was overjoyed at
finding his son safe,
nevertheless Aegeus was
astonished that . . .

153. Temporal conjunctions. Time relationships in subordinate clauses can be expressed by many subordinate conjunctions:

Indicative		*Indicative or Subjunctive*	
ubi	when	**dum**[12]	while; as long as, until
ut	as	**dōnec**	until
quandō	when, at the time when	**antequam**	before
		postquam	after
cum	when	**simul ac** (atque)	as soon as
		cum	when; since, because, although

The conjunctions in the first column *usually* take the indicative in the perfect or the historical present. The conjunctions in the second column *usually* take the indicative if the time element is a fact or a clear possibility; they govern the subjunctive if they indicate purpose or expectancy or vague possibility.

154. Adjectives with the dative case. Certain adjectives like **grātus** (*pleasing to*) and **cārus** (*dear to*) take the dative case. The adjective **ignārus** can take several different constructions in its active meaning of *ignorant of*, *unacquainted with*, but in its passive meaning of *unknown* it takes the dative case.

fīlius **parentī** ignārus   a son unknown *to his father*

155. Irregular comparison of adjectives. Most adjectives follow the rules for the comparative and superlative forms already presented (see **Sec. 124**).

Positive	*Comparative*	*Superlative*
laetus, -a, -um	**laetior, laetius**	**laetissimus, -a, -um**
happy	happier	happiest

A. Several adjectives ending in **-lis** (**facilis, difficilis, similis, humilis, gracilis**), however, are irregular in forming the superlative by adding **-limus, -lima, -limum** *to the base of the word*:

---

[11] **Tamen** in the main clause signals that **cum** means "although."

[12] **Dum** generally is used with the present indicative to denote continued action in past time. **Dum** with the Subjunctive means *as long as* or *until*.

facilis, -e   **facilior, facilius**   **facillimus, -a, -um**
easy   easier   easiest

Other adjectives in **-lis** form their superlatives regularly.

B. All adjectives ending in **-er** (in the masculine) form their superlative by adding **-rimus, -rima, -rimum** *to the whole word*; **miserrimus**.

miser, -era, -erum	**miserior, -ius**	**miserrimus, -a, -um** most wretched
sacer, -cra, -crum	**sacrior, sacrius**	**sacerrimus, -a, -um** most sacred
acer, acris, acre	**acrior, acrius**	**acerrimus, -a, -um** most bitter

C. Review the irregular comparison of the most common adjectives: **bonus, malus, magnus, parvus. multus,** in **Sec. 124.**

Adverbs formed from these irregular superlatives are as follows:

laetissimē   most joyfully
facillimē   most easily
miserrimē   most wretchedly
sacerrimē   most sacredly
acerrimē   most bitterly

156. Word mosaic or arresting word order. Note how effectively tight the word order makes the line and the idea expressed in the following excerpt:

> ... **currū serpentibus pennātīs ablātō**
> ... in her chariot, carried aloft by winged serpents

Although this criss-cross technique is a poetic usage, it is still effective in a line of prose to express an idea in a tight, succinct fashion.

Exercises

I.   Respondete Latine, quaeso.

1. Narrate fabulam de Medea et Iasone.
2. Cur Aegeus Medeam in matrimonium duxerat?
3. Quod facinus Medea temptavit?
4. Cur facinus Medeae non fieri potest?
5. Quibus signis filium recognovit Aegeus?
6. Quomodo Aegeus gratias deis demonstravit?
7. Estne Theseus dignus esse filius regis?

8. Cur Minos bellum facere volebat?

9. Quis erat Androgeus? Cur Athenis erat?

10. Quomodo taurus albus in Graeciam portabatur?

II. Decide which is the best translation for **cum** in each sentence and then translate:

1. Quae cum ita sint, Minos bellum facere desiderat.

2. Cum Aegeus laetus esset quod Theseus adesset, tamen miratus est quod paene filium suum necaverat.

3. Cum in regiam intravisset, Theseus patrem recognovit.

4. Cum venenum in poculum posuisset, Medea id Aegeo dedit.

5. Cum Theseus se similem Herculis esse vellet (*wanted*), per isthmum ire desideravit.

6. Cum Theseus patrem recognosceret, tamen Aegeus filium adhuc non recognovit.

7. Cum Theseus in regno patris adesset, magnum gaudium (*joy*) in urbe erat.

8. Cum Medea venenum secum haberet, facile hoc in poculum vini ponere potuit.

9. Cum Theseus filius Aegeo esset, tamen rex adhuc de filio nescivit.

10. Cum Medea advenam viderat, timuit.

III. Translate the following forms; complete each idea with either **ibam** or **habitabam**:

into English:	into Latin:
1. domi	1. to the island
2. ruri	2. at Athens
3. Athenis	3. in Crete
4. Romae	4. at home
5. in Creta	5. in Greece
6. in urbe	6. home (going home)
7. domum	7. in the country
8. Romam	8. in Sicily
9. Athenas	9. at Carthage
10. Carthagine	10. in Thebes

IV. Translate this epigram of Martial:

> **Non amo te, Sabidi, nec possum dicere quare.**
> **Hoc tantum possum dicere: non amo te.**

Sabidi:	*vocative*, Sabidius
quare:	why
hoc tantum:	only this

Do you know the English version of this epigram?

> I do not love thee, Doctor Fell,
> And why it is I cannot tell,
> But this I know and know full well,
> I do not love thee, Doctor Fell.

It was written by Tom Brown, who, having been expelled from his college in England, was given a chance to be reinstated by the Dean, one Doctor Fell, who required that the young man translate this epigram. The student did so, substituting the name of his dean for Sabidius.

V. In Latinum convertite:

1. Medea tried (use **conor**) to give Theseus poison by means of a cup of wine.
2. When Aegeus recognized his son, he immediately prevented him from drinking it. (**prohibeō** + *acc.* + *infinitive*)
3. Medea fled in her winged chariot (*rephrase in Latin to say*: in her chariot drawn by winged serpents) singing her evil song.
4. Theseus was praised because he was the son of the king and because he had freed the isthmus from many great dangers.
5. The kingdom at Athens, however, was not joyful because Athens was afraid of a war with Crete. (**timeō, -ēre** + *acc.*)

Etymology

BIOLOGICAL, BOTANICAL, AND ZOOLOGICAL LATIN

Latin, the language of scholars and scientists, was widely used as the source for names given to identify objects in the physical world. The following constitutes a *beginning* list of such names in the various disciplines:

Biological Terms

Word	Meaning	Source
lumen	a unit of light, passageway	**lumen**, *light*
locus	place or position	**locus**, *place*
flagellum	whip-like appendage	**flagellum**, *whip*
in vivo	in life, alive	**vivus**, *living*
in vitro	in glass, in a tube, in the laboratory	**vitrum**, *glass*
in situ	in natural position	**situs**, *position*
ovum	egg	**ovum**, *egg*
genus	classification between family and species	**genus**, *kind, clan*
species	classification lower than a genus	**species**, *appearance*
virus	poison or disease	**virus**, *venom*

Consult a standard dictionary for the meanings and source of the following terms:

Botanical Terms		Zoological Terms	
pollen	floral	viscera	villus
stamen	cell	caecum	fossil
arboretum	fungus	cilium	canine
conservatory	order	foetus	leonine
lilium	palm	cloaca	simian
		papilla	

Similar lists could be compiled from the fields of geology, astronomy, physics, or chemistry—all scientific investigation into the physical world. Throughout history, scientists all over the world have given Latin names (sometimes their own names Latinized) to objects identified in the physical universe. Many times local names also exist, but the Latin names have provided an international language for the identification of plants, animals, and other phenomena. **Ficus** (fig tree) and **pinus** (pine tree) provide a clear reference, whether the botanist lives in America, Russia, Greece, or Iran.

*   *   *   *   *

From the vocabulary of the lesson identify the Latin source for the synonyms of the underlined words:

	English Synonym	*Latin Source*
jolly, party mood	c-	
kindness to a guest	h-	
path through the maze	l-	
bull-headed monster	m-	
cloud formations	n-	
thunderous clapping	(ap)p-	
dangerous poison	v-	
sensuous creature	v-	
low degree of poverty	ab-	
perform a ceremony	c-	
please come, don't wait for an	i-	
the process of reproduction	p-	
one's own wishes	v-	
make sacred	s-	
between two seas	b-	
one who does not know	i-	
a powerful agent	p-	

Sententiae

Cui me moribundam deseris, hospes	*To what, my guest, are you leaving me?*
(hoc solum nomen quoniam de	*"Guest"—that is all I may call you*
coniuge restat).	*now, who have called you husband.*
Virgil, *Aen.* IV.323	

Chapter XXIX
THESEUS CRETAE

Neptunus, deus maris, album taurum pulchrum Minoi donaverat ut sibi sacrificaretur; taurus autem erat tam pulcher ut Minos ipse taurum conservaret. Neptunus, qui regem punire voluit, fecit ut Pasiphaē, coniunx eius, taurum amaret; adultera ligno taurum saevum deceperat ut fetum discordem utero ferret.[1] Dum Minos bellum gerit, opprobrium generis creverat et adulterium foedum reginae monstro biformi patebat. Minos hunc pudorem thalamo removere et eum multiplici domo sub regiam celare constituit.

Daedalus, qui celeberrimus in arte aedificandi erat, hunc labyrinthum construxit qui lumina in errorem variarum viarum multis flexibus duceret. Non aliter Maeandrus in agris Phrygiis ludit et ambiguo lapsu fluit et refluit; occurrens nunc ad fontes nunc aquas incertas ad mare apertum ducit. Tantae sunt camerae, tantae sunt viae ut Daedalus ipse vix ad limen revertere possit. Tanta est fallacia tecti.

Quo Minos celaverat geminam figuram tauri iuvenisque et bis monstrum sanguine Atheniensium pastum erat mortis causa Androgei.[2] Tertia sors autem (nam iuvenes Athenienses ad Cretam missi sorte lecti erant) mortem Minotauro dedit. Nam Theseus quamquam filius regis erat, tamen inter alios iuvenes navigare constituit ut patriam a terrore Minotauri liberaret. Si navis, Minotauro necato, reveniat,[3] velo albo naviget;[3] iuvenibus necatis, velo atro. Hoc futurum est signum Aegeo.

Cum navis in Cretam perveniret, familia regalis in litore descendit ut iuvenes Athenienses videret. Minos, qui de factis et parentibus Thesei audiverat, nunc vidit quam formosus et fortis heros esset. "Estne Neptunus vere pater qui te iuvet?" inquit Minos et anulum de digito in mare iecit.

---

[1] Daedalus had constructed a wooden cow into which the adulterous queen crawled to deceive and mate with the bull.

[2] Androgeus, Minos' son, had been allowed to go on a boar hunt while a guest of Aegeus in Athens and had been killed; his death became the pretext for the tribute demanded of Athens to be sent to Crete every nine years.

[3] Subjunctive: *If the ship should return . . ., it would sail . . .* (see **Sec. 170**).

"Refer mihi hunc anulum, signum parentis divini." Theseus, qui virtutem ad fortitudinem addit, orans deis omnibus et magnopere Neptuno se in mare submergit; mox cum anulo a Nereo dato revenit.

Ariadna, filia Minois, quae omnia haec opera spectaverat, statim Theseum amavit. Cum omnes Athenienses spem effugiendi dimitterent, virgo regalis spem novam dedit, nam Theseum quaesivit et consilium ei proposuit quo ambo effugerent. Primo ei filum gladiumque dedit (alii dicunt eum secreto gladium patris retenuisse) et heroi naturam labyrinthi docuit qui a Daedalo aedificatus erat. Oportuit ligare in postem ianuae filum quod Theseus evoluturus est dum errat etiam propius Minotauro. Monstro gladio necato, filum glomerandum est[4] Theseo qui tum omnes amicos educeret. Pro tanto beneficio Aegides promisit se Ariadnam in matrimonium ducturum esse et eam Athenas coniugem portaturum esse. Auxilio virginis ianua difficilis a Theseo iterum inventa est. Consilio secundo Theseus a Creta cum sociis filiaque regis navigavit.

Ariadna rapta, Aegides protinus ad insulam Diam[5] vela dedit. Qua in insula alii dicunt Theseum virginem reliquisse; alii dicunt Ariadnam in litore relictam esse ab heroe qui in navem redeuns subito ab insula tempestate ablatus est. Desertae virgini multa querenti Bacchus amorem opemque tulit et coronam de fronte Ariadnae in caelo posuit ut perennis stella foret clara. Aut forte aut voluntate deorum Ariadna fit coniunx et sacerdos Dionysi.

Verba

NOUNS

adulterium, -iī, *n.*	adultery
ānulus, -ī, *m.*	ring
***Ariadna, -ae,** *f.*	Ariadne, daughter of Minos
***camera, -ae,** *f.*	box, chamber, room
***Daedalus, -ī,** *m.*	Daedalus (*an inventor*)
Dīa, -ae, *f.*	Dia (*an old name for Naxos*)
***Dionȳsus, -ī,** *m.*	Dionysus (*god of wine and the liquid principle in life*)
***error, -ōris,** *m.*	error, wandering, mistake
fallācia, -ae, *f.*	trick, deceit
fētus, -ūs, *m.*	fetus
fīlum, -ī, *n.*	string
flexus, -ūs, *m.*	bending, turning
fortitūdō, -inis, *f.*	strength
frōns, -ntis, *f.*	forehead

---

[4] *The string had to be wound up by Theseus who then would lead out. . . .*

[5] Dia is an ancient name for Naxos, the island in the Aegean on which Theseus abandoned Ariadne.

*iānua, -ae, *f*.	door
lapsus, -ūs, *m*.	gliding, falling
*lignum, -ī, *n*.	wood
līmen, -inis, *n*.	threshold
*lūmen, -inis, *n*.	light, eye, life
Maeandrus, -ī, *m*.	Meander River
Naxos, -ī, *f*.	Naxos (*the island*)
Nērēus, -eī, *m*.	Nereus (*a sea god*)
opprobrium, -iī, *n*.	scandal, disgrace
*opus, -eris, *n*.	work, labor
*Pāsiphaē, -ae, *f*.	Pasiphaë (*wife of Minos*)
*patria, -ae, *f*.	fatherland
socius, -iī, *m*.	companion, ally
*sors, sortis, *f*.	lot, chance, lottery
uterus, -ī, *m*.	uterus, womb
voluntās, -tātis, *f*.	will, wish

VERBS

*conservō (1)	keep, preserve
*constituō, -uere, -uī, -stitūtum	decide, determine
construō, -ere, -struxī, -structum	build, construct
dēcipiō, -ere, -cēpī, -ceptum	deceive
*dīmittō, -ere, -mīsī, -missum	send away, let go, abandon
ēvolvō, -ere, -volvī, -volūtum	roll out
foret (futūrum esset)	would be
*libet, -ēre, libuit	it is pleasing
*licet, -ēre, licuit	it is permitted
*ligō (1)	bind, tie, fasten
*occurrō, -ere, -currī, -cursum + *dat*.	run, run against
*oportet, -ere, oportuit	it is necessary
pascō, -ere, pāvī, pastum	feed
*placet, -ēre, placuit	it is pleasing
prōpōnō, -ere, -posuī, -positum	propose
pūniō, -īre, -īvī, -ītum	punish
queror, -ī, questus sum	complain
refluō, -ere, -fluxī, -fluxum	flow back
*reveniō, -īre, -vēnī, -ventum	come back, return
submergō, -ere, -mersī, mersum	submerge, plunge into

ADJECTIVES

dēsertus, -a, -um	deserted
discors, -cordis	inharmonious, discordant

foedus, -a, -um	abhorrent, abominable
multiplex, -icis	multiple, with many windings and turnings
perennis, -e	perennial, eternal
***rēgālis, -e**	royal
***saevus, -a, -um**	savage, fierce
***varius, -a, -um**	different, varied, various

OTHER WORDS

aliter (ac)	otherwise
***ambō, -ae, -ō**	both (*of two*)
bis	twice
***crūdēliter**	cruelly
***mox**	soon
nōn aliter	not otherwise, *i.e.* just as
propius; etiam propius	closer; closer and closer
prōtinus	immediately
quam	how

Structure

157. Relative clauses with the indicative. The relative pronoun **qui, quae, quod,** which you have already learned in **Section 100,** may be used to introduce adjectival clauses which describe a noun antecedent.

Pāsiphaē, **quae** erat coniunx Mīnōis, taurum amāvit.	Pasiphaë, *who* was the wife of Minos, loved a bull.
Taurus **quem** Neptunus Mīnōī dōnāverat erat pulcher.	The bull *which* Neptune had given to Minos was beautiful.

158. Relative clauses with the subjunctive.
A. Relative clauses of characteristic: When the descriptive nature of the subordinate adjectival clause is not of the simple, factual kind, as in the above sentences, but rather tells the *sort of person* that the antecedent is or may be, then the less definitive mood, the subjunctive, is used to to indicate this less factual nature.

Haec est fēmina **quam** in theātrō vīdī.	She is the woman *whom I saw* in the theater. (*a definite person*)
Haec est fēmina **quam** in theātrō **videam**.	She is the *sort of* woman *whom I may see* in the theater. (*the kind of person* whom I would see in the theater)

Notice the less factual, less definite, less real nature of the second example. Keep this difference in mind and you will understand the subtle change in meaning from the simple relative clause to the relative clause of characteristic.

Estne Neptunus vērē pater **quī** tē **iuvet**?

Is Neptune really the *sort of* father *who may help* you? (*who would help* you)?

B. Relative purpose clause. The relative pronoun introducing a subordinate clause with the subjunctive may be used to give variety to the normal **ut** clause to express purpose.

Thēseūs ēduxit amīcōs **quī effugerent**.

Theseus led out his friends *so that they might escape*.

The same idea could be expressed by using **ut** instead of **quī**.

159. Impersonal verbs: **oportet, licet, libet, placet**. Frequently Latin uses the third person singular of certain verbs to introduce an infinitive construction which may be translated in English in a variety of ways to express necessity, permission, or pleasure.

Oportuit ligāre in postem fīlum quod ēvolverētur.

It was necessary to tie on the doorpost the thread which would be unwound.
(*or*)
He had to tie on the doorpost the thread which would be unwound.
(*or*)
He should tie on the doorpost the thread which would be unwound.

Mē lūdere licet.

It is permitted for me to play. (*I may play*, am allowed to play.)

Mē lūdere libet.

It is pleasant for me to play. (*I like to play*.)

Respondēte, **sī vōbīs placet**.

Reply, *if you please* (*lit., if it is pleasing to you*).

160. Relative Pronouns used to introduce a sentence. The relative pronoun, which normally is used within the sentence to refer to an antecedent, may be used in Latin to introduce a sentence or even a paragraph. Its

antecedent may be found in the preceding sentence and the pronoun is
best translated as a definite pronoun or a demonstrative.

Quō (in locō) Mīnōs cēlāverat geminam figūram taurī iuvenisque.	*In this place (lit., in which place)* Minos had concealed the twin figure of bull and youth.
Quem ē saxō sublātum in mare iēcit.	Then he lifted *him* from the rock and threw *him* into the sea.

161. **Facere ut**. A special causal expression is used to indicate the idea of
bringing about or *making happen* in the phrase **facere ut** with the subjunctive:

Neptūnus **fēcit ut** Pāsiphaē taurum amāret.	Neptune *caused* Pasiphaë to fall in love with the bull. (*brought it about that . . .*) (*made it happen that . . .*)

162. Gerund used in the genitive. The gerund is *a verbal noun* made by adding
-ndī (-ō, -um, -ō) to the stem of the verb. It is a second declension neuter
noun declined *only* in the singular of the genitive, dative, accusative, and
ablative cases, since the infinitive is used in the nominative.

	I	II	III	III-io	IV
	NO NOMINATIVE (Use infinitive)				
Gen.: *of loving*	**amandī**	**videndī**	**dūcendī**	**capiendī**	**sciendī**
Dat.: *to loving*	**amandō**	**videndō**	**dūcendō**	**capiendō**	**sciendō**
Acc.: *loving* (object)	**amandum**	**videndum**	**dūcendum**	**capiendum**	**sciendum**
Abl.: *by loving*	**amandō**	**videndō**	**dūcendō**	**capiendō**	**sciendō**
	loving	*seeing*	*leading*	*taking*	*knowing*

A common use of the gerund is the genitive used to complete an objective
idea in such phrases as:

ars aedificandī	the art of building
spēs effugiendī	the hope of escaping
facultās dīcendī	opportunity of speaking

The use of the gerund is beautifully illustrated in this passage from
Ecclesiastes in the *Old Testament*:

Omnia tempus habent, et suis spatiis transeunt universa sub caelo.
Tempus nascendi et tempus moriendi,
tempus plantandi et tempus evellendi quod plantatum est
tempus occidendi et tempus sanandi,

tempus destruendi et tempus aedificandi,
tempus flendi et tempus ridendi,
tempus plangendi et tempus saltandi,
tempus spargendi lapides et tempus colligendi,
tempus amplexandi et tempus longe fieri ab amplexibus,
tempus adquirendi et tempus perdendi,
tempus custodiendi et tempus abiciendi,
tempus scindendi et tempus consuendi,
tempus tacendi et tempus loquendi,
tempus dilectionis et tempus odii,
tempus belli et tempus pacis.
Quid habet amplius homo de labore suo?

Liber Ecclesiastes III. 1–9

Verba

spatium, -iī, *n.*, *space, prescribed path*
ūniversus, -a, -um, *whole, entire*; the whole world, everything
plantō (1), *plant*
ēvellō, ere, -vellī, -volsum, *tear out*
sanō (1), *heal*
dēstruō, -ere, -ūxī, -ūctum, *destroy*
plangō, -ere, -ānxī, -anctum, *beat, lament, wail*
saltō (1), *dance*
colligō (conligō), -ere, -lēgī, -lēctum, *collect*
amplexor, -ārī, -ātus sum, *embrace*
adquīrō, -ere, -quīsīvī, -quīsītum, *accumulate*
perdō, -ere, -didī, -ditum, *throw away*
custodiō, -īre, -īvī, -ītum, *keep back, preserve, hoard*
scindō, -ere, scidī, scissum, *tear apart, divide*
consuō, -ere, -suī, -sūtum, *sew together, mend*
dilectiō, -ōnis, *f.*, *choosing love*
amplius, *more, further*
*pax, pacis, *f.*, *peace*

Exercises

I.   Respondete Latine, quaeso.

1. Quis taurum Minoi donaverat?
2. Cur Neptunus Minoem punire voluit?
3. Quomodo Neptunus Minoem punivit?
4. Ubi Minos monstrum celare constituit?
5. Cui Minos opus labyrinthum aedificandi dat?

6. Estne facile effugere e labyrintho? Cur non est?
7. Quomodo lecti sunt iuvenes qui missi sunt ad Cretam?
8. Quid erit signum si Theseus monstrum necaverit?
9. Quomodo Theseus Minotaurum superavit?
10. Cuius auxilio Theseus a Creta effugit?

II. Supply the correct form of **qui, quae, quod,** according to the case required in the subordinate clause and the number and gender of the antecedent; then translate the sentence.

1. Pasiphae erat regina _____ est adultera.
2. Minotaurus erat monstrum _____ Minos sub regiam celavit.
3. Daedalus erat artifex _____ Minos opus labyrinthum aedificandi dedit.
4. Iuvenes _____ cum Theseo navigaverunt fortes amici in itinere fiebant.
5. Insula ad _____ iuvenes navigaverunt erat Creta.
6. Minotaurus _____ iuvenes pasti sunt sub regia in labyrintho habitavit.
7. Ariadna statim Theseum amavit _____ filum et gladium dedit.
8. Ariadna Theseo docuit consilium _____ labyrinthus aedificatus erat.
9. Neptunus erat pater _____ filium iuvaret.
10. Aegeus erat pater __(whose)__ filius ad Cretam navigaverat.

III. Write each **ut** clause as a relative purpose clause, after translating:

1. Minos naves Athenas misit ut iuvenes ad Cretam portarent.
2. Aegeum iuvenes mittere oportuit ut Minotauro sacrificerentur.
3. Ariadna Theseo filum dedit ut e labyrintho educeretur.
4. Defessi ad insulam Diam navigant ut dormiant.
5. **Theseum navigare velo albo oportet ut Aegeus filium salvum esse sciat.**

IV. Change each relative clause to a relative clause of characteristic and translate both sentences:

1. Hoc est animal quod in silva *vides*.
2. Quercus est arbor qui in Africa non *crescit*.
3. Theseus est hero quem in hac fabula *invenis*.
                     quem solum in fabulis _____ .
4. Ariadne erat filia quae non *erat* fidelis patri.
5. Haec est fabula quae non credibilis *est*.

V. Supply the correct form of the impersonal verb.

   ·1. _____ Theseum navigare cum iuvenibus aliis. (*Theseus has to . . .*)

   2. _____ Theseum monstrare fortitudinem in litore Cretae. (*It is permitted . . .*)

   3. _____ Ariadnam Theseum adiuvare. (*It is pleasant for Ariadne to help Theseus*)

   4. _____ Bacchum Ariadnam servare. (*It is pleasant for Bacchus to save Ariadne.*)

   5. _____ Theseum velo albo navigare. (*Theseus has to . . .*)

VI. In Latinum convertite:

1. While Minos was waging war (*use the present tense of* **gerō**), the monster grew large in the womb of his wife.
2. Neptune made Pasiphaë fall in love with the bull because Minos had not sacrificed to him.
3. When Minos was no longer able to conceal the disgrace to his marriage couch, he had Daedalus build a labyrinth beneath the palace.
4. Maidens and youths who had no hope of escaping were fed every nine years (**novenis annis**) to the Minotaur.
5. Theseus decided to sail with the other youths to free his country.
6. When Theseus arrived in Crete Minos tried to test his courage and bravery, and hoped that he would drown in the sea.
7. Luckily the gods helped Theseus and caused Ariadne to fall in love with the hero.
8. Ariadne gave Theseus a string by which he might find the way through the many blind passages (**vias caecas**) of the labyrinth.
9. Either by chance or by the will of the gods, Ariadne was left on the island of Dia where she became the priestess of Bacchus.
10. Unfortunately Theseus did not sail home with the white sail on his ship.

Etymology

PSYCHOLOGICAL LATIN

Modern psychiatry, deriving from the investigations of Sigmund Freud and his followers, has given English many words derived from Latin or Greek words and from mythological sources, which took on a new symbolism as applied to human behavior. The following words are typical of the contribution made by this science to the English language.

id (neut. of **is**, *it*)
ego (**ego**, *I*)
psyche (Greek, **psyche**, *soul*)
suppression (**suppressum**, *pressed under*)
subliminal (**sub** + **limen**, *under the threshold*)
libido (**libido**, *desire*)
oral (**os**, **oris**, *mouth*)
anal (**anus**, *anus*, *ring*)

Consult a dictionary for the meaning and etymology of the following words:

complex	dementia precox	eros
neurosis	dementia senilis	Oedipus complex
psychosis	analysis	Electra complex
hysteria	phobia	

*   *   *   *   *

Match the words in the two columns and identity the Latin source for the words in the second column:

1. faithlessness	a. opera (**opus**, pl. **opera**, *work*)
2. an orgy	b. fallacious
3. wandering from the right course	c. janitor
4. tricky, deceitful	d. adultery
5. embryo	e. Meandering
6. great strength of mind	f. punitive
7. family	g. pasture
8. doorman (literally)	h. (sub)liminal
9. a sliding from the path, a slip	i. lapse
10. just under the threshold	j. genus
11. following a winding and turning course	k. Bacchanalia
12. shame or disgrace	l. patriotism
13. great effort in many arts combined in a single program	m. uterus
14. love for the fatherland	n. construction
15. the womb	o. virtue
16. the quality of moral excellence	p. error
17. wishful	q. fortitude
18. save energy	r. conserve
19. punishing action	s. voluntary
20. something made	t. foetus (fetus)
21. place to feed	u. opprobrium

Sententiae
Virtuti sis par, dispar fortunis patris.   *May you be like your father in*
L. Accius, *Armorum iudicium*   *courage, unlike him in fortune.*

Chapter XXX
THESEUS REX

Cum Theseus ad Graeciam rediret, aut commotus cogitatione laetitiae patris aut regis oblitus navem velo albo non ornavit; Aegeus qui velum atrum ex arce vidit se in mare iecit et mortuus est. Mare nominabatur Aegaeum, huius regis causa et exitus maesti.

Ita Theseus fiebat rex, Aegeo mortuo, et sapiens dux per multos annos populo Atheniensi auspicium felicem et iura iusta dedit. Tum Athenae habebantur domus libertatis, urbs prima totae orbis. Non iam Athenae ad Cretam tributum lamentabile mittere debebant. Templa floribus coronantur; populus Minervam cum Iove disque aliis honorat quorum templa sanguine voto muneribusque datis turibusque decorat.

Nomen Thesei per urbes Graecas sparserat et ceteri populi opem huius in magnis periculis imploraverunt. Supplex Calydon, urbs vicina, auxilium huius petivit, quamquam Meleagrum regem habebat. Causa petendi erat ingens sus, monstrum quod agros et pastores et canes et venatores Calydonis vastaverat. Populus effugit nec se esse salvum putavit donec in moenibus urbis esset. Hunc suem Calydon Theseum oravit ut necaret ut terrorem suum finiret. Vicit heros suem multis cum comitibus inter quos erant Iason et Pirithoüs[1] et virgo venatrix Atalanta[2] et princeps Calydonis, Meleager[3] ipse.

Alii Aegidem rogaverunt ut auxilium daret, imprimis septem principes qui bellum contra Thebas gesserunt, quarum rex Creon non permiserat ut hostes corpora militum mortuorum humarent.[4] Victi imploraverunt ut Theseus Thebanos cogeret ne hanc rem facerent. Non solum ille opem fert, sed etiam sapiens non permisit milites suos urbem captam vastare; mortuis sepultis pacem in terra tota fecit.

Oedipum quoque fugientem in exsilio recepit cum hic miserus nunc

---

[1] Pirithoüs, king of the Lapiths, was Theseus' best friend.
[2] See story in Chapters XVII and XVIII.
[3] Meleager loved Atalanta.
[4] Creon's refusal to allow the burial of the dead is central to the plot of the play *Antigone*.

caecus cum filiabus duabus errabat.[5] Herculi amicitiam Theseus fert postquam ille furens coniugem et liberos necaverat et postea in sanitatem mentis
revenerat. Aegides semper Herculem miratus etiam post tantum factum
malum ei persuasit ne se necaret. Hercule comite, traditur, Theseus in terram
Amazonum bellum gessit. Cum Athenas rediret Hippolytam reginam earum
secum rettulit quae maxime amata filium Hippolytum peperit. Haec autem
infelix pugnans iuxta Theseum in proelio necata est.

Verba

NOUNS

Amāzon, -onis, *f.*	Amazon (*female warrior*)
arx, arcis, *f.*	citadel
auspicium, -iī, *n.*	guidance, divination
Calydōn, -ōnis, *f.*	Calydon (*a city in Greece*)
*****canis, canis, -um,** *c.*	dog
cogitātiō, -iōnis, *f.*	thinking
exsilium, -iī, *n.*	exile
*****furor, -ōris,** *m.*	madness, insanity
*****Hippolyta, -ae,** *f.*	Hippolyta (*queen of the Amazons*)
*****Hippolytus, -ī,** *m.*	Hippolytus (*son of Theseus*)
*****iūs, iūris,** *n.*	law, justice
laetitia, -ae, *f.*	joy
*****lībertās, -tātis,** *f.*	liberty
Meleager, -grī, *m.*	Meleager (*king of Calydon*)
moenia, -ium, *n. pl.*	city walls, fortification, ramparts
*****Oedipus, -ī,** *m.*	Oedipus (*king of Thebes*)
pastor, -ōris, *m.*	shepherd
Pīrithoüs, -ī, *m.*	Pirithoüs (*friend of Theseus*)
*****prīnceps, -cipis,** *m.*	chief, leader, prince
*****proelium, -iī,** *n.*	battle
sanguis, -inis, *m.*	blood
sānitās, -tātis, *f.*	sanity, health
sūs, suis, *c.*	sow, swine, pig, boar
tribūtum, -ī, *n.*	tribute
tūs, tūris, *n.*	incense
vēnātrix, -īcis, *f.*	huntress

---

[5] Oedipus wandered in exile after the suicide of his mother/wife, Jocasta.

VERBS

*cōgō, -ere, coēgī, coactum	force, compel
*commoveō, -ēre, -mōvī, -mōtum	shake, move, disturb
*habeor, habērī (*passive of* habeō, habēre)	be held, regarded, considered
implōrō (1)	implore, beg
*mālō, mālle, māluī	prefer
*nōlō, nōlle, nōluī	not wish, not want
*oblīviscor, -viscī, oblītus sum + *gen.*	forget, be forgetful of
*pariō, -ere, peperī, partum	give birth to
*volō, velle, voluī	want, wish

ADJECTIVES

lāmentābilis, -e	deplorable, lamentable
*sapiēns, -ientis	wise
sepultus, -a, -um	buried

OTHER WORDS

*contrā + *acc.*	against
imprīmīs	especially, among the first
iuxtā + *acc.*	beside, next to
*nōn iam	no longer

Structure

163. Irregular verbs **volō, nōlō, mālō**. The conjugation of the irregular verbs based on **volō** is logical, but notice the patterns in the following paradigms:

volō, velle, voluī	nōlō, nōlle, nōluī	mālō, mālle, māluī
wish, want	*not wish, not want*	*prefer*

Indicative

volō	nōlō	mālō
vīs	nōn vīs	māvīs
vult	nōn vult	māvult
volumus	nōlumus	mālumus
vultis	nōn vultis	māvultis
volunt	nōlunt	mālunt

Imperfect Tense	**volēbam, nōlēbam, mālēbam,** etc.
Future Tense	**volam, volēs, volet, volēmus, volētis, volent**
	nōlam, nōlēs; nōlet, nōlēmus, nōlētis, nōlent
	mālam, mālēs, mālet, mālēmus, mālētis, mālent

The perfect system is entirely regular.

Subjunctive

Present:	**velim, velīs, velit, velīmus, velītis, velint**
	nōlim, nōlīs, nōlit, nōlīmus, nōlītis, nōlint
	mālim, mālīs, mālit, mālīmus, mālītis, mālint
Imperfect:	**vellem,** etc.
	nōllem, etc.
	māllem, etc.
Perfect:	**voluerim,** etc.
	nōluerim, etc.
	māluerim, etc.
Pluperfect:	**voluissem,** etc.
	nōluissem, etc.[6]
	māluissem, etc.

Present Participle

volēns	**nōlēns**	———

Imperative

Singular	———	**nōlī**	———
Plural	———	**nōlīte**	———

The imperative forms of **nōlī, nōlīte** are the regular means of expressing a negative command with the infinitives:

Sing.	**Nōlī** in perīculum **īre.**	*Do not go* into danger. (one person)
Plu.	**Nōlīte** in perīculum **īre.**	*Do not go* into danger. (more than one)
Sing.	**Nōlī** mē **tangere.**	*Do not touch* me. (Jesus to Mary Magdalene)

164. Noun clause of desire (also called indirect command or jussive noun clause):

---

[6] In describing Fortunata and her low life before Trimalchio raised her to become his wife, Petronius has one of the guests say of her: "**Noluisses** de manu illius panem accipere." ("*You would not have wished* to take bread from her hand.") The quotation is from Petronius, *Cena Trimalchionis*, ed. by T. Cutt with Introduction to the Revised Edition by J. E. Nyenhuis (Detroit: Wayne State University Press, 1970), p. 53, Sect. 37a.

This formidable array of titles introduces a quite simple construction which is closely related to the purpose clause, differing only in that it is introduced in the main clause by a verb of *asking, begging, requesting,* or *ordering.* The idea which is asked or ordered is the "desired" noun clause and its verb is in the subjunctive, introduced by **ut** or **nē**.

Rēx Herculī imperāvit **ut** leōnem **necāret.**	The king ordered Hercules *to kill* the lion.
Māter ab eō petīvit **ut cavēret.**	The mother begged him *to take care.*
Populus Thēseum ōrāvit **ut** auxilium **ferret.**	The people begged Theseus *to bring* aid
Thēseūs urbī imperāvit **ut** portās **aperīret.**	Theseus ordered the city *to open* the gates.
Prīncipēs dūcem rogāvērunt **ut** fortiter **pugnāret.**	The chiefs asked their leader *to fight* bravely.
Antigonē ōrāvit Creōntem **ut** corpus frātris **humāret.**	Antigone begged Creon *to bury* the body of her brother.
Equum hortātus est **nē verteret.**	He urged the horse *not to turn.*
Thēseūs Herculī persuāsit **nē** sē **necāret.**	Theseus persuaded Hercules *not to kill* himself.

From these examples the principle may be easily seen: a verb of desiring or commanding or persuading or asking, *i.e.* from a request to a command, followed by **ut** or **nē** and the subjunctive. Notice how closely this construction is related to a regular purpose clause. Note also the idiomatic use of certain cases after each verb:

+accusative	+ablative	+dative
ōrō Thēseum ut . . .	**petō ā Thēseō ut . . .**	**imperō Thēseō ut. . .**
rogō Thēseum ut . . .	**quaerō ā Thēseō ut . . .**	**persuādeō Thēseō**
hortor Thēseum ut . . .		**ut . . .**
moneō Thēseum ut . . .		

165. Subjunctive by attraction (or seduction, as one class in Latin preferred to call it). This use involves a change of the verb from indicative to subjunctive whenever a subordinate clause verb occurs within an indirect statement or within another subordinate clause. The logic is that a dependent construction standing within another dependent construction represents a removal from reality that the subjunctive easily expresses:

Thēseūs Thēbānīs persuāsit ut
corpora eōrum, **quī in bellō
mortuī essent**, humārent.

Theseus persuaded the Thebans
to bury the bodies of the men
who had died in the war.

The simple relative clause **quī in bellō mortuī erant** thus becomes the
subjunctive **quī in bellō mortuī essent** by attraction.

166. Subjunctive after verbs of fearing. After verbs indicating fear (**metuō**
and the deponent verb **vereor, vererī, veritus sum**) the subjunctive is used
with the meaning of **ut** and **nē** reversed:

ut   *that . . . not*
nē   *that* or *lest . . .*

Populus metuit **nē** animī,
corporibus nōn sepultīs,
aeternum **errārent**.

The people feared *lest* the souls,
if the bodies were not buried,
would wander eternally.

167. Inverted **cum** clause with the indicative. **Cum** (*when*) is used with the
indicative to make subordinate an idea that would normally in English
be the main clause of the sentence, reversing the emphasis of ideas:

Vix Thēseūs rēx factus erat
cum bellum **incēpit**.

Scarcely had Theseus become
king *when* war *began.*

Usually a word such as **vix** (*hardly, scarcely*) or **nōndum** (*not yet*) introduces the main clause.

Nōndum carmen Hymenis
incēperat **cum** virgō **adest**
aliīs mātribus et puellīs.

The song of Hymen had not yet
begun *when* the maiden *stood
present* with the other matrons
and girls.

168. Accusative of place to which. The accusative is used without a preposition to indicate place to which with names of cities, towns, small
islands and the words **dōmum** (*home*) and **rūs** (*to the country*).

Caesar **Brundisium** vēnit.
Cicerō **dōmum** revēnit.
Crās **rūs** ībō.

Caesar came *to Brundisium.*
Cicero returned *home.*
Tomorrow I shall go *to the
country.*

169. Accusative of extent of time. The accusative is used without a preposition
to indicate the time unit within which an action has occurred.

Graecī **multōs annōs** bellum ▪ contrā Trōiānōs gessērunt.	The Greeks waged war *for many years* against the Trojans.

Exercises

I. Quaestiones. Respondete Latine, quaeso.

1. Cur Theseus rex fiebat?
2. Qualia (*what kind of*) iura populo Theseus dedit?
3. Cur cives Calydonis opem a Theseo petiverunt?
4. Cur septem principes contra Thebas a Theseo petiverunt ut opem sibi daret?
5. Cur Oedipus caecus erat?
6. Cur Oedipus cum filiabus errabat?
7. Quae scenae (*scenes*) in marmore picturae sunt in templo Athenae nomine Parthenone? Ubi nunc sunt scenae in marmore?
8. In quo bello Hippolyta victa est a Theseo?
9. Quid est nomen filio Hippolytae?
10. Quomodo Hippolyta necata est?

II A. Change each of the following statements into a noun clause of desire after the introductory clause "**Rex imperavit ut . . .**" and translate the sentence, as in the example:

Theseus suem necavit.	Rex imperavit Theseo ut suem necaret. The king ordered Theseus to kill the boar.

1. Populus mortuos suos humavit.
2. Cives vitas bonas agebant.
3. Oedipus Thebis excedebat. (**Thēbīs**—*from Thebes*)
4. Hercules poenas pro furore dabat. (*paid the penalties*)
5. Pirithoüs Hippodamiam in matrimoniam ducebat. (Hippodamia was the bride of Pirithoüs at whose wedding the centaur relatives of the bride got drunk and tried to carry her off, the conflict between the centaurs and the Lapiths [the men of Pirithoüs] being the scenes depicted in marble sculpture on many public buildings in Greece.)
6. Hercules se non necavit.
7. Oedipus in exsilio errabat.
8. Septem principes contra Thebas domum ibant.

B. Now change each of the sentences above to primary sequence after "**Rex imperat . . .**" and translate the sentence.

Rex imperat Theseo ut suem necet.	The king orders Theseus to kill the sow.
1.	5.
2.	6.
3.	7.
4.	8.

C. Now substitute **iussit** for **imperavit** and change each subjunctive construction in A. to the infinitive construction, as in the example: Rex iussit Theseum suem necare.

D. Now change **Rex imperavit** to **Rex petivit** and change the object nouns to the proper case (**peto a Theseo, Sec. 164**).

III. Give a synopsis of **volo, nolo, malo,** and **fero** in the indicative, third person singular. What peculiarity of infinitive forms do these verbs have in common? Give the imperatives, singular and plural, where applicable.

IV. Change each of the following short statements into a **cum** clause within indirect discourse (see **Sec. 165**):

Theseus putabat populum futurum esse laetum cum
   1. leges bonas dedit.
   2. bellum finivit.
   3. suem necavit.
   4. Hippolytam in matrimonium duxit.
   5. pacem fecit.

V. Translate into Latin:
   1. Since Aegeus was dead, his son Theseus became king.
   2. Theseus gave good laws to the citizens of Athens and he persuaded them to live in peace.
   3. The seven against Thebes persuaded him to give them aid in their war.
   4. Theseus conquered the Amazons and persuaded one of them to return to Athens as his bride (dative, in apposition with "one of them").
   5. Theseus knew that the Amazons, who were very brave, did not want their queen to go away.

Etymology

DAYS OF THE WEEK

Naming the days of the week in Latin after the sun, moon, Mars, Mercury, Jove, Venus, and Saturn continued into Romance languages, except for the name for Sunday which was considered the Lord's day (**Dominus**). The suffix -di in French and Italian is derived from **dies**. The English equivalents for the first six days come from Germanic roots and Norse mythology: Sun-day; Mo(o)n-day; Tiw(god of war)'s-day; Wodin (king of the Norse gods)'s-day; Thor (thunder god)'s-day; Freya (goddess of love)-day; Satur(n)-day comes from the Latin Saturn, although Spanish and Italian use *Sabbath* as their source for this day's name:

English	Latin	French	Spanish	Italian
Sunday	dies solis	dimanche	domingo	domenica
Monday	dies lunae	lundi	lunes	lunedì
Tuesday	dies martis	mardi	martes	martedì
Wednesday	dies mercurii	mercredi	miércoles	mercoledì
Thursday	dies iovis	jeudi	jueves	jovedì
Friday	dies veneris	vendredi	viernes	venerdi
Saturday	dies saturni	samedi	sábado	sabbato

*   *   *   *   *

Fill in the blank at the right with the English word derived from the Latin root word at the left:

totus	e.g. _____*total*_____ warfare
mens	_____ anguish
navigo	circum _____ the globe
orbis	put a vehicle in _____
pastor	_____ , feed your flock
sanitas	a plumber, a _____ engineer
supplex	a _____ prayer
tributum	not a cent for _____
sapio	a _____ ruler
partum	giving birth, an act of _____
commoveo	such a noisy _____
vasto	a *(de-)*_____ city
imploro	I _____ your aid
corono	attend the _____ of the queen

INTERIM READING IV:
PLUTO ET PROSERPINA

Prima Ceres terram aratro dimovit,[1] prima fruges alimentaque mitia[2] terris dedit, prima leges dedit; omnia sunt dona Cereris. Carmen de Cerere canendum mihi est.[3] Utinam modo[4] dicere possim carmina digna dea. Certe dea carmine digna est.

Vasta insula Sicilia in corpore gigantis Typhoei[5] iacet premitque[6] qui saepe pugnat et surgere[7] temptat. Ingens Aetna pectora et caput premit; resupinus[8] flammas cinesque ex ore vomit[9] dum ceteri montes ceteras partes corporis premunt. Saepe vi magna surgere et magnos montes corpore devolvere[10] temptat. Deinde tellus tremit et ipse rex (Pluto) terret ne, terra fissa,[11] lux in regnum tenebrosum perveniat et trepidantes umbras terreat. Hanc rem metuens,[12] Pluto curru atrorum equorum e tenebroso regno exierat ut terras Sicilianas inspiceret.[13] Dum rex maestus insulam explorat,[14] Venus in monte suo sedens hunc videt. Dea natum volucrem[15] vocans dixit: "Cape illa tela, Cupido, quibus omnes superas, et mitte celeres[16] sagittas tuas in pectus dei. Tu superos ipsumque Iovem et deum maris regnas. Cur Pluto potentiam tuam evitat? In terra et in caelo vires amoris minuuntur.[17]

---

[1] *Ceres was the first to stir* (*first stirred*); **dīmoveō, -ēre, -mōvī, -mōtum,** *move, part, divide, stir, plow*; **arātrum, -ī,** *n., plow.*

[2] **Frux, frūgis,** *f., fruits of the earth*; **alimentum, -ī,** *n., food*; **mītis, -e,** *soft, gentle, kindly.*

[3] *I must sing* (lit., [it] *ought to be sung by me*) passive periphrastic; **canō, -ere, cecinī, cantum.**

[4] *Only.*

[5] **Typhōeūs, -eī,** *m., Typhoeus,* a giant buried beneath Mt. Etna.

[6] **Premō, -ere, pressī, pressum,** *press, lie on.*

[7] **Surgō, -ere, surrexī, surrectum,** *rise.*

[8] *On his back.*

[9] **Vomō, -ere, -uī, -itum,** *vomit forth, throw up.*

[10] *To roll off.*

[11] *When the earth is split apart*; ablative absolute.

[12] **Metuō, -uere, -uī, -ūtum,** *fear, be afraid.*

[13] **Inspiciō, -ere, -spexī, -spectum,** *look into, examine, inspect.*

[14] **Explōrō** (1), *search out, investigate, explore.*

[15] **Volucer, -cris, -cre,** *winged.*

[16] **Celer, -eris, -ere,** *swift.*

[17] *Are being diminished.*

Nonne vides Minervam et Dianam et omnes nymphas me fugitare? Filia quoque Cereris virgo erit, si patiemur.[18] At tu, pro me et pro tuo regno, iunge deam patruo."[19]

Dixit Venus; ille pharetram[20] aperuit et de mille sagittis unam acutissimam in arcu posuit. Flexile arcum curvavit[21] inque cor[22] sagitta acuta Plutonem percussit.[23]

Haud procul lacus[24] est ubi carmina cycnorum[25] audiuntur. Silva aquas frondibus suis coronat; perpetuum ver est.[26] Quo dum Proserpina ludit carpitque aut violas[27] aut candida lilia[28] impletque tunicam[29] floribus, paene simul a Plutone visa amataque raptaque est. Ita est potentia amoris.

Dea territa et matrem et comites (sed matrem saepius)[30] ore maesto clamat, et quod vestimentum laniatur,[31] collecti flores, tunica remissa,[32] ceciderunt. Tanta simplicitas ei adfuit, haec iactura[33] virgineum dolorem movit.

Raptor currus per lacum stagnaque agit et equos hortatur, nomine quemque[34] vocando. In medio stagno nympha Cyane[35] a cuius nomine stagnum dictum est, celeberrima inter nymphas Sicilianas exstitit[36] recognovitque[37] deam. "Nec longius[38] ibitis," inquit. "Non potes gener[39] Cereris invitae. Proserpina roganda, non rapienda fuit. Anapis[40] me dilexit; exorata[41] tamen nec, ut haec, exterrita nupsi.[42]

Dixit et in partes diversas bracchia tendens obstitit. Pluto autem iram non tenuit et sceptro stagnum percussit. Terra viam apertam in Tartarum

---

[18] **Patior, patī, passus sum,** *allow, suffer, endure.*
[19] **Patruus, -ī,** *m., paternal uncle.*
[20] *Quiver.*
[21] **Curvō** (1), *bend, curve.*
[22] **Cor, cordis,** *n., heart.*
[23] **Percutiō, -ere, -cussī, -cussum,** *beat. strike.*
[24] **Lacus, -ūs,** *m., lake;* **haud procul,** *not at a distance;* that is, *close by.*
[25] *Of swans.*
[26] *It is eternal spring.*
[27] *Violets.*
[28] *White lilies.*
[29] **Tunica, -ae,** *f., tunic, garment.*
[30] Comparative of **saepe,** *often.*
[31] **Laniō** (1), *tear, rip.*
[32] **Remittō, -ere, -mīsī, -missum,** *send back, free, loosen.*
[33] *Loss.*
[34] **Quisque, quaeque, quidque,** *each, each one, every one.*
[35] *Cyane,* a nymph and pool in Sicily.
[36] **Exstō, -āre, exstitī,** *stand out, be visible, show oneself, appear.*
[37] **Recognoscō, -ere, -nōvī, -nitum,** *recall, know again, recognize.*
[38] Comparative of **longē,** *no further.*
[39] **Gener, -erī,** *m., son-in-law.*
[40] *Anapis,* a river god.
[41] **Exōrō** (1), *beg, entreat, plead with.*
[42] **Nūbō, -ere, nupsī, nuptum,** *marry, be wed.*

fecit et currum medio cratere[43] recepit. At Cyane dolens et deam raptam et iura fontis sui contempta[44] mente tacita vulnus[45] gerit et omnis in lacrimas convertitur. In ipsas aquas, quarum fuerat nympha, Cyane mutatur. Molliri[46] membra videres: ossa et caerulei crines[47] digitique et crura et pedes lique- scunt;[48] post haec umeri[49] et tergum et pectus in gelidas undas abeunt; denique pro sanguine vivo subit aqua clara; nihil restat[50] quod tangere posses.

Interea filia Cereris a matre territa omnibus terris quaesita est. Aurora[51] et Hesperus[52] illam quaerentem vidit. Illa duabus manibus pinus flammi- feras[53] ab Aetna tulit; sine requiete errabat per terras filiam ab occasu solis ad ortus[54] quaerens. Quas per terras et quas undas dea erraverit longa mora est dicere. Siciliam denique repetit; dum quaerit, venit ad Cyanem; quam- quam nympha in aquas mutata narrare omnia desiderabat, tamen et os et lingua dicere non aderant. Tamen signa dedit: tunicam notam Proserpinae in summis undis natantem.[55] Tum dea capillos laniavit et pectora palmis[56] suis percussit. Nescit adhuc ubi sit filia. Tum omnes terras accusat[57] et eas ingratas vocat nec frugum munere[58] dignas. Ante alias terras maxime damnavit Siciliam in qua tunicam et vestigia filiae invenit. Vastavit agros et herbas et animalia et boves.[59] Avidae volucres semina legunt.[60]

Tum nympha Arethusa[61] caput ex undis tulit et comas a fronte[62] ad aures removit atque ait, "O mater filiae raptae et frugum, siste[63] immensos labores tuos. Terra invita nihil meruit[64] nec digna tantis poenis est. Serva has terras. Dum sub terris Stygio flumine[65] fluo, tua Proserpina oculis meis

---

[43] **Crātēra, -ae,** *f.,* or **crātēr, -ēris,** *m., large bowl, crater of a volcano.*
[44] **Contemnō, -ere, -tempsī, -temptum,** *despise, contemn, scorn.*
[45] **Vulnus, -eris,** *n., wound.*
[46] **Molliō, -īre,** *soften; become soft* (passive).
[47] **Crīnis, -is,** *m.,* (usually pl.) *the hair.*
[48] **Liquescō, -ere, licuī,** *become liquid.*
[49] **Umerus, -ī,** *m., shoulder.*
[50] **Restō, -stāre, -stitī,** *resist, oppose, stay behind, remain.*
[51] *Morning.* Aurora is the goddess of the dawn.
[52] *Evening.* Hesperus is the god of the evening.
[53] *Flame-bearing, burning.*
[54] *From the setting of the sun to its rising.*
[55] **Natō** (1), *swim, float.*
[56] **Palma, -ae,** *f., palm of the hand, hand.*
[57] **Accūsō** (1), *accuse, blame.*
[58] **Mūnus, -eris,** *n., gift;* here, *the gift of fruits of the earth.*
[59] *Cattle.*
[60] *Eager birds pick the seeds.*
[61] *Arethusa,* a nymph of a famous pool in Sicily.
[62] **Frons, -tis,** *f., forehead.*
[63] *Desist.*
[64] **Mereō, -ēre, -uī, -itum,** *deserve.*
[65] *By the River Styx.*

visa est. Illa quidem tristis[66] neque etiam adhuc interrita sed tamen est regina maxima regni obscuri, tamen uxor regis inferni."[67]

Mater haec verba audiens similis saxi fuit, dea pulsa est ira et dolore. Curribus in oras aetherias[68] exit: ibi ante Iovem capillis passis[69] stetit. "Pro mea filia veni supplex tibi, Iuppiter," inquit, "et pro filia tua; si nulla gratia matris est tibi, nata patrem moveat. En filia diu quaesita tandem[70] inventa est, si vocas invenire eam certius amittere, aut si eam invenire vocas, scire ubi sit. Pluto eam reddat. Feremus quod[71] rapta est, si modo eam reddet. Neque tua filia est digna praedone[72] coniuge."

Iuppiter respondit, "Nata tua est cura communis mihi tecum, sed si modo nomina vera rebus dare placet, non iniuria est hoc factum, sed amor. Neque ille erit nobis gener pudori,[73] si tu modo, dea, velis. Si cetera desint, quantum[74] est fratrem Iovis esse. Sed si tanta cupido discidii[75] est tibi, repetet Proserpina caelum, tamen lege certa, si nullos cibos illic ore tetigit.

Dixerat, at Cereri certum est educere natam; non ita fata sinunt,[76] quoniam Proserpina ederat. Dum in hortis cultis[77] errat, pomum poeniceum[78] de arbore curva carpserat et in ore suo septem grana[79] presserat.

At Iuppiter medius fratris sui et sororis maestae annum ex aequo[80] dividit; nunc dea communis duorum regnorum sex menses[81] cum matre, sex menses cum coniuge agit. Facies et oris et mentis vertitur dum filia cum matre est. Proserpina quae maesta Plutoni videbatur nunc laeta est, ut sol qui nubibus[82] obscuris ante tectus fuit, nunc e nubibus exit et terrae lucem dat.   *Metamorphoses* V. 341–571 (adapted)

---

[66]**Tristis, -e,** *sad.*
[67]**Infernus, -a, -um,** *lower, underground, infernal.*
[68] *Aetherial shores,* i.e., *heaven.*
[69] *With disheveled hair.*
[70]**Tandem,** *adv., at last, at length.*
[71]**Quod,** *the fact that.*
[72] *Worthy of a robber husband.*
[73] *A disgrace to us;* double dative.
[74] *How great a thing it is . . .*
[75] *To separate* (lit., *of separating*) *the couple.*
[76]**Sinō, -ere, sīvī, situm,** *let, allow, permit.*
[77]**Cultus, -a, -um,** *cultivated, well-tended, planted.*
[78] *Phoenician;* the fruit is identified as the pomegranate.
[79] *Seeds.*
[80] *Equally.*
[81]**Mensis, -is,** *m., month.*
[82]**Nūbes, -is,** *f., cloud.*

The Trojan War

Probably no war in history has been so far-reaching in its effect on subsequent literature as the real or fictional expedition of the Greeks to bring home from Troy the captured Helen and to destroy the city of Priam, whose son Paris had caused so much suffering to both Trojans and Greeks. Quite familiar is the legend material, probably based on historical events of war and conquest by Hellenic tribes from the Peloponnesus against older cities on the coast of Asia Minor. Such a war for plunder, for revenge, or for carrying off treasure and captive women, provided much material for the bard who sang nightly in the halls of great princes, reciting in chanted verse the adventure of some great chief, the battle between great heroes, the quarrels between rival chieftains, or the beauty of some ancient princess. Added to the affairs of mortal men were the tales of the gods who regularly intervened in the stories to aid a favorite or to pursue an enemy.

The story of the Trojan war begins with the wedding of Peleus and Thetis, to which Eris, the goddess of Discord, has not been invited. The

offended goddess takes revenge for the slight by introducing into the festivi-
ties the golden apple on which is inscribed "To the Fairest." A quarrel ensues
between the three leading goddess-contenders for the title—Juno, Minerva,
and Venus—and Jupiter chooses as judge for the contest the Trojan Paris
who awards the golden apple to the goddess of Love, unfairly bribed by her
on the promise that he is to receive the most beautiful woman in the world to
be his wife.

Complications arise from the unfortunate (for Paris) marital status of
this most beautiful lady, Helen, whose position as wife of Menelaus, King of
Sparta in the Greek Peloponnesus, makes her quite unattainable by legal
means. Her abduction, therefore, has to be admittedly improper, with Paris
breaking the important bonds of host-guest relationship in carrying off his
host's wife while a visitor in Sparta. King Menelaus does not stand alone in
his injury to pride and home, for his relatives and friends have all promised
to help defend his marriage, should it ever be threatened. They all rally to
his cause, assembling a fleet at Aulis to sail to Troy to recover the lost Helen.

Included in the assembly of Greek leaders are Agamemnon, Prince of
Mycenae and brother of Menelaus; the great warrior Achilles, who with his
Myrmidons provided a formidable army himself; the mighty Ajax, son of
Telamon of Salamis; the aged Nestor of Pylos; and the wily Ulysses
(Odysseus), King of Ithaca. The latter's subsequent adventures on the way
home from the war in a ten-year series of detours provide the substance for
the *Odyssey*, the sequel to Homer's first epic poem describing part of the
ten-year war at Troy, the *Iliad*.

The Greek fleet has assembled at Aulis, ready to sail, when the wind
dies down and the becalmed Greeks seek from the priests the reason for the
delay. The explanation given is that a sacred animal of Diana has been killed
and the fleet must remain at Aulis until this affront to deity has been expiated
in the form of the sacrifice of the young Iphigenia, daughter of Agamemnon.
Such a sacrifice is an ancient motif in folk literature, that of human sacrifice
to appease an injured deity. The father naturally is reluctant to accept the
honor of having his daughter sacrificed, but persuasion by the other leaders,
especially Ulysses, finally affects his decision to have the girl brought to the
fleet. Not daring openly to reveal the reason for summoning the girl,
Agamemnon pretends that Iphigenia is being brought to be the bride of
Achilles so that Clytemnestra, his wife, will comply with his request. Then
treacherously he allows the sacrifice to take place. Luckily for the girl, however, Diana relents at the last moment, substituting a deer at the altar, and
wrapping the girl in a cloud, she spirits her away to safety to become priestess
at the temple of Diana in Tauris. The scene is reminiscent of the sacrifice
demanded of Abraham where an animal is substituted for Isaac at the last
moment. Both incidents are probably indicative of a social order in which a
memory of human sacrifice remained at a time when the human blood rite

had become abhorrent, the substitution of the animal making the ritual more acceptable. Ovid, delighting in the visual drama of the scene of Iphigenia being slain, tells the story twice, himself as narrator in Book XII, and in the words of Ulysses again in Book XIII.

Ovid was quite aware that his readers were familiar with the episodes of the Trojan War, both from the *Iliad* and the *Odyssey* in Greek and from early Latin imitations of these epics. Furthermore, Virgil, the giant of court poetry, had recently completed the *Aeneid*, the story of the wanderings of the Trojan prince Aeneas as he comes to Italy to found an Italian nation, an elaborate epic written in frank admiration and imitation of the epics of Homer, with six books of *Odyssey*-like wanderings and six books of *Iliad*-like warfare in Italy between Aeneas and the local prince Turnus. Thus if Ovid was to include the story of the Trojan War, he had to find an original approach, for he had no wish to compete for laurels with Virgil, Rome's greatest epic poet. Though Ovid does include almost three books devoted to Trojan War episodes in the *Metamorphoses* (Books XII–XIV), he handles the material in a unique manner, emphasizing certain stories omitted by other poets and dramatists and neglecting some of the more familiar parts of the tale completely. He does, however, enjoy retelling the sacrifice of Iphigenia, and the reading section begins with this tale.

Note how the poetic devices of richly decorative words, unusual word order, certain shortened verb forms, and the recurrent beat of the meter all create new dimensions of meaning, but demand new skills to master and appreciate. One can almost hear the ancient poet chanting his tale, creating his visual images in serial manner in a time when there was no other nightly entertainment for the telling of tales.

Sententiae

Tantum religio potuit suadere malorum.   *Religion could persuade men to*
   Lucretius, *De rerum natura* I.101   *such evil deeds.*

   A New Format: *Beginning with this chapter a new format will be used.*
A short portion of the reading will be followed by explanatory notes and
vocabulary. For instance, Selection **31a** *in the reading will be accompanied by*
31a *in the notes and vocabulary. Selection* **31b** *of the reading then follows, with*
its corresponding notes and vocabulary. The usual sections of Structure and
Exercises follow. As before, vocabulary words to be acquired are indicated by
an asterisk (*). *The other words and explanatory notes need not be memorized.*
Selections **31a–d** *depart noticeably from Ovid's metrical phrasing to provide a*
transition into the poetry which begins in Selection **31e**.

Chapter XXXI
BELLUM TROIANUM: SACRIFICIUM IPHIGENIAE

31a   Paris, filius Priami regis Troiae, longum bellum in patriam
         attulit cum Helena rapta esset. Mille rates et omnes Pelasgae gentes
         coniuratae sequuntur. Nec poena dilata foret, nisi saevi venti
         fecissent aequora invia et tellus Aulide puppes tenuisset.

31a

*__Paris, Paridis__, *m.*, *Paris*, son of King Priam, was exposed as a child because of a prophecy that
   he would cause disaster to his father's kingdom. The prince, therefore, had been reared as a
   shepherd on the slopes of Mt. Ida near Troy, and he was selected to be the judge in the beauty
   contest between the three goddesses, Juno, Minerva, and Venus.
*__Priamus, -ī__, *m.*, *King Priam* of Troy is supposed to have had fifty sons and fifty daughters.
*__bellum, -ī__, *n.*, *war*.
*__adferō, -ferre, attulī, allātum__, *bring to*, *cause*, *bring about*.
*__Helena, -ae__, *f.*, *Helen*.
*__mīlle, mīlia, mīlium__, *thousand*, indeclinable in singular; abbreviated **M** in Roman numerals:
   MCMLXXII = 1972.
*__ratis, ratis__, *f.*, *ship*, *boat*, *vessel*.
__Pelasgus, -a, -um__, *Pelasgian* or *Greek*. The Pelasgians were the oldest inhabitants of Greece, and
   the name is used poetically to refer to the Greeks.
__gentēs coniūrātae__, all the Greek *tribes sworn together*; *__gēns, gentis__, *f.*, *tribe*.
__nec dīlāta foret__ (= dīlāta futūra esset), a syncopated or shortened form used in poetry: *would not*
   have been delayed; *__differō, differre, distulī, dīlātum__, *carry in different directions*, *delay*, *post-*
   pone.
*__aequor, -oris__, *n.*, *flat or level surface* of land or sea; hence, poetically *the sea* itself (from **aequus**,
   -a, -um).
*__invius, -a, -um__, *impassable*.
__tellūs, -ūris__, *f.*, *land*, *earth*.
__Aulide__, *at Aulis*, locative case; review locative forms, **Sec. 151**.
*__puppis, puppis__, *f.*, *ship*.

305

31b   Hic de more patrio cum Iovi sacra parassent ut ara accensis ignibus incanduit, Danai draconem in arbore videre quae proxima aris sacris stabat. Nidus erat bis quattuor volucrum arbore summa, quas serpens avido ore corripuit et matrem volantem circum sua damna.

31c   Augur "Vincemus" ait "Pelasgi; gaudete! Troia cadet si nos moram longam belli ferre poterimus. Novem volucres in novem annos belli digerit."

31d   At permanet Neptunus violentus in undis et bella non transfert. Sunt qui credant Neptunum Troiae parcere (quia moenia urbi fecerat) et iram virginis deae sanguine virgineo placandam esse. Si Danai Iphigeniam Agamemnonis filiam sacrificaverint, venti rates movebunt.   *Met.* XII.5–29, adapted passim

In Book XIII Ulysses tells how he was responsible for persuading Agamemnon to sacrifice his daughter. Ulysses brags about his eloquence as he recounts his achievements before the Greek chiefs, trying to claim the

---

31b

dē mōre patriō, *according to ancient custom*; *mōs, mōris, *m.*, *custom, habit.*

parāvissent becomes parāssent in its syncopated form; cum circumstantial.

incandēscō, -ere, -canduī, *begin to glow or whiten*, especially with heat or fire (ignibus accensīs, *kindled fires*).

*Danaī, -ōrum, *m.*, *the Danai* or *the Greeks*, a particular tribe being used for all the Greeks.

*vīdēre—syncopated form of vīdērunt, (*they*) *saw.*

nīdus, -ī, *m.*, *nest.*

*bis quattuor volucrum, *eight birds*, (lit., *twice four birds*), gen. of the whole.

*ōs, ōris, *n.*, *mouth* or any opening such as the harbor of a river or the opening of a cave. Do not confuse with os, ossis, *n.*, *bone.*

corripuit, *snatched at.*

damna, a substantive for *her condemned ones*, or *her doomed offspring.*

31c

*augur, -uris, *m.*, *the augur*, fortune teller or prophet who frequently told the future on the basis of interpreting natural phenomena, the flight of birds, or the entrails of animals.

ait, *say, affirm, assert*; *āiō, aïs, aït, āiunt, defective and postpositive.

dīgerō, -ere, -gessī, -gestum, *spread, arrange, interpret.*

31d

*permaneō, -ēre, -mānsī, *remain.*

*Neptūnus, -ī, *m.*, *Neptune*, god of the sea, had helped to build the walls of Troy.

violentus, -a, um, *violent.*

*trānsferō, -ferre, -tulī, -lātus, *carry across, transfer.*

urbī: dat. of reference, the walls *of the city*; *urbs, urbis, *f.*

*sunt quī, *there are those who . . .*

crēdant, *may believe that . . .*; followed by two infinitives in indirect statement, parcere and placandum esse. *parcō, parcere, pepercī, *spare*, followed by the dative case; placandam esse, gerundive with sum, the passive periphrastic implying obligation or necessity, *must be appeased* (see Sec. 184).

virgineus, -a, -um, *maidenly, of the maiden, virgin* (Iphigenīa, -ae, *f.*).

placō (1), *calm, quiet, appease.*

armor of Achilles by virtue of his greater cleverness whereas the other claimant for the armor of dead Achilles, the mighty Ajax, can recite only deeds in battle which he has done in the war with the Trojans. Here are the words of Ulysses:

31e "Ut dolor unius Danaos pervenit ad omnes,
    exspectata diu, nulla aut contraria classi
    flamina erant, duraeque iubent Agamemnona sortes
    inmeritam saevae natam mactare Dianae.
    Denegat hoc genitor divisque irascitur ipsis
    atque in rege tamen pater est; ego mite parentis
    ingenium verbis ad publica commoda verti:
    difficilem tenui sub iniquo iudice causam.
31f Hunc tamen utilitas populi fraterque datique
    summa movet sceptri, laudem ut cum sanguine penset;
    mittor et ad matrem, quae non hortanda, sed astu
    decipienda fuit. Sed si Telamonius isset,
    orba suis essent etiam nunc lintea ventis."

Met. XIII.181–195 passim

31e

*dolor, -ōris, *m.*, grief.
*ūnīus, gen. of ūnus, *of one man*, that is, Agamemnon.
contrārius, -a, -um, *against* + dat.
nūlla, *not (at all)*, i.e., *there were no winds or* . . .
flāmen, -inis, *n., a blowing of the wind, blasts*; exspectāta diū, *long awaited*.
*classis, classis, *f., the fleet*.
sors, sortis, *f., casting of lots, prophecy*; here the plural refers to the harsh prophecy, subject of iubent.
*Agamemnōn, -onis, *m., Agamemnon*. The form Agamemnona is a Greek accusative, subject of mactāre, *to sacrifice*.
*in- or immeritus, -a, -um, *undeserving of punishment* or *innocent*.
dēnegō (1), *refuse*
genitor, -ōris, *m., father, producer*.
*irāscor, -ī, īrātus sum, *be angry*.
dīvus, -ī, *m., a divinity, god*.
*mītis, -e, *mild, soft, kind, gentle*, modifies ingenium.
*ingenium, -iī, *n., nature*.
ad pūblica commoda, *to the common good*.
*vertō, -ere, vertī, versum, *turn*.
causam tenēre, *plead a case*.
sub inīquō iūdice, *before a biased* (unfair) *judge*.

31f

ūtilitās, -tātis, *f., usefulness*.
summā sceptrī datī, *the chief command intrusted* (to him); lit., *the highest part of the scepter having been given*.
pēnsō (1), *weigh, estimate, consider*.
laus, laudis, *f., esteem, fame, glory*.   (31f continues overleaf)

31g   Consilium Ulixis erat dolosum. Si Clytemnestra filiam mittat,
           Achilles princeps eam in matrimonium ducat. Mater laeta
           Iphigeniam mittit ut filia coniunx herois praeclari Danaorum fiat.
31h   . . . postquam pietatem publica causa
           rexque patrem vicit, castumque datura cruorem
           flentibus ante aram stetit Iphigenia ministris,
           victa dea est nubemque oculis obiecit et inter
           officium turbamque sacri vocesque precantum
           supposita fertur mutasse Mycenida cerva.

                    . . . .

31k   Accipiunt ventos a tergo mille carinae
           multaque perpessae Phrygia potiuntur harena.

                                              Met. XII.29–38 passim

---

quae nōn hortanda sed astū dēcipienda fuit, *who was not to be urged, but had to be deceived by
    cunning* (passive periphrastic).
Telamōnius, *Ajax,* the son of Telamon, king of Salamis in Greece. There is another Ajax, a lesser
    hero, in the Trojan war, Ajax, son of Oïleus.
isset, pluperf. subjv. in a contrary-to-fact condition.
linteum, -ī, *n., linen cloth, sail.*
orbus, -a, -um, +gen. or abl., *deprived of, without.*

                              31g
*dolōsus, -a, -um, *tricky, crafty.*
Achillēs, -is, *m., Achilles,* a Greek hero, son of Peleus and Thetis.
praeclārus, -a, -um, *famous.*
*fīō, fierī, factus sum, *become.*

                              31h
pūblica causa, *the common good.*
castumque datūra cruōrem, *about to shed her innocent blood,* **datūra** modifies **Īphigenīa**.
*fleō, -ēre, flēvī, flētum, *weep.*
minister, -trī, *m., attendant, official;* here probably *a priest.*
obiciō, -ere, -iēcī, -iectum, *cast before,* with dat. of compound.
nūbēs, -is, *f., cloud.*
*officium, -iī, *n., ceremonial action, duties.*
*turba, -ae, *f., crowd* (attending the *sacred rite,* **sacrum, -ī,** *n.*).
precantum, *of those praying.*
*fertur, *it is said;* **Mycēnida** (Greek acc.: *the Mycenaean maiden*) is the subject of **mūtāsse** (ind.
    statement).
mūtāsse is **mūtāvisse** syncopated, *replaced, changed places with* (+abl. **cervā**).
*cerva, -ae, *f., a hind, a deer,* modified by **suppositā,** *(having been) put in her place.*

                              31k
carīna, -ae, *f., keel, ship,* use of the part of the vessel to represent the whole ship, a literary device
    called **pars prō tōtō.**
*ā tergō, *at their back.*
multa perpessae, *having suffered many adventures.*
potior, -īrī, potītus sum, *gain possession of, arrive at,* with abl.
Phrygiā harēnā, *the sandy beach of Phrygia,* the land in which Troy is located.

Thus Ovid completes the tale of Iphigenia, but not so the earlier Greek playwright, Euripides, who, like Diana, transports the girl from the scene of the sacrifice to the island of Tauris where she is set down to assume duties as the priestess of Diana in that barbarian region where all strangers are sacrificed to the goddess. The king of the island, Thoas, falls in love with the maiden and wishes to keep her forever in his land. In Euripides' play, Iphigenia's brother Orestes comes to the island, and when the two finally discover their relationship, they plan to escape by sea. Thoas pursues, but he is prevented from apprehending the fugitives by the intervention of the gods in the form of a storm, a "deus ex machina" device of Greek drama to affect the outcome by a force outside the play.

The same material is handled by the eighteenth-century German writer Goethe, who, in a most classically structured drama based on the same story, accounts for the departure of Iphigenia from the land of Tauris by a character change within Thoas who relents in his physical pursuit of the maiden priestess and decides to allow her, whom love cannot hold, to leave of her own free will. Thoas becomes humanly real as a person and grows in stature as a man and as a king. Characters as pawns of fate or as instruments of the gods pale beside this new dimensional portrait.

Structure

170. Conditions. A sentence consisting of a subordinate clause introduced by **sī** (*if*) or **nisi** (*if . . . not*) and a concluding main clause is called a condition. The verbs of both clauses are in the indicative if the condition is a real possibility, but in the subjunctive if the condition is unreal, vague, improbable, or contrary-to-fact.

Real conditions (Indicative Mood in both clauses)

Present:	**Sī** hoc **temptat,** fortis **est.**	*If he tries* this, *he is* brave.
Imperfect:	**Sī** hoc **temptābat,** fortis **erat.**	*If he tried* this, *he was* brave.
Future:	**Sī** hoc **temptābit,** fortis **erit.**	*If he tries* (will try) this, *he will be* brave.
Future Perfect:	**Sī** hoc **temptāverit,** fortis **erit (fuerit).**	*If he will try* (will have tried) this, *he will* be (have been) brave.

The Roman mind delighted in the logic of this last combination of time ideas, for a future act would have had to be completed in the past in order for the conclusion to be logical. The use of the future or future perfect in both clauses is called by some grammarians the *Future More Vivid.*

Unreal Conditions (Subjunctive in both clauses)

Present: **Sī** hoc **temptet**, fortis   *If he should try* this, *he would be*
sit.   brave.

This clause is sometimes called the *should . . . would clause*; some texts
refer to this use as the *Less Vivid*.

Contrary-to-Fact:

Imperfect: **Sī** hoc **temptāret**,   *If he tried* this, *he would be*
fortis **esset**.   brave.

The implication is that *he had not tried it.*

Pluperfect: **Sī** hoc **temptāvisset**,   *If he had tried* this, *he would have*
fortis **fuisset**.   *been* brave.

Again the implication is that *he had not tried it.*
Let us try some sentences from the reading:

Fut. Ind.	Trōia **cadet sī nōs** moram longam bellī ferre **poterimus**.	Troy *will fall if we can* bear the long delay of war (*lit., will be able to* bear).
Pres. Subj.	**Sī** Clytemnēstra fīliam **mittat**, Achillēs eam in mātrimōnium **ducat**.	*If* Clytemnestra *should send* her daughter, Achilles *would marry* her.
Contrary- to-Fact	**Sī** Aiāx **īsset**, sine suīs **essent** etiam nunc lintea ventīs.	*If* Ajax *had gone*, the sails *would* now *be* devoid of winds. The implication is that Ajax had *not* gone.

171. Reading poetry. Reading poetry demands a more imaginative kind of
comprehension than reading prose, since the poet is freed from the con-
ventional language of direct statement and tries to communicate in an
exciting or unusual manner, using any device that he finds effective to
convey an idea. He may condense many ideas into few words; he may
depend on certain rhythms to reflect the mood of his ideas; he may use
unusual word order to gain a certain effect; he may make use of decorative, sensuous, foreign, or unusual words.

a) Let us first explore *the unusual word order* and see what effect is gained
by it.

flentibus ante āram stetit Īphigenīa ministrīs.

Notice how the adjective **flentibus** describing the attendants or priests is separated by the whole of the main sentence (adverbial phrase, verb, subject) from **ministrīs**, the noun modified. There is no possibility of losing the meaning, since the endings (both in the ablative plural) make this absolute phrase a unity, but within the unity is the whole reason for the **ministrī** being there and for their **flentibus**, for their weeping. This is visually arresting word order and it is here very effective. A modern poet like E. E. Cummings uses the physical arrangement of words on a page to gain his effect in the same manner. Notice the image of Iphigenia standing between the weeping priests.

b) Meter. Many times the unusual word order is also the result of the poet fitting his ideas into the meter of the line; in the case of the meter of epic poetry, Ovid uses in the *Metamorphoses*, as Virgil in the *Aeneid*, dactylic hexameter with spondaic alternations. This meter is discussed in the Appendix under Reading Latin Poetry. It consists of six measures or feet to a verse, each a dactyl or spondee.

c) Poetic forms. Several contractions in the spelling of verbs appear in poetry and should be mastered so that confusion is avoided.

vidēre < **vidērunt**	they have seen
parāssent < **parāvissent**	they had prepared
mūtāsse < **mūtāvisse**	to have changed
(dilata) foret < **futūrus, -a, -um, esset**	would have been (delayed or postponed)
fore < **futūrum esse**	to be going to be (about to be)

d) Name and place allusions. The poet delights in giving the genealogy, geography, history, or any other details of local color to enliven his material. Therefore he will call Ulysses the son of Laertes, or Aeneas the son of Venus, or the brothers Agamemnon and Menelaus, the **Atrīdēs**, the sons of Atreus, and he will make allusions to the ancient Pelasgians and the **Danaī** and the Phrygian sands. In giving genealogy, the poet regularly uses the ending **-idēs** to mean "*the son of*" the person to whose name the suffix is attached; just as the English name Stephenson means the son of Stephen. (The *-vich* ending in Russian serves the same purpose.)

Exercises

I.   Respondete Latine:

1. Quis est coniunx rapta a Paride?
2. Quis est pater Paridi?
3. Estne pulcherrima femina virgo aut coniunx? Cui coniunx?

4. Quis est frater regi Spartae?
5. Qui sunt duces qui cum classe Aulide convenerunt?
6. Cur classis non navigavit?
7. Quot rates erant Aulide?
8. Quem Danai viderunt in arbore proxima sacrae arae?
9. Quot annos erit bellum inter Danaos et Troianos?
10. Cur Clytemnestra filiam Iphigeniam ad classem misit?
11. Quis mittitur ad Clytemnestram ut ei persuadeat ut filiam ad classem mittat?

II. Translate the following conditions, noting the shades of meaning indicated by the changes in tense and mood:

Real	1. Si Caesar adest, bene est.
Real	2. Si Caesar aderat, bene erat.
Real	3. Si Caesar aderit, bene erit.
Real	4. Si Caesar adfuerit, bene erit.
Unreal	5. Si Caesar adsit, bene sit.
Unreal	6. Si Caesar adesset, bene esset.
Unreal	7. Si Caesar adfuisset, bene fuisset.

(Rewrite 1–7 using the forms of **veniō** instead of **adsum**)

8. Si me amabit, fidelis erit.
9. Si me amavit, fidelis fuit.
10. Si me amet, fidelis sit.
11. Si me amavisset, fidelis fuisset.
12. Si me vides, te saluto.
13. Si te videbo, te salutabo.
14. Si te videbit, te salutabit.
15. Si te videat, te salutet.
16. Si te viderem, te salutarem.
17. Si te vidissem, te salutavissem.
18. Nisi venti movent, rates non navigare possunt.
19. Nisi venti movebant, rates non navigare poterant.
20. Nisi venti movebunt, rates non navigare poterunt.
21. Nisi venti moverint, rates non navigare potuerint.
22. Nisi venti moveant, rates non navigare possint.
23. Si rex ero, pecuniam pauperibus dabo.
24. Si rex sim, pecuniam pauperibus dem.
25. Si rex essem, pecuniam pauperibus darem.
26. Si rex fuissem, pecuniam pauperibus dedissem.

III. Construct a conditional sentence using the vocabulary of the lesson to demonstrate the real and unreal uses of the Indicative and Subjunctive. See 1–7 above.

IV. Name the meters of a two-foot line
                     a three-foot line
                     a four-foot line
                     a five-foot line
                     a six-foot line

Indicate the schematic length of the following feet:

| iamb | dactyl | |
| trochee | spondee | anapest |

What is the meter of the *Metamorphoses*? Indicate the pattern of the dactyls and spondees in this meter.

Etymology

MONTHS OF THE YEAR

January	**Januarius**	**Janus**, two-headed god of doorways
February	**Februarius**	the **Februa**, days of atonement and cleansing
March	**Martius**	**Mars**, the god of War
April	**Aprilis**	**aperire** (*to open*) or Aphrodite
May	**Maius**	**Maia**, mother of Mercury by Jupiter, or **maiores** (*the older ones*)
June	**Junius**	**Juno**, wife of Jupiter, or **juniores** (*the younger ones*)
July	**Julius**	originally **Quintilis** (*the fifth month*) renamed for Julius Caesar
August	**Augustus**	originally **Sextilis** (*the sixth month*), renamed for Augustus Caesar
September	**September**	**septem**; originally the seventh month
October	**October**	**octo**; originally the eighth month
November	**November**	**novem**; originally the ninth month
December	**December**	**decem**; originally the tenth month

The Kalends (**Kalendae**) were the first of each month.
The Ides (**Ides**) were either the fifteenth or the thirteenth.
The Nones (**Nones**) were either the seventh or the fifth.

Days between these monthly designations were reckoned as so many days *before* the Kalends or the Nones or the Ides. See Appendix for a full account of the Roman calendar.

*   *   *   *   *

What Latin roots account for these English derivatives?

| bellicose | oral |
| turbulence | augury |

rapture

minister

dragon

summit

permanent

transfer

contrary

Sententiae

Pallida Mors aequo pulsat pede pauperum tabernas regumque turres.	*Pale death with impartial foot knocks at the door of poor men's hovels and kings' palaces.*
Horace, *Carmina* IV.13	

Chapter XXXII
BELLUM TROIANUM: MORS CYGNI

The report (**Fama**) of the armada of invasion reached Troy long before the Greek ships appeared off the Phrygian coast. The ships pulled up on to the sandy beaches, and the battle began with great slaughter on both sides. Single combat between heroes is often described by epic writers in the style of Homer, who recounts in the *Iliad* events of a war which may have taken place about three hundred and fifty years before his time. The great wonder is that so much of what Homer tells us is fairly accurate (allowing for anachronisms such as describing weapons that had not yet been made of certain materials), although the conversations and challenges that the heroes exchange are, of course, part of poetic convention. Ovid here, nearly eight hundred years after Homer, describes the same war and a particular battle between Achilles and Neptune's son Cygnus, who is fighting on the side of the Trojans.

32a   Fecerat fama notum Graias cum milite forti
      adventare rates neque inexspectatus in armis
      hostis adest; prohibent aditus litusque tuentur
      Troes, et
              magno quid Achaica dextera posset
      sanguine senserunt, et iam Phrygia rubebant
      litora, iam leto proles Neptunia, Cygnus,

32a

*fāma, -ae, f., report, rumor.
***Grāius, -a, -um**, *Greek*; The Romans gave the many tribes living in Greece the name **Grāiī** or **Graecī**, from the name of a Greek family living in the Naples area of **Magna Graecia**. The name spread to cover all the other tribes—the Achaeans, the Danai, the Pelasgi, and the Hellenes, none of whom ever called themselves **Graecī**.
ratēs Grāiās adventāre, indirect statement telling what rumor had made known. Note the sequence of tenses here: *had made known* that the Greek ships *were arriving.*
inexspectātus, -a, -um, *unexpected.*
***adventō** (1), *arrive, approach.*

(32a continues overleaf)

32b   mille viros dederat, iam curru instabat Achilles
       agmina perque acies aut Cygnum aut Hectora quaerens
       occurrit Cygno (decimum dilatus in annum
       mors Hectoris erat): tum . . .
       exhortatus equos currum direxit in hostem
       concutiensque suis vibrantia tela lacertis
       "quisquis es, o iuvenis" dixit "solamen habeto
       mortis, ab Aeacide quod sis iugulatus Achille!"

---

*aditus, -ūs, *m., approach*; here, accusative plural.

*lītus, lītoris, *n., shore*.

tueor (tuor), tuērī, tūtus sum, *protect*; Tuēbor, "I shall protect," is the motto of the state of Michigan.

Trōes, *the Trojans*, subject of prohibent.

quid . . . posset, an indirect question completing the idea of sensērunt. *They realized what power the Achaean (Greek) army possessed* (lit., what the Achaean hand was able [to do]—what power was in the Achaean hand). Try several different possibilities for this image and you will see the problems of the translator as he tries to approximate the image of the original.

Phrygius, -a, -um, *Phrygian*; Phrygia lītora, *the Phrygian shores*.

rubeō, rubēre, *to be red* (with what?) or perhaps from rubēscō, rubēscere, rubuī, *grow* or *become red*; this verb is inceptive; that is, it has the ending -escō (*to become*) in the present forms. Naturally, after the present tense the inceptive form is not used.

lētum, -ī, *n., death*.

prōles, prōlis, *f., offspring*.

Neptūnius, -a, -um, *Neptunian*.

Cygnus, the name of the Neptunian offspring, *Cygnus* (meaning *swan*, into which the appropriate metamorphosis takes place at the end of the story).

32b

*instō, -stare, -stitī, *stand in, follow closely, press on*.

*agmen, -inis, *n., battle line, column of troops, army ranks*.

aciēs, -ēī, *f., the whole army*.

*Hectora, Greek accusative form.

*decimus, -a, -um, *tenth*.

dīlātus erat, from *differō, *delay*.

exhortātus, perfect participle of a deponent verb is translated as active, *having urged*.

*dīrigō, -rigere, -rexī, -rectum, *direct*.

*in + acc., *against*; in hostem, *against the enemy*.

concutiō, -ere, -cussī, -cussum, *shake violently, agitate*.

vibrantius, -a, -um, *vibrating, quivering*.

*tēlum, -ī, *n., weapon, spear, javelin*.

*lacertus, -ī, *m., arm, shoulder*.

quisquis, *whoever*.

sōlāmen, -inis, *n., comfort, consolation*; here acc. sing.

habētō, future imperative (see Sec. 176); *consider* is a second meaning for habeō, in the sense of "have in mind, hold in your thought."

quod iugulātus sīs, *the fact that you have been butchered by Achilles*, the son of Aeacus (really his grandfather); the whole quod clause is in apposition with sōlāmen, explaining the consolation.

32c   Heros ita fatus est: vocem gravis hasta secuta est,
        sed quamquam certa nullus fuit error in hasta,
        nil tamen mortis cum ferro emisso volavit.
        "Nate dea, nam te fama praenovimus" inquit
        Cygnus "cur a nobis vulnus miraris abesse?"
32d   (mirabatur Achilles enim.) "Nec haec cassis quam vides
        neque scutum, onus sinistrae,
        auxilio mihi sunt; decor est quaesitus ab illis;
        Mars quoque ob hoc capere arma solet! [Si] removebitur huius
        tegminis officium, tamen indestrictus abibo;
        est aliquid non esse natum Nereide, sed qui
        Nereaque et natas et totum temperat aequor."

32c

fatus est, *spoke*, from **fateor** (deponent).
*__hasta__, -ae, *f.*, *spear*, modified by **certa**.
*__nīl mortis__, genitive of the whole.
*__ferrum__, ī, *n.*, *iron weapon, spear*. Iron had not been invented as a metal for use in weapons of war in Trojan war times, but the Romans of Ovid's day had developed iron weapons, as had the smiths of Homeric times.
Nāte deā, *goddess born*, **nāte** is vocative and **deā** ablative.
*__praenoscō__, -ere, *get to know beforehand*.
fāmā, *by reputation*, abl. of means
ā nōbis, *from me*, the plural used for the singular.
mirāris is followed by indirect statement (**abesse**).

32d

nec . . . neque, *neither . . . nor*.
cassis, -idis, *f.*, *helmet of metal*.
*__scūtum__, -ī, *n.*, *shield*.
*__onus__, oneris, *n.*, *burden*.
*__sinistra__, -ae, *f.*, *left hand*; portents on the left were considered unfavorable and therefore were associated with unpleasant, undesirable ideas, hence, the English word *sinister*.
auxiliō mihi, *as an aid for me*, a double dative usage (see Sec. 177).
decor, -ōris, *m.*, *beauty, grace*.
Mars, Martis, *m.*, *Mars*, the god of warfare.
ob hoc, *for this purpose*.
solet, *is accustomed* (to bear arms).
tegminis officium, *the job of protection, the function of protecting* (*me*).
indestrictus, *untouched, unhurt*.
*__abībō__, from *__abeō__, -īre, -iī or -īvī, -itum; *I shall go my way* (conclusion of a future more vivid clause).
nātum Nērēide, *the son of a Nereid*; Cygnus is referring to Achilles being the son of Thetis, a Nereid, a minor goddess of the sea.
quī, (of the one) *who*.
temperō (1), *rule*.
Nērea, *Nereus*, a Greek accusative form.
nātās, *his daughters*.
aequor, acc. *n.* sing., *the sea*.

318 Latin via Ovid

Now the battle rages between the two heroes; Achilles is increasingly frustrated that, with all his strength and experience, he is unable to wound the young son of Neptune. The older hero presses harder and harder against the presumptuous youth, and now finally Cygnus is on the run.

32e   . . . pavor occupat illum,
          ante oculosque natant tenebrae retroque ferenti
          aversos passus medio lapis obstitit arvo;
          quem super inpulsum resupino corpore Cygnum
          vi multa vertit terraeque adfixit Achilles.
          Vincula trahit galeae;
                              victum spoliare parabat;
          arma relicta videt; corpus deus aequoris albam
          contulit in volucrem, cuius modo nomen habebat.

                                    Met. XII.64–145, adapted passim

Structure

172. Review of deponent and semi-deponent verbs. The trick to mastering the deponent verb is to remember that certain verbs with *passive endings* must be translated *actively*.

Trōes **tuentur** lītus.   The Trojans *protect* their
                                        shoreline.

Achilles, equōs **exhortātus** . . .   Achilles, *having urged on* his
                                        horses . . .

(N.B. perfect active translation for the perf. pass. part.)

32e

*pavor, -ōris, *m.*, *fear, trembling.*
*occupō (1), *seize.*
tenebrae, nom. pl., *dark shadows.*
retrō . . . arvō, *a stone blocks him as he steps backward in the middle of the field*; lapis (*a stone*) is subject of obstitit, which has a dat. of compound object (eī) understood, modified by ferenti: bearing his turned steps backward in the middle of the field (mediō arvō).
quem super inpulsum resupīnō corpore, *with his body bent backwards over this* (*stone*).
*vī multā, *with mighty force.*
adfīgō, -ere, -fīxī, -fīxum, *pin to, affix*: with the dat. of compound (terrae) and acc. dir. obj. (Cygnum).
vinculum, -ī, *n.*, *band, cord, chain.* Ovid wrote vincla for metrical reasons.
*galea, -ae, *f.*, *helmet* (of leather).
victum, *the man he had conquered.*
spoliō (1), *despoil, strip of arms.*
relicta (having been left) *empty.*
deus aequoris, *Neptune.*
contulit, *has changed.*
*modo, *now.*

An irregular verb like **gaudeō, gaudēre, gāvīsus sum** is conjugated with active endings in the present system and only has deponent forms in the perfect system. Because of this double nature such verbs are termed semi-deponent:

Gaudēte, Pelasgī . . .	*Rejoice*, Pelasgians . . .
Gaudeāmus, igitur . . .	*Let us* therefore *rejoice* . . .
Mīlitēs **gāvīsī sunt**.	The soldiers *rejoiced*.

173. Deponent verbs have four participles and three infinitives.

Participles

Pres. Active	**hortāns, -antis**	urging
Perf. Passive	**hortātus, -a, -um**	having urged
Fut. Act.	**hortātūrus, -a, -um**	about to urge
Fut. Pass. (*Gerundive*)	**hortandus, -a, -um**	about to be urged

Infinitives

Pres.	**hortārī**	to urge
Perf.	**hortātus esse**	to have urged
Fut.	**hortātūrus esse**	to be about to urge

Imperative Mood

The imperative forms of a deponent verb are similar to the forms of the passive second person singular (the alternate **-re** form) and plural:

Singular	*Plural*
hortāre[1] (urge!)	**hortāminī** (urge!)

Consult the paradigms in the Appendix for the deponent verb forms of the other conjugations.

174. Review of indirect questions. Verbs of asking, knowing, sensing, feeling, perceiving and the like may complete their ideas with a subordinate clause (verb in the subjunctive) introduced by an interrogative word. (What, why, where, how, who, whose, etc.) Reread **Sec. 148**.

Rēx scit **quis sīs**.	The king knows *who you are*.
Rēx rogat **quid dēsīderēs**.	The king asks *what you desire*.
Rēx quaesit **cūr veniant**.	The king asks *why they are coming*.
Trōes sēnsērunt **quid** Achaea manus **posset**.	The Trojans understood *what* the Achaean band *was able* (*to do*).

---

[1] This form looks like an active infinitive, but it is not. It is really the alternate form of **hortāris**.

Trōes sēnsērunt **cūr** Graecī
venīrent. (**vēnissent**)

The Trojans understood *why* the
Greeks *came.* (*had come.*)

Trōes sēnsērunt **quam ob causam**
Graecī **vēnissent.**

The Trojans understood *why*
(*for what reason*) the Greeks
had come.

Trōes sēnsērunt in **quō locō**
ratēs Graecae **sē cēlārent.**

The Trojans realized *where* (*in
what place*) the Greek ships
were hiding.

Trōes sēnsērunt **unde** ratēs
Graecae **ēvēnissent.**

The Trojans realized *from whence*
the Greek ships *had come.*

Trōes sēnsērunt **quōmodo**
Graecī **vēnissent.**

The Trojans realized *how* the
Greeks *had come.*

Notice the *secondary* nature of all the tense sequences in the **Trōes**
sentences above:

Main Verb	*Subordinate Verb*
Past Tense in the Indicative (Imp., Perf., Pluperf.)	Imperfect or Pluperfect Subjunctive

Primary Sequence

Present or Future Indicative	Present or Perfect Subjunctive

Notice the *primary* sequence of the tenses in the first three sentences.
This principle holds true for most subjunctive uses.

175. Further uses of the genitive. You are already familiar with the genitive
to show possession and the objective use of the genitive:

Possession:	fīlius **Priamī**—	the son *of Priam* (or) *Priam's* son
	mors **Hectoris**—	the death *of Hector* (or) *Hector's* death
Objective:	amor **pecūniae**—	love *of money*

The genitive is also used in a partitive sense, also called very logically
Genitive of the Whole, since it represents the whole of which a part is
being referred to:

pars **terrae**	part *of the land*
quid **bonī**?	what *good*? (*lit.*, what *of good*?)
nīl **mortis**	no *death* (*lit.*, nothing *of death*)
octō **volucrum**	eight *birds* (*lit.*, eight *of birds*)
plūs **fortūnae**	more *luck* (*lit.*, more *of luck*)
pars **fortūnae**	part *of the luck*
multa mīlia **virōrum**	many thousands *of men*

In each case there is a word (usually an indeclinable pronoun or a number) followed by the whole of which the preceding word is a quantitative part.

176. Future Imperative. The logic of having a future imperative is clear, since all commands can be fulfilled only in the future, although when the General commands "Attack" or "Halt" the reaction in the future should be instantaneous. Nevertheless, although English cannot make this subtle distinction of time in a command except by an adverbial modifier, Latin had separate forms for a Present Imperative command and a Future Imperative:

	Singular		Plural	
Present	**Habē**	Consider	**Habēte**	Consider
Future	**Habētō**	In the future, consider . . .	**Habētōte**	In the future, consider . . .

(The use of the future, however, is rare and usually poetic.)

177. Double Dative. The double dative involves two dative case nouns, the first explaining a function and the second the person for whom the function occurs.

Auxiliō mihi sunt. They are *an aid to me.*

Exercises

I.   Respondete Latine:

1. Quis fecerat notum Graias rates adventare?
2. Adestne hostis Graecus inexspectatus?
3. Qui aditum Graecorum prohibent?
4. Quis mille viros Graecorum leto dederat?
5. In quem annum mors Hectoris delatus est?
6. Quid erit solamen mortis Cygni? (**solāmen**—*comfort, consolation*)
7. Cur hasta gravis Achillis nil mortis portavit?
8. Quam ob causam Cygnus scutum portavit?

    9. Quid Achilles victo facere parabat?

    10. In quam avem deus Neptunus corpus Cygni contulit?

II.   Change each of these indirect questions to secondary sequence by making the indicative verb perfect and the subjunctive verb either imperfect or pluperfect as the sense requires.

    1. Neptunus sentit cur filius suus immortalis sit.

    2. Cygnus non sentit in quo loco moriatur.

    3. Troes non sentiunt quo modo Graeci bellum gerant.

    4. Achilles miratur cur hasta sua nil mortis portet.

    5. Vos omnes sciunt cur Cygnus in cygnum mutetur.

III.   Change these commands to future imperative:

    1. Scribe, discipule!

    2. Cantate mecum.

    3. Venite, adoremus.

    4. Gaudete, discipuli; ludus finitus est.

    5. Da dona deis.

    6. Ama, non pugna. (or) Fac amorem, non bellum.

IV A. Write an indicative synopsis of **hortor, hortari, hortatus sum** with a synopsis of **morior, mori, mortuus sum** beside it so that you can compare the forms of the verb in the first (and second) conjugation with those of the third. Naturally these will all be passive forms since the verbs are deponent.

	hortor	morior
Indicative:	3rd person singular	
Present	_____	_____
Imperfect	_____	_____
Future	_____	_____
Perfect	_____	_____
Pluperfect	_____	_____
Fut. Perfect	_____	_____
Subjunctive:		
Present	_____	_____
Imperfect	_____	_____
Perfect	_____	_____
Pluperfect	_____	_____

Consult the Appendix for a full conjugation.

B. Write the participles, infinitives, and imperatives of the verbs above and translate each.

V.   Translate into Latin:

1. The Trojans knew why the Greeks were coming to their shores.
2. Both the Greeks and the Trojans had sent many thousands of men to their deaths in this bloody war.
3. Cygnus had no fear because he knew that his father was an immortal god who ruled the sea.
4. Achilles' mother was the goddess Thetis and his father was Peleus, the son of Aeacus.
5. Cygnus was changed into a swan when Achilles tried to despoil (**vastāre** or **spoliāre**) his victim.

Etymology and Roman Life[2]

EDUCATION

In early times Roman children were educated at home either by the father of the family or by a slave, usually Greek, who often was better educated than the master himself. Sometimes neighboring children or those of friends or relatives would also attend the lessons of such a slave, but eventually schools were established in central locations—usually in the entrance to a building in an area roofed but open to the street, where the distractions of public life competed with the lessons of the slave or freedman teacher. Small fees were paid for such lessons, the amount varying with the reputation of the teacher, and often presents took the place of regular tuition. Children from well-to-do families were accompanied to the school by a slave called the **paedagogus** (*child leader* in Greek), and this trusted family servant, usually an elderly man, was in charge not only of conducting his student to the school, but also of supervising his studying, his Greek learning, his moral deportment, and his general behavior. The relationship between **paedagogus** and child often continued informally after the child reached the age of assuming the toga. Our English word *pedagogue* comes from this word.

Pupils learned to write on wax tablets, making an impression on the smooth surface by means of a **stilus**, a pointed tool with a flattened end for

---

[2] The Etymology sections are now expanded to include discussions on various aspects of Roman life to enrich your understanding of the cultural context of the Latin language. The material presented in these sections has been adapted from Jerome Carcopino, *Daily Life in Ancient Rome*, trans. E. O. Lorimer (New Haven: Yale University Press, 1940), and Mary Johnston, *Roman Life* (Chicago: Scott Foresman, 1957). Other references include: William S. Davis, *A Day in Old Rome* (New York: Biblo & Tannen, 1959); W. W. Fowler, *Social Life in Rome in the Age of Cicero* (New York: Macmillan, 1915); Tenney Frank, *Aspects of Social Behavior in Ancient Rome* (Cambridge: Harvard University Press, 1932); Gilbert Picard, *The Ancient Civilization of Rome*, trans. H. S. B. Harrison (Geneva: Nagel, 1969); Helen H. Tanzer, *The Common People of Pompeii* (Baltimore: Johns Hopkins University Press, 1939); Walton Brooks McDaniel, *Roman Private Life and its Survivals* (Boston: Marshall Jones, 1924); and Peter Arnott, *Romans and their World* (New York: St Martin's Press, 1970).

smoothing over errors in the manner of an eraser. Later the pupil learned to write with ink on papyrus, ancient paper made from the papyrus plant. Letters were all capitals, although there was a kind of script called "cursive," which was found on tablets and in various account books. Roman numerals made arithmetic difficult, and complicated problems were computed on an abacus or by means of fingers. Much learning was memory training, the epics of Homer being learned by students in the original Greek language. Because the chief pursuit of the upper-level school (reading, writing, and arithmetic having been learned in the elementary school) was **grammatica**—literature and language—the school was called a "grammar" school and teacher a **grammaticus**. Students were given lessons in many subjects rising out of the careful study of Homer's *Iliad* and *Odyssey*, depending on the skill of the teacher. Latin schools naturally stressed Roman authors, as poetry began to appear, especially the translation of the Homeric epic into Latin by Livius Andronicus in the third century B.C. In both elementary and grammar schools, special emphasis was given to oral recitation and to careful pronunciation of words, since oratory was to be important for many young men in public life. Some of these young men went on to study at schools of rhetoric where they studied prose: history, philosophy, and public speaking, leading to a refining of the art of oratory. The wealthy also could attend famous schools at Athens, to which Roman youths went much as Americans go abroad to Europe to study and complete their education. Young men could also become apprenticed to lawyers and men in the government, especially in the administration of overseas colonies, to prepare themselves for future occupations.

Below are some of the many words connected with education that have come into English from Latin roots:

education (**educare** &/or **educere**)	disciple	elementary
	science	secondary
school (**schola**)	literature	cum laude
curriculum	medicine	summa cum laude
college	letter	B.A. (**Baccalaureus Artium**, Bachelor of Arts)
university	fraternity	
professor	sorority	M.A. (**Magister Artium**, Master of Arts)
confer (a degree)	alma mater	
grade	office	Ph.D. (**Philosophiae Doctor**, Doctor of Philosophy)
student	notes	
discipline		

*   *   *   *   *

What English words are derived from these Latin words in the lesson?

fama	annus	onus
advenio	error	traho (tractum)
tueor	emitto (emissum)	sinister
rubrum	admiror	verto
occurro	absum	

Sententiae

. . . **in corpore nostro**	. . . *in our bodies*
pectora sunt potiora manu.	*the heart (mind) is stronger than the hand.*
Ovid, *Met.* XII.368–9	
Vis consili expers mole ruit sua.	*Force devoid of wisdom falls by its own*
Horace, *Carmina*	*weight.*
IV.65	

Chapter XXXIII
BELLUM TROIANUM: AIAX ET ULIXES

Homer's *Iliad* is the tale of the coming of age of the hero Achilles, whose rash anger in the ninth year of the war, in a quarrel with Agamemnon over a woman captive, results in the disastrous prolonging of the war. The Greeks and Trojans finally consent to a battle of champions, one to represent each side. And who better to fight than Menelaus, the injured husband, and Paris, the amorous abductor? Menelaus wins the battle easily, and is about to drag Paris off by his helmet strap when Venus intervenes and whisks Paris off to Helen's boudoir to be tended by her, and the battle resumes. The Greeks are hard pressed, and they retreat even to the ships, despite heroic action by Ajax and Diomedes. The leaders try to persuade Achilles to rejoin the battle with his Myrmidon army, but the hot-headed Achilles sulks in his tent and will not be moved. Then Patroclus, beloved friend of Achilles, begs the hero to allow him to go into battle wearing Achilles' armor, the sight of which will be enough to reinspire the troops. Achilles agrees and Patroclus, wearing Achilles' armor, for a time breathes new hope into the Greek forces, rallying the troops. Finally the great Trojan hero Hector slays the young man and strips the body of its borrowed armor. When Achilles learns the fate of Patroclus, weeping he regrets his delay in rejoining the battle, and he now furiously seeks Patroclus' slayer, wearing wonderful new armor forged by Hephaestus at the request of his mother, the Nereid Thetis. He demands to meet Hector in single combat. After a tender farewell to his wife Andromache and his young son Astyanax, Hector comes forth to meet the greatest of the Greek warriors. Hector is defeated and begs for his life. Achilles is on the verge of sparing him when he sees his own baldric, which Patroclus had worn, on the shoulder of the fallen hero; and his anger rekindled, Achilles kills Hector. In a terrible show of pride, he drags the body tied to his chariot around the walls of Troy for Priam and all the Trojans to see.

There is a lull in the fighting, and Priam, urged on by the gods, goes through the enemy lines to Achilles to beg for the body of Hector so that it may be buried. Achilles, now more mature, pities the elderly king, remembering his own father, and he returns the corpse for burial, achieving in this single act what he could not achieve on the battle field—his maturity. There is a truce for burial and funeral games, and thus ends the twenty-fourth book of the *Iliad* with the war still unconcluded.

Achilles had been warned by his sea-goddess mother that he himself would die soon after Hector's defeat, but undaunted the Greek hero continues fighting. Eventually he is killed by Paris, who wounds him in the heel, the only part of his body that is vulnerable.[1] After his death, the possession of his wonderful armor becomes the subject of a violent quarrel between Ulysses[2] and Ajax.

Ulysses engages in a mighty verbal battle with Ajax, son of Telamon, who has claimed the armor as his reward, since he is the strongest of all the Greeks. Ajax has recounted his ancestry through Telamon and Aeacus to Jove himself, since Jupiter had been the father of Aeacus, conceived when the king of gods and men had carried off Aegina. Ajax speaks of his massive shield and his brave deeds on the battlefield, while Ulysses, he says, is confined to describing deeds done at night and by stealth. Ajax challenges Ulysses to a contest of arms then and there, in the presence of the assembled Greek chiefs to decide which of them deserves the honor. In reply, Ovid has Ulysses describe his own honored ancestry; then he tells about how he tricked Achilles into betraying his identity when this young Greek hero had hidden as a girl to avoid going to war. Then Ulysses tells how he persuaded Agamemnon to sacrifice Iphigenia and how he went to Troy as an ambassador.

33a   "Mittor et Iliacas audax orator ad arces
          visaque et intrata est altae mihi curia Troiae
          plenaque adhuc erat illa viris; interritus egi,
          quam mihi mandaret communis Graecia, causam
          accusoque Parin praedamque Helenamque reposco
          et moveo Priamum Priamoque Antenora iunctum;
          at Paris et fratres et qui rapuere sub illo
          vix tenuere manus (scis hoc, Menelae) nefandas,
          primaque lux nostri tecum fuit illa pericli.

33a

audax ōrātor, *as a bold orator.*
Īliacās arcēs, note the interlocking word order, *the Trojan citadel.* Ilium is the Greek name for
  Troy; **Īliacus, -a, -um**, *Trojan.*   (33a continues opposite)

---

[1] Achilles had been dipped in the River Styx when he was an infant to make him invulnerable a common motif in epic literature. His mother held him by the heel, thus covering "Achilles' heel."

[2] Ulysses (**Ulixēs**) is the Latin equivalent for the Greek Odysseus.

33b   "Longa referre mora est, quae consilioque manuque
utiliter feci spatiosi tempore belli.
Post acies primas urbis se moenibus hostes
continuere diu, nec aperti copia Martis
ulla fuit; decimo demum pugnavimus anno;
quid facis interea, qui nil nisi proelia nosti?
Quis tuus usus erat? Nam si mea facta requiris,
hostibus insidior, fossa munimina cingo,
consolor socios, ut longi taedia belli
mente ferant placida, doceo, quo simus alendi
armandique modo, mittor, quo postulat usus."

---

*arx, arcis, f., *building*, pl. **arcēs**, *citadel*.
*cūria, -ae, f., *the senate house* (an anachronism, since Ovid is using the name of the Roman assembly for the Trojan senate).
mihi is dat. of agent, *by me*.
*interritus, -a, -um, *unterrified, undaunted*.
*causam accūsō, *accuse* (Paris) and also plead a case (**causam**), as in a senate hearing, continuing the image of the curia; **reposcō**, *demand back*.
*commūnis, -e, shared, common, general, public; therefore, *the state* (here *the Greek state*).
*mandō (1), *intrust*.
Paris, Paridis, *m.*, *Paris*; **Paridin** (shortened to **Parin**) is a Greek acc. obj. of **accūsō**.
*que . . . que, *both . . . and*.
*praeda, -ae, f., *booty*, obj. of **reposcō** with **Helenam**.
Antēnor, -oris, *m.*, *Antenor*, a Trojan **Antenora**, Greek acc. sing.
iunctus, -a, -um, joined to, *together with* + dat. **Priamō**.
sub illō, *helped him in the robbery* (lit., *those who robbed under him*).
*rapuēre = **rapuērunt**, perfect, 3rd. pl.
*tenuēre = **tenuērunt**, perfect 3rd. pl.
Menelāe, vocative.
nefandus, -a, -um, *wicked, evil*, modifying **manus**.
*lux, lūcis, f., *light, day*; *that was the first day of my danger* (**periclī**) *with* (in behalf of) *you*.

33b

*referre, *to recount*, to tell again; *it would cause a long delay to recount (all the things) which . . .*
quae, the antecedent **omnia** is omitted.
*ūtiliter, *usefully, for the common good*.
spatiōsus, -a, -um, *long*.
*post + acc., *after*.
*aciēs, -ēī, f., (acc. pl.), *keenness, edge; a line of battle, the battle* itself, *skirmish*.
*contineō, -ēre, -uī, -tentum, *keep together, hold together, defend* + **sē**, *themselves*.
moenibus, *walls, ramparts, fortifications*; abl. of place where.
*diū, *for a long time*.
*copia, -ae, f., *plenty, abundance, means; opportunity*; pl., *troops*.
nec ulla copia aperti Martis, a poetic way of saying *not any opportunity of open combat*, Mars standing for warfare or fighting.
*demum, *finally*.
*nosti, contraction for **nōvistī**, perf. of **cognoscō**, an inceptive verb meaning *learn* or *begin to know*; the perfect means *know*.
*ūsus, -ūs, m., *use, usefulness, service*.
*requirō, -ere, -quisiī or *-quisīvī, -quisītum*, *ask, look for, inquire after*.
insidior, -ārī, -ātus sum, *lay snares for, lie in ambush for*.   (33b continues overleaf)

Ulysses continues to berate Ajax, describing how Ajax was ready to turn his back on the war and sail home.

33c   "Quid, quod et ipse fugit? Vidi, puduitque videre,
cum tu terga dares inhonestaque vela parares;
nec mora 'quid facitis? Quae vos dementia' dixi
'concitat, o socii, captam dimittere Troiam,
quidque domum fertis decimo, nisi dedecus, anno?' "

Optional Reading

33d   Talibus atque aliis, in quae dolor ipse disertum
fecerat, aversos profuga de classe reduxi.
Convocat Atrides socios terrore paventes:
nec Telamoniades etiamnunc hiscere quicquam
audet. . . .
Orior et trepidos cives exhortor in hostem
amissamque mea virtutem voce repono.
Tempore ab hoc, quodcumque potest fecisse videri
fortiter iste, meum est, [ego] qui dantem terga retraxi."

Met. XIII.196–237 passim

---

cingō mūnīmina fossā, *I surround the fortifications with a trench* (fossā, abl. of means).
consōlor, -ārī, -ātus sum, *console, comfort, encourage.*
ut ferant taedia placidā mente, purpose clause; *so that they may bear the tedium of the long war with equanimity* (mente, lit., *with a calm mind*).
*quō . . . modo, *how we are to be fed and armed*, two indirect questions introduced by doceō, *I taught them*; (alō, -ere, -uī, *feed*).
quō postulat ūsus, *where usefulness demands, wherever there is a mission.*

33c
quid, quod, *what of the fact that . . .*
puduit, *I was ashamed*, impersonal verb (lit., *it shamed me to see it*).
*terga dare, *to turn one's back*; inhonesta vēla, *dishonored sails.*
*nec mora, *without delay* (lit., *and there was not a delay*).
concitō (1), *incite, impel.*
*dīmittō, -ere, -mīsī, -missum, *send out, send away, give up, abandon.*
nisi dēdecus, *except disgrace* (dēdecus, -decoris, *n., disgrace*).
*socii, vocative.

33d
tālisbus atque aliīs, *with such and other words.*
in quae dolor ipse disertum, *to which grief itself had made me eloquent.*
disertus, -a, -um, *eloquent.*
aversōs, *those who had turned in flight* (acc. object of reduxit).
*Atrīdēs, *the son of Atreus assembled his companions trembling* (paventēs) *with fear.*
Telamōniadēs, *the son of Telamon*, i.e., *Ajax.*
etiamnunc, *even now.*
hiscō, -ere, *open his mouth.*
quicquam, *at all* (anything), here used adverbially.
*Orior, *I arose*, historical present (*orior, orīrī, ortus sum*).   (33d continues opposite)

Ulysses acknowledges Ajax's glorious deeds in battle, but he continues to berate him as a claimant for the arms of Achilles, citing his own participation in the actual fighting and also his cunning strategy. He explains his previous reluctance to fight and then tells how *he* brought about the conclusion of the war in favor of the Greeks by gaining the prophecy of the Trojan seer Helenus, who told that the Greeks must bring the weapons of Hercules which were still on the island of Lemnos with Philoctetes, and that they must capture the Palladium, a sacred image of Athena, and carry it from the temple at the citadel of Troy into the Greek lines. In order to accomplish the first prophetic command Ulysses goes with Achilles' young son, Neoptolemus, and tricks Philoctetes into surrendering the weapons of Hercules, the scene at Lemnos being the setting for a play by Sophocles, *Philoctetes*. The stealing of the Palladium, Ulysses accomplishes with Diomedes. Here are Ulysses' own words as he recounts his exploits. Ovid does not have him include the final Trojan Horse venture, but that would have been the final, convincing argument. The Greek leaders are swayed by his eloquence and award Ulysses the armor.

Thus Ulysses sums up the difference between the two: "*You excel only in body, I in mind.* As much as he who captains the ship is superior to the man who rows, as much as the general is greater than the soldier, just so much I surpass you, for in our bodies the heart (mind) is stronger than the hand; for all our strength lies in it."

Further optional reading

Ulysses' description of the Philoctetes and Palladium episodes:

33e   "Sis licet infestus sociis regique mihique,
       dure Philoctete, licet exsecrere meumque
       devoveas sine fine caput cupiasque dolenti
       me tibi forte dari nostrumque haurire cruorem,

---

*trepidus, -a, -um, *trembling*.
*tempore ab hōc, *from this time on*.
*iste, -a, -ud, *that fellow* (spoken in a derogatory manner), *that one over there*.
*vidērī, passive of videō means *seem*.
quodcumque, *whatever*.
*meum est, *is mine, belongs to me*.
*retrahō, -ere, -trāxī, -tractum, *drag back*.
dantem, acc. (modifying Ajax or him), *when he was running away* (lit., *giving his back*).

33e
sīs licet, *although you may be angry with . . .* or *granted that . . .* **licet** is impersonal: *it is permitted that you may be, granted that you may be . . .*
dūre Philoctēte, vocative sing.
licet exsecrēre, *although you may curse me and pile curses on my head without end* (**exsecrēre** is a first conj. deponent verb, second person sing., alternate form, **exsecror, -ārī, -ātus sum**, *curse*; subjv. following **licet**).   (33e continues overleaf)

te tamen adgrediar mecumque reducere nitar
tamque tuis potiar (faveat Fortuna) sagittis,
quam sum Dardanio, quem cepi, vate potitus,
quam responsa deum Troianaque fata retexi,
quam rapui Phrygiae signum penetrale Minervae
hostibus e mediis. Et se mihi comparat Aiax?
Nempe capi Troiam prohibebant fata sine illo:
fortis ubi est Aiax? Ubi sunt ingentia magni
verba viri: cur hic metuis? Cur audet Ulixes
ire per excubias et se committere nocti
perque feros enses non tantum moenia Troum,
verum etiam summas arces intrare suaque
eripere aede deam raptamque adferre per hostes?
Quae nisi fecissem, frustra Telamone creatus
gestasset laeva taurorum tergora septem.
Illa nocte mihi Troiae victoria parta est:
Pergama tunc vici, cum vinci posse coegi."

Met. XIII.328–349

---

cupiāsque, *and desire that I be given to you in your grief to drink my blood* (**cupiās**, second per. sing. subjv. followed by indirect statement).

tamen, *nevertheless*, conclusion from all the "although" clauses preceding.

adgrediar, *I will go to you.*

nītar, *I will strive.*

potiar, *I will get possession of* (with abl.).

faveat, *favor, let fortune favor me.*

tamquam (tamque ... quam), *just as I got possession of the Dardanian* (Trojan) *seer*; the reference here is to Helenus who, having been captured, related the prophecy to Ulysses.

deum = **deōrum**.

quam, *just as* (I rewove).

penetrālis, -e, *inner.*

Phrygius, -a, -um, *Phrygian, Trojan.*

comparō (1), *compare.*

nempe, *truly, certainly, to be sure.*

capī, pres. passive infinitive.

sino illō, without the Palladium.

ingens, ingentis, *huge, mighty.*

hīc, *here* (in this situation).

metuō, -uere, *fear.*

excubiās, *sentinels, guards.*

ferōs ensēs, *wild swords.*

Trōum, *of Troy.*

intrō (1), *enter, go into.*

suā aede, indirect reflexive. Obviously Ovid means that Ulysses is stealing the statue of the goddess from her own shrine.

per hostēs, *through enemy lines.*

Telamōne creātus, *the man created from Telamon*, i.e., *Ajax.*

gestāsset = **gestāvisset**, the concluding verb in a contrary to fact condition, from **gestō** (1), *wear, carry.*

(33e continues opposite)

Structure

178. Further uses of the accusative. The customary uses of the accusative case
are as direct object and as object of certain prepositions:

a) Direct object

Rapuī **signum** Minervae.	I stole *the statue* of Minerva.

b) Object of preposition

Ad īnsulam nāvigāvimus.	We sailed *to the island*.

The latter usage is made even briefer in Latin by omitting the preposition **ad** with names of cities, islands and with the words *home*
(**domum**) and *country* (**rūs**).

Quid decimō annō **domum** fertis?	What are you taking *home* in the tenth year?
Quid decimō annō **Athēnās** fertis?	What are you taking *to Athens* in the tenth year?

N.B.: *Athens* is plural in Latin, just as it is in English.

c) The accusative is also used as the subject of an infinitive, both in
indirect statement and in constructions with certain verbs such as
iubeō and **prohibeō**:

Trōiānī sensērunt **Graecōs** appropinquāre.	The Trojans realized that *the Greeks* were coming.
Trōiānī iubēbant **mīlitēs suōs** adstare.	The Trojans ordered *their soldiers* to stand ready.
Fāta prohibēbant **Trōiam** sine illō signō capī.	The fates forbade *Troy* to be captured without that statue.

d) Accusative of Extent of Time:

Decem annōs bellum contrā Trōiam gessit.	*For ten years* he waged war against Troy.

e) The accusative is also used with impersonal verbs in the following
constructions:

Meum est.	It is *mine*.
Vērum est.	It is *true*.
Certum est mihi.	I am *sure*.

---

laevā, *on his left hand.*
tergōra, *hides* of leather.
parta est, *was gained*, from **pariō, -ere, peperī, partum**, *bring forth, create.*
Pergama, acc., *the citadel of Troy.*
vincī, present passive infinitive.
cum . . . coēgī, *when I forced it* (to be able) *to be conquered.*

179. The pronouns of Latin. The personal pronouns, **is, ea, id**, are not used as frequently as the demonstrative substitutes for these forms: **hic, haec, hoc**, and **ille, illa, illud**. There is a group of adjective-pronouns which are declined much like **ille**, in that they have the genitive singular in **-īus** and the dative singular in **-ī**.

ūnus, -a, -um	one	**tōtus, -a, -um**	whole, all
ūllus, -a, -um	any	**sōlus, -a, -um**	alone, the only, sole
nūllus, -a, -um	no, none	**alius, alia, aliud**	other
		alter, -era, -erum	the other, an other

These words are adjectives when they modify nouns which are expressed; they act as pronouns when they are substantives.

facta **ūnīus**,	the deeds *of one man*
verba **nūllīus**,	the words *of no one*
Dat dōna **sōlī** fēminae.	He gives gifts to *only one* woman.
Perīculum **tōtī** urbī vīdimus.	We saw the danger *to the whole* city.

(The forms of **nēmō** are irregular in that **nūllīus** usually appears in place of the genitive **nēminis**, and **nūllō** in place of **nēmine** in the ablative. Thus the only usual forms are **nēmō, nēminī**, and accusative **nēminem**, *no one*.) Frequently used in place of the personal pronouns are the more intensive forms **īdem, eadem, idem** (*the same*). This pronoun is declined just like **is, ea, id** with the suffix **-dem**, except where **-m** changes to **-n** before **-d** and in the Nom. Masc. Sing.

	Singular			*Plural*		
	M.	*F.*	*N.*	*M.*	*F.*	*N.*
Nom.	**īdem**	**eadem**	**idem**	**eīdem** (**īdem**)	**eaedem**	**eadem**
Gen.	**eiusdem**	**eiusdem**	**eiusdem**	**eōrundem**	**eārundem**	**eōrundem**
Dat.	**eīdem**	**eīdem**	**eīdem**	**eīsdem** (**īsdem**)	**eīsdem** (**īsdem**)	**eīsdem** (**īsdem**)
Acc.	**eundem**	**eandem**	**idem**	**eōsdem**	**eāsdem**	**eadem**
Abl.	**eōdem**	**eādem**	**eōdem**	**eīsdem** (**īsdem**)	**eīsdem** (**īsdem**)	**eīsdem** (**īsdem**)

Another intensive pronoun, based on the forms of **is, ea, id**, is the pronoun **ipse, ipsa, ipsum**, Gen.: **ipsīus**, Dat.: **ipsī**, Acc.: **ipsum, ipsam, ipsum**, Abl.: **ipsō, ipsā, ipsō**. The plural forms are completely regular. The meaning is *himself, herself, itself*, but many times the personal pronouns *he, she, it* may be used for a smoother translation.

Ipse respondit.	*The man himself* replied, (or) *he* replied.

Facta **ipsīus** sē dēmonstrāvit.   The deeds *of the man himself*
reveal him (his true character).

A third intensive pronoun **iste, ista, istud** was used in a rather derogatory manner when the Romans wished to refer to "that man over there," or "that sort of man" (or woman or thing). It is declined like the word **ille** (Gen.: **istīus**, Dat.: **istī**) and appears in situations where the speaker wishes to imply that "that man of yours" is doing something he should not do. See the Appendix for a complete paradigm.

180. **Fīō**, an irregular verb. The verb **faciō** has no regular passive forms beyond the participle **factus**, and the passive conjugation is replaced by the verb **fīō** which means *be made, become, happen.*

fīō, fierī, factus sum

Indicative

Pres.	*Imp.*	*Fut.*	*Perf.*	*Pluperf.*	*Fut. Perf.*
fīō	fīēbam	fīam	factus sum	factus eram	factus erō
fīs	fīēbās	fīēs	factus es	factus erās	factus eris
fit	fīēbat	fīet	factus est	factus erat	factus erit
fīmus	fīēbāmus	fīēmus	factī sumus	factī erāmus	factī erimus
fītis	fīēbātis	fīētis	factī estis	factī erātis	factī eritis
fīunt	fīēbant	fīent	factī sunt	factī erant	factī erunt

Subjunctive

fīam	fīerem	factus sim	factus essem
fīās	fīerēs	factus sīs	factus essēs
fīat	fīeret	factus sit	factus esset
fīāmus	fīerēmus	factī sīmus	factī essēmus
fīātis	fīerētis	factī sītis	factī essētis
fīant	fīerent	factī sint	factī essent

The forms frequently used are the subjunctive **fīat**, as in **fīat lux**, *let there be light*, and **fīeri**, *to happen, to become*.

181. Review of impersonal verb, **licet**. The use of impersonal verbs is restricted to a few constructions in the third person singular followed by an infinitive or a subjunctive clause introduced by **ut**, or simply by the subjunctive. **Licet** means *it is permitted, granted that*, or *although*, depending on the context. (Cf. **Sec. 159**.)

Licet fūmāre.	*It is permitted* to smoke.
Licet sīs infestus mihi, . . .	*Granted that* you are angry with me, . . . (or) *Although* you may be angry with me . . .
Dum **licet** . . .	While *it is permitted* . . .

The principal parts of the verb are **licet, licēre, licuit**. Other impersonal verbs used in a similar manner are **libet, libēre, libuit**, *it is desirable*, and **decet, decēre, decuit**, *it is proper, it is fitting*, **placet, placēre, placuit**, *it is pleasing*, **pudet, pudēre, puduit**, *it shames, it is shameful*.

Fac quod **libet**.	Do what *you wish* (*is desirable*).
Fac quod **decet**.	Do what *is proper*.
Vīdī, **puduitque** vidēre.	I saw it and *I was ashamed* to see it.

182. Questions; **Nōnne** and **Num**. Simple questions in Latin may begin with an interrogative word or by affixing **-ne** to the first word in the sentence (cf. **Sec. 7, 104** and **105**):

Rapuitne Plūto Prōserpinam?　　*Did* Pluto *carry off* Proserpina?

If, however, one wishes to suggest either an affirmative or negative response, one should use either **Nōnne** or **Num** as the first word. When a question is prefaced with **Nōnne**, the implied or suggested answer is "yes":

Nōnne Cerēs **est** misera, Prōserpinā raptā?
　　Is not Ceres unhappy because Proserpina has been carried off?
Answer implied: **Ita** Cerēs misera est. *Yes*, Ceres is unhappy.

When **Num** introduces the question, a "no" answer is implied:

Num Iuppiter **erat** indignātus, cum Prōserpina rapta esset?
　　Jupiter *was not outraged*, when Proserpina had been carried off, *was he*?
Answer implied: **Nōn** erat indignātus. *No*, he was not outraged.

Exercises

I.   Respondete Latine:

1. Nonne Ulixes mittitur orator ad arces Iliacas?
2. Quem Ulixes accusat?
3. Quid Ulixes reposcit?
4. Qui voluerunt manus nefandas in Ulixem ponere?
5. (In) quo anno demum pugnaverunt Graeci et Troiani?
6. Num Aiax socios consolatur?
7. Num voluit Ulixes domum redire, Troia non capta?
8. Nonne voluit Aiax domum redire?
9. Qua cingit munimina Ulixes?
10. Quid Ulixes docuit sociis?

II. Change the following commands with **iubeo** into noun clauses of desire using **ut** (or **ne**) and the subjunctive: (Use **impero** and remember that it takes the dative case.)

Agamemnon iussit milites domum redire.
Agamemnon militibus imperavit ut domum redirent.

1. Agamemnon iussit milites domum redire.
2. Priamus iussit Achillem corpus Hectoris reddere.
3. Laocoön iussit Troianos equum ligneum in urbem non trahere.
4. Menelaus iussit Pariden Helenam reddere.
5. Hector iussit coniugem suam non lacrimare.
6. Iuppiter iussit Agamemnonem bellum Troianum non gerere.
7. Ulixes iussit Aiacem terga non dare.
8. Ulixes iussit Philoctetem arma Herculis Troiam ferre.
9. Agamemnon Achillem iussit servam (ancillam) tradere.
10. Thetis iussit Hephaestum arma nova Achilli facere.

III. Change each personal pronoun to an intensive pronoun or a demonstrative pronoun. *Translate* each pronoun.

Helen   Eam in muros vidimus. Hanc in muros vidimus. Ipsam in muros vidimus. Eandem vidimus. Istam vidimus.

Achilles   1. Eum in curru vidimus. Eundem, Hunc, Ipsum, Istum.
Priamus   2. Corpus ei dedit. Huic corpus dedit. Ipsi, eidem, isti.
Corpus   3. Achilles id Priamo dedit. idem, hoc, ipsum, istud.
Equos   4. Achilles eos concutit. hos, eosdem, ipsos, istos.
servus   5. Ab eo arma portantur. eodem, hoc, ipso, isto.

IV. Rephrase these English sentences into impersonal constructions and translate them into Latin:

I am allowed to go home.   It is permitted for me to go home.
Licet mihi (*or* me) domum redire.

1. I am permitted to smoke. (fumare)
2. I like to read and write. (libet)
3. I do not like to wage war.
4. They are permitted to enter the citadel.
5. You are not permitted to touch the statue of the goddess.
6. Reply, please.

V. Scribite Latine, quaeso.

1. The leaders are not able to persuade Achilles to rejoin the battle.
2. The death of Patroclus persuades Achilles finally to fight again.
3. Ulysses entered the senate of Troy which was full of men.
4. He demanded that they return the booty and Helen to the Greeks.
5. Ajax fights with his body, Ulysses with his mind.
6. Finally in the tenth year of the war Agamemnon, at the command of Jove, ordered his troops to go home.
7. Ajax prepared to obey, but Ulysses warned his companions not to leave without Troy being captured (*use an abl. abs.*).
8. Ulysses persuaded Philoctetes to bring the weapons of Hercules to the war at Troy.
9. Ulysses entered the citadel of Troy at night and carried off the statue of Minerva, the Palladium.
10. Ulysses persuaded the leaders of the Greeks to give the arms of Achilles to him.

Etymology and Roman Life

ROMAN NAMES AND FAMILIES

In legendary times one name seems to have sufficed for people; even kings and the earliest heroes were known by one name alone—Aeneas, Romulus, Remus, Latinus, Evander. By the time of the monarchy described by Livy, however, two names are given for the early kings: Ancus Martius, Numa Pompilius, Tullius Hostilius, Tarquinius Priscus, Servius Tullius, and Tarquinius Superbus. The second of the names seemed to be a descriptive element in the names of the Tarquins, and perhaps that element was the origin of the added name. By the time of the Republic and the Empire, however, citizens usually had at least three names:

Praenomen	*Nomen*	*Cognomen*
Gaius	Julius	Caesar
Publius	Ovidius	Naso
Marcus	Tullius	Cicero

Publius   Cornelius   Scipio Africanus[1]

The **Praenomen** was given by the father to the son nine days after his birth, and it was usually the father's own **praenomen** handed down to the first-born male. Originally these names had meaning: **Lucius**, related to **lux**, **lucis**, *light*; **Gaius**, from **gaudere**, *to enjoy*; **Marcus**, related to **Mars**. But these original meanings were later lost, as evidenced by Cicero's only brother being given the name **Quintus** (*fifth*). There was not too great a variety in these **praenomina**, and they were usually indicated by an initial or abbreviation: **Appius (App.); Aulus (A.); Decimus (D.); Gaius (C.); Gnaeus (Cn.[2]); Lucius (L.); Marcus (M.); Publius (P.); Quintus (Q.); Servius (Ser.); Sextus (Sex.); Tiberius (Ti.)** and **Titus (T.).** A man was called this **praenomen** by his friends.

The **Nomen** was the family generic name, the name of the clan, and it was equivalent to our "last name." The Julian clan to which Caesar belonged was an old family claiming descent from Iulus, the son of Aeneas, the Trojan hero whose divine mother Venus had protected him on his trip from Asia Minor to Italy. On such slim evidence Caesar traced his ancestry back to the goddess Venus. When Caesar and the subsequent Caesars were deified, the justification for such elevation of status was conveniently obvious in the divine origin of the family.

The **Cognomen** was an added name given as a nickname, a descriptive appendage, or a conferred honor: **Caesar**, referring to the cutting (**caesus**) at birth to deliver the child safely,[3] **Naso** (*nose*) referring to a prominent facial feature of a member of the family; **Cicero** (*vetch*) referring perhaps to an identifying mark on the face or body; **Africanus**, a name given to honor the general on the successful completion of a campaign. This inherited **cognomen** also indicated the branch of the **gens** or clan, the descriptive origin eventually becoming lost: **Barbatus** (*Bearded*), **Cincinnatus** (*Curly*), **Longus** (*Long*), **Benignus** (*Kind*), **Severus** (*Severe*), **Sabinus** (*Sabine*), **Tuscus** (*Tuscan*). Some freedmen added **cognomina** of their own, and sometimes additional names were acquired through adoption, since a man when adopted assumed the names of his adopted father as well as keeping his own as an adjective **cognomen** in **-ānus**, the most famous example[4] being that of Octavian who

---

[1] An additional cognomen granted after the success of the African campaign in the Second Punic War.

[2] The letter C was related to the Gamma, Γ, the third letter of the Greek alphabet, as evidenced in the abbreviation.

[3] Even today we refer to a birth which involves cutting into the abdomen of the mother as a Caesarean section.

[4] Almost as famous was Cicero's friend M. Pomponius Atticus, who became Q. Caecilius Pomponianus Atticus when adopted by Caecilius.

became **Gaius Julius Caesar Octavianus**, and subsequently **Augustus** when he became emperor.

Women were sometimes given feminine (first declension) equivalents of the **praenomina**, but there was not great variety and often the name merely referred to number: **Secunda** (*Second*); **Tertia** (*Third*); **Virginia** (*Maidenly*); **Caelia** (*Heavenly*); **Tarquinia** (*the Tarquin*). Until marriage a woman many times was known by the feminine equivalent of her father's **nomen**: Augustus' daughter was Julia; Cicero's daughter was Tullia; Cornelius' daughter Cornelia. In early times when a woman married she came under jurisdiction of her husband and assumed his **nomen**, but under the Empire this custom seemed not to have continued. A woman could add her mother's **nomen** to that of her father's.

Slaves originally had no names of their own and were called **puer** which became **-por**, an enclitic added to the master's name and given to the young slave: **Lucipor**, Lucius' boy; **Quintipor**, Quintus' boy. This lamentable lack of identity existed until a need to refer to slaves as individuals caused names to be given, sometimes identifying places of origin (**Britannicus**) followed by the name of the master in the genitive case and the word **servus** following. Freedmen at manumission were given the **Nomen** of the master with an assigned **praenomen** and the man's own name as a **cognomen**. A master frequently gave his own **praenomen** to a favorite or selected a name for him, but descendants of a freedman often dropped any name identifying the family as once slave. A naturalized Roman took his name, much as did a freedman, from the name of the Roman who sponsored his citizenship, adding a **praenomen** of his own choosing and his name as a **cognomen**.

The **cognomen** was generally used by patrician families, less frequently by plebeians. Consider the following genealogy:

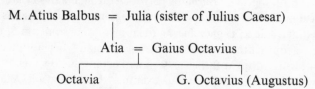

M. Atius Balbus = Julia (sister of Julius Caesar)

Atia = Gaius Octavius

Octavia   G. Octavius (Augustus)

Below are the meanings of some of the most common English names derived from Latin names or words:

Augustus	*majestic*	Alma	*nourishing,*
Christopher	*bearer of Christ*		*cherishing*
Claudius	*lame*	Amanda	*worthy to be loved*
Constantine	*firm, faithful*	Amy	*beloved*
Dexter	*right-handed*	Angela	*angel*
Felix	*lucky*	Aurelia	*golden*
Hilary	*cheerful, merry*	Barbara	*foreign, wild*

Horace	name of a poet and a gens
Julian	related to Julius
Justin	just
Leo	the lion
Leonard	strong as a Lion
Lucius	shining
Mark	related to Mars
Martin	warlike
Sylvester	woodsy
Urban	citified
Valentine	strong
Patrick	patrician
Paul	little
Pius	pious
Quentin	fifth
Rex (Roy)	king
Rufus	red
Victor (Vincent)	conqueror

Beata	blessed
Beatrice	she that makes happy
Belle	beautiful
Clara	bright, shining
Constance	firm
Diana	goddess of moon, hunt
Estella (Stella)	star
Felicia	happy
Flora	flower
Gloria	glory
Grace	favor, grace
Julia	related to Julius
June	related to Junius, a gens
Laura	laurel
Lucy	light
Marcia	related to Mars
Miranda	admirable
Norma	pattern, form, guide
Octavia	eighth
Patience	patience
Prudence	discretion
Regina	queen
Rose	rose
Silvia	forest
Serena	calm
Ursula	shebear (diminutive)
Victoria	victor
Viola	violet
Virginia	virgin

*   *   *   *   *

The following words in the lesson supply English cognates and derived words:

curia	The Roman Senate House, the Curia
communis	common, communal
contineo	continent, continence
copia	cornucopia (the horn of plenty)

usus	*use, usable, useful, usage*
factum	*fact, factual*
requiro	*require, requirement, requisition*
trepidus	*trepidation*
retraho	*retract, retraction, retractable*
penetralis	*penetrable, penetrate*

Silent leges inter arma.

Cicero, *Pro Milone*

In time of wars, laws are silent.

"Vae victis" vox intoleranda Romanis.

Livy, *Ab Urbe Condita*

"Woe to the vanquished," a cry intolerable to Romans.

Chapter XXXIV
BELLUM TROIANUM: TROIA CAPTA

After Troy had fallen, its ramparts breached, its buildings in ruins, and its leaders slain or fled, the Trojan women suffered either death or captivity. The epilogue of the fate of the women has been eloquently told by the playwright Euripides in the *Trojan Women*, *Hecuba*, and *Helen*. Ovid, as usual at his best when writing from the female point of view, also has an eloquent section in Book XIII as he describes the death of the youngest Trojan princess, Polyxena, and the transformation of Hecuba into a dog. The tragic Cassandra begins the section in her role as priestess.

34a   Cassandra tracta atque comis antistita Phoebi
non profecturas tendebat ad aethera palmas.
Dardanidas matres patriorum signa deorum
dum licet amplexas succensaque templa tenentes
invidiosa trahunt victores praemia Grai;
mittitur Astyanax illis de turribus, unde
pugnantem pro se proavitaque regna tuentem
saepe videre patrem monstratum a matre solebat.

. . . .

34a

*Cassandra, **-ae,** *f.*, *Cassandra*, daughter of Priam and Hecuba was beloved of Apollo, who gave her his gift of prophecy, but when she refused to bear him children, added that no one would ever believe her. Taken as a war prize by Agamemnon, she was later killed in Mycenae by Clytemnestra and Aegisthus.

coma, -ae, *f.*, *hair* (of the head).
antistita, -ae, *f.*, *priestess.*
nōn prōfectūrās palmās, *unavailing* (lit., *not about to be effective*) *hands*; **palmas, pars pro toto.**
aether, -eris, *m.*, *the upper air, heaven.*
Dardanidās, *Dardanian = Trojan.*
*patrius, -a, -um, *paternal, ancestral.*
*signum, -ī, *n.*, here, *a figure, image,* or *statue.*
*dum licet, *while they could* (lit., *while it was permitted*).
amplexās, participle of **amplector, -plectī, -plexus sum,** *embrace.*
succensa templa tenentēs, *holding onto the burning temples.*

(34a continues overleaf)

34b "Troia, vale, rapimur" clamant; dant oscula terrae
Troades et patriae fumantia tecta relinquunt.
Ultima conscendit classem—miserabile visu!—
in mediis Hecuba natorum inventa sepulcris:
[eam] prensantem tumulos atque ossibus oscula dantem
Graecorum traxere manus, tamen unius hausit
inque sinu cineres secum tulit Hectoris haustos;
Hectoris in tumulo crinem lacrimasque reliquit.

Achilles' Ghost

34c   Est, ubi Troia fuit, Phrygiae contraria tellus;
litore Threicio classem religarat Atrides
dum mare pacatum dum ventus amicior esset:
hic subito, quantus, cum viveret, esse solebat,
exit humo late rupta similisque minanti
temporis illius vultum referebat Achilles,
quo ferus iniusto petiit Agamemnona ferro
"immemores" que "mei disceditis" inquit "Achivi,
obrutaque est mecum virtutis gratia nostrae?
Ne facite! utque meum non sit sine honore sepulcrum,
placet Achilleos mactata Polyxena manes!"

---

invidiōsus, -a, -um, *hate-producing*, modifying **praemia** (*booty*) in apposition to **mātrēs**.
Graī, *the Greeks*.
Astyanax, *Astyanax, son of Hector*.
mittitur (ad mortem).
*turris, -is, *f.*, *tower*.
proavītus, -a, -um, *ancestral*.
*soleō, -ēre, solitus sum, *be accustomed to*.

34b

Trōadēs, *the Trojan women*.
fūmantia, *smoking* (from **fūmō** [1], *smoke*).
*conscendō, -ere, -dī, -sum, *climb into, climb up, ascend, go aboard*.
miserābile vīsū, *a pitiful sight*.
*sepulcrum, -ī, *n.*, *grave*.
prensantem, alternate form of **prehensantem**, *grasping*.
*tumulus, -ī, *m.*, *grave, hill, mound*.
*os, ossis, *n.*, *bone*.
traxēre = traxērunt (eam) (*her*).
hauriō, -īre, hausī, haustum, *drink up, take in*.
ūnīus [fīliī], *of one son* (Hector).
haustōs cinerēs, *a handful of ashes*.
*crīnis, crīnis, *m.*, *hair*; women cut their hair as a sign of grief and mourning for the dead.
Hector, -oris, *m.*, *Hector, son of Priam*.

34c

Phrygia, -ae, *f.*, *the land of Phrygia* in which Troy was a major city.
contrārius, -a, -um, *opposite*.

(34c continues opposite)

34d   Dixit, et inmiti sociis parentibus umbrae,
rapta sinu matris, . . .
fortis et infelix et plus quam femina virgo
ducitur ad tumulum. . . .
Utque Neoptolemum stantem ferrumque tenentem [vidit],
[dixit:] "Conde meo iugulo vel pectore telum."
Nulla mora est. Iugulumque simul pectusque retexit
scilicet haud ulli servire Polyxena vellet!

. . . .

. . . si quos tamen ultima nostri
verba movent oris (Priami vos filia regis,
non captiva rogat), genetrici corpus inemptum
reddite, neve auro redimat ius triste sepulcri,
sed lacrimis! tunc, cum poterat, redimebat et auro."
Dixerat, at populus lacrimas, quas illa tenebat,
non tenet; ipse etiam flens invitusque sacerdos
virginis ferrum in pectore condit.

---

*tellus, tellūris, *f., land.*
Thrēicius, -a, -um, Thracian.
religō (1), *tie up, moor;* religārat = religāverat.
Atrides, *Agamemnon.*
*dum, *until,* here with subjunctive.
quantus cum vīveret, *as large as life.*
*humus, -ī, *f., ground, earth.*
lātē ruptā, *split widely.*
vultum referebāt, *and he reproduced a threatening expression like the one on that day when as a
   wild young man . . .* (N.B. similis actually modifies Achilles and governs the dat. minanti).
immemorēs, *forgetful* (of me).
obruta, *buried.*
Nē facite—nōlite facere. *Do not let this be* (happen).
mactō (1), *slay, smite.*
*mānēs, -ium, *m., shades of the dead, ghost.*

34d

sociīs parentibus, abl. abs. *his companions obeying the heartless shade* (inmītī umbrae is dat. with
   pareō).
*sinus, -ūs, *m., fold, bend, breast, bosom.*
*conde, imperative, *plunge* (lit., *hide,* condō, -ere, -didī, -ditum).
*iugulum, -ī, *n., throat.*
*simul, *at the same time, at once, as soon as.*
*retegō, -ere, -texī, -tectum, *uncover, lay bare, reveal.*
*scīlicet, *obviously.*
*haud, *not at all.*
ūllī, dat. *to anyone.*
*serviō, -īre, -īvī, -ītum + dat., *be a slave to.*
*volō, velle, voluī, *wish, want.*
*os, oris, *n., mouth.*
*captīva, -ae, *f., a captive woman.*   (34d continues overleaf)

Hecuba's Lament

34e   Troades [corpus] excipiunt deploratosque recensent
Priamidas et quot tulerit domus una cruores,
teque gemunt, virgo, teque, o modo regia coniunx
regia dicta parens, Asiae florentis imago;
haec mater maestas lacrimas in vulnera fundit
osculaque ore tegit consuetaque pectora plangit
canitiemque suam concreto in sanguine verrens
plura quidem, sed et haec laniato pectore, dixit:
"nata, tuae—quid enim superest?—dolor ultime matris,
nata, iaces, videoque tuum, mea vulnera, vulnus:

34f   . . . cecidisti et femina ferro,
totque tuos idem fratres, te perdidit idem,
exitium Troiae nostrique orbator, Achilles;
at postquam cecidit Paridis Phoebique sagittis,
'nunc certe' dixi 'non est metuendus Achilles':
nunc quoque mi metuendus erat; cinis ipse sepulti
in genus hoc saevit, tumulo quoque sensimus hostem,
Aeacidae fecunda fui! Iacet ingens Troia."

Met. XIII.410–505 adapted passim

---

genetrīcī, *to my mother.*
inemptus, -a, -um, *unbought.*
redimō, -ere, -dēmi, -demptum, *buy back, redeem.*
nēve, *and . . . not.*
flēns, from **fleō, -ēre, -ēvī, -tum**, *weep.*
invītus, -a, -um, *unwilling, against his will.*

34e

*excipiō, -ere, -cēpī, -ceptum, *take up.*
recenseō, -ēre, *recount, retell.*
dēplōrātōs, *lamented* (modifies **Priamidās**).
Priamidās, *sons of Priam* (Greek acc.).
quot cruōrēs, *how many slaughters.*
tulerit ūna domus, *one house has suffered* (indirect question).
*gemō, -ere, uī, -itum, *groan, mourn, weep, lament, bemoan.*
*modo, *just a while ago.*
dicta, *called, spoken of as, referred to as royal* (**rēgius, -a, -um**).
imāgo Asiae flōrentis, *the image of flowering Asia*; the wealth and abundance of Asia may once have been symbolized by the Queen of Troy.
consuēta, *accustomed* (to woes).
*plangō, -ere, planxī, planctum, *beat, strike.*
cānitiemque suam concrētō in sanguine verrens, . . . et laniātō pectore, dixit, *sweeping her white hair in the clotted* (hardened) *blood and tearing her breast, she cried this and much more*; **cānitiēs, f.**, *gray hair*; **verrō, -ere**, *sweep*; **concrētus, -a, -um**, *hardened.*

Structure

183. Review of participles. Participles may be either active or passive and appear in the present, perfect and future tenses, but only in the following *four* instances:

	ACTIVE	PASSIVE
Present	**gerēns, -entis** *waging* (declined like 3rd decl. adj.)	———
Perfect	———	**gestus, -a, -um** *having been waged*
Future	**gestūrus, -a, -um** *about to wage*	**gerendus, -a, -um** *about to be waged* This future passive participle is called the *gerundive* and functions, as do all participles, as *a verbal adjective*, that is, *an adjective with action* describing a noun or pronoun.

Cēna **afferenda** ā cocō parābātur.	The dinner *about to be carried in* was being prepared by the cook.
Bella **gerenda** ab omnibus terrēbantur.	The wars *about to be waged* were feared by all.

184. Passive periphrastic with the gerundive. An even more common use of the gerundive is with a form of **sum**, a use called the passive periphrastic. *Periphrastic* means talking around or a roundabout way of expressing an idea. The Romans enjoyed many roundabout ways of expressing the idea of obligation or necessity.

They could say for *I ought to love you*

simply:	**Dēbeō tē amāre.** (or)
passively:	**Tū ā mē amārī dēbēs.**

34f

et **fēmina**, *even though you are a woman.*
tot, *so many.*
perdō, -ere, -didī, -ditum, *ruin, destroy, do away with.*
orbātor, -ōris, *m., a bereaver, one who deprives another of children or parents.*
sepeliō, -īre, -iī or **-īvī, sepultum**, *bury;* **sepultī**, *of the buried man.*
saevit in genus hoc, *rages against this race.*
tumulō, *even in the tomb* (***tumulus, -ī**, m., a mound of earth, grave, tomb).*
Aeacidae, *the son* (really grandson) *of Aeacus, i.e.*, Achilles.
fēcunda, *fruitful, productive.*
iacet, *lies* (destroyed), *lies low, has fallen.*

or, also passively:

Tū amandus mihi es.
This is a roundabout or
periphrastic way of saying, *you
ought to be loved by me.*

In other words, the gerundive used with a form of **sum**, gives the idea of
obligation or necessity. We could also translate the sentence as, *You
should be loved by me.*
The sophisticated Romans could also say:
Necesse est mē tē amāre, but the meaning is a bit more urgent:

I have to love you.
It is necessary that I love you.

N.B. When the passive periphrastic is used, the agent by whom the
action is performed is expressed *by the dative* of agent, **mihi**, *not by the
ablative* of agent with a preposition (**ā mē**).
In the Lesson:

Dixī: **nōn mihi metuendus est
Achillēs.**

I said (to myself): *I don't have to
fear* Achilles; *or,* Achilles
doesn't have to be feared by me.

Nunc quoque **mi**[1] **metuendus
erat.**

And even now *he did have to be
feared* by me; *or,* And even
now *I still have to fear him.*

185. Review of numbers. Earlier you studied the numbers 1–100. Of these
only *one, two,* and *three* are declined. All other numbers are indeclinable:

haec **ūna** domus
cinis **ūnīus (ūnius)**

This *one* house
The ashes of this *one* man
    (Hector)

ūnus	**ūndecim**
duo	**duodecim**
trēs	**tredecim**
quattuor	**quattuordecim**
quīnque	**quīndecim**
sex	**sēdecim**
septem	**septendecim**
octō	**duodēvīgintī**
novem	**ūndēvīgintī**
decem	**vīgintī**

---

[1] **mi** is shortened form of **mihi**.

186. Review of ablative usage. Because of its blend of several case functions that existed in the parent Indo-European language, the ablative combines a variety of uses that can be profitably organized as follows (see **Sec. 80**):

A. True ablative

    Separation—with prepositions: **dē, ex, ab, sub,** *etc.*

ab īnsulā	*from the island*
ex urbibus	*out of the cities*

        —with verbs: **līberō**

Cīvēs **(ē) terrōre** līberāvit.	He freed the citizens *from fear.*

        —with adjectives: **līber, nūdus, vacuus, orbus**

vacua **perīculō**	free *from danger*
orba **ventīs**	deprived *of winds*

    Source—parentage or origin

nātus **deā**	born *from a goddess*
ortus **ā Germānīs**	descended *from the Germans*

        —material

equus **(ē) lignō** factus	a horse made *of wood.*

    Place from which

Athēnīs	*from Athens*
ab urbe	*away from the city*

    Comparison: (without **quam**)

maior **frātre suō**	greater *than his brother*

B. Instrument

Means

Cassandra **ferrō** necāta est.	Cassandra was killed *by a dagger.*

Manner

magnō (cum) gaudiō	*with great joy.*

Accompaniment

cum mātre	*with his mother.*

Description

multīs flōribus	*with many flowers.*

Agent with passive voice

Ab ursō necātus est.	He was killed *by a bear.*

C. Locative—in place and time

    In place: **in Lydiā**

in Lydiā	*in Lydia*
omnibus casīs	*in all the houses*
Athēnīs	*in Athens*

With names of cities and small islands the name in the ablative is sufficient and no preposition is required.

In time: **paucīs hōrīs**   *in a few hours*
            decimō annō   *in the tenth year*
            tribus diēbus   *in three days*

D. Ablative absolute: Two ablative words making up an independent construction which accompanies the main thought of the sentence, but which has its own subject and verbal or descriptive element both expressed in the ablative case.

Nāve vastātā, bellum fīnītum   *The ship having been destroyed,*
est.   the war was finished.
                                        When the ship had been destroyed,
                                        the war was over.
                                        Because the ship had been
                                        destroyed, the war was over.

Caesare duce, nōs salvī sumus.   *With Caesar as leader*, we are
                                        safe.

E. Ablative of specification (in what respect)

Virtūte praestat.   He excels *in bravery.*

F. With verbs **ūtor, fungor,** and **vescor**

Magnīs vīribus male ūsus est.   He used *his great strength* badly.

Exercises

I.   Primo respondete Anglice, quaeso; deinde Latine, quaeso.

1. Quot filios et quot filias Priamus habet?
2. Quis erat sacerdos Apollonis?
3. Cur Apollo fecit ut nemo verba Cassandrae crederet?
4. Qui Dardanidas matres trahunt?
5. Quis de turribus Troiae mittitur? A quibus?
6. In quo loco Hecuba inventa erat?
7. Quae (*n. plu.*) Hecuba ossibus natorum dedit?
8. In quo loco cineres Hectoris secum tulit?
9. Cuius manes in terra Phrygiae subito humo exit?
10. Quid placet manibus Achilli (*to Achilles' ghost*)?
11. Quis Polyxenam necavit?
12. Sagittane aut ferro Polyxenam necavit?
13. Achillesne metuendus est Hecubae? Cur?

14. Cur Achilles Hecubae metuendus est?
15. Quam ad finem adducta est urbs Troia?

II. Change each of these constructions of obligation or necessity into passive periphrastic expressions.

    1. Debeo litteras scribere.
    2. Debet Hecuba Achillem non metuere.
    3. Neoptolemus debet Polyxenam non necare.
    4. Debes urbem condere in hoc loco. (**condere**—*to establish*)
    5. Populi verba Cassandrae credere debent.

III. Form the participles for each of the following verbs:

    ago, agere, egi, actum
    do, dare, dedi, datum
    moneo, monere, monui, monitum
    incipio, incipere, incepi, inceptum

Sample:

	ACTIVE	PASSIVE
Present	**agēns, -entis** doing	——
Perfect	——	**actus, -a, -um** having been done
Future	**actūrus, -a, -um** about to do	**agendus, -a, -um** about to be done (what is an *agenda* in English?)

IV. Supply the proper form of the number in each of the following:

    1. (*one*) equus
    2. (*with three*) sagittis
    3. (*from five*) urbibus
    4. by (*two*) viris
    5. (*out of ten*) domibus
    6. on (*one*) insula
    7. (*with a hundred*) militibus
    8. (*five hundred*) urbes
    9. (*twelve*) arbores
    10. (*Three blind*) mures (**mūs, mūris,** *mouse; blind* = **caecus, -a, -um**)

V. Scribite Latine, quaeso.

    1. Cassandra told the Trojans (*ind. obj.*) about the war, but they did not believe her.
    2. Little Astyanax was thrown (**mittō**) from the towers of Troy by the Greeks.
    3. Achilles had to be feared (*passive periphrastic*) by Hecuba, even from the grave.

Etymology and Roman Life

TOMBSTONE LATIN

Ideas of afterlife are reflected in how the Romans buried their dead, either by cremation or inhumation or both. Burial was very necessary because the shades of the dead (**Manes**) had to be appeased in a satisfactory manner so that the dead could rest comfortably and not return to disturb the living. The shades went to the Underworld as so many bloodless shadows to be ferried across the River Styx by Charon: this concept of death was inherited from the Greeks. Burials, therefore, were usually outside the walls of towns or cities, many times separated by walls or running water. Tombs were more or less elaborate depending on the wealth and importance of the deceased and his family. The most extensive were those erected for the families of rulers; the tombs of Augustus and Hadrian with their distinctive circular architectural plans still may be seen in Rome. Since the tomb was considered the residence for the dead, great pains were taken by wealthy nobles to make the "residence" appropriate to one's station in life. Elaborate sarcophagi were housed in temple-like structures whose façades lined the roads leading out of town. Extensive property going back into fields beyond the limited plot on the road might be developed into parks with formal gardens, sculptural decoration, sundials, and benches for mourners. Some tombs contained foods and utensils to make the afterlife more comfortable, but in many tombs mere sculptural representations of these objects sufficed.

The middle and lower classes in Rome, who could ill afford private residences in their earthly existence and lived in multiple dwellings or apartments (**insulae**), reflected this pattern in the afterlife, since they were usually buried in large common underground chambers (called **columbaria**, bird houses) with niches in the walls for corpses or ossuaries.[2] Cooperative societies, craft guilds, or fraternal orders sponsored such burial projects so that the cost of funerals could be kept at a reasonable price when shared by members. The very poor, the unknown, and foreigners were dumped with little if any ceremony into common open pits without markers or identifying stones, but they too were buried.

The graves and the beautifully carved markers provide much evidence for our knowledge of the Roman concepts of death and afterlife. So that the shades might be properly appeased, most markers began with the phrase: DIS MANIBUS, *to the shades of the dead* abbreviated D.M. The **Manes** (pl.) were considered as an individual or group divinity later identified as **Di parentes**, one's ancestors whose shades must be reverenced. Portrait busts of the important ancestors stood in the **alae** of the **atrium** of the home,

---

[2] An ossuary was a container for the bones (**ossa**) of the dead. Often it resembled a hut or a house, since it was the "house of the dead"; sometimes it was an urn.

indicating a respect for parents and ties with deceased members of the family, who remained in the home as guardian spirits or divinities. Next on the marker appeared the name of the deceased (in the dative case) with the names of those erecting the stone in the nominative. A marker at the Kelsey Museum in Ann Arbor, Michigan, has the following inscription under DIS MANI-BUS:

D M	D(IS) M(ANIBUS)	"To the Shades of the Dead
CORNELIAE	CORNELIAE	To Cornelia Hermione,
HERMIONENI	HERMIONENI	their mother,
CORNELIVS	CORNELIUS	who well deserved it,
HERMOGENES	HERMOGENES	Cornelius Hermogenes and
ETCORNELIVS	ET CORNELIUS	Cornelius Aquilinus
AQUILINVS	AQUILINUS	have erected (this stone)."
MATRI	MATRI	
B M F	B(ENE) M(ERENTI)	
	F(ECIT)	

Other Latin mottos include:

REQUIESCAT IN PACE!	May he rest in peace!
SIT TIBI TERRA LEVIS!	May the earth be light on you!
HIC IACET FULVIA.	Here lies Fulvia.
FLOS IPSA JULIA SICUT	Julia, herself a flower, has died
FLORES PERIIT	just as the flowers die.

Petronius satirized the nouveau riche freedman Trimalchio giving directions for his tomb at the end of his elaborate dinner party. Trimalchio tells that he wants the following words inscribed:

C. POMPEIUS TRIMALCHIO MAECENATIANUS HIC REQUI-ESCIT. HUIC SEVIRATUS ABSENTI DECRETUS EST. CUM POSSET IN OMNIBUS DECURIIS ROMAE ESSE, TAMEN NOLUIT. PIUS, FORTIS, FIDELIS, EX PARVO CREVIT; SES-TERTIUM RELIQUIT TRECENTIES, NEC UMQUAM PHILO-SOPHUM AUDIVIT. VALE, ET TU.[3]

Cena 71e

This inscription follows direction for the tomb he envisions for his remains: statues of his little dog, garlands of flowers, all the exploits of his favorite gladiator are to be depicted on the tomb a hundred feet wide along the road and extending two hundred feet into the field. He asks for all kinds

---

[3] Gaius Pompey Trimalchio Maecenatianus lies here. He was decreed a Sevir (Priest) in his absence. Although he could have held any office in Rome, nevertheless he didn't want any. Pious, brave, faithful, he grew from a small boy; he left thirty million sesterces, and never studied any philosophy. Farewell, and (farewell to) you too.

of fruit trees to surround the tomb and "lots of grapevines." A specific inscription should be added that the tomb not be allowed to be inherited outside the family: **Hoc monumentum heredem non sequitur** (which appeared on ancient tombs abbreviated H.M.H.N.S.). He directs one of his slave boys to have the permanent job of keeping trespassers, especially those who would use the tomb as a toilet, off the property. He further orders ships under full sail to be carved on the tomb, with himself represented as sitting on a dais wearing the purple bordered toga, distributing cash to the people out of a bag; and he wants all the people sitting in a dining room having a good time. Then he wants his wife depicted holding a dove and leading a little dog on a leash, and he directs that his pet slave boy also be sculpted along with sealed jars of wine, a broken urn with a weeping boy bending over it, and a sundial with his name so that anyone passing by will see whose tomb it is when he reads the time.

*   *   *   *   *

Answer the following questions using the vocabulary of the lesson as your etymological source:

1. Why did no one ever believe *Cassandra's* prophecies?
2. Why is a *signal* a sign?
3. The *turret* is what part of a castle?
4. Who is buried in Grant's *sepulchre*?
5. What is a *tumulus*?
6. What is an *ossuary*?
7. What is a *cinerary* urn?
8. What is made of rock, sand, clay, and *humus*?
9. What is the vein in the neck called?
10. Why is Hecuba called the **imago Asiae florentis**?

"Nil mihi rescribas, tu tamen ipse veni!"   *"Write me nothing, just come*
     Ovid, *Heroides* (Penelope   *yourself!"*
     to Ulysses), I.2

Chapter XXXV
FILMING THE ODYSSEY

The reading section of this lesson is a very abbreviated Latin version of Homer's *Odyssey*, the ancient epic recounting the wanderings of the Greek hero-adventurer, Odysseus/Ulysses. It was written as a script to accompany a film of shadow puppets made by students in a junior-college art class, as part of a project exploring the forms of the ancient Greek vases and black-figure vase paintings.

The characters in the film are shadow puppets made from black cardboard and animated from below with rods attached to their moving parts. A vertical stage front, of heavy black cardboard, supported on the sides by wings, concealed the student puppeteers. This front panel, about ten feet long and seven feet high, was perforated by the outlines of six Greek vase shapes. The students' careful research insured that the forms for each opening were accurate.

These openings were covered by layers of colored tissue paper which, when lighted from behind, would provide the transparent backgrounds against which the shadow puppets, also behind the stage, would move in the manner of figures on a vase painting.

From each student's choice of a character from the *Odyssey*, one member of the class worked out the brief, somewhat choppy, but connected narrative which embraces several of the generally known parts of the story. Music was added in the form of a single-line flute, to suggest the music which may have accompanied the voice of an ancient bard recounting to his listeners the hero's adventures. The Latin text was prepared for a special showing of the film at an all-Latin program, but can be read independently.

Latin Text for The Odyssey

Ecce urnae Graecae—crater, hydria, calix

Artifex coloribus urnas pingit; format picturas de deis et de heroe Graeco, Ulixe.

Ecce dea Minerva
Ecce deus Mercurius
   deus Iuppiter cum fulminibus
   deus Neptunus, currum trans mare agens
Ecce classis Graecorum, biremis, triremis
     servi remos ducentes
     duces ventum secundum sperantes.

Nautae ad terram ignotam navigant. Ibi cyclops Polyphemus agnos curat. Polyphemus gigas crudelissimus erat qui solum unum oculum habebat. Videte—nautam devorat! Sed sagax Ulixes unum oculum telo acuto transfodit. Tum se et suos sub agnos celat. Effugiunt!

Iterum naves ventis trans mare transportantur ad terram in qua Aeolus, rex ventorum, habitat. Ulixes ventos in sacco, dono a rege Aeolo, accepit. "Noli aperire hoc donum," dixit Aeolus. Trans mare tranquillum naves paene ad litus Ithacae adveniunt. Sed saccum ventorum a nautis curiosis aperitur et venti effugiunt. Magna tempestas furit. Ecce Iuppiter cum fulminibus; ignes fulgent. Neptunus e mari surgit et classis Graeca fracta est, pulsa a deo et ventis et undis.

Laestrygones quoque barbari ceteras naves in fundum maris demittunt; navis Ulixis sola effugit. Nunc appropinquant Harpyiae—aves biformes, capite feminae; tum Ulixes iubet se ad navem ligari dum nautae, auribus clausis, Sirenes effugiant. Nunc Scylla, monstrum maris sex capitibus nautam carpit; ecce Charybdis—cur tam vorax?—naves, undas, aves, vada, monstra devorat revomitque.

Sed Ulixes effugit et pervenit ad insulam Circae. Circe maga est quae potestatem malam habet; viros in procos transformat. Videte—nunc viri, nunc porci. Ulixes autem de periculo audit. Deus Mercurius eum iuvat. Ulixes ad regiam Circae venit et Circae persuadet ut viros, nunc porcos, in homines iterum transformet. Circe Ulixem et viros retinere desiderat, sed oportet eos navigare domum.

Quae domus est in Ithaca; in regia Ithacae fida Penelope texit dum coniunx viginti annos errat. Tempus est longum; et multi proci desiderant Penelopam in matrimonium ducere. Sed Ulixes adest! Omnes hos viros sagittis necat et Penelopam coniugem fidam salutat.

Minerva signum facit: finis fabulae.

Artifex fabulam finit.

Spectate fabulas in urnis, discipuli.

Hae scenae moventes factae sunt a discipulis de Collegio Highland Park; magistra eorum, Cyril Miles et coniunx Arnold, picturam moventem fecerunt.

Si pictura vobis grata est, plaudite nunc!

Verba

NOUNS

Aeolus, -ī, *m.*	Aeolus, *king of winds*
*agnus, -ī, *m.*	lamb
*artifex, -icis, *m.*	artist, painter
*barbarus, -ī, *m.*	a barbarian
calix, -icis, *m.*	wine cup
Circē, -ae, *f.*	Circe, *the sorceress*
*color, -ōris, *m.*	color
crātēr, -ēris, *m.*	a large mixing bowl
Cyclops, -is, *m.*	Cyclops
*fulmen, -inis, *n.*	lightning, thunderbolt
fundus, -ī, *m.*	bottom
gigās, -antis, *m.*	giant
Harpyiae, -ārum, *f.*	the Harpies, *half-woman, half-bird*
*historia, -ae, *f.*	story
hydria, -ae, *f.*	large water jar
*Ithaca, -ae, *f.*	*the island of* Ithaca
Laestrȳgōn, -onis, *m.*	Laestrygonians, *a race of giants*
maga, -ae, *f.*	witch
*nauta, -ae, *m.*	sailor
*Pēnelopē, -ae, *f.*	Penelope, *wife of Ulysses*
*Polyphēmus, -ī, *m.*	Polyphemus, *the Cyclops*
porcus, -ī, *m.*	pig, swine (*in pl.*)
*potestās, -tātis, *f.*	power
*rēmus, -ī, *m.*	oar
*saccus, -ī, *m.*	sack, bag
Scylla, -ae, *f.*	Scylla, *a monster with six dog heads*
Sīrēnēs, -um, *f.*	Sirens
*tempestās, -ātis, *f.*	storm, tempest
*Ulixēs, -is, *m.*	Ulysses
*unda, -ae, *f.*	wave, water, sea
vadum, -ī, *n.*	shallows, bottom of the sea

VERBS

dēvorō (1)	devour, swallow
fīniō, -īre, -īvī, -ītum	finish, limit
fulgeō, -ēre, fulsī, -sum	flash
*frangō, -ere, frēgī, fractum	break
furō, -ere, furī	rage

ligō (1)	tie
*pellō, -ere, pepulī, pulsum	drive
pingō, -ere, pinxī, pictum	paint, depict, draw
plaudō, -ere, plausī, plausum	applaud
*salūtō (1)	greet
*texō, -ere, texuī, textum	weave
transfodiō, -ere, -fōdī, -fossum	stab, transfix
vomō, -ere, -uī, -itum	disgorge, vomit, spew

ADJECTIVES

birēmis, -e	two-oared, with two banks of oars
*cūriōsus, -a, -um	curious
*ignōtus, -a, -um	unknown, strange
sagax, -ācis	wily, shrewd
trirēmis, -e	three-oared
vorax, -ācis	hungry, gluttonous

Exercises

Respondete Latine, quaeso.

1. Quae sunt nomina urnarum Graecarum?
2. Quibus signis Iuppiter intrat?
3. Quis coloribus urnas pingit?
4. Quem ventum duces sperant?
5. Quos Polyphemus curat?
6. Quot oculos Polyphemus habet?
7. Quomodo Ulixes e spelunca Polyphemi effugit?
8. Quomodo socii Ulixis e spelunca Polyphemi effugiunt?
9. Quis Ulixi saccum ventorum dedit?
10. A quibus saccus ventorum apertus est?
11. Quis e mari surgit dum tempestas furit?
12. Qui ceteras naves in fundum maris demittunt?
13. Suntne Harpyiae feminae?
14. Quomodo Ulixes Sirenes effugit?
15. Quot capita Scylla habet?
16. Quae Charybdis edit?
17. In quos Circe homines transformavit?
18. Quis Ulixem iuvat ut potestatem malam Circae evitaret?
19. Ubi est domus Ulixis?
20. Qui Penelopam in matrimonium ducere desiderabant?

Etymology and Roman Life

FOODS

The terraced hillsides and fertile valleys of Italy supplied the ancients with the staples of grain, fruits, and vegetables, just as they do today. The temperate climate and plentiful rainfall was and is conducive to all kinds of produce. Most of the same crops that were grown in antiquity still are brought to market in Italy today.[1] Flocks of sheep and goats still graze the meadows; cows, pigs, poultry continue to be cared for on farms, and the "fruits of the sea" have changed little from the delicacies that were supplied to the tables of Rome.

The Romans usually ate three meals a day, as we do, but in the early Republic the midday meal was usually the heaviest, as it still is in some areas of Europe today, particularly in rural communities. Served about the time of our lunch, this meal, the **cena**, could be more or less elaborate, depending on the wealth of the family and the social situation. Breakfast (**jentaculum**) was served early in the morning, while supper (**vesperna**) was served as an evening meal. In classical and imperial Rome the **cena** was served later in the day, crowding out the **vesperna**, and a luncheon called the **prandium** took the place of the noon **cena**. This evening **cena**, as described by Roman authors, began with an appetizer (variously called an **ante cenam** or **gustus** or **gustatio**), consisting of eggs, shellfish, oysters, snails, vegetables (cooked or raw). Imagine the hors d'oeuvres cart at a restaurant in France or Italy today with its artistically arranged variety of appetizers and the display would be much the same. Obviously, in a private home the normal meal would have more limited choices.

For the **cena** proper, a main course (**mensae primae**) of roasted or stewed meat, poultry, game, or fish was followed by a dessert course (**mensae secundae**) of pastry, fruits (raw or cooked), and nuts. Each course was accompanied by an appropriate drink: a light **mulsum** (like a mead of wine and honey) with the **gustatio**; wine mixed with water so as not to dull the taste of the food for the main course and the dessert; unmixed wine served liberally after the dinner. Since meals frequently began with eggs and ended with apples, the phrase **ab ovo ad mala** is equivalent to English "from soup to nuts."

Breakfasts and lunches were usually simple meals. Breakfast could be bread, dry or dipped in wine or honey, accompanied by raisins, salt, and cheese.[2] A luncheon might have included bread, salad, olives, cheese, fruits, nuts, and cold meats left over from the **cena** of the previous night. Raw or

---

[1] Except for tomatoes, potatoes, and American corn (maize), which were introduced much later.

[2] The Romans did not have butter; olive oil was used wherever fat was needed.

cooked vegetables may have also been served, much as in a present-day luncheon, depending on the circumstances. A siesta generally followed luncheon, even as it does in most Mediterranean countries today. The austere life characteristic of early Republican times would have precluded such elaborate meals, whereas the difficulties of transporting and storing food also would have limited soldiers' fare to simple foods, such as porridge and bread.

In classical times, the late-afternoon or evening **cena** became an opportunity for social gathering and entertainment; the wealthy Roman gathered (**in convivium**) with friends and family around a central table (**mensa**) on couches, which replaced benches or stools. These couches, three in number, on which guests reclined (**reclinare**) in a fixed position of honor and courtesy, gave the name to the dining room (**triclinium**) in the Roman house. One propped himself on his elbow (**discumbere**) and partook of the same delightful variety of foods that would appear at a banquet in Italy today, with several interesting additions: all kinds of fish, as well as sea urchins, oysters, clams, mussels, jellyfish, octopus; meats including goat, pork, veal, boar's head, whole roast pig, sow's udder, duck, goose, chicken, hare, sausages, tiny birds, such as thrushes, stuffed dormice, all prepared by roasting or stewing in a variety of ways. Beef seems to have been more rare, since the size of the animal and the problems of keeping meat fresh demanded that it be used quickly. During the Republic the heart, liver, and lungs were given to the priests for prophecy and the flesh provided the subsequent banquet. A garlanded master of revels introduced the eating and drinking courses.

Food was cut by a server, but one generally ate with the fingers; servants supplied water and towels for rinsing the hands at the table. Food was served on a discus, any of many sizes of flat dishes or plates of circular shape; large platters, shallow bowls of silver, bronze or pewter, often incised with patterns or relief work were used. Bronze, silver, fine pottery bowls, cups, open drinking vessels, pitchers, glass jars of extraordinary sophistication in color and design, all attest the skill of the metal worker, the potter and the glass blower.

Sources for our knowledge of Roman cooking include many authors whose references to foods and their preparation and consumption are valuable, but probably no **cena** in history is as celebrated as the hilarious burlesque that the author Petronius described as having been served in the **triclinium** of the nouveau riche Trimalchio, during the Empire. This **cena** consisted of course after course of elaborately decorated trays of food in all disguises: hares done up to resemble Pegasus, fish swimming in sauces, whole pigs stuffed with sausages attacked by the carver dressed up in a hunting costume, all the courses interrupted by acrobatics, songs, dancing, and tricks played on the guests, even to a dropped ceiling that opened to sprinkle guests with small gifts. The book is a treasury of gastronomical information, even if one allows for deliberate exaggeration.

Another fine source of information about Roman foods is a cookbook attributed to Apicius,[3] a compilation of several works on various household subjects: a book on housekeeping, one on sauces, a farmer's manual of household tips (e.g., one for liquefying honey which has sugared), and a medicinal guide for the use of herbs. The last section makes the work valuable to the medical world. A translation by Barbara Flower and Elisabeth Rosenbaum, *Apicius: The Roman Cookery Book* (London: Peter Nevill, 1958) makes the recipes for many exotic Roman dishes available to the average cook. The authors have tried out the recipes themselves, and in addition there is a fine introductory section on sauces, wine preparation, cheeses, and on Roman kitchens and cooking utensils. Latin and English appear on facing pages for the benefit of people with limited facility in Latin.

*   *   *   *   *

Match the following etymological items from the lesson:

	Synonym
1. Christ, the lamb of God (Answer: a)	a. agnus dei
2. A foreigner.	b. urn
3. The bowl-shaped interior of a volcano.	c. siren
4. A bowl for mixing wine and water.	d. pork
5. Half woman, half bird; a shrewish woman.	e. fractile
6. Men who sailed on the *Argo*.	f. barbarian
7. Meat from a pig.	g. crater
8. A bag.	h. sack
9. An irresistible female.	i. Argonauts
10. Shakespeare's storm.	j. picture
11. A pot for holding food or ashes.	k. Tempest
12. Something depicted.	l. finished
13. Something woven.	m. hydria
14. Something broken.	n. textile
15. Something ended.	o. Harpy

---

[3] Evidently there were several gourmets of this name, one in the first century A.D. who, having made a science of his skill as a cook, is referred to by Pliny, Seneca, and Juvenal. The book, *De Re Coquinaria*, however, is a later work compiled by Caelius Apicius, probably in the fourth century A.D.

Sententiae
Equo ne credite, Teucri;
Quicquid id est, timeo Danaos et dona ferentes.
Virgil, *Aen*. II.48

Chapter XXXVI
AENEAS

Ovid does not try to compete with Virgil in recounting the voyages of the Trojan hero Aeneas, whose wanderings in the manner of Ulysses over the same areas of the Mediterranean occupy the twelve books of the *Aeneid*. Ovid uses the Aeneas episodes to shift the setting of his myth materials to the Italian scene, for he is much concerned with bringing his tale of the changes in all of existence to his own country and to his own times. He is especially anxious to flatter Augustus, whose deification occurs at the end of the work. On the way to this transformation are the earlier deifications of Aeneas, Romulus, and Caesar. The story of Aeneas' wanderings is choppy and uneven. Below are parts of the Ovid tale; for comparison we will read some of Virgil's epic, written in the same meter.

36a   Non tamen eversam Troiae cum moenibus esse
        spem quoque fata sinunt: sacra et, sacra altera patrem
        fert umeris, venerabile onus, Cythereius heros.
        De tantis opibus praedam pius eligit illam
        Ascaniumque suum profugaque per aequora classe . . . .
        intrat Apollineam sociis comitantibus urbem.
        Tunc Anius illum temploque domoque recepit
        urbemque ostendit haec templaque nota duasque
        Latona quondam arbores pariente retentas.
        Ture dato flammis vinoque in tura profuso, . . .
        regia tecta petunt, positisque tapetibus altis
        munera cum liquido capiunt Cerealia Baccho.
    . . . .

36a

ēversam (esse), *to be overturned.*
fāta nōn sinunt, *The fates do not allow* . . .; sinō, -ere, sīvī, situm, *permit, allow.*
umerīs, *on his shoulders.*
venerābile, this is a pun, either intentional or accidental; *a venerable burden* reminds us of Anchises' relationship with Venus (**Venus, Veneris,** *f.*). (36a continues overleaf)

The giving of gifts upon the departure of the Trojan wanderers reflect the patterns of heroic society.

36b   Talibus atque aliis postquam convivia dictis
         implerunt, mensa somnum petiere remota
         cumque die surgunt adeuntque oracula Phoebi,
         qui petere antiquam matrem cognataque iussit
         litora; prosequitur rex et dat munus ituris,
         Anchisae sceptrum, chlamydem pharetramque nepoti
         cratera Aeneae, quem quondam transtulit illi
         hospes ab Aoniis Therses Ismenius oris:
         miserat hunc illi Therses, fabricaverat Alcon
         Hyleus et longo caelaverat argumento.
         Urbs erat, et septem posses ostendere portas:
         hae pro nomine erant, et quae foret illa, docebant;
         ante urbemque exequiae tumulique ignesque pyraeque
         effusaeque comas et apertae pectora matres
         significant luctum.

                                     Met. XIII.623–689 adapted passim

---

*onus, oneris, *n.*, *burden.*

Cythereïus hērōs, "Cytherian" is an epithet identifying Aphrodite (Venus) who, born from the genitals of castrated Uranus and the foam of the sea, floated by the island of Cytherea on her way to Cyprus. *Aeneas* is her son.

*ops, opis, *f.*, *might, power, resources, strength, help, wealth.*

*pius, -a, -um, *pious, devoted,* the standard epithet of Aeneas.

*ēligō, -ere, -lēgī, -lectum, *pick out, choose.*

profugā classe, ablative absolute.

Apollonineam urbem is *the island of Delos* where Latona is said to have given birth to the twins Apollo and Diana by holding on to a palm tree (here two trees).

comitantibus, *accompanying* (him).

ostendō, -ere, -tendī, -tentum, *show, display.*

pariente, *while giving birth.*

rēgia tecta, *royal palace.*

tapetia, -ium, *n. pl.*, *drapery, draped couch for dining.*

mūnera Cereālia, *the gifts of Ceres,* that is, *food.*

liquidō Bacchō, the drink that Bacchus symbolizes, that is, *wine* (lit., *the flowing Bacchus*).

36b

implērunt convīvia, *they filled up the feast.*

*petiēre = **petīvērunt**.

*surgō, -ere, surrexī, surrectum, *rise, arise, get up.*

cognāta lītora, *kindred shores,* a reference to Italy which is soon to be "related."

prosequitur, *follows them out, escorts them out.*

itūrīs, *to them upon departure* (lit., *to those about to depart*; future active participle used as a substantive).

Anchisēs, -ae, *m.*, *Anchises,* father of Aeneas.

chlamydem, *the chlamys,* a garment of wool, worn by soldiers.

pharetra, -ae, *f.*, *a quiver of arrows.*

nepōs, -ōtis, *m.*, *nephew,* here *grandson,* i.e., to Ascanius. (36b continues opposite)

You can recognize the scene depicted here on the goblet as the city of Thebes with its seven gates.

The wanderers go on to Crete, but leave soon for a trip up along the western shore of Greece, past Ithaca, past Epirus to the land of the Phaeacians, sometimes identified as Corfu. From here Ovid has Aeneas sail across to:

36c   Siciliam: tribus haec excurrit in aequora pennis.
. . . .
Scylla latus dextrum, laevum inrequieta Charybdis
infestat; vorat haec raptas revomitque carinas;
illa feris canibus succingitur, illa etiam nunc
virginis ora gerens, et, si non omnia vates
ficta reliquerunt, aliquo quoque tempore virgo.

Met. XIII.724–734 adapted passim

---

crātēra, -ae, *f., goblet.*
*hospes, -itis, *m., host, visitor, guest;* **hospes . . . argūmentō:** . . . *which Ismenian Therses, when a guest, brought from Aonian* (Boeotian) *shores; Therses was the donor, but Alcon from Hyle* (in Boeotia) *had crafted it and engraved it with a lengthy pictorial narrative* (**argūmentum, -ī,** *n., matter, subject, theme;* **caelō** (1), *engrave).*
*fabricō (1), *make, craft, fashion.*
*porta, -ae, *f., gate.*
*foret = futūra esset.
exequiae, -ārum, *f., funeral procession.*
pyra, -ae, *f., funeral pyre.*
effūsae mātrēs comās, *matrons with dishevelled hair* (lit., *pouring out their hair).*
apertae pectora, *bare breasted,* a Greek accusative of respect (lit., *opened in respect to their breasts).*
*significō (1), *indicate, notify.*
luctus, -ūs, *m., mourning, lamentation.*

36c
tribus pennīs, *in three tips, in three promontories.*
haec, *this land* (Sicily).
*latus, lateris, *n., side.*
laevum, *the left side.*
inrequiēta, *never resting.*
infestō (1), *infest.*
*vorō (1), *suck down.*
revomit, *vomits forth again.*
*carīna, -ae, *f., keel,* here = **nāvis** (part for the whole).
illa, *the former,* i.e., Scylla.
succingitur, *is girt around.*
gerēns, *having* (lit., *wearing).*
vātēs, -is, *c., bard, poet.*
fictus, -a, -um, *false, made up, fictitious.*
relīquērunt, *left behind, given, told;* (*if poets tell the truth).*
aliquis, aliqua, aliquid, *some, any.*

Of the tale of Aeneas and Dido, Ovid tells a brief summary synopsis:

36d   Hunc ubi Troianae remis avidamque Charybdin
         evicere rates, cum iam prope litus adessent
36e   Ausonium, Libycas vento referuntur ad oras.
         Excipit Aenean illic animoque domoque
         non bene discidium Phrygii latura mariti
         Sidonis; inque pyra sacri sub imagine facta
         incubuit ferro deceptaque decipit omnes.

Met. XIV.75–81

Virgil begins his monumental epic, the *Aeneid*, with this description of Aeneas and his tribulations escaping the wrath of Juno.

36Va   Arma virumque cano, Troiae qui primus ab oris
         Italiam fato profugus Lavinaque venit
         litora; multum ille et terris iactatus et alto
         vi superum saevae memorem Iunonis ob iram
         multa quoque et bello passus, dum conderet urbem
         inferretque deos Latio, genus unde Latinum
         Albanique patres atque altae moenia Romae.

Virgil, *Aen.* I.1–7

36d

Hunc, this man, *Polyphemus.*
Trōiānae ratēs, *The Trojan ships.*
***ēvīcēre** = ēvicērunt, overcame, escaped from.*

36e

Ausonium, an old name for Italy, poetically, *the Italian shore.*
Libycās, *Libyan;* **illic,** *in that place,* refers to the Libyan shores, Carthage.
nōn bene lātūra discidium Phrygiī marītī, *not about to bear well the departure of her Phrygian husband.*
Sidonis, -idis, *adj., f., Sidonian;* here, *Dido,* queen of Carthage, who came from Phoenicia in Asia Minor, of which Sidon was a chief city.
***imāgo, -inis,** f., image, copy, likeness, pretext.*
incumbō, -ere, -cubuī, -cubitum, *fall upon.*
***dēcipiō, -ere, -cēpī, -ceptum,** deceive.*

36Va

***Arma virumque,** arms and the man,* a phrase which G. B. Shaw adopted as the title of a play; it announces the theme of the epic: war and a hero's adventures.
profugus, *driven* by fate (**fātō**).
Ītaliam, *to Italy.*
Lāvina lītora, *the Lavinian shores;* Lavinia is the name of the Italian princess Aeneas is destined to marry.
iactātus (est) multum, *he was much tossed about.*
altō, *on the sea.*
***superum** = superōrum, the gods.*

(36Va continues opposite)

Virgil tells in detail how Dido, queen of Carthage, received the Trojans and fell in love with Aeneas. The bare thread of the kindly reception (**animo domoque**) in Ovid's version had earlier been expanded by Virgil into an elaborate love story set against the bustling city being constructed on the shores of Africa by the Phoenician queen. Before Dido knows who her guests really are, they tell her that they are Trojans fleeing from the destroyed city of Troy and that Aeneas is their king. She answers:

36Vb   "Quis genus Aeneadum, quis Troiae nesciat urbem
         virtutesque virosque aut tanti incendia belli?
         Non obtunsa adeo gestamus pectora Poeni,
         nec tam aversus equos Tyria Sol iungit ab urbe.
         Seu vos Hesperiam magnam Saturniaque arva
         sive Erycis finis regemque optatis Acesten,
         [vos] auxilio tutos dimittam opibusque iuvabo.
         Vultis et his mecum pariter considere regnis?

36Vc   Urbem quam statuo, vestra est; subducite navis;
         Tros Tyriusque mihi nullo discrimine agetur.
         Atque utinam rex ipse Noto compulsus eodem
         adforet Aeneas: equidem per litora certos
         dimittam et Libyae lustrare extrema iubebo,
         si quibus eiectus silvis aut urbibus errat."

                                  Virgil, *Aen.* I.565–578

---

ob memorem īram, *on account of the remembering wrath*; note the interlocking word order.
*passus, *having endured*; the perfect passive participle of **patior, patī, passus sum,** *endure, suffer.*
dum conderet, *until he might establish* the city (Rome).
*inferō, -ferre, -tulī, illātum, *carry in*; **Latiō** (*dat.*) *to Latium,* the country in Italy where Aeneas landed.
genus Latīnum, *the Latin race.*
Albānus, -a, -um, *Alban,* referring to an ancient city in Italy, Alba Longa.

36Vb

Quis . . . nesciat, *what man doesn't know. . . .*
genus Aeneadum, *the Aeneid race.*
*incendium, -iī, *n., fire.*
Nōn . . . Poenī, *we Phoenicians do not have such hard hearts*; **obtunsus, -a, -um,** *dull.*
tam adversus, *so far from* the Tyrian city; that is, they are not so far off the beaten track.
magnam Hesperiam, *Spain.*
arva Sāturnia, *Saturnian fields,* i.e., Italy.
seu . . . sive, *whether . . . or perhaps.*
Acesten Erycis fīnis, *King Acestes of the territory of Eryx.*
opibus, *with my wealth.*
et vultis, *and do you wish.*
cōnsīdere hīs rēgnīs, *to settle in this kingdom.*

36Vc

*statuō, -uere, -uī, -ūtum, *establish.*
*subdūcō, -ere, -duxī, -ductum, *beach, draw up on shore.*   (36Vc continues overleaf)

Now that Venus is sure of Aeneas' welcome, she discloses the identity of the handsome stranger and makes him seem almost like a god. Dido is overwhelmed and urges the visitors to stay in Carthage.

36Vd   "Quare agite, o tectis, iuvenes, succedite nostris:
me quoque per multos similis fortuna labores
iactatam hac demum voluit consistere terra:
non ignara mali miseris succurrere disco."
Sic memorat; simul Aenean in regia ducit
tecta.

Dido gives Aeneas gifts for himself and for his young son Ascanius, who is still on the ship. Aeneas sends swift Achates back to the ship to bring little Ascanius with gifts for the Carthaginian queen. But Venus has a better idea.

36Ve   Aeneas rapidum ad naves praemittit Achaten, [ut]
Ascanio ferat haec, ipsumque ad moenia ducat;
omnis in Ascanio cari stat cura parentis.
[eum] Munera praeterea Iliacis erepta ruinis
ferre iubet. . . .

---

nāvis = **nāvēs**.
nūllō discrīmine agētur, *will be considered with no difference* or discrimination.
*__utinam__, *would that . . .!*
Notō compulsus eōdem, *driven by the same South Wind.*
*__adforet__ = **adfutūrus esset**.
certōs, *trusty men.*
*__equidem__, *indeed.*
lustrāre, *to search.*
*__ēiciō__, **ēicere**, **ēiēcī**, **ēiectum**, *cast out*; **ēiectus**, *if he, as an outcast . . .*
*__quibus__, *any, some.*

36Vd

quārē, *therefore.*
*__agite__, *come now*, imperative pl.
succēdite, *enter*, imperative pl.
similis fortūna, *a like fortune*, similar experience.
iactātam, *tossed about.*
voluit, *caused me to* (lit., *wanted me to*).
consistere hāc terrā, *to settle in this land.*
miserīs succurrere, *to help wretched ones*; **miserīs** is dat.
*__memorō__ (1), *recount*, tell a tale.

36Ve

rapidum Achāten, *swift Achates.*
ut ferat haec, *to tell these things.*
ipsum, *the boy himself.*
Īliacīs ērepta ruīnīs, *snatched from Trojan ruins.*
praetereā, *besides, moreover, in addition.*
Cytherēa, *Venus.*

(36Ve continues opposite)

> At Cytherea novas artes, nova pectore versat
> consilia, ut faciem mutatus et ora Cupido
> pro dulci Ascanio veniat, donisque furentem
> incendat reginam atque ossibus implicet ignem.

Virgil, *Aen.* I.627–660 passim

Aeneas tells the assembled guests at the court of Dido the story of the fall of Troy, how the Greek fleet pretended to leave and abandoned on the shore the wooden horse, which when brought inside the walls of Troy caused the ultimate ruin of the city. He tells in detail the words of the priest Laocoön, who had warned the Trojans not to bring the horse inside the walls.

36Vf   Laocoön ardens summa decurrit ab arce,
> et procul: "O miseri, quae tanta insania, cives?
> Creditis avectos hostes, aut ulla putatis
> dona carere dolis Danaüm? sic notus Ulixes?
> Aut hoc inclusi ligno occultantur Achivi,
> aut haec in nostros fabricata est machina muros
> inspectura domos venturaque desuper urbi,
> aut aliquis latet error: equo ne credite, Teucri.
> Quicquid id est, timeo Danaos et dona ferentes."

Virgil, *Aen.* II.41–49

---

versat, *turn over in the mind, twist around, meditate over.*
faciem et ora, *changed in appearance and features*, Greek acc. of respect.
*****dulcis, -e**, *sweet.*
ut . . . veniat, incendat (*enflame*); **implicet** (*enfold*); three subjunctive verbs in three purpose clauses introduced by **ut**; **ut . . . furentem incendat reginam**, *that he may fire the queen to mad passion*: the participle here anticipates the result of the action of the verb.
*****os, ossis**, *n., bone.*

36Vf

*****ardēns, -dentis**, *eager, spirited.*
*****dēcurrō, -ere, -currī, -cursum**, *run down.*
*****procul**, *from a distance*, *said* (supply **ait**).
quae tanta insānia, *what great madness is this.*
āvectōs (esse), *have been carried away* (on their ships).
ūlla dōna Danaüm, *any gifts of the Greeks* (**Danaüm**, gen. pl.).
careō, -ēre, caruī + dat., *be lacking, be free from* (**dolis**, *tricks* or *deceit*).
nōtus (est), *famous for.*
*****occultō** (1), *hide.*
inclūsī, *shut up.*
*****lignum, -ī**, *n., wood*, here, *wooden horse.*
in nostrōs mūrōs (as a plot) *against our walls.*
inspectūra, *about to overlook.*
ventūraque, *and about to come down.*
*****dēsuper**, *from above.*
error, here, *deception.*
*****lateō, -ēre, latuī**, *lie hidden.*

(36Vf continues overleaf)

Structure

187. Supine to express purpose. The supine (identical in form to the perfect passive participle in **-um**) is a verbal noun of the fourth declension, but appears only in the accusative and ablative singular: **amātum, amātū; vīsum, vīsū; conditum, conditū**. The most common use of the supine is the accusative to express purpose, following a verb of motion.

Vēnit mē **vīsum**.	He came *to see* me.
Aeneās vēnit rēgīnam **visitātum**.	Aeneas came *to visit* the queen.

The supine is generally used as the fourth principal part for intransitive verbs, although the future active participle occasionally replaces it in the vocabulary (e.g., **sum, esse, fuī, futūrum**).

188. The many ways to express purpose. The Romans had a variety of ways to express purpose, that idea which in English we most easily express by an infinitive phrase:

He sent his son *to see the queen.*

Purpose Clause:	Fīlium mīsit **ut rēgīnam vidēret**.
Relative Purpose Clause:	Fīlium mīsit **quī rēgīnam vidēret**.
Gerund after **ad**:	Fīlium mīsit **ad rēginam videndum**.[1]
Gerundive after **ad**:	Fīlium mīsit **ad rēginam videndam**.[1]
causā + Gerundive:	Fīlium mīsit **rēgīnae videndae causā**.[2]
gratiā + Gerundive:	Fīlium mīsit **rēgīnae videndae gratiā**.[2]
Supine:	Fīlium mīsit **rēgīnam vīsum**.

Exercises

I A. Express this simple idea of purpose in the seven different ways suggested above.

The king sent soldiers to save the city.

1. Purpose Clause: Rex milites misit ut urbem servarent.
2. Relative Clause:

---

nē crēdite, poetic imperative pl. in a negative command.
Teucrī, *Trojans*, voc.
Danaōs, *the Greeks*, acc.
*et **dōna ferentēs**, *even bearing gifts* (**ferentēs** is a pres. act. part., acc. pl. modifying **Danaōs**);
et = etiam.

---

[1] When a noun is required to complete the idea expressed by the gerund, it is more common to substitute the gerundive construction.
[2] **Causā** and **gratiā** (*for the sake of*) are both in the ablative case, preceded by the genitive of the gerundive.

3. Gerund after **ad**:
4. Gerundive after **ad**:
5. **causa** + Gerundive:
6. **gratia** + Gerundive:
7. Supine:

B. Express the purpose idea in each of the following sentences in the seven different ways. The sentence will be given in the purpose clause form. You will need to supply the other six.

1. Aeneas Achaten mittit ut Ascanium ducat. (**dūcō, -ere, dūxī, ductum**)
2. Venus Cupidinem misit ut reginam incenderet. (**incendō, -ere, -censī, censum**)
3. Polyphemus saxum dimisit ut Graecos necaret. (**necō** [1])

Etymology and Roman Life

CLOTHING

Roman clothing was simple, graceful, and elegant. Men and boys wore a practical tunic (**tunica**) for everyday dress and a draped toga for formal or social occasions. The **tunica**, a long straight shirt, consisted of two lengths of fabric caught at each shoulder and attached down the sides with openings for head and arms. It extended to the calves and could be shortened by means of a belt (**cingulum**). Sleeves were achieved by extending the shoulder area of the cloth over and down the arm. In cloth of suitable weight for warm or cold weather and varied by being designed as an under-tunic or an over-tunic for the very old or very cold (who wore both), it was usually of white wool and served as the all-around practical garment for all occasions within the home. If any undergarment (**subligaculum**) was worn, it was a simple loin cloth tied around the groin or put on like shorts. Trousers (**bracae**) were copied from the **barbari** of the northern areas conquered by the Romans, and soldiers returning from these lands sometimes wore them as riding breeches, but they were out of style and a sign of a foreigner in Rome.

The **toga** for formal occasions was the characteristic clothing for a Roman all during the history of the country. Falling to the feet, it was made of heavy white wool and was wound or draped about the body, instead of being put on over the head, as was the **tunica**. It was worn wherever social and state occasions demanded—in the forum, the senate, the court, the market place, at public games, to and from the baths. It was the Roman's symbol of citizenship (he assumed it once he reached manhood at seventeen years of age), and the Roman boy of a wealthy family wore the **toga praetexta** from the age of thirteen until manhood four years later. Only citizens were permitted to wear the **toga**, and if exiled, one had to leave his **toga** behind.

Slaves wore only the **tunica** and added a rough cloak for severe weather, as probably did the poor also. Soldiers later adopted the cloak, and then the rich also in imitation of the soldier.

The toga had to be carefully draped by a slave who adjusted the complex folds over shoulders and under arms so that the fold in the front (**sinus**) could serve as a sort of carry-all purse. Sometimes the ends were weighted with lead to cause the drape to fall more securely. An ordinary citizen wore a natural-colored wool toga (**toga pura** or **virilis**). Fuller's chalk could give a bright whiteness to the toga, and such a whitened toga was called **candida**. Those running for office wore such a toga and were called **candidati**. A crimson (purple) border edged the **toga praetexta** worn by government officials and young boys, and a fancy **toga picta**, crimson with gold embroidery, was worn by emperors or those in triumphs.

The cloak first worn by soldiers (**lacerna**) and held together by a pin (**fibula**) became popular with the wealthy and was sometimes worn in place of the toga. The **fibula**, first developed by the Etruscans, was the ancestor of the modern safety pin, its spring and clasp working on the same principle. The upper portion of the pin was bowed into a high gentle curve and was decorated with precious woods and metals. Samples of these beautifully designed **fibulae** appear in museums all over Europe and America.

Footgear consisted of sandals (**soleae**) and shoes (**calcei**). Sandals were soles with straps and were worn indoors with the **tunica**. **Calcei** or outdoor shoes were generally of leather with sturdy uppers and straps. Senators wore **calcei** with an ivory crescent on the outside of the ankle holding together thongs wound around the legs and tied twice in front. No stockings were ever worn. The soldier's boot (**caliga**) was of very sturdy material, and the diminutive of the word, **caligula**, gave the name to the Emperor Gaius who, raised in his brother's army barracks, was given the nickname "Little Boots," a name which he retained when he became emperor.

Women's wear was not greatly different from men's. Women also wore a tunic which differed little from that of the men, save that it might be woven of finer fabric, but they generally wore a **subligaculum** or undergarment. In addition, women wore a **stola**, a long full garment fastened by a girdle or belt, indoors. For outdoor wear there was added a **palla**, a woolen shawl which could cover the upper portion of the body or go over the head when needed. Men and women wore rings (**anuli**) both for decoration and for sealing, as a signature. Boys wore a ceramic or stone central bead on a thong of leather. This single decoration, called the **bulla**, was worn by the sons of nobles and freedmen until they reached maturity, at which time it was consecrated to the **Lares**, the household gods.

*   *   *   *   *

Give the etymological source for these underlined words from the vocabulary:

1. a pious man
2. a general insurrection
3. laws of hospitality
4. fabricate a lie
5. infest the area with disease
6. came to (de)vour us
7. a large funeral pyre
8. image of his father
9. deceptive means
10. infer that you will be here
11. incendiary bomb
12. a statute of the constitution
13. eject the capsule on the flight
14. ardent admirer
15. occult practices
16. inspect the walls for sabotage

Heu fuge crudelis terras, fuge litus avarum. *Alas, flee from this cruel land,*
Virgil, *Aen.* III.44 *from this harsh shore.*

Chapter XXXVII
ACHAEMENIDES

Near Aetna off the coast of Sicily, Aeneas took aboard a Greek named Achaemenides who had been left behind when Ulysses escaped from the Cyclops Polyphemus. Achaemenides later tells a Greek friend what happened on the island after Ulysses sailed away and then he is told about the subsequent adventures of Ulysses with the bag of winds given by Aeolus, the sinking of the ships by the Laestrygonians and the adventure with Circe. The friend wondered why a Greek had traveled on a Trojan ship.

37a   Dixit Achaemenides: "iterum Polyphemon et illos
adspiciam fluidos humano sanguine rictus,
hac mihi si carior domus est Ithacaque carina,
si minus Aenean veneror genitore, nec umquam
esse satis potero, non si dedero omnia, gratus.
Quod loquor et spiro caelumque et sidera solis
respicio, possimne ingratus et immemor esse?
Ille dedit, quod non anima haec Cyclopis in ora
venit, et ut iam nunc lumen vitale relinquam,
aut tumulo aut certe non illa condar in alvo.

37a

Achaemenides, *m.*, *Achaemenides.*
*Polyphēmon, Greek acc.
*adspiciam, subjunctive, *may I look upon.*
illōs rictūs fluidōs, *those jaws dripping*; **rictus, -ūs**, *m.*, *jaw.*
*cārior, comparative + abl., *dearer than* (**hāc carīnā**).
* veneror, -ārī, -ātus sum, *respect, revere, honor, worship.*
genitore = **parente**.
*spirō (1), *breathe.*
sīdera, *constellations of the sun, stars.*
quod, *the fact that I. . . .*
immemor, *forgetful, unmindful.*
ille dedit, *it is due to him that . . .* (lit., *he gave it that . . .*)
ut iam nunc relinquam, *when I now shall leave the light of life*; i.e., *when I die.*
nōn illā condar in alvō, *and I shall not be buried in that stomach* (**alvus, -ī,** *f.*).

37b   Quid mihi tunc animi (nisi si timor abstulit omnem
       sensum animumque) fuit, cum vos petere alta relictus
       aequora conspexi? volui inclamare, sed hosti
       prodere me timui; vidi, cum monte revulsum
       immanem saxum medias permisit in undas;
       vidi iterum veluti tormenti viribus acta
       [eum] vasta Giganteo iaculantem saxa lacerto.
37c   Ille quidem totam gemebundus obambulat Aetnam
       praetemptaque manu silvas et luminis orbus
       rupibus incursat foedataque bracchia tabo
       in mare protendens gentem exsecratur Achivam
       atque ait: 'o si quis referat mihi casus Ulixen,
       aut aliquem e sociis, in quem mea saeviat ira,
       viscera cuius edam, cuius viventia dextra
       membra mea laniem, cuius mihi sanguis inundet
       guttur, et elisi trepident sub dentibus artus.'

37b

quid mihi animī fuit, *what was my state of mind.*
nisi sī, *except that.*
vōs, *you* (Aeneas and his men).
alta aequora, *the deep sea*, with **petere**, *sailing on* (lit., *seeking*).
conspexī, *I caught sight of.*
*****inclāmō** (1), *shout out.*
prōdere, *to hand myself over.*
revulsus, -a, -um, *m., torn away.*
*****immānis, -e**, *huge.*
velutī tormentī vīribus acta, *just as if driven by the force of a catapult.*
vastus, -a, -um, *huge.*
Gigantēō lacertō, *with his giant arm.*
iaculantem, pres. part. of **iaculor** (1), *throw, hurl.*

37c

gemebundus, -a, -um, *groaning, moaning, sighing.*
*****obambulō** (1), *wander over, stumble over, prowl about.*
*****Aetna, -ae**, *f., Mt. Aetna.*
*****praetemptō** (1), *feel, try out.*
orbus, -a, -um + gen., *deprived of*; **luminis**, *light* (of the eye).
*****rūpēs, rūpis**, *m., rock.*
incursō (1) + dat., *stumble against, bump into.*
foedāta, perf. pass. part., *fouled, stained with.*
tābum, -ī, *n., gore.*
*****prōtendō, -ere, -tendī, -tentum** or **-sum**, *stretch out.*
exsecror, -ārī, -ātus sum, *curse.*
*****Achīvus, -a, -um**, *Greek.*
*****cāsus, -ūs**, *m., chance, accident*; **quis = aliquis.**
saeviō, -īre, -iī, -ītum, *rage, be violent.*
viscera, -um, *n. pl., inner organs, heart, entrails.*
*****edō, -ere, ēdī, ēsum**, *eat, devour.*

(37c continues opposite)

37d   Mors erat ante oculos, me luridus occupat horror.

. . . .

     Perque dies multos latitans omnemque tremiscens
     ad strepitum mortemque timens cupidusque moriri,
     glande famem pellens et mixta frondibus herba
     hanc procul adspexi longo post tempore navem
     oravique fugam gestu ad litusque cucurri,
     et movi: Graiumque ratis Troiana recepit."

37e   Aeolon ille dixit Italico regnare profundo
     Aeolon regem omnes cohibentem carcere ventos;
     quos bovis inclusos tergo, memorabile munus,
     [Aenean] Iliacum sumpsisse ducem flatuque secundo
     lucibus isse novem et terram aspexisse petitam;
     proxima post nonam cum sese aurora moveret
     invidia socios praedaeque cupidine victos
     esse; ratos aurum dempsisse ligamina ventis;
     cum quibus isse retro, per quas modo venerat undas,
     Aeoliique ratem portus repetisse tyranni.

                   Met. XIV.167–232 adapted passim

---

*lanió (1), *tear to pieces.*
*inundō (1), *overflow, inundate.*
ēlisi artūs, *mangled limbs, torn-out limbs.*
*guttur, -uris, *n., throat* + mihi, dat. of reference.
trepidō (1), *quiver.*

                        37d

lūridus, -a, -um, *pale, ghastly.*
*occupō (1), *seize.*
latitō (1), *hide.*
tremiscō, -ere, *tremble.*
*strepitus, -ūs, *m., noise.*
*cupidus, -a, -um, *desiring.*
morīrī = morī, *morior, morī, mortuus sum, *die.*
glāns, glandis, *f., acorn, chestnut.*
*famēs, famis, *f., hunger.*
*adspiciō, -ere, -spexī, -spectum, *catch sight of.*
gestus, -ūs, *m., gesture.*
mōvī, *I moved* (*them to compassion*).

                        37e

ille, *that man*: Achaemenides' Greek friend, who now tells him a story.
Aeolon, *Aeolus*, king of the winds, Greek accusative, subject of regnāre.
*aiō, defective (ais, ait, aiunt), *say, tell,* introducing a series of infinitives in indirect statement
     to tell the whole story of Aeolus.
Ītalicō profundō, *the Italian sea* (*deep*).
*regnō (1), *rule over.*   (37e continues overleaf)

Structure

189. Ablative of comparison. After a word of comparison the "than" idea may be expressed by **quam** or by the *ablative of comparison*. With **quam** the two words compared are in the same case.

Honor est grātior **opibus**.	Honor is more pleasing *than* wealth.
or	
Honor est grātior **quam opēs**.	Honor is more pleasing *than* wealth.
Hāc mihi sī cārior domus est Ithacaque **carīnā**.	. . . if my home and Ithaca are dearer to me *than this ship*.
Caesar minor est **quam Cicero**.	Caesar is younger *than Cicero*.
or	
Caesar minor est **Cicerōne**.	Caesar is younger *than Cicero*.

The ablative of comparison is regularly used in negative sentences.

Nihil est pēior **servitūte**.	Nothing is worse *than slavery*.

190. Verbs of remembering and forgetting with the genitive case. The verbs of remembering and forgetting—**meminī, oblīviscor**—usually take an objective genitive, but may also take the accusative in poetry.

Vīvōrum meminī.	I remember *the living*. (am mindful of . . .)
Virtūtis mīlitum meminit.	He remembered *the courage* of the soldiers.

---

*cohibeō, -ēre, -uī, -itum, *hold together, confine.*
*carcer, -eris, *m., *prison (originally the barrier or starting gate of the race course).*
*bōs, bovis, *c., *ox, cow.*
*inclūdō, -ere, -sī, -sum, *shut up, confine, imprison.*
*tergum, -ī, *n., *skin, hide.*
*mūnus, -eris, *n., *gift.*
Īliacum, *Trojan.*
*sūmō, -ere, -psī, -ptum, *take.*
*flātus, -ūs, *m., *blowing wind, breeze.*
lūcibus novem, *nine days.*
aspexisse, *had caught sight of.*
nōnus, -a, -um, *ninth.*
aurōra, -ae, *f., *the dawn.*
invidius, -a, -um, *envious.*
reor, rērī, ratus sum, *think.*
dempsisse ligamina, *had untied the bands* (unloosing the winds from the bag).
*retrō, *backward.*
*tyrannus, -ī, *m., *king.*

Flammārum oblītus est.   He was forgetful *of the flames.*

or

Flammās oblītus est.   He was forgetful *of the flames.*
(occasionally)

The verb **meminī, meminisse** is defective, having no present system.
The verb **oblīviscor, oblīviscī, oblītus sum** is deponent.

191. Aids in translation. Now that the format of the reading provides the
vocabulary and notes immediately below the section to be translated,
the pleasure of being able to read the Latin fluently and get the ideas
quickly is within your grasp. The following suggestions may implement
the process. First read the Latin once or twice, either a portion or an
entire passage, to hear the sound of the words and to feel the meter. You
may understand only a few words here and there, but get into the habit
of *reading the Latin first.* Then begin your translation by letting your
eye travel along the line until the verb or verb phrase appears. If it is in
first or second person, then translate it accordingly and assume that the
other nouns in the sentence will be objects or modifiers. If the verb is
third person, then possibly the subject will be along the line somewhere
before the verb. Know the possible endings for subjects, direct objects,
objects of prepositions, possessives, indirect objects, in all genders, and
be prepared, especially in poetry for words which ordinarily stand together to be separated for the sake of meter, chiasmus, or interlocking
word order. It is assumed that you will be able to translate any tense of
the verb and any voice that occurs. Look for words that introduce sub-
ordination, and be prepared for indirect statement after verbs of saying,
thinking, feeling and the like. It may help to read through the notes first,
so that you have a general idea of the material that is to appear.

Exercises

I.   Quaestiones
      1. Ubi olim habitabat Achaemenides? Ubi erat domus ei?
      2. Quales rictus Polyphemus habet? (*What kind of jaws* . . .)
      3. Quem Achaemenides veneratus est?
      4. Cum Achaemenides navem Troianam videret, quid voluit facere?
      5. Cur non inclamavit?
      6. Quid Polyphemus faciebat eo tempore?
      7. Quibus Achaemenides famem pellit dum latet?
      8. Quale munus Aeolus Ulixi dedit?
      9. Qui donum Aeoli aperuerunt?
      10. Cur aperuerunt hoc donum?

II A. Supply the correct form of the ablative of comparison.

1. Sanguis est densior _____ . (water)
2. Amici sunt meliores _____ . (relatives: **cognatus, -i**, *m.*)
3. Consilia tua sunt clariora _____ . (light)
4. Nemo est laetior _____ . (I)
5. Quis est crudelior _____ ? (you)
6. Quis est clarior _____ ? (Ulysses)
7. Quid est carius _____ ? (gold)
8. Exegi monumentum perennius _____ . (bronze)
   Actually the word order of Horace's rather immodest summary of his creative work goes as follows, **Exegi monumentum aere perennius. . . .**
   I have created a monument more lasting than bronze.[1]
9. Verba eius dulciora _____ erant. (honey: **mel, mellis**, *n.*)
10. Estne patria carior _____ ? (life)

B. Now change each of the above to a "**quam**" idea.

III. Supply the infinitive subjects for these impersonal verbs and translate each sentence.

1. Mihi (*to speak*) libet.
2. Mihi (*to ask*) licet?
3. Amicos (*to forget*) non oportet.
   One should not forget friends.
4. (*To be away*) non mihi placebat.
5. (*To wage war*) mihi paenitet.

IV. Supply the correct form of the objective *genitive* for each of these verbs:

1. (*Friends*) meminit semper.
2. (*Enemies*) numquam oblitus est.
3. (*Greeks*) meminerat.
4. (*Food and wine*) obliti sunt.
5. (*Fatherland*) obliti erant. (**patria, -ae**, *f.*)

V. Translate into English.

1. "I remember Polyphemus and his jaws flowing with human blood," said Achaemenides.
2. When I saw your ship, I wanted to shout out, but I was afraid.
3. I saw Polyphemus hurling rocks with giant arms.

---

[1] Ovid concludes his last book of the *Metamorphoses*, lines 871–879, with much the same image: "Iamque opus exegi, quod nec Iovis ira nec ignis nec poterit ferrum nec edax abolere vetustas."

4. I ran down to the shore and begged you to accept me, a Greek, in your Trojan ship.
5. Aeolus had given the winds enclosed in the skin of a cow to Ulysses.

Etymology and Roman Life

AN INSULA IS NOT A DOMUS

To generalize about an average Roman house (**domus**) would be as misleading as to postulate floor plans for an average American house, since individual houses differed according to climate and social function; but there were distinctive features which made the construction of Roman houses unique. First was the lack of frontal space or landscape architecture, because houses or apartments fronted directly on the street or sidewalk with no area between the road and the front door, just as in European city architecture today. One entered immediately into an entrance hall (**vestibulum** or **ostium**) flanked in a larger home or apartment by alcoves (**fauces**, *jaws*) where the janitor or butler might watch the people who came to the door (**janua**), much in the manner of the French concierge. The floor of the entrance hall many times was decorated with beautiful mosaics, perhaps of a fierce dog who might be the vestigial remains of his real counterpart who once guarded the entrance. One such floor in Pompeii bears the warning, **Cave canem!** Such embellishments of mosaic decoration, usually designed and executed by Greek artists, attested the wealth and taste of the owner.

Beyond the entrance was the **atrium**, the most characteristic feature of the Roman house. In early times this name applied to the single important room of the house when the society was simple and the family gathered about the central hearth for all of its activities. The name **atrium** was later given to the large interior reception room which still was the focus for family gathering when the house had become more elaborate with separate rooms designed for serving functions of eating, sleeping, and food preparation. This **atrium** in the more elaborate house contained the central pool (**impluvium**) filled through a rectangular opening (**compluvium**) in the roof through which the rain (**pluvium**) came to fill the pool beneath. The pool could be unadorned or, in the homes of the wealthy, decorated with pillars of wood or marble extending up to and helping support the roof. Wings (**alae**) led off the **atrium** in the form of alcoves, and in these were the ancestral portrait busts. Rooms led off to the sides and the rear: the **tablinum** or study of the master which might hold the account books (**tabulae**), the family treasure chest and books for study; the **triclinium** (dining room) for formal meals, with its three couches grouped around the central table (**mensa**); bedrooms (**cubicula**); the kitchen (**culina**); possibly a library; the toilet (**latrina**); storerooms; and servant quarters.

Beyond these rooms, the house opened out into a peristyle or garden court with a portico for outdoor activities including dining, possibly a small fountain or pool in the center, with formal gardens and, in the rear, a small vegetable and herb garden with fruit trees and perhaps even a pool for fresh fish for the table. All this was surrounded by a high wall to screen it from the street or from other adjacent garden areas. Along the street, on either side of the entrance hall, shops could be rented out. These did not connect with the interior of the house, unless they belonged to the owner and were part of his business. Other rooms along the street might be rented out as separate apartments, and the upper floors that did not contain bedrooms for the main house were frequently rented out as apartments.

As crowding forced people into congested living patterns, the **insula** or apartment house provided a solution to multiple dwelling. Soaring to four, five, six, even seven stories, these wood, brick, or stone[2] structures sometimes occupied a whole city block, with a central court in the interior to provide light. Built flush to the street with shop stalls facing the road, they probably resembled their dreary counterparts in France or Italy today with narrow stairs in dimly lit corridors leading to upper floors with smaller and less desirable apartments. Built cheaply for investment, these **insulae** were often firetraps, and many times they collapsed because of poor construction. Unscrupulous men often appeared at moments of fire or collapse to buy up the apartment for very little and then put their own men to work to reconstruct the building for small investment and great return.

In contrast, as wealth and luxury spread in the late Republic and the Empire, homes of the rich reflected the desire for splendor in marble veneer and fluted columns, elaborately painted walls resembling stage sets with panels depicting scenes that seemed to retreat into **trompe-l'oeil** vistas, cleverly enlarging the size of the room. Walls sometimes had panels painted with scenes of the outdoors, as if a window opened onto a country scene. Floors were constructed of marble or mosaic tile; ceilings and walls were decorated with ivory and gold. Furniture became elaborate and expensive with precious woods and fine fabrics imported from colonies abroad designed into couches for sleeping and entertaining.

Even in the relatively mild climate of Italy, the houses needed heat in the winter, and although the poor moved with the sun into warmer areas of the house and added cloaks to keep warm, or huddled about a central hearth, the very rich could enjoy the comforts of heat supplied beneath the floors by an arrangement called the **hypocaust**. The steam rooms of the great public baths were heated by this same device. Heated air was channeled into an area of squat brick pillars on which the floor rested. The warm air circulated

---

[2] A durable type of wall construction called **opus incertum** ("random" work), named from the random fill of stone or rubble in cement, was popular in the building trade.

through tile pipes or in hollow walls to provide a comfortable temperature for the room above, as well as heating the floor directly. Examples of these hypocausts have been excavated in Italy and throughout all areas of Europe, Britain and the Near East where Romans built. Such sophisticated devices as running water which, coming from aqueducts, was piped under the roads and into the houses, made plumbing and sewers part of Roman life for the wealthy. As engineers, builders of structures in stone, concrete, marble, wood, and tile, the Romans were unexcelled in the ancient world.

* * * * *

What English words are derived from the following words from the lesson?

veneror	trepido
spiro	occupo
Giganteo	cupidus
damno	fames
inundo	gestus
vastus	bovis
viscera	retro

Sententiae

In nova fert animus mutatas   *My mind is bent to sing of forms changed*
dicere formas corpora.   *into new bodies.*
    Ovid, *Met.* I.1

Chapter XXXVIII
CIRCE

A Greek is still telling the story of the adventures of Ulysses. He continues with the adventure at the city of the Laestrygonians:

38a   "Inde autem veterem Laestrygonis" inquit "in urbem
    venimus: Antiphates terra regnabat in illa.
    Missus ad hunc ego sum, numero comitante duorum
    vixque fuga quaesita salus comitique mihique, [est]
    tertius e nobis Laestrygonis impia tinxit
    ora cruore suo. Fugientibus instat et agmen
    concitat Antiphates; coeunt et saxa trabesque
    coniciunt merguntque viros merguntque carinas.
    Una tamen, quae nos ipsumque vehebat Ulixen,
    effugit.

38a

*inde, from there, thence.
*vetus, -eris, old, ancient.
Laestrȳgōn, -gonis, m., the Laestrygonians, a race of giants and cannibals.
Antiphatēs, -ae, m., Antiphates, king of the Laestrygonians.
*comitō (1), join as a companion, accompany.
*salus, -ūtis, f., safety, health.
*impius, -a, -um, impious, godless.
*tingō, -ere, -nxī, -nctum, wet, dye.
*instō, -āre, -stitī, -stātum, pursue, follow eagerly, +dat.
*agmen, -inis, n., army, troop, band.
*concitō (1), incite.
*coeō, -īre, -īvī or -iī, -itum, come together, converge (on us).
trabs or trabes, -is, f., timber, beam; tree.
*coniciō, -ere, -iēcī, -iectum, throw together, hurl (upon us).
ūna (supply carina).
*vehō, -ere, vexī, vectum, carry, convey.

385

A Warning about Circe

38b   Amissa sociorum parte dolentes
multaque conquesti terras advenimus illas,
quas procul hinc spectas (procul est, mihi crede, videnda
insula visa mihi!) tuque o iustissime Troum,
nate dea, (neque enim finito Marte vocandus
hostis es, Aenea) moneo, fuge litora Circes!
Nos quoque Circaeo religata in litore nave,
Antiphatae memores tum crudelisque Cyclopis,
ire negabamus; sed tecta ignota subire
sorte sumus lecti:

Circe's Palace

38c   . . . sors me fidumque Politen
Eurylochumque simul nimioque Elpenora vino
bisque novem socios Circaea ad moenia misit.
Quae simul attigimus stetimusque in limine tecti,
mille lupi mixtaeque lupis ursaeque leaeque
occursu fecere metum, sed nulla timenda
nullaque erat nostro factura in corpore vulnus;

38b

*doleō, -ēre, -uī, dolitum, *suffer pain, grieve, bewail.*
multa conquestī, *complaining of many things;* **conqueror, -ī, -questus sum,** *complain of.*
videnda est, the passive periphrastic, which has the force of "ought to" (see **Sec. 184**).
Trōum, *of the Trojans,* gen. pl.
nāte deā, vocative of *nātus, -ī, *m., *born from, son of;* **deā** is abl. sing.; "goddess born" is a
  usual term for Aeneas; the Trojan hero here is being warned by a Greek who knows Circe.
*Mars, Martis, *m., *Mars,* god of war, here standing for war itself; **Marte fīnītō,** abl. abs.: *the war
  now over,* now that the war has ended.
neque vocandus es, passive periphrastic, implying obligation.
Aenēa, voc. sing.
Circēs, gen. sing.
Circaeus, -a, -um, *of Circe.*
*religō (1), *moor.*
Antiphatae memorēs, *mindful of Antiphates and of the cruel Cyclops;* *memor, -oris, *mindful of,
  remembering,* takes the genitive case.
*legō, -ere, lēgī, lectum, *pick, choose; read.*

38c

fīdum Polīten, *the faithful Polites.*
Eurylochum, *Eurylochus,* one of the Greek comrades of Ulysses.
Elpēnora, *Elpenor,* another companion; form is a Greek acc.
*nimius, -a, -um, *very much, excessive;* *too much* (supply *who drank . . .*).
sors . . . mīsit, *the lot sent. . . .*
Quae, refers to **moenia,** *there.*
attingō, -ere, -tigī, -tactum, *arrive* (at a place).
*līmen, -inis, *n., *threshold.*
*lupus, -ī, *m., *wolf.*
*lea, -ae, *f., *lioness.*

(38c continues opposite)

38d   quin etiam laetas movere per aëra caudas
nostraque adulantes comitant vestigia, donec
[nos] excipiunt famulae perque atria marmore tecta
ad dominam ducunt: pulchro sedet illa recessu
sollemni solio, pallamque induta nitentem
insuper aurato circumvelatur amictu.
Nereides nymphaeque simul, quae vellera motis
nulla trahunt digitis nec fila sequentia ducunt,
herbas disponunt sparsosque sine ordine flores
secernunt calathis variasque coloribus herbas;
ipsa, quod hae faciunt, opus exigit, ipsa, quis usus
quove sit in folio, quae sit concordia mixtis,
novit et advertans pensas examinat herbas.

Met. XIV.233–270 adapted passim

---

*occursus, -ūs, *m.*, meeting, running up* (to us).
*metus, -ūs, *m.*, fear, horror.*
*nullus, -a, -um, *none, not one of them.*
*timenda (erat), passive periphrastic implying obligation.
*factūra (erat), active periphrastic, implying futurity.

38d

quīn, *but.*
*mōvēre = mōvērunt, poetic 3rd pl., perf.
cauda, -ae, *f.*, *tail* of an animal.
adulō (1), *fawn, cringe.*
*vestīgium, -iī, *n.*, footsteps.*
famula, -ae, *f.*, *servant girl.*
*atrium, -iī, *n.*, entrance hall, reception room.*
*marmor, -oris, *n.*, marble.*
*sedeō, -ēre, sēdī, sessum, *sit.*
recessus, -ūs, *m.*, nook, corner, recess.*
*sollemnis, -e, *solemn.*
solium, -iī, *n.*, throne.*
palla, -ae, *f.*, *long, wide garment*; *robe.*
nītentem, *shining, gleaming.*
insuper, *from above.*
circumvēlō (1), *envelop.*
aurātō amictū, *a golden veil.*
Nērēidēs, *the daughters of Nereus*, sea nymphs.
*fīlum, -ī, *n.*, thread*; fīla sequentia dūcunt, *weave.*
*dispōnō, -ere, -posuī, -positum, *sort out*; *place down.*
sēcernō, -ere, -crēvī, -crētum, *separate.*
calathīs, *in wicker baskets.*
exigō, -ere, -ēgī, -actum, *examine.*
*ūsus, -ūs, *m.*, use, value.*
quove, *in each . . .*; -ve, enclitic conjunction, *or.*
*folium, -iī, *n.*, leaf.*
*concordia, -ae, *f.*, *harmony, union.*
*misceō, -ēre, -uī, mixtum, *mix, mingle, blend*; *which ingredients blend well together.*
*pendō, -ere, pependī, pensum, *weigh.*
examinō (1), *consider.*

The Men Changed Into Swine

38e   Haec ubi nos vidit, dicta acceptaque salute,
nec mora tum accipimus sacra data pocula dextra.
Quae simul arenti sitientes hausimus ore,
et tetigit summos virga dea dira capillos,
(et pudet et referam) saetis horrescere coepi
nec iam posse loqui, pro verbis edere raucum
murmur et in terram toto procumbere vultu,
osque meum sensi tum magno crescere rostro,
colla tumere toris, et qua modo pocula parte
sumpta mihi fuerant, illa vestigia feci;

38f   cumque eadem passis (tantum medicamina possunt!)
claudor hara, solumque suis caruisse figura
vidimus Eurylochum: solus data pocula fugit;
quae nisi vitasset, pecoris pars una manerem
nunc quoque saetigeri, nec tantae cladis ab illo
certior ad Circen ultor venisset Ulixes.

38e

haec (rēgīna), *this queen Circe.*
***salūs, -ūtis,** f., health, safety; greeting, good wish.*
mec mora: supply **est**, *there is no delay.*
***pōculum, -ī,** n., drinking goblet, a drink, cup.*
sacrā dextrā (manū), abl. of means; note interlocking word order.
ārentī ōre, *with thirsty mouth.*
sitientēs, *parched, dry*, modifying **nōs** understood.
***hauriō, -īre, hausī, haustum**, drink, swallow, absorb.*
***dīrus, -a, -um**, cruel, horrible.*
virga, -ae, f., *magic wand, rod.*
***pudet**, impersonal verb, it shames (me) (to speak of it), and (yet)*; **et . . . et**, *both . . . and.*
***referō, -ferre, -tulī, -lātum**, carry back, tell a tale.*
saeta, -ae, f., *bristle, stiff hair.*
horrescō, -ere, horruī, *grow rough.*
raucus, -a, -um, *rough, harsh.*
murmur, -uris, n., *murmur, growl.*
prōcumbō, -ere, -cubuī, -cubitum, *bend forward.*
***rostrum, -ī,** n., beak.*
collum, -ī, n., *neck* (**colla**, *our necks*).
tumeō, -ēre, *swell* (with muscles: **torus, -ī,** m., *muscle, knot*).
quā parte, *with that part of me* (my hands) *with which drinking cups had been taken.*
***sūmō, -ere, sumpsī, sumptum**, take, pick up.*

38f

passīs, perf. part. of **patior**, *suffer; with those who had suffered the same things.*
tantum medicamina possunt, *so great was the power of her drugs* (or *magic potions*).
hara, -ae, f., *pig-pen, sty.*
careō, -ēre, -uī + abl., *be lacking* + **figūrā**, *the figure.*
suis, from **sūs, suis**, c., *a pig.*
fugit, *avoid, shun, escape.*
***vītō** (1), *avoid, escape*; **vītāsset** = **vītāvisset**, *if he had not avoided*, contrary-to-fact condition.

(38f continues opposite)

Ulysses to the Rescue

38g   Pacifer huic dederat florem Mercurius album:
        moly vocant superi, nigra radice tenetur;
        tutus eo monitisque simul caelestibus intrat
        ille domum Circes et ad insidiosa vocatus
        pocula conantem virga mulcere capillos
        reppulit et stricto pavidam deterruit ense.

38h   Inde fides dextraeque datae thalamoque receptus
        coniugii dotem sociorum corpora poscit.
        Spargimur ignotae sucis melioribus herbae
        percutimurque caput conversae verbere virgae,
        verbaque dicuntur dictis contraria verbis.
        Quo magis illa canit, magis hoc tellure levati
        erigimur, saetaeque cadunt, bifidosque relinquit
        rima pedes, redeunt umeri et subiecta lacertis
        bracchia sunt; flentem flentes amplectimur ipsi
        haeremusque ducis collo, nec verba locuti
        ulla priora sumus quam nos testantia gratos.
        Annua nos illic tenuit mora, multaque praesens
        tempore tam longo vidi, multa auribus hausi.

Met. XIV.271–309 adapted passim

---

pecus, pecoris, *n., herd*; modified by **saetiger, -era, -erum,** *bristly.*
***ūnā,** together, in one.*
clādēs, -is, *f., damage, disaster, ruin.*
ab illō, *by that man* (Eurylochus).
certior, *made aware,* modifying **Ulixes.**
ūltor, -ōris, *m., (as an) avenger.*

38g

Pācifer Mercurius, *peace-bringing Mercury.*
huic, i.e., **Ulixī.**
moly, *moly,* the name of the plant.
***superī, -ōrum,** *m., the gods, the heavenly ones.*
***niger, -gra, -grum,** *black.*
***rādix, -īcis,** *f., root.*
monitīs caelestibus, *heavenly warnings.*
***insidiōsus, -a, -um,** *treacherous, deceitful.*
vocātus, *here invited* (*to drink*).
conantem (supply **eam**) *her attempting,* a present participle of a deponent verb.
mulceō, -ēre, *stroke, touch lightly.*
***strictus, -a, -um,** *drawn.*
pavidus, -a, -um, *frightened.*
***deterreō, -ēre, -uī, -itum,** *thoroughly terrify.*

38h

***fidēs, -eī,** *f., pledge, promise, faith, assurance.*
***dextrae datae (sunt),** *right hands were given* (to bind the pledge).

(38h continues overleaf)

Structure

192. Gerund and gerundive. Considering the *gerund* as a *verbal noun* and the *gerundive* as a *verbal adjective* greatly helps to clarify the difference between them. The *gerund, as noun*, occurs only in the neuter singular, but without a nominative, since the infinitive serves that function (for forms, see **Sec. 162**). The *gerundive, as adjective*, is fully declined (like **bonus, -a, -um**) in all three genders (see **Secs. 183–84**). The following examples illustrate usages of the gerund:

Gen.:	Gaudium **audiendī** dēsīderāmus.	We desire the pleasure *of listening.*
Dat.:	**Docendō** sē dedit.	He devoted himself *to teaching.*
Acc.:	Sē exercuit **ad dūcendum**.	He trained himself *for leading.*
Abl.:	Amāre discit **amandō**.	He learns to love *by loving.*

Notice that in each case the *gerund is an active verbal noun*, although the gerund appears without an object like an intransitive verb. When the gerund would require a direct object, the Romans preferred to change the phrasing of the idea into a noun in the case of the gerund with the gerundive modifying the noun. The following examples are an expansion of the previous examples to include the idea of the gerund with an object, but they are therefore recast in the gerundive construction:

Gen.:	Gaudium **tuī audiendī** dēsīderāmus.	We desire the pleasure *of hearing you.* (of you being heard)

---

thalamus, -ī, *m., marriage couch.*
*****coniugium, -iī**, *n., marriage, wedding.*
dōs, dōtis, *f., dowry.*
sūcus, -ī, *m., juice.*
percutimur caput . . . verbere, *we are struck on the head by a blow.*
virgae conversae, *of her wand turned around.*
*****canō, -ere, cecinī, cantum**, *sing.*
*****magis . . . magis**, *the more . . . the more.*
*****levō** (1), *lift, free, make light.*
ērigō, -ere, -rēxī, -rectum, *raise up, lift.*
rīma, -ae, *f., crack, cleft* (+ **pedēs bifidōs** = *cloven hoof*); **bifidus, -a, -um**, *split in two.*
*****umerus, -ī**, *m., shoulder.*
subiciō, -ere, -iēcī, -iectum, *attach, append* (to upper arms: **lacertus, -ī**, *m.*).
*****fleō, -ēre, flēvī, flētum**, *weep.*
amplector, -plectī, -plexus sum, *embrace.*
haereō, -ēre, -sīvī, -situm, *cling to, hang on.*
priora quam . . . gratos, *before* (*words*) *declaring that we were grateful.*
annuus, -a, -um, *of a year's duration.*
praesēns, -entis, *being present.*

Dat.:	**Līberīs docendīs** sē dedit.	He devoted himself *to teaching children.* (to children being taught)
Acc.:	Sē exercuit **ad mīlitēs dūcendōs.**	He trained himself *for leading soldiers.* (for soldiers being led)
Abl.:	Amāre discit **aliīs amandīs.**[1]	He learns to love *by loving others.* (by others being loved)

Remember that the gerundive is a *passive* verbal adjective.

193. Review of the passive periphrastic. A common use of the gerundive is in the passive periphrastic (see **Sec. 184**), that round-about manner of expressing obligation or necessity by combining the future passive participle with a form of **sum**. The reading contains several examples:

Procul **est**, mihi crēde, **videnda** insula vīsa mihi!

Despite the problems posed by the poetic word order, the meaning here is quite clear:

Believe me, the island already seen *ought to be seen* by me from a distance.

| Neque fīnītō Marte **vocandus** hostis **es**, Aenēa. | Now that the war is over, *you should* not *be called* an enemy, Aeneas. |

Exercises

I. Respondete latine, quaeso:

1. Quis in terra Laestrygonis regnabat?
2. Quot Graecorum ad Antiphatem missi sunt?
3. Quae navis Laestrygones effugit?
4. Quae terra procul videnda est?
5. Qui occursu metum fecerunt?
6. Ubi sedit illa regina?
7. Quomodo Graeci in sues transformati sunt?
8. Cur Eurylochus non mutatus est in suem?
9. Quis Ulixi florem album dedit?
10. Quomodo Graeci iterum in homines transformati sunt?

II. Make each of these **debeo** constructions into their equivalent passive periphrastic ideas. Remember to use the dative of agent.

---

[1] N.B. the name Amanda in English, formed from the feminine singular.

1. Navem aedificare debeo.   1. Navis aedificanda est mihi.
2. Ulixes amicos servare debet.
3. Graeci vinum Circes bibere non debent.
4. Troiani terram Circes evitare debent.
5. Regina sues in homines iterum mutare debet.

III A. Decline the gerund forms of each of these verbs:

                levo   doceo   sequor   conor   ago
   Gen.
   Dat.
   Acc.
   Abl.

B. Supply the correct form of the gerund in the following sentences:

1. Se dedit (*to singing*).   **canto** (1)
2. Discimus (*by reading*).   **lego**
3. Venit ad (*to give aid*).   **iuvo** (1)
4. Nuntium misimus ad (*to deliberate*).   **consulto** (1)
5. Causa (*of listening*) in aulam venimus. **audio, -ire**
6. Semper habet metum (*of flying*).   **volo** (1)
7. Librum scripsit de (*cooking*).   **coquo, -ere**
8. Romam venimus ad (*to visit*).   **visito** (1)
9. Odi[2] (*moving*).   **moveo, -ere**
10. In scholam Latinam ad (*to learn*) venimus. **disco, -ere**

IV.   Change each active gerund construction into the passive gerundive modifying the noun object; then translate the sentence.

1. Se dedit pecuniam faciendo.   1. Se dedit pecuniae faciendae. He devoted himself to making money (to money about to be made).
2. Discimus libros legendo.
3. Venit ad homines iuvandum.
4. Nuntium misimus ad pacem petendum.
5. Causa musicam bonam audiendi in aulam venimus.
6. Semper habemus metum videndi malum factum.
7. Librum scripsit de bonam vitam vivendo.
8. Romam venimus ad ludos Romanos videndum. (**ludos**—games)
9. Romam venimus ad pacem faciendum.
10. In scholam Latinam, linguam ad discendum venimus.

---

[2] **Odī**, *I hate.*

V.   Translate into Latin:

1. Antiphates dyed his wicked mouth with the blood of my friend.
2. The Laestrygonians sunk our ships, and only the ship that carried Ulysses escaped.
3. I warn you, Aeneas, stay far away from the land of Circe because she has drugs which can turn men into pigs.

Etymology

LATIN IN MATHEMATICS AND GEOMETRY

Few words in the English language so clearly show their Indo-European roots as the word *mathematics*. Its source is Latin **mathematicus** (a mathematician or astrologer), which in turn is derived from Greek **mathematikos**, coming from **manthanein**, *to learn*. The word is related to Gothic **mundon**, *to pay attention* and Sanscrit **medha**, *intelligence*. Geometry is from two Greek words, **ge**, *earth* and **metrein**, *to measure*. Most of the words used in the system of computing numbers come from Latin roots, and many of them originate in Greek roots, just as did the concepts they embrace.

Term	Source
add (addition)	**addere** (to add) or **additio** (addition)
angle	**angulus** (corner)
arc	**arcus** (bow, curved as an arc)
calculate, calculus, calculator	**calculus** (a stone used in reckoning, *from* **calx**, **calcis**, limestone)
circle	**circus** (circle, ring)
circumference	**circumferre** (to carry around)
cube	**cubus** (from Gr. **kybos**, cube, vertebra)
curve	**curvare** (to curve)
decimal	**decem** (ten)
denominator	**denominare** (to name or designate)
difference (differential)	**differre** (to carry down)
diameter	**diametros** (from Gr. **dia** + **metron**, measure through)
digit	**digitus** (finger)
divide, division	**dividere** (divide, separate)
equal, equation	**aequus** (equal)
exponent	**exponere** (to put or place out)
factor	**facere** (to make or do) or **factum** (made)
figure	**figura** (figure, image)
fraction	**fractum** (broken)
integer, integral	**integer** (whole)
line	**linum** (flax, thread)

maximum	**maximum** (greatest)
minimum	**minimum** (least)
minus	**minus** (less)
multiply	**multiplicare** (to fold many times)
number, numerator	**numerus** (number)
percent, percentage	**per** + **centum** (by a hundred)
plus	**plus** (more)
proportion	**pro** (before) + **portio** (share, portion)
quotient	**quotiens** (how many)
radius	**radius** (staff, rod, ray)
ratio	**ratio** (rational thought, reasoning)
segment	**segmentum** (a cutting, *from* **secare**, to cut)
square	**ex** + **quadrare** (to make four-sided)
subtract	**subtractum** (dragged under, *from* **subtrahere**)
sum	**summus** (highest, total)
tangent	**tangere** (to touch)
triangle	**tri** (three) + **angulus** (corner)

*   *   *   *   *

What Latin word is the source for the underlined words in the following phrases? Give the English meaning and the Latin source, as in the example:

a fugitive from justice
   someone who flees

fuga, -ae, *f.* flight or **fugito** (1), flee

salutary exercise
impious act
tincture of iodine
merge to the right
(in)vective against my opponent
hear dolorous complaints
martial music of the band
lupine gait
ursine tracks
leonine appetite
words that occur often
nullify that law

vulnerable place on his body
vestigial remains
sedentary work
solemn procession
disposition of the goods
dire outcome or event
(ex)hausting work
the rostrum in the Forum at Rome
pecuniary laws
floral arrangements
insidious remarks
succulent plant

INTERIM READING V:
CEYX ET ALCYONE

Ceyx, rex Thracius,[1] ad oraculum ire parat ut sortes sacras consultat.[2] Antequam tamen relinquit, uxori fidissimae Alcyoni de consilio suo itineris narrat. Cui statim frigus[3] ossa receperunt pallorque ora transit lacrimisque profusis genae maduerunt.[4] Ter loqui conata est; ter querellas pias lacrimae prohibuerunt.

"Quae mea culpa, carissime," dixit, "tuam mentem vertit? Ubi est illa cura mei prior esse solebat? Iam securus abesse potes, Alcyone relicta? Iam tibi via longa placet? Iam absens sum tibi carior? At puto, per terras iter est; non etiam metuam curaeque timore carebunt. Aequora me terrent et ponti[5] tristis imago. Nam ventos saevos novi (saepe parva domo paterna vidi). Quo magis[6] hos novi, magis hos reor[7] timendos esse. Si autem tua sententia[8] precibus nullis flecti potest, care coniunx, tuque es certus eundi, me quoque tolle[9] simul. Certe iactabimur una.[10] Quicquid erit, pariter super aequora lata feremur."

Talibus dictis lacrimisque coniunx movetur, neque enim minor ignis amoris in illo est. Sed neque cursus propositos dimittere vult, nec vult Alcyonem in periculo ducere; itaque multa solantia[11] respondit. "Longa quidem est nobis omnis mora, sed tibi iuro per ignes patrios, si me modo fata remittant, me reversurum esse antequam luna bis orbem impleat. Protinus[12]

---

[1] **Thrācius, -a, -um,** *Thracian, of Thrace*; **Ceyx, Ceycis,** *m., Ceyx*, king of Thrace.
[2] **Consultō** (1), *consult, ask advice of.*
[3] **Frīgus, -oris,** *n., coldness*; here acc.
[4] *Her cheeks became wet.*
[5] **Pontus, -ī,** *n., the deep sea.*
[6] **Quo magis . . . magis,** *the more . . . the more.*
[7] **Reor, rērī, ratus sum,** *think, reckon, judge.*
[8] **Sententia, -ae,** *f., way of thinking, opinion, sentence, thought.*
[9] **Tollō, -ere, sustulī, sublātum,** *take up, take away* or *along.*
[10] **Ūna,** *in one, together.*
[11] **Sōlor, -ārī, -ātus sum,** *comfort, console.* **Solantia** is neut. pl. substantive.
[12] **Prōtinus,** *adv., forward*; (of time) *continuously, immediately.*

Ceyx navem eductam aequore tingi iubet et navalibus armamentis aptari.[13]
Qua visa, Alcyone horruit lacrimasque emisit amplexusque[14] dedit tristique
miserrima tandem ore "vale" dixit et conlapsa[15] corpore toto est. Deinde
illa oculos sustulit videtque maritum stantem in nave recurva[16] dantemque
sibi signa manu. Ut nec vela videt, vacuum lectum petit seque toro[17] ponit.
Lectus locusque lacrimas eius renovat.

Interim magna tempestas nocte prima navem egit. Mare undis tumidis[18]
albescere[19] coepit. Omnia parte feroces venti bella gerunt. Nautae navem
fragilem servare temptaverunt, sed frustra. Tota nocte sonant clamore viri,
undarum vi gravis unda, tonitribus aether.[20] Credas totum caelum descendere inque regiones caeli tumefactum ascendere pontum.[21] Navis fracta est;
Ceyx in mare jactata est. In ore Ceycis nulla nisi Alcyone est et cum desiderat
unam, tamen abesse gaudet. Quoque ad oras patriae vellet respicere inque
domum supremos vultus vertere, verum, ubi sit, nescit. Tenet ipse manu,
qua sceptra teneri solebat, fragmina navigii[22] Ceyx socerumque[23] patremque
invocat heu, frustra; sed plurima in ore eius Alcyone coniunx est. Nominat
Alcyonen ipsisque immurmurat undis ut unda magna caput Ceycis mersum
obruit.

Interea filia Aeoli, ignara tantorum malorum noctes numerat et iam
vestes ille induat tegit, iam quas, ubi ille venerit, ipsa gerat. Illa pia omnibus
superis tura ferebat, tamen ante omnes Iunonis templa colebat proque viro
(qui nullus erat) ad aras veniebat.

At dea non iam sustinet pro morte rogari et Morpheum[24] ad Alcyonen
infelicem imagine Ceycis misit ut veros casus in somno narraret. In faciem
Ceycis venit exanimi similis, sine vestibus ullis ante torum coniugis miserae
stetit et haec ait: Cognoscis Ceyca,[25] miserrima coniunx, an mea facies
nece[26] mutata est? Respice; nosces inveniesque tuo pro coniuge coniugis
umbram. Nil opis mihi,[27] Alcyone, tua vota tulerunt. Occidi!"

Alcyone gemit, lacrimas movet atque per somnum corpus petens
amplectitur auras exclamatque: "Mane! Quo tu abis? Ibimus una." Alcyone

---

[13] *To be fitted with naval equipment.*
[14] **Amplexus, -ūs**, *m.*, *embrace.*
[15] **Conlābor, -ārī, -lapsus sum**, *sink down, collapse.*
[16] *Curved.*
[17] **Torus, -ī**, *m.*, *mattress, couch, bed.*
[18] **Tumidus, -a, -um**, *swollen.*
[19] *To grow white.*
[20] *The air with thunder.*
[21] **Tumefactus, -a, -um**, *made swollen*; **pontus, -ī**, *n.*, *the sea.*
[22] *Fragments of the ship*; perhaps a broken spar.
[23] **Socer, -erī**, *m.*, *father-in-law.*
[24] **Morpheus, -eī**, *m.*, *Morpheus*, god of sleep.
[25] *Greek acc.*
[26] **Nex, necis**, *f.*, *death.*
[27] *No help to me.*

voce sua et imagine viri ex somno surgit. Ministri voce moti lumen intulerunt. Postquam eum non usquam invenit, vestes a pectore laniat et ait: "Nulla est Alcyone, nulla est. Occidit una cum Ceyce suo. Naufragus[28] interiit. Eum vidi cognovique manusque ad discedentem cupiens retinere tetendi. Umbra fuit, sed et umbra tamen vera mei viri.

Mane[29] erat; egreditur tectis ad litus, et maesta illum locum repetit, de quo euntem spectaret. Dumque moratur ibi dumque "hic vela retinacula[30] solvit, hoc litore mihi discedens dedit oscula" dicit, spectat spatio distante in unda nescioquid corpus, naufragum. "Heu, miser," inquit, "quisquis es, et si qua est coniunx tibi." Iamque propinquae admotus terrae, iam quod cognoscere posset, recognovit: erat coniunx! "Ille est!" exclamat et una ora, comas, vestem lacerat tendensque trementes manus ad Ceyca. "Sic, o carissime coniunx, sic ad me, miser, redis?" ait. Alcyone se iacit in undas. Volabat per aera pennis natis.[31] Ut corpus sine sanguine tetigit, artus[32] amplexa recentibus alis, oscula frigida duro rostro dedit. Hoc Ceyx sensit et tandem deis miserantibus,[33] ambo in aves mutantur. Coerunt et fiunt parentes perque septem dies placidos hiberno tempore incubat Alcyone pendentibus aequora nidis.[34] Tunc mare est placidum nam Aeolus ventos custodit praestatque nepotibus aequor.[35]

---

[28] **Naufragus, -ī**, *m.*, *shipwrecked person, castaway.*

[29] **Māne**, indecl. noun or adv., *morning, early in the morning, early.*

[30] *Ropes.*

[31] **Nātus, -a, -um**, *newly created;* participle of **nascor**, *be born, be produced.*

[32] **Artus, -ūs**, *m.*, *limbs.*

[33] *Having compassion.*

[34] *Sits on her nest floating on the surface of the sea.*

[35] *Guarantees the safety of the sea for his grandchildren.*

Having left the unfortunate Dido to her dramatic suicide in Carthage, Aeneas then visited Sicily where he paid honors at his father's tomb. He then sailed past the lands of Aeolus and escaped the dangers of Circe to arrive finally in Italy. At Cumae, the setting for his descent to the Underworld, his guide is the Sibyl, that aged prophetess whose powers of divination and oracular vision are a gift of Apollo. Ovid has her tell her own story, as well as prophesying Aeneas' adventures. The marshy land around Cumae with its sacred grove is the background for Aeneas' entrance into Hades, the Underworld. The Sibyl bids Aeneas strip from a tree in the grove a "golden bough" which will act as a magic talisman of entrance and safe conduct in the trip down to the Underworld. (Frazer, in naming his gigantic work of initiation into the myths of all peoples, uses this name as the talisman "induction" into the realm of myth materials from all over the world. His twelve-volume compendium has now been republished in a single comprehensive volume called *The New Golden Bough*.)

Sententiae

Facilis descensus Averno. *The descent to Avernus is easy.*
Virgil, *Aen.* VI.126
Invia virtuti nulla est via.
Ovid, *Met.* XIV.113

Chapter XXXIX
SIBYLLA CUMAE

The Grotto of the Sibyl

39a   [Aeneas] . . . loca feta palustribus undis,
litora Cumarum vivacisque antra Sibyllae
intrat, et [ut] ad manes veniat per Averna paternos
orat. At illa diu vultum tellure moratum
erexit tandemque deo furibunda recepto
"magna petis," dixit, "vir factis maxime, cuius
dextera per ferrum, pietas spectata per ignes.
Pone tamen, Troiane, metum: potiere petitis
Elysiasque domos et regna novissima mundi
me duce cognosces simulacraque cara parentis.
invia virtuti nulla est via."

39a

*__fētus, -a, -um__ + abl., *full of, teeming with, pregnant.*
paluster, -tris, -tre, *marshy.*
*__Cūmae, -ārum,__ *f., Cumae,* ancient city in Italy, famous for the Sibyl.
*__antrum, -ī,__ *n., cave.*
*__vīvax, -ācis,__ *long-lived, lively.*
Sibylla, -ae, *f., the sibyl,* a wise prophetess.
mānēs, mod. by **paternōs.**
*__paternus, -a, -um,__ *paternal, of a father.*
Averna, -ōrum, *n. pl., region or cave of Avernus,* legendary entrance to the Underworld.
*__moror, -ārī,__ morātus sum, *delay.*
*__tellus, -ūris,__ *f., the earth.*
ērexit, *raised* (her face).
furibunda, *inspired in mad divination.*
*__vir maxime,__ vocative, although the **maxime** more logically goes with **factīs,** *o man of greatest deeds* or *mighty deeds.*
spectāta (est), with a double subject of *hand* (**dextera**) and *piety* (**pietās**).
*__pōnō, -ere, posuī, positum,__ *lay down, put aside.*
potiēre (-iēris) petītīs, *you will have your wish*; lit., *you will gain the things sought*; **potior** takes the abl.   (39a continues overleaf)

39b   dixit et auro
fulgentem ramum silva Iunonis Avernae
monstravit iussitque suo divellere trunco.
Paruit Aeneas et formidabilis Orci
vidit opes atavosque suos umbramque senilem
magnanimi Anchisae; didicit quoque iura locorum,
quaeque novis essent adeunda pericula bellis.

The wars referred to are the ones Aeneas is destined to fight in Italy with
Turnus for the hand of Lavinia, the daughter of Latinus, king of Latium.
Turnus, king of the neighboring Rutulians, had been promised the hand of
this princess in marriage long before Aeneas' arrival in Italy, and this valiant
local chief contends for her hand in a long bloody war against Aeneas and his
followers. King Latinus favors Aeneas, but Queen Amata, Latinus' wife,
favors the local man. Virgil describes the climax of this war, a battle of
champions, in his Twelfth Book of the *Aeneid*, and the epic poem closes with
the defeat of Turnus and the departure of his angry shade to the underworld.
    Before all this strife in Italy, however, the Sibyl conducts Aeneas through
Hades, and on the way out she tells the hero her story:

---

*domos Ēlysiās, *Elysian abodes.*
*mundus, -ī, *m., the universe, world.*
*cognoscō, -ere, -nōvī, -nitum, *recognize, see.*
simulacrum, -ī, *n., likeness, image.*
*invius, -a, -um, *impassable.*

                                                        39b
*fulgeō, -ēre, fulsī, *shine, gleam, glitter.*
silvā = in silvā.
Iūnōnis Avernae, *Avernal Juno.*
dīvellere, with **eum** as subject, *him to remove it from its trunk.*
*truncus, -ī, *m., trunk.*
*pāreō, -ēre, -uī + dat., *obey.*
*formīdābilis, -e, *terrible, fearful.*
*Orcus, -ī, *m., Orcus, the Underworld.*
atavus, -ī, *m., ancestor.*
*senīlis, -e, *old, aged.*
*magnanimus, -a, -um, *greathearted.*
*Anchīsēs, -ae, *m., Anchises, the father of Aeneas.*
quae . . . bellīs, *what dangers he must undergo in new wars* (lit., *what dangers would have to be
    undergone*).

39c   "Nec dea sum," dixit, "nec sacri turis honore
       humanum dignare caput; neu nescius erres,
       lux aeterna mihi carituraque fine dabatur,
       si mea virginitas Phoebo patuisset amanti.

A Foolish Request

39d   "Dum tamen hanc sperat, dum praecorrumpere donis
       me cupit, 'elige,' ait 'virgo Cumaea, quid optes:
       optatis potiere tuis.' Ego pulveris hausti
       ostendi cumulum: quot haberet corpora pulvis,
       tot mihi natales contingere vana rogavi;
       excidit, ut peterem iuvenes quoque protinus annos.
       Hos tamen ille mihi dabat aeternamque iuventam,
       si Venerem paterer: contempto munere Phoebi,
       innuba permaneo; sed iam felicior aetas
       terga dedit, tremuloque gradu venit aegra senectus,
       quae patienda diu est.

39c

*dignor, -ārī, dignātus sum, *consider worthy*; **nec dignāre** is a mild imperative, *do not consider a human head worthy*.

tūs, tūris, *n., incense.*

*nescius, -a, -um, *not knowing,* here *unknowing, ignorant.*

*errēs, subjunctive of *errō (1), *lest you err, so that you not err.*

*careō, -ēre, -uī, -itūrum, *be without.*

*virginitās, -tātis, *f., virginity.*

Phoebō amantī, *to Phoebus as a lover.*

39d

sperat, understand **Phoebus** as subject.

praecorrumpere, *bribe, persuade.*

optēs, subjunctive in indirect question.

*pulvis, -eris, *m., sand.*

haustī, perf. pass. part. of **hauriō**, modifying **pulveris**, *collected, drawn up.*

*ostendō, -ere, -tendī, -tentum, *point out, show.*

cumulus, -ī, *m., pile, heap.*

*corpus, -oris, *n., body; grains* (of sand).

nātālis, -is, *m., birthday;* here with **contingere**, *to reach as many birthdays.*

*vānus, -a, -um, *silly, idle, vain.*

excidit, ut peterem = **oblīta sum petere.**

prōtinus, *continuous.*

*iuvenis, -e, *young, youthful.*

quot . . . tot, *as many . . . so many.*

*Venus, -eris, *f.,* Venus, but here *love,* and probably *his love.*

contemptō mūnere Phoebī, abl. abs., *having scorned the gift of Phoebus.*

innubus, -a, -um, *unwed.*

*aetās, aetātis, *f., age, time of life.*

*aeger, -gra, -grum, *weak, sick.*

tremulō gradū, *with trembling step.*

Only a Voice Remains

39e   Tempus erit, cum de tanto me corpore parvam
      longa dies faciet, consumptaque membra senecta
      ad minimum redigentur onus: nec amata videbor
      nec placuisse deo, Phoebus quoque forsitan ipse
      vel non cognoscet, vel dilexisse negabit:
      usque adeo mutata ferar nullique videnda,
      voce tamen noscar; vocem mihi fata relinquent."

Met. XIV.103–153 passim

   Thus the Sibyl ends her tale with the grim reminder that in the world of change even one who has been touched by a divinity is subject to decay and dissolution. The whole idea of prophetic voices which speak the words of prophecy at sacred spots in the ancient world (at Delphi, at Samos, in Libya, and here at Cumae) still poses a question of wonder and mystery. How does the voice of a prophet speak—through an inspired book, through a chosen individual, through a dedicated scholar, or as here, through one beloved of a god?

   Cassandra, princess of Troy, also had been given the gift of prophecy by Apollo, but when she refused to bear him children he added that no one would ever believe her. In both instances, the recipient of the gift is a mortal beloved of the god. We still speak of an inspired person as one whom a god loves, although we no longer attribute the love as the profane or personal kind of possession described in these myths, nor do we associate the inspired words with the maddened intoxication or drugged state that the inhaling of fumes would produce, a trance into which the prophet entered. But there are seemingly magic areas of the world—caves, grottos, crevices, places where the underworld and its secrets bubble up and spill out into the upper world, places of magic smell and color and atmosphere—where it is easy to believe a divine spirit could emerge to conduct a hero into the mysteries of the unknown world beneath the earth.

39e

longa diēs, *length of days*, i.e., *old age.*
*****senectus, -a, -um**, *old, aged.*
*****consumō, -ere, -sumpsī, -sumptum**, *consume, destroy, waste.*
*****redigō, -ere, -ēgī, -actum**, *bring back, reduce.*
*****forsitan**, *perhaps.*
dīlexisse, *that he loved me.*
*****vel . . . vel**, *either . . . or.*
usque adeō, *all the way to that point.*
videnda nūllī, *though visible to no one*; lit., *about to be seen by no one.*
noscō, -ere, nōvī, nōtum, *know.*

Structure

194. Review of the vocative. The case of direct speech, direct address, where a person is directly spoken to is the vocative case, the endings of which are identical with those of the nominative case, except for masculine singular of the second declension: **-us** becomes **-e.**

    vir maxime factīs—*o greatest man* in deeds

    Also irregular is the form for words in **-ius**, which become **-ī**:

    Gāius becomes **Gaī**
    Vergilius becomes **Vergilī**

    All other forms are regular and identical with the nominative.

	I	II	III	IV	V
Sing.	puella	amīce	fīlī	māter	exercitus	diēs
Pl.	puellae	amīcī	fīliī	mātrēs	exercitūs	diēs

195. Effective repetition: **seu ... seu**; **nec ... nec**; **vel ... vel**; **et ... et**. Latin frequently employs repeated conjunctions to introduce parallel ideas, either words, phrases or clauses with the same effective balance as would occur from the same use in English: *either ... or*; *neither ... nor*; *both ... and*.

196. Review of passive forms and deponent verbs. It is important to be able to recognize passive forms, both for their regular use with verbs in the passive voice and also for their use in deponent verbs. Especially the alternate form for the second person singular should be mastered so as not to be a stumbling block in translating. The forms for the deponent verbs will serve to review the passive endings:

1st Conj.:	**mīror, mīrārī, mīrātus sum**	admire
2nd Conj.:	**vereor, verērī, veritus sum**	fear
3rd Conj.:	**loquor, loquī, locūtus sum**	speak
4th Conj.:	**potior, potīrī, potītus sum**	get, obtain

INDICATIVE MOOD

Present Tense

mīror	vereor	loquor	potior
mīrāris (-re)	verēris (-re)	loqueris (-re)	potīris (-re)
mīrātur	verētur	loquitur	potītur
mīrāmur	verēmur	loquimur	potīmur
mīrāminī	verēminī	loquiminī	potīminī
mīrantur	verentur	loquuntur	potiuntur

Imperfect (add -ba-)

mīrābar	verēbar	loquēbar	potiēbar
mīrābāris (-re)	verēbāris (-re)	loquēbāris (-re)	potiēbāris (-re)
etc.	etc.	etc.	etc.

Future

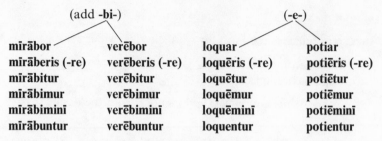

(add -bi-)   (-e-)

mīrābor	verēbor	loquar	potiar
mīrāberis (-re)	verēberis (-re)	loquēris (-re)	potiēris (-re)
mīrābitur	verēbitur	loquētur	potiētur
mīrābimur	verēbimur	loquēmur	potiēmur
mīrābiminī	verēbiminī	loquēminī	potiēminī
mīrābuntur	verēbuntur	loquentur	potientur

The Perfect System is regular

Perfect: mīrātus, veritus, locūtus, potītus sum, es, est, mīrātī, -ae, -a, etc. sumus, estis, sunt

Pluperf.: mīrātus, veritus, locūtus, potītus eram, erās, erat, mīrātī, -ae, -a, etc. erāmus, erātis, erant

Fut. Perf.: mīrātus, veritus, locūtus, potītus erō, eris, erit, mīrātī, -ae, -a, etc. erimus, eritis, erunt

SUBJUNCTIVE MOOD

Present

mīrer	verear	loquar	potiar
mīrēris (-re)	vereāris (-re)	loquāris (-re)	potiāris (-re)
mīrētur	vereātur	loquātur	potiātur
mīrēmur	vereāmur	loquāmur	potiāmur
mīrēminī	vereāminī	loquāminī	potiāminī
mīrentur	vereantur	loquantur	potiantur

Imperfect

mīrārer	verērer	loquerer	potīrer
mīrārēris (-re)	verērēris (-re)	loquerēris (-re)	potīrēris (-re)
mīrārētur	verērētur	loquerētur	potīrētur
mīrārēmur	verērēmur	loquerēmur	potīrēmur
mīrārēminī	verērēminī	loquerēminī	potīrēminī
mīrārentur	verērentur	loquerentur	potīrentur

Perfect: mīrātus, veritus, locūtus, potītus sim, sīs, sit, mīrātī, -ae, -a, etc. sīmus, sītis, sint

Pluperf.: mīrātus, veritus, locūtus, potītus essem, essēs, esset, mīrātī, -ae, -a, etc. essēmus, essētis, essent

PARTICIPLES

mīrāns	verēns	loquēns	potiēns
mīrātus	veritus	locūtus	potītus
mīrātūrus	veritūrus	locūtūrus	potītūrus
mīrandus	verendus	loquendus	potiendus

INFINITIVES		IMPERATIVES	
Pres.	mīrārī, *to admire*	*Sing.*	mīrāre
Perf.	mīrātus esse, *to have admired*	*Pl.*	mīrāminī
Fut.	mīrātūrus esse, *to be about to admire*		

Consult Appendix for forms in other conjugations.

Exercises

I. Respondete Latine, quaeso:

1. Ubi est antrum Sibyllae?
2. Quid orat Aeneas ut Sibylla faciat?
3. Quid Sibylla monstravit in silva Avernae Iunonis?
4. Cuius umbram Aeneas vidit in Orco?
5. Estne Sibylla dea?
6. Quis Sibyllam amavit?
7. Quid rogavit Sibylla ut Apollo daret?
8. Quid Sibylla rogare oblita est?
9. Ducitne Apollo Sibyllam in matrimonium?
10. Cum Sibylla minima fuerit, quid permanebit?

II. Give a synopsis of **hortor**, indicative and subjunctive, 3rd per. sing.
 sequor, indicative and subjunctive, 2nd per. sing.
 (use the **-re** forms)

III. Translate into Latin:

1. I was trying	6. he has suffered
2. he followed	7. we will urge
3. they spoke	8. we will follow
4. he tried	9. you (pl.) have feared
5. we will get possession of	10. you (pl.) were suffering

IV. Fill in the vocative forms, in the following sentences:

1. (*Boys*), venite ad me.
2. (*Marcus*), mane in schola.
3. (*Vergilius*), carmina tua sunt dulcissima.
4. (*Mothers*), audite mea verba.
5. (*Night*), veni celeriter.

V. Translate into Latin:

1. Aeneas entered the cave of the Sibyl on the shores of Cumae.
2. The Trojan hero sought to visit his father's shade in Orcus.
3. With the Sibyl as his guide (*abl. abs.*), Aeneas was able to recognize the likeness of his father.
4. No road is impassable for a good man.
5. The Sibyl ordered Aeneas to take the bough gleaming with gold from the trunk of the tree.
6. Phoebus loved the Sibyl and wanted to give her eternal life (**lux**), if she would open herself to his love.
7. The Sibyl asked for as many years as were in a pile of sand, but she forgot to ask also for young years.
8. The Sibyl grew older and older and smaller and smaller.
9. Even Phoebus Apollo himself no longer loved her.
10. Only her voice remained.

Etymology

LATIN ABBREVIATIONS IN ENGLISH

MEDICAL

NPO (**nihil per os**) nothing by mouth
h.s. (**hora somni**) at bedtime (hour of sleep)
bid (**bis in die**) two times daily
c̄ (**cum**) with
R$_x$ (**recipe**) take
a.c. (**ante cenam**) before meals
p.c. (**post cenam**) after meals
up ad lib (**ad libidinem**) patient may get up when he wishes

CHEMICAL

Au (**Aurum**) gold
Cu (**Cuprum**) copper
Fe (**Ferrum**) iron
Pb (**Plumbum**) lead
Aq (**Aqua**) water
Ag (**Argentum**) silver
K (**Kalium**) potassium
Te (**Tellurium**) tellurium

TEMPORAL

A.M. (**ante meridiem**) before noon
P.M. (**post meridiem**) after noon
pro tem (**pro tempore**) for the time being
A.D. (**Anno Domini**) in the year of our Lord
ad. inf. (**ad infinitum**) to infinity
c. (**circa**) about
fl. (**floruit**) he flourished, lived

RELIGIOUS

INRI (**Iesus Nazarenus, Rex Iudaeorum**) Jesus of Nazareth, King of the Jews
DV (**Deo volente**) God willing

LITERARY

P.S. (**post scriptum**) written after
etc. (**et cetera**) and others
e.g. (**exemplum gratia**) for example
i.e. (**id est**) that is
ibid. (**ibidem**) in the same place
viz. (**videlicet**) you may see, namely
cf. (**confer**) compare
ex lib. (**ex libris**) from the books
  of . . .
loc. cit. (**loco citato**) in the place
  cited
non seq. (**non sequitur**) it does not
  follow
N.B. (**nota bene**) note well

MISCELLANEOUS

QED (**quod erat demonstrandum**)
  that which was to be
  demonstrated or proved
RSVP (**Répondez, s'il vous plaît**
  from **Respondete, si vobis placet**)
  Reply, if you please
Vox pop (**vox populi**) voice of the
  people
Verb sap (**verbum sapienti satis est**)
  a word to the wise is sufficient
v.v. (**vice versa**) turned to the
  opposite position
SPQR (**Senatus Populusque
  Romanus**) the senate and the
  people of Rome

*   *   *   *   *

Define the following English words and tell what their etymology is,
basing your choice of source words on the vocabulary of the lesson:

vivacious	lively	**vivax, vivacis,** *lively*
paternal		
position		
mundane		
cognition		
trunk		
formidable		
senile		
magnanimous		
dignify		
lucifer		
virginity		
patent		
(a)spirations		
elect		
ostentatious		

(ac)cumulate
vain
juvenile
contemptuous
permanent
temporal
cognition

Sententiae

Tantae molis erat Romanam condere gentem.   *So massive a task it was to*
            Virgil, *Aen.* I.33   *found the Roman race.*

Chapter XL
AENEAS IN ITALIA

40a   [Aeneas] . . . domo potitur nataque Latini,
         non sine Marte tamen. Bellum cum gente feroci
         suscipitur, pactaque furit pro coniuge Turnus.
         Concurrit Latio Tyrrhenia tota, diuque
         ardua sollicitis victoria quaeritur armis.
         Auget uterque suas externo robore vires,
         et multi Rutulos, multi Troiana tuentur
         castra, neque Aeneas Evandri ad moenia frustra [ivit
         nam Pallas, filius Evandri ad bellum pugnandum missus est.]
         . . . .
         [Bellum] perstat, habetque deos pars utraque, quodque deorum est
         instar, habent animos. . . .
         Bella gerunt, tandemque Venus victricia natri
         arma videt, Turnusque cadit.
                                         Met. XIV.449–573 adapted passim

---

40a

*nāta, -ae, f., daughter, i.e., Lavinia, daughter of Latinus, king of Latium.
pacta, *agreed upon, promised.*
furō, -ere, -uī (rare), *rage, be furious.*
*concurrō, -ere, -currī, -cursum, *rush to battle* with or against (with dat. **Latiō**).
Tyrrhenia, -ae, f., Etruria.
*sollicitus, -a, -um, *anxious.*
*augeō, -ēre, auxī, auctum, *increase.*
*uterque, utraque, utrumque, *each side, each* (of two).
*externus, -a, -um, *outside, external, foreign.*
rōbur, -oris, *n., strength.*
*vīs, acc. **vim**, abl. **vī**, pl. **vīrēs**, *strength.*
Rutulōs, *the Rutulians*, a tribe in Italy of which Turnus is chief.
*tueor, -ērī, tutus sum, *aid, protect.*
neque . . . frustra, *and Aeneas did not go in vain to the city of Evander;* **moenia** are *city walls*
      or *fortifications.* Evander is king of a nearby city who sends his son Pallas to fight for the
      Trojans.
*perstō, -are, -stitī, -staturus, *stand firm, continue.*   (40a continues overleaf)

The following description of the end of the battle between Aeneas and
Turnus is taken from the conclusion of the *Aeneid,* an episode which Virgil
describes most vividly. The two heroes have come out to meet in single
combat, and the Rutulians with a groan watch their leader, who has fallen
to the ground, beg for mercy.

40Vb   Ille humilis supplexque oculos dextramque precantem
           protendens "equidem merui, nec deprecor" inquit;
           "utere sorte tua. Miseri te si qua parentis
           tangere cura potest, oro (fuit et tibi talis
           Anchises genitor), Dauni misere senectae,
           et me, seu corpus spoliatum lumine mavis,
           redde meis.
40Vc   Vicisti et [me] victum tendere palmas
           Ausonii videre; tua est Lavinia coniunx."
           Aeneas, volvens oculos, dextramque repressit;
           et iam iamque magis cunctantem flectere sermo
           coeperat, infelix umero cum apparuit alto
           balteus et notis fulserunt cingula bullis
           Pallantis pueri, victum quem vulnere Turnus
           straverat atque umeris inimicum insigne gerebat.

       .   .   .   .

---

*instar + gen., *equivalent to.*
*tandem, *at length, at last, finally.*
victricia, *conquering, victorious,* modifying **arma.**

40Vb

humilis supplexque, *humble and suppliant.*
precantem, *pleading* (hand).
merui, *I have deserved* (death).
dēprecor, dep. (1), *nor do I beg for mercy.*
ūtere sorte tuā, *press* (use) *your luck;* **utere** is imperative singular of ***ūtor.**
*genitor, -ōris, *m., parent.*
Daunī . . . senectae, *pity the old age of Daunus* (father of Turnus).
et . . . meīs, *and return me or my body, deprived of life, if you wish, to my family.*

40Vc

*palma, -ae, *f., hand, palm* of the hand.
vidēre = vidērunt.
Ausoniī, *the Ausonians,* another name for the early Italians.
*volvō, -ere, volvī, volūtum, *roll.*
repressit, *restrained, held back.*
iam iamque magis, *and every moment more and more.*
sermō, -ōnis, *m., words, talk, speech* (of Turnus).
*flectō, -ere, flexī, flexum, *influence, bend, change;* supply **eum**; **eum cunctantem,** *as he hesitated;*
    lit., *him hesitating.*
umerō altō, *high on his shoulder.*   (40Vc continues opposite)

[Tum dixit Aeneas,] "Pallas te hoc vulnere, Pallas
immolat et poenam scelerato ex sanguine sumit."
Hoc dicens ferrum adverso sub pectore condit
fervidus. Ast illi solvuntur frigore membra,
vitaque cum gemitu fugit indignata sub umbras.

                              Virgil, *Aen.* XII.930–952 adapted passim

Ovid concludes his episode with Aeneas being made divine, a transformation which Ovid will extend to other famous Romans—Romulus,
Caesar, Augustus, and finally himself—in the final books of the *Metamorphoses.*

40d   Iamque deos omnes ipsamque Aeneia virtus
           Iunonem veteres finire coegerat iras,
           cum, bene fundatis opibus crescentis Iuli,
           tempestivus erat caelo Cythereius heros.
           Ambieratque Venus superos colloque parentis
           circumfusa sui, "numquam mihi" dixerat, "ullo
           tempore dure, pater, nunc sis mitissimus, opto,

---

balteus infēlix, *the unfortunate baldric.*
***appāreō, -ēre, -uī, -itum**, appear, become visible.*
cingula, -ōrum, *n. pl., belt, sword-belt, girdle.*
nōtīs . . . puerī, *and the belt of the boy Pallas gleamed with its well-known ornaments;* Turnus had
   killed Pallas in battle and had taken this emblem of his victory. Because he is wearing this
   belt now, Aeneas in anger does not spare his life. Compare the similar slaying of Hector by
   Achilles for the same kind of battle trophy being worn. Obviously Virgil is imitating Homer
   in having the young Pallas, son of Evander, correspond to Patroclus.
***victum quem**, repeat Pallas *whom, overcome by a wound,* Turnus had destroyed.
sternō, -ere, strāvī, strātum, *spread out, flatten, level, destroy.*
***insigne, -nis**, *n., badge, insignia.*
***inimīcus, -a, -um**, *enemy's, unfriendly.*
immolō (1), *slay.*
poenam sūmit, *exacts punishment.*
***scelerātus, -a, -um**, *wicked.*
sūmō, -ere, sumpsī, sumptum, *take, exact.*
condit ferrum, *buries his sword.*
adversō sub pectore, *in his opponent's heart; in his hateful* (or, *hostile*) *heart.*
ast = **at**, used before words beginning with a vowel: *but, but meanwhile, and.*
illī . . . membra, *his limbs were* (dissolved) *weakened with the cold of death;* **illī** is dat. of reference;
   frigore is abl. of means.
***gemitus, -ūs**, *m., groan.*
***indignātus, -a, -um**, *angry, indignant.*

                              40d
Aenēia, *of Aeneas,* an adjective modifying **virtus** (*f.*).
fundō (1), *found, establish, confirm.*
cum . . . hēros, an inverted **cum** clause.
bene . . . Iūlī, *now that the fortunes of the maturing Iulus were well established.*
tempestīvus, -a, -um, *timely, ripe, mature, ready.*
Cytherēius hēros, *Aeneas,* the Cytherian hero; Cytherea is a name for Venus.

                              (40Vd continues overleaf)

Aeneaeque meo, qui te de sanguine nostro
fecit avum, quamvis parvum des, optime, numen,
dummodo des aliquod! . . .
Tum pater "estis" ait, "caelesti numine digni,
quaeque petis pro quoque petis: cape, nata, quod optas!"

. . . .

40e   Quicquid in Aenea fuerat mortale, repurgat
et respersit aquis; pars optima restitit illi.
lustratum genetrix divino corpus odore
unxit et ambrosia cum dulci nectare mixta
contigit os fecitque deum.

Met. XIV.581–607 passim

Structure

197. The many uses of the dative case.

(1) The dative case is primarily the case of the *indirect object*, the person
to or for whom the action of the verb occurs:

Puer librōs **mātrī** mīsit.   The boy sent books *to his mother.*
Mīlitēs pontem **Caesarī**   The soldiers built a bridge *for*
aedificāvērunt.   *Caesar.*

---

*ambiō, -īre, -īvī or -iī, -itum, *approach, go around, entreat.*
*superus, -ī, *m., god.*
circumfūsa collō parentis suī, *throwing her arms around the neck of her father.*
*dūre, *harsh,* vocative with **pater,** "never-at-any-time-harsh-to-me-father."
*avus, -ī, *grandfather;* Aeneas has made Jupiter a *grandfather* by being the son of Venus; Venus
  is sometimes said to be the daughter of Jupiter.
quamvīs . . . nūmen, *may you give some little measure of divinity, whatever you wish.*
*dummodo, *provided that.*
*aliquod, *something.*
caelestī numine dignī, *worthy of heavenly favor* or *divine majesty.*
prō (quō), *also for whom you seek.*

40e

*mortālis, -e, *mortal.*
repurgat et respersit, *she washed away and dissolved.*
*restō, -stāre, -stitī, *remain, survive, be left over.*
illī, dative of possession.
unxit, *anointed.*
corpus lustrātum, *his purified body.*
*ambrosia, -ae, *f., ambrosia;* here ablative.
cum dulcī nectare, *with sweet nectar.*
*contingō, -ere, -tigī, -tactum, *touch.*

(2) Familiar also is the use of the *dative with certain adjectives*:

cārus, grātus, benignus—   dear (to), pleasing (to), kind (to)
Nympha est **deō** cara.   The nymph is dear *to the god.*

(3) Equally familiar is the *dative of possesion* with the verb **sum**:

Fīlia **rēgī** erat.   *The king* had a daughter. (A daughter was *to the king.*)

Erat **eī** cōnsilium.   *He* had a plan.

Frondēs **arborī** erant.   *The tree* had leaves.

(4) In the passive constructions the *agent* by whom the action is done is expressed by a *dative of agent*:

Pax **tibi** quaerenda est.   Peace ought to be sought *by you.*

(5) The *dative* is used *with certain verbs* whose meanings end in a "to" or "for" idea:

crēdō + dat., *trust, believe* (in) (give trust to)
ignōscō + dat., *forgive, pardon* (give pardon to)
imperō + dat., *command* (give orders to)
noceō + dat., *harm, injure* (do harm to)
parcō + dat., *spare* (be lenient to)
pāreō + dat., *obey* (be obedient to)
persuādeō + dat., *persuade* (be persuasive to)
placeō + dat., *please* (be pleasing to)
serviō + dat., *serve* (be servant to)
studeō + dat., *study* (be eager for)

Deō crēdunt.   They believe *in God.*
Inimīcīs ignōscunt.   They forgive *their enemies.*
Mīlitibus imperant.   They command *the soldiers.*
Amīcīs suīs nocent.   They harm *their own friends.*
Hostibus parcunt.   They spare *the enemy.*
Mātrī pārent.   They obey *their mother.*
Patrī persuāsit.   He persuaded *his father.*
Respondēte, sī **vōbīs** placet.   If it pleases *you,* reply.
Caesarī servit.   He was in service *to Caesar.*
Librīs studet.   He is eager *for books.*

(6) The dative is used to denote the person in whose interest the action of the verb occurs, the *dative of reference.*

Erit ille **mihi** semper deus.   He will always be a god *to me.*
Quod **mihi** est fortūna?   What is fortune, *as far as I am concerned*?

Pars optima restitit **illī**.   The best part **of him** remained.

(7) The dative is used twice in the sentence as the so-called *double dative*.

> Hoc dōnum erit **auxiliō** **mihi**.
>
> This gift will be (for) *an aid to me.*

(8) Another use of the dative occurs with certain verbs compounded with the prepositions **ad, ante, circum, con- de, in, inter, ob, post, prae, sub,** and **super,** *the dative of Compound Verbs*:

> Caesar **exercituī** praeerat.
>
> Caesar was in charge of *the army.*
>
> **Fīnitimīs** bellum inferēbant.
>
> They made war on *their neighbors.*
>
> **Omnibus rēbus** amor antevenit.
>
> Love comes before *all things.*

Not all verbs compounded with these prepositions listed above take the dative case:

> **Hostem** interfēcit.
>
> He killed *the enemy.*
>
> **Urbem** circumstetit.
>
> He surrounded *the city.*

Exercises

I.   Respondete Latine, quaeso.

1. Cuius filia in Italia Aeneas potitur?
2. Potiturne Aeneas ea sine Marte?
3. Quis pro coniuge pacta pugnat?
4. Quis ad bellum pugnandum missus est?
5. Quis erat victor belli inter Rutulos et Troianos? Quis cecidit?
6. Cuius cingula Aeneas in umeris Turni vidit?
7. Quid Aeneas sub pectore Turni condit?
8. Quis oravit patrem filio vitam aeternam dare?
9. Quae dea iras veteres finivit?
10. Quae pars heroi restitit?

II.   Make up two sentences demonstrating each use of the dative:

1) Indirect object:
2) With certain adjectives:
3) Dative of possession:
4) Dative of agent:
5) Dative with certain verbs:
6) Dative of reference:
7) Double Dative:
8) Dative of Compound Verbs:

Translate each sentence into English.

III. Translate into Latin:

1. Forgive me.
2. Believe me.
3. Trust me.
4. Spare me.
5. Serve me.

6. I forgive you.
7. I believe you.
8. I trust you.
9. I will spare you.
10. I will serve you.

IV. Supply the correct form of the dative:

1. Servus (*to his master*) carus est.
2. Puer (*to his teacher*) gratus est.
3. Eurydice (*to Orpheus*) cara est.

V. Translate into Latin:

Aeneas killed Turnus who was wearing (**gerō**) the belt of Pallas on his shoulder. Turnus had killed this friend of the Trojan hero in battle and had taken the belt as a mark of victory. Because Turnus was wearing this belt, Aeneas did not spare him. You ought to read this story in Virgil (**apud Virgilem**). (Use the passive periphrastic.)

Etymology

LATIN MOTTOS, WORDS, AND PHRASES IN ENGLISH

ab urbe condita (AUC)	from the founding of the city
addendum	to be added
ad hoc	to (or for) this
ad extremum	to the extreme
ad nauseum	to the point of nausea
advocatus diaboli	devil's advocate
agenda	things to be done
alter ego	another I
anguis in herba	snake in the grass
annuit coeptis	he has smiled on our undertakings (motto on the dollar bill of U.S. currency)
ante bellum	before the war
ars est celare artem	the skill is to conceal the art
ars longa vita brevis	art is long; life is short
ars poetica	the art of poetry
aut Caesar aut nihil	either Caesar or nothing
ave atque vale	hail and farewell
bis dat qui cito dat	he gives twice who gives quickly
carpe diem	seize the day
causa belli	the cause of war
cave canem	beware the dog

de gustibus non disputandum est	there is no quarrelling about taste
de mortuis nil nisi bonum	speak only well of the dead
deus ex machina	god (let down) from a machine heavenly intervention
dramatis personae	characters in a play
exeunt omnes	all leave (the stage is empty)
ex libris	from the books (of a certain person); bookplate device
in aeternum	eternally
in memoriam	in memory
lapsus linguae	slip of the tongue
modus operandi	method of operation
passim	from here and there
pax vobiscum	peace be with you
per capita	by or for each person (head count)
per diem	by the day
per se	in or of itself
post bellum	after the war
post mortem	(examination) after death
pro tem(pore)	for the time being
reductio ad absurdum	reduced to the absurd
res gestae	things accomplished
sic	thus (it was in the original)
sine qua non	without which not (necessary ingredient)
summum bonum	the greatest good
tempus fugit	time flies
ut infra	as below
ut supra	as above
verbatim	word for word

*   *   *   *   *

Fill in the blank with the derived word from the Latin source at the left:

augeo	_____ my salary
appareo	the _____ cause of his misfortune
concurro	a play running _____ with ours
arduus	_____ work
externus	_____ causes of recession
volvo	the re-_____ of the earth on its axis
reprehendo	a _____ act
sermo	_____ on the Mount

flecto	(de) _____ the arrow
inimicus	_____ to our interests
indignatus	_____ at your behavior
mortalis	all that was _____ in him
unguo (ungo)	a jar for _____
contingo	send a _____ of marines
ambrosia	the gods feast on nectar and _____

Nouns

FIRST DECLENSION SECOND DECLENSION

Singular   *Singular*

	puella, *f.*, girl	animus, *m.*, soul	puer, *m.*, boy	ager, *m.*, field	vir, *m.*, man	oppidum, *n.*, town
Nom.	puella	animus	puer	ager	vir	oppidum
Gen.	puellae	animī	puerī	agrī	virī	oppidī
Dat.	puellae	animō	puerō	agrō	virō	oppidō
Acc.	puellam	animum	puerum	agrum	virum	oppidum
Abl.	puellā	animō	puerō	agrō	virō	oppidō

Plural   *Plural*

Nom.	puellae	animī	puerī	agrī	virī	oppida
Gen.	puellārum	animōrum	puerōrum	agrōrum	virōrum	oppidōrum
Dat.	puellīs	animīs	puerīs	agrīs	virīs	oppidīs
Acc.	puellās	animōs	puerōs	agrōs	virōs	oppida
Abl.	puellīs	animīs	puerīs	agrīs	virīs	oppidīs

First declension nouns are feminine, except for a few that refer to males like **nauta**, **pīrāta**, **poēta**, and **agricola**. Second declension nouns are masculine or neuter, except for a few referring to trees or cities. Third declension nouns exist in all three genders, and numerically this is the largest declension. Fourth declension nouns are mostly masculine (except for **manus** and **domus**) with a few neuters, and fifth declension is limited to feminine nouns, with the exception of **diēs**.

The vocative forms of nouns in all declensions are identical to the nominative singular and plural (**puella**, *O girl*, **puellae**, *O girls*), except in the **-us** form of masculines in second declension which ends in **-e** (**anime**, *O soul*; **Marce**, *O Marcus*). Nouns ending in **-ius** form their vocative in **-ī** (**fīlī**, *O son*; **Vergilī**, *O Virgil*).

THIRD DECLENSION

	māter, *f.*, mother	homō, *m.*, man	vīctor, *m.*, victor	prīnceps, *m.*, chief	tempus, *n.*, time
			Singular		
Nom.	māter	homō	vīctor	prīnceps	tempus
Gen.	mātris	hominis	vīctōris	prīncipis	temporis
Dat.	mātrī	hominī	vīctōrī	prīncipī	temporī
Acc.	mātrem	hominem	vīctōrem	prīncipem	tempus
Abl.	mātre	homine	vīctōre	prīncipe	tempore
			Plural		
Nom.	mātrēs	hominēs	vīctōrēs	prīncipēs	tempora
Gen.	mātrum	hominum	vīctōrum	prīncipum	temporum
Dat.	mātribus	hominibus	vīctōribus	prīncipibus	temporibus
Acc.	mātres	hominēs	vīctōrēs	prīncipēs	tempora
Abl.	mātribus	hominibus	vīctōribus	prīncipibus	temporibus

THIRD DECLENSION I-STEM

NEUTERS IN -e, al, -r

	cīvis, *m.*, citizen	urbs, *f.*, city	nox, *f.*, night	mare, *n.*, sea	animal, *n.*, animal
			Singular		
Nom.	cīvis	urbs	nox	mare	animal
Gen.	cīvis	urbis	noctis	maris	animālis
Dat.	cīvī	urbī	noctī	marī	animālī
Acc.	cīvem	urbem	noctem	mare	animal
Abl.	cīve	urbe	nocte	marī	animālī
			Plural		
Nom.	cīvēs	urbēs	noctēs	maria	animālia
Gen.	cīvium	urbium	noctium	marium	animālium
Dat.	cīvibus	urbibus	noctibus	maribus	animālibus
Acc.	cīvēs (-īs)	urbēs (-īs)	noctēs (-īs)	maria	animālia
Abl.	cīvibus	urbibus	noctibus	maribus	animālibus

FOURTH DECLENSION

	exercitus, *m., army*		cornū, *n., horn*	
	Singular	*Plural*	*Singular*	*Plural*
Nom.	exercitus	exercitūs	cornū	cornua
Gen.	exercitūs	exercituum	cornūs	cornuum
Dat.	exercituī	exercitibus	cornū	cornibus
Acc.	exercitum	exercitūs	cornū	cornua
Abl.	exercitū	exercitibus	cornū	cornibus

FIFTH DECLENSION

	diēs, *m. & f., day*		rēs, *f., thing*	
	Singular	*Plural*	*Singular*	*Plural*
Nom.	diēs	diēs	rēs	rēs
Gen.	diēī	diērum	reī	rērum
Dat.	diēī	diēbus	reī	rēbus
Acc.	diem	diēs	rem	rēs
Abl.	diē	diēbus	rē	rēbus

IRREGULAR NOUNS

	vīs, *f., force*		dea, *f., goddess*		domus, *f., house*	
	Sing.	*Plural*	*Sing.*	*Plural*	*Sing.*	*Plural*
Nom.	vīs	vīrēs	dea	deae	domus	domūs
Gen.	——	vīrium	deae	deārum	domūs, domī	domuum, domōrum
Dat.	——	vīribus	deae	deābus	domuī, domō	domibus
Acc.	vim	vīrēs (-īs)	deam	deās	domum	domōs, domūs
Abl.	vī	vīribus	deā	deābus	domū, domō	domibus

Loc. domī

Filia is declined like **dea**.

Domus has forms of both the second and fourth declensions.

Adjectives

FIRST AND SECOND DECLENSION

bonus, *good*

	Singular			*Plural*		
Nom.	bonus, *m.*	bona, *f.*	bonum, *n.*	bonī	bonae	bona
Gen.	bonī	bonae	bonī	bonōrum	bonārum	bonōrum
Dat.	bonō	bonae	bonō	bonīs	bonīs	bonīs
Acc.	bonum	bonam	bonum	bonōs	bonās	bona
Abl.	bonō	bonā	bonō	bonīs	bonīs	bonīs

Adjectives in -er, -era, -eram
miser, *wretched*

Adjectives in -er, -ra, -rum
pulcher, *beautiful*

	Singular			*Singular*		
Nom.	miser, *m.*	misera, *f.*	miserum, *n.*	pulcher	pulchra	pulchrum
Gen.	miserī	miserae	miserī	pulchrī	pulchrae	pulchrī
Dat.	miserō	miserae	miserō	pulchrō	pulchrae	pulchrō
Acc.	miserum	miseram	miserum	pulchrum	pulchram	pulchrum
Abl.	miserō	miserā	miserō	pulchrō	pulchrā	pulchrō

Plural

Endings like the plural of **bonus** retaining the **-e-**

Plural

Endings like the plural of **bonus**, dropping the **-e-**

THIRD DECLENSION

One Termination
ingēns, *huge*

Two Terminations
gravis, grave, *heavy*

Three Terminations
acer, acris, acre, *sharp*

	Singular						
Nom.	ingēns, *m., f.*	ingēns, *n.*	gravis, *m., f.*	grave, *n.*	acer, *m.*	acris, *f.*	acre, *n.*
Gen.	ingentis	ingentis	gravis	gravis	acris	acris	acris
Dat.	ingentī	ingentī	gravī	gravī	acrī	acrī	acrī
Acc.	ingentem	ingēns	gravem	grave	acrem	acrem	acre
Abl.	ingentī	ingentī	gravī	gravī	acrī	acrī	acrī

	Plural						
Nom.	ingentēs	ingentia	gravēs	gravia	acrēs	acrēs	acria
Gen.	ingentium	ingentium	gravium	gravium	acrium	acrium	acrium
Dat.	ingentibus	ingentibus	gravibus	gravibus	acribus	acribus	acribus
Acc.	ingentēs (-īs)	ingentia	gravēs (īs)	gravia	acrēs (-īs)	acrēs (-īs)	acria
Abl.	ingentibus	ingentibus	gravibus	gravibus	acribus	acribus	acribus

In the vocabulary adjectives of one termination appear with the genitive singular following (**ingēns, -entis**); adjectives of two terminations appear with the combined masculine and feminine singular followed by the neuter ending (**omnis, -e**); adjectives of three terminations are listed with all three endings (**acer, acris, acre**).

The present active participle is declined like an adjective of one termination: **amāns, amantis; tenēns, tenentis; dūcēns, dūcentis; capiēns, capientis; audiēns, audientis.** The ablative singular ends in **-e** when it is used as a participle; in **-ī** when used as an adjective (**Iūliā eum amante,** *since Julia loves him;* but **cum coniuge amantī,** *with a loving spouse*).

DECLENSION OF COMPARATIVE OF ADJECTIVES

grātior, grātius, *more pleasing*

	Singular		Plural	
Nom.	grātior, *m., f.*	grātius, *n.*	grātiōrēs	grātiōra
Gen.	grātiōris	grātiōris	grātiōrum	grātiōrum
Dat.	grātiōrī	grātiōrī	grātiōribus	grātiōribus
Acc.	grātiōrem	grātius	grātiōrēs (-īs)	grātiōra
Abl.	grātiōre	grātiōre	grātiōribus	grātiōribus

Comparison of Adjectives

POSITIVE	COMPARATIVE	SUPERLATIVE
Regular		
clārus, -a, -um, *clear*	clārior, clārius	clārissimus, -a, -um
gravis, -e, *heavy*	gravior, gravius	gravissimus, -a, -um
fēlīx, *gen.* fēlīcis, *happy*	fēlīcior, -ius	fēlīcissimus, -a, -um
amāns, *gen.* amantis, *loving*	amantior, amantius	amantissimus, -a, -um
celer, -eris, -ere, *swift*	celerior, celerius	celerrimus, -a, -um
pulcher, -ra, -rum, *beautiful*	pulchrior, pulchrius	pulcherrimus, -a, -um
acer, acris, acre, *sharp*	acrior, acrius	acerrimus, -a, -um
facilis, -e, *easy*	facilior, facilius	facillimus, -a, -um
Irregular		
bonus, -a, -um, *good*	melior, -ius	optimus, -a, -um
magnus, -a, -um, *large*	maior, -ius	maximus, -a, -um
malus, -a, -um, *bad*	peior, -ius	pessimus, -a, -um
multus, -a, -um, *much*	——, plūs	plūrimus, -a, -um
parvus, -a, -um, *small*	minor, minus	minimus, -a, -um
superus, -a, -um, *that above*	superior, -ius	summus (supremus), -a, -um

DECLENSION OF **PLŪS**

	Singular		Plural	
Nom.	——, *m., f.*	plūs, *n.*	plūrēs, *m., f.*	plūria, *n.*
Gen.	——	plūris	plūrium	plūrium
Dat.	——	——	plūribus	plūribus
Acc.	——	plūs	plūrēs	plūria
Abl.	——	plūre	plūribus	plūribus

IRREGULAR ADJECTIVES

These adjectives are irregular in that the genitive singular ends in **-īus** and the dative singular in **-ī**. Otherwise they are declined like **bonus, miser,** and **pulcher.**

alius, alia, aliud, *other, another*
alter, altera, alterum, *the other*
ūllus, -a, -um, *any*
nūllus, -a, -um, *not any, no*
sōlus, -a, -um, *alone*

tōtus, -a, -um, *all, the whole*
ūnus, -a, -um, *one*
uter, -tra, -trum, *which (of two)*
uterque, -traque, -trumque, *each, both*

Numerals

Declension of **duo**, **trēs**, *and* **mīlle**

	M.	*F.*	*N.*	*M. & F.*	*N.*	*M., F., & N.*	*N.*
Nom.	duo	duae	duo	trēs	tria	mīlle	mīlia
Gen.	duōrum	duārum	duōrum	trium	trium	mīlle	mīlium
Dat.	duōbus	duābus	duōbus	tribus	tribus	mīlle	mīlibus
Acc.	duōs (duo)	duās	duo	trēs (trīs)	tria	mīlle	mīlia
Abl.	duōbus	duābus	duōbus	tribus	tribus	mīlle	mīlibus

Comparison of Adverbs

POSITIVE	COMPARATIVE	SUPERLATIVE
Regular		
clārē, *clearly*	clārius	clārissimē
graviter, *heavily*	gravius	gravissimē
fēlīciter, *happily*	fēlīcius	fēlīcissimē
celeriter, *swiftly*	celerius	celerrimē
pulchrē, *beautifully*	pulchrius	pulcherrimē
acriter, *keenly*	acrius	acerrimē
facile, *easily*	facilius	facillimē
Irregular		
bene, *well*	melius	optimē
magnopere, *greatly*	magis	maximē
malē, *badly*	peius	pessimē
multum, *much*	plūs	plūrimum
parum, *little*	minus	minimē

Pronouns

PERSONAL

PERSONAL AND DEMONSTRATIVE

Singular

	I	*you*	*he*	*she*	*it*
Nom.	ego	tū	is	ea	id
Gen.	meī	tuī	eius	eius	eius
Dat.	mihi	tibi	eī	eī	eī
Acc.	mē	tē	eum	eam	id
Abl.	mē	tē	eō	eā	eō

Plural

	we	*you*	*they*		
Nom.	nōs	vōs	eī	eae	ea
Gen.	nostrum (nostrī)	vestrum (vestrī)	eōrum	eārum	eōrum
Dat.	nōbīs	vōbīs	eīs	eīs	eīs
Acc.	nōs	vōs	eōs	eās	ea
Abl.	nōbīs	vōbīs	eīs	eīs	eīs

REFLEXIVE

For first and second person the forms are the same as the personal pronoun, without a nominative case. For third person the forms below are used:

Singular and Plural (himself, herself, itself, themselves)

Gen.	suī
Dat.	sibi
Acc.	sē (sēsē)
Abl.	sē (sēsē)

INTENSIVE

ipse, ipsa, ipsum, *self*

	Singular			Plural		
Nom.	ipse, *m.*	ipsa, *f.*	ipsum, *n.*	ipsī	ipsae	ipsa
Gen.	ipsīus	ipsīus	ipsīus	ipsōrum	ipsārum	ipsōrum
Dat.	ipsī	ipsī	ipsī	ipsīs	ipsīs	ipsīs
Acc.	ipsum	ipsam	ipsum	ipsōs	ipsās	ipsa
Abl.	ipsō	ipsā	ipsō	ipsīs	ipsīs	ipsīs

DEMONSTRATIVE

hic, haec, hoc, *this*

	Singular			Plural		
Nom.	hic, *m.*	haec, *f.*	hoc, *n.*	hī	hae	haec
Gen.	huius	huius	huius	hōrum	hārum	hōrum
Dat.	huic	huic	huic	hīs	hīs	hīs
Acc.	hunc	hanc	hoc	hōs	hās	haec
Abl.	hōc	hāc	hōc	hīs	hīs	hīs

ille, illa, illud, *that*

Nom.	ille, *m.*	illa, *f.*	illud, *n.*	illī	illae	illa
Gen.	illīus	illīus	illīus	illōrum	illārum	illōrum
Dat.	illī	illī	illī	illīs	illīs	illīs
Acc.	illum	illam	illud	illōs	illās	illa
Abl.	illō	illā	illō	illīs	illīs	illīs

iste, ista, istud, *that, that of yours*

Nom.	iste, *m.*	ista, *f.*	istud, *n.*	istī	istae	ista
Gen.	istīus	istīus	istīus	istōrum	istārum	istōrum
Dat.	istī	istī	istī •	istīs	istīs	istīs
Acc.	istum	istam	istud	istōs	istās	ista
Abl.	istō	istā	istō	istīs	istīs	istīs

īdem, eadem, idem, *same*

Nom.	īdem, *m.*	eadem, *f.*	idem, *n.*	eīdem(īdem)	eaedem	eadem
Gen.	eiusdem	eiusdem	eiusdem	eōrundem	eārundem	eōrundem
Dat.	eīdem	eīdem	eīdem	eīsdem	eīsdem	eīsdem
Acc.	eundem	eandem	idem	eōsdem	eāsdem	eadem
Abl.	eōdem	eādem	eōdem	eīsdem	eīsdem	eīsdem

In the dative and ablative plural **īsdem** is an alternate form for **eīsdem**.

INTERROGATIVE PRONOUN

quis, quid, *who, what*

	Singular			*Plural*	
Nom.	quis, *m., f.*	quid, *n.*	quī	quae	quae
Gen.	cuius	cuius	quōrum	quārum	quōrum
Dat.	cui	cui	quibus	quibus	quibus
Acc.	quem	quid	quōs	quās	quae
Abl.	quō	quō	quibus	quibus	quibus

RELATIVE PRONOUN

qui, quae, quod, *who, which, that*

	Singular			*Plural*	
Nom.	quī, *m.*	quae, *f.*	quod, *n.*	quī	quae	quae
Gen.	cuius	cuius	cuius	quōrum	quārum	quōrum
Dat.	cui	cui	cui	quibus	quibus	quibus
Acc.	quem	quam	quod	quōs	quās	quae
Abl.	quō	quā	quō	quibus	quibus	quibus

THE INTERROGATIVE ADJECTIVE

The interrogative adjective is the same as the relative pronoun (see above), except that the nominative singular masculine form may be either **quis** or **quī**.

INDEFINITE PRONOUNS

aliquis, *someone, some*

	Singular			*Plural*	
aliquis, *m. & f.*	aliquid, *n.*	aliquī	aliquae	aliqua
alicuius	alicuius	aliquōrum	aliquārum	aliquōrum
alicui	alicui	aliquibus	aliquibus	aliquibus
aliquem	aliquid	aliquōs	aliquās	aliqua
aliquō	aliquō	aliquibus	aliquibus	aliquibus

The forms **aliquī, aliqua, aliquod** are used as adjectives.

quīdam, *a certain one, a certain*

	Singular	
quīdam, *m.*	quaedam, *f.*	quiddam (quoddam), *n.*
cuiusdam	cuiusdam	cuiusdam
cuidam	cuidam	cuidam
quendam	quandum	quiddam (quoddam)
quōdam	quādam	quōdam

	Plural	
quīdam, *m.*	quaedam, *f.*	quaedam, *n.*
quōrundam	quārundam	quōrundam
quibusdam	quibusdam	quibusdam
quōsdam	quāsdam	quaedam
quibusdam	quibusdam	quibusdam

The forms in parentheses are used as adjectives.

quisque, *each*

Singular only

Pronoun		*Adjective*		
quisque, *m., f.*	quidque, *n.*	quisque, *m.*	quaeque, *f.*	quodque, *n.*
cuiusque	cuiusque	cuiusque	cuiusque	cuiusque
cuique	cuique	cuique	cuique	cuique
quemque	quidque	quemque	quamque	quodque
quōque	quōque	quōque	quāque	quōque

quisquam, *anyone* (*at all*)

Singular only

quisquam, *m., f.*	quicquam (quidquam), *n.*
cuiusquam	cuiusquam
cuiquam	cuiquam
quemquam	quicquam (quidquam)
quōquam	quōquam

Possessives

SINGULAR POSSESSOR

1st person	meus, -a, -um	my
2nd person	tuus, -a, -um	your
3rd person	suus, -a, -um (reflexive)	his, her, its
	eius (gen. sing. of **is**)	his, her, its

PLURAL POSSESSOR

1st person	noster, -tra, -trum	our
2nd person	vester, -tra, -trum	your
3rd person	suus-, -a, -um (reflexive)	their
	eōrum, eārum, eōrum	their
	(gen. pl. of **is**)	

Numerals

ROMAN NUMERALS	CARDINALS	ORDINALS
I	1. ūnus, -a, -um	prīmus, -a, -um
II	2. duo, duae, duo	secundus, alter
III	3. trēs, tria	tertius
IIII; IV	4. quattuor	quārtus
V	5. quīnque	quīntus
VI	6. sex	sextus
VII	7. septem	septimus
VIII	8. octō	octāvus
VIIII; IX	9. novem	nōnus
X	10. decem	decimus
XI	11. ūndecim	ūndecimus
XII	12. duodecim	duodecimus
XIII	13. tredecim	tertius decimus

XIIII; XIV	14. quattuordecim	quārtus decimus
XV	15. quīndecim	quīntus decimus
XVI	16. sēdecim	sextus decimus
XVII	17. septendecim	septimus decimus
XVIII	18. duodēvīgintī	duodēvīcēsimus
XVIIII; XIX	19. ūndēvīgintī	ūndēvīcēsimus
XX	20. vīgintī	vīcēsimus (vīcēnsimus[1])
XXI	21. vīgintī ūnus; ūnus et vīgintī	vīcēsimus prīmus
XXVIII	28. duodētrīgintā	duodētrīcēsimus
XXIX	29. undētrigintā	undētrīcēsimus
XXX	30. trīgintā	trīcēsimus
XXXX; XL	40. quadrāgintā	quadrāgēsimus
L	50. quīnquāgintā	quīnquāgēsimus
LX	60. sexāgintā	sexāgēsimus
LXX	70. septuāgintā	septuāgēsimus
LXXX	80. octōgintā	octōgēsimus
LXXXX; XC	90. nōnāgintā	nōnāgēsimus
C	100. centum	centēsimus
CI	101. centum ūnus	centēsimus prīmus
CC	200. ducentī, -ae, -a	ducentēsimus
CCC	300. trecentī	trecentēsimus
CCCC	400. quadringentī	quadringentēsimus
D	500. quīngentī	quīngentēsimus
DC	600. sescentī	sescentēsimus
DCC	700. septingentī	septingentēsimus
DCCC	800. octingentī	octingentēsimus
DCCCC	900. nōngentī	nōngentēsimus
M	1000. mīlle	mīllēsimus
MM	2000. duo mīlia	bis mīllēsimus

Verbs

REGULAR VERBS

Principal Parts

1st Conjugation	vocō	vocāre	vocāvī	vocātum	*call*
2nd Conjugation	teneō	tenēre	tenuī	tentum	*hold*
3rd Conjugation	dūcō	dūcere	dūxī	ductum	*lead*
3-io Conjugation	capiō	capere	cēpī	captum	*take*
4th Conjugation	audiō	audīre	audīvī	audītum	*hear*

Indicative Active

Present

vocō	teneō	dūcō	capiō	audiō
vocās	tenēs	dūcis	capis	audīs
vocat	tenet	dūcit	capit	audit
vocāmus	tenēmus	dūcimus	capimus	audīmus
vocātis	tenētis	dūcitis	capitis	audītis
vocant	tenent	dūcunt	capiunt	audiunt

---

[1] All of the ordinals from **vīcēsimus, trīcēsimus, quadrāgēsimus**, etc., through **centēsimus** and **mīllēsimus** are also spelled **vīcēnsimus, trīcēnsimus, quadrāgēnsimus, centēnsimus, mīllēnsimus**, etc.

Imperfect

vocābam	tenēbam	dūcēbam	capiēbam	audiēbam
vocābās	tenēbās	dūcēbās	capiēbās	audiēbās
vocābat	tenēbat	dūcēbat	capiēbat	audiēbat
vocābāmus	tenēbāmus	dūcēbāmus	capiēbāmus	audiēbāmus
vocābātis	tenēbātis	dūcēbātis	capiēbātis	audiēbātis
vocābant	tenēbant	dūcēbant	capiēbant	audiēbant

Future

-bi-   -e-

vocābō	tenēbō	dūcam	capiam	audiam
vocābis	tenēbis	dūcēs	capiēs	audiēs
vocābit	tenēbit	dūcet	capiet	audiet
vocābimus	tenēbimus	dūcēmus	capiēmus	audiēmus
vocābitis	tenēbitis	dūcētis	capiētis	audiētis
vocābunt	tenēbunt	dūcent	capient	audient

Perfect

vocāvī	tenuī	dūxī	cēpī	audīvī
vocāvistī	tenuistī	dūxistī	cēpistī	audīvistī
vocāvit	tenuit	dūxit	cēpit	audīvit
vocāvimus	tenuimus	dūximus	cēpimus	audīvimus
vocāvistis	tenuistis	dūxistis	cēpistis	audīvistis
vocāvērunt	tenuērunt	dūxērunt	cēpērunt	audīvērunt

Pluperfect

vocāveram	tenueram	dūxeram	cēperam	audīveram
vocāverās	tenuerās	dūxerās	cēperās	audīverās
vocāverat	tenuerat	dūxerat	cēperat	audīverat
vocāverāmus	tenuerāmus	dūxerāmus	cēperāmus	audīverāmus
vocāverātis	tenuerātis	dūxerātis	cēperātis	audīverātis
vocāverant	tenuerant	dūxerant	cēperant	audīverant

Future Perfect

vocāverō	tenuerō	dūxerō	cēperō	audīverō
vocāveris	tenueris	dūxeris	cēperis	audīveris
vocāverit	tenuerit	dūxerit	cēperit	audīverit
vocāverimus	tenuerimus	dūxerimus	cēperimus	audīverimus
vocāveritis	tenueritis	dūxeritis	cēperitis	audīveritis
vocāverint	tenuerint	dūxerint	cēperint	audīverint

Present Imperative Active[2]

vocā	tenē	dūc[3]	cape	audī
vocāte	tenēte	dūcite	capite	audīte

---

[2] Present imperative passive forms also exist, identical to the present passive alternate second person singular and the regular second person plural: **vocāre, vocāminī**, *be called*, etc., but the *usage is generally limited to deponent verbs*: **cōnāre, cōnāminī**, *try*; **verēre, verēminī**, *fear*; etc. Future imperative forms are usually poetic: **vocātō, vocātōte**, *in the future, call*; **tenētō, tenētōte**, *in the future, hold*; **dūcitō, dūcitōte**, *in the future, lead*; **capitō, capitōte**, *in the future, take*; **audītō, audītōte**, *in the future, hear*.

[3] Regular imperative singular in third conjugation ends in **-e** (**pete**, *seek*; **lege**, *read*), but the very commonly used verbs **dīc, dūc**, and **fac** (*say, lead, make*) drop the **-e**.

Indicative Passive

Present

vocor	teneor	dūcor	capior	audior
vocāris (-re)	tenēris (-re)	dūceris (-re)	caperis (-re)	audīris (-re)
vocātur	tenētur	dūcitur	capitur	audītur
vocāmur	tenēmur	dūcimur	capimur	audīmur
vocāminī	tenēminī	dūciminī	capiminī	audīminī
vocantur	tenentur	dūcuntur	capiuntur	audiuntur

Imperfect

vocābar	tenēbar	dūcēbar	capiēbar	audiēbar
vocābāris (-re)	tenēbāris (-re)	dūcēbāris (-re)	capiēbāris (-re)	audiēbāris (-re)
vocābātur	tenēbātur	dūcēbātur	capiēbātur	audiēbātur
vocābāmur	tenēbāmur	dūcēbāmur	capiēbāmur	audiēbāmur
vocābāminī	tenēbāminī	dūcēbāminī	capiēbāminī	audiēbāminī
vocābantur	tenēbantur	dūcēbantur	capiēbantur	audiēbantur

Future

vocābor	tenēbor	dūcar	capiar	audiar
vocāberis (-re)	tenēberis (-re)	dūcēris (-re)	capiēris (-re)	audiēris (-re)
vocābitur	tenēbitur	dūcētur	capiētur	audiētur
vocābimur	tenēbimur	dūcēmur	capiēmur	audiēmur
vocābiminī	tenēbiminī	dūcēminī	capiēminī	audiēminī
vocābuntur	tenēbuntur	dūcentur	capientur	audientur

Perfect

vocātus sum	tentus sum	ductus sum	captus sum	audītus sum
vocātus es	tentus es	ductus es	captus es	audītus es
vocātus est	tentus est	ductus est	captus est	audītus est
vocātī sumus	tentī sumus	ductī sumus	captī sumus	audītī sumus
vocātī estis	tentī estis	ductī estis	captī estis	audītī estis
vocātī sunt	tentī sunt	ductī sunt	captī sunt	audītī sunt

Pluperfect

vocātus eram	tentus eram	ductus eram	captus eram	audītus eram
vocātus erās	tentus erās	ductus erās	captus erās	audītus erās
vocātus erat	tentus erat	ductus erat	captus erat	audītus erat
vocātī erāmus	tentī erāmus	ductī erāmus	captī erāmus	audītī erāmus
vocātī erātis	tentī erātis	ductī erātis	captī erātis	audītī erātis
vocātī erant	tentī erant	ductī erant	captī erant	audītī erant

Future Perfect

vocātus erō	tentus erō	ductus erō	captus erō	audītus erō
vocātus eris	tentus eris	ductus eris	captus eris	audītus eris
vocātus erit	tentus erit	ductus erit	captus erit	audītus erit
vocātī erimus	tentī erimus	ductī erimus	captī erimus	audītī erimus
vocātī eritis	tentī eritis	ductī eritis	captī eritis	audītī eritis
vocātī erunt	tentī erunt	ductī erunt	captī erunt	audītī erunt

Note: The indicative asserts a world of fact and actuality. Even in subordinate constructions introduced by **dum**, *while*; **postquam**, *after*; **antequam**, *before*; **quamquam**, *although*; **ut**, *as*; **cum**, *when*; **quod**, *because*, the indicative is used if the action referred to is real, possible, or understandable as the occasion for the action expressed by the verb in the main clause.

Subjunctive Active

Present

vocem	teneam	dūcam	capiam	audiam
vocēs	teneās	dūcās	capiās	audiās
vocet	teneat	dūcat	capiat	audiat
vocēmus	teneāmus	dūcāmus	capiāmus	audiāmus
vocētis	teneātis	dūcātis	capiātis	audiātis
vocent	teneant	dūcant	capiant	audiant

Imperfect

vocārem	tenērem	dūcerem	caperem	audīrem
vocārēs	tenērēs	dūcerēs	caperēs	audīrēs
vocāret	tenēret	dūceret	caperet	audīret
vocārēmus	tenērēmus	dūcerēmus	caperēmus	audīrēmus
vocārētis	tenērētis	dūcerētis	caperētis	audīrētis
vocārent	tenērent	dūcerent	caperent	audīrent

Perfect

vocāverim	tenuerim	dūxerim	cēperim	audīverim
vocāverīs	tenuerīs	dūxerīs	cēperīs	audīverīs
vocāverit	tenuerit	dūxerit	cēperit	audīverit
vocāverīmus	tenuerīmus	dūxerīmus	cēperīmus	audīverīmus
vocāverītis	tenuerītis	dūxerītis	cēperītis	audīverītis
vocāverint	tenuerint	dūxerint	cēperint	audīverint

Pluperfect

vocāvissem	tenuissem	dūxissem	cēpissem	audīvissem
vocāvissēs	tenuissēs	dūxissēs	cēpissēs	audīvissēs
vocāvisset	tenuisset	dūxisset	cēpisset	audīvisset
vocāvissēmus	tenuissēmus	dūxissēmus	cēpissēmus	audīvissēmus
vocāvissētis	tenuissētis	dūxissētis	cēpissētis	audīvissētis
vocāvissent	tenuissent	dūxissent	cēpissent	audīvissent

Subjunctive Passive

Present

vocer	tenear	dūcar	capiar	audiar
vocēris (-re)	teneāris (-re)	dūcāris (-re)	capiāris (-re)	audiāris (-re)
vocētur	teneātur	dūcātur	capiātur	audiātur
vocēmur	teneāmur	dūcāmur	capiāmur	audiāmur
vocēminī	teneāminī	dūcāminī	capiāminī	audiāminī
vocentur	teneantur	dūcantur	capiantur	audiantur

Imperfect

vocārer	tenērer	dūcerer	caperer	audīrer
vocārēris (-re)	tenērēris (-re)	dūcerēris (-re)	caperēris (-re)	audīrēris (-re)
vocārētur	tenērētur	dūcerētur	caperētur	audīrētur
vocārēmur	tenērēmur	dūcerēmur	caperēmur	audīrēmur
vocārēminī	tenērēminī	dūcerēminī	caperēminī	audīrēminī
vocārentur	tenērentur	dūcerentur	caperentur	audīrentur

Perfect

vocātus sim	tentus sim	ductus sim	captus sim	audītus sim
vocātus sīs	tentus sīs	ductus sīs	captus sīs	audītus sīs
vocātus sit	tentus sit	ductus sit	captus sit	audītus sit
vocātī sīmus	tentī sīmus	ductī sīmus	captī sīmus	audītī sīmus
vocātī sītis	tentī sītis	ductī sītis	captī sītis	audītī sītis
vocātī sint	tentī sint	ductī sint	captī sint	audītī sint

Pluperfect

vocātus essem	tentus essem	ductus essem	captus essem	audītus essem
vocātus essēs	tentus essēs	ductus essēs	captus essēs	audītus essēs
vocātus esset	tentus esset	ductus esset	captus esset	audītus esset
vocātī essēmus	tentī essēmus	ductī essēmus	captī essēmus	audītī essēmus
vocātī essētis	tentī essētis	ductī essētis	captī essētis	audītī essētis
vocātī essent	tentī essent	ductī essent	captī essent	audītī essent

Participles

Active

Pres.	vocāns	tenēns	dūcēns	capiēns	audiēns
Fut.	vocātūrus	tentūrus	ductūrus	captūrus	audītūrus

Passive

Perf.	vocātus	tentus	ductus	captus	audītus
Fut.	vocandus	tenendus	dūcendus	capiendus	audiendus

Infinitives

Active

Pres.	vocāre	tenēre	dūcere	capere	audīre
Perf.	vocāvisse	tenuisse	dūxisse	cēpisse	audīvisse
Fut.	vocātūrus esse	tentūrus esse	ductūrus esse	captūrus esse	audītūrus esse

Passive

Pres.	vocārī	tenērī	dūcī	capī	audīrī
Perf.	vocātus esse	tentus esse	ductus esse	captus esse	audītus esse
Fut.	vocātum īrī	tentum īrī	ductum īrī	captum īrī	audītum īrī

DEPONENT VERBS

Principal parts

1st Conjugation	conor	conārī	conātus sum	*attempt*
2nd Conjugation	vereor	verērī	veritus sum	*fear*
3rd Conjugation	loquor	loquī	locūtus sum	*speak*
3-io Conjugation	patior	patī	passus sum	*suffer*
4th Conjugation	orior	orīrī	ortus sum	*rise*

Indicative

Present

conor	vereor	loquor	patior	orior
conāris (-re)	verēris (-re)	loqueris (-re)	pateris (-re)	orīris (-re)
conātur	verētur	loquitur	patitur	orītur
conāmur	verēmur	loquimur	patimur	orīmur
conāminī	verēminī	loquiminī	patiminī	orīminī
conantur	verentur	loquuntur	patiuntur	oriuntur

Imperfect

conābar	verēbar	loquēbar	patiēbar	oriēbar
conābāris (-re)	verēbāris (-re)	loquēbāris (-re)	patiēbāris (-re)	oriēbāris (-re)
conābātur	verēbātur	loquēbātur	patiēbātur	oriēbātur
conābāmur	verēbāmur	loquēbāmur	patiēbāmur	oriēbāmur
conābāminī	verēbāminī	loquēbāminī	patiēbāminī	oriēbāminī
conābantur	verēbantur	loquēbantur	patiēbantur	oriēbantur

Future

conābor	verēbor	loquar	patiar	oriar
conāberis (-re)	verēberis (-re)	loquēris (-re)	patiēris (-re)	oriēris (-re)
conābitur	verēbitur	loquētur	patiētur	oriētur
conābimur	verēbimur	loquēmur	patiēmur	oriēmur
conābiminī	verēbiminī	loquēminī	patiēminī	oriēminī
conābuntur	verēbuntur	loquentur	patientur	orientur

Perfect

conātus sum	veritus sum	locūtus sum	passus sum	ortus sum
conātus es	veritus es	locūtus es	passus es	ortus es
conatus est	veritus est	locūtus est	passus est	ortus est
conātī sumus	veritī sumus	locūtī sumus	passī sumus	ortī sumus
conātī estis	veritī estis	locūtī estis	passī estis	ortī estis
conātī sunt	veritī sunt	locūtī sunt	passī sunt	ortī sunt

Pluperfect

conātus eram	veritus eram	locutus eram	passus eram	ortus eram
conātus erās	veritus erās	locūtus erās	passus erās	ortus erās
conātus erat	veritus erat	locūtus erat	passus erat	ortus erat
conātī erāmus	veritī erāmus	locūtī erāmus	passī erāmus	ortī erāmus
conātī erātis	veritī erātis	locūtī erātis	passī erātis	ortī erātis
conātī erant	veritī erant	locūtī erant	passī erant	ortī erant

Future Perfect

conātus erō	veritus erō	locūtus erō	passus erō	ortus erō
conātus eris	veritus eris	locūtus eris	passus eris	ortus eris
conātus erit	veritus erit	locūtus erit	passus erit	ortus erit
conātī erimus	veritī erimus	locūtī erimus	passī erimus	ortī erimus
conātī eritis	veritī eritis	locūtī eritis	passī eritis	ortī eritis
conātī erunt	veritī erunt	locūtī erunt	passī erunt	ortī erunt

Subjunctive

Present

coner	verear	loquar	patiar	oriar
conēris (-re)	vereāris (-re)	loquāris (-re)	patiāris (-re)	oriāris (-re)
conētur	vereātur	loquātur	patiātur	oriātur
conēmur	vereāmur	loquāmur	patiāmur	oriāmur
conēminī	vereāminī	loquāminī	patiāminī	oriāminī
conentur	vereantur	loquantur	patiantur	oriantur

Imperfect

conārer	verērer	loquerer	paterer	orīrer
conārēris (-re)	verērēris (-re)	loquerēris (-re)	paterēris (-re)	orīrēris (-re)
conārētur	verērētur	loquerētur	paterētur	orīrētur
conārēmur	verērēmur	loquerēmur	paterēmur	orīrēmur
conārēminī	verērēminī	loquerēminī	paterēminī	orīrēminī
conārentur	verērentur	loquerentur	paterentur	orīrentur

Perfect

conātus sim	veritus sim	locūtus sim	passus sim	ortus sim
conātus sīs	veritus sīs	locūtus sīs	passus sīs	ortus sīs
conātus sit	veritus sit	locūtus sit	passus sit	ortus sit
conātī sīmus	veritī sīmus	locūtī sīmus	passī sīmus	ortī sīmus
conātī sītis	veritī sītis	locūtī sītis	passī sītis	ortī sītis
conātī sint	veritī sint	locūtī sint	passī sint	ortī sint

Pluperfect

conātus essem	veritus essem	locūtus essem	passus essem	ortus essem
conātus essēs	veritus essēs	locūtus essēs	passus essēs	ortus essēs
conātus esset	veritus esset	locūtus esset	passus esset	ortus esset
conātī essēmus	veritī essēmus	locūtī essēmus	passī essēmus	ortī essēmus
conātī essētis	veritī essētis	locūtī essētis	passī essētis	ortī essētis
conātī essent	veritī essent	locūtī essent	passī essent	ortī essent

Imperative

Present

conāre	verēre	loquere	patere	orīre
conāminī	verēminī	loquiminī	patiminī	orīminī

Participles

Pres.	conāns	verēns	loquēns	patiēns	oriēns
Perf.	conātus	veritus	locūtus	passus	ortus
Fut.	conātūrus	veritūrus	locūtūrus	passūrus	ortūrus
Ger.	conandus	verendus	loquendus	patiendus	oriendus

Infinitives

Pres.	conārī	verērī	loquī	patī	orīrī
Perf.	conātus esse	veritus esse	locūtus esse	passus esse	ortus esse
Fut.	conātūrus esse	veritūrus esse	locūtūrus esse	passūrus esse	ortūrus esse

IRREGULAR VERBS

Principal Parts

to be	*to be able*	*to go*	*to want*	*not to want*	*to prefer*
sum	possum	eō	volō	nōlō	mālō
esse	posse	īre	velle	nōlle	mālle
fuī	potuī	iī *or* īvī	voluī	nōluī	māluī
futūrus		itum			

Indicative

Present

sum	possum	eō	volō	nōlō	mālō
es	potes	īs	vīs	nōn vīs	māvīs
est	potest	it	vult	nōn vult	māvult
sumus	possumus	īmus	volumus	nōlumus	mālumus
estis	potestis	ītis	vultis	nōn vultis	māvultis
sunt	possunt	eunt	volunt	nōlunt	mālunt

Imperfect

eram	poteram	ībam	volēbam	nōlēbam	mālēbam
erās	poterās	ībās	volēbās	nōlēbas	mālēbas
erat	poterat	ībat	volēbat	nōlēbat	mālēbat
erāmus	poterāmus	ībāmus	volēbāmus	nōlēbāmus	mālēbāmus
erātis	poterātis	ībātis	volēbātis	nōlēbātis	mālēbātis
erant	poterant	ībant	volēbant	nōlēbant	mālēbant

Future

erō	poterō	ībō	volam	nōlam	mālam
eris	poteris	ībis	volēs	nōlēs	mālēs
erit	poterit	ībit	volet	nōlet	mālet
erimus	poterimus	ībimus	volēmus	nōlēmus	mālēmus
eritis	poteritis	ībitis	volētis	nōlētis	mālētis
erunt	poterunt	ībunt	volent	nōlent	mālent

Perfect

fuī	potuī	iī	voluī	nōluī	māluī
fuistī	potuistī	īstī	voluistī	nōluistī	māluistī
fuit	potuit	iit	voluit	nōluit	māluit
fuimus	potuimus	iimus	voluimus	nōluimus	māluimus
fuistis	potuistis	īstis	voluistis	nōluistis	māluistis
fuērunt	potuērunt	iērunt	voluērunt	nōluērunt	māluērunt

Pluperfect

fueram	potueram	ieram	volueram	nōlueram	mālueram
fuerās	potuerās	ierās	voluerās	nōluerās	māluerās
fuerat	potuerat	ierat	voluerat	nōluerat	māluerat
fuerāmus	potuerāmus	ierāmus	voluerāmus	nōluerāmus	māluerāmus
fuerātis	potuerātis	ierātis	voluerātis	nōluerātis	māluerātis
fuerant	potuerant	ierant	voluerant	nōluerant	māluerant

Future Perfect

fuerō	potuerō	ierō	voluerō	nōluerō	māluerō
fueris	potueris	ieris	volueris	nōlueris	mālueris
fuerit	potuerit	ierit	voluerit	nōluerit	māluerit
fuerimus	potuerimus	ierimus	voluerimus	nōluerimus	māluerimus
fueritis	potueritis	ieritis	volueritis	nōlueritis	mālueritis
fuerint	potuerint	ierint	voluerint	nōluerint	māluerint

Subjunctive

Present

sim	possim	eam	velim	nōlim	mālim
sīs	possīs	eās	velīs	nōlīs	mālīs
sit	possit	eat	velit	nōlit	mālit
sīmus	possīmus	eāmus	velīmus	nōlīmus	mālīmus
sītis	possītis	eātis	velītis	nōlītis	mālītis
sint	possint	eant	velint	nōlint	mālint

Imperfect

essem	possem	īrem	vellem	nōllem	māllem
essēs	possēs	īrēs	vellēs	nōllēs	māllēs
esset	posset	īret	vellet	nōllet	māllet
essēmus	possēmus	īrēmus	vellēmus	nōllēmus	māllēmus
essētis	possētis	īrētis	vellētis	nōllētis	māllētis
essent	possent	īrent	vellent	nōllent	māllent

Perfect

fuerim	potuerim	ierim	voluerim	nōluerim	māluerim
fuerīs	potuerīs	ierīs	voluerīs	nōluerīs	māluerīs
fuerit	potuerit	ierit	voluerit	nōluerit	māluerit
fuerīmus	potuerīmus	ierīmus	voluerīmus	nōluerīmus	māluerīmus
fuerītis	potuerītis	ierītis	voluerītis	noluerītis	māluerītis
fuerint	potuerint	ierint	voluerint	nōluerint	maluerint

Pluperfect

fuissem	potuissem	īssem	voluissem	nōluissem	māluissem
fuissēs	potuissēs	īssēs	voluissēs	nōluissēs	māluissēs
fuisset	potuisset	īsset	voluisset	nōluisset	māluisset
fuissēmus	potuissēmus	īssēmus	voluissēmus	nōluissēmus	māluissēmus
fuissētis	potuissētis	īssētis	voluissētis	nōluissētis	māluissētis
fuissent	potuissent	īssent	voluissent	nōluissent	māluissent

Imperative

Present

es	_____	ī	_____	nōlī	_____
este	_____	īte	_____	nōlīte	_____

Future

estō	_____	ītō	_____	nōlītō	_____
estōte	_____	ītōte	_____	nōlītōte	_____

Participles

_____	potēns *pres.*	iēns *gen.* euntis	volēns	nōlēns
_____	_____	itum *perf.*	_____	_____	_____
futūrus *fut.*	_____	itūrus	_____	_____	_____
_____	_____	eundus *ger.*	_____	_____	_____

Infinitives

esse *pres.*	posse	īre	velle	nōlle	mālle
fuisse *perf.*	potuisse	īsse	voluisse	nōluisse	māluisse
futūrus esse *or* fore *fut.*	_____	itūrus esse	_____	_____	_____

PRINCIPAL PARTS: ferō, ferre, tulī, lātum, *bear*

Indicative

Present		Imperfect		Future	
Act.	*Pass.*	*Act.*	*Pass.*	*Act.*	*Pass.*
ferō	feror	ferēbam	ferēbar	feram	ferar
fers	ferris (-re)	ferēbās	ferēbāris (-re)	ferēs	ferēris (-re)
fert	fertur	ferēbat	ferēbātur	feret	ferētur
ferimus	ferimur	ferēbāmus	ferēbāmur	ferēmus	ferēmur
fertis	feriminī	ferēbātis	ferēbāminī	ferētis	ferēminī
ferunt	feruntur	ferēbant	ferēbantur	ferent	ferentur

Perfect		Pluperfect		Future Perf.	
Act.	*Pass.*	*Act.*	*Pass.*	*Act.*	*Pass.*
tulī	lātus sum	tuleram	lātus eram	tulerō	lātus erō
tulistī	lātus es	tulerās	lātus erās	tuleris	lātus eris
tulit	lātus est	tulerat	lātus erat	tulerit	lātus erit
tulimus	lātī sumus	tulerāmus	lātī erāmus	tulerimus	lātī erimus
tulistis	lātī estis	tulerātis	lātī erātis	tuleritis	lātī eritis
tulērunt	lātī sunt	tulerant	lātī erant	tulerint	lātī erunt

Subjunctive

	Present		Imperfect
Act.	Pass.	Act.	Pass.
feram	ferar	ferrem	ferrer
ferās	ferāris (-re)	ferrēs	ferrēris (-re)
ferat	ferātur	ferret	ferrētur
ferāmus	ferāmur	ferrēmus	ferrēmur
ferātis	ferāminī	ferrētis	ferrēminī
ferant	ferantur	ferrent	ferrentur

	Perfect		Pluperfect
Act.	Pass.	Act.	Pass.
tulerim	lātus sim	tulissem	lātus essem
tulerīs	lātus sīs	tulissēs	lātus essēs
tulerit	lātus sit	tulisset	lātus esset
tulerīmus	lātī sīmus	tulissēmus	lātī essēmus
tulerītis	lātī sītis	tulissētis	lātī essētis
tulerint	lātī sint	tulissent	lātī essent

Pres. Imperative		Participles			Infinitives	
Act.	Pass.		Act.	Pass.	Act.	Pass.
fer		Pres.	ferēns		ferre	ferrī
		Perf.		lātus	tulisse	lātus esse
ferte		Fut.	lātūrus	ferendus	lātūrus esse	lātum īrī

PRINCIPAL PARTS: fīō, fierī, factus sum, *be made, be done, become*

Indicative

Pres.	Impf.	Fut.	Perf.	Pluperf.	Fut. Perf.
fīō	fīēbam	fīam	factus sum	factus eram	factus erō
fīs	fīēbās	fīēs	factus es	factus erās	factus eris
fit	fīēbat	fīet	factus est	factus erat	factus erit
fīmus	fīēbāmus	fīēmus	factī sumus	factī erāmus	factī erimus
fītis	fīēbātis	fīētis	factī estis	factī erātis	factī eritis
fīunt	fīēbant	fīent	factī sunt	factī erant	factī erunt

Subjunctive

Pres.	Impf.	Perf.	Pluperf.	Participles	Infinitives
fīam	fierem	factus sim	factus essem	Pres.	fierī
fīās	fierēs	factus sīs	factus essēs	Perf. factus	factus esse
fīat	fieret	factus sit	factus esset	Fut. faciendus	factum īrī
fīāmus	fierēmus	factī sīmus	factī essēmus		
fīātis	fierētis	factī sītis	factī essētis	Imperative: fī, fīte	
fīant	fierent	factī sint	factī essent		

Resumé of the Subjunctive

Your ability to interpret the uses of the subjunctive will greatly facilitate your reading of Latin. Unlike the indicative, which assumes a world of fact and actuality, the subjunctive supposes an unreal or hypothetical situation. Used in both independent (main) clauses and in dependent (subordinate) clauses, it expresses ideas or actions that are circumstantial, invitational, resultant, unreal, indirect, or downright contrary-to-fact.

Remember that there are only four tenses in the subjunctive. There are no future tenses because all subjunctive tenses may imply futurity.

	Active	*Passive*
Pres.	amet	amētur
Imp.	amāret	amārētur
Perf.	amāverit	amātus sit
Pluperf.	amāvisset	amātus esset

Independent

1. Jussive or hortatory (*let . . .*)
   Vivamus, mea, Lesbia, atque amemus.
   Miser Catulle, desinas ineptire (only in
   poetry; in prose use imperative for
   second person).
   Requiescat in pace.

2. Deliberative (surprise, indignation,
   perplexity).
   Quid faciam? Quid agam? Quid dicam?

3. Optative (wish) (*would that . . .* !)
   Utinam auxilio tibi sit!
   Utinam di auxilium ferant!
   Ne vivam, captiva misera.

4. Potential (possibility) (*may, might, can,
   could, would*)
   Nemo dicat me esse latro.

Dependent

1. Purpose (neg, *ne*)
   Ulixes socios misit ut naturam terrae
   cognoscerent.

2. Result (neg. *non*)
   Tanta tempestas coorta est ut nulla
   navium cursum tenere posset.

3. Conditions (should-would: Less Vivid)
   Si Ulixes Polyphemum necet, socii
   effugiant.
   Conditions (Contrary-to-fact)
   Si Ulixes Polyphemum necaret
   (necavisset), socii effugere possent
   (potuissent).

4. Cum clauses
   Circumstantial
   Cibum novum cum Graeci gustavissent,
   patriae suae obliti sunt.
   Causal
   Quae cum ita essent, nuntii redierunt.
   Concessive
   Cum nulla facultas effugiendi maneat,
   tamen Ulixes spem non deponit.

5. Noun clause of desire (after **rogo, peto,
   quaero, persuadeo, oro,** etc.)
   Oravit ut abire liceret.

6. Indirect question (after interrogative
   word)
   Polyphemus quaesivit ubi esset navis.

7. Relative clauses
   Purpose: Ulixes socios misit qui aquam
   referrent.
   Characteristic: Hi erant homines qui
   patriae obliti essent.

8. After verbs of fearing (**vereor** and
   metuo).
   Ulixes veritus est ne Polyphemus dolum
   cognosceret.

9. Subordinate clause in Indirect Discourse
   Populus scivit Theseum esse ducem
   quem exspectaret.

APPENDIX B

I. The Roman Calendar

Our present calendar is a descendant of the Roman calendar as revised by Julius Caesar in 45 B.C. and further amended by Pope Gregory in 1582 A.D. According to Ovid in his *Fasti*, an almanac-like work on the Roman festivals, the calendar of Romulus, who founded the city of Rome in 753 B.C., was divided originally into ten months beginning with **Martius** (March). Numa, one of the subsequent kings, is said to have inserted at the beginning of the year the months of **Ianuarius** (January) and **Februarius** (February), which like the other months were based on the lunar cycle from one new moon to the next. Thus, centuries later, Caesar inherited a twelve-month year based on the lunar year of 355 days, which unfortunately did not correspond to the solar year, so that by Caesar's time **Ianuarius** was occurring several months out of season. Adding to the complexity of the situation was the fact that the calendar had become a tool for power to be used by one class against another because the priests had in their power the appointing of days lawful (**fas**) or unlawful (**nefas**) for business or legal and political activity. The resulting confusion and abuses influenced Caesar, as Pontifex Maximus, to effect a calendar reform which established the same twelve months in a solar year of $365\frac{1}{4}$ days, the extra day being added every fourth year.

The months of Caesar's calendar were **Ianuarius, Februarius, Martius, Aprilis, Maius, Iunius, Quintilis, Sextilis, September, October, November,** and **December.**[1] **Ianuarius** was appropriately named for the double-faced god of doorways, **Ianus** (Janus), who looked backward to the old and forward to the new. **Februarius** contained the **februa,** the feast of purification, and took its name from that holiday. **Martius** was named for the god Mars, who had sired the twins Romulus and Remus, and according to Ovid, **Aprilis** was named for Venus, being a corruption of the Greek name Aphrodite. Ovid further tells us that **Maius** was named for the "elders" (**maiores**), and that Iunius was named for the "younger ones" (**iuniores**), a most interesting etymology, unfortunately not further substantiated.[2] The remaining months were named for their original numerical position; **quintus** (fifth), **sextus** (sixth), **septem** (seven), **octo** (eight), **novem** (nine), **decem** (ten). **Quintilis** subsequently was renamed **Iulius** (July) in honor of Julius Caesar, and **Augustus** (August) replaced **Sextilis** in honor of the deified Emperor Augustus. Thus our present month names have had continuous use for about two thousand years.

Since dates in the pre-Christian era obviously could not have been reckoned relative to the birth of Christ, another significant event was used as the date point from which to calculate events: dates were reckoned from the traditional date of the founding of the city of Rome, 753 B.C., in Latin **ab urbe condita**, abbreviated **AUC.** Thus **AUC** 54 was 53 years after the founding of the city or 700 B.C.[3] Another way the Romans expressed the year was in terms of the consuls who served during a particular year—thus an event was said to have occurred "in the consulship of Piso and Gabinius."[4]

---

[1]The months in Latin are considered either as adjectives or as substantives: the ones in **-ius** are declined like **bonus, -a, -um;** the others are third declension (**Aprilis, -e**) or (**September, -bris**).

[2]Other sources list **Aprilis** as derived from **aperire** (*to open*), the month opening to spring, or from **apero** (*second*), since originally it was the second month. Most dictionaries give the goddess Maia as the derivation of **Maius** and call **Iunius** a Roman family name, the Junius gens.

[3]The extra year is added since the Romans counted the founding year and the indicated year, so that one must consider the number 754 when converting B.C. or A.D. dates to **AUC** or vice versa.

[4]Given as an ablative absolute construction: **Pisone et Gabinio consulibus.**

The dates within the month were reckoned by counting backwards from three points of time in each month—the Nones, the Ides, and the Kalends of the following month.[5] These three names of days divided the Roman month into sections, with the date being counted either as on or as so many days before each point of time. The Kalends fell on the first day of the month. Thus the phrase **Kalendae Apriles** (abbreviated **Kal. Apr.**) indicates the first day of April. The Ides and Nones are separated by eight days (or nine Roman days) and can best be remembered by the following rhymed verse:

> In March, July, October, May
> The Ides come on the 15th day,
> The Nones the 7th, and all besides
> Have two days less for Nones and Ides.

To these three names of days, the names of the months were attached as adjectives: **Idibus Martiis (Id. Mar.)**, *on the 15th of March.*

To convert a Roman date with its inclusive and backward reckoning one must apply the following principles: add 1 to the number of the day on which the Nones or Ides fall, then subtract the number of the given day; when converting Kalends, add 2 to the number of days in the preceding month, then subtract the number of the given day. Note the following examples:

1) **ante diem III Non. Iun.**, *the 3rd day before the Nones of June.* In June the Nones are on the 5th. Add 1 to 5: 5 + 1 = 6. Subtract 3 from 6: 6 − 3 = 3. Hence, the date is June 3.
2) **a.d. VI Id. Mar.**, *the 6th day before the ides of March.* In March the Ides are on the 15th. Add 1 to 15: 15 + 1 = 16. Subtract 6 from 16: 16 − 6 = 10. Hence, the date is March 10.
3) **a.d. VIII Kal. Mai.**, *the 8th day before the Kalends of May.* Since the Kalends are the 1st day of the month, this date will be in April. April has 30 days. Add 2 to 30: 30 + 2 = 32. Subtract 8 from 32: 32 − 8 = 24. Hence, the date is April 24.

The day before each point of reference was called **pridie**. Thus, **pr. Non. Iun.** would be June 4, **pr. Id. Mar.** would be March 14, and **pr. Kal. Mai.** would be April 30. Notice also that the day before the day designated as **pridie** is always **a.d. III** (as in ex. 1).

There are actually several ways to express a date such as June 3 in the first example:

a) **ante diem tertium Nonas Iunias**, shortened to **a.d. III Non. Iun.** Ante diem came to be treated as an indeclinable noun which could be used with other prepositions and thus **ad a.d. III Non. Iun.** means *up to the 3rd of June.* Cicero and Livy commonly use this expression.
b) by the ablative of time:
   tertio die ante Nonas Iunias
c) omitting **die ante** from the above example in b):
   tertio Non. Iunias

Convert the following Roman dates to present dates:[6]

1. **Kal. Iun.**	4. **Pridie Id, Mar.**
2. **Non. Feb.**	5. **a.d. IV Non. Ian.**
3. **a.d. VIII Id. Mar.**	6. **a.d. III Non. Ian.**
7. **Pridie Kal. Mai.**	

---

[5] **Nones**; **Idus, Iduum**, *f.*; and **Kalendae**, the last being the source of our English word *calendar.*

[6] The answers are given below:

1. June 1	4. Mar. 14
2. Feb. 5	5. Jan. 2
3. Mar. 8	6. Jan. 3
7. Apr. 30	

Time during the day was divided from sunrise to sunset into twelve parts or **horae**. The length of these **horae** varied with the season. One can approximate the Roman hour by adding our six hours from midnight to sunrise to the given Roman hour. Thus the third hour (Roman time) would be about 9:00 AM. The night from sunset to sunrise was divided into four watches of three **horae** each.

II. The Olympians

Jupiter, Jove (Zeus)—god the father, god of sky and weather, cloud gatherer, god of sky phenomena, rain, thunder, lightning, but also of open, clear sky.

Attributes and/or symbols:
eagle, oak tree, thunderbolt, lightning, scepter, aegis, bull

Neptune (Poseidon)—Earth-shaker, god of all waters, seas, ocean, god of horses, earthquakes

trident, bull, horse, dolphin

Pluto, Dis (Hades)—the Unseen, god of the Underworld (Tartarus), receiver of many guests; carried off Proserpina, daughter of Ceres.

dark chariot, wife Proserpina

Juno (Hera)—ox-eyed, goddess of marriage, childbirth, fertility in marriage, bonds of wedlock; wife of Jupiter

peacock, cow, lily, fleur-de-lys

Vesta (Hestia)—goddess of the hearth

sacred fire

Ceres (Demeter)—earth mother, goddess of grain, corn, vegetation, harvest, fertility of the soil, sorrow over a lost child, joy at annual rebirth; seasonal change

shaft of wheat, vegetation

Venus (Aphrodite)—Cyprian, Cytherean goddess of love, beauty, marriage, protectress of sailors; birth from sea foam and genitalia of Uranus.

swan, cosmetics, mirror, dove, apple

Minerva (Pallas, Athena)—gray-eyed goddess of wisdom, war, justice, goddess of the city, crafts, skills, patron of Athens, unmarried girls, born fully grown and clothed from head of Zeus; gave olive tree, horse taming; goddess of weaving.

Aegis with Medusa head, owl, tree, Nike, spindle, snake, helmet

Mercury (Hermes)—slayer of Argos, messenger of the gods, conductor of souls of the dead, guide and protector of travelers, bringer of good luck to merchants; commerce, thieves, shepherd

winged sandals, caduceus, broad-brimmed hat

Vulcan, Mulciber (Hephaestus)—god of fire and the forge, artisan god of smiths; lame god, neglected husband of Venus

metalcraft, hammer, anvil, bellows, fire, limp

Mars (Ares)—bloody god of wars and weapons; lover of Venus

vulture, helmet, shield, arms

Apollo (Phoebus)—Pythian god of sun, identified with earlier Helios and Hyperion, god of prophecy, medicine, fine arts, flocks, herds, rational thought, courage, order, but also capable of the irrational act

tripod, omphalos (navel stone placed at Delphi), lyre, bow and arrows, laurel wreath, palm tree, wolf, crow

Diana (Artemis)—goddess of hunt, patron of small animals, wild beasts, virginity, the moon and monthly cycles in women; twin of Apollo

bow, quiver of arrows, torch, hunting dress, stag, palm tree

Bacchus, Liber (Dionysus)—the liquid principle, god of wine, the vine, cultivation of vine, excesses from wine; song, dance, poetry, fertility, drama, excesses, mysticism, Silenus and the satyrs

ivy, grapes, vines, deer, thyrsos, drinking cup, leopard, Maenads and satyrs

*   *   *   *   *

In his long, colorful career, Jupiter (Zeus) had many consorts to produce the younger Olympians, minor divinities, and the heroes:

ZEUS'S CONSORTS AND THEIR PROGENY

Metis	Minerva (Athena), born from the head of Zeus
Themis	Justice, Hours, Order
Eurynome	The Three Graces
Ceres (Demeter)	Proserpina (Kore, Persephone)
Mnemosyne	The Nine Muses
Latona (Leto)	Apollo and Diana (Artemis)
Juno (Hera)	Vulcan (Hephaestus), Mars (Ares), Hebe
Maia	Mercury (Hermes)
Semele	Dionysus (Bacchus)
Alcmena	Hercules (Heracles)
Callisto	Arcas
Danaë	Perseus

III. The Lesser Deities

1. The *Muses*, the mythological embodiment of the cultural arts, were nine in number, the daughters of Zeus and Mnemosyne (Memory). They provide the inspiration for the arts they represent: Clio is the Muse of history; Calliope, of epic poetry; Terpsichore, of the dance; Thalia, of comedy; Urania, of astronomy; Melpomene, of tragedy; Euterpe, of lyric poetry; Polyhymnia, of sacred song; and Erato, of profane love poetry. Their mountain haunts were Helicon, Pierus, and Parnassus in Greece, and of course, Olympus.

2. The *Graces* were three—Aglaia (Splendor), Euphrosyne (Mirth), and Thalia (Good Cheer). They were the daughters of Jupiter and Eurynome, an Oceanid. Not usually separately identified, they were the embodiment of grace and beauty.

3. The *Fates* (*Parcae* or *Moirae*) were also three in number: Clotho spins the thread of life; Lachesis, the disposer of lots, weaves it; and Atropos cuts the thread of each man's existence.

4. The *Furies* (*Erinyes*) were the ministers of justice, the punishers of evil. They were Tisiphone, Megaera, and Allecto.

5. The *Hesperides*, called variously the daughters of Night or of Atlas, guarded the golden apples; the eleventh labor of Hercules was to obtain these apples.

6. The *Oceanids* were the daughters of Oceanus and Tethys. The Nereids were the children of Nereus, son of the sea (Pontus). Only one Nereid (Thetis) is listed by name and she is important since it is from her marriage with King Peleus that the hero Achilles was born.

7. The *Gorgons* were earth creatures, sometimes represented as female with snakey locks, sometimes as dragon-like with wings. Their look turned men to stone. The hero Perseus slew Medusa, the Gorgon, using his polished shield as a mirror to avoid being turned to stone. From the drops of blood which fell into the sea the winged horse, Pegasus, is said to have sprung.

8. The *Winds*, headed by King Aeolus, lived on earth. The four Winds represent the directions: Boreas (Latin, **Aquilo**) was the North Wind; Zephyr (Latin, **Favonius**) was the West Wind; Notus (Latin, **Auster**) was the South Wind; and Eurus was the East Wind.

9. The *Satyrs* or *Sileni* were the spirits of the wild life of the woodlands and the hills. They are bestial in their nature and desires, usually represented in art as male creatures with goat hoofs, pointed ears, and a horse's tail emerging from the center of the back. They follow in the procession of Bacchus in vase paintings and sculptural relief, many times playing the aulos or flute-like "pipes of Pan."

10. The *Nymphs* represent the female divine spirits of natural phenomena: woods, rivers and streams, mountain regions, trees, caves, towns, and cities. They are considered as young, fair, unwed, and usually reside in the locality which they represent. Pursued by gods, men, and satyrs, they many times are considered the female counterpart of the Satyrs, roaming the woods in the band of Diana's followers.

IV. Genealogy of the Gods

(Olympians in Bold face Type)

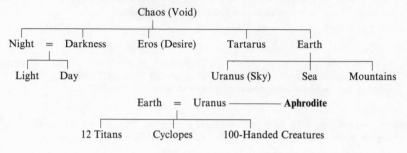

```
                    Chaos (Void)
        ┌───────────────┼───────────────────┐
Night = Darkness    Eros (Desire)    Tartarus    Earth
  ┌─────┴─────┐                        ┌──────────┼──────────┐
Light      Day                    Uranus (Sky)   Sea    Mountains
```

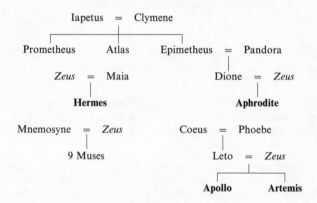

```
            Earth = Uranus ──────── Aphrodite
        ┌──────────┼──────────────────┐
   12 Titans    Cyclopes      100-Handed Creatures
```

(Titans include Iapetus, Mnemosyne, Coeus, Phoebe, Cronus, Rhea)

```
            Iapetus = Clymene
        ┌──────────┼──────────────┐
Prometheus       Atlas       Epimetheus = Pandora
        Zeus = Maia               Dione = Zeus
            Hermes                   Aphrodite

Mnemosyne = Zeus              Coeus = Phoebe
        9 Muses                  Leto = Zeus
                              ┌──────┴──────┐
                           Apollo        Artemis
```

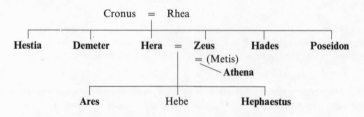

```
                Cronus = Rhea
   ┌───────┬───────────┼──────────┬──────────┐
Hestia  Demeter      Hera = Zeus  Hades   Poseidon
                          = (Metis)
                              ╲ Athena
          ┌───────────────────┼───────────┐
        Ares               Hebe        Hephaestus
```

Source: Hesiod, *Theogony*

V. Bibliography on Mythology

The following titles offer a starting place for the student who wishes to explore in greater depth the stories told by Ovid or to investigate the general subject of mythology. For further suggestions, consult the bibliographies in these books or consult the bibliography by Peradotto listed below.

Grant, Michael. *Myths of the Greeks and the Romans.* New York: New American Library, 1964 (copyright 1962).

Morford, Mark P. O. and Robert J. Lenardon. *Classical Mythology.* New York: David McKay, 1971.

Mayerson, Philip. *Classical Mythology in Literature, Art, and Music.* Waltham, Mass.: Xerox College Publishing, 1971.

Hamilton, Edith. *Mythology.* New York: Grosset & Dunlap, n. d. (copyright 1940).

Godolphin, F. R. B. (ed.) *Great Classical Myths.* New York: Random House, 1964.

Guthrie, W. K. C. *The Greeks and Their Gods.* Boston: Beacon Press, 1955 (copyright 1950).

Campbell, Joseph. *The Masks of God III: Occidental Mythology.* New York: Viking Press, 1964.

Murray, Henry A. (ed.). *Myth and Mythmaking.* New York: George Braziller, 1960.

Sebeok, Thomas A. *Myth: A Symposium.* Bloomington: Indiana University Press, 1965 (copyright 1955).

Kirk, G. S. *Myth: Its Meaning and Functions in Ancient and Other Cultures.* Berkeley: University of California Press; Cambridge: Cambridge University Press, 1970.

Stanford, W. B., and J. V. Luce. *The Quest for Ulysses.* New York and Washington: Praeger Publishers, 1974.

Ward, Anne G. (ed.). *The Quest for Theseus.* London: Pall Mall Press, 1970.

Humphries, Rolfe (trans.). *Ovid: Metamorphoses.* Bloomington: Indiana University Press, 1955.

For examples of the retelling of ancient myths by modern writers, see:

Ayrton, Michael. *The Maze Maker.* New York, Chicago and San Francisco: Holt, Rinehart & Winston, 1967. Also, New York: Avon Books, 1975.

O'Neill, Eugene. *Three Plays: Desire Under the Elms, Strange Interlude, and Mourning Becomes Electra.* New York: Vintage Books, 1961 (copyright 1924, 1928 and 1931, respectively).

Renault, Mary. *The King Must Die.* New York: Pantheon Books, 1958; Pocket Books, 1959.

Renault, Mary. *The Bull from the Sea.* New York: Pantheon Books, 1962; Pocket Books, 1963.

For an annotated bibliography of mythology, see:

Peradotto, John. *Classical Mythology: An Annotated Bibliographical Survey.* Urbana, Ill.: The American Philological Association, 1973.

VI. Roman Chronology

HISTORY	LITERATURE

B.C. 753–509   THE KINGS

753	Foundation of Rome (tradition)
750	Cumae founded by Greeks
750–509	Etruscans establish hill-top City-States; expansion in Latium, Campania, and Po area
509	Tarquinius Superbus expelled

B.C. 509–264   EARLY REPUBLIC

493	Battle of Lake Regillus	B.C. 451	*Twelve Tables*
466	Tribunate established	445	*Lex Canuleia*, legalizing marriage between classes
444–442	Decemvirate; Codification of the Law	312	Appius Claudius, censor, orator
390	Rome sacked by the Gauls		
326–290	Samnite Wars	272	Livius Andronicus brought to Rome
281–275	Wars with Pyrrhus of Epirus		

B.C. 264–134   MIDDLE REPUBLIC

264–241	First Punic War with Carthage	270–201	Naevius
		239–169	Ennius "father of Roman poetry"
234–149	Cato, conservative senator	250–150	Roman Comedy
218–202	Second Punic War: Scipio	254–184	Plautus
149–146	Third Punic War: Carthage destroyed	220–132	Pacuvius
		200–117	Polybius
146	Corinth destroyed	185–150	Terence
		170–85	Accius

B.C. 133–27   LATE REPUBLIC   **GOLDEN AGE: LATE REPUBLIC**

133	Tiberius Gracchus, Tribune		
123	Gaius Gracchus, Tribune		
111–105	War with Jugurtha		
104–100	Consulships of Marius		
82–81	Sulla dictator		
70	Consulate of Pompey & Crassus		
66–62	Pompey in the East		
63	Cicero Consul: Catiline conspiracy	B.C. 106–43	Cicero
60	First Triumvirate: Pompey Crassus, Caesar	102–44	Caesar
		96–55	Lucretius
		84–54	Catullus
59	Caesar Consul; Gallic Wars	116–27	Varro
49–45	Civil Wars	99–24	Nepos
44	Caesar assassinated	86–34	Sallust
44–27	Wars of Octavian to establish Empire		
33	Battle of Actium: Anthony and Cleopatra defeated		

B.C. 27–14 A.D.   EMPIRE OF
                  AUGUSTUS
                  Establish, rule, and
                  maintain colonial
                  empire in Asia Minor,
                  Europe, and North
                  Africa: "The
                  Principate"

GOLDEN AGE: AUGUSTAN OR
IMPERIAL
B.C. 70–19   Virgil
B.C. 65–8   Horace
B.C. 59–17 A.D.   Livy
B.C. 54–2 A.D.   Propertius
B.C. 43–17 A.D.   Ovid
B.C. 20–40 A.D.   Philo
B.C. f. 25–23   Vitruvius

A.D. 14–284   CONTINUATION OF
              PRINCIPATE
    14–37   Tiberius
    37–41   Caligula ⎫
    41–54   Claudius ⎬ Julio-Claudians
    54–68   Nero   ⎭
    68–69   Galba, Otho, Vitellius
    69–79   Vespasian (Flavian)
    70   Capture of Jerusalem
    79–81   Titus (Flavian)
    79   Eruption of Vesuvius
    81–96   Domitian (last of Flavians)
    96–98   Nerva
    98–117   Trajan
    117–138   Hadrian
    138–161   Antoninus Pius   ⎫
    161–180   Marcus Aurelius ⎬ Antonines
    180–193   Commodus   ⎭
    198–211   Septimius Severus
    211–217   Caracalla
    222–235   Alexander Severus
    227   Sassanians in Persia
    235–84   Barracks Emperors
    259   Valerian captured by
              Sassanians
    284–305   Diocletian
    306–337   Constantine

SILVER LATIN
B.C.   4–65 A.D.   Seneca
A.D.   23–79 A.D.   Pliny, the Elder
        c. 39–95 A.D. Quintilian
        ?–65   Petronius
        37–100 A.D.   Josephus
        62–114   Pliny, the Younger
        54–105   Martial
        46–126   Plutarch
        55–120   Tacitus
        c. 60–140   Juvenal

A.D.   69–150   Suetonius
        95–165   Appian
        125–171   Apuleius

CHURCH FATHERS
        155–222   Tertullian

        340–420   St. Jerome
        c. 340–397   St. Ambrose, Bishop
                      of Milan
        354–430   St. Augustine

VII. Reading Roman Poetry

Roman poets regularly wrote their verses[7] in formal patterns which they felt suited the nature of the ideas being expressed. The most familiar of these patterns is probably the hexameter of epic literature, and indeed the proper reading of Roman epic literature has the effect of waves of repeated action, like the beat of marching feet, the roll of the drum, the coming of invading armies, or the waves of the sea; and since heroic, epic literature dealt with such subjects, the meter did indeed aptly suit the ideas being expressed.

---

[7] A *verse* is a single line of poetry (**versum**, *turned*); a *stanza* is a group of verses.

Another popular verse form, elegy or elegiac couplet, consists of alternating lines of hexameter and pentameter.[8] This meter was early used by poets to express many different moods and ideas when epic hexameter proved too heavy or formal. Elegiac couplet was used as a vehicle for personal reflection on a great variety of subjects, both serious and gay. Ovid, in his monumental accumulation of legends and seasonal calendar events, *The Fasti,* employs this meter, perhaps because of its alternations, to emphasize the contrast of one day against the next, for he would like to communicate in all his works the changes in life—in seasons, in ages, in people, in the gods themselves.

It is difficult to read into the meter of the various patterns of lyric poetry a reflection of the meaning of the poems; rather an association of the meter with a certain kind of verse (e.g., the use of Sapphics[9] with love poetry) in imitation of Greek meters in use by Roman poets has resulted in certain meters being identified with certain types of poetic expression. Whether the psychological effect of such meter is the result of the meter itself or of the poems already written in the meter and quite familiar to poets is a difficult subject to discuss with certainty. However, the clever, tight fit of the hendecasyllabic line[10] seems most appropriate for the love poem that Catullus chose to cast in its form, for with all its limitations it still allows Catullus to express a most delightful invitation to love in a kind of voluntary surrender to the meter with the compensating fulfillment of idea:

Da mi basia mille, deinde centum!

Of the many other lyric forms, the scazon, also called limping iambs,[11] provides another verse form that seems to reflect its meaning. A line contains six feet, all iambic except for the last one which changes to a trochee. This abrupt change acts as a sort of brake pedal to the line and slows the otherwise repetitious flow of rhythm:

Miser Catulle, desinas ineptire

To read the poems properly, you should read aloud, delighting in the alternation of long and short vowels producing in turn the long and short syllables. Relax into the rhythm of the poem, and the sense, the emphasis of words, and the meaning will develop naturally. The poet planned it that way, choosing his words and his word order to fit his ideas and the meter he had selected. Pronounce the words carefully, giving the proper quantity to the long and short vowels, and you will emerge with a compromise of beat and accent that is neither tedious nor exaggerated. But of course you must be able to identify long and short syllables[12] and to read them properly in the meter. The following rules may help:

Long and Short Vowels. A vowel is either long or short.

Study the paradigms in your grammar to remind yourself of the stem vowels and ending vowels that are usually long. All the others are short. A diphthong is always long.

Long and Short Syllables. A syllable is long:

1) if it contains a long vowel or a diphthong. Such a syllable is called *long by nature.*

a·mā·mus   lau·dā·re   a·mī·cō·rum

---

[8]Hexameter is a verse with six beats to the line; pentameter with five.
[9]Sapphics are described on p. 00.
[10]A hendecasyllabic line is one containing eleven syllables.
[11]An iamb is a ∪ — foot; a trochee is the opposite — ∪.
[12]Consult the introductory material on pronunciation for rules about how to divide a word into syllables.

2) if it contains a short vowel followed by two consonants or x (ks).[13] Such a syllable is called **long by position**.

a·gun·tur   se·cun·da   pu·el·la   Les·bi·a

All other syllables are short.

Elision. There is elision or cutting off of a final vowel (or diphthong) before a word beginning with a vowel (or diphthong) or **h**. Also, final **-m** is elided along with its preceding vowel before a word beginning with a vowel (or diphthong) or **h**.

Vivamus, mea Lesbia, atque amemus

Meters. Once you have identified the long and short syllables, you can mark a verse into its units of measure, called feet. The most commonly used feet in Latin poetry are as follows:

iamb (or iambus)	∪ —	dactyl	— ∪ ∪
trochee	— ∪	anapest	∪ ∪ —
spondee	— —		

The adjectives from these terms are *iambic, trochaic, dactylic, anapestic,* and *spondaic.* The beat (**ictus**) usually falls on the long syllable, and sometimes differs from the normal prose accent of the word, which is determined by the antepenultimate rule.[14] Your reading should be a compromise of beat and accent.

The number of measures or feet in the line usually identifies the meter:

trimeter:	three feet to a line (or six iambic or trochaic feet)[15]
tetrameter:	four feet to a line
pentameter:	five feet to a line
hexameter:	six feet to a line

HENDECASYLLABLES

As the name implies (**hendeca** means *eleven* in Greek), *hendecasyllable* means a line of eleven syllables repeated until the thought is completed. The poems vary in length. Catullus' famous love poem to Lesbia is in this meter, and each line is marked as follows:

— —|— ∪∪| — ∪|— ∪ |— ∪
Vivamus, mea Lesbia, atque amemus

— —|— ∪ ∪|— ∪|–∪|— ∪
rumoresque senum severiorum

— —|–∪∪|—∪| — ∪|—∪
omnes unius aestimemus assis?

spondee   dactyl   trochee   trochee   trochee

---

[13] A mute (**p, b, d, t, k, s**) followed by a liquid (**l** or **r**) counts as a single consonant and the syllable that contains a short vowel followed by such a combination can be either long or short to suit the meter.

[14] Antepenultimate Rule: A word of two syllables is accented on the first syllable (the penult); a word of three or more syllables is accented on the penult *if it is long,* on the antepenult if the penult is short.

[15] Iambic and trochaic verses are measured, not by single feet, but by pairs: for example, six iambic feet make a trimeter. This doubling occurs because two longs were needed to make up a full measure.

The poet must surrender much to so limiting a form, but his gains are rewardingly great. Notice that the eleven syllables can be grouped into a pentameter line of feet: spondee, dactyl, and three trochees following. Notice also that there is elision between words according to the rules for elision. It is a good idea to mark elisions before trying to read a line. Ignore punctuation within a line when eliding. Practice reading each line with its elisions until you understand how elisions work. The Romans probably sounded each vowel ever so slightly to fit the meter, but it is easier to drop the final syllable of the first word and fuse the two words together as one, pronouncing only the initial vowel of the second word. Elisions occur in all meters, but you can practice them first in Catullus' love poem:

$$-\,-|-\,\cup\cup|\,-\,\,\cup|-\cup|-\,-$$
soles occidere et redire possunt:

nobis cum semel occidit brevis lux
nox est perpetua una dormienda.

da mi basia mille, deinde centum,
dein mille altera, dein secunda centum,

deinde usque alter mille, deinde centum,

dein, cum milia multa fecerimus,
conturbabimus illa, ne sciamus,
aut ne quis malus invidere possit,
cum tantum sciat esse basiorum.

SAPPHICS

The meter Sapphics, so named because it copies the meter of Sappho, the seventh-century Greek poetess of the island of Lesbos, is easily learned once you are familiar with hendecasyllables, for the meter consists of a four-verse stanza, the first three lines of which are a variety of hendecasyllables and the last short verse a two-foot dactyl-and-spondee combination.

$$-\cup|-\,\,-|-\cup\,\cup|-\cup|-\,\cup$$
Ille mi par esse deo videtur,
$$-\cup|-\,-|-\,\,\cup\cup|-\cup|-\,-$$
ille, si fas est, superare divos,
$$-\,\,\cup|\,-\,-|-\,\,\cup\cup|-\cup|\,-\,-$$
qui sedens adversus identidem te
$$-\,\,\cup\,\,\cup|-\cup$$
spectat et audit

dulce ridentem, misero quod omnes
eripit sensus mihi; nam simul te,
Lesbia, aspexi, nihil est super mi
vocis in ore,

lingua sed torpet, tenuis sub artus
flamma demanat, sonitu suopte
tintinant aures, gemina teguntur
lumina nocte.

This poem is a translation of an original poem by Sappho in Greek.

HEXAMETER

The Latin hexameter consists of six feet arranged as follows:

$$— \cup \cup \,|\, — \cup \cup \,|\, — \cup \cup \,|\, — \cup \cup \,|\, — \cup \cup \,|\, — —$$

The first four feet may be either dactyls or spondees, the fifth foot is regularly a dactyl, and the sixth a spondee (like the last two-foot line in the Sapphic stanza). The roll of the hexameter is beautifully used by Lucretius in his *De Rerum Natura* and by Virgil in the *Aeneid*. Ovid too uses the hexameter for the *Metamorphoses*. Below are the opening lines of the *Aeneid*. Once you have mastered them you will be able to read any hexameter line with ease. If the line does not seem to scan easily, mark the last two feet first and then the first four will be easier to read.

$$— \cup \cup \,|\, — \quad \cup \cup \,|\,—\,\|\,—\,|\,— —\,|\, — \cup \cup \,|\,— —$$
Arma virumque cano, Troiae qui primus ab oris
Italiam fato ‖ profugus ‖ Lavinaque venit
litora multum ille et terris ‖ iactatus et alto

vi superum, ‖ saevae memorem ‖ Iunonis ob iram,
multa quoque et bello ‖ passus, dum conderet urbem

inferretque deos ‖ Latio; genus unde Latinum
Albanique patres ‖ atque altae moenia Romae.

Somewhere along the hexameter line the poet paused for a breath, usually at the end of a word within a foot where the meaning required a cutting of the verse into parts. This pause is called the *caesura* (from **caedo**, *cut*) and it may occur within the second, third, or fourth foot, but most often in the third. It is marked by a double line written vertically (‖). Note the pauses as marked in these opening lines of the *Aeneid*.

Ending a word at the end of a foot, rather than within a foot, is called *diaeresis* (dividing). Thus, diaeresis can be considered the opposite of caesura. It, too, is a pause in the line, and is marked like a sharp in music (♯).

litora ♯ multum ille et terris iactatus et alto

ELEGIAC COUPLET

Elegiac couplet contains two alternating lines, one hexameter followed by one pentameter consisting of two sections, each with two and a half feet.

$$— \cup \cup \,|\, — \; —\,|\, — \quad —\,|\, — \cup \cup \,|\, — \cup \cup \,|\, — —$$
Forsitan et quaeras, cur sit locus ille Lupercal
$$— \cup \cup \,|\, — \; —\,|\, — \,\|\, — \cup \cup \,|\, — \cup \cup \,|\, —$$
quaeve diem tali nomine causa notet.
Silvia Vestalis caelestia semina partu
ediderat, patruo ‖ regna tenente suo.

SCAZONS (LIMPING IAMBS)

The true iambic trimeter (six iambic feet) was the favorite verse of the playwrights; their lines are all variations on this type of rhythm, for it most nearly duplicated human speech. The scazon added the variety of reversing the last foot of the trimeter to act as a brake in the rush of the line, as in this poem of Catullus:

$$\cup - | \cup - | \cup - | \cup - | \cup - | - \cup$$

Miser Catulle, desinas ineptire
et quid vides perisse perditum ducas
fulsere quondam condidi tibi soles,
cum ventitabas quo puella ducebat
amata nobis quantum amabitur nulla.

Enjoy reading the meters; you will be able to do so only after you are so familiar with the beat that you stop marking the long and short syllables and start responding with your body to the rhythm, as you would to a samba or a rumba. After all, they are Latin (American) rhythms.

Gaudeamus Igitur

(FOR MIXED VOICES)

Anonymous, c. 1710   Old German Melody

1. Gau - de - a - mus   i - gi - tur,   Iu - ve - nes   dum   su - mus;
2. U - bi   sunt, qui   an - te   nos   In mun - do   fu -   e - re?
3. Vi - ta   nos - tra   bre - vis est,   Bre - vi   fi - ni - e - tur;
4. Vi - vat   a - ca - de - mi - a,   Vi - vant pro - fes - so - res,

Post   iu - cun - dam   iu - ven - tu - tem, Post mo - les - tam   se - nec - tu - tem
Va - di - te   ad   su - pe - ros,   Tran - si - te   ad   in - fe - ros,
Ve - nit mors ve - lo - ci - ter,   Ra - pit nos   a - tro - ci - ter;
Vi - vat mem-brum quod - li - bet,   Vi - vant mem - bra quae - li - bet;

Nos ha - be - bit   hu - mus, Nos ha - be - bit   hu - mus.
U - bi iam   fu - e - re,   U - bi iam   fu - e - re.
Ne - mi - ni   par - ce - tur,   Ne - mi - ni   par - ce - tur.
Sem - per sint   in   flo - re,   Sem - per sint   in   flo - re.

5 Vivat et respublica
Et qui illam regit,
Vivat nostra civitas,
Maecenatum caritas,
Quae nos hic protegit.

6 Vivant omnes virgines,
Faciles, formosae,
Vivant et mulieres,
Tenerae, amabiles,
Bonae, laboriosae.

7 Pereat tristitia,
Pereant osores,
Pereat diabolus
Quivis antiburschius,
Atque irrisores.

From *Latin Songs, Classical, Medieval, and Modern*, ed. Calvin S. Brown (New York and London, 1914).

LATIN–ENGLISH VOCABULARY

Parts of speech are indicated in the following manner: only adverbs, conjunctions, and interjections are specifically identified; nouns are listed in the nominative case, followed by the genitive singular ending and the gender; verbs appear with their principal parts, with first conjugation forms summarized by the symbol (1); adjectives appear in masculine, feminine, and neuter singular forms, as do pronouns; and prepositions are followed by the case they govern (+acc., or +abl.).

a, *interj.,* ah

ā (ab) + *abl.* from, away from

abeō, īre, -iī *or* **-īvī, -itum,** go away, depart

abiciō, -ere, -iēcī, -iectum, throw away, aside

absum, -esse, āfuī, āfutūrus, be absent, be away

ac. *See* **atque**

accendō, -ere, -cendī, -censum, kindle, set on fire

accipiō, -ere, -cēpī, -ceptum, receive

accūsō (1), accuse

ācer, -cris, -cre, bitter, hard, harsh, rough

Acestēs, -ae, *m.,* Acestes, king in Sicily

Achaemenidēs, Achaemenides, a Greek companion of Ulysses

Achātēs, -ae, *m.,* Achates, faithful friend of Aeneas

Achillēs, -is, *n.,* Achilles, Greek hero

Achīvus, -a, -um, Greek

aciēs, -eī, *f.,* keenness, edge, a line of battle, the battle itself

Acis, -idis, *m.,* Acis, the lover of Galatea

aconītum, -ī, *n.,* aconite, a poisonous herb

acūtus, -a, -um, sharp

ad + *acc., with verbs of movement,* to, toward; *with verbs of rest,* near

addō, -ere, -didī, ditum, place upon, join, attach, add

addūcō, ere, dūxī, -ductum, bring to, draw to, lead to, induce

adeō, *adv.,* to this point, thus far

adeō, -īre, -iī *or* **īvī, -itum,** go near, approach

adferō, -ferre, attulī, allātum, bring, carry in (alternate spelling: **afferō**)

adficiō, -ere, -fēcī, -fectum, affect, afflict, weaken

adfīgo, -ere, -fīxī, -fixum + *dat.,* pin to, affix, fasten to

adforet = adfutūrum esset

adgredior, -gredī, -gressus sum, go to, approach

adhūc, *adv.,* up to this time, to this point in time or space, here

aditus, -ūs, *m.,* approach, access

adiuvō (1), **-iūvī, -iūtum,** help, bring help to, aid

admittō, -ere, -mīsī, missum, send to, admit

adōrō (1), worship

adquīrō, -ere, -quīsīvī, -quīsīturs, acquire

adspiciō, -ere, -spexi, -spectum, look upon

adsum, -esse, adfuī, adfuturum, be present, be at hand, be here

adultera, -ae, *f.,* adulteress

adulterium, -iī, *n.,* adultery

adulterius, -a, -um, adulterous

advena, -ae, *c.,* stranger

adventō (1), arrive, approach

adversus, -a, -um, unfavorable

advertō, -ere, -tī, -sum, turn to

Aeacidēs, -ae, *m.,* the son (really grandson) of Aeacus, i.e., Achilles

aedēs, -is *f.,* building, shrine

aedificō (1), build, construct

aeger, -gra, -grum, weak, sick

Aegēus, -eī, *m.,* Aegeus, King of Athens

Aegīdēs, -ae, *m.,* son of Aegeus

Aegyptus, -ī, *f.,* Egypt

Aenēas, -ae, *m.,* Aeneas

aēneus, -a, -um, brass, bronze, brazen

aēnus, -ī, *m.,* brass pot

Aeolus, -ī, *m.,* Aeolus, king of the winds

aequor, -oris, *n.,* flat or level surface of land or sea; *poetically,* the sea itself (from **aequus, -a, -um**)

aequus, -a, -um, equal, level, fair, just

āēr, āeris, *m.,* the air, the atmosphere; **aëra,** Greek accusative

Aesōn, -onis, *m.,* Aeson, father of Jason

Aesonides, the son of Aeson, Jason

aetās, aetātis, *f.,* age, life, time

aeternō, aeternum, *adv.*, eternally, forever
aether, -eris, *m.*, the upper air, heaven
Aethiopia, -ae, *f.*, Ethiopia
Aethra, -ae, *f.*, Aethra, princess of Troezen
Aetna, -ae, *f.*, Mt. Aetna in Sicily
afferō, -ferre, attulī, allātum, carry to, bring to, bring in
affirmō (1), affirm
Āfrica, -ae, *f.*, Africa
Agamemnōn, -onis, *m.*, Agamemnon, King of Mycenae; Agamemnona *is Greek acc.*
ager, -grī, *m.*, field
agere grātiās, to give thanks
agmen, -inis, *n.*, battle line, column of troops, army ranks, band of men
agnus, -ī, *m.*, lamb
agō, agere, ēgī, actum, do, drive, spend time, live, discuss
agricola, -ae, *m.*, farmer
ait; *pl.* **aiunt,** say, tell, assert; *defective verb used mainly in the present and imperfect indicative*
Āiax, -ācis, *m.*, Ajax, Greek warrior, son of Telamon
āla, -ae, *f.*, wing
Albānus, -a, -um, Alban—*referring to an ancient city in Italy*
albeō, ēre, be white; **albescō, -ere,** become white
albus, -a, -um, white
Alcyonē, -ēs, *f.*, Alcyone, wife of Ceyx, daughter of Aeolus
aliquī, aliqua, aliquod, some
aliquis, aliquid, someone, somebody, something
aliter, *adv.*, otherwise; **nōn aliter,** not otherwise, just like
alius, -ia, -iud, other, another; **aliī . . . aliī,** some . . . others
alō, -ere, -uī, altum, feed, nourish
alter, -era, -erum, the other (of two), second
altus, -a, -um, high, tall, lofty, deep, old; **altō,** on the deep sea
alvus, -ī, *f.*, belly
amāns, amantis, *c.*, lover
Amāzon, -onis, *f.*, Amazon, woman warrior
ambiguus, -a, -um, moving from side to side, uncertain, doubtful
ambiō, -īre, -iī *or* **-īvī, -ītum,** approach, go around, entreat
ambō, -ae, -ō, both, two together
ambrosia, -ae, *f.*, ambrosia
ambulō (1), walk
amīca, -ae, *f.*, friend

amīcitia, -ae, *f.*, friendship
amictus, -ūs, *m.*, veil, garment
amīcus, -ī, *m.*, friend
āmittō, -ere, -mīsī, -missum, lose
amō (1), love, like
amoenus, -a, -um, pleasant
amor, amōris, *m.*, love
amplector, -ī, -plexus sum, embrace
amplexor, -ārī, -ātus sum, embrace
amplexus, -ūs, *m.*, embrace
amplius, *adv.*, more
an, *conj.*, whether, or, perhaps
Anchīsēs, -ae, *m.*, Anchises, father of Aeneas
ancilla, -ae, *f.*, servant girl
angulus, -ī, *m.*, corner
anima, -ae, *f.*, spirit, soul
animal, -ālis, *n.*, animal
animus, -ī, *m.*, mind, soul; *pl.*, courage
annus, -ī, *m.*, year; **annuus, -a, -um,** of a year's duration
anser, -eris, *m.*, goose
ante + *acc.*, before, in front of
antea, *adv.*, beforehand
antequam, *conj.*, before, sooner than
antīquus, -a, -um, ancient, olden
Antēnor, -oris, *m.*, Antenor, a Trojan
Antiphatēs, -ae, *m.*, Antiphates, king of the Laestrygonians
antrum, -ī, *n.*, cave
ānulus, -ī, *m.*, ring
aperiō, -īre, -uī, apertum, open
apertus, -a, -um, open
Apollineus, -a, -um, pertaining to Apollo
Apollo, Apollinis, *m.*, Apollo, god of music and the arts
Apollōnius, -iī, *m.*, Apollonius, a writer from Rhodes
appāreō, -ēre, -uī, -itum, appear, become visible
appellātus, -a, -um, called
appellō (1), call, name
appropinquō (1) + *dat.*, approach, draw near to
aptō (1) + *dat.*, fit to, adapt to
aptus, -a, -um, suitable, fitting
apud + *acc.*, among
aqua, -ae, *f.*, water
āra, -ae, *f.*, altar
Arabia, -ae, *f.*, Arabia
Arachnē, -ēs, *f.*, Arachne
arānea, -ae, *f.*, spider
arātrum, -ī, *n.*, plough
arbitror, -ārī, -ātus sum, think, judge

arbor, -oris, *f.*, tree
Arcadia, -ae, *f.*, Arcadia, land in the center of the Peloponnesus
Arcas, -adis, *m.*, Arcas, son of Jupiter and Callisto
arcus, -ūs, *m.*, bow
ardēns, -dentis, eager, hot, burning
ardeō, -ēre, -arsī, arsum, burn, be on fire
ardor, ōris, *m.*, burning heat, eagerness
arduus, -a, -um, hard, difficult
āreō, -ēre, by dry, thirsty
argenteus, -a, -um, made of silver, silver
argentum, -ī, *n.*, silver
Argonautae, -ārum, *m. pl.*, sailors on the *Argo*, Argonauts
argūmentum, -ī, *n.*, proof, subject matter, tale
Argus, -ī, *m.*, Argus, the builder of the Argo
Ariadna, -ae, *f.*, Ariadne, daughter of Minos
aridus, -a, -um, dry, barren
ariēs, arietis, *m.*, a ram
arma, ōrum, *n.*, weapons, arms
armātus, -a, -um, armed
Armenia, -ae, *f.*, Armenia, a country in Asia Minor
arō (1), plough, cultivate
ars, artis, *f.*, art, skill
artifex, -icis, *m.*, artist, painter
artus, -ūs, *m.*, joints, limbs
arvum, -ī, *n.*, ploughed land, a field
arx, arcis, *f.*, building; *pl.* **arcēs,** citadel
ascendō, -ere, ascendī, ascensum, ascend
Asia, -ae, *f.*, Asia
Asia Minor, Asia Minor
astus, -ūs, *m.*, cleverness, cunning
astūtus, -a, -um, clever, cunning; **astūtē,** cunningly
Astyanax, -actis, *m.*, Astyanax, son of Hector
at, *conj.*, *introd. contrary idea,* but, yet, but meanwhile
atavus, -ī, *m.*, ancestor
āter, ātra, ātrum, black, dark, gloomy, sad
Athēnae, -ārum, *f.*, Athens, a city in Attica
Athēnaeus, -a, -um, Athenian
Athēneus, -ī, *m.*, an Athenian
atque (ac), *conj.*, and, and also
atrium, -iī, *n.*, the atrium, main hall or room of the house
Atrīdēs, *m.*, the son(s) of Atreus; Agamemnon (and Menelaus), *pl.*, **Atrīdae**
attingō, -ere, -tigī, -tactum, touch, come in contact with
auctor, -ōris, *m.*, author, causer, originator, doer

audācia, -ae, *f.*, boldness, daring
audax, ācis, bold, daring
audeō, -ēre, ausus sum, *semi-deponent,* dare
audiō, -īre, -īvī, -ītum, hear
aufero, -ferre, abstulī, ablātum, carry away, carry off
augeō, -ēre, auxī, auctum, increase
augur, -uris, *c.*, the augur or fortune teller or prophet
aula, -ae, *f.*, hall
Aulis, -idis, *f.*, Aulis
aura, -ae, *f.*, breeze, air
aurātus, -a, -um, golden
aureus, -a, -um, golden
auris, -is, *f.*, ear
Aurōra, -ae, *f.*, Aurora, goddess of the dawn
aurum, -ī, *n.*, gold
Ausonius, -a, -um, *subst.* **Ausoniī,** the Ausonians, an old name for the Italians
auspicium, -iī, *n.*, guidance, divination
aut, *conj.*, or; **aut . . . aut,** either . . . or
autem, *post. pos., conj.*, but, however
auxilium, -iī, *n.*, aid
āvehō, -ere, -vexī, -vectum, carry off
Avernus, -a, -um, Avernal
Avernus, -ī, *m.*, Avernus, the cave of the Underworld
aversus, -a, -um, *perf. pass. part. of* **avertō**
avertō, -ere, -vertī, -versum, turn away
avidus, -a, -um, eager
avis, avis, *f.*, bird
avus, -ī, *m.*, grandfather
axis, -is, *m.*, axle, chariot, car, wagon; axis of the earth, the heavens

Baccha, -ae, *f.*, (also **Bacchantes**), a Bacchante, a follower of Bacchus
Bacchus, -ī, *m.*, Bacchus
bālātus, -ūs, *m.*, bleating
barba, -ae, *f.*, beard
barbarus, -a, -um, rough, rude, foreign
barbarus, -ī, *m.*, a barbarian
Baucis, -cidis, *f.*, Baucis, wife of Philemon
beātus, -a, -um, happy
bellum, -ī, *n.*, war
bene, *adv.*, well
benignus, -a, -um + *dat.*, kind
bibō, -ere, bibī, bibitum, drink
bifidus, -a, -um, split in two
biformis, -e, two-formed
bimaris, -e, lying on two seas
birēmis, -e, having two banks of oars

bis, *adv.,* twice
bonus, -a, -um, good
bōs, bovis, *c.,* ox, cow
brācchium, -iī, *n.,* arm
brevis, -e, short
Britannia, -ae, *f.,* Britain

Cadmus, -ī, *m.,* Cadmus, founder of Thebes
cadō, -ere, cecidī, cāsum, fall, fall down
cādūcifer, *m.,* Caducifer, carrier of caduceus, Mercury
caecus, -a, -um, blind
caelestis, -e, heavenly
caelō (1), engrave, carve
caelum, -ī, *n.,* sky
calceus, calceī, *m.,* shoe
callidus, -a, -um, clever, skillful, cunning
Callistō, *f.,* Callisto, a nymph
Calydōn, -ōnis, *f.,* Calydon, a city
camera, -ae, *f.,* room, vaulted chamber
campus, -ī, *m.,* field
canis, canis, *c.,* dog; *gen. pl.* **canum**
cānitiēs, -em, -e, *f.,* whitish gray, gray hair
canō, -ere, cecinī, cantum, sing
cantō (1), sing, make music
capillus, -ī, *m., usually pl.,* hair
capiō, -ere, cēpī, captum, take, capture
captīva, -ae, *f.,* a captive woman
caput, capitis, *n.,* head
carcer, -eris, *m.,* prison
careō, -ēre, caruī, itūrum + *abl.,* be lacking, be free from
carīna, -ae, *f.,* keel, ship, vessel
carmen, -inis, *n.,* song, chant, incantation, charm
caro, carnis, *f.,* flesh, meat
carpō, -ere, -psī, -ptum, pick, pluck
carta, -ae, *f.,* piece of paper; **carta geōgraphica,** map; *also* **charta**
Carthāgō, -inis, *f.,* Carthage, a city on the coast of North Africa
cārus, -a, -um + *dat.,* dear (to)
casa, -ae, *f.,* small house, cottage, hut
Cassandra, -ae, *f.,* Cassandra, daughter of Priam and Hecuba
cassis, -idis, *f.,* helmet of metal
castus, -a, -um, pure, innocent
casus, ūs, *m.,* chance, accident
cauda, -ae, *f.,* tail
causa, -ae, *f.,* cause, reason, case (*in law court*); **causā,** for the sake of; **causam accūsō,** accuse, plead a case
celeber, -bris, -bre, celebrated, crowded, filled, famous

celebrō (1), praise, honor, celebrate
celeriter, *adv.,* quickly
cēlō (1), hide, conceal
cēna, -ae, *f.,* dinner, meal
centum, *indecl.,* hundred
cēra, -ae, *f.,* wax
Cerberus, -ī, *m.,* Cerberus, three-headed dog of the Underworld
Cereālis, -e, relating to Ceres
Cerēs, Cereris, *f.,* Ceres, goddess of agriculture
certāmen, -inis, *n.,* contest
certē, *adv.,* surely
certō (1), contend, fight, struggle
certus, -a, -um, trustworthy, certain, sure
cerva, -ae, *f.,* a hind, a deer
cervus, -ī, *m.,* stag
cēterus, -a, -um, other, the rest (of)
Ceyx, Ceycis, *m.,* Ceyx, king of Thrace
charta, -ae, *f.,* map, piece of paper; **charta geōgraphica,** map
Charybdis, -is, *f.,* whirlpool
chlamys, -ydis, *f.,* garment of wool, worn by soldiers
cibus, -ī, *m.,* food
cingō, -ere, cinxī, cinctum, surround, encircle
cinis, -eris, *m.,* ashes
Circē, -ae, *f.,* Circe
Circaeus, -a, -um, Circean
circum + *acc.,* around, about
circumeō, -īre, -iī *or* **īvī, -itum,** go around, encircle
circumspectō (1), look about, cast a glance
circumvēlō (1), envelop
clādēs, -is, *f.,* damage, disaster, ruin
clāmō (1), shout, exclaim, cry
clāmor, -ōris, *m.,* shout, clamor, noise
clārus, -a, -um, bright, shining, famous
classis, classis, *f.,* fleet of ships
claudō, -ere, clausī, -sum, close, shut, shut up
clausus, -a, -um, closed
clāva, -ae, *f.,* club
coeō, -īre, -iī *or* **īvī, -itum,** come together, go together, assemble
coepī, coepisse, *in perfect system only,* began
cōgitātiō, -ōnis, *f.,* thinking, reasoning, idea
cognātus, -a, -um, related
cognoscō, -ere, -nōvī, -nitum, recognize, see, get to know, become acquainted with, learn; *in perfect tenses,* know
cōgō, -ere, coēgī, coactum, force, compel
cohibeō, -ēre, -uī, -itum, confine
Colchis, -idis, *f.,* Colchis on the Black Sea

collectus, -a, -um, gathered, collected
collum, -ī, *n.*, neck
colō, -ere, coluī, cultum, till, honor, cultivate
color, -ōris, *m.*, color
coma, -ae, *f.*, *generally pl.*, hair
comes, comitis, *m.*, companion
comitō (1), accompany
comitor, -ārī, -ātus sum, accompany
committō, -ere, -mīsī, -missum, commit (as a crime), undertake, entrust, unite, begin
commodum, -ī, *n.*, opportunity, advantage, suitable time
commoveō, -ere, -mōvī, mōtum, shake, move, disturb
commūnis, -e, shared, common, general, public; *hence*, the state (*here*, the Greek state)
comparō (1), compare
compellō, -ere, -pulī, -pulsum, drive, compel
complexus, -ūs, *m.*, embrace
concilium, -iī, *n.*, union, coming together
concinō, -ere, -uī, sound in chorus
concipiō, -ere, -cēpī, -ceptum, conceive, hold together
concitō (1), stir up, rouse, excite
concordia, -ae, *f.*, agreement, union
concrescō, -ere, -crēvī, -crētum, grow; become stiff, harden; collect, increase
concrētus, -a, -um, thickened, hardened, congealed
concurrō, -ere, -currī, -cursum + *dat.*, meet, come up against, rush to battle
concutiō, -ere, -cussī, -cussum, shake violently, agitate
condō, -ere, -didī, -ditum, build, establish; hide, bury (a weapon in someone)
conferō, -ferre, -tulī, -collātum, bring together, collect, take oneself to
confiteor, -ērī, -fessus sum, confess
congelō (1), freeze, stiffen, congeal
coniciō, -ere, -iēcī, -iectum, throw together, unite, collect, draw together
coniugium, -iī, *n.*, marriage
coniungō, -ere, -iūnxī, -iūnctum, join together
coniūnx, -iugis, *c.*, husband, wife, spouse
coniurō (1), swear an oath together
conlābor, -ī, -lapsus sum, collapse, sink down
conligō, -ere, -lēgī, -lectum, gather, collect
cōnor, -ārī, -ātus sum, try, attempt
conqueror, -querī, -questus sum, complain of, bewail, lament
conscendō, -ere, -dī, -sum, go on board ship, embark

conservō (1), keep, preserve
consīdō, -ere, -sēdī, -sessum, settle
consilium, iī, *n.*, plan, advice
consistō, -ere, -stitī, -stitum, agree, stay, halt, stop
consōlor, -ārī, -ātus sum, comfort, encourage, console
conspiciō, -ere, -spexī, -spectum, catch sight of
constituō, -uere, -uī, -stitūtum, decide, determine, appoint, establish
construō, -ere, -struxī, -structum, heap together, construct, build
consuescō, -ere, -suēvī, -suētum, accustom
consuētus, -a, -um, accustomed to
consultō (1), consult, ask advice of
consuō, -suere, -suī, -sūtum, sew, mend
contemnō, -ere, -psī, -temptum, value little, disdain
contemptor, -ōris, *m.*, a despiser
contendō, -ere, -dī, -tum, struggle, vie
contentus, -a, -um, satisfied, happy, contented, held together
contineō, -ēre, -uī, -tentum, keep together, hold together
contingō, -ere, -tigī, -tactum, touch
contrā + *acc.*, against
contrārius, -a, -um + *dat.*, against
conveniō, -īre, -vēnī, -ventum, meet, come together, convene, assemble
convertō, -ere, -vertī, -versum, turn around, alter, change, turn
convīvium, -iī, *n.*, banquet, party
convocō (1), call together, summon
cōpia, -ae, *f.*, plenty, abundance, means, opportunity, *pl.*, troops
Corinthus, -ī, *f.*, Corinth, a city at the isthmus
Corinthiacus, -a, -um, Corinthian
cornū, -ūs, *n.*, horn
corōna, -ae, *f.*, crown
corōnō (1), crown
corpus, corporis, *n.*, body
corripiō, -ripere, -ripuī, -reptum, snatch, seize violently
Corsica, -ae, *f.*, Corsica
crātēr, -ēris, *m.*, bowl
crātēra, -ae, *f.*, cup
crēdō, -ere, -didī, -ditum + *dat.*, believe, trust
creō (1), make, create, produce
crescō, -ere, crēvī, crētum, grow large, increase, arise
Crēta, -ae, *f.*, Crete
crīmen, crīminis, *n.*, sin, crime, fault, accusation

crīnis, crīnis, *m.*, *usually pl.*, hair
crūdēlis, -e, cruel
crūdēliter, *adv.*, cruelly
cruentus, -a, -um, bloody, covered with blood
cruor, -ōris, *m.*, blood, gore
cubiculum, -ī, *n.*, bedchamber, room
culpa, -ae, *f.*, guilt, fault
culpō (1), blame
cum, *prep.* + *abl.*, with
cum, *conj.*, when, since, because
Cūmae, -ārum, *f.*, Cumae, a city in southern Italy, home of the Sibyl
cumulus, -ī, *m.*, heap, pile, mass
cupidē, *adv.*, eagerly
Cupīdō, -inis, *m.*, Cupid, Eros, Amor, son of Venus
cupidus, -a, -um + *gen.*, desirous of, eager, keen
cupiō, -ere, -īvī, cupitum, desire, wish, try
cūr, *adv.*, why?
cūra, -ae, *f.*, care, concern
cūria, -ae, *f.*, the senate house
cūriōsus, -a, -um, curious
cūrō (1), care for
currō, -ere, cucurrī, cursum, run
currus, -ūs, *m.*, chariot
cursor, -ōris, *m.*, runner
cursus, cursūs, *m.*, running, race, course
curvō (1), curve, bend, arch
custōdiō, -īre, guard, keep, hoard
custos, -tōdis, *c.*, custodian, keeper, guard
Cyclops, -ōpis, *m.*, Cyclops
cygnus, -ī, *m.*, swan
Cyprus, -ī, *f.*, Cyprus
Cytherēa, -ae, *f.*, Cythera, i.e., Venus
Cytherēius, -a, -um, Cytherean

Daedalus, -ī, *m.*, Daedalus, an inventor
damnō (1), curse, condemn
damnōsus, -a, -um, ruinous, harmful
damnum, -ī, *n.*, loss, injury, doomed one
Danaī, -ōrum, *m.*, The Danaans or the Greeks
Dānuvius, -ī, *m.*, Danube, a river
Daphnē, -nēs, *f.*, Daphne, a nymph
de + *abl.*, about, from, down from, away from, concerning
dea, -ae, *f.*, goddess; *dat. and abl. pl.*, deābus
dēbeō, dēbēre, dēbuī, dēbitum, ought (to), must, owe
decem, *indecl.*, ten
decimus, -a, -um, tenth
dēcipiō, -ere, -cēpī, -ceptum, deceive, cheat
decor, -ōris, *m.*, beauty, grace

decorō (1), decorate
dēcurrō, -ere, -currī, -cursum, run down
dēdecus, -oris, *n.*, shame, disgrace
dēfessus, -a, -um, tired, worn out
deinde, *adv.*, then
dēlectāmentum, -ī, *n.*, delight, pleasure, amusement
dēligō, -ere, -lēgī, -lectum, pick, choose, select
Delphī, -ōrum, *m.*, Delphi, the site of Apollo's oracle
dēmittō, -ere, -mīsī, -missum, send down, send away, lower
dēmō, -ere, dempsī, demptum, take away, subtract
dēmonstrō (1), show
dēmum, *adv.*, finally, at last
dēnegō (1), refuse
dēnique, *adv.*, finally
dēns, dentis, *m.*, tooth
densus, -a, -um, thick, dense
dēplōrō (1), weep, lament
depōnō, -ere, -posuī, -positum, lay down, place down, deposit
dēsertus, -a, -um, deserted
dēsiderō (1), desire, wish, want
dēstruō, -ere, -strūxī, -strūctum, destroy
dēsum, dēesse, dēfuī, dēfutūrus, be lacking
dēsuper, *adv.*, from above
dēterior, -ius, worse, lower
dēterreō, -ēre, -uī, -itum, frighten, discourage, deter, terrify
dēterritus, -a, -um, deterred, frightened away, discouraged
deus, -ī, *m.*, god; *nom. pl.*, dī, the gods
dēvorō (1), devour, swallow
dēvoveō, -ēre, -vōvī, -vōtum, devote, consecrate
dexter, -tra, -trum, right; dextera (dextra), -ae, *f.*, right hand; dextrā, on the right
dī. *See* deus
Dīa, -ae, *f.*, Dia, old name for Naxos
Diāna, -ae, *f.*, Diana, goddess of the moon, the chase
dīcō, -ere, dīxī, dictum, say, tell, speak; dīcunt, they say, people say
dictum, -ī, *n.*, word, saying, speech
dīcunt. *See* dīco
Dīdō, -ūs, *f.*, Dido, queen of Carthage
diēs, diēī, *m.* & *f.*, day; longa diēs, length of days, old age
differō, differre, distulī, dīlatum, delay, postpone, carry in different directions, scatter
difficilis, -e, difficult
dīgerō, -ere, -gessī, -gestum, spread; arrange, interpret

digitus, -ī, *m.,* finger
dignor, -ārī, -ātus sum, consider worthy
dignus, -a, -um + *abl.,* worthy
dīlectiō, -ōnis, *f.,* choosing love, loving
dīligō, -ere, -lexī, -lectum, love, esteem
dīmittō, -ere, -mīsī, -missum, send forth, send away, disband, give up, abandon
Dionȳsus, -ī, *m.,* Dionysus, god of wine
dīrigō, -rigere, -rexī, -rectum, direct
dīripiō, -ere, -uī, -reptum, snatch apart, tear away
dīrus, -a, -um, cruel, horrible, frightful
discēdō, -ere, -cessī, -cessum, depart, go away
discidium, -iī, *n.,* parting, separation
discipulus, -ī, *m.,* pupil, student
discō, -ere, didicī, learn
discors, -cordis, inharmonious, discordant
discrīmen, -inis, *n.,* difference, discrimination
disertus, -a, -um, eloquent
dispōnō, -ere, -posuī, -positum, sort out, place down
diū, *adv.,* for a long time; by day
dīvellō, -ere, -vellī, -vulsum, tear apart
dīversus, -a, -um, turned in different directions, scattered, spread out
dīvīnus, -a, -um, divine
dō, dare, dedī, datum, give
doceō, -ēre, docuī, doctum, teach
doleō, -ēre, -uī, dolitūrum, suffer pain, grieve, bewail
dolor, -ōris, *m.,* grief
dolōsus, -a, -um, tricky, crafty
domina, -ae, *f.,* lady
dominus, -ī, *m.,* master, lord
domus, -ūs, *or* **-ī,** *f.,* house; **domōs Ēlysiās,** Elysian abodes
dōnec, *conj.,* until
dōnō (1) give, present
dōnum, -ī, *n.,* gift
dormiō, -īre, -iī *or* **-īvī, -itum,** sleep
dracō, -ōnis, *m.,* dragon, serpent
dubitō (1), doubt, hesitate
dūcō, -ere, dūxī, ductum, lead
dulcis, -e, sweet
dum, *conj.,* while; **dum licet,** while they may, *lit.,* while it is permitted
dummodo, *conj.,* provided that
duo, duae, duo, two
duodecim, *indecl.,* twelve
duodēvīgintī, *indecl.,* eighteen
dūrus, -a, -um, hard, rough, harsh
dux, ducis, *m.,* leader

ē (ex) + *abl.,* out of, from, out from
ea, she
ebur, -oris, *n.,* ivory
eburneus (-us), -a, -um, ivory, made of ivory
ecce, *demonstrative adv.,* lo, behold
Ēchō,-ūs, *f.,* Echo, a nymph
edō, -ere, ēdī, ēsum, eat
ēdō, -ere, ēdidī, ēditum, put forth, give out
ēducō, -ere, -duxī, -ductum, lead out
efflō (1), breathe out, blow out
effodiō, -ere, -fōdī, -fossum, dig, dig out
effugiō, -ere, -fugī, -fugitum, flee from, escape
effundō, -ere, -fūdī, -fūsum, pour out, pour forth
ego, I
ēgredior, -gredī, -gressus sum, step out, go out, disembark
ēiciō, ēicere, ēiēcī, ēiectum, cast out
eius, his, her, its (*poss.*); *gen. of* **is, ea, id**
ēlectrum, -ī, *n.,* amber
ēlīdō, -ere, -līsī, -līsum, strike, dash to pieces
ēligō, -ere, -lēgī, -lectum, pick out, choose
Elpēnor, -oris, *m.,* Elpenor, companion of Ulysses
Ēlysius, -a, -um, Elysian
ēmittō, -ere, -mīsī, -missum, send forth, let go, dispatch
ēn, *interj.,* lo, behold, see
enim, *conj.,* for, to be sure, indeed, in fact
ensis, ensis, *m.,* sword
eō, īre, iī *or* **īvī, itum,** go
equidem, *adv.,* indeed
equus, ī, *m.,* horse
ergō, *adv.,* therefore, consequently, accordingly, then
ērigō, -ere, -rexī, -rectum, lift up, raise up, make upright
Erīnȳs, -yos, *f.,* Erinys, a Fury
ēripiō, -ere, -ripuī, -reptum, snatch away, tear out
errō (1), wander
error, -ōris, *m.,* error, wandering, mistake
Eryx, -rycis, *m.,* Eryx, a mountain in Sicily
esse, to be, *the infinitive of* **sum**
estó, let (this) be
et, *conj.,* and, also, even; **et . . . et,** both . . . and
etiam, *adv.,* still, yet
etiamnunc, *adv.,* yet, still, even now
Eurōpa, -ae, *f.,* Europe, the continent; Europa, the maid, princess of Tyre
Eurydicē, -ēs, *f.,* Eurydice, wife of Orpheus
Eurylochus, -ī, *m.,* Eurylochus, one of the Greek companions of Ulysses

Ēvander, -drī, *m.*, Evander, an Arcadian king
ēvellō, -ere, -vellī, -vulsum, pluck out
ēveniō, īre, -vēnī, -ventum, turn out, come about
ēvertō, -ere, -vertī, -versum, eject, overturn
ēvincō, -ere, -vīcī, -victum, conquer, overcome
ēvītō (1), avoid
ēvolvō, -ere, -volvī, -volūtum, roll out
exanimis, -e *or* **exanimus, -a, -um,** lifeless, dead; dead with fear, terrified
excidō, -ere, -cidī, fall out, slip out, escape, forget, lose, fail to obtain
excubiae, -ārum, *f.*, sentinels, guards
exemplī gratiā, for example
exeō, -īre, -iī *or* **-īvī, -itum,** go out, depart
ex(s)equiae, -ārum, *f.*, *funeral procession*
exerceō, -ēre, -uī, -item, train, exercise
exhortor, -ārī, -hortātus sum, urge, exhort
exigō, -ere, -ēgī, -actum, direct, demand, complete, examine
existimō (1), think
exitus, -ūs, *m.*, end, exit, finish, outcome, conclusion
expellō, -ere, -pulī, -pulsum, drive out, expel
experientia, -ae, *f.*, experience
experior, -īrī, -pertus sum, try, find out, test, prove, make trial of
expetō, -ere, -iī *or* **-īvī, -ītum,** seek out
expōnō, -ere, -posuī, -positum, put forth, explain
exsiliō, -īre, -uī, leap up or out
exsilium, -iī, *n.*, banishment, exile
exspectō (1), await
exstinctus, -a, -um, put out, extinguished
exstinguō, -ere, -stinxī, -stinctum, extinguish, put out
exstō, -āre, stitī, stand forth
externus, -a, -um, foreign, outside
extrēmus, -a, -um, furthest, last

fabricō (1), make, depict, design, form, forge
fābula, -ae, *f.*, story, tale
faciēs, -ēī, *f.*, shape, form, figure, face, appearance
facilis, -e, easy; **facile,** *adv.*, easily
facinus, -oris, *n.*, bad deed, crime
faciō, -ere, fēcī, factum, do, make
factum, -ī, *n.*, deed, exploit
fallācia, -ae, *f.*, trick, deceit
fallō, -ere, fefellī, falsum, deceive, cheat, lead astray
fāma, -ae, *f.*, reputation, fame, report
fames, famis, *f.*, hunger

familia, -ae, *f.*, family
fāmōsus, -a, -um, famous
famula, -ae, *f.*, household servant *(fem.)*
fateor, -ērī, fassus sum, confess, speak, admit, allow
fātum, -ī, *n.*, fate
faveō, -ēre, fāvī, fautum, favor, help
favor, -ōris, *m.*, favor, good will
fax, facis, *f.*, torch
fēcundus, -a, -um, fruitful, productive
fēlix, fēlīcis, happy, fortunate
fēmina, -ae, *f.*, woman
ferō, ferre, tulī, lātum, bear, carry, bring, endure, report
ferox, -ōcis, savage, wild, fierce
ferreus, -a, -um, iron
ferrum, -ī, *n.*, iron, weapon, sword
fertur, it is said, reported
ferus, -a, -um, wild, courageous
fētus, -a, -um + *abl.*, full of, teeming with, pregnant
fētus, -ūs, *m.*, fetus, offspring
fibula, -ae, *f.*, pin
fidēlis, -e + *dat.*, faithful (to)
fides, -eī, *f.*, pledge, trust, confidence, faith, belief
fīdus, -a, -um, true, faithful
fīgō, -ere, fixī, fixum, pierce, transfix, fasten
figūra, -ae, *f.*, form, shape
fīlia, -ae, *f.*, daughter; *dat. and abl. pl.*, **fīliābus**
fīlius, -iī, *m.*, son
fīlum, -ī, *n.*, string
fingō, -ere, finxī, fictum, shape, form, invent
fīniō, -īre, -īvī, -ītum, finish, limit, end
finis, fīnis, *m. & f.*, end, boundary, territory
fīō, fierī, factus sum, become, be made, happen
fissum, -ī, *n.*, crack, hole, cleavage
fistula, -ae, *f.*, pipes of Pan
fixus, -a, -um, fixed
flāmen, -inis, *n.*, blowing, blast
flamma, -ae, *f.*, flame
flectō, -ere, flexī, flexum, influence, bend, change
fleō, -ēre, flēvī, flētum, weep
flexus, -ūs, *m.*, bending, turning
flōrens, -entis, blooming, flourishing
flōreō, -ēre, -uī, bloom, flower
flōs, flōris, *m.*, flower, plant
fluidus, -a, -um, flowing, dripping
flūmen, flūminis, *n.*, river
fluō, -ere, fluxī, fluxum, flow
foedus, -a, -um, abhorrent, abominable

foedus, -eris, *n.*, covenant, agreement, treaty

folium, -iī, *n.*, leaf

fons, fontis, *m.*, fountain

for, fārī, fātus sum, speak, say

foret = **futūrum esset,** would be

fōrma, -ae, *f.*, shape, appearance

formīdābilis, -e, terrible, fearful

fōrmō (1), shape, make, fashion

fōrmōsus, -a, -um, beautiful

forsitan, *adv.*, perhaps

forte, *adv.*, by chance; *abl.* of **fors,** luck, chance

fortis, -e, strong, brave

fortitūdo, -inis, *f.*, strength

fortūna, -ae, *f.*, fortune

fossa, -ae, *f.*, ditch

fragilis, -e, fragile, weak, easily broken

fragmen, -inis, *n.*, broken piece, fragment

frangō, -ere, frēgī, fractum, break

frāter, -tris, *m.*, brother

frēna, -ōrum, *n. pl.*, reins, bridle

frīgidus, -a, -um, cold

frīgus, -oris, *n.*, cold, coldness

frondeō, -ēre, grow leafy, put out leaves

frons, frondis, *f.*, leaf, foliage

frons, -ntis, *f.*, forehead, brow

frustrā, *adv.*, in vain

frutex, -ticis, *m.*, shrub, bush

frux, frūgis, *f.*, fruit

fuga, -ae, *f.*, flight

fugiō, ere, fūgī, fugitum, flee

fugitō (1), flee, shun, avoid

fugō (1), put to flight

fulgeō, -ēre, fulsī, flash, shine, glow, gleam

fulmen, -inis, *n.*, thunderbolt

fūmō (1), smoke

fūmus, -ī, *m.*, smoke

fundō (1), found, establish, confirm

fundus, -ī, *m.*, bottom, ground

fūnus, eris, *n.*, funeral

furibundus, -a, -um, raging, inspired

furō, -ere, rage, rave

furor, -ōris, *m.*, madness, insanity

galea, -ae, *f.*, helmet

Gallia, -ae, *f.*, Gaul

gaudeō, -ēre, gāvīsus sum, *semi-deponent verb*, rejoice, enjoy

gemebundus, -a, -um, groaning, sighing

geminus, -a, -um, twin

gemitus, -ūs, *m.*, groan

gemma, -ae, *f.*, gem

gemō, -ere, -uī, -itum, groan, mourn, weep, lament, bemoan

gena, -ae, *f.*, cheek, eyes

genetrīx, -trīcis, *f.*, mother

genitor, -ōris, *m.*, parent, father

gens, gentis, *f.*, family, nation, people, tribe, clan

genus, -eris, *n.*, race, kind, family

germāna, ae, *f.*, sister

gerō, -ere, gessī, gestum, do, make, experience, wear, carry

gestō (1), carry, wear

gestus, -ūs, *m.*, gesture

Gigantēus, -a, -um, giant

Gigās, -antis, *m.*, giant

gladius, -iī, *m.*, sword

glans, -ndis, *f.*, chestnut, acorn

glomerō (1), wind into a ball

Gnossus, -ī, *f.*, Knossos, the city; the palace of Minos

gradus, -ūs, *m.*, step

Graecia, -ae, *f.*, Greece

Grāius, -a, -um, Greek

Grāius, -iī, *m.*, a Greek

grātus, -a, um + *dat.*, pleasing (to)

gravis, -e, heavy

gravō (1), load, burden, weigh down

guttur, -uris, *n.*, throat

habeō, -ēre, habuī, habitum, have, hold, consider

habeor, -ērī, habitus sum, be regarded, be considered

habitō (1), live, dwell

haereō, -ēre, -sīvī, -situm, cling to, hang on

hara, -ae, *f.*, pig sty, pen

harēna, -ae, *f.*, sand

Harpȳiae, -ārum, *f.*, Harpies

hasta, -ae, *f.*, spear, javelin

haud, *adv.*, not, not at all

hauriō, -īre, hausī, haustum, drink, swallow, absorb, draw up

haustus, -ūs, *m.*, a drinking, a draught, inhaling (of air), a handful

Hebrus, -brī, *m.*, Hebron, a river

Hecatē, -ēs, *f.*, Hecate, a goddess

Hector, -oris, *m.*, Hector, son of Priam

Hecuba, -ae, *f.*, Hecuba, queen of Troy, wife of Priam

Helena, -ae, *f.*, Helen

herba, -ae, *f.*, grass

herbōsus, -a, -um, grassy

Hercules, -is, *m.,* Hercules, the hero
hērōs, -ōis, *m.,* hero
Hesperia, -ae, *f.,* Spain
heu, *interj.,* alas!
hic, haec, hoc, this; this man, woman, thing, the latter
hīc, *adv.,* here
hinc, *adv.,* here, on this side, hence
Hippolyta, -ae, *f.,* Hippolyta, queen of Amazons
Hippolytus, -ī, *m.,* Hippolytus
hiscō, -ere, open, gape, open the mouth
Hispānia, -ae, *f.,* Spain
historia, -ae, *f.,* story
hōc modō, *adv.,* in this way, in this manner, thus
hodiē, *adv.,* today
homō, hominis, *m.,* man
honōrō (1), honor
hōra, -ae, *f.,* hour
horrendus, -a, -um, horrible, terrible
horrescō, -ere, -uī, grow, rough; *also* **horreō, -ēre, -uī,** stand on end, bristle, be rough; shiver, shudder with fright
hortor, -ārī, hortātus sum, urge, incite
hospes, -itis, *c.,* a guest, host
hospitium, -iī, *n.,* hospitality
hostis, hostis, *c.,* foe, enemy
hūc, *adv.,* to this place, here
hūmānus, -a, -um, human
humō (1), bury
humus, -ī, *f.,* ground, earth
hydria, -ae, *f.,* large water jar
Hymēn, -menis, *m.,* Hymen, god of marriage

iaceō, -ēre, -uī, lie (at rest), lie on the ground
iaciō, -ere, iēcī, iactum, throw, hurl, cast
iactō (1), throw, toss about, cast
iaculum, -ī, *n.,* javelin
iam, *adv.,* now, already
iānua, -ae, *f.,* door
Iāsōn, -onis, *m.,* Jason
ibi, *adv.,* there
Īcarus, -ī, *m.,* Icarus, son of Daedalus
ictus, -ūs, *m.,* blow
idcirco, *adv.,* for that reason
īdem, eadem, idem, same
idōneus, -a, -um + *dat.,* suitable, fitting
igitur, *adv.,* therefore
ignārus, -a, -um + *gen.,* unaware, unknowing; + *dat.,* unknown to
ignis, ignis, *m.,* fire
ignoscō, -ere, -nōvī, -nōtum + *dat.,* forgive, grant pardon to, overlook

ignōtus, -a, -um, unknown, strange
Īliacus, -a, -um, Trojan
ille, illa, illud, that; that man, woman, thing, the former
illinc, *adv.,* on that side, thence, from that place; **illūc,** to that place
imāgō, -inis, *f.,* image, reflection
immensus, -a, -um, immense
immolō (1), slay, sacrifice
immortalis, -e, immortal
immōtus, -a, -um, unmoving
immurmurō (1), whisper into, murmur
imperō + *dat.* (1), command
impius, -a, -um, wicked, impious
impleo, -ēre, -plēvī, plētum, fill, fill up
implicō (1), enwrap, enfold
implōrō (1), implore
imprīmis, *adv.,* especially, first of all
īmus, -a, -um, lowest, bottom of
in + *acc.,* into, toward, against; + *abl.,* in, on
incandescō, -ere, -canduī, begin to whiten, *esp.* with heat or fire
incendium, -iī, *n.,* fire, conflagration
incendō, -ere, -cendī, -censum, inflame
incertus, -a, -um, uncertain
inclāmō (1), shout out
inclīnō (1), bend, incline
inclūdō, -ere, -clūsi, -clūsum, shut up, block, enclose, obstruct
incola, -ae, *c.,* inhabitant
incumbō, -ere, -cubuī, -cubitum, fall down
incursus, -ūs, *m.,* attack, influx
inde, *adv.,* from there, thence
indestrictus, -a, -um, untouched, unhurt
indignātus, -a, -um, offended, indignant
induō, -ere, duī, -dūtum, put on, wear
inemptus, -a, -um, unbought
inexspectātus, -a, -um, unexpected, unawaited
īnfēlīx, -icis, unhappy, unfortunate, miserable, wretched, ill-fated
inferō, -ferre, -tulī, -lātum, carry in, place on, bear in
infestō (1), infest, attack
ingenium, -iī, *n.,* talent, skill, natural ability
ingēns, -entis, huge, mighty
ingrātus, -a, -um, unpleasant, unpleasing
inhonestus, -a, -um, dishonored, disgraceful
inimīcus, -a, -um, enemy; unfriendly, hostile
inīquus, -a, -um, uneven, unfair
iniūria, -ae, *f.,* injury, hurt
iniustus, -a, -um, unjust, unfair
in- *or* **immānis, -e,** huge
in- *or* **immemor, -oris,** unmindful, forgetful

in- *or* **immeritus, -a, -um,** undeserving of punishment, innocent

in *or* **immītis, -e,** harsh, cruel, stern

innocens, -entis, innocent, harmless

innuba, -ae, *f.,* unmarried woman, unwed woman, without a husband

in- *or* **impellō, -pellere, -pulī, -pulsum,** strike upon, urge, impel

inquit, he or she says or said; **inquiunt,** they say, reply, respond, answer, affirm

inrequiētus, -a, -um, never resting, restless, troubled

insānia, -ae, *f.,* madness

insānus, -a, -um, maddened, insane

insequor, -sequī, -secūtus sum, follow after, follow on

insidior (1), lay snares for

insidiōsus, -a, -um, treacherous, deceitful

insigne, -nis, *n.,* badge, insignia, mark, token

inspiciō, -ere, -spexī, -spectum, examine, look into

instar + *gen.,* equivalent to, corresponding to, like

instō, -stare, -stitī + *dat.,* stand in, follow closely, press on, pursue

īnsula, -ae, *f.,* island

insuper, *adv.,* from above

inter + *acc.,* between, among

intereā, *adv.,* meanwhile

intereō, -īre, -iī *or* **-īvī, -itum,** die, perish

interficiō, -ere, -fēcī, -fectum, kill

interim, *adv.,* meanwhile

interritus, -a, -um, unterrified

intrā, *adv.,* inside; *also* + *acc.,* within

intrō (1), enter

inundō (1), overflow, pour into

inveniō, -īre, -vēnī, -ventum, find, discover

invidiōsus, -a, -um, hate-producing, causing envy

invidus, -a, -um, envious, unfavorable

invītō (1), invite

invītus, -a, -um, unwilling

invius, -a, -um, impassable

invocō (1), invoke

love, by Jupiter

Īphigenīa, -ae, *f.,* Iphigenia, daughter of Agamemnon

ipse, ipsa, ipsum, self

īra, -ae, *f.,* wrath

īrācundus, -a, -um, angry

īrascor, -ī, -īrātus sum, be angry

īrātus, -a, -um, angry

is, ea, id, he, she, it; **eī, eae, ea,** they

iste, -a, -ud, *spoken in a derogatory manner,* that fellow of yours

Isthmus, -ī, *m.,* the Isthmus of Corinth

ita, *adv.,* so, thus

Ītalia, -ae, *f.,* Italy

Ītalus, -a, -um, Ītalicus, -a, -um, Italian

itaque, *adv.,* and so, therefore

iter, itineris, *n.,* road, path, way, journey, search

iterum, *adv.,* again

Ithaca, -ae, *f.,* the island of Ithaca

itūrus, -a, -um, *fut. act. part. of* **eō**

iubeō, -ēre, iussī, iussum, order, command, bid

iūdex, -icis, *m.,* judge

iūdicium, -iī, *n.,* judgment

iugulō (1), to cut the throat of, butcher

iugulum, -ī, *n.,* throat

iugum, -ī, *n.,* yoke

iungō, -ere, iūnxī, iūnctum, join

Īūno, -ōnis, *f.,* Juno, queen of the gods

Iuppiter, Iovis, *m.,* Jupiter, Jove, king of the gods

iūrō (1), swear, take an oath

iūs, iūris, *n.,* law, justice, right

iussum, -ī, *n.,* command, order

iustus, -a, -um, just, true, fair

iuvenis, -e, young, youthful

iuvenis, iuvenis, *c.,* youth, maiden, young person; *gen. pl.,* **iuvenum**

iuventa, -ae, *f.,* age of youth, youth

iuventās, -ātis, *f.,* youth

iuventus, -ūtis, *f.,* youth

iuvō, -āre, iūvī, iūtum, help, aid

iuxtā + *acc.,* beside, next to; *adv.,* close by

Kalendae, -ārum, *f.,* the Kalends, first day of the month

labōrō (1), work

labyrinthus, -ī, *m.,* labyrinth

lac, lactis, *n.,* milk

lacerō (1), tear to pieces, maim

lacertus, -ī, *m.,* upper arm, shoulder

lacrima, -ae, *f.,* tear

lacrimō (1), cry, weep

Laestrygōn, -onis, *m.,* Laestrygonians, a race of giants

laetitia, -ae, *f.,* joy

laetus, -a, -um, joyful, happy

laeva, -ae, *f.,* the left hand, the left

laevum, -ī, *n.,* the left side

laevus, -a, -um, left

lāmentābilis, -e, deplorable, lamentable

lāna, -ae, *f.,* wool, spinning

laniō (1), tear to pieces

lapis, -idis, *m.,* stone

lapsus, -ūs, *m.,* gliding, falling

lātē, broadly, widely

lateō, -ēre, latuī, lie hidden

Latīnus, -a, -um, Latin; **Latīnus, -ī,** *m.,* King Latinus of Latium; **Latīnē,** in Latin

latitō (1), hide, be concealed

Lātōna, -ae, *f.,* Latona, mother of Apollo and Diana

lātrātus, -ūs, *m.,* barking

latro, -ōnis, *m.,* robber

lātūrus, -a, -um. *See* **ferō**

lātus, -a, -um, broad wide

latus, lateris, *n.,* side

laudō (1), praise

laurus, -ī, *f.,* laurel

laus, laudis, *f.,* praise, glory, esteem

Lāvīnia, -ae, *f.,* Lavinia, daughter of Latinus, king of Latium

Lāvīnus, -a, -um, Lavinian

lavō, -āre, lāvī, lautum, *or* **lōtum,** wash

lea, -ae, *f.,* lioness

lectus, -ī, *m.,* bed, couch

legō, -ere, lēgī, lectum, pick, choose, read

leō, leōnis, *m.,* lion

Lēthē, -ēs, *f.,* Lethe, a river in the Underworld

lētum, -ī, *n.,* death

levis, -e, light

levō (1), lift, free, make light, raise, lift up

lex, lēgis, *f.,* law

liber, -brī, *m.,* book

liber, -era, -erum, free

liberī, -ōrum, *m.,* children

līberō (1), free, set free

lībertās, -tātis, *f.,* freedom

Libya, -ae, *f.,* Libya, a country in Africa

Libycus, -a, -um, Libyan

libet, -ēre, libuit, it is pleasing, it is pleasant

licet, licēre, licuit, it is permitted, it is allowed

ligāmen, -inis, *n.,* string, tie, bandage

lignum, -ī, *n.,* wood, timber, wooden horse

ligō (1), tie

līmen, -inis, *n.,* threshold

lingua, -ae, *f.,* tongue, language

liquidus, -a, -um, liquid

lītus, -oris, *n.,* shore

locus, -ī, *m.,* **loca,** *n. pl.,* place

longē, *adv.,* for a long time, far away, far, at a distance

longus, -a, -um, long

loquor, loquī, locūtus sum, speak

luctus, -ūs, *m.,* grief, mourning

lūdō, -ere, lūsī, lusum, play

lūmen, -inis, *n.,* light

lūna, -ae, *f.,* moon

lupus, -ī, *m.,* wolf

lustrō (1), search, examine

lux; lūcis, *f.,* light, day, light of life

Lȳdia, -ae, *f.,* Lydia, a country in Asia Minor

lyra, -ae, *f.,* lyre

mactō (1), slay, smite

madeō, -ēre, -uī, be wet

Maeander *or* **Maeandrus, -ī,** *m.,* the Maeander River in Asia Minor

Maenas, -adis, *f.,* a Bacchante, a maddened woman

maestitia, -ae, *f.,* sadness

maestus, -a, -um, gloomy, sad

maga, -ae, *f.,* witch, magical person

magicus, -a, -um, magic

magis, -e, *adv.,* more; **magis . . . magis,** the more . . . the more

magister, -trī, *m.,* teacher (male)

magistra, -ae, *f.,* teacher (female)

magnanimus, -a, -um, great-hearted

magnopere, *adv.,* very much, especially

magnus, -a, -um, large, great

magus, -ī, *m.,* a learned man of Persia; a magician, one who works magic

maior, maiōris, greater

male, *adv.,* badly

mālō, malle, māluī, prefer

malus, -a, -um, bad

mandō (1), trust, entrust

māne, *indecl. noun or adv.,* morning, early in the morning, early

maneō, -ēre, mansī, remain

mānēs, -ium, *m. pl.,* shade, ghost

mānō (1), flow

Mantō, -ūs, *f.,* Manto, a woman of Thebes

manus, -ūs, *f.,* hand; band (of people)

Marathōn, ōnis, *f.,* Marathon, a coast city in Attica

mare, maris, *n.,* sea

Mare Euxīnum, Black Sea

Mare Internum, Mediterranean Sea

marītus, -ī, *m.,* husband

marmoreus, -a, -um, marble

Mars, Martis, *m.,* Mars, god of war

māter, mātris, *f.,* mother

mātricīdium, -iī, *n.,* matricide

mātrimōnium, -iī, *n.,* marriage

Mauritānia, -ae, *f.,* Mauritania, a country in Africa

maximē, *adv.,* very much

maximus, -a, -um, very great; *superl. of* **magnus**

mē, me, *acc.* and *abl. sing.*

Mēdēa, -ae, *f.,* Medea, princess of Colchis

medicāmen, -inis, *n.,* drug, medicine

medicīna, -ae, *f.,* medicine

Mediterrāneus, -a, -um, Mediterranean, lands and the Sea

medius, -a, -um, middle (of)

Megarēus, -ēī, *m.,* Megareus, son of Neptune; father of Hippomenes

Meleager, -ī, *m.,* Meleager, King of Calydon

melior, -ius, *adv.,* better

melius quam, *adv.,* better than

membrāna, -ae, *f.,* membrane, skin

membrum, -ī, *n.,* leg (of a table), limb of the body, part

meminī, -isse + *gen.,* remember, be mindful of

memor, -oris + *gen.,* mindful, remembering

memoria, -ae, *f.,* memory

memorō (1), recount, tell a tale

Menelāus, -ī, *m.,* Menelaus, brother of Agamemnon

mens, mentis, *f.,* mind

mensa, -ae, *f.,* table

Mercurius, -iī, *m.,* Mercury

mergō, -ere, mersī, mersum, sink, overwhelm, submerge, immerse

Mesopotamia, -ae, *f.,* Mesopotamia

mēta, -ae, *f.,* goal

metuō, -ere, uī, -ūtum, fear, be afraid

metus, -ūs, *m.,* fear, apprehension

meum est, is mine, belongs to me

meus, -a, -um, my

micō, -āre, -uī, glitter, twinkle, flicker, vibrate

mihi, to me

mīles, mīlitis, *m.,* soldier

mille; mīlia, mīlium; thousand, *indeclinable in singular;* abbrev. **M** in Roman numerals

Minerva, -ae, *f.,* Minerva

minimē, *adv.,* least, not at all

minimus, -a, -um, smallest, least, very little; *superl. of* **parvus**

minister, -tri, *m.,* attendant, official

minor, minus, smaller; *comparative of* **parvus**

Mīnōs, -ōis, *m.,* Minos, king of Crete

Mīnōtaurus, -ī, *m.,* the Minotaur

mīrāculum, -ī, *n.,* miracle

mīror, -ārī, -ātus sum, admire, wonder at

mīrus, -a, -um, wonderful, amazing

misceō, -ēre, miscuī, mixtum, mix, mingle

miser, -era, -erum, wretched, miserable, unhappy

miserābilis, -e, wretched, pitiful

misericordia, -ae, *f.,* pity

mītis, -e, mild, soft, kind, gentle

mittō, -ere, mīsī, missum, send

modo, *adv.,* just now, only now

modus, -ī, *m.,* manner, style; **quōmodo,** in what manner, how

moenia, moenium, *n. pl.,* walls, ramparts, fortification

molliō, -īre, -iī *or* **-īvī, -ītum,** soften, make soft, make pliant

mollis, -e, soft

mōly, -yos, *n.,* moly, the name of a plant

moneō, -ēre, monuī, monitum, warn

mōns, montis, *m.,* mountain

mōnstrō (1), point out, show

mōnstrum, -ī, *n.,* monster

monumentum, -ī, *n.,* memorial, reminder

mora, -ae, *f.,* delay

mordeō, -ēre, momordī, morsum, bite

morīrī = morī

morior, morī, mortuus sum, die

moror, -ārī, -ātus sum, delay

Morpheus, eī, *m.,* Morpheus, god of sleep

mors, mortis, *f.,* death

mortālis, -e, mortal

mortuus, -a, -um, dead

mos, mōris, *m.,* custom

mōtus, -a, -um, moved, stirred, influenced

moveō, -ēre, mōvī, mōtum, move

mox, *adv.,* soon

mulceō, -ēre, mulsī, mulsum, stroke, touch lightly

Mulciber, -eris *or* **erī,** *m.,* Mulciber, another name for Vulcan, god of the forge

multiplex, -icis, multiple, with many turnings

multus, -a, -um, much, *pl.,* many

mundus, -ī, *m.,* the universe, the world

mūnimen, -inis, *n.,* fortification

mūnus, -eris, *n.,* gift

murmur, -uris, *n.,* murmur, roaring

murmurō (1), murmur

mūrus, -ī, *m.,* wall

Mūsa, -ae, *f.,* Muse

mūsica, -ae, *f.,* music

mūtō (1), change

nam, *conj.,* for

Narcissus, -ī, *m.,* Narcissus, a youth

narrō (1), tell, relate

nāscor, -ī, nātus sum, be born

nāsus, -ī, *m.,* nose; **Nāso,** cognomen of Ovid

nāta, -ae, *f.,* daughter

nātālis, -e, of or relating to birth, natal; **diēs nātālis,** birthday

nātio, -ōnis, *f.,* birth; race, tribe, people, nation; sort, kind

natō (1), swim

nātūra, -ae, *f.,* nature, property, quality

nātus, -ī, *m.,* son, offspring; **nāte deā,** *voc.,* goddess born

naufragium, -iī, *n.,* shipwreck

nauta, -ae, *m.,* sailor

nāvigātiō, -iōnis, *f.,* sailing

navigium, -iī, *n.,* sailing; vessel, ship

nāvigō (1), sail

nāvis, -is, *f.,* ship

Naxos, -ī, *f.,* Naxos, the island

-ne, *interrogative enclitic, attached to verb to ask a question*

nē, so that . . . not, lest

nebulae, -ae, *f.,* cloud

nec (neque), *conj.,* and that . . . not, and not; **nec . . . nec,** neither . . . nor, not; **nec mora,** without delay

necō (1), kill

nefandus, -a, -um, wicked, evil, not to be spoken of, unspeakable

nefārius, -a, -um, impious, wicked, abominable, evil

nefas, *n. indecl.,* a wicked deed, sin

neglectus, -a, -um, neglected

negō (1), deny

negōtium, -iī, *n.,* business, affair

nēmō, (nūllius), nēminī, nēminem, nēmine, *no pl.,* no one

nempe, *conj.,* truly, certainly, to be sure

nepos, -ōtis, *m.,* grandson, nephew

neque, and not. *See* **nec**

Neptūnius, -a, -um, Neptunian

Neptūnus, -ī, *m.,* Neptune, god of the sea

Nērēis, -idis, *f.,* a Nereid, daughter of Nereus

Nērēus, -ī, *m.,* Nereus, a sea god

nesciō, -īre, -īvī, -ītum, not know, be ignorant of

nesciō quis, nesciō quid, I do not know who or what; somebody or something; **nesciō quis advena,** some stranger or other

nescius, -a, -um, not knowing, ignorant, unaware

neve, *adv.,* or not, and not

nex, necis, *f.,* death

nīdus, -ī, *m.,* nest

niger, nigra, nigrum, black

nihil (nil), nothing

nimius, -a, -um, too much, very much, excessive

Ninus, -ī, *m.,* Ninus

Niobē, -ēs, *f.,* Niobe, queen of Thebes

nisi, *conj.,* unless

nītor, nītī, nīsus sum, strive

noceō, ēre, uī + *dat.,* harm, do harm to

nōlīte + *inf.,* do not

nōlō, nōlle, nōluī, refuse, be unwilling, wish not

nōmen, -inis, *n.,* name

nōminō (1), name, call

nōn, *adv.,* not

Nōnae, -ārum, *f.,* the Nones

nōnāgintā, *indecl.,* ninety

nōn aliter, *adv.,* not otherwise, i.e. just as

nōn dum, *adv.,* not yet

nōn iam, *adv.,* no longer

nōnnullus, -a, -um, some, several

nōn procul, *adv.,* nearby (not a distance away)

nōn sōlum. . . . sed etiam, not only . . . but also

nōnus, -a, -um, ninth

nōs, us (*acc.*)

noscō, -ere, nōvī, nōtum, come to know, know

noster, -tra, -trum, our

nōstī, *contraction for* **nōvistī,** *perf. of* **cognoscō,** *an inceptive verb,* learn or begin to know; *perf.* know

nōtus, -a, -um, well-known

notus, -ī, *m.,* south wind

novem, *indecl.,* nine

novus, -a, -um, new, strange, novel

nox, noctis, *f.,* night

nūbes, nūbis, *f.,* cloud

nūdus, -a, -um, naked

nūllus, -a, -um, no one, none

num, *interr. adv., asks a question implying a "no" reply*

numerō (1), count, recount, relate, number

nūmen, -inis, *n.,* divine power, divine will, divinity, god

Numidia, -ae, *f.,* Numidia, country in Africa

numquam, *adv.,* never

nunc, *adv.,* now, at present, at this time

nūntiō (1), announce, report

nūntius, -iī, *m.,* messenger

nūper, *adv.,* recently

nupta, -ae, *f.,* bride

nympha, -ae, *f.,* nymph

rēgius, -a, -um, royal
rēgnō (1), rule, rule over
rēgnum, -ī, *n.,* kingdom, rule
relevō (1), lighten
relictus, -a, -um. *See* **relinquō**
religō (1), moor
relinquō, -ere, -līquī, -lictum, leave, leave behind, leave unchanged, abandon
remittō, -ere, -mīsī, -missum, send back, let go back, drive away, relax, set free, loosen
remoror, -ārī, -ātus sum, delay, hinder, detain
removeō, -ēre, -mōvī, -mōtum, remove, take away, put off
rēmus, -ī, *m.,* oar
renovō (1), renew
reor, rērī, ratus sum, think, suppose, judge
repellō, -ere, reppulī, -pulsum, drive back, away, push away, spurn
repleō, -ēre, -plēvī, -plētum, fill again, fill up
repōnō, -ere, -posuī, -positum, replace, put back
reportō (1), carry back, report
reposcō, -ere, demand back
repugnō (1), fight back
requiēs, -iētis, *f.,* rest
requīrō, -ere, -quīsiī *or* **-quīsīvī, -quīsītum,** ask, look for, inquire after
rēs, reī, *f.,* thing, object, situation
resecō, -āre, -secuī, -sectum, cut off
resonō (1), resound, sound again
respiciō, -ere, -spexī, -spectum, look back, look behind; see plain
respondeō, -ēre, -spondī, -sum, reply, answer back, respond
restō, -stāre, -stitī, remain, survive, be left over, stand still, stay behind
resupīnus, -a, -um, bent backwards, on one's back
retegō, -ere, -texī, -tectum, uncover, lay bare, reveal
retineō, -ēre, -uī, -tentum, retain, hold
retrahō, -ere, -trāxī, tractum, drag back
retrō, *adv.,* backwards
revellō, -ere, -vellī, -vulsum, tear up, pull, pluck back
reveniō, -īre, -vēnī, -ventum, come back again, return
revertor, (revertō), -ī, -versus sum, return, come back
revīvīscō, -ere, -vixī, revive, come to life again
revocō (1), call back, revoke, call again
revomō, -ere, -vomuī, vomit forth again
rēx, rēgis, *m.,* king

Rhodanus, -ī, *m.,* the Rhone, a river in Gaul
rictus, -ūs, *m.,* open mouth, jaws
rideō, -ēre, -rīsī, rīsum, laugh
rīma, -ae, *f.,* a cleft, crack, fissure
rīpa, -ae, *f.,* bank
rōbur, -oris, *n.,* oak, hardwood, strength, power, force
rogō (1), beg for, ask
Rōma, -ae, *f.,* Rome
rostrum, -ī, *n.,* beak (of a bird or ship); **rostra, -ōrum,** speakers' platform in the Forum
rota, -ae, *f.,* wheel
rubeō, -ēre, to be red
rubescō, -ere, rubuī, grow red, become red, redden
ruīna, -ae, *f.,* disaster
rūmor, -ōris, *m.,* rumor
rumpō, -ere, rūpī, ruptum, break, shatter, split
ruō, -ere, -uī, -utum, fall with violence, rush, go to ruin
rūrsus, *adv.,* backwards, in turn, on the other hand, again
rūs, rūris, *n.,* the country; **rūrī,** *loc.,* in the country

saccus, ī, *m.,* sack, bag
sacer, -cra, -crum, sacred, holy
sacerdōs, -dōtis, *c.,* priest (ess)
sacrificium, -iī, *n.,* sacrifice
sacrificō (1), sacrifice
saepe, *adv.,* often
saeta, -ae, *f.,* bristle, stiff hair; **saetiger, -gera, -gerum,** bristly
saevio, -īre, -iī, -ītum, rage, be furious
saevus, -a, -um, savage, fierce
sagax, -ācis, wily, shrewd
sagitta, -ae, *f.,* arrow
saltō (1), dance
salus, -ūtis, *f.,* safety, health, soundness
salūtō (1), greet
salveō, -ēre, be well; **salvēte,** greetings, hello
salvus, -a, -um, safe
sanctus, -a, -um, holy, sacred
sanguineus, -a, -um, bloody
sanguis, -inis, *m.,* blood
sānitās, -tātis, *f.,* sanity, health
sānō (1), heal, cure
sapiēns, -entis, wise
sapientia, -ae, *f.,* wisdom
sapiō, -ere, īvī *or* **-iī,** think, discern
Sardinia, -ae, *f.,* Sardinia
Sarmatia, -ae, *f.,* Sarmatia

satis, *adv.*, enough
Sāturnus, -ī, *m.*, Saturn; **Saturnius, -a, -um,** referring to Saturn
satyrus, -ī, *m.*, satyr
saxum, -ī, *n.*, rock, stone
scelerātus, -a, -um, wicked
scelestus, -a, -um, wicked
scelus, -eris, *n.*, wicked deed
sceptrum, -ī, *n.*, sceptre
schola, ae, *f.*, school, class
scīlicet, *adv.*, obviously, of course, certainly naturally
scindō, -ere, scidī, scissum, cut, tear
sciō, -īre, -īvī *or* **-iī, -ītum,** know, perceive, understand
Scīron, -ōnis, *m.*, Sciron, a brigand
scrībō, -ere, scrīpsī, scrīptum, write
scūtum, -ī, *n.*, shield
Scylla, -ae, *f.*, Scylla, a rock and a six-headed monster, originally a maiden
sē (sēsē), himself, herself, itself, themselves
sēcernō, -ere, -crēvī, -crētum, separate
secō, -āre, -uī, sectum, cut
sēcrētō, *adv.*, secretly, apart
sēcrētus, -a, -um, secret
secundus, -a, -um, second, following, favorable
sēcūrus, -a, -um, secure
sed, *conj.*, but
sēdecim, *indecl.*, sixteen
sedeō, -ēre, sēdī, sessum, sit
sēdēs, sēdis, *f.*, seat, bench, chair; *gen. pl.*, **sedum** *or* **sedium**
sēmen, -inis, *n.*, seed
semper, *adv.*, always
senectūs, -ūtis, *f.*, old age
senex, senis, *c.*, old man, old woman; *gen. pl.* **senum**
senīlis, -e, old, aged
sēnsa, -ōrum, *n.*, sense, perceptions, ideas
sēnsus, -ūs, *m.*, sensation; perception, sense
sententia, -ae, *f.*, sentence, thought
sentiō, -īre, sēnsī, sēnsum, feel, perceive, know, sense
septem, *indecl.*, seven
septendecim, *indecl.*, seventeen
septimus, -a, -um, seventh
septuāgintā, *indecl.*, seventy
sepulcrum, -ī, *n.*, grave
sepultus, -a, -um, buried
sequor, sequī, secūtus sum, follow
sermō, -ōnis, *m.*, words, talk, speech
serpēns, -entis, *c.*, snake, serpent

servātrix, -īcis, *f.*, savior (fem.)
serviō, -īre, -īvī, -ītum + *dat.*, be a slave to, serve
servō (1), save
servus, -ī, *m.*, slave, servant
seu (sīve), *conj.*, or; **seu . . . seu,** whether . . . or
sex, *indecl.*, six
sexāgintā, *indecl.*, sixty
sextus, sixth
sī, if
sīc, *adv.*, thus, so, in this manner, in this way
Sicilia, -ae, *f.*, Sicily
sīdus, -eris, *n.*, constellation
significō (1), notify, indicate, signify
signum, -ī, *n.*, signal, sign; a figure, image, statue
silva, -ae, *f.*, forest
similis, -e + *gen. or dat.*, like, as
simul, *adv.*, at the same time, at once; **simul . . . simul,** not only . . . but at the same time
simul ac, *adv.*, as soon as, immediately after
simulō (1), assume the shape of, copy, simulate
sine + *abl.*, without
sinister, -tra, -trum, left (hand), adverse
sinistra, ae, *f.*, the left hand
sinō, -ere, sīvī, situm, allow, permit
sinus, -ūs, *m.*, fold, bend, breast, bosom
Sīrēnēs, -um, *f.*, Sirens
sitiō, -īre, -īvī, be thirsty
socer, -erī, *m.*, father-in-law
socius, -iī, *m.*, companion, ally
sōl, sōlis, *m.*, sun
sōlāmen, -inis, *n.*, comfort, consolation
solea, -ae, *f.*, shoe, sandal
soleō, -ēre, solitus sum, to be accustomed
solium, -iī, *n.*, throne
sollemnis, -e, solemn, festive, religious
sollicitus, -a, -um, anxious
sōlor, -ārī, -ātus sum, comfort, console
sōlum, *adv.*, only, alone, merely
sōlus, -a, -um, only, sole, lone, alone, one
solvō, -ere, solvī, solūtum, set sail, untie, release, free
somnus, -ī, *m.*, sleep; **in somnō,** asleep
sonō, -āre, -uī, -itum, sound, make a sound
sonus, -ī, *m.*, sound, noise
soror, -ōris, *f.*, sister
sors, sortis, *f.*, luck, chance, lot, lottery; **sorte,** by lot, by chance
spargō, -ere, sparsī, sparsum, scatter, sprinkle
sparsus, -a, -um, scattered
spatiōsus, -a, -um, long

spatium, -iī, *n.*, space, room, extent
spectātor, -ōris, *m.*, spectator
spectō (1), look at, watch, see
spēlunca, -ae, *f.*, cave, cavern
spērō (1), hope
spēs, speī, *f.*, hope
spīrō (1), breathe
spolium, -iī, *n.*, booty, plunder, spoils
spūma, -ae, *f.*, foam, froth
stagnum, -ī, *n.*, pool
statim, *adv.*, immediately
statua, -ae, *f.*, statue
statuō, -uere, -uī, -ūtum, establish
stella, -ae, *f.*, star
stō, stāre, stetī, statum, stand
strepitus, -ūs, *m.*, noise
strictus, -a, -um, drawn (as a sword)
studeō, -ēre, -uī + *dat.*, be eager, strive after, study
stultus, -a, -um, foolish
stupeō, -ēre, -uī, be amazed
Styx, Stygis, *f.*, Styx, a river, in the Underworld
suādeō, -ēre, suāsī, suāsum + *dat.*, persuade, be sweet to
sub + *acc. or abl.*, under, beneath
subdūcō, -ere, -duxī, -ductum, beach, draw up on shore
subeō, -īre, -iī *or* **-īvī, itum,** go under, pass under
subiciō, -ere, -iēcī, -iectum, attach, append, put in place of, substitute
subitō, *adv.*, suddenly
submergo (summergō), -ere, -mersī, -mersum, submerge, plunge into, immerse
subveniō, -īre, -vēnī, -ventum, come to the aid of, help, relieve
submittō, -ere, -mīsī, -missum, let down, send under, lower
succēdō, -ere, -cessī, -cessum, enter, follow, ascend, come after, mount
succendo, -ere, -cendī, -censum, set on fire from below, kindle, inflame
succingō, -ere, -cinxī, -cinctum, gird around
sucurrō, -ere, -currī, -cursum, come to the aid
sūcus, -ī, *m.*, juice
suī, sibi, sē, sē, himself, herself, itself, themselves
sulfur, -uris, *n.*, sulphur
sum, esse, fuī, futūrus, be, exist
summus, -a, -um, top of, highest
sūmō, -ere, sumpsī, sumptum, take
super + *acc. or* + *abl.*, over, above

superbia, -ae, *f.*, pride
superbus, -a, -um, proud
superī, -ōrum, *m. pl.*, the gods
superō (1), win, beat, conquer, overcome, surpass
supersum, -esse, -fuī, -futūrum, be left, remain
superus, -a, -um, highest, upper
supplex, -icis, suppliant
supplicium, -iī, *n.*, supplication
suppōnō, -ere, -posuī, -positum, put, put in place of
sūprēmus, -a, -um, highest, uppermost, last
surgō, -ere, surrēxī, surrēctum, rise, arise, get up
sūs, suis, *c.*, sow, swine, pig
suscipio, -ere, -cēpī, -ceptum, undertake, offer
suspīrō (1), breathe
sustineō, -ēre, -uī, -tentum, bear, hold up
suus, -a, -um, her, his, its; their (own)
Syriae, -ae, *f.*, Syria
Syringa, -ae, *f.*, Syrinx

tabula, -ae, *f.*, table, board, blackboard
tābum, -ī, *n.*, corrupt matter, plague, pestilence
taceō, -ēre, -uī, -itum, be silent
taedium, -iī, *n.*, disgust, boredom, weariness
tālis, -e, such (a)
Tālus, -ī, *m.*, Talux, the bronze man of Crete
tam, *adv.*, so
tamen, *adv.*, nevertheless, however, yet, still
tamquam, *adv.*, as much as, just as, as if
tandem, *adv.*, at length, at last, finally
tangō, -ere, tetigī, tactum, touch
tantus, -a, -um, so great, such great
tardus, -a, -um, late, slow; **nōn tardius,** not more slowly, just as fast as
taurus, -ī, *m.*, bull
tē, you, *acc. of* **tū**
tectum, -ī, *n.*, covered building, house, home
tegmen, -inis, *n.*, cover, protection
tegō, -ere, tēxī, tēctum, cover, cover over; hide, conceal
tēla, -ae, *f.*, loom
Telamōn, -ōnis, *m.*, Telamon, son of Aeacus
Telamōniadēs, -ae, *m.*, son of Telamon, i.e., Ajax
Telamōnius, -iī, *m.*, the son of Telamon (Ajax); grandson of Aeacus
tellus, -ūris, *f.*, earth, land
tēlum, -ī, *n.*, weapon, spear, javelin
temerārius, -a, -um, rash
temperō (1), rule, control, set bounds, govern

tempestās, -ātis, f., storm, tempest

tempestīvus, -a, -um, timely, ripe, ready, mature, seasonable

templum, -ī, n., temple

temptō (1), try, attempt

tempus, -oris, n., time; tempore ab hōc, from this time on

tendō, -ere, tetendī, tentum (tensum), stretch out, extend

tenebrae, -ārum, f. pl., darkness, dark shadows

teneō, -ēre, -uī, -tum, hold, keep, grasp

ter, adv., three times, thrice

tergum, -ī, n., back; terga dare, give his back (in flight), turn his back, run away

tergus, -oris, n., skin, hide

terminō (1), end, finish

terquīnque, indecl., three times five, fifteen

terra, -ae, f., land

terreō, -ēre, -uī, -itum, terrify, frighten

terribilis, -e, terrible

territus, -a, -um, terrified

tertius, -a, -um, third

testis, -is, c., witness

testor, -ārī, -ātus sum, bear witness, give evidence

Teucrī, -ōrum, m., Trojans

textile, -is, n., weaving

texō, -ere, texuī, textum, weave

thalamus, -ī, m., marriage couch, marriage, bedroom

Thēbae, -ārum, Thebes, a city of Boeotia

Thēseūs, -eī, m., Theseus, son of Aegeus

Thessalia, -ae, f., Thessaly, a region in northern Greece

Thisbē, -ēs, f., Thisbe

Threicius, -a, -um, or Thrācius, Thracian

tibi, to you

tigris, -idis, c., a tiger

timeō, -ēre, -uī, fear, be afraid of

timidus, -a, -um, timid, fearful

timor, -ōris, m., fear

tingō, -ere, -xī, -ctum, dye, wet

tollō, -ere, sustulī, sublātum, raise, lift up, take along

tonitrus, -ūs, m., thunder

tormentum, -ī, n., catapult, rack, windlass

torus, -ī, m., muscle, knot; mattress, couch, bed

tot, indecl., so many

tōtus, -a, -um, whole

trabs (trabes), -is, f., timber, tree; ship, vessel

trādō, -ere, -didī, -ditum, hand over, betray, hand down; trāditur, trādunt, it is handed down, the story goes

trahō, -ere, -trāxī, tractum, drag

trans + acc., across

transeō, -īre, -iī, -itum, go across, pass over, cross

transferō, -ferre, -tulī, -lātum, carry across, transfer

transfodiō, -ere, -fōdī, -fossum, stab, transfix

transformō (1), transform, change

transmittō, -ere, -mīsī, -missum, transmit, send through, pass through, send over

transportō (1), carry across

tredecim, indecl., thirteen

tremō or tremescō, -ere, tremble, quake, shiver

tremulus, -a, -um, shaking, trembling

trepidō (1), be agitated, waver confusedly, quiver

trepidus, -a, -um, trembling

trēs, tria, three

tribūtum, -ī, n., tribute

triformis, -e, three-formed

trigintā, indecl., thirty

trirēmis, -e, having three banks of oars

tristis, -e, sad

Trōas, -ādos, f., Trojan woman

Trōes, -um, m. pl., Trojans

Troezēn, -ēnis, f., Troezen, a city of Argolis

Trōia, -ae, f., Troy, a city in Asia Minor

Trōiānus, -a, -um, Trojan

Trōs, Trōis, m., a Trojan

truncus, -ī, m., trunk (of a tree)

tū, tuī, tibi, tē, tē, you

tueor (tuor), -ērī, tūtus sum, aid, protect

tum, adv., then

tumeō, -ēre or tumescō, -ere, -uī, swell, be swollen, begin to swell; tumidus, -a, -um, swollen

tumulus, -ī, m., mound, grave

turba, -ae, f., crowd

turbō (1), stir, disturb

turris, is, f., tower

turtur, -uris, m., turtle

tūs, tūris, n., incense

tūtō, adv., safely, in safety

tūtus, -a, -um, safe

tuus, -a, -um, your (sing.)

tympanum, -ī, n., tambourine, drum

tyrannus, -ī, m., tyrant, king

Tyrius, -a, -um, Tyrian
Tyrrhēnia, -ae, *f.*, Etruria
Tyrus, -ī, *f.*, Tyre

ubi, *adv.*, where, in what place; when, as soon
    as
Ulixēs, -is, *m.*, Ulysses
ūllus, -a, -um, any; **nec ūlla,** not any
ultimus, -a, -um, last
ultor, ōris, *m.*, avenger
umbra, -ae, *f.*, shade, spirit, shadow
umbrōsus, -a, -um, shady
umerus, -ī, *m.*, shoulder
umquam, *adv.*, ever
ūnā, together, in one
unda, -ae, *f.*, wave, water, river
unde, *adv.*, whence, from where
undecim, *indecl.*, eleven
undētrīgintā, twenty-nine
undēvīgintī, nineteen
ūniversum, -ī, *n.*, the whole world
ūnus, -a, -um, one; **ūnīus,** *genitive of* **ūnus,** of
    one man
urbs, -bis, *f.*, city
urna, -ae, *f.*, urn, pot, vessel
ursa, -ae, *f.*, bear
Ursa Maior, Big Bear (Callisto), Big Dipper
Ursa Minor, Little Bear (Arcas), Little Dipper
usque, *adv.*, as far as; **usque adeō,** all the way
    to that point
ūsus, -ūs, *m.*, use, usefulness, service
ut, *conj.* + *ind.*, when, as; + *subjv. in purpose
    and result clauses*, in order that, to, so that
uterque, utraque, utrumque, each of two;
    utrimque, *adv.*, on both sides
uterus, -ī, *m.*, uterus, womb
ūtiliter, *adv.*, usefully, for the common good
utinam, *adv.*, would that . . . !
ūtor, ūtī, ūsus sum + *abl.*, use
utrimque, *adv.*, on each side, on both sides
uxor, -ōris, *f.*, wife

vadum, -ī, *n.*, shallows, bottom of the sea
valeō, -ēre, -uī, be strong, be well; **valē, valēte,**
    farewell
validus, -a, -um, strong
valva, -ae, *f.*, *usually pl.*, door, a folding door
vānus, -a, -um, silly, idle, vain
varius, -a, -um, different, varied, various
vastō (1), destroy, lay waste
vātes, -is, *c.*, bard, singer, poet, seer

vehō, -ere, vexī, vectum, carry, convey
vel, *conj.*, or; **vel . . . vel,** either . . . or
vēlāmen, -inis, *n.*, robe, garment, clothing, veil
vellus, -eris, *n.*, fleece, wool
vēlum, -ī, *n.*, sail
velut (velutī), *adv.*, just as, even as
vēnātor, -ōris, *m.*, hunter
vēnātrix, -rīcis, *f.*, huntress
venēnum, -ī, *n.*, poison
veneror, -ārī, -ātus sum, respect, revere, honor,
    worship
venia, -ae, *f.*, favor, pardon
veniō, īre, vēnī, ventum, come
ventus, -ī, *m.*, wind
Venus, -eris, *f.*, Venus, goddess of love
verbum, -ī, *n.*, word
vērē, *adv.*, truly, really, actually
vereor, verērī, veritus sum, fear
Vergilius, -iī, *m.*, P. Vergilius Maro, Virgil
verrō, -ere, verrī, versum, drag, trail, sweep
versō (1), twist around, meditate
vertō, -ere, vertī, versum, turn, twirl, whirl
vērus, -a, -um, true
vester, -tra, -trum, your (*pl.*)
vestīgium, -iī, *n.*, trace, track, footstep
vestīmentum, -ī, *n.*, clothes, garment
vestis, -is, *f.*, clothing, clothes
vetus, veteris, old, ancient
via, -ae, *f.*, street, roadway
vibrō (1), vibrate, quiver
vīcīnus, -a, -um + *dat.*, neighboring
victor, -ōris, *m.*, victor
victōria, -ae, *f.*, victory
victus, -a, -um, conquered
videō, -ēre, vīdī, vīsum, see, observe, discern,
    look at, understand
videor, vidērī, vīsus sum, seem; **vidētur,** it
    seems
vīgintī, twenty
vigor, -ōris, *m.*, vigor
villōsus, -a, -um, shaggy-haired, hairy
villus, -ī, *m.*, shaggy hair
vincō, -ere, vīcī, victum, conquer
vinculum, -ī, *n.*, band, cord, chain
vīnum, -ī, *n.*, wine
vir, virī, *m.*, man, husband
virga, -ae, *f.*, green twig, magic wand
Virgilius. *See* **Vergilius**
virgineus, -a, -um, maidenly, of the maiden
virginitās, -tātis, *f.*, virginity
virgo, -inis, *f.*, maiden

viridis, -e, green
virtus, -tūtis, *f.,* courage, bravery, virtue
vīs, vīs, *f.,* power, force, *pl.* **vīrēs,** strength;
    vīs aurea, the golden touch
viscus, -eris, *n.,* flesh, internal organs
vīsitō (1), visit
vīta, -ae, *f.,* life
vītō (1), avoid, escape
vitta, -ae, *f.,* fillet
vīvax, -ācis, long-lived, lively
vīvēns, -entis, living, alive
vīvō, -ere, vīxī, vīctum, live, be alive
vīvus, -a, -um, alive
vix, *adv.,* scarcely, hardly, with difficulty
vōbīs, to you
vocō (1), call, summon

volō (1), fly
volō, velle, voluī, wish, want
volucris, -is, *f.,* bird; *gen. pl.* **volucrum;**
    volucer, -cris, -cre, winged, flying
voluntās, -tātis, *f.,* will, wish
voluptās, -tātis, *f.,* pleasure, delight
volvō, -ere, volvī, volūtum, roll
vorax, -ācis, hungry, gluttonous
vorō (1), suck down
vōs, *nom. and acc. pl.,* you
vōtum, -ī, *n.,* prayer, offering
vox, vōcis, *f.,* voice
vulnerō (1), wound
vulnus, -eris, *n.,* wound
vultus, -ūs, *m.,* expression of the face, the
    countenance, face

ENGLISH–LATIN VOCABULARY

abandon, **relinquō, -ere, -līquī, -lictum**
able, be, **possum, posse, potuī**
about, **dē** + *abl.*
accept, **accipiō, -ere, -cēpī, -ceptum**
Achaemenides, **Achaemenidēs, -is,** *m.*
Achilles, **Achillēs, -is,** *m.*
Aeacus, **Aeacus, -ī,** *m.*
Aeëtes, **Aeētēs, -ae,** *m.*
Aegeus, **Aegēūs, -eī,** *m.*
Aeneas, **Aenēas, -ae,** *m.*
Aeson, **Aesōn, -onis,** *m.*
Aethra, **Aethra, -ae,** *f.*
afraid, be, **vereor, verērī, veritus sum**
after (*prep.*), **post** + *acc.*
after (*conj.*), **postquam** + *ind.*
again, **iterum, rursus**
against, **contrā** + *acc.*
Agamemnon, **Agamemnōn, -onis,** *m.*
age, **aetās, aetātis,** *f.*; **iuventus, -ūtis,** *f.*
aid, **auxilium, -iī,** *n.*
Ajax, **Āiax, -ācis,** *m.*
all, **omnēs, omnia,** *pl. of* **omnis, -e,** each, every
allow, **permittō, -ere, -mīsī, -missum; sinō, -ere, sīvī, situm**
almost, **paene**
already, **iam**
also, **quoque**
altar, **āra, -ae,** *f.*
always, **semper**
Amazon, **Amāzon, -onis,** *f.*
and, **et**
announce, **nuntiō** (1)
angry, **īrātus, -a, -um**
animal, **animal, -ālis,** *n.*
answer, **respondeō, -ēre, -spondī, -sponsum**
Antiphates, **Antiphatēs, -ae,** *m.*
Apollo, **Apollo, -inis,** *m.*
apple, **pomum, -ī,** *n.*
approach, **appropinquō** (1) + *dat.*
Arachne, **Arachnē, -ēs,** *f.*
Arcadia, **Arcadia, -ae,** *f.*
Arcas, **Arcas, -adis,** *m.*
Argonauts, **Argonautae, -ārum,** *m. pl.*
Ariadne, **Ariadna, -ae,** *f.*
arm, **lacertus, -ī,** *m.*; **bracchium, -iī,** *n.*
armed, **armātus, -a, -um**
arms, **arma, -ōrum,** *n.pl.*; **tēla, -ōrum,** *n.pl.*

arrive, **perveniō, -īre, -vēnī, -ventum**
arrow, **sagitta, -ae,** *f.*
art, **ars, -tis,** *f.*
ash(es), **cinis, -eris,** *n.* (*usually pl.*)
ask (for), **orō** (1); **rogō** (1); **petō, -ere, -iī** *or* -**īvī, -ītum; quaerō, -ere, quaesīvī, quaesītum**
asleep, **in somnō**
as many . . . so many, **quot . . . tot; quam . . . tam**
ass, **asellus, -ī,** *m.*
Astyanax, **Astyanax, -actis,** *m.*
at, **ad** + *acc.*
Atalanta, **Atalanta, -ae,** *f.*
Athens, **Athēnae, -ārum,** *f. pl.*
attempt, **temptō** (1)
Attica, **Attica, -ae,** *f.*
avoid, **ēvītō** (1)
away, be, **absum, abesse, āfuī, āfutūrum**

Bacchus, **Bacchus, -ī,** *m.*
bad, **malus, -a, -um**
bard, **vātes, -is,** *m.*
battle, **pugna, -ae,** *f.*; **proelium, -iī,** *n.*
Baucis, **Baucis, Baucidis,** *f.*
be, **sum, esse, fuī, futūrum**
be able (can), **possum, posse, potuī**
be afraid, **vereor, verērī, veritus sum**
be away, **absum, abesse, āfuī, āfutūrum**
bear (*noun*), **ursa, -ae,** *f.*; **ursus, -ī,** *m.*
bear (*verb*), **ferō, ferre, tulī; lātum**
beat (conquer), **vincō, -ere, vīcī, victum; superō** (1)
beautiful, **pulcher, -chra, -chrum**
beauty, **forma, -ae,** *f.*; **pulchritūdō, -inis,** *f.*
because, **quod** + *ind.*; **cum** + *subjv.*
because of, **ob** + *acc.*; **propter** + *acc.*; **causā** + *gen.*
become, **fīō, fierī, factus sum**
bed, **lectus, -ī,** *m.*
before, **prō** + *abl.*
beg, **ōrō** (1); **rogō** (1); **precor, -ārī, precātus sum**
behold, **ecce**
believe, **crēdō, -ere, credidī, creditum** + *dat.*
belt, **balteus, -eī,** *m.*; **cingulum, -ī,** *n., usually pl.*
beneath, **sub** + *abl. or acc.*
bend over, **sē inclīnō** (1)

be present, **adsum, -esse, -fuī, -futūrum**

best, **optimus, -a, -um**

betray, **trādō, -ere, -didī, -ditum**

better, **melior, melius**

bid, **iubeō, -ēre, iussī, iussum; imperō** (1) +
   dat.

bind, **retineō, -ēre, -uī, -tentum**

bind together, **coniungō, -ere, -iunxī, -iunctum**

bite, **mordeō, -ēre, momordī, morsum**

blood, **cruor, -ōris,** *m.*; **sanguis, -inis,** *m.*

bloody, **cruentus, -a, -um; sanguineus, -a, -um**

body, **corpus, -oris,** *n.*

booty, **praeda, -ae,** *f.*

born, **nātus, -a, -um**

both . . . and, **et . . . et**

bough, **rāmus, -ī,** *m.*

bow, **arcus, -ūs,** *m.*

bowl, **crātēr, -ēris,** *m.*; **crātēra, -ae,** *f.*

boy, **puer, -erī,** *m.*

branch, **rāmus, -ī,** *m.*

brass, **aes, aeris,** *n.*

brave, **fortis, -e**

bravery, **fortitūdo, -inis,** *f.*

breathe, **suspīrō** (1)

breathe out, **efflō** (1)

bride, **nūpta, -ae,** *f.*

bright, **clārus, -a, -um**

bring, **ferō, ferre, tulī, lātum**

bronze, brass, **aes, aeris,** *n.*; **aēneus, -a, -um**

brother, **frāter, -tris,** *m.*

build, **aedificō** (1)

bull, **taurus, -ī,** *m.*

but, **sed; autem** (*postpos.*)

by, **ā (ab)** + *abl.*; *or abl. of means*

Cadmus, **Cadmus, -ī,** *m.*

call, **vocō** (1)

call together, **convocō** (1)

Callisto, **Callistō, -ūs,** *f.*

can, **possum, posse, potuī**

capture, **capiō, -ere, cēpī, captum**

careless, **neglectus, -a, -um**

carry, **portō** (1); **ferō, ferre, tulī, lātum; gerō,
   -ere, gessī, gestum**

carry off, **auferō, -ferre, abstulī, ablātum;
   rapiō, -ere, -uī, raptum**

Carthage, **Carthāgō, -inis,** *f.*

Cassandra, **Cassandra, -ae,** *f.*

cause (*verb*), **facere ut**

cave, **spēlunca, -ae,** *f.*

chance, by, **forte**

change, **transformō** (1); **mūtō** (1)

chariot, **currus, -ūs,** *m.*

charm (*verb*), **capiō, -ere, cēpī, captum**

charm (*noun*), **carmen, -inis,** *n.*

children, **līberī, -ōrum,** *m., pl.*

choose, **legō, -ere, lēgī, lectum**

Circe, **Circē, -ae,** *f.*

citadel, **arx, arcis,** *f.*

citizen, **cīvis, -is,** *m.*

city, **oppidum, -ī,** *n.*; **urbs, urbis,** *f.*

close, **claudō, -ere, clausī, clausum**

club, **clāva, -ae,** *f.*

Colchis, **Colchis, -chidis,** *f.*

color, **color, colōris,** *m.*

come, **veniō, -īre, vēnī, ventum**

command, **iussum, -ī,** *n.*

commit, **committō, -ere, -mīsī, -missum**

companion, **comes, -itis,** *c.*

complaint, **querella, -ae,** *f.*

conceal, **tegō, -ere, texī, tectum**

condemn, **damnō** (1)

condition, **lex, lēgis,** *f.*

conquer, **vincō, -ere, vīcī, victum**

contend, **certō** (1)

contest, race, **certāmen, -inis,** *n.*

Corinth, **Corinthus, -ī,** *f.*

costly, **pretiōsus, -a, -um**

cottage, **casa, -ae,** *f.*

country, **rūs, rūris,** *n.*; in the country, **rūrī**

country (fatherland), **patria, -ae,** *f.*

courage, **animī, -ōrum,** *m.*; **virtus, virtūtis,** *f.*

cover, **tegō, -ere, texī, tectum**

covered, **tectus, -a, -um**

Crete, **Crēta, -ae,** *f.*

crowd, **turba, -ae,** *f.*

Cumae, **Cūmae, -ārum,** *f.*

cup, **poculum, -ī,** *n.*

Cupid, **Cupīdo, -inis,** *m.*

custodian, **custos, -ōdis,** *c.*

cut (up), **resecō** (1), **-uī, -tum**

Cygnus, **Cygnus, -ī,** *m.*

Daedalus, **Daedalus, -ī,** *m.*

danger, **perīculum, -ī,** *n.*

dangerous, **perīculōsus, -a, -um**

Daphne, **Daphnē, -ēs,** *f.*

daughter, **fīlia, -ae,** *f.*; *dat. and abl. pl.* **fīliābus**

day, **diēs, diēī,** *m. & f.*

dead, **mortuus, -a, -um**

dear (to), **cārus, -a, -um** + *dat.*

death, **mors, mortis,** *f.*

deceive, **fallō, -ere, fefellī, falsum**

decide, **constituō, -uere, -uī, -stitūtum**

decorate, **decorō** (1); **ornō** (1)
deed, **factum, -ī,** *n.*
delay, **mora, -ae,** *f.*
demand, **imperō** (1) + *dat.*; **iubeō, -ere, iussī, iussum; poscō, -ere, poposcī**
descend, **descendō, -ere, descendī, -censum**
desire, **dēsīderō** (1)
Dia, **Dīa, -ae,** *f.*
Diana, **Diāna, -ae,** *f.*
die, **morior, morī, mortuus sum**
dig, **effodiō, -ere, -fōdī, -fossum**
disembark, **ēgredior, -gredī, -gressus sum**
disgrace, **opprobrium, -iī,** *n.*
dragon, **serpēns, serpentis,** *c.*; **draco, -ōnis,** *c.*
drink (*verb*), **bibō, -ere, bibī, bibitum**
drown, **submergō, -ere, -mersī, -mersum**
drug, **medicāmen, -inis,** *n.*
dull, **obtūsus, -a, -um**
dye, **tingō, -ere, tinxī, tinctum**

ear, **auris, -is,** *f.*
earlier, **prior, prius**
earth, **terra, -ae,** *f.*; **humus, -ī,** *f.*
eat, **edō, -ere, ēdī, ēsum**
Echo, **Ēchō, -ūs,** *f.*
eight, **octō**
either . . . or, **aut . . . aut**
end, **fīnis, -is,** *m.* & *f.*
enemy, **hostis, -is,** *m.*
enough, **satis**
enter, **intrō** (1)
Epidaurus, **Epidaurus, -ī,** *f.*
escape, **fugiō, -ere, fūgī, -itum**
especially, **magnopere, maximē**
eternal, **aeternus, -a, -um**
Europa, **Eurōpa, -ae,** *f.*
Eurydice, **Eurydicē, -ēs,** *f.*
even, **etiam**
even if, **etiam sī**
even now, **etiam nunc, etiam hodiē**
even today, **etiam hodiē**
ever watchful, **pervigil, -ilis**
evil, **malus, -a, -um**
evil deed, **facinus, -oris,** *n.*; evil deeds, **facta mala,** *n.pl.*
except, **praeter** + *acc.*
experience, **experientia, -ae,** *f.*
eye, **oculus, -ī,** *m.*

faithful, **fīdus, -a, -um; fidēlis, -e**
fall in love, **amō** (1)
false, **falsus, -a, -um**

famous, **nōtus, -a, -um; clārus, -a, -um**
far, **longē**
far away, **procul**
farmer, **agricola, -ae,** *m.*
father, **pater, -tris,** *m.*
fatherland, **patria, -ae,** *f.*
favorable, **secundus, -a, -um**
fear (*verb*), **timeō, -ēre, -uī; metuō, -ere, -uī**
fear (*noun*), **timor, -ōris,** *m.*; **metus, -ūs,** *m.*
feed, **pascō, -ere, pāvī, pastum**
feel, **sentiō, -īre, sensī, -sum**
feelings, **sensus, -ūs,** *m.*
field, **ager, agrī,** *m.*
fifteen, **ter quīnque; quīndecim**
fifty, **quīnquāgintā**
fight, **pugnō** (1)
fillet, **vitta, -ae,** *f.*
finally, **dēnique**
find, **inveniō, -īre, -vēnī, -ventum**
fire, **ignis, -is,** *m.*
first, **prīmus, -a, -um;** *adv.* **prīmō, prīmum**
fish, **piscis, -is,** *m.*
fit, **aptō** (1) + *dat.*
five, **quīnque**
flee, **fugitō** (1); **fugiō, -ere, fūgī, fugitum**
fleece, **vellus, -eris,** *n.*
flow, **fluō, -ere, fluxī, fluxum**
flower, **flōs, flōris,** *m.*
follow, **sequor, -ī, secūtus sum**
food, **cibus, -ī,** *m.*
foolish, **stultus, -a, -um**
foot, **pēs, pedis,** *m.*
for (*prep.*), **prō** + *abl.*
for (*adv.*), **enim**
forest, **silva, -ae,** *f.*
forever, **aeternō, aeternum**
forget, **oblīviscor, -ī, oblītus sum** + *gen.*
forgive, **ignoscō, -ere, -nōvī, -nōtum** + *dat.*
former, the, **ille, illa, illud**
fortune, **fortūna, -ae,** *f.*
four, **quattuor**
free, **līberō** (1)
friend, **amīcus, -ī,** *m.*; **amīca, -ae,** *f.*
friendship, **amīcitia, -ae,** *f.*
from, **dē, ē (ex), ā (ab)** + *abl.*
from a distance, **procul**
fruit, **pōmum, -ī,** *n.*
full (of), **plēnus, -a, -um** + *gen.*

garment, **vestīmentum, -ī,** *n.*
gaze back, **respiciō, -ere, -spexī, -spectum**
get possession of, **potior, -īrī, potītus sum** + *abl.*

gift, **dōnum, -ī,** *n.*
giant, **gigantēus, -a, -um**
girl, **puella, -ae,** *f.*
give, **dō, dare, dedī, datum; dōnō** (1)
give back, **reddō, reddere, reddidī, redditum**
gleam, **fulgeō, -ēre, fulsī, fulsum**
go, **eō, īre, iī** *or* **īvī, itum**
go away, **discēdō, -ere, -cessī, -cessum; abeō, -īre, -iī** *or* **īvī, - itum**
god, **deus, -ī,** *m.*
goddess, **dea, -ae,** *f.*; *dat. and abl. pl.* **deābus**
gold, **aurum, -ī,** *n.*
golden, **aureus, -a, -um**
good, **bonus, -a, -um**
goose, **anser, -eris,** *m.*
grave, **tumulus, -ī,** *m.*
great, **magnus, -a, -um**
greater, **maior, maius**
Greece, **Graecia, -ae,** *f.*
Greek (*noun*), **Graecus, -ī,** *m.*
green, **viridis, -e**
ground, **terra, -ae,** *f.*, **humus, -ī,** *f.*
grow, **crescō, -ere, crēvī, crētum**
guest, **hospes, -itis,** *m.*
guardian, **custos, -ōdis,** *c.*
guide, **dux, ducis,** *c.*

hair, **capillus, -ī,** *m.*, *usually pl.*
hand, **manus, -ūs,** *f.*
handsome, **pulcher, -chra, -chrum; formōsus, -a, -um**
hang, **pendeō, -ēre, pependī**
harsh, **dūrus, -a, -um; acer, -cris, -cre; sevērus, -a, -um**
have, **habeō, -ēre, -uī, -itum**
have to, **dēbeō, -ēre, -uī, -itum; oportet, -ēre, -uit** (*impers.*)
he, **is;** *or use personal ending* **-t**
hear, **audiō, -īre, -īvī, -ītum**
heaven, **caelum, -ī,** *n.*
Hecate, **Hecatē, -ēs,** *f.*
Helen, **Helena, -ae,** *f.*
help (*noun*), **auxilium, -iī,** *n.*
help (*verb*), **iuvō, -āre, iūvī, iūtum**
her, **eius**
her (own), **suus, -a, -um**
Hercules, **Hercules, -is,** *m.*
here, **hīc; in hōc locō**
hero, **hērōs, -ōis,** *m.*
herself, **suī, sibi, sē, sē**
hesitate, **dubitō** (1)
hide, **cēlō** (1)

himself, **suī, sibi, sē, sē**
Hippomenes, **Hippomenēs, -ae,** *m.*
his, **eius**
his (own), **suus, -a, -um**
hoarse, **raucus, -a, -um**
hold, **habeō, -ēre, -uī, -itum; teneō, -ēre, -uī, tentum**
hold back, **retineō, -ēre, -uī, -tentum**
hole (split, cleft), **fissum, -ī,** *n.*
home, **domus, -ūs,** *f.*; at home, **domī**; to go home, **domum īre**
hope (*verb*), **spērō** (1)
hope (*noun*), **spēs, -eī,** *f.*
hour, **hōra, -ae,** *f.*
house, **casa, -ae,** *f.*; **domus, -ūs,** *f.*
how, **quōmodo**
however, **autem,** *postpos.*
human, **humānus, -a, -um**
hundred, **centum**
hunter, **vēnātor, -ōris,** *m.*
hurl, **iaciō, -ere, iēcī, iactum**
husband, **vir, virī,** *m.*; **coniunx, coniugis,** *c.*
Hymen, **Hymēn, -enis,** *m.*

I, **ego (meī, mihi, mē, mē)**
if, **sī**
image, **imāgō, -inis,** *f.*
immediately, **statim**
immortal, **immortālis, -e**
impassable, **invius, -a, -um**
in, **in** + *abl.*
inflame, **incendō, -ere, -cendī, -censum**
inhabitant, **incola, -ae,** *c.*
in like manner, **pariter**
in place of, **prō** + *abl.*
insane, **insānus, -a, -um**
into, **in** + *acc.*
is, **est**
is, are, was, were, **sum, esse, fuī, futūrum**
island, **īnsula, -ae,** *f.*
isthmus, **isthmus, -ī,** *m.*
it, **id**
Italy, **Ītalia, -ae,** *f.*
it is necessary, **oportet, -ēre, -uit** (*impers.*); **necesse est; opus est**
it is permitted, **licet, -ēre, -uit,** (*impers.*)
it is pleasant, **libet, -ēre, libuit** (*impers.*)
it is said, **trāditur**
its, **eius;** its own, **suus, -a, -um**

Jason, **Iāsōn, -ōnis,** *m.*

javelin, **iaculum, -ī,** *n.*; **hasta, -ae,** *f.*; **tēlum, -ī,** *n.*

jaw, **rictus, -ūs,** *m.*

join, **iungō, -ere, iūnxī, iūnetum**

journey, **iter, itineris,** *n.*

Jove, **Iuppiter, Iovis,** *m.*

joyful, **laetus, -a, -um**

judge, **iūdex, iūdicis,** *m.*

judgment, **iūdicium, -iī,** *n.*

Juno, **Iūno, -ōnis,** *f.*

Jupiter, **Iuppiter, Iovis,** *m.*

kill, **necō** (1); **interficiō, -ere, -fēcī, -fectum**

kind, **benignus, -a, -um**

king, **rēx, rēgis,** *m.*

kingdom, **rēgnum, -ī,** *n.*

know, **sciō, -īre, -īvī, -ītum**

labyrinth, **labyrinthus, -ī,** *m.*

laden, **onustus, -a, -um**

Laestrygonians, **Laestrygonēs, -um,** *m.*

lake, **stagnum, -ī,** *n.*; **lacus, -ūs,** *m.*

land, **terra, -ae,** *f.*

large, **magnus, -a, -um**

last, **ultimus, -a, -um**

later, **post** + *acc.*; **tardius**

later (after many days), **post multōs diēs**

Latona, **Lātōna, -ae,** *f.*

latter, the, **hic, haec, hoc**

laurel, **laurus, -ī,** *f.*

law, **lex, lēgis,** *f.*

lead, **dūcō, -ere, duxī, ductum**

lead away, **abdūcō, -ere, -dūxī, -ductum**

leader, **dux, ducis,** *c.*

leave, **relinquō, -ere, -līquī, -lictum**

leg, **membrum, -ī,** *n.*

left, **sinister, -tra, -trum**

let, **permittō, -ere, -mīsī, -missum** *or use subjunctive*

let it be, **esto**

level, **plānus, -a, -um**

lie asleep, **iaceō, -ēre, iacuī, iactum (in somno)**

life, **vīta, -ae,** *f.*

light, **lux, lūcis,** *f.*

likeness, **imāgō, -inis,** *f.*

lion, **leō, leōnis,** *m.*

little, **parvus, -a, -um**

live, **habitō** (1); **vīvō, -ere, vīxī, vīctum**

locks (of hair), **capillī, -ōrum,** *m.*, *usually pl.*

long, **longus, -a, -um**

look about, **spectō** (1)

look back, **respiciō, -ere, -spexī, -spectum**

lose, **amittō, -ere, -mīsī, -missum**

love (*verb*), **amō** (1)

love (*noun*), **amor, -ōris,** *m.*

lover, **amāns, -ntis,** *c.*

luckily, **fēlīciter**

Lydia, **Lydia, -ae,** *f.*

lyre, **lyra, -ae,** *f.*

Maenad, **Maenas, -adis,** *f.*

magic, **magicus, -a, -um**

maiden, **puella, -ae,** *f.*; **virgō, virginis,** *f.*

make, **faciō, -ere, fēcī, factum**

man, **vir, virī,** *m.*; **homō, -inis,** *m.*

manner, **modus, -ī,** *m.*

many, **multī, -ae, -a**

Marcus, **Marcus, -ī,** *m.*

mark, **insigne, -is,** *n.*

marriage, **mātrimōnium, ii,** *n.*

marriage couch, **thalamus, -ī,** *m.*

marry, **in mātrimōnium dūcere; sē coniungere**

master, **magister, -trī,** *m.*; **dominus, -ī,** *m.*

matricide, **mātricīdium, -iī,** *n.*

may, *use subjunctive*

Medea, **Mēdēa, -ae,** *f.*

medicine, **medicīna, -ae,** *f.*; **medicāmen, -inis,** *n.*

meet, **conveniō, -īre, -vēnī, -ventum**

Mercury, **Mercurius, -iī,** *m.*

messenger, **nuntius, -iī,** *m.*

Midas, **Midās, -ae,** *m.*

mind, **mēns, mentis,** *f.*

Minerva, **Minerva, -ae,** *f.*

Minos, **Mīnōs, -ōis,** *m.*

Minotaur, **Mīnōtaurus, -ī,** *m.*

miracle, **mīrāculum, -ī,** *n.*

monster, **mōnstrum, -ī,** *n.*

mother, **māter, -tris,** *f.*

mountain, **mōns, montis,** *m.*

mouth, **ōs, ōris,** *m.*

move, **moveō, -ēre, mōvī, mōtum**

mulberry (tree), **mōrus, -ī,** *f.*

muse, **mūsa, -ae,** *f.*

music, **mūsica, -ae,** *f.*

my, **meus, -a, -um**

myself (*intensive*), **ipse, -a, -um**

myself (*reflexive*), **mē**

name (*noun*), **nōmen, -inis,** *n.*

name (*verb*), **nōminō** (1); **appellō** (1)

Narcissus, **Narcissus, -ī,** *m.*

nature, **natūra, -ae,** *f.*

near, **ad** + *acc.*; **propinquus, -a, -um** + *dat.*; **nōn procul** necessary, it is, **oportet, -ere, -uit; opus est; necesse est**

neighboring, **vīcīnus, -a, -um** + *dat.*

neither . . . nor, **nec . . . nec**

Neptune, **Neptūnus, -ī,** *m.*

new, **novus, -a, -um**

night, **nox, noctis,** *f.*,; at night, **nocte**

nine, **novem**

Ninus, **Ninus, -ī,** *m.*

Niobe, **Niobē, -ēs,** *f.*

no, **nūllus, -a, -um**

no longer, **nōn iam**

no one, **nēmō, -inis,** *c.*; **nūllus, -a, -um**

not, **nōn**

not know, **nesciō, -īre, -īvī, -ītum**

now, **nunc**

nymph, **nympha, -ae,** *f.*

obey, **pāreō, -ēre, -uī** + *dat.*

o, oh, **ō**

old (person), **senex, senis,** *c.*; *gen. pl.* **senum; vetus, veteris,** *usually pl.*

old (thing), **antīquus, -a, -um**

omen, **ōmen, -inis,** *n.*

on, **in** + *abl.*

on each side, **utrimque**

on that side, **illinc**

on the left (hand, side), **sinistrā (manū)**

on the right (hand, side), **dextrā (manū)**

on this side, **hinc**

once, once upon a time, **ōlim**

one, **ūnus, -a, -um**

only, **sōlus, -a, -um; sōlum**

open, **aperiō, -īre, -uī, -pertum**

open(ed), **apertus, -a, -um**

oracle, **ōrāculum, -ī,** *n.*

Orcus, **Orcus, -ī,** *m.*

order, **imperō** (1) + *dat.*; **iubeō, -ēre, iussī, iussum**

Orpheus, **Orpheus, -eī,** *m.*

other, **cēterus, -a, -um; alius, -a, -ud**

ought to, **dēbeō, -ēre, -uī, -itum**

over, **trāns** + *acc.*

overcome, **vincō, -ere, vīcī, victum; superō** (1)

overjoyed, **laetissimus, -a, -um**

owe, **dēbeō, -ēre, -uī, -itum**

palace, **rēgia, -ae,** *f.*

palladium, **palladium, -iī,** *n.*

Pallas, son of Evander, **Pallās, -antis,** *m.*

Pān, **Pān, -os,** *m.*

pardon, **venia, -ae,** *f.*

parents, **parēns, -entis,** *c.*

part, **pars, partis,** *f.*

Pasiphaë, **Pāsiphāa, -ae,** *f.*; **Pāsiphaē, -ēs,** *f.*

passion, **amor, -ōris,** *m.*

Patroclus, **Patroclus, -ī,** *m.*

peace, **pax, pācis,** *f.*

Peleus, **Pēleūs, -eī,** *m.*

Pelias, **Peliās, -ae,** *m.*

penalty, **poena, -ae,** *f.*

people, **populus, -ī,** *m.*

Periphetes, **Periphetes, -is,** *m.*

permitted, it is, **licet, -ēre, licuit** (*impers.*)

persuade, **persuādeō, -ēre, -suāsī, -suāsum** + *dat.*

Philemon, **Philēmōn, -mōnis,** *m.*

Philoctetes, **Philoctētēs, -ae,** *m.*

Phoebus, **Phoebus, -ī,** *m.*

Phoenicia, **Phoenicia, -ae,** *f.*

Phrygia, **Phrygia, -ae,** *f.*

pick, **carpō, -ere, carpsī, carptum**

picture, **pictūra, -ae,** *f.*

pig, **sūs, suis,** *c.*; **porcus, -ī,** *m.*

pile, **cumulus, -ī,** *m.*

pin, **fibula, -ae,** *f.*

pipes (of Pan), **fistula, -ae,** *f.*

Pittheus, **Pitthēūs, -eī,** *m.*

place (*noun*), **locus, -ī,** *m.*; **loca, -ōrum,** *n.pl.* (geographical places)

place (*verb*), **pōnō, -ere, posuī, positum**

plan, **consilium, -iī,** *n.*

pleasant, **grātus, -a, -um** + *dat.*; **amoenus, -a, -um**

pleasant, it is, **libet, -ēre, libuit** (*impers.*)

please (*verb*), **placeō, -ēre, -uī, -itum** + *dat.*

please (I ask you), **quaesō**

pleasing (to), **grātus, -a, -um** + *dat.*

pledge, **fidēs, -eī,** *f.*

plow, **arō** (1)

pour, **infundō, -ere, -fūdī, -fūsum**

poet, **poēta, -ae,** *c.*

poison, **aconītum, -ī,** *n.*; **venēnum, -ī,** *n.*

Polyphemus, **Polyphēmus, -ī,** *m.*

possess, **potior, -īrī, potītus sum** + *abl.*

power, **potentia, -ae,** *f.*

praise, **laudō** (1)

pray, **ōrō** (1); **precor, -ārī, -ātus sum**

prayer, **prex, precis,** *f.*; *usually pl.*

prepare, **parō** (1)

pretty, **pulcher, -chra, -chrum**

prevent, **prohibeō, -ēre, -hibuī, -hibitum**

price, **pretium, -iī,** *n.*

priestess, **sacerdōs, -dōtis,** *c.*

prize, **praemium, -iī,** *n.*

Procrustes, **Procrustēs, -ae,** *m.*

promise, **prōmittō, -ere, -mīsī, -missum**

proud, **superbus, -a, -um**

punishment, **poena, -ae,** *f.*
purple, **purpureus, -a, -um**
put, **pōnō, -ere, posuī, positum**
put out leaves, **frondeō, -ēre**
Pyramus, **Pȳramus, -ī,** *m.*

queen, **rēgīna, -ae,** *f.*

race course, running, **cursus, -ūs,** *m.*
rash, **temerārius, -a, -um**
read, **legō, -ere, lēgī, lēctum**
realize, **sentiō, -īre, sēnsī, sēnsum**
reason, **ratiō, -ōnis,** *f.*
recall (remember), **in memoriam tenēre**
received, **receptus, -a, -um**
recognize, **recōgnōscō, -ere, -nōvī, -nitum**
reed, **papȳrus, -ī,** *m.*
refuse, **negō** (1)
rejoice, **gaudeō, -ēre, gāvīsus sum**
rejoin, **redeō, -īre, -iī** or **-īvī, -itum; sē referre**
  (to take oneself back)
remain, **maneō, -ēre, mānsī, mānsum**
remember, **meminī, meminisse,** defective verb
remove, **removeō, -ēre, -mōvī, -mōtum**
reply, **respondeō, -ēre, -spondī, -spōnsum**
report, **reportō** (1)
repulse, **repellō, -ere, -pulsī, -pulsum**
respond, **respondeō, -ēre, -spondī, -spōnsum**
rest, **requiēs, -iētis,** *f.*; also *acc.* **requiem**
restore (give back), **reddō, -ere, -didī, -ditum**
restrain, **retineō, -ēre, -uī, -tentum**
return (give back), **reddō, -ere, -didī, -ditum**
return (go back), **redeō, -īre, -iī** or **-īvī, -itum;**
  reveniō, -īre, -vēnī, -ventum; sē referre
right, **dexter, -tra, -trum**
river, **flūmen, -inis,** *n.*
road, **via, -ae,** *f.*
rock, **saxum, -ī,** *n.*
rule, **rēgnō** (1)
run down, **dēcurrō, -ere, -currī, -cursum**
rushes, **harundō, -inis,** *f.*

sacred, **sacer, -cra, -crum**
sacrifice (*verb*), **sacrificō** (1)
sacrifice (*noun*), **sacrificium, -iī,** *n.*
sadness, **maestitia, -ae,** *f.*
safety, **salūs, salūtis,** *f.*
said, **dīxit, inquit; ait;** it is said, **trāditur**
sail (*verb*), **nāvigō** (1)
sail (*noun*), **vēlum, -ī,** *n.*; **linteum, -eī,** *n.*
same, **īdem, eadem, idem**
seem, **videor, -ērī, vīsus sum**

sand, **harēna, -ae,** *f.*; **pulvis, -eris,** *n.*
sandal, **solea, -ae,** *f.*; **calceus, -eī,** *m.* (= shoe)
satyr, **satyrus, -ī,** *m.*
say, **dīcō, -ere, dīxī, dictum**
scatter, **spargō, -ere, sparsī, -sum**
Sciron, **Scīron, -ōnis,** *m.*
sea, **mare, -is,** *n.*; **aequor, -oris,** *n.*
secretly, **sēcrētō**
see, **videō, -ēre, vīdī, vīsum; spectō** (1)
seek, **quaerō, -ere, quaesīvī, quaesītum; petō,**
  -ere, -iī or **-īvī, -ītum**
seem, **videor, vidērī, vīsus sum;** it seems, **vidētur**
senate, **cūria, -ae,** *f.*
send, **mittō, -ere, mīsī, missum**
serpent, **serpēns, -entis,** *c.*
servant, **servus, -ī,** *m.*
serve, **serviō, -īre, -īvī, -ītum** + *dat.*
set out, **ēgredior, -dī, -gressus sum; proficīscor,**
  -ī, -fectus sum
seven, **septem**
shade, **umbra, -ae,** *f.*; **mānēs, -ium,** *m.* (shades
  of the dead)
shape, **forma, -ae,** *f.*
sharp, **acūtus, -a, -um**
she, **ea**
shine, **splendeō, -ēre; radiō** (1)
ship, **nāvis, -is,** *f.*; **ratis, -is,** *f.*; **puppis, -is,** *f.*
shoe, **calceus, -eī,** *m.*; **solea, -ae,** *f.* (=sandal)
shore, **rīpa, -ae,** *f.*; **lītus, -oris,** *n.*
shoulder, **umerus, -ī,** *m.*
shout, **clāmō** (1)
shout, **clāmor, -ōris,** *m.*
shout out, **inclāmō** (1)
show, **mōnstrō** (1)
Sibyl, **Sibylla, -ae,** *f.*
Sicily, **Sicilia, -ae,** *f.*
side, to the, **oblīquē**
since, **cum** + *subjv.*; *abl. abs.*
sing, **cantō** (1); **canō, -ere, cecinī, cantum**
sink, **mergō, -ere, mersī, mersum**
sister, **soror, -ōris,** *f.*
sit (down), **sedeō, -ere, sēdī, sessum**
situation, **rēs, reī,** *f.*
six, **sex**
sky, **caelum, -ī,** *n.*
slave, **servus, -ī,** *m.*
sleep (*noun*), **somnus, -ī,** *m.*
sleep (*verb*), **dormiō, -īre, -uī, -ītum**
small, **parvus, -a, -um**
smaller, **minor, minus**
so, **tam; ita**
so great, **tantus, -a, -um**

some, **aliquis, aliquid**
so that, **ut** + *subjv.*
son, **fīlius, -iī,** *m.*
song, **carmen, -inis,** *n.*
sound (*noun*), **sonus, -ī,** *m.*
sound (*verb*), **sonō** (1)
sow, **serō, -ere, sēvī, satum**
spare, **parcō, -ere, pepercī, parsum** + *dat.*
speak, **dīcō, -ere, dīxī, dictum; loquor, loquī, locūtus sum**
spectator, **spectātor, -ōris,** *m.*
spider, **arānea, -ae,** *f.*
stand, **stō, -āre, stetī, statum**
star, **stella, -ae,** *f.*
statue, **imāgō, -inis,** *f.*
stay, **maneō, -ēre, mānsī, mānsum**
stiffen, **congelō** (1)
still, **etiam**
stone, **saxum, -ī,** *n.*
story, **fābula, -ae,** *f.*
stranger, **advena, -ae,** *c.*
stretch out, **tendō, -ere, tetendī, tentum** *or* **tēnsum**
string, **fīlum, -ī,** *n.*
strong, **fortis, -e; validus, -a, -um**
suffer, **patior, patī, passus sum**
suitable, **idōneus, -a, -um**
suitor, **procus, -ī,** *m.*
summon, **convocō** (1)
sun, **sōl, sōlis,** *m.*
supper, **cēna, -ae,** *f.*
supplication, **supplicium, -iī,** *n.*
supposed to, be, **dēbeō, -ēre, -uī, -itum**
surrender (hand over), **trādō, -ere, -didī, -ditum**
surpass, **superō** (1); **supersum, -esse, -fuī, -futūrum**
swan, **cygnus, -ī,** *m.*
sword, **gladius, -iī,** *m.*
Syrinx, **Sȳringa, -ae,** *f.*

table, **mēnsa, -ae,** *f.*
tablet, **tabula, -ae,** *f.*
take, **capiō, -ere, cēpī, captum**
take the form of, **simulō** (1)
task, **opus, -eris,** *n.*
teach, **doceō, -ēre, -uī, doctum**
teacher, **magister, -trī,** *m.*; **magistra, -ae,** *f.*
tears, **lacrima, -ae,** *f.*
tell, **narrō** (1); **dīcō, -ere, dīxī, dictum**
temple, **templum, -ī,** *n.*
ten, **decem**
tenth, **decimus, -a, -um**

terrify, **terreō, -ēre, -uī, -itum**
terrified, **territus, -a, -um**
test, **temptō** (1); **experior, -īrī, -pertus sum**
than, **quam;** *abl. of comparison*
that, **ille, illa, illud;** *omit in indirect statement*
Thebes, **Thēbae, -ārum,** *f.*
their, **eōrum, eārum; suus, -a, -um** (*refl.*)
them, **eōs, eās, ea**
themselves, **ipsī, ipsae, ipsa**
then, **deinde**
Theseus, **Thēseūs, -eī,** *m.*
Thetis, **Thetis, -idis,** *f.*
they, **eī, eae, ea; hī, hae, haec; illī, illae, illa**
think, **putō** (1); **cogitō**
third, **tertius, -a, -um**
thirty-five, **trīgintā quinque** *or* **quinque et trīgintā**
this, **hic, haec, hoc**
Thisbe, **Thisbē, Thisbēs,** *f.*
thousand, **mille,** *indecl.; pl.* **mīlia, -ium,** *n.*
thread, **fīlum, -ī,** *n.*
three, **trēs, tria**
through, **per** + *acc.*
throw, **iaciō, -ere, iēcī, iactum**
thus, **ita; sīc**
time, **tempus, -oris,** *n.*
Tmolus, **Tmōlus, -ī,** *m.*
to, **ad** + *acc.*
tomb, **tumulus, -ī,** *m.*
too + *adj., use comparative of adj.*
tooth, **dēns, dentis,** *f.*
touch, **tangō, -ere, tetigī, tactum**
touch (golden), **vīs aurea,** *acc.* **vim,** *abl.* **vī;** *pl.* **vīrēs**
town, **oppidum, -ī,** *n.*
tower, **turris, -is,** *f.*
transfix, **trānsfodiō, -ere, -fōdī, -fossum**
transform, **trānsformō** (1)
transport, **trānsportō** (1)
traveller, **peregrīnātor, -ōris,** *m.*
tree, **arbor, -oris,** *f.*
Troezen, **Troezēn, ēnis,** *f.*
Trojan, **Trōiānus, -a, -um; Trōiānus, -ī,** *m.*
troops, **cōpiae, -ārum,** *f.*
Troy, **Trōia, -ae,** *f.*
true, **vērus, -a, -um**
truly, **vērē**
trunk, **truncus, -ī,** *m.*
trust, **crēdō, -ere, credidī, creditum** + *dat.*
try, **temptō** (1); **conor, -ārī, -ātus sum**
turn (into), **mūtō** (1); **trānsformō** (1)
Turnus, **Turnus, -ī,** *m.*

two, **duo, duae, duo**
tyrant, **tyrannus, -ī,** *m.*
Ulysses, **Ulixēs, -is,** *m.*
under, **sub** + *acc.* or *abl.*
unfair, **iniustus, -a, -um**
unfavorable, **infēlix, -īcis; adversus, -a, -um**
unfortunately, **infēlīciter**
unless, **nisi**
until, **dōnec** + *ind.*; **ad** + *acc.*; dum + *subjv.*
up to, **usque**
urge, **hortor, -ārī, -ātus sum**
urn, **urna, -ae,** *f.*
us, **nōs**
utter, **dīcō, -ere, dīxī, dictum; ēdō, ēdere, ēdidī,
    ēditum**

veil, **vēlāmen, -inis,** *n.*
Venus, **Venus, -eris,** *f.*
Vergil, **Vergilius (Virgilius), -iī,** *m.*
very much, **maximē, valdē**
very small, **minimē**
victim, **victima, -ae,** *f.*
victor, **victor, -ōris,** *m.*
victory, **victōria, -ae,** *f.*
Virgil. *See* Vergil.
visit, **visitō** (1)
voice, **vox, vōcis,** *f.*

wage, **gerō, -ere, gessī, gestum**
walk, **ambulō** (1)
wall, **pariēs, -ietis,** *m.*
wander, **errō** (1)
want, **volō, velle, voluī; dēsīderō** (1)
war, **bellum, -ī,** *n.*
warn, **moneō, -ēre, -uī, -itum**
was, **erat**
wash, **lavō, -āre** or **-ere, lāvī, lautum** or **lōtum**
watch, **spectō** (1)
water, **aqua, -ae,** *f.*
wax, **cēra, -ae,** *f.*
way, **via, -ae,** *f.*; **iter, itineris,** *n.*
we, **nōs**
weapon, **tēlum, -ī,** *n.*; **ferrum, -ī,** *n.*
wear, **induō, -ere, -uī, -ūtum; gerō, -ere, gessī,
    gestum; portō** (1)
well-known, **nōtus, -a, -um**
weep, **lacrimō** (1); **plōrō** (1)

well, **bene**
were, **erant; fuērunt**
what? (*interrog. pron.*), **quid?**
when, **cum** + *ind.* or *subjv.*; **ubi** + *ind.*
where, **ubi; in quō locō**
whether, **an**
which, **quī, quae, quod**
while, **dum** + *pres. ind.*
whisper, **murmurō** (1)
white, **albus, -a, -um**
who, **quī, quae, quod; quis, quid**
why, **cūr**
wicked, **malus, -a, -um; impius, -a, -um**
wife, **coniūnx, -iugis,** *c.*; **uxor, -ōris,** *f.*
wild, **ferus, -a, -um**
will, **voluptās, -tātis,** *f.*
win, **vincō, -ere, vīcī, victum; supersum, -esse,
    -fuī, -futūrum; superō** (1)
wind, **ventus, -ī,** *m.*
wine, **vīnum, -ī,** *n.*
winged, **pennātus, -a, -um**
wisdom, **sapientia, -ae,** *f.*
wish, **dēsīderō** (1); **volō, velle, voluī; optō** (1)
with, **cum** + *abl.*; *or abl. of means*
witness, **testis, -is,** *c.*
woman, **fēmina, -ae,** *f.*
womb, **uterus, -ī,** *m.*
wonder, **mīror, -ārī, -ātus sum**
woods, **silva, -ae,** *f.*
word, **verbum, -ī,** *n.*
work, **labōrō** (1)
worship, **ōrō** (1); **colō, -ere, coluī, cultum**
wrath, **īra, -ae,** *f.*
wretched, **miser, -era, -erum**
write, **scrībō, -ere, scrīpsī, scrīptum**
year, **annus, -ī,** *m.*
yoke, **iungō, -ere, iūnxī, iūnctum**
you, *sing.*: **tū, tuī, tibi, tē, tē;** *pl.*: **vōs, vestrī,
    vōbīs, vōs, vōbīs**
young, **iuvenis, -is**
young man *or* woman, **iuvenis, -is,** *c.*;
    gen. pl. **-um**
your, *sing.*: **tuus, -a, -um;** *pl.*: **vester, -tra,
    -trum**
youth (young person), **iuvenis, iuvenis,** *c.*;
    gen. pl. **-um**
youth (time of life), **iuventus, iuventūtis,** *f.*

INDEX

Norma Goldman is adjunct assistant professor of Latin at Wayne State University, with thirty years' experience in teaching Latin at both high school and college levels. Co-author Jacob E. Nyenhuis, former head of the Department of Greek and Latin, Wayne State University, is professor of Classics and dean for the Humanities at Hope College.

The book was designed by Richard Kinney. Illustrations were done by Bernard Goldman and Betty Hanson. The typeface for the text is Times Roman, designed under the supervision of Stanley Morison about 1931. The display face is Optima, designed by Hermann Zapf about 1958.

The text is printed on EB Natural text paper. The book is bound in Joanna Mills' XK cloth over binder's boards. Manufactured in the United States of America.